Microsoft Foundation Class Primer

PROGRAMMING WINDOWS 3 AND NT WITH MFC

Jim Conger

Publisher: *Mitchell Waite*
Editorial Director: *Scott Calamar*
Managing Editor: *John Crudo*
Content Editor: *Harry Henderson*
Technical Reviewers: *Jeff Harbors, David Calhoun*
Design: *Michael Rogondino*
Production: *Cecelia Morales*
Illustrations: *Carl Yoshihana*
Cover Design: *Michael Rogondino*
Production Director: *Julianne Ososke*

© 1993 by The Waite Group, Inc.®
Published by Waite Group Press™, 200 Tamal Plaza, Corte Madera, CA 94925.

Waite Group Press is distributed to bookstores and book wholesalers by Publishers Group West, Box 8843, Emeryville, CA 94662, 1-800-788-3123 (in California 1-510-658-3453).

Printed in the United States of America
93 94 95 • 10 9 8 7 6 5 4 3 2 1

Conger, Jim.
   Microsoft foundation class primer : programming Windows 3 and NT with MFC / Jim Conger.
      p.   cm.
   Includes bibliographical references and index.
   ISBN: 1-878739-31-X : $29.95
   1. Windows (Computer programs)   2. Microsoft Windows (Computer file)   3. C++ (Computer program language)   I. Title.
QA76.76.W56C66   1993
005.4'3--dc20   92-46999
                                                          CIP

FOR Shirley

Acknowledgments

I am again in debt to Harry Henderson and David Calhoun, who edited this book and provided excellent guidance as to its content and organization. Thanks also to Jeff Harbers of Microsoft, who edited the book for technical accuracy, and to Erin Carney, also from Microsoft, for her assistance in the early stages of this book. Finally, I would like to thank the entire team at Microsoft who particpated in creating the *Microsoft Foundation Class Primer* and who significantly advanced the art of computer programming.

About the Author

Jim Conger began programming in 1972 while studying engineering at the University of Southern California. He has been writing programs ever since for a variety of computers. Most of his early work was done on mainframe computer systems using FORTRAN and BASIC for process simulation work. Jim started programming microcomputers in the early 1980s while living in London. These projects were primarily financial models, using BASIC, Pascal, and assembly language. His first C programs were written in 1983 while under the CP/M operating system, and he has continued using C and C++ under MS-DOS and Windows.

Jim's hobby of playing woodwind instruments lead to his interest in computer music. He is the author of two books on the subject, *C Programming for MIDI* (M&T Books, 1988), and *MIDI Sequencing in C* (M&T books, 1989). He also wrote *The Waite Group's Windows API Bible* (Waite Group Press, 1992) and *Windows Programming Primer Plus* (Waite Group Press, 1992). Jim lives in California with his wife and two children.

Introduction

This book is an effort to share my enthusiasm for the Microsoft Foundation Classes with other programmers. The Microsoft C++ 7.00 compiler was released about the time we were finishing work on The *Waite Group's Windows Programming Primer Plus*. Having just finished a C language book on Windows, I decided to try out Microsoft's new C++ compiler by converting several example programs from the Primer to C++. Looking through the documentation, I discovered that Microsoft had included an extensive collection of C++ classes called the Microsoft Foundation Classes (MFC) with the compiler. They had not been heavily advertised, so I had overlooked the MFC classes until I started working on the examples.

After working a few days, I gradually realized that the MFC classes encapsulated the Windows programming environment in a few powerful C++ objects. I was able to make every example behave exactly as it had with the C language version, but with far fewer lines of program code. The classes took care of many of the mundane details of Windows programming, but without abstracting the problem so much that I could not exercise complete control over Windows. The classes gradually became my "alternative universe" for Windows programming.

Another strong argument for using the MFC classes became apparent when Microsoft released the first beta version of its new 32-bit operating system, Windows NT. The examples for this book compiled to make Windows NT applications without any effort other than recompiling. The internal differences between Windows 3.1 and Windows NT are so completely hidden by the MFC classes that you can create most programs without any thought as to which platform the program will eventually use.

Because C++ and the MFC classes are a complete and alternative approach to Windows programming, we decided to start this book at the beginning. This book does not assume that you have programmed for Windows before, and it assumes only a modest familiarity with the C++ language. Most of us have been slow to use C++, perhaps because there was not a strong incentive to switch from C or other languages. The MFC classes change all of that. Using the MFC classes puts thousands of lines of code from Microsoft's programmers at your disposal. Best of all, you will probably never need to look at their code. The classes hide the inner workings, leaving you to concentrate on the overall program logic.

Chapter 1 begins with an introduction to how Windows works, and the underlying differences between Windows and Windows NT. The MFC classes are designed primarily to create Windows 3.1 and Windows NT applications, so an understanding of Windows is necessary background before working with the MFC classes. Chapter 1 includes an outline of how Windows is able to run more than one program at a time, and how Windows programs use the Windows environment to do many tasks. The concept of Windows messages is introduced, along with the different elements that make up a Windows program, such as resource data and module definition files. If you have created Windows programs in C or another computer language, you may want to skip Chapter 1 and move directly to the specifics of the MFC classes, which are introduced in Chapter 2.

Chapter 2 focuses on how the MFC classes are used to create Windows applications. The C++ approach to combining functions and data into class objects is first reviewed. The two most important MFC classes are introduced with a very short program called MINIMAL1, which displays a simple window with a caption bar. Chapter 2 also discusses the setup of the Microsoft compiler, and tests your computer's setup by compiling the example program. Common problems and their solutions are discussed, including several examples showing the compiler's output when various mistakes are made. When you finish this chapter, you will have the compiler working and you will be comfortable with the Microsoft C++ environment.

Chapter 3 starts with the simple MINIMAL1 program and improves it in three steps to create a complete Windows application. The changes include separation of the program into a C++ header file and program file, the addition of message processing logic, and finally the addition of a program menu. These steps are fully explained, allowing you to see what each of the specialized MFC classes accomplishes. This approach is different from most Windows programming tutorials, which start out with a fairly lengthy "first" program. The stepwise approach, building up to the full program, gives you a chance to see clearly how the different parts of a Windows program operate.

The extensive graphics functions provided by the MFC classes are introduced in Chapter 4. The initial examples focus on output of text, followed by painting objects like rectangles and ellipses. Painting brings up the subject of how Windows programs update the center of each program's window, which is important in an environment where one program's window can be covered up by another program. The last program in Chapter 4 demonstrates animated graphics, producing a ball that continually bounces around inside the program's window.

Window controls, such as buttons, scroll bars, and list boxes, are discussed in Chapter 5. Controls are the building blocks of most applications. These ready-to-use tools are a big time saver. Each type of control is demonstrated with a separate example program. Chapter 6 focuses on the mouse. Many mouse functions are built into the default logic for window controls. Sometimes it is necessary to deal more directly with the mouse. Examples that track the mouse and change the mouse cursor shape are provided. The latter is also used to introduce menus that include drop-down (or pop-up) menus with additional items.

Chapter 7 discusses the Windows character set, character fonts, and dealing with the keyboard. Windows uses a different character set than DOS, so the distinction between the two character sets is important, particularly if you are writing programs that may be translated into different languages. Several techniques in dealing with character fonts are covered, again using example programs.

Child and pop-up windows are discussed in Chapter 8. They are small windows that can be used for utility functions within a program. Creating child and pop-up windows provides insight into how the Windows environment manages the screen, and separates activities between different running programs. The examples in Chapter 8 also demonstrate the important programming technique of sending messages between different window elements of the same program.

Chapters 9 through 11 focus on different types of resource data that Windows programs use to store information. Chapter 9 covers menus, including menus with multiple levels of pop-up menus, and menu items consisting of bitmap pictures. Chapter 10 discusses dialog boxes. The Windows programming environment provides partial automation in creating dialog box windows using the dialog box editor. Chapter 11 covers the remaining resource types, which can be used to store character strings and other data in the program's resource data.

Chapter 12 covers the Windows memory management functions. C++ programmers frequently take advantage of the *new* and *delete* operators for memory management, but these operators do not make full use of Windows. Windows includes its own sophisticated memory management functions, which can be used to allocate blocks of memory for use by the application. Two new classes for managing local and global memory blocks are developed in the course of the chapter, demonstrating both Windows memory management and the general process of creating your own C++ classes.

Chapter 13 looks at Windows' graphics functions in more detail, focusing on the role of the "device context" settings in controlling the size and position of the finished output. This leads to the discussion of sending output to the printer in Chapter 14. The examples allow the user to set up the printer, and to cancel a printer job while it is in progress.

Disk file operations are discussed in Chapter 15. The MFC classes provide several alternative ways of dealing with disk files, so each technique is demonstrated with an example. This chapter includes an example text editor which uses a file selection dialog box. Chapter 16 covers bitmaps, which are one of Windows' techniques for storing graphical data. The examples demonstrate displaying bitmaps, stretching and shrinking bitmap images, using various binary operations when copying a bitmap to the screen, and drawing on the bitmap image in memory. The latter is a technique used in animating drawings, which is demonstrated with an example that animates an image using two different drawing techniques.

The Windows Clipboard is discussed in Chapter 17. The Clipboard allows different Windows applications to exchange data, usually via cut-and-paste operations. Examples are given using the Clipboard to exchange text, graphics, and user-defined data. The simple text editor developed in Chapter 15 is also expanded to include cut, copy, and paste operations.

Chapter 18 concludes the book with a discussion of dynamic link libraries (DLLs). DLLs provide the Windows programmer with the ability to store frequently used functions in libraries, which can be accessed by more than one program during a single Windows session. Besides providing a useful programming tool, creating a DLL provides insights into how Windows works internally, as most of the Windows environment consists of functions residing in DLLs. The conventional C language approach to DLLs and a C++ based DLL are demonstrated with separate examples.

After completing this text, you will have experience with the MFC classes that are used in all Windows and Windows NT applications, and have a sound background in C++. You will have created programs with animated graphics, and written your own simple word processor. The examples should provide starting points for a wide variety of programs.

Good luck with your Windows projects!

Jim Conger

Table ofContents

Contents

How Windows Works

The MFC classes are designed primarily as a basis for creating Windows 3.1 and Windows NT applications. You will need to have a general understanding of Windows programming to make sense out of the MFC classes. This chapter provides an overview of how Microsoft Windows works internally, and the different elements that make up a Windows program. We will look at the differences between Windows and DOS programs, and examine how the Windows environment appears to run more than one program at a time. Some of the unique aspects of creating Windows programs, such as processing Windows messages and using resources to store the program's data, are also discussed.

Built-in memory management functions are vital to the ability of Windows to run many applications at the same time. As a programmer, you will be able to control how different portions of a program are managed in memory. This control is specified in parts of a Windows program that do not have equivalents when compiling a DOS program, such as the module definition file or resource script file. We will look at these files in preparation for compiling your first Windows program in Chapter 2, *Using the MFC Classes*.

All of the subject matter in this chapter applies to any Windows program, regardless of the language you choose to create the program. If you are an experienced Windows programmer with C or another language, you may want to skip ahead to Chapter 2, which introduces the C++ approach to Windows programming.

Concepts covered: How Windows programs work, messages, resource data, structure of a Windows application program, compiling and linking, program instances, resources, client area, static data, local heap, module definition files.

Key words covered: GUI, PRELOAD, LOADONCALL, MOVEABLE, FIXED, MULTIPLE, SINGLE.

WHAT IS MICROSOFT WINDOWS?

If you have been using Microsoft Windows for some time, you probably take its ease of use for granted. You do not need to understand how Windows works internally to use it or run complex Windows programs. In fact, the Windows environment does an excellent job of shielding the user from the underlying workings. The situation is different when you decide to write your own Windows programs. You will need to look "under the hood" and see how Windows works.

When you get down to fundamentals, Microsoft Windows is a DOS program that has the ability to run other programs written in a special way. That probably sounds odd, as Windows looks different on the screen than most DOS programs. When you think about it, Windows is started from DOS like any DOS program. To start Windows you type WIN (ENTER) from the DOS prompt. What you are doing is running the DOS program WIN.COM, which is the core of Windows. WIN.COM loads several other files into memory, displays the Windows logo, and gets the Windows Program Manager application running. At that point, you are in the "Windows Graphical Environment," as shown in Figure 1-1. It is called "graphical" because Windows uses graphics to organize the workspace and present the user with intuitive ways to accomplish tasks. It is called an "environment" because you can run other programs from within Windows. Environments like Windows are sometimes called "GUI" for "Graphical User Interface."

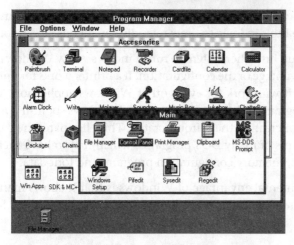

Figure 1-1 The Windows Graphical Environment

Once you have Windows running, you can run Windows programs, such as Excel and Write. A number of these programs can be run at the same time and share the screen. The Windows environment makes sure that each program gets its own portion of the screen, that the programs do not interfere with each other, and that each receives a slice of the computer's time.

THE ADVANTAGES OF WINDOWS

Windows is fundamentally just a big DOS program. The programs that you run from within Windows, such as Paintbrush and Windows Write, are definitely *not* DOS programs. These applications will run only within Windows. Why is that?

The answer lies in the internal structure of Windows. Windows includes a huge collection of built-in functions and data. For example, Windows includes functions with the ability to draw text in different sizes and styles using font data. Windows has a broad range of graphical functions for drawing lines and geometric shapes in color. Windows programs (like Excel) use these built-in functions, and do not need to supply the program logic to do these tasks. Excel uses these functions by requesting them from Windows.

Because Windows programs use built-in Windows functions, the programs end up smaller than they would be if each program had to include all of that logic. There are a number of advantages to this approach:

▶ Windows programs (called "application programs" or just "applications") take up less disk space, and less room in memory, once Windows is already running.

▶ All Windows applications tend to have the same "look and feel" because they are using the same built-in logic to draw text, display menus, and so on.

▶ Once the user sets up his or her system to run Windows, every Windows application can take advantage of the configuration. If a printer works for one Windows application, it will work for every other Windows application. That is because every program will take advantage of Windows' built-in printing functions instead of creating them from scratch. This eliminates the complex installation programs of many DOS programs, which had to have their own printer installation, memory configuration program, and font data.

Finally, the fundamental advantage of Windows is that it allows many programs to operate at the same time. We will have more to say about this later in the chapter.

WHAT IS WINDOWS NT?

Windows NT is basically a rewritten version of Windows. Although Windows NT looks and acts just like Windows 3.1 (Figure 1-1), the underlying structure of the environment is somewhat different. The biggest differences are:

▶ Windows NT is *not* an MS-DOS application like Windows 3.1. Instead, Windows NT is a complete operating system including all file operations. If you have a computer loaded with Windows NT, you can start up (boot) the computer directly into NT without loading MS-DOS. You can think of Windows NT as replacing both MS-DOS and Windows 3.1 with one streamlined package. Windows NT continues to support the underlying disk file structure used by MS-DOS (and Windows 3.1) so that disk files can be easily exchanged between the two systems.

▶ Windows NT takes advantage of the advanced memory management features built into the Intel 80386 and higher CPU chips. This makes programs more efficient, and less likely to crash. It also means that Windows NT will not run on the older 80286 family of computers.

Despite these underlying differences, Windows 3.1 and Windows NT are very similar to both users and programmers. Microsoft went to great pains to make NT look and behave as much like Windows 3.1 as possible. The two operating systems are so similar that throughout this book we will use the term "Windows" to refer to both systems. Information boxes that document details specific to Windows NT are included where there are underlying differences that you need to understand.

One bit of confusion stems from Microsoft's use of two terms to describe one operating system. You may see the programming environment referred to as "Win32" rather than "Windows NT." Win32 is the 32-bit application programming interface (API) for the Windows NT operating system. In other words, Win32 is the part of Windows NT that only programmers see. To keep things simple, this book uses the term "Windows NT" for both the operating system and the programming environment.

HOW WINDOWS PROGRAMS WORK

All programs function by telling the computer's hardware what to do. The difference between a Windows application and a DOS program lies in how direct the connection is between the running program and the actual hardware. Most DOS programs have a structure as shown in Figure 1-2. Besides the program logic (do this first, that second, and so on), DOS programs deal directly with the computer's hardware to access the screen, read the keyboard, and to perform other "low-level" functions. The main support the DOS operating system provides is for disk file access.

Figure 1-2 is a bit simplified. There are some limited functions within DOS for dealing with the screen and communications devices. Most DOS programs do not use these features because it is usually faster to deal directly with the computer's hardware.

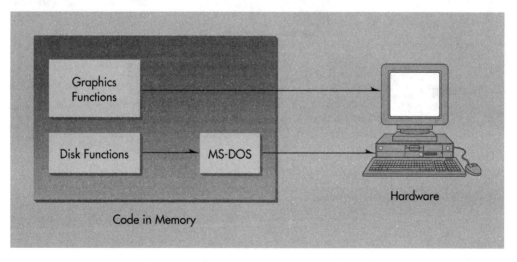

Figure 1-2 How a DOS Program Works

Figure 1-3 shows how a Windows program operates. Windows applications interact with the Windows environment, not directly with the hardware. If an application decides to write or draw something on the screen, it calls a function within Windows. Internally, Windows decodes the function call and translates it into hardware commands. If Windows was installed specifying a VGA video system, VGA hardware commands are sent out. If an IBM 8514 video adapter was specified when Windows was installed, IBM 8514 video hardware commands are sent out. The application program does not necessarily know or care what type of hardware the user has installed. The Windows environment takes care of the hardware for the program.

Note in Figure 1-3 that disk file commands are still done via DOS. Because Windows is a DOS program, DOS is always running before Windows is started. All of the DOS file support functions are available to Windows, just as they are available to any DOS program. Windows designers took advantage of DOS to do what it does best—disk file access. Files created by Windows programs are really DOS files. This means that you can save a text file created by the Windows Notepad application on a floppy disk, and hand it to a coworker who uses a DOS word processor. The DOS word processor will have no trouble reading the file, even though it was created by a Windows program. Using the DOS file functions has the disadvantage of limiting file names to eight characters, plus a three character extension, like "ANEWFILE.TXT."

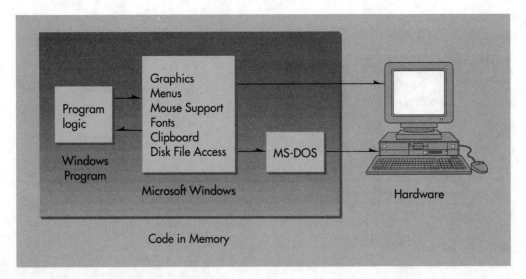

Figure 1-3 How a Windows Program Works

Windows NT differs from Windows in that it does not use the MS-DOS file system for file access. Windows NT has its own built-in file functions. This does not affect programming under Windows NT because the functions provided by NT work identically to their equivalents under Windows.

Running Several Programs at One Time

Windows allows you to run many application programs at the same time. "Running" means that the program is loaded into memory. It does not mean that the program is necessarily doing anything. Most of the time Windows applications just sit in memory. They only do something when requested to by the Windows environment. A well-designed Windows program constantly tries to finish what it is doing and give control back to Windows. Think of Windows programs as being incredibly polite. They only act when commanded to do so by Windows, and then they promptly give control back to their host, the Windows environment.

To understand why Windows applications must be so polite, consider a situation where you have several applications running at the same time. Figure 1-4 shows a typical Windows screen image with several programs running. The Program Manager, Notepad, Control Panel, and Calculator are all visible. This means that these four applications are loaded into memory. We will see later that Windows has the ability to load just parts of a program to conserve memory space. Any running program will be at least partly loaded into memory.

Note that each of the running applications in Figure 1-4 occupies its own rectangular area on the screen. These areas are said to be the program's "window."

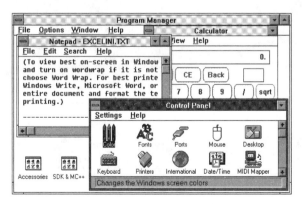

Figure 1-4 Windows Session with Several Programs Running

The Windows environment gets its name from the concept of these program windows. Each program window is an independent entity. Each program can write only on its own window area, not on another program's window. You can think of each window's border as being a fence that restricts output from the program to an individual little "screen" dedicated to that one program.

Two Meanings of "Window"

The word "window" has two meanings in this book. When the first letter is capitalized ("Windows"), it means the complete Microsoft Windows environment. This includes the Program Manager, File Manager, and all of the Windows API (Application Programming Interface) functions. In small letters ("a window"), it refers to an individual program window on the screen.

Looking Into Memory

If you could look into the memory chips of the computer that is shown in Figure 1-4, you would find things organized roughly as shown in Figure 1-5. Prior to loading Windows 3.1, DOS is loaded from the disk drive and stays in memory

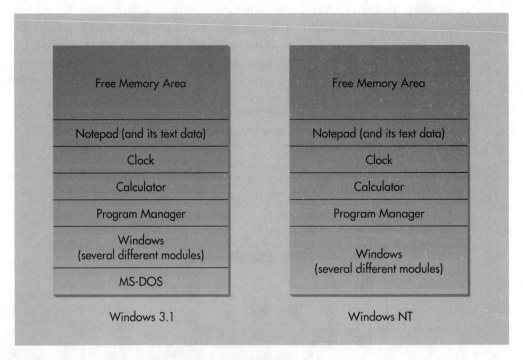

Free Memory Area	Free Memory Area
Notepad (and its text data)	Notepad (and its text data)
Clock	Clock
Calculator	Calculator
Program Manager	Program Manager
Windows (several different modules)	Windows (several different modules)
MS-DOS	
Windows 3.1	Windows NT

Figure 1-5 Memory Organization for a Windows Session

while Windows operates. Windows 3.1 is loaded into memory when the user types `WIN` (ENTER). (Windows NT starts running immediately when the computer is turned on, without going through the step of loading MS-DOS.)

Windows consists of several files, each called a "program module." Starting Windows automatically loads the Program Manager program into memory. Windows applications that the user starts are also loaded into memory, along with the data that each application uses, such as the text file Notepad may be editing.

At any one time, the computer's CPU will be executing instructions residing in one of these memory areas. The program with "control" of the system is the one whose code is currently being executed. Those instructions are in the memory block occupied by the program. If the user does not do anything, the Windows environment has "control" of the "system." "System" is just another word for a running computer, including all of the programs that are currently active. When a program is processing instructions, the program is said to have "control of the system." When Windows has control, instructions in the portion of memory occupied by Windows are being executed. Windows just keeps checking to see if any key was pressed, if the mouse was used, etc.

MESSAGES

Now imagine that the user moves the mouse cursor (the little arrow that moves when you move the mouse) over to the Calculator program's window area and clicks the left mouse button. Windows contains the logic for decoding the hardware signals sent from the mouse. The functions containing this hardware decoding logic are in the block of memory occupied by a portion of Windows called a "driver" (because it "drives" the mouse). Once the hardware information from the mouse is decoded, Windows must figure out which program the user selected with the mouse cursor. Windows does this by comparing where the mouse cursor is located to the location of the program windows on the screen. The top-most window under the mouse cursor must be the one that the user wants to activate. Again, the logic for figuring out which application the user has selected is built into the Windows environment, and is always ready to run.

Next, Windows must tell the Calculator program what has happened, so that the Calculator can do something, such as display a new digit. Windows does this by sending the Calculator application a "message." The message tells Calculator something like "The user has clicked the right mouse button over point X,Y on your (the Calculator application's) window. Do whatever is appropriate, then return control back to Windows."

Of course, computers do not really have internal message systems like telephones and telexes. Computers just execute instructions in memory. To pass the message data to a running program, Windows writes some data into a memory block, and then lets the program receiving the message data start running. The program reads the memory block, does whatever is required, and then returns control to Windows.

To pass the message data to a program, Windows writes the information into a memory area set aside for each running program. Once Windows has written the message data into memory, Windows allows the program that is receiving the message to execute its instructions. The program reads the message data from the memory block, decodes all of the data bytes, decides what to do, and then returns control back to Windows. This cycle is shown in Figure 1-6.

The message cycle shown in Figure 1-6 allows Windows to send messages to any number of programs in memory. If the user moves the mouse cursor over one program's window and clicks a mouse button, that program will receive messages. The messages will be information from Windows such as "the mouse moved," "the left mouse button was depressed," or "the left mouse button was released." If the user then moves the mouse over another window on the screen and clicks a mouse button, that program will start receiving the messages from Windows.

The channeling of message data to different applications is the secret of Windows' ability to appear to run more than one application at the same time. The computers that Windows runs on can really only execute one instruction at a time. Either Windows itself is executing instructions (has control), or one of the programs in memory is executing its instructions. Windows can rapidly switch which program is getting the messages, to reflect which application the user has selected with a mouse action or keystroke. The switching of messages

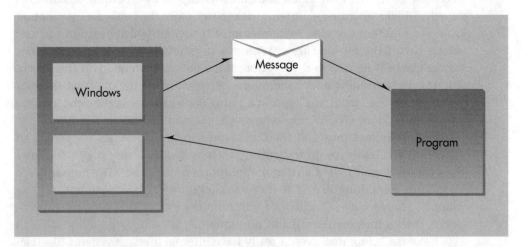

Figure 1-6 The Message Cycle

from one program to the next is the sleight of hand that Windows uses to make it appear that all of the programs are running at once. Figure 1-7 shows two applications receiving different messages from Windows. Keep in mind that each message is sent at a different time, and that only one program can process a message at any one time.

AN ANALOGY

If you want to draw an analogy at this point, think of Windows as the boss and the running programs as workers. Each program worker sits behind a desk with an "In" box. To begin with, the Windows boss is active, but all of the program workers are frozen in place. The boss determines which worker needs to do a task, writes the message on a piece of paper, and puts it in the worker's "In" box. The boss goes back to his desk and stops moving. The worker begins moving, reads the message, and does whatever is required. Unlike a normal office, none of the other workers or the boss can move while another worker processes a message. When the worker is done, the boss becomes active again, and all of the workers are frozen.

You may be wondering if the workers (programs) have both "In" and "Out" boxes. Absolutely! Windows programs can both send and receive messages. We will use the ability to send messages to allow a program to communicate with other windows, such as editing windows and list boxes. Windows application

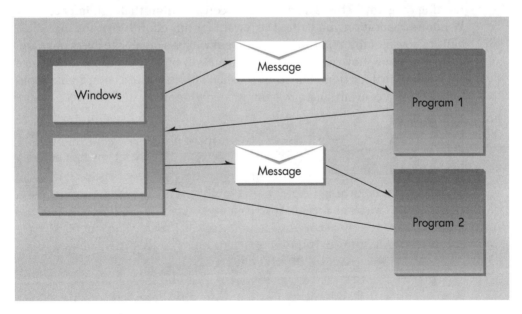

Figure 1-7 Two Application Programs Receiving Messages

programs can also exchange data with each other by sending messages. This is called "Dynamic Data Exchange," or DDE.

The office analogy points out the importance of writing Windows programs correctly. You can write a Windows program that includes CPU instructions that directly access the computer's hardware, takes over the entire screen, keeps other programs from running, and generally behaves like a wild dog. A poorly written Windows program can act like a very slow worker in an otherwise efficient office—the other workers cannot get any work done while they wait for the slow worker to finish his or her task. Generally speaking, Windows does not stop the programmer from doing things wrong. It is up to the programmer to write a well-behaved program that will coexist with other running programs in memory.

This all sounds intimidating. You may be thinking, "If I write my program wrong, I could make all the other programs running under Windows fail." This is basically true, and every Windows programmer has the responsibility of writing "well-behaved" programs. However, writing well-behaved Windows programs is not difficult, particularly when using the Microsoft Foundation Classes. We will see in the next chapter that a program with fewer than 30 lines of code can be a perfectly acceptable and well-mannered Windows program. This book will guide you through the process of designing programs that will coexist with any other Windows application.

The bottom line is: Windows applications are written to coexist with other running programs. This is a basic design consideration that will impact every Windows application you write. The reward for this effort is that the incredible built-in power of the Windows environment will be available to every program. Once you know how to use Windows, you will be able to create impressive applications in a fraction of the time it would take to create a comparable application using a conventional programming environment, such as DOS.

 Windows NT has several advanced features for controlling program execution that do not exist in Windows 3.1. Windows NT will interrupt a running application if it attempts to "hog" the entire system, allowing the user to gracefully terminate the errant program. Windows NT also has the ability to split execution of a program into pieces, called "threads" of execution. A computer with more than one CPU can route different "threads" to different CPU chips so that the computer can literally do more than one thing at one time.

The MFC classes were designed for compatibility between Windows 3.1 and Windows NT and, therefore, do not support the unique programming

continued on next page

continued from previous page

features of Windows NT. However, many of the advantages of Windows NT (such as the ability to interrupt an errant program) are built into Windows NT and require no special effort on the part of the programmer. The vast majority of applications can be created without any need to use multithreaded execution and can use the MFC classes without modification.

THE STRUCTURE OF WINDOWS PROGRAMS

You have seen how a Windows program behaves and what shows up on the screen. Now let's look at the parts that make up a Windows program, and why compiling a Windows program has different requirements and results than compiling a DOS program.

Windows programs basically do two things:

▶ Initial activities when the program is first loaded into memory. These activities consist of creating the program's own window and any startup chores, such as setting aside some memory space.

▶ Processing messages from Windows.

The key item in the first step is creating the program's window, which is the piece of the screen that the program will control. Application programs only write inside their own window, not in other program windows, or on the background of the screen. Restricting output to the program's window is one of the keys to having several programs coexist on the same screen. Program windows are always rectangular and will contain various elements, such as menus and captions, depending on what the program does. Figure 1-8 shows a typical program window, with the elements labeled.

Windows uses a standard set of names to describe the various parts of a program's window area. The *client area* of the window is the central portion in which the program can draw graphics and text. If a program tries to write outside of the client area, nothing shows up on the screen. This is how Windows keeps programs from interfering with each other on the screen. If the window has a thick border (like the border in Figure 1-8), the window size can be changed by positioning the mouse cursor over a corner, depressing the left mouse button, dragging the corner to a new location, and releasing the mouse button. Changing the window's size changes the size of the client area. If the client area is increased in size, the program will be able to write on all of the area, but not outside of the client area.

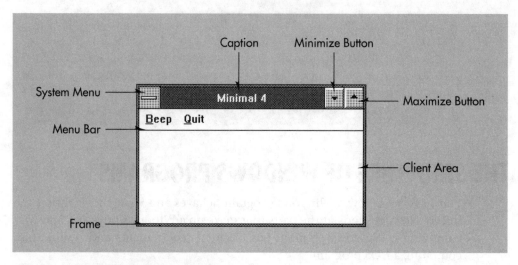

Figure 1-8 Program Window Elements

Code and Resources

Most programmers think of a program as a series of instructions that the computer executes. Actually, programs consist of both instructions and static data. Static data is any portion of the program that is not executed as a machine instruction, and which does not change as the program executes. Examples of static data are character strings for messages to the user, menu definitions, and character data to create fonts.

Static data is different from dynamic data. Dynamic data changes as the program runs. Usually dynamic data is stored in separate files, and is the data that the program reads and writes. For example, Microsoft Excel stores the (dynamic) worksheet data in .XLS spreadsheet files, but has static data defining its menu structure as part of the Excel program.

Resource Data

The designers of Windows wisely decided that static data should be handled separately from the program code. The Windows term for static data is "resource data," or just "resources." Resource data can include any of the items listed in Table 1-1. By separating static data from the program code, the creators of Windows were able to use a standard C++ compiler to create the code portion of the finished Windows program, and only had to write a "resource compiler" to create the specialized resources that Windows programs use. Separating the code from the resource data has other advantages in reducing memory demands

Data Type	Meaning
Accelerators	Definition of keyboard shortcuts for executing menu items, or other commands using the keyboard instead of the mouse.
Bitmaps	Picture data defining larger images. Bitmaps can be used to display many types of images in a program, including graphical menu items (for selecting pens, brushes, etc.), pictorial information in the program's client area, etc.
Cursors	Picture (bitmap) data defining the shapes of mouse cursor shape.
Dialog box definitions	Defines the layout of dialog boxes. Dialog boxes are small windows that a program "pops up" to display information, or to ask for specific input. A typical example is a dialog box to request the user to type a word before starting a search operation in a word processor.
Fonts	Data defining the size and style of characters.
Icons	Picture (bitmap) data defining small images. Icons are most often used for displaying a small image when the program is minimized.
Menu	Defines the menu structure for the program. This includes the top menu bar (shown in Figure 1-8) and all drop-down menus.
String tables	Tables of character strings. They are used for messages and other static character data used within the program.
User-defined resources	Any static data that the programmer may need in the application, such as tables of numbers.

Table 1-1 Resource Data Types

and making programs more portable. It also means that a programmer can work on the program's logic, while a designer works on how the program looks.

Program Instances

Windows allows you to run more than one copy of a program at a time. This is handy for cutting and pasting between two copies of Notepad, or when running more than one terminal session with a terminal emulator program. Each running copy of a program is called a "program instance." There are a few programs that allow only one instance to be run at a time, but most Windows applications allow any number of instances.

An interesting memory optimization trick that Windows 3.1 performs is to share a single copy of the program's code between all running instances. For example, if you get three instances of Notepad running, there will only be one copy of Notepad's code in memory. All three instances share the same code, but they will have separate memory areas to hold the text data being edited. The difference between the handling of the code and data is logical, as each instance of Notepad will be able to edit a different file, so the data must be unique to each instance. The program logic to edit the files is the same for every instance, so there is no reason a single copy of Notepad's code cannot be shared.

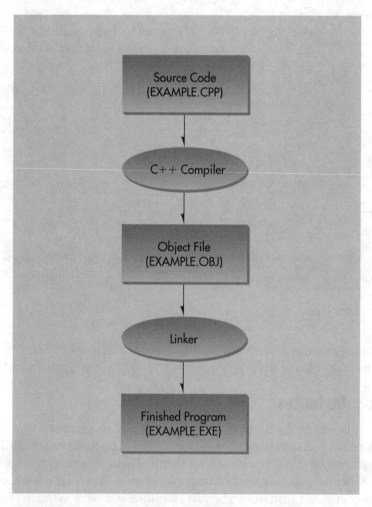

Figure 1-9 Steps in Creating a DOS Program

 Although you can run multiple copies of the same program under Windows NT, each instance is loaded separately into memory and has its own separate memory areas. Windows NT uses this approach to provide more protection for errant programs that may attempt to write to other programs' areas of memory.

Compiling a Windows Program Versus a DOS Program

Because Windows programs store resource data in separate files, the process of putting together a complete Windows program is a little more involved than compiling a DOS program. Figure 1-9 shows how a C++ program written to run under DOS is compiled and linked to create a finished program. The C++ compiler converts the source code file into an object file. A linker converts the object file into the finished executable program. This two-step link/compile process is used so that more than one source code (.CPP) file can be used to create a large finished program. The source code files can be separately compiled, and then linked together by the linker. If a change is made to just one of the source code files, only that one file must be compiled and then linked to the other object files to create the new executable program. This method saves a lot of time during the development of large programs.

Figure 1-10 shows a flow diagram for the creation of a Windows program. The compilation of the source code files to make object files is the same in both DOS and Windows. In creating a Windows program, the linker gets some additional information from a small file called the "module definition file," with the file name extension ".DEF." This file tells the linker how to assemble the program. We will examine the module definition file later in this chapter. The linker combines the module definition file information and the object files to make an unfinished .EXE file. The unfinished .EXE file lacks the resource data.

The biggest difference in compiling Windows programs as opposed to DOS programs is in the compilation of the resource data. The resource data is compiled by the resource compiler to make a resource data file with the extension ".RES." The resource data is added to the unfinished .EXE file to create the finished executable program. The resource data is basically stuck onto the end of the program's code and becomes part of the program file. In addition to adding the resource data, the resource compiler writes the Windows version number into the program file. This version data is how Windows tells whether a program was compiled for the 2.0 version of Windows or under a more recent version. If you try to

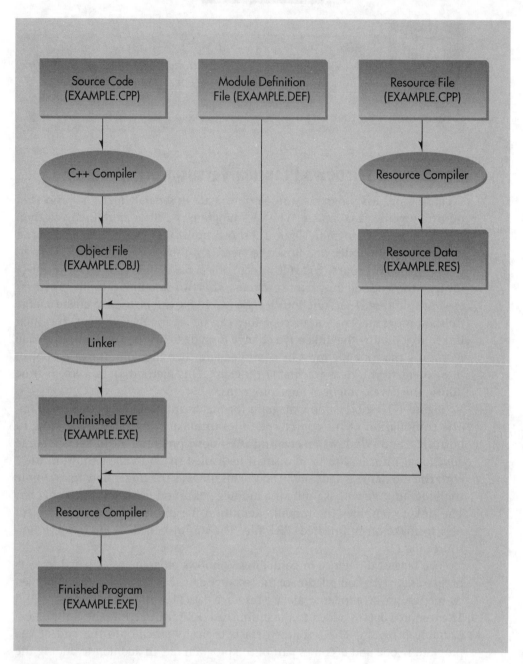

Figure 1-10 Steps in Creating a Windows Program

run a Windows 2.0 program under Windows 3.0 or 3.1, you will get a warning message telling you that the program needs to be updated.

WINDOWS MEMORY MANAGEMENT

Computer memory is like money—you can never have too much. No matter how much memory you install on your computer, sooner or later you will run out. Windows goes to a lot of trouble to make the best possible use of whatever amount of memory is installed. For the most part, these memory management functions are automatic. However, as a programmer you will need to understand the basics of what Windows is doing so that you can properly design the program.

The first thing you need to know about Windows memory management is that almost everything in memory can be moved. Windows moves objects (code and data) automatically to make room for new programs and data. To understand why this is necessary, consider the example in Figure 1-11. To begin with, there are three programs loaded into memory. If the user stops (terminates) Program 2, its block of memory is free for use. The total free memory on the system ends up being fragmented into two sections. If the user decides to load another large program, the largest available single block of memory may not be big enough. To

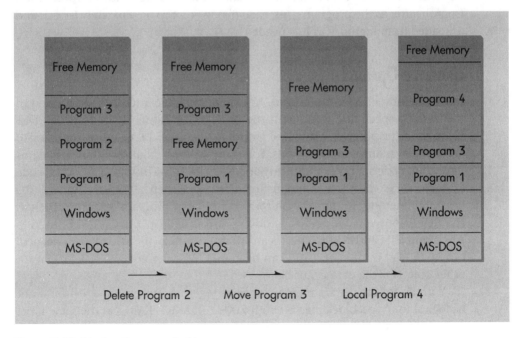

Figure 1-11 Moving Programs in Memory

make room for Program 4, Windows moves Program 3 down in memory. This makes a larger section of memory available for Program 4 to load.

Memory shifts, as shown in Figure 1-11, happen all of the time when you run Windows application programs. This is the reason that programs take longer to start running if you already have several other Windows applications running. Windows must make room for the next program, which frequently involves shifting things around in memory.

For simplicity, Figure 1-11 shows the programs as single big blocks. In reality, Windows handles program files in a much more sophisticated manner. If you compile a big Windows program consisting of many C++ program files, each of the C++ program files ends up turned into a separate piece of the final program, called a "segment." Windows can load and remove each segment of a program to and from memory separately. If you have five C++ program files, there will be five program segments. At any one time, Windows may have between one and five of these segments loaded in memory. If a function is called in a segment that is not already loaded, Windows will automatically load the segment before it tries to execute the function.

Windows manages data with a similar degree of sophistication. Each piece of data in the program's resource data will be separately managed. For example, if you define a series of small windows (called "dialog boxes") to get information from the user as the program runs, each dialog box can be separately loaded and unloaded from memory as it is needed.

Memory Options

As a programmer, you can control how program code and data is managed in memory by specifying options in the program's module definition file (.DEF file) and in the program's resource script file (.RC file). Table 1-2 shows some of the memory management options. For example, most small Windows programs have their code set up as PRELOAD and MOVEABLE. This loads all of the code into memory when the program first starts, but then allows the code to be moved in memory to make room for other objects. Program resources, such as the definitions for dialog box windows, are usually LOADONCALL, MOVEABLE, and DISCARDABLE. This means that the data is not loaded until needed, can be moved in memory, and can be erased from memory to make room for other objects if the data is not being used.

You cannot use certain memory options together. For example, it would not be logical to have a block marked both FIXED and MOVEABLE at the same time. To be DISCARDABLE, a block must also be marked as MOVEABLE. DISCARDABLE is the ultimate form of MOVEABLE—moving the block right out of memory. This

Option	Meaning
PRELOAD	The code or data is loaded into memory when the program first starts.
LOADONCALL	The code or data is not loaded into memory until it is needed.
MOVEABLE	The code or data can be moved in memory. This is the most common option.
FIXED	The code or memory remains at a fixed address in memory. This restricts Windows' ability to manage memory, so the FIXED option is used only in rare situations, such as interrupt driven interfaces with hardware devices.
DISCARDABLE	The code or memory can be temporarily removed from memory to make room for other objects. The code or data will then be reloaded if it is needed.
MULTIPLE	Applies only to program data. MULTIPLE means that if the same program is started several times (several instances), each will have a different set of data.
SINGLE	Applies only to program data. SINGLE means that all instances share the same data.

Table 1-2 Memory Management Options in Windows

means that the block will have to be reloaded if that portion of the program is again needed. This takes a little time, but gives Windows the maximum flexibility to optimize memory. DISCARDABLE blocks are not removed from memory unless simply moving blocks does not make enough room. FIXED memory blocks are to be avoided. A few FIXED blocks scattered about in memory will make it impossible for Windows to properly optimize memory.

One final bit of optimization that Windows does is possible only in "enhanced" mode. Windows starts up in enhanced mode automatically if you are running on an 80386 or 80486 based computer. With these advanced CPU chips, Windows is capable of using the hard disk to store data and code if Windows runs out of RAM memory room. This is called "virtual memory management." All of this is done automatically by Windows. If you are running a lot of applications at the same time, you may notice the hard disk running periodically. That is Windows reading and writing memory blocks to and from the hard disk.

Windows NT can run only on 80386 and higher CPU chips and, therefore, can always take advantage of the virtual memory managment features of these advanced CPUs. Windows NT will automatically copy areas of memory off to the computer's hard disk if Windows NT runs short of RAM.

Stacks and Heaps

If you have been programming with the C++ or C languages, you are probably familiar with automatic, static, and global variables. Listing 1-1 shows a simple program with all three types of variables defined. The function **CountByTen()** just adds 10 to the static variable *nKeep* 10 times. This is trivial, but it does demonstrate the three variable types. Automatic variables (*n* in Listing 1-1) are defined inside a function, but only retain their values while the function's code is being executed. If you call the function a second time, the automatic variable's last value is forgotten. Static variables (*nKeep* and *cBuf[]* in Listing 1-1) are defined inside of a function, but with the prefix "static." These values are stored in a permanent memory block and are not forgotten each time the function exits. Global variables are defined outside of any function (*nGlobal* in Listing 1-1). Global variables are known to every function in the program and retain their values as functions in the program execute.

You can use automatic, static, and global variables in a Windows program. Physically, automatic variables are stored in a memory area called the "stack." Global and static variables are stored in a memory area called the "local heap." Each Windows program has its own memory area to hold its stack and local heap. The combined size of the stack and local heap is limited to 64K because they are physically stored in a single memory "segment." This 64K limit is due to the limitations of the 80286 processors, with a maximum segment size of 64K. The 80386 and 80486 processors do not have this limit, but Windows 3.1 maintains compatibility with the older CPUs (Windows NT does not have these limitations, so segments can be far larger than 64K).

Figure 1-12 shows how a Windows program exists in memory. The program's code is in one or more segments. A separate segment holds the stack and local heap. The stack is used by every function that uses automatic variables. Each time a new function executes, the stack holds that function's automatic variables,

Listing 1-1 Automatic, Static, and Global Variables

```
int nGlobal = 10 ;          // a global variable

int CountByTen ()           // start a function
{
    int    n ;              // an automatic variable
    static int nKeep ;      // a static integer
    static char   cBuf [] = "This is static text.";

    for (n = 0 ; n < nGlobal ; n++)
        nKeep += 10 ;
    return (nKeep) ;
}
```

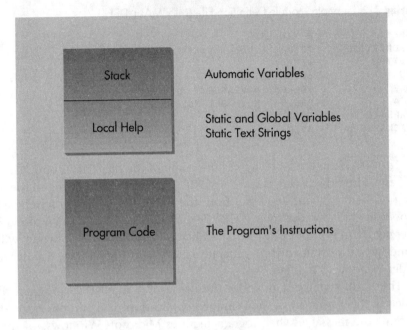

Figure 1-12 A Windows Program in Memory

writing over the values from the previous function. In contrast, the static and global variables in the local heap occupy fixed positions within the segment. These variables do not get written over when a new function is called.

Windows programs can also request blocks of memory as the program runs. This is similar to a C program running under DOS calling the **alloc()** function, or a C++ program using the *new* operator. Windows programs call similar functions to request memory blocks either in the local memory heap, or outside of the local heap in main memory called the "global heap." You can request blocks that are fixed, moveable, or discardable as the program runs. Most of the time, Windows applications set aside memory blocks that are moveable, so that Windows can continue to optimize memory space by moving things around. We will discuss allocating memory blocks in Chapter 12, *Managing Memory*.

An Example Module Definition File

Listing 1-2 shows a typical module definition file for a Windows program. The module definition file tells the linker how to organize the program's use of memory. There is no equivalent to a module definition file when compiling a DOS program. The data in the module definition file controls memory options that are specific to Windows.

Listing 1-2 Example Module Definition File (MINIMAL1.DEF)

```
NAME          MINIMAL1
DESCRIPTION   'Basic Windows application'
EXETYPE       WINDOWS
STUB          'WINSTUB.EXE'
CODE          PRELOAD MOVEABLE
DATA          PRELOAD MOVEABLE MULTIPLE
HEAPSIZE      1024
STACKSIZE     5120
```

The NAME statement just gives the name of the file. This is optional, but it makes reading the listing easier. DESCRIPTION adds a text string to the beginning of the file (about 760 bytes from the start). This is handy for embedding copyright notices in the code. EXETYPE marks the program as a Windows 3.0 or later program. Without EXETYPE specified as WINDOWS, the program will be a Windows 2.0 version and will generate a nasty warning message if a user runs it under Windows 3.0 or later.

The STUB statement provides the name of a small DOS program that is added to the beginning of the Windows application. The purpose of the stub is to print the message "The program requires Microsoft Windows." if the user attempts to run the program from DOS. The WINSTUB.EXE program is provided with the Microsoft C++ compiler. (The STUB and EXETYPE statements are not necessary when compiling Windows NT programs and will be ignored if present. These statements can be included in the .DEF file to allow the same .DEF file to be used for both Windows and Windows NT, which is the case for all of the examples in this book.)

The CODE statement controls the memory options for the program's instructions. In MINIMAL1.DEF the code will be loaded into memory when the program starts, and will be moveable in memory. The program's data segment will also be preloaded into memory and will be moveable. If more than one instance of the program is started at the same time, each copy will have its own data (MULTIPLE statement). The module definition file also sets the size of the program's data segment with the HEAPSIZE and STACKSIZE statements. The minimum stack size for a windows program is 5,120 bytes. The HEAPSIZE statement sets the starting size of the local memory heap. The heap will be expanded automatically if the program stores more data in the local memory area as it runs.

SUMMARY

Windows applications are designed to allow many running programs to coexist in memory at the same time. Windows manages switching between applications by sending message data to the program when the program needs to do something. Each Windows program waits to receive a message, acts on messages it receives, and returns control to Windows as soon as possible.

Windows programs are compiled differently than DOS programs. Both DOS and Windows programs use a C++ compiler to convert the source code files into object files. In addition to the source code files, Windows programs have separate resource files that contain static data, such as menus and bitmaps. Resource data is compiled by a separate compiler, called the resource compiler. The compiled resource data is combined with the object files to create the finished Windows program.

Each program will have access to a data segment containing both the stack and the local heap. Windows uses the stack for automatic variables and the local heap to store static and global variables. Windows can move program code and data in memory to make room for new objects. The program's module definition file (.DEF file) sets the memory options used for code and data.

QUESTIONS

1. What is the minimum number of files needed to create a DOS program? How many for a Windows program? Count only the files the programmer writes, not the output of compilers and linkers.

2. What does a Windows program do when it is done processing a message?

3. Draw a picture of a program window. Show the location of the client area, frame, caption, system menu, menu bar, minimize button, and maximize button.

4. If a Windows program's client area is 100 pixels wide and 200 pixels high, and the program outputs graphics commands to draw a 200 by 300 rectangle, what size and shape ends up drawn? Where does the rest of the rectangle show up?

5. The DISCARDABLE memory option is always used with the _____ option.

6. If more than one copy of a Windows application is running, each is said to be a separate _____ of the application.

7. The _____ combines the object files to build an unfinished .EXE program file.

8. When more than one application is running in the same Windows session, two or more applications can process separate messages at the same time. (True/False)

9. Each application will have its own local data segment containing
   a. the application's stack
   b. the application's local data heap
   c. resource data
   d. a and b

ANSWERS TO QUESTIONS

1. A DOS program needs only one program file, a C++ source code file. A Windows program needs a minimum of *two* files: a C++ source code file and a .DEF module definition file. Almost all Windows programs also have an .RC resource script file, containing resource data, so *three* is also a correct answer.

2. Windows programs return control to Windows when they have processed a message.

3. The picture should look roughly as shown in Figure 1-13.

4. Only the portion of the rectangle within the client area will be visible. The portions of the rectangle that extend beyond the client area do not show up at all.

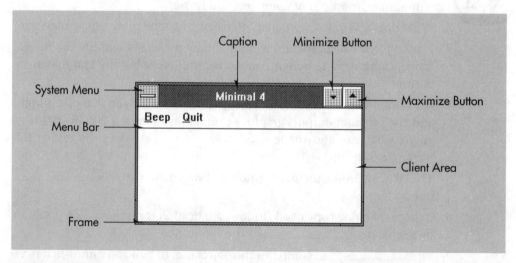

Figure 1-13 Elements of a Window

5. MOVEABLE.

6. instance.

7. linker.

8. False. At any one time, only one application can have code that is being executed by the computer's CPU.

9. d.

Chapter **2**

Using the MFC Classes

Before you can start creating Windows programs using the MFC classes, you need to be familiar with how C++ classes are used to collect functions and data into easy-to-use objects. This chapter starts out with a brief review of C++ classes, and then examines the predefined MFC classes that are provided with the Microsoft C++ 7.0 compiler. The MFC classes encapsulate essentially all of the functions needed to build Windows applications programs. By using the MFC classes, you get immediate access to thousands of lines of programming code written by Microsoft's programmers. The classes make it possible to create working Windows applications with a minimum of effort, as much of the underlying workings are hidden away within the class definitions. Later in the book we will explore extending the MFC classes by writing our own classes.

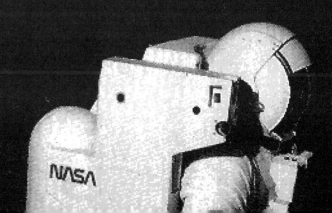

This chapter also discusses how to compile and run a simple example program. Using the MFC classes requires a few special settings for the C++ compiler to run properly. The Programmer's Workbench will be used in the examples, as this tool simplifies creating a Windows program.

Size limitations make it impossible for this book to provide a complete introduction to the C++ language. Check the bibliography for additional references if you need more help with C++ syntax. If you are already an experienced C++ programmer, skip ahead to the section titled *Applying C++ to Windows* in this chapter.

Concepts covered: C++ classes, derived classes, Microsoft Foundation Classes, application object, window object, project files, compiler setup, external functions, unresolved externals, DOS environment variables, AUTOEXEC.BAT.

Key words covered: struct, class, public, private.

Functions covered: CWinApp::InitInstance(), CFrameWindow::Create().

Classes covered: CWinApp, CFrameWindow.

A REVIEW OF C++ CLASSES

Although C++ is a separate computer language, C++ has its roots in the C language. Among the several differences between the C and C++ languages, the most fundamental change is the introduction of *classes*. Classes are an extension of C language structures. In C (and C++) you can collect a group of different variable types in a structure. Listing 2-1 shows a typical structure definition, creating a structure to hold the dimensions of a rectangle. The rectangle is described in terms of the location of the upper left and lower right corners.

Structures make it possible to treat the data defining an object as a single data entity. For example, you can make one rectangle equal to another with an assignment statement (=), or access individual members of the structure using the period operator. Listing 2-2 shows examples.

Listing 2-1 An Example C Language Structure

```
struct RECT
{
    int top ;
    int left ;
    int bottom ;
    int right ;
} ;
```

Listing 2-2 Using a Structure

```
struct RECT r1, r2 ;        /* declare two RECT objects */

r1.top = 10 ;               /* assign values to each member of r1 */
r1.left = 20 ;
r1.bottom = 100 ;
r1.right = 67 ;

r2 = r1 ;                   /* assign r2 equal in all values to r1 */
```

Classes are similar to structures, but more flexible. In C++ you can collect not only data, but functions in a class. For example, Listing 2-3 shows a class definition for a class called **CRect**, which includes not only the integer data defining the rectangle, but also two functions that return information about the rectangle. Two slant characters together begin a comment in C++. The comment extends to the end of the line. C++ also allows the traditional /* */ comments introduced with the C language.

The *private* and *public* key words control how the data and functions in the class can be accessed. Public members (functions and data) can be accessed by parts of the program outside of the class definition. Private members can only be used within the class. In Listing 2-3, the integers *top*, *left*, *bottom*, and *right* are private to the class. However, the **Initialize()**, **GetWidth()** and **GetHeight()** functions can be used to indirectly access this data. Figure 2-1 shows a conceptual model of a class, with both public and private members. Classes default to having all of their member functions and data *private*, so you could skip the *private* key word. Normally, you will show both the *public* and *private* key words in the class definition for clarity. (C++ also supports an intermediate level of protection called *protected*, but this aspect of C++ is not used in the examples in this book.)

Listing 2-3 An Example C++ Language Class

```
class CRect
{
private:         // the private members of the class are defined here
    int top ;
    int left ;
    int bottom ;
    int right ;
public:          // public members of the class are defined here
    void Initialize (int tp, int lf, int bot, int rt)
        {top = tp ; left = lf ; bottom = bot ; right = rt ; }
    int GetWidth () {return (right - left) ; }
    int GetHeight () {return (bottom - top) ; }
} ;
```

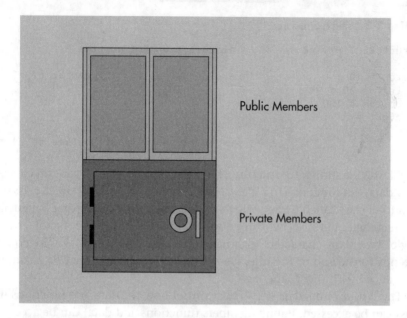

Public Members

Private Members

Figure 2-1 Public and Private Members of a Class

Accessing functions and data in a C++ class is done exactly the same way as with data accessed in a C language structure. Listing 2-4 shows an example that creates a **CRect** object, initializes it, and determines the width of the rectangle. Note that the period operator is used to link an object to a function name, just as it links an object to a data member in both structures and classes.

Listing 2-4 Using a C++ Class

```
CRect r ;                    // declare a CRect object
int width ;                  // and an integer

r.Initialize (2, 5, 100, 62) ;  // call Initialize() function
width = r.GetWidth () ;      // call GetWidth() function
```

Implications of C++ Classes

Although it may appear that classes are a simple extension to the C language, having classes with private and public members has a profound impact on the way programs are created using C++. This is particularly true when several programmers are involved with different portions of a program. A common problem with large C projects is that different programmers can write code that changes the same global variable. For example, a global variable might be used to store the current record number in a database. If different parts of the program independently change the current record number, the database will behave unpredictably, and the program will probably crash.

C++ allows different portions of the program to be isolated by collecting related functions and data in classes. Each programmer creates separate classes that manage data and provide public access functions (like **GetWidth()** and **GetHeight()** earlier). Only the public members of the classes are available for use by other parts of the program outside of the class definition. The private portions of each class are only accessible within the class definitions. Classes with controlled public access replace the need for global variables for shared data. Instead, each class manages and protects its own data. Thus, the record number of a database class would be a private data member, and could not be changed directly from outside of the class.

Separating parts of the program into well-protected classes is the heart of "object oriented" programming. The collection of related data and functions into a single "object" changes the way programmers do their work. The goal becomes writing objects that can be reused without modification. Objects can be used with much more confidence than regular C functions, as the creator of the object can "hide" critical portions of the code in private functions and data, and provide safe access functions for use of the object.

Constructors and Destructors

It is frequently useful to perform some automatic operations when a class object is first created. For example, our lowly **CRect** class could be improved by initializing the private data elements to some predefined values. Listing 2-5 shows an improved **CRect** class, which automatically initializes the data elements to zero values when the class is created.

The trick to getting a function to be executed when an object is first created is to give the function the same name as the class itself. In C++, a function with the same name as the class is called a "constructor." This name is a little misleading, as the constructor function does not *construct* the object. The constructor function simply gets executed when an object is first created. For example, Listing 2-6 shows the creation of a **CRect** object. Because the constructor function sets all of the private data members to zero, the initial width and height of the rectangle are sure to be zero.

Without the constructor function's initialization, the initial values for the **CRect** object would have been whatever values happened to be in the memory area where the compiler set aside a few bytes to hold the **CRect** object. Having the values automatically set to zero when the object is created is a significant

Listing 2-5 Adding a Constructor to CRect

```
class CRect          // improved CRect class with a constructor
{
private:             // private members of the class are defined here
    int top ;
    int left ;
    int bottom ;
    int right ;
public:              // public members of the class are defined here
    void CRect ()    // constructor function - same name as class
        {top = left = bottom = right = 0 ; }
    void Initialize (int tp, int lf, int bot, int rt )
        {top = tp ; left = lf ; bottom = bot ; right = rt ; }
    int GetWidth () {return (right - left) ; }
    int GetHeight () {return (bottom - top) ; }
} ;
```

Listing 2-6 Using the Improved CRect Class

```
CRect r ;                      // create a CRect object
int width = r.GetWidth () ;    // width will equal zero
```

improvement to the **CRect** class. You can imagine that in more complex classes the constructor can be used to do a lot of processing when an object is first created. All of the processing can then be performed by just creating an object of the class and letting the constructor do its work. This is one of the keys to the Foundation Classes hiding much of the complexity of Windows in well-designed classes. The constructor functions automatically take care of a wide variety of tasks required by Windows.

Although we will not use them now, it is worth noting that C++ also allows you to add a function to the class that is automatically run just before an object created from the class is destroyed. These functions are called "destructors." Again the name is misleading, as destructors do not *destroy* the object. Destructor functions are just a handy place to do any cleanup activities before the object is removed from memory. In C++, destructor functions are created by naming the function the same name as the class, but preceded by a tilde character (~). We will look at destructors later in the book.

Class Inheritance

Another important part of the C++ language is the ability to use existing classes as the basis for creating new ones. The new class is said to "inherit" from the old class. For example, a new class called **cColorRect** could be defined that inherits the properties of the **CRect** class, and then adds new functions and data.

Listing 2-7 shows an example that defines a new class **cColorRect**, which is derived from **CRect**. The new class adds the *color* private member to store the color of the rectangle. Three new functions are also declared: **SetColor()** to change the *color* value, **GetColor()** to determine the *color* value, and **FillRect()** to paint the interior of the rectangle. For simplicity the **FillRect()** implementation is not shown here, and only the declaration of the function is included in the **cColorRect** class definition.

The **cColorRect** class in Listing 2-7 will automatically have access to the public members of the **CRect** class, such as **GetWidth()** and **GetHeight()**. This saves the programmer creating the **cColorRect** class from needing to duplicate the functionality of the **CRect** class. Well-designed base classes can be reused many times for different purposes, with large savings in programming time. Note that the **cColorRect** class inherits only the public members of the **CRect** class, which is shown by the *public* declaration in the top line of Listing 2-7. (It is possible to derive classes that have access to both the public and private members of a class. However, these techniques are generally reserved for advanced uses of C++, and not used in any of the examples in this book. See the bibliography for references on the C++ language if you are interested in learning more about class inheritance.

When one class is created from another, the original class is called the "base class" and the new class the "derived class." Figure 2-2 shows the relationship. The derived class can use the public members of the base class, but it *cannot* directly access the private members. This maintains the integrity of the private members of the base class. The public members of both the base and derived classes can be accessed from outside of the class definitions. In some cases, the derived class may create a function that has the same name as a function in the base class. In this case, the derived class function is said to "override" the base class function. If the function names are different, both the base class and derived class public functions are available for use outside of the class definitions.

Listing 2-7 Inheritance of Class Members

```
class cColorRect : public CRect    // class cColorRect inherits public
{                                   // data and functions from CRect
private:
    DWORD   color ;                 // and adds a new data member
public:                             // and new public functions
    DWORD GetColor () {return color ; }
    void SetColor (DWORD InputColor) { color = InputColor ; }
    void FillRect () ;
} ;
```

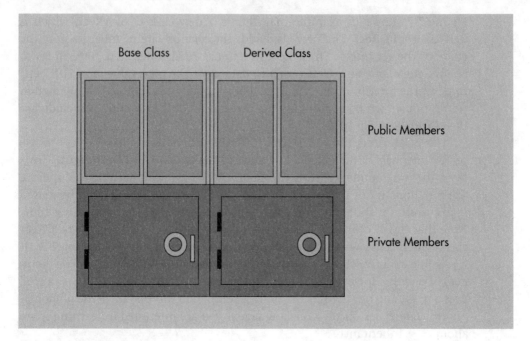

Figure 2-2 Base and Derived Classes

You can imagine from Figure 2-2 that it is possible to keep deriving new classes based on other derived classes. Gradually adding new functionality by deriving new classes from old ones is the key to efficient programming under C++. The MFC classes provide several excellent examples of class hierarchies involving as many as five levels of class derivations. We will look at the full derivation of the most commonly used MFC classes in the next chapter.

APPLYING C++ TO WINDOWS

The Microsoft Foundation Classes take full advantage of the C++ language to organize related data and functions. As you will discover in the course of the book, there are many different parts of the Windows application programming interface (API), resulting in a number of different classes. For now we will focus on the classes needed to create a simple working Windows application, such as the MINIMAL1 program shown in Figure 2-3.

Although MINIMAL1 does not do anything useful, it does have a resizable main window, which can be minimized and maximized. MINIMAL1 also has a system menu button at the upper left corner, which displays the standard

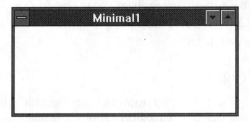

Figure 2-3 The MINIMAL1 Program

Windows system menu when clicked with the mouse. Selecting the "Close" item from the system menu is the easiest way to stop the MINIMAL1 program.

It is helpful to think about the MINIMAL1 program as two separate but connected objects. The visible window with the caption "MINIMAL1" is one object. The visible window is the part of the program that the user sees. However, underneath the surface are the inner workings of the program. The inner workings contain the programming instructions to minimize the MINIMAL1 window when the minimize button is pressed, to change the title area color when another program's window is selected, and so on. This hidden part that does all of the work is called the "application." Figure 2-4 shows a conceptual model of the two parts of a complete Windows application program.

The MFC classes deal with the visible program window and the hidden internal application as two separate classes. Fortunately for us, Microsoft has already

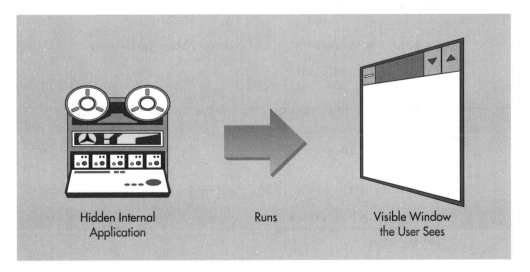

Hidden Internal
Application

Runs

Visible Window
the User Sees

Figure 2-4 The Two Parts of a Windows Application

written fairly complete class definitions for each of these objects. To create a simple program like MINIMAL1 (Figure 2-3) simply requires that we take advantage of these existing classes in our program.

First Look at an MFC Program

You are now ready to look at your first programming example of a Windows application created in C++ using the MFC Classes. Listing 2-8 shows the entire C++ source code needed to create the MINIMAL1 program (shown in Figure 2-3). Each part of the listing will be explained in a moment, but for now just admire the brevity of the example. Remember that this program creates an application with a resizable window that can be minimized and restored, moved on the screen, and has a working system menu (top left button).

Even if you are an experienced C++ programmer, the MINIMAL1.CPP program listing may look a bit unfamiliar. The reason is that MINIMAL1.CPP makes heavy use of inheritance from the MFC classes. The next section explains

Listing 2-8 The MINIMAL1.CPP C++ Program

```
// minimal1.cpp                  // minimal windows application

#include <afxwin.h>              // class library header file

class CMainWindow : public CFrameWnd    // derive main window class
{
public:
    CMainWindow () ;             // declare a constructor
} ;

CMainWindow::CMainWindow ()      // constructor for window
{
    Create (NULL, "Minimal1") ;
}

class CTheApp : public CWinApp  // derive an application class
{
public:
    BOOL InitInstance () ;       // override default InitInstance()
} ;

BOOL CTheApp::InitInstance ()    // override default InitInstance()
{
    m_pMainWnd = new CMainWindow () ;       // create a main window
    m_pMainWnd->ShowWindow (m_nCmdShow) ;   // make it visible
    return TRUE ;
}

CTheApp theApp ;         // create one CTheApp object - runs program
```

how two new classes are derived from MFC classes and used to create MINI-MAL1. MINIMAL1 will then be tested by compiling and running the program.

The CFrameWnd Class

The Microsoft Foundation class for a main program window is called **CFrameWnd**. The "Frame" part of the name comes from the thick border that programs like MINIMAL1 use for resizing the window. The **CFrameWnd** class is defined in a header file called AFXWIN.H, which is supplied with the C++ 7.0 compiler. AFXWIN.H is a BIG header file, adding up to over 300K of data if you add up all of the files that AFXWIN.H includes. Most of the classes that we will be using in this book are defined in AFXWIN.H, and it is included at the top of every program that uses the MFC classes to create a Windows application.

The first step in creating the MINIMAL1 program is to derive a new window class from the **CFrameWnd** class. Listing 2-9 shows how this is done, starting with the inclusion of the AFXWIN.H header file. You can call the new derived class anything you like, but all of the main program windows in this book will be called "CMainWindow" for consistency. Remember that by deriving a class from **CFrameWnd**, all of the public functions defined in the **CFrameWnd** class are available to our new **CMainWindow** class. The only new function defined in our simple **CMainWindow** class is a constructor function. The **CMainWindow()** constructor function will be called when a **CMainWindow** object is created.

It appears in Listing 2-9 that the **CMainWindow** class is derived simply from the **CFrameWnd** MFC class. Actually, the **CFrameWnd** class is also a derived class, derived from the **CWnd** class, which contains most of the logic concerning windows. The full derivation of the classes used in MINIMAL1.CPP will be explained in the next chapter. For now, let's concentrate on the big picture.

You can write the definition for the **CMainWindow()** constructor function right in the class definition, as was shown earlier for the **CRect** class. However, the usual practice is to show all but very simple functions outside of the class definition. To do this you must tell the C++ compiler that the function you are defining

Listing 2-9 Deriving a Program Window Class

```
#include <afxwin.h>                          // class library header file

class CMainWindow : public CFrameWnd         // derive main window class
{
public:
    CMainWindow () ;                          // declare a constructor
} ;
```

belongs to the **CMainWindow** class. Listing 2-10 shows how this is done to define the **CMainWindow**() constructor. The double colon (called the "scope resolution operator" in C++) tells the compiler that the function on the right of the double colon is a part of the class named to the left of the double colon.

The **CMainWindow**() constructor just calls one function: **Create**(). **Create**() is a function that is defined as part of the **CFrameWnd** MFC class, so our new **CMainWindow** class gets access to the **CFrameWnd::Create**() function by inheritance. The **CFrameWnd::Create**() function creates the MINIMAL1 program's main window. The first parameter is set to NULL, specifying that we want to use standard properties for the window. These properties include a white color for the window interior and a standard arrow cursor shape when the mouse cursor is over the program's window area. Normally, these default values are just what you will want, but you can change the defaults (explained in Chapter 8, *Child and Pop-Up Windows*). The second parameter just specifies the title for the window and is set as the string "Minimal1."

The CWinApp Class

The only other class we need to derive is an application class to build the internal engine that will run the MINIMAL1 program. The foundation class that defines a Windows application is **CWinApp**, again defined in the AFXWIN.H header file. The **CWinApp** class is the real backbone of any application written using the Foundation Classes. **CWinApp** takes care of starting the application, processing messages from Windows, and performing all of the default activities for a program. The default activities do *not* include creating a program window, as program windows are defined in the **CFrameWindow** class that we just examined. To make the **CWinApp** class useful for the MINIMAL1 program, you will need to derive your own class from **CWinApp**, and use the derived class to initiate creating the program's main window.

Listing 2-11 shows how a new class called **CTheApp** is derived from the **CWinApp** Foundation Class. Again, you can call the new derived class anything you like, but the examples in this book stick with the name **CTheApp**. Only one public function is added to the **CTheApp** class, called **CWinApp::InitInstance**(). If you dig through the **CTheApp** definition in the AFXWIN.H header file, you will find that **CWinApp::InitInstance**() is defined in the **CWinApp** as a *virtual*

Listing 2-10 Constructor Definition for CMainWindow Class

```
CMainWindow::CMainWindow ()        // constructor for window
{
    Create (NULL, "Minimal1") ;
}
```

Listing 2-11 Deriving a New Class from CWinApp

```
class CTheApp : public CWinApp   // derive an application class
{
public:
    BOOL InitInstance () ;       // override default InitInstance()
} ;
```

function. This means that the **CWinApp** class is designed to have other classes derived from it, and expects that the derived classes will define their own **InitInstance()** functions. For all practical purposes, you must define your own **InitInstance()** function, as otherwise the application will not create a visible window that the user can see. The application would be loaded into memory when started, but you would have no way of interacting with it.

You may be wondering why the **InitInstance()** function is added to the **CTheApp** class, but no new constructor function is added as we did for the **CMainWindow** class. The reason is that the constructor function for **CWinApp** is complex, and does all sorts of things automatically for the benefit of programs like MINIMAL1. If you defined a constructor function for the **CTheApp** class, the new constructor would override the default constructor inherited from the **CTheApp** class, and you would lose all of the built-in operations. To get around this, the **CWinApp** default constructor is designed so that it always calls the virtual function **InitInstance()** when a class object is created (when the program is started). **InitInstance()** is, therefore, an ideal place to put the extra logic that you will need your program to perform when the application is first started.

Listing 2-12 shows the **InitInstance()** function definition for the **CTheApp** class. The only things that MINIMAL1 needs to do when the application is created is to create a main program window and make it visible on the screen. The **CMainWindow** class is already defined, so you can create a **CMainWindow** object with the C++ *new* operator. The returned value from the *new* operator is a pointer to the **CMainWindow** object in memory. This is saved in the variable *m_pMainWnd*, which was inherited from the **CWinApp** class. The prefix "m_" is used in the Foundation classes to label variables that

Listing 2-12 Defining an InitInstance() Function

```
BOOL CTheApp::InitInstance ()                // override default InitInstance()
{
    m_pMainWnd = new CMainWindow () ;        // create a main window
    m_pMainWnd->ShowWindow (m_nCmdShow) ;    // make it visible
    return TRUE ;
}
```

are defined in the class definitions. *m_pMainWnd* is defined in the **CWinApp** class, as all Windows applications will need to keep track of the main program window for the application.

After the new **CMainWindow** object is created with the *new* operator, the window must be made visible on the screen. This is done by calling the **CWnd::ShowWindow()** function. **CWnd::ShowWindow()** is passed an integer value *m_nCmdShow* that is defined in the **CWinApp** class. *m_nCmdShow* tells the **ShowWindow()** function whether to start the window minimized, maximized, or normally sized. The *m_nCmdShow* value is passed to the application from the Windows environment when the application is started. (You can change this value by using the Program Manager "File/Run" menu item to start an application.) The **CWinApp** class defines the *m_nCmdShow* value, so the **CTheApp** class inherits it. Finally, the **InitInstance()** function returns TRUE, signifying that everything went well.

You may be wondering why the Foundation Classes do not go ahead and include the code to create a main program window and make it visible. That would save us from adding these rather cryptic lines to the **CWinApp::InitInstance()** function. The problem is, you can name the main program class derived from **CFrameWindow** anything you like. In MINIMAL1, the main window class happens to be called **CMainWindow**, but you could call it **MyWindow** or **Sally**. The Foundation Classes have no way of knowing in advance what name you will use, so you are stuck with putting a few lines in an **InitInstance()** function for every program. This is not too much to ask, considering the thousands of lines of C++ code that were avoided by using the MFC classes.

With all of the classes defined, the MINIMAL1.CPP program can start. This turns out to be very simple. You simply create a **CTheApp** object, as shown in Listing 2-13. In this case, the object is called **theApp**, although you can name it anything you like. Creating the object results in the object's constructor function being called, which calls the **InitInstance()** function, which creates the main program window, and so on. The exact sequence of events that are initiated by creating a **CTheApp** object is discussed in the next section.

The last line of MINIMAL1.CPP, shown in Listing 2-13, is worth thinking about for a moment. By deriving new classes from the Foundation Classes, MINIMAL1 manages to encapsulate its entire existence into the **theApp** object. Hidden away behind the single line of code (Listing 2-13) are thousands of lines of coding in the MFC classes, plus the lines defined in MINIMAL1.CPP.

Listing 2-13 Starting the Application Running

```
CTheApp theApp ;        // create one CTheApp object - runs program
```

MINIMAL1.CPP Startup Sequence

There is so much built-in logic behind the classes in MINIMAL1.CPP that it is a bit difficult to follow the logic that gets the program running. Figure 2-5 shows the sequence of events that culminates in the program's window being created. The only statement that is directly called is the creation of the **theApp** object. Everything else happens as a consequence of this one function call.

Once the program window is visible, message processing is handled automatically by the default logic in the **CWinApp** and **CFrameWnd** base classes. As no messages are intercepted by MINIMAL1.CPP, all of the messages are passed to the default message processing logic. Somewhere deep in the definition of the **CFrameWnd** class is the call to the **DefWindowProc()** function, directly accessing the default logic for windows. The C++ classes do such a good

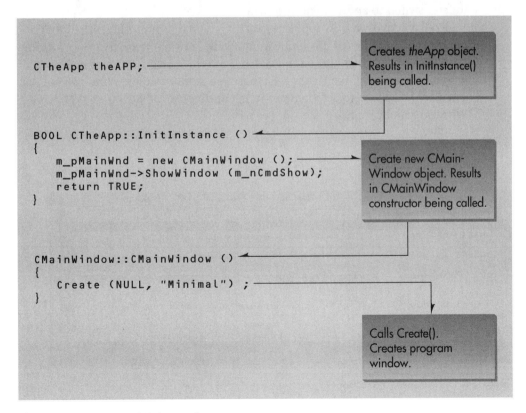

Figure 2-5 MINIMAL1.CPP Startup Sequence

job of encapsulating the window and application objects that you do not need to be concerned about where this action is taking place.

COMPILING MINIMAL1.CPP WITH PWB

Now for the acid test, creating and running the MINIMAL1.CPP example program. Microsoft provides an integrated editor/compiler with the C++ 7.0 package called the Programmer's Workbench (PWB). The PWB will be used in the examples, as this is the simplest way to compile Windows programs. If you have another editor that you prefer to use, you may want to review Appendix D, *Command Line Compilation*, which covers the use of the NMAKE utility which is also provided with the C++ 7.0 compiler. If you are compiling under Windows NT, review Appendix A, *Windows NT*, for specific directions. It is probably best to follow the first example or two using PWB and Windows 3.1 even if you plan to later switch to another editor or to Windows NT.

PWB is actually a DOS application. This is a bit disappointing, but it does not reduce the usefulness of the application. PWB is normally run in a DOS window from within Windows, although you can run it full screen. Either way, PWB will look approximately like Figure 2-6 when you start it. Under Windows 3.1 you can use the mouse to select menu items and edit text, just as if PWB were a Windows application.

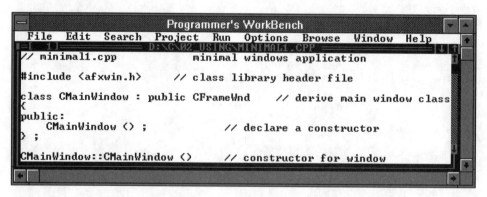

Figure 2-6 Programmer's Workbench

The first step is to create the MINIMAL1.CPP file, which was shown back in Listing 2-8. You can either type in the file using PWB or another editor or take advantage of the optional source code disks which include every file used in the example programs. In this discussion, it is assumed you are using the PWB and creating all of the files from scratch. Using PWB to create the first few examples wil help you to gain experience with the tools and the details of C++ syntax, even if you plan to use the source code disks later to save time.

If some other file is showing in the PWB screen, select the "File/Close" menu item to get rid of the old file, and then select "File/New" to create a blank editing area. Type in the MINIMAL1.CPP listing exactly as shown, and use the "File/Save As..." menu item to save the file in a convenient working directory.

Module Definition File

As mentioned in Chapter 1, Windows programs also require a module definition file. Listing 2-14 shows the MINIMAL1.DEF file for the MINIMAL1 program. Create this file using PWB, and save it in the same directory with MINIMAL1.CPP. These are the only two source code files needed to create the MINIMAL1 program, so you are now set to compile your first Foundation Class Windows application.

Project File

Although the PWB automates many aspects of creating a program, you still need to tell PWB what to do. This is done by creating a project file for the program. The project file keeps track of the names of all of the source code files and

Listing 2-14 MINIMAL1.DEF Module Definition File

```
NAME            minimal1
DESCRIPTION     'minimal1 C++ program'
EXETYPE         WINDOWS
STUB            'WINSTUB.EXE'
CODE            PRELOAD MOVEABLE
DATA            PRELOAD MOVEABLE MULTIPLE
HEAPSIZE        1024
STACKSIZE       5120
```

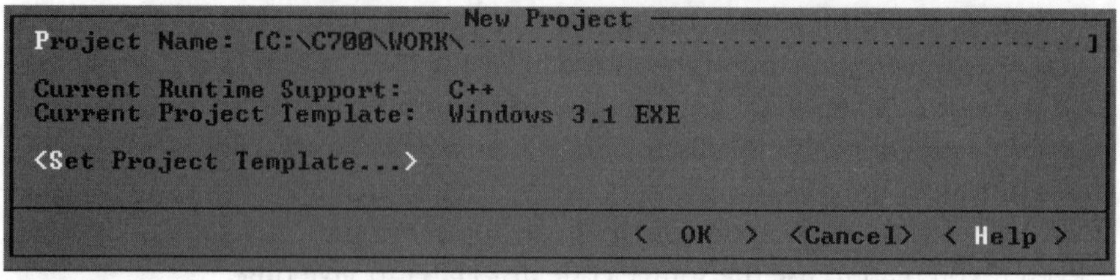

```
———————————————————— New Project ————————————————————
Project Name: [C:\C700\WORK\· · · · · · · · · · · · · · · · · · · · · · · · · · · · · · · · · · · · ]

Current Runtime Support:    C++
Current Project Template:   Windows 3.1 EXE

<Set Project Template...>

                                  <  OK  >  <Cancel>  < Help >
```

Figure 2-7 The New Project Dialog Box in PWB

which compiler options to use when creating the program. To create a project file, select the "Project/New Project..." menu item in PWB. A small window (dialog box) will appear, similar to the one shown in Figure 2-7.

If the New Project dialog box shows C++ as the "Runtime Support" and "Windows 3.1 EXE" and the "Project Template," just click the "OK" button and continue. Otherwise, select the "Set Project Template..." button, and pick "Windows 3.1 EXE" from the list provided. The project template tells PWB what type of program you are creating. Also select C++ runtime support to let PWB know that you will be using the C++ language, not just C. Finally, back on the "New Project" dialog box, select the "Project Name:" item at the top, and make the project file name MINIMAL1.MAK. This file should be in the same subdirectory with MINIMAL1.CPP and MINIMAL1.DEF. Click the "OK" button to create the project file.

Because you are creating a new project file, PWB does not know which files to include when creating the finished program. Another dialog box appears, this time allowing you to select files for the project. Figure 2-8 shows the appearance of this dialog box. You will want to add both MINIMAL1.CPP and MINIMAL1.DEF to the project, so select each of these files by double-clicking the file name with the mouse. Both files will show up in the lower list, as members of the project. Select the "Save List" button to save your project file.

Compiler Options

At this point, PWB know that you will be creating a Windows 3.1 application using C++ from the two selected files. However, you will also need to tell PWB to use the Foundation Classes when creating the program. Choose the

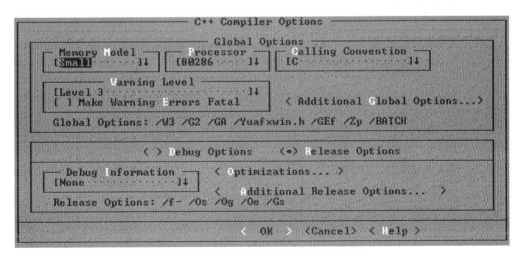

Figure 2-8 Selecting Files into a Project File

"Options\Language Options...\C++ Compiler Options" menu item, and a dialog box similar to Figure 2-9 will appear. For this small example, use the small memory model, the 80286 processor option, C calling conventions (not Pascal), and Warning Level 3. Unless you are planning to try out the debugger, select the "Release Options" button.

Figure 2-9 Choosing the C++ Compiler Options in PWB

Segments, Offsets, and Memory Models

C and C++ compilers for DOS and Windows programs come with all sorts of options. A number of the possibilities revolve around the "memory model" the compiler will use. To understand memory models requires an understanding of how the computer's CPU (central processing unit) deals with memory. Let's take a brief detour to look at how memory is organized under MS-DOS and Windows.

The Intel 80X86 family of CPU chips uses what is called the "segmented" memory model. The idea is that any location in memory is described by two addresses, the segment and the offset. The segment describes a portion of the memory in the computer system. The offset specifies an individual location within the segment. As shown in Figure 2-10, the full address is the combination of the segment and the offset. This is similar to describing a person's address in terms of a street and an address number. The name of the street localizes the address to a given street, and the address number provides the location (offset) from the beginning of the street.

The advantage of the segmented memory model is that you can describe an address within a single segment by just specifying the offset. This is faster than specifying the full segment + offset for every address, as long as the addresses are all within the same segment. Again, this is just like specifying a street number once you know the street name. There is no need to keep repeating the street name, as long as you know a group of addresses are all on the same street.

Your C++ compiler can take advantage of the segmented memory model to make the program more efficient. For small programs, all of the program's code can be put in a single segment. This is called the "small memory model." This means that all of the function addresses can use just the offset value, as the segment will always be the same. Windows limits the maximum

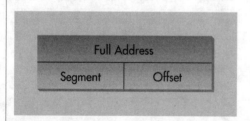

Figure 2-10 Segmented Memory Model

continued on next page

continued from previous page

size of a segment to 64K because Windows maintains compatibility with the older 80286 CPU chips, which could not handle segments larger than 64K. The largest small memory model program has 64K of compiled code.

The other option is to break the program's code up into multiple segments. If you compile with the "medium" or "large" memory models, each C program file will end up compiled into a separate segment. This means that the function addresses must be the full offset + segment values. Figure 2-11 shows a comparison of the three memory models. Although the medium and large memory models make the program a little larger and a tiny bit slower, there is an advantage. Windows can move each segment of the program in memory individually. This allows much greater freedom for memory optimization. If your program is over 15K in size, use the medium memory model, as the benefits of Windows' memory management far outweigh the slight increase in program size.

In the C and C++ languages, "pointers" are memory locations used to hold the numeric value of another memory address. Because of the difference in size between an address that just contains an offset, and a full address that

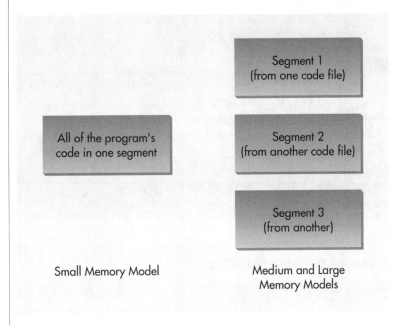

Figure 2-11 Small, Medium, and Large Memory Model Programs

continued on next page

continued from previous page

contains both the segment and offset, you will need to specify what type of pointer you want to use. This is done with two compiler key words, NEAR and FAR. NEAR pointers just contain the offset portion of the address. FAR pointers contain both the segment and the offset. For example, to declare a near pointer to an integer, and a far pointer to a character, you would use the following statements:

```
int  NEAR *n ;   // near pointer to an address containing an integer
char FAR  *c ;   // far pointer to an address containing a character
```

If you study the compiler's documentation, you will also find reference to other memory models, such as "compact," "huge," and "tiny." They control how the program handles data in one or more segments of memory. Table 2-1 summarizes the differences between the memory models. We will use the small memory model in every example in the book until Chapter 18, which has examples that use the large memory model to create and use Dynamic Link Libraries (DLLs). The tiny memory model is a hold-over from the MS-DOS .COM file format and is not suitable for Windows. The compact memory model is used only for MS-DOS programs, and offers no advantages in Windows programming.

Windows NT takes advantage of the 80386 and higher chips to define a "flat" memory space. This means that instead of segments and offsets, all memory addresses are in one continuous space and use a single 32-bit address value to specify a location in memory. This does away with all of the complexity of segments and offsets, and eliminates the need for different compiler memory models. Near and far addresses have no meaning under Windows NT, as every address has a 32-bit value.

Additional Compiler Options

Before closing the C++ Compiler Options dialog box, select the "Additional Global Options..." button. Another dialog box will appear, as shown in Figure 2-12. This dialog box is where you inform PWB that you will be using the

Model	Code Segments	Maximum Code	Data Segments	Maximum Data	OK For Windows?
Tiny	One, shared with Data	64K	One, shared with Code	64K less Code size	No
Small	One	64K	One	64K	Yes
Medium	Many	No limit	One	64K	Yes
Compact	One	64K	Many	No limit	No
Large	Many	No limit	Many	No limit	Yes
Huge	Many	No limit	Many	No limit (Individual Blocks > 64K)	Yes, but rarely used

Table 2-1 Compiler Memory Models

Microsoft Foundation Classes (MFC) by selecting the "Use MFC Libraries" button. To save compiling time, also select the "Use Pre-compiled Header" button, and type in the "Include File" name as AFXWIN.H. This tells PWB to save the compiled version of the AFXWIN.H header file, so that it can be used again without recompiling, thus saving a lot of time on all subsequent compilations. This technique will work for all of the examples in this book, as long as the AFXWIN.H header file is always the first file included at the top of a program listing (such as in MINIMAL1.CPP).

Close the dialog boxes by selecting the "OK" buttons, and you are all set to compile your first C++ program for Windows.

COMPILING AND LINKING

With the source code and project files defined, compiling the program is simple. Just select the "Project\Rebuild All" menu item. You will be able to watch the compiler and linker execute in the PWB window. PWB will take a little extra time the first time you compile while it generates the pre-compiled header file AFXWIN.PCH. This file will be saved in the same subdirectory with your source code. Any subsequent compilations of MINIMAL1.CPP or any other program that references the AFXWIN.H pre-compiled header (see Figure 2-12) will read the

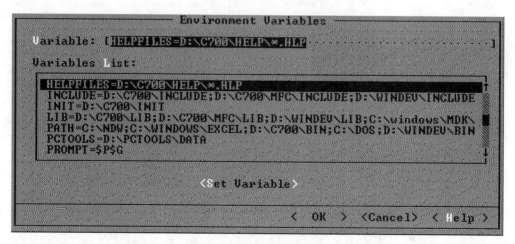

Figure 2-12 The PWB Additional Global Options Dialog Box

AFXWIN.PCH file rather than recompiling AFXWIN.H from scratch. This speeds up compile times tremendously as the compiled form of AFXWIN.H occupies over 800K. The only time you will need to generate a new pre-compiled header file is if you change compiler options, such as picking a different memory model. If you are following the examples in this book, you will not switch to a different memory model until Chapter 18, *Dynamic Link Libraries*, so the pre-compiled header file you generate with MINIMAL1.CPP will work for all the examples until Chapter 18.

Besides the pre-compiled header file, compiling MINIMAL1.CPP will produce the object file MINIMAL1.OBJ and the executable file MINIMAL1.EXE. MINI-MAL1 is so simple that it does not have any resource data, so none is included in the compilation. When the compilation is complete, the compiler will show a message with the total number of errors. If all went well you will get a message saying that there were zero errors. You can then run the MINIMAL1.EXE program. You will not be able to do this by selecting the "Run/Execute: MINIMAL1.EXE" menu item from PWB because this menu item assumes that you want to execute a DOS program. Use the Windows File Manager application to select the subdirectory containing MINIMAL1, and double-click the MINIMAL1.EXE program name to start the application. Figure 2-13 shows the File Manager window and the subdirectory containing the MINIMAL1.EXE program file, as well as the other files created when MINIMAL1.CPP was compiled.

If everything went as planned—Congratulations! Do not expect this to happen every time, as there are a lot of little things that can go wrong in compiling

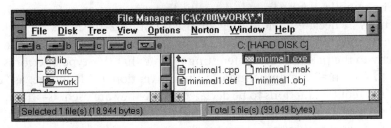

Figure 2-13 Starting MINIMAL1.CPP from the File Manager

a program. The next section discusses the most common problems and their solutions, in case you ran into a glitch.

TRACKING DOWN ERRORS

There are a number of things that can go wrong in the process of compiling a program. Most of them are easy to track down and correct, but a few can be confusing the first time you run into them. This section examines the most common errors, including problems with the setup of your compiler. The main rule in tracking down errors is: Don't give up! Computers are stupid machines. You cannot let them get the upper hand.

Most of the time you will make a simple typing mistake when entering the source code, and the compiler will detect it and specify which line has the error. These errors are easy to fix, particularly in an integrated editor/compiler system like PWB. For example, Listing 2-15 shows the top portion of the MINIMAL1.CPP program, with a typing error. The last "e" in the **Create()** function was left off.

Listing 2-15 Typo in a C++ File

```
// minimal1.cpp                     minimal windows application

#include <afxwin.h>            // class library header file

class CMainWindow : public CFrameWnd    // derive main window class
{
public:
    CMainWindow () ;            // declare a constructor
} ;

CMainWindow::CMainWindow ()    // constructor for window
{
    Creat (NULL, "Minimal1");
}
```

The compiler has no trouble detecting this type of error, as C++ requires that functions be declared before they are used. Listing 2-16 shows the error messages that PWB will display for this typing error. The error messages lead you directly to the problem. It is interesting to note that this type of error is not as easy to find in a program written in the conventional C language, as "old" C does not require functions to be declared before they are used. C++ (and "modern" versions of C such as ANSI C) enforce declaring functions before they are used to make sure that the correct function name and parameter types are used. The function declaration for the **Create()** function is defined in the AFXWIN.H header file, which is included at the top of MINIMAL1.CPP.

Some typing errors confuse the compiler, leading to error messages that are not particularly helpful. A classic example is to omit a semicolon. In C++, the class definitions end in a semicolon, while function definitions do not. Listing 2-17 shows the top portion of the MINIMAL1.CPP program, which has both a class definition and a function definition.

If you leave out the semicolon at the end of the **CMainWindow** class definition, the compiler will detect an error and display the messages shown in

Listing 2-16 PWB Error Messages for a Misspelled Function Name

```
Microsoft (R) Program Maintenance Utility   Version 1.20
Copyright (c) Microsoft Corp 1988-92. All rights reserved.

Microsoft (R) C/C++ Optimizing Compiler Version 7.00
Copyright (c) Microsoft Corp 1984-1992. All rights reserved.

cl /Ycafxwin.h /c /W3 /G2 /GA /Yuafxwin.h /GEf /Zp /BATCH
    /f- /Os /Og /Oe /Gs /FoMINIMAL1.obj MINIMAL1.CPP
minimal1.cpp
minimal1.cpp(13) : error C2065: 'Creat' : undeclared identifier
minimal1.cpp(14) : error C2064: term does not evaluate to a function

NMAKE : fatal error U1077: 'CL' : return code '2'
Stop.
```

Listing 2-17 Correct Semicolon Placement in C++

```
class CMainWindow : public CFrameWnd     // class definition
{
public:
    CMainWindow () ;
} ;         // <---- semicolon, end of class definition

CMainWindow::CMainWindow ()              // function definition
{
    Create (NULL, "Minimal1") ;
}           // <---- no semicolon here, end of function definition
```

Listing 2-18. The confusing thing about these error messages is that they suggest that there is an error in the **CMainWindow()** function definition, not in the class definition that has the missing semicolon. The reason for this is that the **CMainWindow** class definition is correctly written, but it happens to be missing the ending semicolon. The compiler does not detect that you are finished defining the **CMainWindow** class because the compiler uses semicolons to mark the ends of all types of declarations. Without the semicolon, the compiler blunders into the **CMainWindow()** function definition without realizing that it has entered a new portion of the code.

Another type of source code error that can be tricky to find is where you misspell a word in the program's module definition file. Listing 2-19 shows the MINIMAL1.DEF file with a typo. The word STACKSIZE has been misspelled, omitting the letter "K."

Listing 2-18 Compiler Errors—Missing Semicolon

```
Microsoft (R) Program Maintenance Utility   Version 1.20
Copyright (c) Microsoft Corp 1988-92. All rights reserved.

Microsoft (R) C/C++ Optimizing Compiler Version 7.00
Copyright (c) Microsoft Corp 1984-1992. All rights reserved.

cl /Ycafxwin.h /c /W3 /G2 /GA /Yuafxwin.h /GEf /Zp /BATCH
   /f- /Os /Og /Oe /Gs /FoMINIMAL1.obj MINIMAL1.CPP
minimal1.cpp
minimal1.cpp(12) : error C2533: 'CMainWindow::CMainWindow' :
constructors not allowed a return type

minimal1.cpp(12) : error C2556: 'CMainWindow::CMainWindow' :
overloaded functions  only differ in return type

minimal1.cpp(25) : error C2264: 'CMainWindow::CMainWindow' : error in
function definition or declaration; function not called

NMAKE : fatal error U1077: 'CL' : return code '2'
Stop.
```

Listing 2-19 Error in a Module Definition File

```
NAME            minimal1
DESCRIPTION     'minimal1 C++ program'
EXETYPE         WINDOWS
STUB            'WINSTUB.EXE'
CODE            PRELOAD MOVEABLE
DATA            PRELOAD MOVEABLE MULTIPLE
HEAPSIZE        1024
STACSIZE        5120
```

The module definition file is not used during the compiling step, so the compiler does not detect an error. The error does not show up until PWB invokes the linker, which uses the module definition file to supply information used in assembling the finished program. Listing 2-20 shows the resultant error messages. The only clue as to where the error lies is the line number (8) that shows up in parentheses after the MINIMAL1.DEF file name. Fortunately, module definition files are so short that this type of error is easy to find and correct.

COMPILER SETUP ERRORS

Another category of errors involves problems with the compiler installation or choice of compiler options. For example, a single error in selecting compiler options will result in a list of 26 errors shown in Listing 2-21. It can be pretty discouraging when the list of errors is longer than the program's source code.

The problem that caused all of the errors shown in Listing 2-21 is that the linker could not find a long list of functions. When a function is referenced in a source code file, but not defined in the file, it is called an "external" function. An "unresolved external" is a function that was used in the source code file, but which the linker could not find in a library file or another .OBJ file. All of the

Listing 2-20 Error Messages for Incorrect Module Definition File

```
Definitions File [nul.def]: MINIMAL1.DEF /BATCH /ONERROR:NOEXE /NOF;
MINIMAL1.DEF(8) : fatal error L1035: syntax error in module-definition file
NMAKE : fatal error U1077: 'LINK' : return code '2'
```

Listing 2-21 Unresolved External Linkage Errors

```
MINIMAL1.obj(minimal1.cpp) : error L2029: 'public: virtual class
CFrameWnd near pascal CFrameWnd::GetChildFrame(void)near' : unresolved external

MINIMAL1.obj(minimal1.cpp) : error L2029: 'public: virtual int near
pascal CWinApp::Run(void)__near' : unresolved external

MINIMAL1.obj(minimal1.cpp) : error L2029: 'protected: virtual long
(far pascal CWnd::GetSuperWndProcAddr(void)__near)(unsigned
int,unsigned int,unsigned int,long)' : unresolved external

MINIMAL1.obj(minimal1.cpp) : error L2029: 'public: virtual struct
CRuntimeClass(void)const near' : unresolved external

MINIMAL1.obj(minimal1.cpp) : error L2029: 'public: virtual void near
pascal CObject::AssertValid(void)const near' : unresolved external

// etc. 26 total errors
```

unresolved external errors in Listing 2-21 were caused by forgetting to tell the compiler that the MFC functions were going to be used. This should have been done by selecting the "Use MFC Libraries" option from the PWB "Additional Global Options" dialog box (Figure 2-12). If this option is selected, the linker will include an extra library file in the linking step which has all of the functions from the MFC classes. These are the external functions that the linker needs to complete the program. The linker will extract only the functions that are needed by the program from the library file, and will add them to the finished .EXE program.

A similar problem occurs if you do not have the correct DOS environment variables set before PWB is started. For example, Listing 2-22 shows some of the error messages in a first attempt to compile MINIMAL1.CPP. The key to the problem is given in the top two LINK warning messages. The linker could not find the LIBW.LIB and SAFXCW.LIB files. These are the library files the linker needs for the external functions MINIMAL1.CPP accesses. Because the library files were not found, 35 unresolved external errors are generated.

The reason the LIBW.LIB and SAFXCW.LIB library files could not be found is that the linker did not know where to look. Microsoft C++ uses DOS "environment variables" to store the location of key subdirectories that the compiler and linker will need to access. These DOS environment variables are normally put in a file called AUTOEXEC.BAT in the root directory (C:\ directory) of your hard disk. AUTOEXEC.BAT is a program file that runs automatically when your computer is first turned on, so any commands in AUTOEXEC.BAT will apply every time you use your computer.

Listing 2-22 PWB Errors—Cannot Find Library

```
Definitions File [nul.def]: MINIMAL1.DEF /BATCH /ONERROR:NOEXE /NOF;
LINK : warning L4051: LIBW.LIB : cannot find library
LINK : warning L4051: SAFXCW.lib : cannot find library

MINIMAL1.obj(minimal1.cpp) : error L2029: 'public: virtual class
CFrameWnd near pascal CFrameWnd::GetChildFrame(void) near' : unresolved external

MINIMAL1.obj(minimal1.cpp) : error L2029: 'public: virtual int __near
_pascal CWinApp::Run(void) near' : unresolved external

MINIMAL1.obj(minimal1.cpp) : error L2029: 'protected: virtual long
(far pascal CWnd::GetSuperWndProcAddr(void)__near)(unsigned int,unsigned
int,unsigned int,long)' : unresolved external

MINIMAL1.obj(minimal1.cpp) : error L2029: 'public: virtual struct
CRuntimeClass void)const near' : unresolved external

MINIMAL1.obj(minimal1.cpp) : error L2029: 'public: virtual void near pascal
CObject::AssertValid(void)const near' : unresolved external

// etc. 35 total errors
```

When you install the C++ 7.00 compiler, the SETUP program will modify your AUTOEXEC.BAT file. The SET and PATH commands are used in the AUTOEXEC.BAT file to pass these values to DOS. Listing 2-23 shows a typical AUTOEXEC.BAT file, which establishes path names for the INCLUDE, INIT, LIB, and HELPFILES values.

When you install the Microsoft C++ 7.00 compiler, the INSTALL program will modify the AUTOEXEC.BAT file with the proper settings for you. However, you may find that your AUTOEXEC.BAT file has been corrupted, or that another .BAT file is changing the environment variables before the compiler and linker get them. You can check the current status of your environment variables with PWB by selecting the "Options/Environment Variables..." menu item. Figure 2-14 shows a typical example for a system that has two hard drives (C: and D:).

Listing 2-23 An Example AUTOEXEC.BAT File

```
PATH C:\WINDOWS\EXCEL;D:\C700\BIN;C:\DOS;D:\WINDEV\BIN;
Set LIB=D:\C700\LIB;D:\C700\MFC\LIB;D:\WINDEV\LIB;
Set INCLUDE=D:\C700\INCLUDE;D:\C700\MFC\INCLUDE;D:\WINDEV\INCLUDE;
Set HELPFILES=D:\C700\HELP\*.HLP
Set INIT=D:\C700\INIT
C:\WINDOWS\SMARTDRV.EXE
SET COMSPEC=C:\DOS\COMMAND.COM
PROMPT $P$G
```

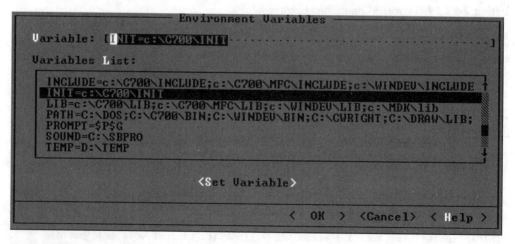

Figure 2-14 PWB "Options/Environment Variables" Dialog Box

For the C++ 7.00 compiler to work properly using the MFC classes, your environment variables will need to pass the correct directory names for four types of subdirectory:

1. The INCLUDE variable should pass the name of the subdirectories containing header files for the C++ compiler, MFC classes, and Windows Software Development Kit (SDK) header files. These are typically C:\C700\INCLUDE, C:\C700\MFC\INCLUDE, and C:\WINDEV\INCLUDE, respectively.

2. The LIB variable should pass the name of the subdirectories containing the C++ compiler library files, MFC library files, and SDK library files. These are typically C:\C700\LIB, C:\C700\MFC\LIB, and C:\WINDEV\LIB.

3. The INIT variable should pass the name of the subdirectory containing compiler initialization files. This is typically C:\C700\INIT.

4. The HELPFILES variable should pass the name of the subdirectory containing the help files for PWB and other utilities. This is typically C:\C700\HELP.

Only the INCLUDE and LIB variables are absolutely required. If you find that the environment variables do not give the correct directory names for your system, you have a couple of choices. One is to edit the AUTOEXEC.BAT file to add the correct subdirectory names, and then reboot your computer. The other option is simply to reinstall the C++ 7.00 compiler and then reboot.

There is one last pitfall you might run into with the MS-DOS environment variables. MS-DOS must store all of the environment variables in memory, and MS-DOS defaults to having room for only 256 bytes of storage for *all* environment variables. If you have several long SET commands, you can easily exceed 256 bytes and will see the MS-DOS error message:

```
Out of environment space
```

This means that the last SET command exceeded the room set asside by MS-DOS, and will, therefore, not have any effect. To get around this problem, you need to tell MS-DOS to set aside more than the default 256 bytes. This is best done by modifying your CONFIG.SYS file, which is located in the root directory (C:\) of your hard disk. For example, the following line in CONFIG.SYS sets up a 1,024 byte buffer to hold all of the environment variable data:

```
SHELL=C:\DOS\COMMAND.COM C:\DOS\ /E:1024 /p
```

The SHELL command tells MS-DOS that the file COMMAND.COM contains the user interface for MS-DOS. This is the standard command-line shell that comes with MS-DOS. The COMMAND.COM file is expected to be in the directory C:\DOS. The environment size is set with the /E: command to 1,024 bytes.

Finally, the /p switch tells MS-DOS that the changes should be permanent and continue to work even after the user uses the EXIT command. Changes to your CONFIG.SYS file will not take effect until you reboot your computer.

OTHER ERRORS

There are certainly many other possible errors that you may run into. The key to success is perseverance. If the error message does not make sense to you, look it up in your compiler's manual, or use the on-line help provided with the Microsoft C++ compiler. Sometimes the description of the error will give you an idea of where to look in your program. If you are really stuck, try to go back to a previous situation where you did not run into the error, and then add one change at a time until the error pops up. You can also get help by taking advantage of the support provided by Microsoft and other software vendors on the CompuServe network.

SUMMARY

C++ classes allow you to collect a group of related functions and data into a single object. The *public* and *private* key words make it possible to control which parts of a class can be accessed from outside of the class, and which parts are kept hidden. Classes make it possible to design objects that other programmers can safely use without any knowledge of how the class works internally.

A key to the efficient use of C++ is to derive new classes from existing ones. All of the functions in the base class are inherited by the derived class. In addition, the derived class can add new data and functions for special features that were not included in the base class. Microsoft includes a library of classes called the Microsoft Foundation Classes (MFC) with the C++ 7.00 compiler. These classes are ideal starting points for deriving new classes. The MINIMAL1.CPP program derived a new application class from the **CWinApp** MFC class, and a new window class from the **CFrameWnd** MFC class.

Compiling a Windows application using the Foundation Classes requires that you use a number of special settings so that the compiler and linker can find the files needed to build the finished application. Most of these settings can be made using the PWB menu items and dialog boxes. However, C++ 7.00 also requires that DOS environment variables be set to contain the subdirectory names for the header and library files. These environment variables are normally set by the AUTOEXEC.BAT program when your computer is first turned on.

QUESTIONS

1. Private members of a class can be accessed only by functions that are defined within the body of the class definition. (True/False)

2. Write the syntax for a new class, **CMyClass**, which derives from the base class **CClassOne**.

3. When an object of a given class is first created, the _____ function is called. Right before the object is destroyed the _____ function is called.

4. The full name of the constructor function for the **COneClass** class is _____. The full name for the destructor function is _____.

5. In the MINIMAL1.CPP program (Listing 2-8), which function actually makes the program's window visible? To which class does that function belong?

6. Functions that are used in a program's code and are defined outside of the program are called _____ functions.

7. What does "unresolved external" mean?

EXERCISES

1. Separate the class definitions into a separate header file with the extension .HPP. Include this header file at the top of the CPP source code and recompile the program. Does this change the program's operation in any way? Do you need to change the project file?

2. Change the value of the parameter passed to the **CMainWindow::Show-Window()** function in MINIMAL1.CPP from *m_nCmdShow* to SW_SHOWMINIMIZED and recompile. What happens to the program? Can you guess where the SW_SHOWMINIMIZED value is defined?

ANSWERS TO QUESTIONS

1. False. Private members can only be accessed by functions within the class. However, the functions of a class can be defined either within the class definition, or separately using the **ClassName::FuncName()** syntax.

2. class **CMyClass : public CClassOne** { } ;.

3. Constructor, destructor.

4. **COneClass::COneClass(), COneClass::~COneClass()**

5. **ShowWindow()**. The full name of the function is **CMainWindow::Show-Window()**. The **CMainWindow** class is derived from the **CFrameWnd** class.

6. External.

7. "Unresolved external" means that a function or data object was used in the source code for a program, but the linker could not find the function or data during the linking process.

SOLUTIONS TO EXERCISES

1. Moving the class definitions to a separate header file is the normal programming technique for C++ programs. The rearranged files are provided on the source code disks under the file name C2EXER1. Listing 2-24 shows the new header file, C2EXER1.HPP.

    Listing 2-25 shows the modified C++ program, which includes the C2EXER1.HPP file at the top of the listing. Note that the creation of the **theApp** object has been moved to the top of the file. This is only for clarity. The program will function the same with the line "CWinApp theApp ;" at the top, middle, or bottom of the listing because this is the only line

Listing 2-24 C2EXER1.HPP Header File

```
// c2exer1.hpp       header file

class CMainWindow : public CFrameWnd      // derive main window class
{
public:
    CMainWindow () ;                      // declare a constructor
} ;

class CTheApp : public CWinApp           // derive an application class
{
public:
    BOOL InitInstance () ;               // override default InitInstance()
} ;
```

in the program that is executed directly. The rest of the program is function and class definitions, which are executed as a consequence of creating the theApp object.

Moving the class definitions to a separate header file does not change the behavior of the program in any way. You will not need to change the project file because header files are not included in the list of files that make up a project. The header file will be included during the compilation step because of the *#include* directive in the source code.

2. Listing 2-26 shows the modified MINIMAL1.CPP program using the SW_SHOWMINIMIZED value for the **CWnd::ShowWindow**() function. The result of this change is that the window is minimized at the bottom of the screen at startup. The window can be restored to normal size or maximized to fill the screen by clicking the minimized window to display its system menu.

The SW_SHOWMINIMIZED value is known to the compiler because the AFXWIN.H header file is included at the top of the listing. If you search through AFXWIN.H using a text editor (it is in the C:\C700\MFC\INCLUDE subdirectory by default), you will not find the value SW_SHOWMINIMIZED. However, you will find that AFXWIN.H includes a number of other header files. One of them is WINDOWS.H, which defines the SW_SHOWMINIMIZED value.

Listing 2-25 C2EXER1.CPP Program File Using a Header File

```
// c2exer1.cpp          // solution to chapter 2, exercise 1

#include <afxwin.h>      // class library header file
#include "c2exer1.hpp"   // new header file

CTheApp theApp ;         // create one CTheApp object - runs program

CMainWindow::CMainWindow ()     // constructor for window
{
    Create (NULL, "C2exer1") ;
}

BOOL CTheApp::InitInstance ()    // override default InitInstance()
{
    m_pMainWnd = new CMainWindow () ;       // create a main window
    m_pMainWnd->ShowWindow (m_nCmdShow) ;   // make it visible
    return TRUE ;
}
```

Listing 2-26 C2EXER2.CPP—Modified MINIMAL1.CPP Program

```
// c2exer2.cpp          // solution to chapter 2, exercise 2

#include <afxwin.h>      // class library header file

class CMainWindow : public CFrameWnd    // derive main window class
{
public:
    CMainWindow () ;             // declare a constructor
} ;

CMainWindow::CMainWindow ()      // constructor for window
{
    Create (NULL, "Minimal1") ;
}

class CTheApp : public CWinApp  // derive an application class
{
public:
    BOOL InitInstance () ;       // override default InitInstance()
} ;

BOOL CTheApp::InitInstance ()    // override default InitInstance()
{
    m_pMainWnd = new CMainWindow () ;        // create a main window
    m_pMainWnd->ShowWindow (SW_SHOWMINIMIZED) ;// start minimized
    return TRUE ;
}

CTheApp theApp ;         // create one CTheApp object - runs program
```

## Chapter 3

First Programming Experiments

This chapter explains more of the details behind the MINIMAL1 program from the previous chapter, and then it expands the program in three steps. Each addition to the program will explain more of the fundamentals behind Windows programming using the MFC classes. You will add message processing logic and resource data. By the end of the chapter, you will have a complete Windows application with its own icon and menu. This program will serve as an excellent starting point for other programming projects, including other programs in this book.

Besides improving the MINIMAL1 application, the additions will introduce two new types of files that will be used in all of the remaining example programs. The first is a header file, which will store definitions of constants and function declarations. The second is a resource file, containing the program's menu definition and icon image. Many other uses for resource data will be explored in subsequent chapters.

Concepts covered: AFXWIN.H, pre-compiled headers, WINDOWS.H, Hungarian notation, handles, adding icons and menus, processing messages, command-line strings.

Key words covered: ICON, MENU, BEGIN_MESSAGE_MAP, END_MESSAGE_MAP, DECLARE_MESSAGE_MAP, HANDLE, UINT, **m_pszAppName**, **m_hInstance**, **m_hPrevInstance**, **m_lpCmdLine**, **m_nCmdShow**.

Functions covered: **::MessageBeep()**, **CWnd::SetWindowText()**, **CWnd::DestroyWindow()**.

Messages covered: WM_SIZE, WM_MOVE, WM_COMMAND, WM_DESTROY.

THE AFXWIN.H FILE

The MINIMAL1.CPP program introduced in the last chapter started with the inclusion of the AFXWIN.H header file. You will include this header file in every C++ program you write using the MFC classes. If you are curious, take a look at the AFXWIN.H file using a text editor. By default AFXWIN.H is located in a directory named C:\C700\MFC\INCLUDE.

AFXWIN.H contains a number of class definitions. This is how the compiler knows about the **CWinApp** and **CFrameWnd** classes that are used in the MINIMAL1 program. AFXWIN.H also contains a number of *#include* directives, which bring in other header files. For example, AFXWIN.H includes AFX.H, which in turn includes five other header files. Simply including the AFXWIN.H file in a program results in a total of 12 header files being read by the compiler before it gets to your code. Table 3-1 shows the complete list of header files and their sizes.

As shown in Table 3-1, AFXWIN.H adds up to about 300K of header files. If you do nothing but include the AFXWIN.H file at the top of your C++ listings, the compiler will end up spending far more time reading AFXWIN.H than your code. Fortunately, the 7.00 release of the Microsoft C++ compiler has the ability to store a compiled version of the header file information on disk. This is called using a "pre-compiled header," and is one of the PWB options you turned on while setting up PWB to compile MINIMAL1.CPP in Chapter 2, *Using the MFC*

File	Contents	Size
AFXWIN.H	MFC header file for Windows	(60K)
AFX.H	MFC header file for utility functions	(35K)
STRING.H	C runtime library for string functions	(6K)
STDIO.H	C runtime library for input/output	(7K)
STDLIB.H	Standard C runtime library	(7K)
TIME.H	C runtime library for time functions	(3K)
AFX.INL	Inline function definitions for AFX.H	(12K)
WINDOWS.H	Windows standard header file	(64K)
COMMDLG.H	Header file for Windows common dialogs	(12K)
AFXRES.H	Standard resource names for MFC	(1K)
AFXMSG.H	Message map table for MFC	(23K)
AFXWIN.INL	Inline function definitions for AFXWIN.H	(76K)
Total AFXWIN.H header file size		(299K)

Table 3-1 Contents of the AFXWIN.H Header File

Classes. For most work with the MFC classes, it is sufficient to pre-compile AFXWIN.H. The first time you use the pre-compiled header option, the compiler will read AFXWIN.H and all of its include files and write a compiled version of the data into the file AFXWIN.PCH. From then on the compiler will just read AFXWIN.PCH, rather than compiling all of the data each time you run the compiler. This saves a lot of time, although you will need to create a new header file if you change memory models, or decide to add other header files to the pre-compiled header.

The file name you list in PWB under the pre-compiled header name will be the last file in the source code listing that will be added to the pre-compiled header. For example, if you specify AFXWIN.H as the pre-compiled header file, but list it after other header files at the top of the listing, all of the header files up to and including AFXWIN.H will be added to the pre-compiled header. For example, if your C++ program starts with the list of files shown in Listing 3-1 and AFXWIN.H is the pre-compiled header file name you specified in PWB, the pre-compiled header will also include the header file data from STRSTREA.H and FSTREAM.H, but not from FILESTRM.HPP. This gives you the flexibility to pre-compile all of the "standard" header files that your projects will use, while compiling files specific to each project separately ("on the fly").

Listing 3-1 Multiple Files Added to a Pre-Compiled Header

```
// program.cpp            example using several header files

#include <strstrea.h>      // streams header file
#include <fstream.h>       // file streams header file
#include <afxwin.h>        // class library header file
#include "filestrm.hpp"    // header file for this program
```

Header Files Versus Library Files

Although the AFXWIN.H header file and its included files amount to a lot of source code, this is not the entire code for the MFC classes. The header files only include definitions of constants and functions that can be written on one line (C++ inline functions). The remaining code resides in library files that the linker reads when making the .EXE program. For example, the library file that has most of the MFC code is called SAFXCW.LIB. You can find this file in the MFC library subdirectory, which is called C:\C700\MFC\LIB by default.

The letter "S" in SAFXCW.LIB designates that this library was created to be used with small memory model programs. MAFXCW.LIB is for the medium memory model, LAFXCW.LIB is for the large memory model, and so on. There are also debugging versions of the libraries that include CodeView information that will allow you to trace through the execution of functions in the MFC classes. They are indicated by adding a "D" to the file name, such as SAFXCWD.LIB for the small memory model library with debugging information.

If you use the PWB to do your compiling and linking, the PWB automatically will pick the correct library file based on the memory model you are using. Do not forget to tell PWB that you will be using the MFC classes in the PWB "Additional Global Options" dialog box, as explained in the last chapter. If you are using another editor, you will need to specify the library name. This is explained in Appendix D, *Command-Line Compilation*.

One other little complication is that Microsoft only provides small and medium memory model libraries with the C++ 7.00 compiler. If you want to use the large memory model, you will need to create it from the MFC source code files. This is easy to do, although it takes upwards of 20 minutes to create a library. Creating a library is explained in Chapter 18, *Dynamic Link Libraries*, because DLLs use the large memory model.

The WINDOWS.H File

One of the files that AFXWIN.H includes is WINDOWS.H. This is the standard header file that C programmers use when creating Windows applications. This is only part of the header information you will need when creating Windows applications using the MFC classes. Nevertheless, WINDOWS.H is an important file, and one that we will refer to many times in this book. Listing 3-2 shows a small portion of WINDOWS.H

WINDOWS.H makes heavy use of the C (and C++) language *typedef* statement. For example, the new type WORD is not defined in the C language, but is defined in WINDOWS.H as an unsigned integer. This means that in a program that includes WINDOWS.H (singly or as part of AFXWIN.H), you can use "WORD" anywhere that you would otherwise have to type out "unsigned int." At the end of Listing 3-2, you will see that WORD is then used to create the HANDLE data type, which is then used to create HWND, a handle of a window. The result is that WORD, HANDLE, and HWND are all unsigned integers, even though each has a different purpose. These new names will make declarations of variable types more obvious than always using the declaration "unsigned int." We will see examples of this in a moment.

Hungarian Notation

Back before C++, C programmers frequently ran into program bugs created by passing the wrong type of data to a function. This is less of a problem today due to the improved type checking that has been added to the C language. C++ provides elegant means of avoiding passing the wrong type of data, but it can

Listing 3-2 WINDOWS.H Excerpt

```
typedef int              BOOL;
typedef unsigned char    BYTE;
typedef unsigned int     WORD;
typedef unsigned long    DWORD;
typedef char near        *PSTR;
typedef char near        *NPSTR;
typedef char far         *LPSTR;
typedef BYTE near        *PBYTE;
typedef BYTE far         *LPBYTE;
typedef int near         *PINT;
typedef int far          *LPINT;
typedef WORD near        *PWORD;
typedef WORD far         *LPWORD;
typedef long near        *PLONG;
typedef long far         *LPLONG;
typedef DWORD near       *PDWORD;
typedef DWORD far        *LPDWORD;
typedef void far         *LPVOID;

typedef WORD             HANDLE;
typedef HANDLE           HWND;
```

still happen. It is a good idea to use variable names that make it obvious what type of data the object contains. Windows programmers use a naming convention called "Hungarian notation" in honor of its inventor, Charles Simonyi. The idea is to precede variable names with key letters that describe what type of data the variable represents, including many of the specialized types defined in WINDOWS.H. Table 3-2 shows the basic system of prefixes.

Figure 3-1 shows an example using Hungarian notation. The variable *lpszBigName* is a long pointer to a zero terminated string (l = long, p = pointer, sz = zero terminated string). Also note the use of capital letters in the name to make the word breaks obvious without wasting space.

Listing 3-3 shows some additional examples of variables named using Hungarian notation. The bottom two declarations show pointers to strings. Pointers to character strings are used so frequently that WINDOWS.H includes typedef statements for PSTR (char *), a near pointer to a string, and LPSTR (char FAR *), a far pointer to a string. These definitions just save a bit of typing.

Handles

The one unusual data type in the WINDOWS.H list of variable types is HANDLE. Handles are unsigned integers that Windows uses internally to keep track of

Prefix	Data Type
b	BOOL (int, use only TRUE and FALSE values, 1 and 0)
by	BYTE (unsigned char)
c	char
dw	DWORD (double word, a four-byte unsigned long integer)
fn	function
h	handle. This is an ID value that Windows uses internally to keep track of memory blocks, window ID values, etc.
l	long
n	short (int) or near pointer (np)
p	pointer
s	character string
sz	character string terminated by zero
w	word (two bytes)

Table 3-2 Variable Name Prefix Codes Used in Hungarian Notation

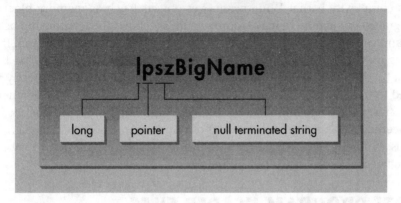

Figure 3-1 Hungarian Notation Example

Listing 3-3 Hungarian Notation Used in Declaring Variable Types

```
int        nMyValue ;              // an integer
int        *pnPointerOne ;         // near pointer to an integer
int FAR    *fpnPointerTwo ;        // far pointer to an integer
WORD       wOtherValue ;           // WORD = unsigned integer
WORD FAR   *fpwPointerThree ;      // far pointer to a word
CHAR FAR   *fpChar ;               // far pointer to a character
PSTR       pszNearString ;         // near pointer to a null term. string
LPSTR      lpszFarString ;         // far pointer to a null term. string
```

objects in memory. For example, every window on the screen has a unique window handle. Handles are also used to keep track of running applications, of allocated memory blocks, and a host of other objects.

We will be using handles frequently while programming in Windows to keep track of various objects in memory. You can think of handles as being similar to the "handle" (nickname) that truck drivers call themselves when using the CB radio. If you use the radio, you contact another driver using his or her handle. When you get a response, you will not know where that driver is located, unless you specifically ask. The location of the driver is not important to getting the information, but the handle is. You will get the information from Windows by using Windows function calls (instead of a CB radio), and by using the handle of the object you want to contact.

Internally, a portion of Windows called the "Kernel" maintains tables that allow Windows to convert from handles to physical memory addresses. A handle is actually a pointer to a pointer to a memory location. The reason for this complexity is that Windows moves objects (such as memory blocks and programs) in memory to make room. Figure 3-2 shows the relationship between a handle used in a Windows program, and a physical memory location. If Windows moves the object in memory, the handle table is updated. The handle used by the program does not need to change, as it always gets correctly translated to the right physical address by the Windows Kernel no matter where the object is moved in memory. As a Windows programmer, you will not need to be concerned with the internal workings of Windows' memory management functions. Windows keeps the handles valid, and the handle is all that you will need to locate and access any object in memory.

SEPARATE PROGRAM HEADER FILES

Our first foray into programming in this chapter is a simple improvement to the MINIMAL1 program. In Chapter 2, *Using the MFC Classes*, the MINIMAL1.CPP program included both the class definitions and the class member functions. Having everything in one source code file is fine for small programs like MINIMAL1.CPP, but becomes unworkable as the classes become more complex. Most C++ programs keep the class definitions in a separate header file with the extension .HPP. Listings 3-4 to 3-6 show the revised MINIMAL1 source code files, with separation of the class definitions in the MINIMAL1.HPP file.

One of the benefits of separating the class definitions from the functions is that it is easier to keep track of which ones end in a semicolon. All of the class definitions in the HPP header file end in a semicolon. All of the function

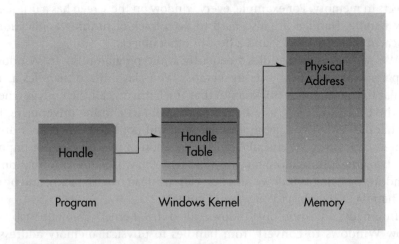

Figure 3-2 How Handles Point to Memory

Listing 3-4 MINIMAL1.CPP—Note Inclusion of MINIMAL1.HPP

```
// minimal1.cpp        reorganized to use a header file

#include <afxwin.h>    // class library header file
#include "minimal1.hpp" // program's own header file

CTheApp theApp ;        // create one CTheApp object - runs program

CMainWindow::CMainWindow ()    // constructor for window
{
    Create (NULL, "Minimal1") ;
}

BOOL CTheApp::InitInstance ()   // override default InitInstance()
{
    m_pMainWnd = new CMainWindow () ;       // create a main window
    m_pMainWnd->ShowWindow (m_nCmdShow) ;   // make it visible
    return TRUE ;
}
```

Listing 3-5 MINIMAL1.HPP—Header File for Class Definitions

```
// minimal1.hpp        header file for minimal1.cpp

class CMainWindow : public CFrameWnd     // derive main window class
{
public:
    CMainWindow () ;             // declare a constructor
} ;

class CTheApp : public CWinApp  // derive an application class
{
public:
    BOOL InitInstance () ;       // override default InitInstance()
} ;
```

Listing 3-6 MINIMAL1.DEF Module Definition File (Unchanged)

```
NAME            minimal1
DESCRIPTION     'minimal1 C++ program'
EXETYPE         WINDOWS
STUB            'WINSTUB.EXE'
CODE            PRELOAD MOVEABLE
DATA            PRELOAD MOVEABLE MULTIPLE
HEAPSIZE        1024
STACKSIZE       5120
```

definitions in the CPP file do not. (You can probably guess that the author has made this type of error more than once....)

Note in Listing 3-4 that the creation of the **CTheApp** object has been moved to the top of the file. The **CTheApp** class is defined in the MINIMAL1.HPP header file, so the compiler has read the definition of the **CTheApp** class before it attempts to create the object. Although you can put the line

```
CTheApp theApp ;
```

anywhere in the listing you like (outside of function declarations), the usual practice is to put this line at the top of the file. Creating the **theApp** object starts the entire program running, so having this pivotal line easily visible at the top of the listing makes the program easier to understand.

No change to the project file is needed to compile the new version of MINI-MAL1. PWB does not allow header files to be added to project lists, so the only files in the project are MINMAL1.CPP and MINIMAL1.DEF. The compiler and linker options are unchanged from those specified in the last chapter.

MFC Base Classes

If you look in the MFC documentation, you will find descriptions of both the **CWinApp** and **CFrameWindow** classes that are the base classes for the **CTheApp** and **CMainWindow** classes derived in MINIMAL1.HPP. It turns out that both **CWinApp** and **CFrameWindow** are derived classes themselves. Figure 3-3 shows the relationship between the base and derived classes for these two types of objects.

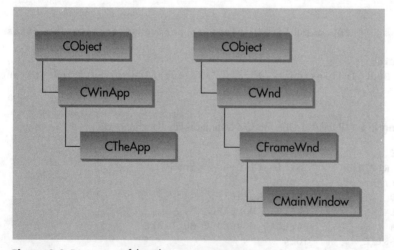

Figure 3-3 Derivation of the Classes in MINIMAL1.HPP

The MFC **CWinApp** and **CFrameWnd** classes are both based on a common class called **CObject**. The **CObject** class contains low-level functionality that is used in many classes, such as support of debugging features. The **CWinApp** class is derived directly from **CObject** and, therefore, inherits these debugging features. The **CFrameWnd** class is derived from the **CWnd** class, which also inherits from **CObject**. **CWnd** is the class that defines all of the functions that a window can perform. We will use the **CWnd** class extensively throughout the book. The **CFrameWnd** class just adds a few features that are unique to the program's main window, such as defaulting to a thick border for the window.

As you can see from Figure 3-3, the simple **CTheApp** and **CMainWindow** classes derived in the MINIMAL1.HPP header file have a lot of power behind them. The beauty of C++ is that all of that power is hidden away in the classes themselves. You do not need to dig into the source code for the **CObject**, **CWnd** and **CFrameWnd** classes to use their functionality in the derived **CMainWindow** class.

With its revised organization including the MINIMAL1.HPP header file, MINIMAL1 is complete. It is time to move on and create a more complicated example that processes specific messages from Windows. This new program will be called MINIMAL2, and it will build on the structure of MINIMAL1, adding message processing logic.

Class Member Function Naming Conventions

Throughout this book, we will discuss member functions of various MFC classes. It is important to remember which class each function belongs to, because the functions will be accessed by objects of that class. To make the relationship clear, this book precedes the function name with the class name such as **CFrameWnd::Create()**. This makes it obvious that the **Create()** function is a member of the **CFrameWnd** class. It also makes it easier to look up the **Create()** function in the MFC documentation because it is listed under "**CFrameWnd::Create()**," not simply "**Create()**." This is logical because there are several "**Create()**" functions in different MFC classes.

Occasionally, you will need to use global functions that are not tied to any particular class. For example, Windows provides the **lstrcpy()** (string copy) function as a global function. To make the global nature of the function obvious, global functions are preceded by the C++ scope resolution operator (::), so **::lstrcpy()** is the form used in this book. The double colon just makes it obvious that **::lstrcpy()** is not tied to any particular class.

continued on next page

---

continued from previous page

One point of confusion occurs when you use derived classes. If a function is defined as *public* in a base class, it is available to all derived classes. This makes it possible to refer to the function by either the name of the base class or the name of the derived class. In this book, the derived class name will be used if the text refers to a specific derived class in a program example. The base class name will be used if the function is being described in general terms.

Message Processing

MINIMAL1 has the virtue of brevity, but it does not represent a typical Windows application. Normally, you will want to intercept messages from Windows, such as menu selections and keyboard actions, and have the program respond to the message. It is not obvious how to do this from the MINIMAL1.CPP example, as the example lacks a means to trap a message from Windows.

The MFC approach to processing messages is to divert each message that the program will process to a separate function. The function does whatever action is appropriate in the program for that one message, and then returns. The diversion of messages to individual functions is done with a "message map." The message map specifies which functions get called for specific messages, and then lets any other messages pass on to the default message processing logic. Figure 3-4 shows how the message map diverts functions.

The creation of a message map is done using several macros that are defined in the AFXWIN.H header file. Listing 3-7 shows a typical example, which processes three messages. The BEGIN_MESSAGE_MAP macro starts the definition of the message map, and END_MESSAGE_MAP ends it. Between these two macros can be any number of references to messages that will be processed by the program. Listing 3-7 shows an example where the WM_SIZE, WM_MOVE, and WM_DESTROY messages are processed. All other messages are not diverted by the message map and, therefore, end up being sent to the default Windows message processing logic.

Listing 3-7 Defining a Message Map

```
BEGIN_MESSAGE_MAP (CMainWindow, CFrameWnd)
    ON_WM_SIZE ()               // WM_SIZE message
    ON_WM_MOVE ()               // WM_MOVE message
    ON_WM_DESTROY()             // WM_DESTROY message
END_MESSAGE_MAP ()
```

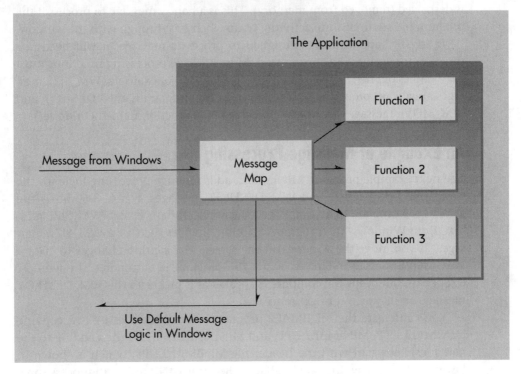

Figure 3-4 Message Mapping

The syntax of the message map is completely arbitrary, and not particularly elegant or consistent with C++ conventions. However, message mapping has a number of important virtues. Message mapping breaks up the logic for processing messages into a series of separate functions. The message map itself (Listing 3-7) provides simple documentation as to which messages are processed. Even though the syntax of the message map is arbitrary, it provides a workable method of coding Windows applications in C++.

In case you are curious, the WM_SIZE, WM_MOVE, and WM_DESTROY messages have simple purposes. The Windows environment sends the WM_SIZE message to the program's window when the window is created and when the window's size is changed (usually by the user dragging a border with the mouse). Many applications process WM_SIZE messages to keep track of the client area size. The WM_MOVE message is sent every time the window is relocated. This is important in some applications that are designed to be positioned only on certain parts of the screen (or certain parts of the parent window's client area in the case of child windows). WM_DESTROY is sent right before a window is destroyed (removed from memory). This is a handy message to process if the program has some cleanup activities to do when it is through with the window.

If an MFC application is designed to process a message, it will need one function for each message processed. Most message processing functions must have names defined in the AFXWIN.H header file. For example, WM_SIZE messages are always processed by a function in the program named **OnSize()**, and WM_MOVE messages are always processed by a function named **OnMove()**.

An Example of Message Processing

The next example program, MINIMAL2, adds message processing logic for the WM_SIZE, WM_MOVE, and WM_DESTROY messages. Figure 3-5 shows the MINIMAL2 program in action. When the application receives a WM_SIZE message from Windows, the program's caption changes to "Got a WM_SIZE message." If you move the window on the screen, the caption changes to "Got a WM_MOVE message." Finally, when the program is terminated the window disappears, but beeps the computer's speaker as it processes the WM_DESTROY message on its way out of existence.

You can create the MINIMAL2 program source code files by just copying MINIMAL1.CPP, MINIMAL1.HPP, and MINIMAL1.DEF and then adding to the new files. Let's start with the header file MINIMAL2.HPP, which is shown in Listing 3-8. The new lines are boldfaced. Because MINIMAL2 will process three messages, there will need to be three message processing functions. These functions have predefined names and parameter lists that are declared in the AFXWIN.H file, so you do not have any choice as to the function name or list of parameters (unless you go to the trouble of defining your own function names). This sounds arbitrary, but it makes it much easier to read someone else's C++ program if he or she used the MFC classes.

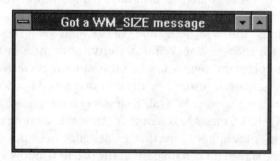

Figure 3-5 The MINIMAL2 Program

Listing 3-8 MINIMAL2.HPP Header File

```
// minimal2.hpp    header file for minimal2.cpp

class CMainWindow : public CFrameWnd  // derive a main window class
{
public:
    CMainWindow () ;                    // declare a constructor
private:                               // message response functions
    void OnSize (UINT nType, int cx, int cy) ;
    void OnMove (int x, int y) ;
    void OnDestroy () ;

    DECLARE_MESSAGE_MAP()              // prepare for message processing
} ;

class CTheApp : public CWinApp        // derive an application class
{
public:
    BOOL InitInstance () ;             // declare new InitInstance()
} ;
```

At this point, you should look up each of the message processing functions in the MFC *Class Library Reference* provided with the Microsoft C++ compiler. Each of these functions is a member of the **CWnd** class, so the full function names are **CWnd::OnSize()**, **CWnd::OnMove()**, and **CWnd::OnDestroy()**. The MFC reference spells out the meaning of each of the parameters passed along with the message. For example, the *x* and *y* values passed with the **CWnd::OnMove()** message provide the location of the upper left corner of the window on the screen. The *cx* and *cy* parameters passed with the **CWnd::OnSize()** message provide the width and height of the window on the screen. These values are not used in the simple MINIMAL2 program.

The **CWnd::OnSize()** function declaration also introduces another new data type: UINT. This type is defined in WINDOWS.H as an unsigned integer. The reason for using the UINT type is to flag values that will be 16-bit values in Windows, but will be 32-bit values under Windows NT. You do not need to concern yourself with the size of the data object. The compiler will choose the appropriate number of bytes for a UINT object at compile time. The same C++ source code will automatically compile to the correctly sized UINT objects depending on whether the target is Windows or Windows NT.

The other important addition to MINIMAL2.HPP is the macro DECLARE_MESSAGE_MAP(), which is also defined in AFXWIN.H. This macro tells the compiler that the program will be mapping specific messages to message processing functions. Although the DECLARE_MESSAGE_MAP() macro is required, you will still need to define a message map in the program. The message map itself is normally part of the CPP portion of the program, as shown in Listing 3-9. The message map specifies exactly which messages will be processed by the program. In this case, only the WM_SIZE, WM_MOVE, and WM_DESTROY messages are processed. Any other messages are sent on to the default message processing logic that Windows maintains for all programs.

Listing 3-9 MINIMAL2.CPP

```
// minimal2.cpp        first example processing messages

#include <afxwin.h>      // class library header file
#include "minimal2.hpp" // header file for this program

CTheApp theApp ;          // create one CTheApp object - runs program

BOOL CTheApp::InitInstance ()    // override default InitInstance()
{
    m_pMainWnd = new CMainWindow () ;        // create a main window
    m_pMainWnd->ShowWindow (m_nCmdShow) ;    // make it visible
    m_pMainWnd->UpdateWindow () ;            // paint center
    return TRUE ;
}

CMainWindow::CMainWindow ()       // constructor for window
{
    Create (NULL, "Minimal2") ;
}

BEGIN_MESSAGE_MAP (CMainWindow, CFrameWnd)  // process messages
    ON_WM_SIZE ()                // WM_SIZE message
    ON_WM_MOVE ()                // WM_MOVE message
    ON_WM_DESTROY()              // WM_DESTROY message
END_MESSAGE_MAP ()

                                 // WM_SIZE message processing
void CMainWindow::OnSize (UINT nType, int cx, int cy)
{
    this->SetWindowText ("Got a WM_SIZE message") ;
}

void CMainWindow::OnMove (int x, int y) // WM_MOVE message
{                                       // processing function
    this->SetWindowText ("Got a WM_MOVE message") ;
}

void CMainWindow::OnDestroy ()          // WM_DESTROY message
{                                       // processing function
    ::MessageBeep (0) ;
}
```

The bottom of MINIMAL2.CPP shows the three message processing functions. Although the message processing functions are defined as part of the **CWnd** MFC class, MINIMAL2.CPP derived a new class named **CMainWindow**, and the message response functions are shown as members of this new derived class.

Calling Functions in a Class (The this Pointer)

The **CMainWindow::OnSize()** and **CMainWindow::OnMove()** message processing functions both call the **CWnd::SetWindowText()** function to change the program window's caption when the appropriate message is received. **CWnd::SetWindowText()** is another member function of the **CWnd** MFC class, and it is used to change the text of any type of window that has a title. The **CMainWindow** class is derived from **CWnd**, so **CMainWindow** objects can call the **SetWindowText()** function. There are several ways to do this. One way is to explicitly call the function using the following syntax:

```
void CMainWindow::OnSize (UINT nType, int cx, int cy)
{
    CMainWindow::SetWindowText ("Got a WM_SIZE message") ;
}
```

This makes it clear to the compiler that the **SetWindowText()** function is a member of the **CMainWindow** class. The other way to call **SetWindowText()** is to take advantage of the C++ *this* pointer. Within the body of a function that is a member of a class, the *this* pointer points to the object itself. This sounds like double-talk, but it is simple once you get the hang of it. For example, to use the *this* pointer to call the **SetWindowText()** function:

```
void CMainWindow::OnSize (UINT nType, int cx, int cy)
{
    this->SetWindowText ("Got a WM_SIZE message") ;
}
```

The *this* pointer is used within a function of the **CMainWindow** class, so the pointer contains the address of the **CMainWindow** object. You can think of the *this* pointer from the point of view of the **CWnd::SetWindowText()** function. **SetWindowText()** must be called by a window object because otherwise the function would not know which window object should receive the text string. Because *this* is a pointer, you must use the -> operator to access a member. Do not worry if the *this* pointer seems a bit obscure at this time. Many of the examples in the book take advantage of the *this* pointer, so you will be able to see how it is used in different circumstances.

The last function put to use in MINIMAL2.CPP is the **::MessageBeep()** function. **::MessageBeep()** just beeps the speaker. If you are using the multimedia version of Windows, ::**MessageBeep**() produces a sound using the currently selected sound device. ::**MessageBeep**() is an interesting function in that it is not a member of any MFC class. There is no reason that ::**MessageBeep**() should be added to a class, as it basically functions on its own and is unlikely to be used to derive any new class. In C++, this type of function is called a "global" function because it is available inside or outside of any class definition or class member function.

The ::**MessageBeep**() function is declared in the WINDOWS.H header file that is included in AFXWIN.H. There are two ways to call ::**MessageBeep**(). One is to use standard C syntax, and the other is to use the C++ scope resolution operator "::" to explicitly mark ::**MessageBeep**() as global in scope. Listing 3-10 shows both methods being used to call ::**MessageBeep**().

The C++ syntax will be used throughout this book to clearly mark global functions. It is a good practice to always use the C++ extensions to the language rather than drifting back and forth between C and C++. C++ practices tend to be more rigorous, and reduce the chance of errors in your code.

Listing 3-10 Calling the MessageBeep() Function in C and C++

```
void CMainWindow::OnDestroy ()
{
    ::MessageBeep (0) ;        // C++ language, global function
    MessageBeep (0) ;          /* C language syntax, same effect */
}
```

Completing MINIMAL2

The last file you will need to create to compile MINIMAL2 is the module definition file. Listing 3-11 shows MINIMAL2.DEF, which is copied directly from the MINIMAL1.DEF file created in the last chapter. You will also need to define a project file in order to compile MINIMAL2, consisting of MINIMAL2.CPP and MINIMAL2.DEF.

Listing 3-11 MINIMAL2.DEF Module Definition File

```
NAME            minimal2
DESCRIPTION     'minimal2 C++ program'
EXETYPE         WINDOWS
STUB            'WINSTUB.EXE'
CODE            PRELOAD MOVEABLE
DATA            PRELOAD MOVEABLE MULTIPLE
HEAPSIZE        1024
STACKSIZE       5120
```

Where Are the Messages Received?

MINIMAL2 provides a good example of how MFC programs process messages. The MFC classes do such a good job of hiding the complexity behind Windows applications that you may wonder how the messages end up getting to the program. Do the messages end up going to the **CWinApp** or **CFrameWindow** based object?

When Windows "sends" a message to an application, all that Windows really does is copy the message data into a memory block that the application can access, and then alerts the application to read the memory block. When the application reads the memory block it is said to have "received" the message. The logic that reads the message data is defined in the **CWinApp** MFC class. This is why it is critical to derive a class from **CWinApp** and create an object from this class in the program, so that the message reading logic is added to the program by inheritance.

This does not mean that the message was "sent to" the **CWinApp** based object. The message is "sent to" a window in all cases. At a low level this means that the block of data that Windows uses to write the message includes the handle (ID value) for the window that is to "receive" the message. In MINIMAL2, the program's main window is the only window object the program creates, and this window "receives" all of the messages. More complex applications will have many window objects, each of which can send and receive messages to/from other windows.

Throughout the book, we will talk about messages being "sent" and "received" by window objects. This is a convenient abstraction of a fairly complex process that is being handled by the MFC classes. Unlike using the C language to create Windows applications, C++ and the MFC classes allow us to ignore the low-level details of receiving messages and concentrate on what the program should do when a message is received.

ADDING A MENU AND ICON

To close out this chapter, we will do one more improvement to MINIMAL. After this, we will not be able to call the program "minimal" any more, as it will be a complete Windows application. This final example is called MINIMAL3, and is shown in Figure 3-6. Note that MINIMAL3 has a menu bar containing two menu items, "Beep" and "Quit."

The main additions to our new MINIMAL3 program are a menu and an icon that is displayed when MINIMAL3 is minimized. These items are defined in the

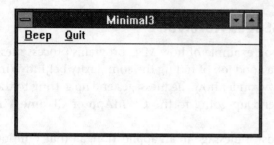

Figure 3-6 The MINIMAL3 Program

resource script file MINIMAL3.RC. As we saw in Chapter 1, *How Windows Works*, the data in the resource script file gets compiled by the resource compiler to make an .RES resource data file. The linker combines the data in the .RES file with the rest of the program to make a finished Windows application. Resources allow static data (data that does not change as the program runs) to be maintained separately from the program code. You can change the wording of the menu items, even translate them into another language, without changing the program code. Resources will be explored in more detail later in the book. For now, let's just add an icon and a menu to the MINIMAL3 program's resource script file, as shown in Listing 3-12.

MINIMAL3.RC introduces the three most common elements in resource script files. The first is a resource ID header file (named MINIMAL3.H) included at the top of the file. There is also a program icon and the definition of a simple menu. Each of these elements is discussed in the following sections.

Resource ID Header Files

The header file MINIMAL3.H is included at the top of the resource script file MINIMAL3.RC (and in the C++ program file MINIMAL3.CPP) to provide definitions of constants. Each menu item must have an ID number so that the program logic can determine which menu item was selected. Rather than use integer values in the program files, the menu item IDs are given names. IDM_BEEP is the ID for the "Beep" menu item, while "IDM_QUIT" is the ID for the "Quit" menu item. This makes the program files easier to read, and reduces the chance of using the wrong ID value for a menu item. The header file MINIMAL3.H (shown in Listing 3-13) is included at the top of both the .RC and .CPP programs so that the same ID values are known to both the C++ compiler and the resource compiler.

The examples in this book stick with the convention that header files that define C++ classes are given the file name extension .HPP, while header files that

Listing 3-12 MINIMAL3.RC Resource Script File

```
// minimal3.rc resource script file

#include <afxres.h>
#include "minimal3.h"

AFX_IDI_STD_FRAME    ICON    minimal3.ico    // the program's icon

MyMenu MENU                                  // define the menu
{
    MENUITEM "&Beep",        IDM_BEEP
    MENUITEM "&Quit",        IDM_QUIT
}
```

Listing 3-13 MINIMAL3.H Resource ID Header File

```
// minimal3.h  header file for resource ID numbers

#define IDM_BEEP     1       // menu items
#define IDM_QUIT     2
```

define ID values have the extension .H. The .CPP and .HPP file types date from the days that C++ programs were created by first running a "Pre-Processor" program that converted the C++ programs into a C program that a regular C compiler could handle. C++ compilers are now stand-alone programs, but the file name conventions remain. Note that the MFC header files such as AFXWIN.H use the simple .H file name extension.

Creating a Program Icon

The MINIMAL1 and MINIMAL2 programs do not include resource data. Both programs display the default Windows logo icon when minimized. Most programs create their own icon images so that the program is easy to identify when minimized at the bottom of the screen. The icon is first "drawn" using the Image Editor application that comes with the C++ 7.00 compiler, and then saved as a separate file with the extension .ICO. The icon image file is then added to the resource script file so that the icon data ends up as part of the finished program. Figure 3-7 shows the MINIMAL3.ICO icon supplied with the source code disks. Creating an icon image like Figure 3-7 is delightfully simple with the Image Editor application.

The individual steps needed to create the icon file are:

1. Select the "File/New..." menu item. A dialog box will appear giving you a choice of editing a bitmap, cursor, or icon. Select icon, and click the "OK" button.

Figure 3-7 Editing the MINIMAL3.ICO Icon Image in the Image Editor

2. A dialog box giving you a choice of the icon size and colors will appear. Select the default "4-Plane 16 COLORS 32x32 Pixels" and click the "OK" button. A blank editing area and the editing tools will appear in the work area.

3. Use the drawing tools and color palette to draw an icon image. This works just like other "paint" programs.

4. When you are done, select the "File/Save File As..." menu item. A dialog box will appear. Make sure that the directory name matches the "work" area where you are saving your program files. Enter the file name MINIMAL3.ICO, and then click the "OK" button.

5. The MINIMAL3.ICO icon file will be saved on your hard disk, ready to be included in the program's resource data.

With the icon image saved as MINIMAL3.ICO, you can include the icon in the program's resources. The MFC classes provide a convenient way to do this. If the program's icon is given the name AFX_IDI_STD_FRAME, the window derived from the **CFrameWindow** class will automatically use this icon image when the window is minimized. The icon data in the MINIMAL3.ICO file is assigned the name AFX_IDI_STD_FRAME in the MINIMAL3.RC resource script file. The key word ICON is used to label the data as icon image data so that the resource compiler knows which format to use when compiling the data. You will also need to include the AFXRES.H header file in your resource script file, to make sure the AFX_ID_STD_FRAME constant is defined.

```
AFX_IDI_STD_FRAME    ICON      minimal3.ico      // the program's icon
```

Defining a Menu

Menus are defined in the .RC file with a few lines of text. MINIMAL3 defines a menu called "MyMenu" that contains two menu items (see Listing 3-14). The first item is "Beep" and the second is "Quit." Note that the ID values (IDM_BEEP and IDM_QUIT) defined in the MINIMAL3.H header file are assigned to each menu item. These menu ID values are used to determine which menu item has been selected in the body of the C program.

The menu character strings that will be displayed on the menu bar are both preceded by ampersand (&) characters. This results in the first letter of each menu item being underlined. Pressing (ALT)-(B) will result in the "Beep" menu item being activated, while pressing (ALT)-(Q) will result in the "Quit" menu item being activated. This a quick way to provide keyboard alternatives for menu item selections.

Compiling the Resource Data

The resource script file MINIMAL3.RC cannot be compiled by the C++ compiler, as it is not a C++ language file. Instead a separate compiler called a "resource compiler" is used to convert the raw data in MINIMAL3.RC into a form that Windows will be able to use. The resource compiler reads the MINIMAL3.RC file, and creates the compiled resource data file MINIMAL3.RES, which is added to the final Windows program MINIMAL3.EXE.

All that is required to compile MINIMAL3.RC is to add that file name to the project list. The PWB project for MINIMAL3 will consist of MINIMAL3.CPP, MINIMAL3.DEF, and MINIMAL3.RC. PWB recognizes the .RC extension and automatically activates the resource compiler to compile MINIMAL3.RC.

Remaining MINIMAL3 Program Files

With the resource data and resource header file defined, the only files left to create for MINIMAL3 are the .CPP, .HPP, and .DEF files. They closely follow the MINIMAL2 example. Listing 3-15 shows the MINIMAL3.HPP header file which includes the class definitions for the CMainWindow and CTheApp classes. Note

Listing 3-14 The Menu Definition

```
MyMenu          MENU
{
    MENUITEM "&Beep",       IDM_BEEP
    MENUITEM "&Quit",       IDM_QUIT
}
```

Listing 3-15 MINIMAL3.HPP Header File

```
// minimal3.hpp    header file for minimal3.cpp

class CMainWindow : public CFrameWnd // derive a main window class
{
public:
    CMainWindow () ;              // declare a constructor
private:
    void OnBeep () ;             // respond to menu items
    void OnExit () ;

    DECLARE_MESSAGE_MAP()         // prepare for message processing
} ;

class CTheApp : public CWinApp  // derive an application class
{
public:
    BOOL InitInstance () ;        // declare new InitInstance()
} ;
```

that the **OnBeep()** and **OnExit()** functions have been declared as members of the CMainWindow class. These functions will respond to menu selections. Unlike functions that respond to specific messages like WM_MOVE and which have predefined names like **OnMove()**, functions that respond to menu items can have any name. MINIMAL3.HPP happens to choose function names that are similar to the predefined function names, but you could call the two functions anything you like.

The DECLARE_MESSAGE_MAP() macro is again included within the CMainWindow class definition in MINIMAL3.HPP to alert the compiler that messages will be processed. Listing 3-16 shows the MINIMAL3.CPP program that includes the message map.

Attaching the Menu

MINIMAL3 has a menu attached to the main program window. Defining a menu in the program's resource script file does not automatically attach the menu to the program's main window. You must do this by specifying the name of the menu (as defined in the resource script data) when you create the main program window. The previous examples did not have a main program menu and were able to use a very simple call to **CFrameWnd::Create()** to build the main program window:

```
Create (NULL, "Program Caption") ;
```

Listing 3-16 MINIMAL3.CPP

```cpp
// minimal3.cpp            first example with a menu

#include <afxwin.h>           // class library header file
#include "minimal3.h"         // header file for resource data
#include "minimal3.hpp"       // header file for this program

CTheApp theApp ;             // create one CTheApp object - runs program

BOOL CTheApp::InitInstance ()   // override default InitInstance()
{
    m_pMainWnd = new CMainWindow () ;          // create a main window
    m_pMainWnd->SetWindowText (m_lpCmdLine) ; // title == cmd line
    m_pMainWnd->ShowWindow (m_nCmdShow) ;      // make it visible
    m_pMainWnd->UpdateWindow () ;              // paint center
    return TRUE ;
}

CMainWindow::CMainWindow ()        // constructor for window
{
    Create (NULL, "", WS_OVERLAPPEDWINDOW, rectDefault,
        NULL, "MyMenu") ;
}

BEGIN_MESSAGE_MAP (CMainWindow, CFrameWnd)  // message map
    ON_COMMAND (IDM_BEEP, OnBeep)    // WM_COMMAND messages are
    ON_COMMAND (IDM_QUIT, OnExit)    // from menu items
END_MESSAGE_MAP ()

void CMainWindow::OnBeep ()      // respond to menu item "Beep"
{
    ::MessageBeep (0) ;          // beep the speaker
}

void CMainWindow::OnExit ()      // respond to menu item "Quit"
{
    this->DestroyWindow () ;     // destroy main window,
}                                // this stops application
```

You probably assumed that there were only two parameters passed to the **CFrameWnd::Create()** function. Actually, the function accepts six parameters. The last four parameters have default values defined in the AFXWIN.H file, so these default values can be used implicitly by simply not entering any values for the parameters when calling **CFrameWnd::Create()**. In the C++ language, default values can be used for parameters, as long as they are the last one or more parameters passed to the function. You cannot omit parameters in the middle of the list of parameters because the C++ compiler would not have any way of knowing which ones had been omitted.

The **CFrameWnd::Create()** function call that creates the MINIMAL3 main program window with the "MyMenu" menu attached is shown here. The menu name is the last parameter, so all six parameter values must be specified.

```
Create (NULL, "", WS_OVERLAPPEDWINDOW, rectDefault,
    NULL, "MyMenu") ;
```

Table 3-3 summarizes the parameter meanings for all six parameters passed to the **CFrameWnd::Create()** function. One unusual aspect of the MINIMAL3.CPP program is that the main program window's caption is not specified in the call to **CFrameWnd::Create()**. The null string ("") is used as a place holder for the caption. MINIMAL3 displays the command line string passed to the program when MINIMAL3 is started up and uses this character string as the caption. Passing a command line argument to a program will be explained a bit later in this chapter.

As you can see from Table 3-3, a lot of complexity is hidden away in the **CFrameWnd::Create()** function. Creating windows is a fundamental part of programming in the Windows environment. We will spend a good portion of the next several chapters exploring how windows are created and destroyed, and how the parameters passed to the **Create()** function can be used to change the properties of the window. For now let's concentrate on how the MINIMAL3 program processes messages from the Windows environment.

Processing Messages

Windows sends the MINIMAL3 program a WM_COMMAND message when a menu item is selected. A WM_COMMAND message is sent regardless of which menu item was selected, so there needs to be a way to decide which menu item was chosen. This is done using the menu item's ID number that we specified in the menu definition in MINIMAL3.RC. For example, the menu item titled "Beep" has the ID number IDM_BEEP. Windows sends this ID number along with the WM_COMMAND message sent to the program. The message map then specifies which function gets executed depending on the ID value passed with the WM_COMMAND message. Listing 3-17 shows the message map for MINIMAL3.CPP, which specifies that the **CMainWindow::OnBeep()** function should be executed if a WM_COMMAND message with the ID value IDM_BEEP

Listing 3-17 Message Map for MINIMAL3.CPP

```
BEGIN_MESSAGE_MAP (CMainWindow, CFrameWnd)  // message map
    ON_COMMAND (IDM_BEEP, OnBeep)    // WM_COMMAND messages are
    ON_COMMAND (IDM_QUIT, OnExit)    // from menu items
END_MESSAGE_MAP ()
```

BOOL **CFrameWnd::Create** (const char FAR* *lpClassName*, const char FAR* *lpWindowName*, DWORD *dwStyle*, const RECT& *rect*, const CWnd* *pParentWnd*, const char FAR* *lpMenuName*) ;

Parameter	Meaning
lpClassName	A pointer to a null-terminated character string containing the name of the window class upon which the window will be based. Window classes have nothing to do with C++ classes. Classes define basic data about a family of windows, such as the color of the window background. Use a value of NULL to specify a standard window with a white client area. Registering new classes of windows is explored in Chapter 8, *Child and Pop-Up Windows*.
lpWindowName	A pointer to a null-terminated character string containing the caption to be displayed at the top of the window.
dwStyle	A DWORD (32-bit) value consisting of a series of binary flag values that specify properties of the window, such as if the window should have a minimize and maximize button, thick or thin window border, etc. Use the value WS_OVERLAPPEDWINDOW to specify a standard program window with a thick border (for sizing the window), minimize, maximize buttons, system menu, and caption bar. Other *dwStyle* values are explored in Chapter 8, *Child and Pop-Up Windows*.
rect	A reference to a RECT structure that contains the initial size of the window when it is created. Use the predefined rectangle *rectDefault* to let Windows decide the initial size and position of the window. The RECT structure is explained in more detail in Chapter 5, *Window Controls*.
pParentWnd	A pointer to the parent window of the window being created. This will be NULL for a main program window. Child and parent windows are discussed in Chapter 5, *Window Controls*.
lpMenuName	A pointer to a null-terminated character string containing the name of the window's menu data in the resource script file.

Table 3-3 CFrameWnd::Create() Function Parameters

is received, and the **CMainWindow::OnExit()** function should be executed if a WM_COMMAND message with the ID value of IDM_QUIT is received.

You can imagine that in a program with a complex menu there would a long list of entries in the message map for all of the menu items. However, the logic for dealing with the actions that should occur as a result of the different menu items being selected is distributed among a series of functions. There will be one function in the window object's class definition for each menu item the window contains. Separating the logic for each menu item into separate functions makes the program easy to read and debug. This is another advantage of the message mapping approach used in the MFC classes.

As always you will need to create a module definition file for the program, as shown in Listing 3-18. The complete PWB project list to compile MINIMAL3.EXE will consist of MINIMAL3.CPP, MINIMAL3.RC, and MINIMAL3.DEF.

Passing a Command Line Argument

An interesting improvement to MINIMAL3.CPP is that the program can read information passed to the program when the program is started. This information is called a "command line string" because it is a string of characters that is passed to the application as part of the command that starts the program operating. There are a couple of ways to establish a command line string when starting a Windows program. One is to select the "File/Run" menu item from the Windows Program Manager. You will be presented with a dialog box similar to Figure 3-8. Enter the full path name where the MINIMAL3.EXE program is stored, followed by the command line string. In Figure 3-8 the string "Hi There!" is passed with the function name.

Any characters following the file name in the "File/Run" dialog box are passed to MINIMAL3.EXE. This string is then used to create the MINIMAL3 window title, as shown in Figure 3-9. This is a trivial use for the command line string. Normally, the command line string is used to pass a file name to the program so that the program can load the file on startup. All of the applications bundled with Windows such as NOTEPAD and WRITE, support this feature.

Another way to pass a command line string to a program is by associating the command line with a program icon. To do this, open up one of the groups in the Program Manager application, such as the Accessories group, and select

Listing 3-18 MINIMAL3.DEF Module Definition File

```
NAME            minimal3
DESCRIPTION     'minimal3 C++ program'
EXETYPE         WINDOWS
STUB            'WINSTUB.EXE'
CODE            PRELOAD MOVEABLE
DATA            PRELOAD MOVEABLE MULTIPLE
HEAPSIZE        1024
STACKSIZE       5120
```

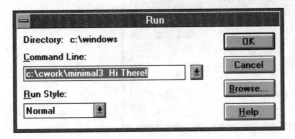

Figure 3-8 The Program Manager "File/Run" Menu Dialog Box

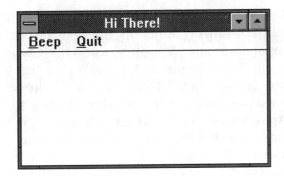

Figure 3-9 MINIMAL3 After Receiving the "Hi There!" Command Line

the "File/New" menu item from the Program Manager menu. A dialog box will appear, similar to that shown in Figure 3-10, allowing you to enter the program's description (which will appear under the icon in the Program Manager group window), the command line string including the program name, and the working directory. You can also select either the program's icon, or another of the stock icon images supplied with Windows. When you select the "OK" button, the program will appear iconized in the Program Manager group window. Double-clicking the icon image will start the program, again passing the command line string on as the *m_lpCmdLine* value when the program starts.

One last way to pass a command line argument to a Windows program is to do it while starting Windows. For example, if you start Windows with the following line, Windows will start running, and start the MINIMAL3.EXE program at the beginning of the Windows session.

```
win c:\msc\work\minimal4 Hi There!
```

Now that you know how to pass a command line string to a program on startup, how do you get the program to read the string? The answer is that the

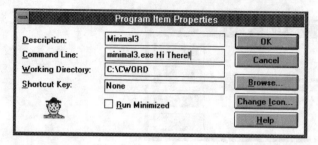

Figure 3-10 Setting a String for a Program Icon in a Program Manager Group

MFC class **CWinApp** automatically takes care of this chore for us. Listing 3-19 shows the **CTheApp::InitInstance()** function from MINIMAL3.CPP. MINIMAL3.CPP sets the main program's caption using the **CWnd::Set-WindowText()** function. The command line string is passed to **CWnd::SetWindowText()** as the *m_lpCmdLine* value. In the previous examples, *m_lpCmdLine* would point to the character string "Hi There!"

Recall that the **CTheApp** class is derived from the **CWinApp** MFC class. The **CWinApp** class defines six public data members that are available to any derived class, which are summarized in Table 3-4. Normally you will only use the *m_nCmdShow* and *m_lpCmdLine* data members in a program. It is also critical to set the *m_pMainWnd* data member equal to a pointer to the main program window. This value is returned when the program's main window is created with the *new* operator, as shown in Listing 3-19.

This is a good time to look up the **CWinApp** class definition in the MFC documentation. Although the **CWinApp** does all sorts of complex things for all MFC applications, the class interface (the parts of the class you will use as a programmer) is quite small. At this point you have been exposed to about half of the class interface. The other commonly used member functions will be introduced in the course of the next few chapters.

Listing 3-19 Setting the Windows Caption

```
BOOL CTheApp::InitInstance ()    // override default InitInstance()
{
    m_pMainWnd = new CMainWindow () ;              // create a main window
    m_pMainWnd->SetWindowText (m_lpCmdLine) ;      // title == cmd line
    m_pMainWnd->ShowWindow (m_nCmdShow) ;          // make it visible
    m_pMainWnd->UpdateWindow () ;                  // paint center
    return TRUE ;
}
```

Variable Name	Meaning
m_pszAppName	A pointer to a character string containing the application's name.
m_hInstance	The program's instance handle. This is a unique ID value that identifies the instance of the program. This value is seldom used with the MFC functions.
m_hPrevInstance	The instance handle of the previous instance of the program. If this is the only instance of the program running, *m_hPrevInstance* will equal NULL. Checking for NULL is the best way to check if another instance of the same program is already running.
m_lpCmdLine	A pointer to a character string containing the command line passed to the application. This is usually used to pass a data file name so that the application can read and display the file immediately on startup.
m_nCmdShow	An integer value that is passed to the **CWnd::ShowWindow()** function to specify if the window should be initially displayed minimized, maximized, or normally sized. These integer values are defined in WINDOWS.H as SW_SHOWMINIMIZED, SW_SHOWNORMAL, etc.
m_pMainWnd	Holds a pointer to the program's main window. A key task you need to perform in the **CWinApp::InitInstance()** function is to create the program's main window, and set *m_pMainWnd* equal to the window object's address.

Table 3-4 CWinApp Public Data Members

SUMMARY

This chapter improved the MINIMAL1 program in three steps to build a complete Windows application. First the program was split into a separate .CPP and .HPP file, which is the standard way C++ programs are constructed. Next a message map was added, which processed the WM_SIZE, WM_MOVE, and WM_DESTROY messages sent to the program from Windows. Finally, we added an icon and a simple menu to the program's resource data, and the message map changed to respond to WM_COMMAND messages generated when menu items are selected.

The final version, MINIMAL3, does nothing special other than beep the computer's sound device. However, it has all of the elements of a normal Windows program. It creates its own application class and main window class, processes several messages, and makes use of data in a resource file. MINIMAL3 is an ideal starting point for many Windows projects.

QUESTIONS

1. Write in standard C++ notation the following Windows types:
   a. WORD
   b. LPSTR
   c. PINT
   d. BOOL

2. Add a Hungarian notation prefix to each of the following variable names to reflect its type. For example, if the variable "MyInt" is an integer, it would be labeled "nMyInt."
   a. Name, a near pointer to a null-terminated character string.
   b. Toggle, an unsigned integer that is either zero or one.
   c. Window, a handle of a window.

3. You must include the AFXWIN.H header file at the top of any C++ listing, as it contains all of the class library functions. (True/False)

4. The Windows data element that is used to keep track of an object in memory is a _____.

5. The **CObject** class is the MFC base class for both **CWinApp** and **CWnd**. (True/False)

6. The message map started with the _____ macro and ended with the _____ macro. In addition, the window class for the window processing the messages will need the _____ macro to alert the compiler that the class contains a message map.

7. The name of the function that will respond to WM_MOVE messages is always _____.

8. The *this* pointer points to
   a. the object for which the function containing *this* is a member
   b. the program's window object
   c. the program's **CWinApp** object

9. The **MessageBeep()** function belongs to which class?
   a. **CWinApp**
   b. **CWnd**
   c. **CFrameWnd**
   d. no class

10. Windows always sends a WM_COMMAND message when the user selects a menu item, regardless of which item was selected. (True/False)

EXERCISES

1. Modify MINIMAL3 so that the first menu item is entitled "Show Title." When this menu item is selected, the program window's caption should change to "Menu item clicked!"

2. Change the STACKSIZE and HEAPSIZE values in MINIMAL3.DEF to zero and recompile. What happens to the application? What if only one of the two values is zero? What if either of the two values is set to a low number like 100 bytes?

ANSWERS TO QUESTIONS

1. a. unsigned int
   b. char FAR *
   c. int *
   d. int

2. a. pszName
   b. bToggle
   c. hWindow

3. False. The AFXWIN.H file is only needed if you use the MFC classes to create a Windows application. The header file does not contain all of the functions, as much of the MFC class code is stored in library files that accessed in the link stage of building the finished program.

4. handle.

5. True.

6. BEGIN_MESSAGE_MAP(), END_MESSAGE_MAP(), DECLARE_MESSAGE_MAP().

7. **OnMove()**.

8. a.

9. d. **MessageBeep()** is a global function.

10. True.

SOLUTIONS TO EXERCISES

1. You will need to modify the resource script file and the .CPP program file. You may want to change the name of the function that responds to the menu item selection from **CMainWindow::OnBeep()** to **CMainWindow::OnShow()**, although this is not strictly necessary. It is also appropriate to change the label given to the menu item from IDM_BEEP to something like IDM_SHOW. This ID value is defined in the resource ID header file. The complete solutions are given under the file name C3EXER1 on the source code disks. Excerpts from the solution are shown in Listings 3-20 to 3-23.

2. MINIMAL3 will not run if either the STACKSIZE or HEAPSIZE value in the MINIMAL3.DEF module definition file is set to zero. The program will terminate on startup with a "Memory Protection Error." This is caused by the program attempting to write on a memory area that is not assigned to the program. The program will run normally if both STACKSIZE and HEAPSIZE are set to nonzero values. This is because the stack will be increased to 5,120 bytes automatically as long as a stack is created, and the heap is expanded as needed to hold the program's data.

Listing 3-20 C3EXER1.RC Changes to the Menu Definition

```
// c3exer1.rc  resource script file

#include <afxres.h>
#include "c3exer1.h"

AFX_IDI_STD_FRAME  ICON  c3exer1.ico   // the program's icon

MyMenu MENU                            // define the menu
{
    MENUITEM "&Show Title", IDM_SHOW
    MENUITEM "&Quit",       IDM_QUIT
}
```

Listing 3-21 C3EXER1.H Modified Resorce ID Header File

```
// c3exer1.h  header file for resource ID numbers

#define IDM_SHOW   1   // menu items
#define IDM_QUIT   2
```

Listing 3-22 C3EXER1.HPP

```
// c3exer1.hpp    header file for c3exer1.cpp

class CMainWindow : public CFrameWnd // derive a main window class
{
public:
    CMainWindow () ;              // declare a constructor
private:
    void OnShow () ;             // respond to menu items
    void OnExit () ;

    DECLARE_MESSAGE_MAP()        // prepare for message processing
} ;

class CTheApp : public CWinApp  // derive an application class
{
public:
    BOOL InitInstance () ;       // declare new InitInstance()
} ;
```

Listing 3-23 C3EXER1.CPP Excerpt—Changes to CPP Program

```
BEGIN_MESSAGE_MAP (CMainWindow, CFrameWnd)  // message map
    ON_COMMAND (IDM_SHOW, OnShow)    // WM_COMMAND messages are
    ON_COMMAND (IDM_QUIT, OnExit)    // from menu items
END_MESSAGE_MAP ()

void CMainWindow::OnShow ()      // respond to menu item "Beep"
{
    this->SetWindowText ("Menu item clicked!") ;
}
```

## Chapter 4

Text and Graphics Output

Unlike most MS-DOS programs that use character-mode displays, Windows programs output everything to the screen using graphics functions. This chapter explains how to output text and graphic images using the rich collection of graphics functions that Windows provides. Windows allows programmers to write programs without concern about the specifics of the video hardware. A Windows program that works on a VGA display will work without modification on an EGA, Super VGA, IBM 8514, or any other video display that Windows supports. The key to this "device independence" is that Windows uses a "device context." We will explore how the device context can be used for both text and graphics output, and how using the device context keeps our programs from interfering with each other on the screen. The last example program will sum things up by demonstrating animated graphics, creating a ball that bounces around inside the program's window.

The MFC classes do an excellent job of encapsulating the Windows text and graphics functions in a few objects. The **CDC** class includes essentially all of the device context functions you will need to use. Although the **CDC** class automates a number of low-level tasks that C programmers must do for themselves, there are still a few traps to avoid. This chapter will guide you through the correct use of the graphics functions in the **CDC** class.

Concepts covered: Device independence, device context, GDI, device drivers, changing device context settings, RGB color model, freeing graphics objects from memory, animation.

Key words covered: OPAQUE, TRANSPARENT.

Classes covered: CDC, CClientDC, CPaintDC, CString, CPen, CBrush, CRect.

Functions covered: CString::GetLength(), CDC::TextOut(), CWinApp::OnPaint(), CDC::SetTextColor(), CDC::SetBkColor(), CDC::SetBkMode(), CDC::SelectStockObject(), CDC::SelectObject(), CDC::Rectangle(), CDC::Ellipse(), CWinApp::OnIdle(), CWnd::GetClientRect(), CRect::Width(), CRect::Height().

Messages covered: WM_PAINT, WM_CLOSE.

CHARACTER VERSUS GRAPHICS MODE

When you start a program under MS-DOS, the computer's screen is in character mode. The dot pattern for each character shown on the screen is stored in the video board's memory chips. The usual display configuration allows 80 characters across each line and 25 lines of characters. Each character occupies a fixed position on the screen. The characters always have the same font (character shapes), although the color of each letter and its background can be changed.

Character mode displays have the advantage of being relatively fast. However, character mode displays limit what you can show on the screen. There is no good way to show different character fonts, such as italics and boldface letters of different sizes, with a character mode display. Nor is there a way to show pictures, unless the pictures are crudely formed from colored characters and character-sized symbols.

To get around the limitations of character mode displays, all modern video boards support one or more graphics modes. In graphics modes, everything is drawn one dot (pixel) at a time. A typical VGA display will show 640 pixels horizontally by 480 pixels vertically. Each pixel can be any of 16 colors. Less expensive displays, such as the older CGA and EGA types, display fewer pixels and have fewer simultaneous colors. More expensive displays, such as super VGA boards, typically show 1,028 by 760 pixels with 256 simultaneous colors. Even higher resolutions are available at a price.

Many DOS programs switch to a graphics mode to show charts and graphs. This method is more flexible, but requires that the DOS program use different commands if the output is to a CGA, EGA, VGA, or Super VGA display, or to a printer, plotter, or some other graphics device. MS-DOS programs must be continually updated to keep up with the evolution of computer hardware. If you have five MS-DOS programs on your computer that support graphics, each of the programs will come with its own code for supporting the different types of displays. This adds up to a lot of duplicate code.

Windows always runs in a graphics mode. This is slower than using a character mode display, but much more flexible. Because everything (even letters and numbers) is drawn one pixel at a time, any shape or size is possible. Windows has no trouble displaying characters in different sizes, with italics and boldface letters. Windows is also free to draw any desired shape or color on the screen at any location. This freedom allowed the designers of Windows 3.0 and 3.1 the flexibility to come up with attractive "three-dimensional" shapes for buttons and scroll bars, and attractive color combinations for the window elements.

The Device Context

During the original design of Windows, one of the goals was to provide "device independence." This means that the same program should be able to work using different screens, keyboards, and printers without modification to the program. Windows takes care of the hardware, allowing the programmer to concentrate on the program itself. If you have ever had to update the code of an MS-DOS program for the latest printer, plotter, video display, or keyboard, you will recognize that device independence is a huge advantage for the developer.

Windows programs do not send data directly to the screen or printer. Instead, the program obtains a handle (ID value) for the screen or printer's *device context*. The output data is sent to the device context (DC), and then Windows takes care of sending it to the real hardware. The advantage of using the DC is that the graphics and text commands you send to the DC are always the same, regardless of whether the physical output is showing up on a VGA screen, IBM 8514 video device, printer, or some device that was invented the day after you shipped your program.

Windows GDI

There are two parts of Windows that do the conversion from the Windows graphics function calls to the actual commands sent to the hardware. One part is the GDI, or Graphics Device Interface. Most of the GDI resides in a program file called GDI.EXE that is stored in the Windows System directory. The Windows environment will load GDI.EXE into memory when it is needed for graphical output. Windows will also load a "device driver" program if the hardware conversions are not part of GDI.EXE. Common examples are VGA.DRV for a VGA video screen, and HPPLC.DRV for the HP LaserJet printer. Drivers are just programs that assist the GDI in converting Windows graphics commands to hardware commands. Figure 4-1 shows the relationship between the program and the physical hardware for a Windows application.

Output of Text

To get started, we will output some text to the screen. The program called TEXT1 is similar in appearance to MINIMAL3 from the last chapter. When the "Show

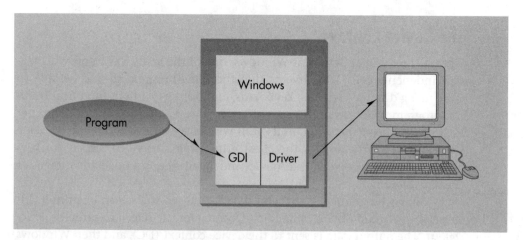

Figure 4-1 Output to a Device by a Windows Program

Text" menu item is clicked, the string "This string is displayed when a menu item is selected." is displayed below the menu bar. Figure 4-2 shows the result.

You can create the TEXT1 program quickly by copying and then modifying the files from MINIMAL3. Listing 4-1 shows the header file for TEXT1. The **CMainWindow** class declares the **OnShowText()** function, which will output the line of text when the "Show Text" menu item is selected.

TEXT1 also needs a header file to store the ID numbers for the program's resources. The TEXT1.H file (Listing 4-2) is pretty simple, as there are only two menu items that need ID numbers.

The menu itself is defined in the TEXT1.RC resource script file (Listing 4-3). Note that TEXT1.RC includes an icon file named TEXT1.ICO for the program's

Listing 4-1 TEXT1.HPP Header File

```
// text1.hpp     header file for text1.cpp
                                // derive a main window class
class CMainWindow : public CFrameWnd
{
public:
    CMainWindow () ;                // declare a constructor
    void OnShowText () ;           // display text function
    void OnExit () ;               // stop application function

    DECLARE_MESSAGE_MAP()          // prepare for message processing
} ;

class CTheApp : public CWinApp    // derive an application class
{
public:
    BOOL InitInstance () ;         // declare new InitInstance()
} ;
```

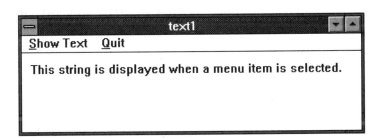

Figure 4-2 The TEXT1 Program

Listing 4-2 TEXT1.H Resource ID Header File

```
// text1.h  header file for resource ID numbers

#define IDM_SHOW      1
#define IDM_QUIT      10
```

Listing 4-3 TEXT1.RC Resource Script File

```
// text1.rc  resource script file

#include <afxres.h>
#include "text1.h"

AFX_IDI_STD_FRAME   ICON    text1.ico   // the program's icon

MyMenu MENU                              // define the menu
{
    MENUITEM "&Show Text",   IDM_SHOW
    MENUITEM "&Quit",        IDM_QUIT
}
```

icon. The icon image is shown in Figure 4-3. You will need to use the Image Editor application to create this file.

Don't forget to create a module definition file for TEXT1. The TEXT1.DEF file is shown in Listing 4-4.

Finally, there is the program file, TEXT1.CPP. As you can see from Listing 4-5, most of TEXT1.CPP is just like MINIMAL3.CPP. The significant changes are all boldfaced. The big change is the addition of the **CMainWindow::On-ShowText()** function, which is executed when a WM_COMMAND message with the ID value IDM_SHOW is received. The WM_COMMAND message is mapped to **CMainWindow::OnShowText()** in the message map.

Using the Device Context

The key part of TEXT1.CPP to notice is the **CMainWindow::OnShowText()** function. Two new MFC classes are introduced here, **CString** and **CClientDC**.

Figure 4-3 TEXT1.ICO Icon Image

Listing 4-4 TEXT1.DEF Module Definition File

```
NAME            text1
DESCRIPTION     'text1 C++ program'
EXETYPE         WINDOWS
STUB            'WINSTUB.EXE'
CODE            PRELOAD MOVEABLE
DATA            PRELOAD MOVEABLE MULTIPLE
HEAPSIZE        1024
STACKSIZE       5120
```

Listing 4-5 TEXT1.CPP

```cpp
// text1.cpp            simple example displaying text string

#include <afxwin.h>     // class library header file
#include "text1.h"      // header file for resource data
#include "text1.hpp"    // header file for this program

CTheApp theApp ;        // create one CTheApp object - runs program

BOOL CTheApp::InitInstance ()    // override default InitInstance()
{
    m_pMainWnd = new CMainWindow () ;        // create a main window
    m_pMainWnd->ShowWindow (m_nCmdShow) ;    // make it visible
    m_pMainWnd->UpdateWindow () ;            // paint center
    return TRUE ;
}


CMainWindow::CMainWindow ()       // constructor for window
{
    Create (NULL, "text1", WS_OVERLAPPEDWINDOW, rectDefault,
        NULL, "MyMenu") ;
}


BEGIN_MESSAGE_MAP (CMainWindow, CFrameWnd)   // send selected messages
    ON_COMMAND (IDM_SHOW, OnShowText)        // text display function
    ON_COMMAND (IDM_QUIT, OnExit)            // to exit function
END_MESSAGE_MAP ()

void CMainWindow::OnShowText ()  // respond to menu item "Message"
{
    CString string = "This string is displayed when a menu item is selected." ;
    CClientDC dc (this) ;         // client area device context

    dc.TextOut (10, 10, string, string.GetLength ()) ; // show string
}

void CMainWindow::OnExit ()       // respond to menu item "Quit"
{
    this->DestroyWindow () ;    // destroy main window,
}                              // this stops application
```

The **CString** class is a collection of many functions relating to manipulating character strings. In **CMainWindow::OnShowText()**, a **CString** object named *string* is created and initialized with a character string. You can create a **CString** object without immediately setting it equal to a string, but in this case it is easier to create *string* and fill it with character data all in one step. The only **CString** function that is used in TEXT1.CPP is **CString::GetLength()**, which returns the number of characters in the string object. The **CString** class has many other functions and operators, which will be put to use throughout this book.

The other new class is **CClientDC**, which is used to work with the device context for the client area of a window. The **CClientDC** class is derived from **CDC**, the base MFC class that contains most of the text and graphics output functions. Figure 4-4 shows the class derivation.

The **CClientDC** class does not add any new functions or operators to the **CDC** class. Instead, **CClientDC** is designed to initialize a device context to the settings for a computer screen. This is done in the **CClientDC** constructor function which gets passed a pointer to the window object which will receive graphics output. The line

```
CClientDC dc (this) ; // construct client area device context
```

passes a pointer to the window handle to the constructor function for the **CClientDC** class. The *this* pointer points to the **CMainWindow** class object, as *this* is used within the body of a **CMainWindow** class function. The **CClientDC** object created is given the name *dc*. After you have created a **CClientDC** object, you can do all sorts of output to the device. In TEXT1.CPP, only the **CDC::TextOut()** function is used to output a single line of text.

```
dc.TextOut (10, 10, string, string.GetLength ()) ;
```

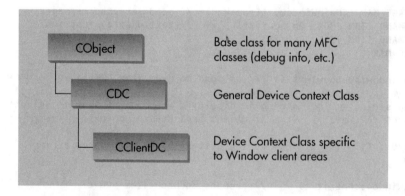

Figure 4-4 Derivation of the CClientDC MFC Class

The text automatically shows up in the window's client area, as *dc* is a **CClientDC** object for the program's main window. The string is started at a position 10 pixels to the right and 10 pixels below the upper left corner of the window's client area. The **CDC::TextOut()** function expects to get the number of characters in the string to output as the fourth parameter, which is conveniently fetched using the **CString::GetLength()** function.

Compile TEXT1 and give it a try. Note that the text appears when you click the "Show Text" menu item, but it is not repainted if you resize the window, minimize it, and then restore it, or cover TEXT1's window with another program's window and then uncover it. These are all commonplace activities for a Windows application, so the text needs to be made more permanent.

THE WM_PAINT MESSAGE

The reason that the text painted in the client area (center) of the TEXT1 window keeps disappearing is that Windows repaints the window every time it is uncovered or changed in size. This automatic repainting logic is what keeps your window from vanishing from the screen once it is covered up by another application. When Windows is about to repaint the client area of an application program's window, Windows sends the application a WM_PAINT message. In TEXT1, this message is not processed by the program's message mapping logic, so the WM_PAINT message just gets passed on to the default message processing logic built into Windows. The default processing just repaints the client area without regard to its contents, which has the effect of re-creating a blank client area.

To avoid having the text disappear, we can intercept the WM_PAINT message and repaint the text. The text lines will be redrawn right after the client area is painted with the window's class brush. Listing 4-6 shows TEXT2.CPP, which is very similar to TEXT1.CPP (the changes are boldfaced).

The message map in TEXT2.CPP has been expanded to include processing of the WM_PAINT message. The function that processes WM_PAINT must be called **OnPaint()**. The WM_PAINT message is sent every time the window's client area needs repainting, so the **OnPaint()** function is the ideal place to put the program's painting logic. TEXT2.CPP is so simple that only a single line of text is output in **OnPaint()**, but the examples that follow will demonstrate more complex output including text and graphics.

In the **CMainWindow::OnShowText()** function, TEXT1.CPP uses the **CClientDC** class to output text to the window's client area device context.

Listing 4-6 TEXT2.CPP

```
// text2.cpp            example with WM_PAINT repainting logic

#include <afxwin.h>    // class library header file
#include "text2.h"     // header file for resource data
#include "text2.hpp"    // header file for this program

CTheApp theApp ;        // create one CTheApp object - runs program

BOOL CTheApp::InitInstance ()    // override default InitInstance()
{
    m_pMainWnd = new CMainWindow () ;      // create a main window
    m_pMainWnd->ShowWindow (m_nCmdShow) ;   // make it visible
    m_pMainWnd->UpdateWindow () ;           // cause painting
    return TRUE ;
}


CMainWindow::CMainWindow ()      // constructor for window
{
    Create (NULL, "text2", WS_OVERLAPPEDWINDOW, rectDefault,
        NULL, "MyMenu") ;
}


BEGIN_MESSAGE_MAP (CMainWindow, CFrameWnd)
    ON_WM_PAINT ()
    ON_COMMAND (IDM_SHOW, OnShowText)
    ON_COMMAND (IDM_QUIT, OnExit)
END_MESSAGE_MAP ()

void CMainWindow::OnShowText ()  // respond to menu item "Message"
{
    CString string = "This string is displayed when a menu item is selected." ;
    CClientDC dc (this) ;       // client area device context

    dc.TextOut (10, 10, string, string.GetLength ()) ;  // show string
}


void CMainWindow::OnPaint ()     // custom window painting function
{                                // called when window need repainting
    CString string = "This string is output as part of painting logic." ;
    CPaintDC dc(this) ;          // get client area device context
            // output starts at 30, 30, missing other text
    dc.TextOut (30, 30, string, string.GetLength ()) ;  // show string
}


void CMainWindow::OnExit ()      // respond to menu item "Quit"
{
    this->DestroyWindow () ;     // destroy main window,
}                                // this stops application
```

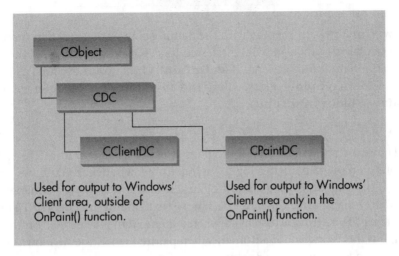

Figure 4-5 Class Derivation of CPaintDC and CClientDC

CMainWindow::OnShowText() is activated when the user selects the "Show Text" menu item. The **CClientDC** class works everywhere *except* in **OnPaint()** functions. When processing the WM_PAINT in an **OnPaint()** function, the specialized **CPaintDC** class must be used. The **CPaintDC** class is also derived from the **CDC** MFC class, so all of the same output functions are available in **CPaintDC**. Figure 4-5 shows how the **CPaintDC** and **CClientDC** classes are related. All of the output functions like **TextOut()** are inherited from the **CDC** base class, so both the **CClientDC** and **CPaintDC** classes use the same set of inherited functions.

The CWnd::OnPaint() Function

You will need to create an **OnPaint()** function as part of your main program window class to process WM_PAINT messages. If you dig through the MFC documentation, you will find that **OnPaint()** is defined as part of the **CWnd** class, which is the base class for all of the derived window classes. Writing your own **OnPaint()** function overrides the default **CWnd::OnPaint()** function, giving your program a chance to do whatever painting operations are appropriate. In TEXT2.CPP, the new **OnPaint()** function is **CMainWin-**

continued on next page

---

continued from previous page

dow::OnPaint(). In keeping with the naming conventions used in this book, the **OnPaint()** function will be referred to as **CWnd::OnPaint()** if the function is referred to in general. If an **OnPaint()** function is declared as part of the **CMainWindow** class, then the function will be referred to as **CMainWindow::OnPaint()**.

Figure 4-6 shows the TEXT2 program in action. The text line "This string is output as part of painting logic." is repainted whenever Windows sends a WM_PAINT message. This gives the illusion of the text being permanently on the TEXT2 client area. Clicking the "Show Text" menu item on TEXT2 outputs the string "This string is displayed when a menu item is selected." on the client area, but this string is not automatically repainted when the window is resized, covered and uncovered, and so on.

Listings 4-7 to 4-10 show the TEXT2 header, resource script, module definition, and project files. The program's icon is shown in Figure 4-7.

Although it is a simple example, TEXT2 gives you an outline of the structure of any Windows application program that needs to keep the client area painted. The **CMainWindow::OnPaint()** function repaints the client area every time a WM_PAINT message is received. Windows detects when the client area needs to

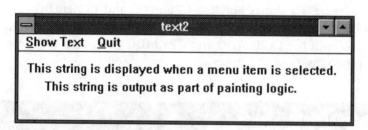

Figure 4-6 TEXT2 Updated by Processing WM_PAINT Messages

Figure 4-7 TEXT2.ICO Icon Image

Listing 4-7 TEXT2.HPP Header File

```
// text2.hpp     header file for text2.cpp
                                // derive a main window class
class CMainWindow : public CFrameWnd
{
public:
    CMainWindow () ;            // declare a constructor
    void OnPaint() ;           // custom painting function
    void OnShowText () ;       // display text function
    void OnExit () ;           // stop application function
    DECLARE_MESSAGE_MAP()      // prepare for message processing
} ;

class CTheApp : public CWinApp     // derive an application class
{
public:
    BOOL InitInstance () ;         // declare new InitInstance()
} ;
```

Listing 4-8 TEXT2.H Resource ID Header File

```
// text2.h  header file for resource ID numbers

#define IDM_SHOW        1
#define IDM_QUIT        10
```

Listing 4-9 TEXT2.RC Resource Script File

```
// text2.rc  resource script file

#include <afxres.h>
#include "text2.h"

AFX_IDI_STD_FRAME   ICON    text2.ico    // the program's icon

MyMenu MENU                              // define the menu
{
    MENUITEM "&Show Text",   IDM_SHOW
    MENUITEM "&Quit",        IDM_QUIT
}
```

Listing 4-10 TEXT2.DEF Module Definition File

```
NAME            text2
DESCRIPTION     'text2 C++ program'
EXETYPE         WINDOWS
STUB            'WINSTUB.EXE'
CODE            PRELOAD MOVEABLE
DATA            PRELOAD MOVEABLE MULTIPLE
HEAPSIZE        1024
STACKSIZE       5120
```

be repainted and sends WM_PAINT messages to the application. The only tricky thing to remember is that you must use the specialized **CPaintDC** class for the client area device context when programming the **OnPaint()** function. Everywhere else in a program you will use the **CClientDC** class to manage a window's client area device context.

Changing the Device Context

So far we have just used the **CDC::TextOut()** function to output character strings to the client area of a window. The default settings for a window's client area device context show the characters in black and white, using the system character font. We can change the color and character font by selecting new values into the device context before the characters are output. TEXT3.CPP in Listing 4-11 shows two examples of this being done, both within the OnPaint() function, and in response to a menu selection.

The result of these changes is shown in Figure 4-8. The upper line, which is displayed when the "Show Text!" menu item is clicked, now uses the small ANSI_VAR_FONT character font. This is a stock font that is always available within Windows. The second line, painted each time a WM_PAINT message is processed, uses the standard font, but shows the text with red letters on a blue background. **CDC::SetTextColor()** changes the color of the text characters, but not their background. **CDC::SetBkColor()** changes the color of the background around each character. Changing the background color does not affect the color of the entire client area, but only the color of a rectangle surrounding each character drawn with the new background color.

CDC::SetBkMode() changes the background painting mode to either OPAQUE or TRANSPARENT. The TRANSPARENT mode is the default, which allows any color or pattern already on the device context to "show through" around the characters. The OPAQUE mode causes the entire rectangle around

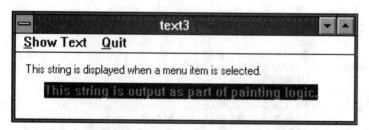

Figure 4-8 The TEXT3 Program

Listing 4-11 TEXT3.CPP

```cpp
// text3.cpp            changing the text color and background

#include <afxwin.h>      // class library header file
#include "text3.h"       // header file for resource data
#include "text3.hpp"     // header file for this program

CTheApp theApp ;          // create one CTheApp object - runs program

BOOL CTheApp::InitInstance ()    // override default InitInstance()
{
    m_pMainWnd = new CMainWindow () ;        // create a main window
    m_pMainWnd->ShowWindow (m_nCmdShow) ;    // make it visible
    m_pMainWnd->UpdateWindow () ;            // paint center
    return TRUE ;
}

CMainWindow::CMainWindow ()       // constructor for window
{
    Create (NULL, "text3", WS_OVERLAPPEDWINDOW, rectDefault,
        NULL, "MyMenu") ;
}

BEGIN_MESSAGE_MAP (CMainWindow, CFrameWnd)
    ON_WM_PAINT ()
    ON_COMMAND (IDM_SHOW, OnShowText)
    ON_COMMAND (IDM_QUIT, OnExit
END_MESSAGE_MAP ()

void CMainWindow::OnShowText ()  // respond to menu item "Message"
{
    CString string =
        "This string is displayed when a menu item is selected." ;
    CClientDC dc (this) ;        // client area device context

    dc.SelectStockObject (ANSI_VAR_FONT) ;  // select different font
    dc.TextOut (10, 10, string, string.GetLength ()) ;  // show string
}

void CMainWindow::OnPaint ()       // custom window painting function
{                                  // called when window need repainting
    CString string =
        "This string is output as part of painting logic." ;
    CPaintDC dc(this) ;            // get client area device context

    dc.SetTextColor (RGB (255, 0, 0)) ;       // text color to red
    dc.SetBkMode (OPAQUE) ;                    // opaque painting mode
    dc.SetBkColor (RGB (0, 0, 255)) ;          // text backround blue
    dc.TextOut (30, 30, string, string.GetLength ()) ;  // show string
}

void CMainWindow::OnExit ()        // respond to menu item "Quit"
{
    this->DestroyWindow () ;       // destroy main window,
}                                  // this stops application
```

the character to be repainted with the current background color.
CDC::SetBkColor() is usually used with **CDC::SetBkMode()** to color the background around each character.

The support files for TEXT3.CPP are shown in Listings 4-12 to 4-15. These files are identical to the TEXT2 equivalents. Figure 4-9 shows the program's icon.

Listing 4-12 TEXT3.HPP Header File

```
// text3.hpp    header file for text3.cpp

class CMainWindow : public CFrameWnd  // derive a main window class
{
public:
    CMainWindow () ;                   // declare a constructor
    void OnPaint() ;                   // custom painting function
    void OnShowText () ;               // display text function
    void OnExit () ;                   // stop application function
    DECLARE_MESSAGE_MAP()              // prepare for message processing
} ;

class CTheApp : public CWinApp        // derive an application class
{
public:
    BOOL InitInstance () ;            // declare new InitInstance()
} ;
```

Listing 4-13 TEXT3.H Resource ID Header File

```
// text3.h   header file for resource ID numbers

#define IDM_SHOW       1
#define IDM_QUIT       10
```

Listing 4-14 TEXT3.RC Resource Script File

```
// text3.rc   resource script file

#include <afxres.h>
#include "text3.h"

AFX_IDI_STD_FRAME   ICON    text3.ico  // the program's icon

MyMenu MENU                            // define the menu
{
    MENUITEM "&Show Text",   IDM_SHOW
    MENUITEM "&Quit",        IDM_QUIT
}
```

Listing 4-15 TEXT3.DEF Module Definition File

```
NAME            text3
DESCRIPTION     'text3 C++ program'
EXETYPE         WINDOWS
STUB            'WINSTUB.EXE'
CODE            PRELOAD MOVEABLE
DATA            PRELOAD MOVEABLE MULTIPLE
HEAPSIZE        1024
STACKSIZE       5120
```

Figure 4-9 TEXT3.ICO Icon Image

Windows RGB Color Model

Windows uses 32-bit (four-byte) numbers to represent colors. This data type is called COLORREF, a DWORD value declared in WINDOWS.H.

```
typedef DWORD          COLORREF;
```

Only the least significant three bytes are used to store color data. The most significant byte is used to distinguish between the Windows RGB color model, and color palettes for devices that support more than 16 simultaneous pure colors. For now, we can assume that the most significant byte is zero, and that the user is using a video device showing only 16 simultaneous pure colors, as with VGA.

The basic color data consists of three values that represent the intensity of the red, green, and blue contributions to color. Each value can vary from 0 to 255. This provides 256*256*256 = 16,777,216 possible colors. The storage format is shown in Figure 4-10.

To create a color value, and set it to pure blue, use the code shown in Listing 4-16.

continued on next page

continued from previous page

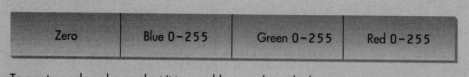

To create a color value, and set it to pure blue, use the code shown in Listing 4-16.

Figure 4-10 RGB Color Data Format

Listing 4-16 Declaring and Initializing a COLORREF Value

```
COLORREF     cr ;
cr = RGB (0, 0, 255) ;
```

Listing 4-17 Setting the Text Color to Blue

```
CPaintDC dc(this) ;
dc.SetTextColor (RGB (0, 0, 255)) ;
```

RGB() is a macro defined in WINDOWS.H that puts the red, green, and blue intensity values in the correct byte positions. RGB (0, 0, 0) encodes black, as black is created by using zero intensity for all three color elements. RGB (255, 255, 255) encodes white, which is the combination of equal (maximum) amounts of red, green, and blue colors. Note that the RGB macro follows the convention of having the red value on the left, even though the actual byte value is stored on the right (least significant) end of the COLORREF block in memory.

In many cases, you can skip declaring a COLORREF value and use the RGB macro right inside a function call. For example, to create blue text, Listing 4-17 uses RGB() in a call to the **CDC::SetTextColor()** function.

With the default color model, Windows assumes that the device (such as a video screen) is limited to 20 "system" colors. If fewer than 20 are available, some of the 20 will be identical. This is the case for most VGA systems, which have only 16 simultaneous colors. If a color value is specified with RGB() that does not match one of the system colors, Windows will approximate the requested color by "dithering." Dithering puts pixels of available colors in a

continued on next page

continued from previous page

pattern to create the illusion of a color between the two colors being mixed. The dithering logic in Windows is very fast, and it does not slow down painting operations appreciably.

Windows versions 3.0 and above support devices with more than 20 colors via color palettes. The same RGB color encoding is used, but the high-order byte contains a code for either an index into a palette, or a color value. The subject of color palettes is beyond the scope of this book. See Chapter 12 in *The Waite Group's Windows API Bible* if you need to use these advanced features.

Device Context Settings

In TEXT3, both of the changes to the device context were made *before* the text was output. You can think of the device context as "remembering" the current settings for the character font, character color, background color, etc. In the case of fonts, pens, brushes, and palettes, the device context is changed by "selecting an object into the device context." This just means that the data for the pen, brush, etc. is made available to the device context for immediate use. Table 4-1 shows the range of objects and settings that can be selected into a device context. The **CDC::SelectObject()** function does this for the graphics objects.

Setting	Selected By	Meaning
Stock Font	**SelectStockObject()**	Sets the font used by **CDC::TextOut()** and related text output functions.
Character Color	**SetTextColor()**	Sets the color of the text.
Character Background	**SetBkColor()**	Sets the background color that surrounds each character.
Background Mode	**SetBkMode()**	Sets if the painting of text and graphics covers everything underneath (OPAQUE) or if the white areas are transparent (TRANSPARENT).
Text Alignment	**SetTextAlign()**	Sets how characters are aligned when output. The default alignment is based on the upper left corner of the character.

Table 4-1 CDC Class Functions Changing Device Context Settings

continued on next page

continued from previous page

Setting	Selected By	Meaning
Text Spacing	SetTextCharacterExtra()	Sets the amount of extra space between each character.
Text Justification	SetTextJustification()	Justifies a string prior to output by **CDC::TextOut()**. Used with **CDC::GetTextExtent()** to determine the amount of space needed to make a character string exactly fill a space.
Pen	SelectObject()	The pen used to draw lines and outlines of objects. **CPen::CreatePen()** is used to create new pens.
Stock Pen	SelectStockObject()	Selects predefined stock pens WHITE_PEN, BLACK_PEN, and NULL_PEN.
Brush	SelectObject()	The pattern used to fill the interior of objects. Use **CBrush::CreateSolidBrush()** and **CBrush::CreatePatternBrush()** to create the brushes prior to calling **CDC::SelectObject()**.
Stock Brush	SelectStockObject()	Selects predefined stock brushes such as BLACK_BRUSH, WHITE_BRUSH, GRAY_BRUSH, etc.
Origin	SetWindowOrg() and SetViewportOrg()	Moves the logical origin (0,0 point).
Mapping Mode	SetMapMode()	Changes the scaling of the device context. Scaling can be used to expand or shrink images, or to base the system of units on inches or millimeters rather than pixels.
Raster Drawing Mode	SetROP2()	Determines how the existing pixels on the device (screen) are combined with the new pixels in drawing lines.
Polygon Filling Mode	SetPolyFillMode()	Determines how polygons are filled. This only changes the image if the polygon lines cross.
Clipping Region	SelectClipRgn()	Limits the area within which output will be displayed.

Table 4-1 CDC Class Functions Changing Device Context Settings

We will explore selecting pens and brushes into the device context in the next section. Logical origins, mapping modes, and raster modes are discussed in Chapter 13, *The Device Context.* Raster drawing operations are covered in Chapter 16, *Bitmaps.*

GRAPHICS OUTPUT

So far the example programs have displayed only text. The next example program will output graphics images. The process is similar to output of text (remember that Windows does all output to the screen in graphics mode, so text and graphics operations are very similar).

1. Create a device context object with either the **CClientDC** or **CPaintDC** class. (**CPaintDC** is used only when processing WM_PAINT messages in the **CWnd::OnPaint()** function.)

2. Select any pens or brushes into the device context.

3. Draw the lines, ellipses, rectangles, arcs, chords, pies, etc. using the Windows graphics functions.

4. Delete any pens or brushes created after displacing them from the device context. Graphics objects should not be deleted if they are currently selected into the device context.

The GRAPHIC1 program was designed to demonstrate how this is done. Figure 4-11 shows the GRAPHIC1 program in action. A turquoise rectangle and

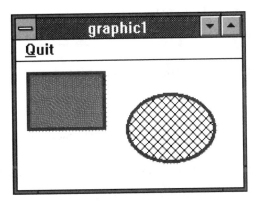

Figure 4-11 The GRAPHIC1 Program

hatched ellipse are drawn in the GRAPHIC1 program's client area. Both the rectangle and ellipse are bordered with a thick red line. Because all of the painting is done within the **CMainWindow::OnPaint()** function in response to WM_PAINT messages from Windows, the ellipse and rectangle reappear if the GRAPHIC1 window is covered up and then uncovered. Listing 4-18 shows the GRAPHIC1.CPP program file.

The support files for GRAPHIC1 are shown in Listings 4-19 to 4-22. Figure 4-12 shows the icon image for the GRAPHIC1 program icon.

Listing 4-18 GRAPHIC1.CPP

```
// graphic1.cpp                demonstrate drawing graphics

#include <afxwin.h>      // class library header file
#include "graphic1.h"    // header file for resource data
#include "graphic1.hpp"  // header file for this program

CTheApp theApp ;              // create one CTheApp object - runs program

BOOL CTheApp::InitInstance ()                // override default
{                                            // InitInstance()

    m_pMainWnd = new CMainWindow () ;     // create a main window
    m_pMainWnd->ShowWindow (m_nCmdShow) ; // make it visible
    m_pMainWnd->UpdateWindow () ;         // paint center
    return TRUE ;
}


CMainWindow::CMainWindow ()       // constructor for window
{
    Create (NULL, "graphic1", WS_OVERLAPPEDWINDOW, rectDefault,
        NULL, "MyMenu") ;
}


BEGIN_MESSAGE_MAP (CMainWindow, CFrameWnd)
    ON_WM_PAINT ()
    ON_COMMAND (IDM_QUIT, OnExit)
END_MESSAGE_MAP ()

void CMainWindow::OnPaint ()    // custom window painting function
{                               // called when window needs repainting
    CPaintDC dc(this) ;         // get client area device context
    CPen Rpen (PS_SOLID, 3, RGB (255, 0, 0)) ;  // red pen 3 wide
    CBrush Sbrush (RGB (0, 128, 128)) ;         // solid turq. brush
                                                // hatched blue brush
    CBrush Hbrush (HS_DIAGCROSS, RGB (0, 0, 255)) ;

        // select the red pen and solid brush into the device context
    CPen* pOldPen = dc.SelectObject (&Rpen) ;
    CBrush* pOldBrush = dc.SelectObject (&Sbrush) ;
    dc.Rectangle (10, 10, 80, 60) ; // rectangle using pen and brush
```

```
    dc.SelectObject (&Hbrush) ;        // select brush, but use old pen
    dc.Ellipse (100, 30, 180, 90) ; // to draw an ellipse
        // select old pen and brush into dc to free new ones
    dc.SelectObject (pOldPen) ;
    dc.SelectObject (pOldBrush) ;
}    // pen and two brushes are deleted here (go out of scope)

void CMainWindow::OnExit ()     // respond to menu item "Quit"
{
    this->DestroyWindow () ;    // destroy main window,
}                               // this stops application
```

Listing 4-19 GRAPHIC1.HPP Header File

```
// graphic1.hpp    header file for graphic1.cpp
                                    // derive a main window class
class CMainWindow : public CFrameWnd
{
public:
    CMainWindow () ;              // declare a constructor
    void OnPaint() ;             // custom painting function
    void OnExit () ;             // stop application function
    DECLARE_MESSAGE_MAP()        // prepare for message processing
} ;

class CTheApp : public CWinApp     // derive an application class
{
public:
    BOOL InitInstance () ;         // declare new InitInstance()
} ;
```

Listing 4-20 GRAPHIC1.H Resource ID Header File

```
// graphic1.h   header file for resource ID numbers

#define IDM_QUIT        1
```

Listing 4-21 GRAPHIC1.RC Resource Script File

```
// graphic1.rc   resource script file

#include <afxres.h>
#include "graphic1.h"

AFX_IDI_STD_FRAME    ICON    graphic1.ico    // the program's icon

MyMenu MENU                                   // define the menu
{
    MENUITEM "&Quit",              IDM_QUIT
}
```

Listing 4-22 GRAPHIC1.DEF Module Definition File

```
NAME            graphic1
DESCRIPTION     'graphic1 C++ program'
EXETYPE         WINDOWS
STUB            'WINSTUB.EXE'
CODE            PRELOAD MOVEABLE
DATA            PRELOAD MOVEABLE MULTIPLE
HEAPSIZE        1024
STACKSIZE       5120
```

Figure 4-12 GRAPHIC1.ICO Icon Image

CREATING PENS AND BRUSHES

All of the logic to paint the window's client area in GRAPHIC1 is done in the **CMainWindow::OnPaint()** function. Before the rectangle is drawn, a **CPen** object and a **CBrush** object are created. **CPen** and **CBrush** are both MFC classes that are used to create the specialized pen and brush objects that Windows uses for all graphics output. Whenever a Windows graphics function like **CDC::Rectangle()** is called, the interior is painted using the currently selected brush, and the border is painted with the currently selected pen. These pens and brushes can have different colors and patterns. In the **CMainWindow::OnPaint()** function of GRAPHIC1, the **CPen** object *Rpen* is a solid red pen 3 pixels wide. The **CBrush** object *Sbrush* is a solid turquoise brush, and *Hbrush* is a hatched blue brush. "Hatched" means that a cross pattern is used instead of a solid color.

One of the interesting things about the **CBrush** and **CPen** classes is that the constructor functions are overloaded. This means that there are several constructor functions that the compiler differentiates depending on the type of data being passed to the function. For example, Listing 4-23 compares the two calls to the **CBrush** constructor in GRAPHIC1.CPP. The first call to the constructor passes only the RGB color value. The constructor defaults to assuming that the programmer wants to create a solid brush (not a hatched pattern brush) because no hatch value was specified. The second call to the constructor specifies the HS_DIAGCROSS value in addition to the RGB color. This time the compiler calls a constructor for a hatched pattern brush because both values were specified as the function parameters.

The HS_DIAGCROSS value is defined in the WINDOWS.H header file (included with AFXWIN.H). HS_DIAGCROSS is an integer value. The RGB macro creates a DWORD value. The compiler can tell the difference between an integer and a DWORD, so the compiler can tell which constructor function needs to be called in each case.

The brush and pen object must be selected into the device context before they have any impact on the drawing functions. Selecting an item "into" the device context just means that the device context is given access to the pen and brush data in memory. Subsequent painting operations use the pen and brush data to perform the output functions. Listing 4-24 shows the pen and brush being selected into the device context using the **CDC::SelectObject()** function. The **CDC::Rectangle()** function which uses the pen and brush to draw the rectangle on the program window's client areas is then called.

An important property of the **CDC::SelectObject()** function is that it returns a pointer to the previously selected object in the device context of the same type. For example, if you are selecting a **CPen** object into a device context, **CDC::SelectObject()** returns a pointer to the **CPen** object that was selected previously. Note in Listing 4-24 that the returned pointers to the "old" pen and brush objects are saved as the *pOldPen* and *pOldBrush* variables. They will be used in a moment to restore the device context to its previous state prior to deleting the new pen and brush objects.

Next the hatched brush is selected into the device context (Listing 4-25), prior to calling **CDC::Ellipse()** to draw an ellipse. Selecting the hatched brush displaces the previous brush (the turquoise *Sbrush*), so the ellipse ends up drawn with a hatched pattern for the interior. The red pen used to draw the rectangle was not displaced from the device context, so it is also used by the **CDC::Ellipse()** function.

Listing 4-23 Overloaded Constructor for CBrush Class

```
CBrush Sbrush (RGB (0, 128, 128)) ;
CBrush Hbrush (HS_DIAGCROSS, RGB (0, 0, 256)) ;  // overloading
```

Listing 4-24 Selecting a Pen and Brush Object into the Device Context

```
CPen* pOldPen = dc.SelectObject (&Rpen) ;
CBrush* pOldBrush = dc.SelectObject (&Sbrush) ;
dc.Rectangle (10, 10, 80, 60) ; // rectangle using pen and brush
```

Listing 4-25 Drawing the Ellipse and Restoring the Device Context

```
dc.SelectObject (&Hbrush) ;      // select brush, use old pen
dc.Ellipse (100, 30, 180, 90) ; // to draw an ellipse
    // select old pen and brush into dc to free new ones
dc.SelectObject (pOldPen) ;
dc.SelectObject (pOldBrush) ;
```

The final activity in the **CMainWindow::OnPaint()** function of GRAPHIC1.HPP (repeated in Listing 4-25) is to select the old pen and brush object back into the device context. This restores the device context to its previous state. This is not an optional activity, as will be explained in the next section.

Safely Deleting Pen and Brush Objects

There is a subtle operation going on in the **CMainWindow::OnPaint()** function of GRAPHIC1.CPP that needs some explanation. Listing 4-26 shows an outline of the **OnPaint()** function, highlighting the creation of the **CPaintDC**, **CPen**, and **CBrush** objects. All three of these objects are created within the body of the **CMainWindow::OnPaint()** function. In C++ (and C), objects created within a function are stored on the program's stack. When the function finishes, the objects are destroyed so that the stack can be reused by the next function.

In C++, an object is destroyed by calling its destructor function. The destructor functions for the **CPaintDC**, **CPen**, and **CBrush** objects are called automatically at the end of the **CMainWindow::OnPaint()** function. This is convenient, as it means that any memory consumed by the objects is released automatically. If you have done any Windows programming in C, you will recognize that this is an extremely convenient feature, as C programmers must do their own deletion operations to free the memory consumed by device contexts, pens, brushes, and other GDI objects.

There is a catch to the simplicity of C++ automatically calling the destructor functions. **Windows may crash if you destroy GDI objects, such as pens and**

Listing 4-26 Creation and Destruction of Three Local Objects

```
void CMainWindow::OnPaint ()
{                                    // create dc, pen, brush
    CPaintDC dc(this) ;              // all are local (automatic)
variables
    CPen Rpen (PS_SOLID, 3, RGB (255, 0, 0)) ;
    CBrush Sbrush (RGB (0, 128, 128)) ;

    // use the objects in the OnPaint() function here
}                                    // local objects all destroyed here
```

Listing 4-27 Selecting the "Old" Pen and Brush

```
void CMainWindow::OnPaint ()      // custom window painting function
{                                 // called when window needs repainting
    CPaintDC dc(this) ;           // get client area device context
    CPen Rpen (PS_SOLID, 3, RGB (255, 0, 0)) ;  // red pen 3 wide
    CBrush Sbrush (RGB (0, 128, 128)) ;    // and a solid turq. brush

    CPen* pOldPen = dc.SelectObject (&Rpen) ;
    CBrush* pOldBrush = dc.SelectObject (&Sbrush) ;
        // use the Rpen and Sbrush objects here to do graphics output
        // select old pen and brush into dc to free new ones
    dc.SelectObject (pOldPen) ;
    dc.SelectObject (pOldBrush) ;
}                                 // dc, Rpen, Sbrush all destroyed here
```

brushes, while they are selected into the device context. The program will intermittently crash when Windows attempts to use the device context which contains pointers to deleted pens and brushes. Needless to say, this is something to avoid.

To stay away from this problem, you must make sure that all GDI objects are displaced out of the device context before they are deleted. There are two ways to do this. The elegant way is demonstrated in the **CMainWindow::OnPaint()** function of GRAPHIC1.CPP and repeated in outline in Listing 4-27. The trick is to save the pointers to the "old" pen, brush, etc. when a new one is selected. The "old" objects can then be selected back into the device context to displace your "new" ones, making the "new" ones safe to delete.

A less elegant but equally effective way to make sure that a pen or brush is not selected into the device context is to select a "stock" pen or brush. Stock objects are common GDI elements that Windows keeps available at all times. You do not need to create stock objects, and you should never attempt to delete them. Selecting a stock pen displaces the current pen from the device context Selecting a stock brush displaces the current brush from the device context, and so on. Listing 4-28 shows how **CDC::SelectStockObject()** can be used to make a device context safe to delete.

Besides providing an easy way to displace pens and brushes out of a device context, stock objects are useful in their own right. This is the subject of the next section.

Stock GDI Objects

In many programs, you will be able to take advantage of the stock objects that Windows always has available as a shortcut means of generating graphics and text output. When you first create a device context, the default selected

Listing 4-28 Selecting a Stock Object into a Device Context

```
void CMainWindow::OnPaint ()      // custom window painting function
{                                 // called when window needs repainting
    CPaintDC dc(this) ;           // get client area device context
    CPen Rpen (PS_SOLID, 3, RGB (255, 0, 0)) ;  // red pen 3 wide
    CBrush Sbrush (RGB (0, 128, 128)) ;         // solid turq. brush

    dc.SelectObject (&Rpen) ;     // don't bother saving old pen/brush
    dc.SelectObject (&Sbrush) ;
        // use the Rpen and Sbrush objects here to do graphics output

        // select stock pen and brush into dc to free new ones
    dc.SelectStockObject (BLACK_PEN) ;
    dc.SelectStockObject (WHITE_BRUSH) ;
}                                 // dc, Rpen, Sbrush all destroyed here
```

objects are a black line one pixel wide, a solid white brush, and black text on a white background using the variable pitch system font. **CDC::Select-StockObject()** is used to retrieve a handle to one of the other stock objects, so that it can be selected into the device context. Table 4-2 shows the complete list of stock objects.

The NULL pen and NULL brush are handy for modifying the behavior of graphics functions. The most common use is to select the NULL_BRUSH and a custom pen. The drawing function will then draw only the outline. Selecting the NULL_PEN and a custom brush allows the center of the object to be filled without drawing a border. Of the stock character fonts, the default SYSTEM_FONT serves well for most purposes. You may want to select a fixed font, such as ANSI_FIXED_FONT, if you have tables of characters that need to line up vertically. The ANSI_VAR_FONT is handy if space is limited, as it is the smallest of the fonts.

Object Type	Choices
Pen	BLACK_PEN, WHITE_PEN (both one pixel wide), NULL_PEN
Brush	DKGRAY_BRUSH, GRAY_BRUSH, BLACK_BRUSH, LTGRAY_BRUSH, NULL_BRUSH, WHITE_BRUSH
Font	ANSI_FIXED_FONT, ANSI_VAR_FONT, DEVICE_DEFAULT_FONT, OEM_FIXED_FONT, SYSTEM_FIXED_FONT, SYSTEM_FONT

Table 4-2 Stock Objects that Can Be Selected with CDC::SelectStockObject()

Other Graphics Functions

Table 4-3 provides a summary of the graphics functions supported by Windows. All of these functions are part of the **CDC** class and are available with both the **CPaintDC** and **CClientDC** derived classes. All of these functions use

Function	Example	Comments
Arc()		Draws portions of an ellipse.
Chord()		Draws the filled portion of an ellipse, bounded by the ellipse border and a line.
Ellipse()		Draws an ellipse.
MoveTo(), LineTo()		**CDC::MoveTo()** establishes a position to start the line. **CDC::LineTo()** draws a line from the starting point to a second point.
Pie()		Draws a filled ellipse. The cut out portion is defined by the interception of two points and the center of the ellipse.
Polygon()		Paints one or more closed polygons. The example uses a white brush for painting the interior.
Polyline()		Paints a series of one or more connected lines. This is equivalent to a call to **CDC::MoveTo()** for the first point, followed by a series of one or more **CDC::LineTo()** function calls.
PolyPolygon()		Paints one or more polygons. The polygons are filled based on the current polygon filling mode, using the selected brush of the DC.
Rectangle()		Paints a rectangular region based on the location of the upper left and lower right corners.
RoundRect()		Paints a rectangular region with rounded corners.

Table 4-3 Windows Graphics Functions in the CDC Class

the currently selected pen and brush. Objects such as lines and arcs are not closed and are not filled with the currently selected brush.

ANIMATED GRAPHICS

The last example in this chapter uses what you have learned about selecting objects into a device context and drawing shapes. Rather than just draw a fixed picture, the program creates a moving graphics image of a ball bouncing around inside the program's window. Figure 4-13 shows the GRAPHIC2 program in action.

The illusion of a moving ball is created by continually redrawing the ball at new locations. The ball is drawn using the **CDC::Ellipse()** function. The **CDC::Ellipse()** function uses the currently selected brush to fill the center and the currently selected pen to draw the ellipse outline. A solid red brush is selected prior to calling **CDC::Ellipse()**, so the ball ends up painted red on the interior. A thick white brush is selected into the device context to draw the ellipse outline. The thick white border erases the "old" part of the ball's image as the ball is moved in the window's client area.

A small rectangle is also drawn on the upper right portion of the ball to simulate a point of reflected light from a three-dimensional ball. This could be further enhanced by using the **CDC::Arc()** function to shade the bottom left of the ball with a darker shade of red.

The interesting part of programming an animated graphic under Windows is the problem of how to make the program repeatedly draw the ball at new locations without taking over the Windows environment. In a DOS application, we would probably program this as shown in Listing 4-29. You can write a loop like this in a Windows program. The result will be that no other program will be

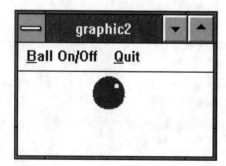

Figure 4-13 GRAPHIC2 Bouncing Ball Program

able to run while the loop is executing. Windows programs must keep giving control back to the Windows environment to allow other programs to operate. (Windows NT does allow errant programs to be interrupted.)

Animation Using the MFC Classes

The key to animation and other repeating actions is to do the repetitive portion of the program during periods when Windows is idle. The **CWinApp** class provides a convenient function called **OnIdle()**, which only gets called if Windows is not busy doing anything else. **CWinApp::OnIdle()** is a virtual function, meaning that although the function is declared in the **CWinApp** class definition, the function only gets executed if you create an **OnIdle()** function in the class you derive from **CWinApp** for your program. For all of the examples in this book, the derived application class is called **CTheApp**, so the **CTheApp** class will need to have a **CTheApp::OnIdle()** function defined if you want to do animation.

The structure of a typical **OnIdle()** function is shown in Listing 4-30. The **CTheApp::OnIdle()** function will be called when Windows runs out of other things to do. The total number of milliseconds since the last time Windows sent the program a message is passed to the **OnIdle()** function as the *lCount* parameter. It is usually a good idea not to start a repetitive activity unless a significant amount of time has passed. In Listing 4-30 the repetitive action is not started unless a second (1,000 milliseconds) has elapsed since the last messages was sent to the application.

Listing 4-29 Program Loop in a DOS Application

```
while (TRUE)
{
    /* quit the loop if a key is pressed */
    /* erase the old ball image */
    /* draw the ball at the new location */
}
```

Listing 4-30 CWinApp::OnIdle() Example

```
BOOL CTheApp::OnIdle (LONG lCount)  // override idle time processing
{
    if (lCount > 1000)              // if no activity for a second
    {
        // do some repetitive activity here
    }
    return TRUE ;                   // OnIdle() returns a BOOL value
}
```

The returned value from the **OnIdle()** function must be either TRUE or FALSE. If TRUE is returned, Windows will continue to call the **OnIdle()** function during idle periods. If FALSE is returned, Windows will stop calling the **OnIdle()** function until a new message is sent to the application. Once the application receives another message from Windows (perhaps because the user moved the mouse cursor over the program window's client area), the **OnIdle()** function will start being called again during idle periods. Occasionally you may run into situations where you want to do a single long calculation during an idle period, but the calculation only needs to be done once. Just return FALSE within **OnIdle()** when the calculation is completed and Windows will stop passing control to the **OnIdle()** function.

Use the **CWinApp::OnIdle()** function with discretion. While the activities within the **OnIdle()** function are being performed, all other message processing is suspended. If the calculation is lengthy but repetitive, it is best to structure **OnIdle()** so that the calculation is performed in small steps during a series of calls to **OnIdle()**. This way the user will be able to perform other activities while the calculation is taking place.

Creating a Moving Ball Class

Before writing the application and window portions of the GRAPHIC2 application, let's look at the functions that draw the moving ball on the GRAPHIC2 window's client area. A moving ball is a physical object, so it is intuitive to encapsulate the programming code into a single class. The **MovingBall** class is defined in the files BALL.CPP and BALL.HPP. They are compiled separately and then linked into the GRAPHIC2 program to create the finished GRAPHIC2.EXE application. This is the first example in the book that has more than one source code (.CPP) file, and also the first that creates a new C++ class from scratch rather than deriving a class from an MFC base class.

Listing 4-31 shows the BALL.HPP header file. The header file defines several constants that control the size and speed of the ball. The **MovingBall** class is also defined in BALL.HPP. The class has six public functions and six data members. The public functions include a constructor, two functions for turning the ball on and off (**MovingBall::BallOn()** and **MovingBall::BallOff()**), a function to check whether the ball is on or off (**MovingBall::IsBallOn()**), and two utility functions that move and draw the ball (**MovingBall::MoveBall()** and **MovingBall::DrawBall()**).

Three of the public functions in the **MovingBall** class are so short that they are defined in the BALL.HPP header file as inline functions (**Moving-Ball::BallOn()**, **MovingBall::BallOff()**, and **MovingBall::IsBallOn()**). The

Listing 4-31 BALL.HPP Header File

```
// ball.hpp  header file for moving ball routines in ball.cpp

#define BALLRAD      20              // ball radius
#define VELOCITY     5               // pixels per move velocity
#define MINRAD       15              // how close ball gets to edge

class MovingBall                     // moving ball class definition
{
public:
    MovingBall (CWnd* pWnd) ;            // constructor
    void BallOn () {bBallOn = TRUE ;}    // turns ball on
    void BallOff () {bBallOn = FALSE ;}  // turns ball off
    BOOL IsBallOn () {return bBallOn ;}  // query status of ball
    void MoveBall () ;                   // move ball to next location
    void DrawBall () ;                   // draw ball at location
private:
    BOOL bBallOn ;                       // true if ball is visible
    int nX, nY ;                         // current ball position
    int nVelX, nVelY ;                   // current ball velocity
    CWnd* pWindow ;                      // pointer to window
} ;
```

remaining three functions are defined in the BALL.CPP program file shown in Listing 4-32. The constructor function for the **MovingBall** class takes one argument, a pointer to a **CWnd** window object. This value is saved in the private *pWindow* data member. The constructor also initializes the other data members to their starting values.

The **MovingBall::DrawBall()** function draws the image of the ball on a window's client area. **MovingBall::DrawBall()** uses the *pWindow* data member to create a **CClientDC** device context object. This device context is then used for all of the graphics operations. The **MovingBall::DrawBall()** function uses a trick to speed up painting the moving ball. The ball is drawn with a solid red brush to fill the interior and a thick white pen for the exterior border. The border pen is so thick that it erases the previous image of the ball at its last location. This works as long as the background of the window's client area is the same color as the pen used to draw the ball's border (white).

The **MovingBall::DrawBall()** function in BALL.CPP shows the creation and deletion of a pen and a brush. Initially a red brush, *Rbrush*, and a thick white pen, *Wpen*, are created and selected into the device context. When **CDC::Ellipse()** is used to draw the ball, the white pen is used by the function to outline the ball, as shown in Figure 4-14. This is not visible against the white background of the window's client area, but has the desirable effect of erasing the portion of the "old" ball that would be visible after the "new" ball is drawn at the next location.

Listing 4-32 BALL.CPP

```cpp
// ball.cpp    moving ball routines

#include <afxwin.h>              // class library header file
#include "ball.hpp"              // header for this program file

MovingBall::MovingBall (CWnd* pWnd) // constructor for moving ball
{
    pWindow = pWnd ;             // just initialize private variables
    bBallOn = FALSE ;
    nX = nY = BALLRAD ;
    nVelX = nVelY = VELOCITY ;
}

void MovingBall::DrawBall ()     // draw ball at current nX,nY location
{
    CPen*   pOldPen ;            // pointers to save old pen and brush
    CBrush* pOldBrush ;

    if (!bBallOn)                // do nothing if ball is not to move
        return ;

    CClientDC dc(pWindow) ;      // get client area device context
                // construct a thick white pen (covers old ball edge)
    CPen Wpen (PS_SOLID, VELOCITY + VELOCITY/2, RGB (255, 255, 255)) ;
    CBrush Rbrush (RGB (255, 0, 0)) ;        // solid red brush
    pOldPen = dc.SelectObject (&Wpen) ;      // select red pen, brush
    pOldBrush = dc.SelectObject (&Rbrush) ; // into device context
                                 // draw ball using ellipse()
    dc.Ellipse (nX - BALLRAD, nY - BALLRAD, nX + BALLRAD,
        nY + BALLRAD) ;
                // thin pen and solid white brush for highlight mark
    CPen Tpen (PS_SOLID, 3, RGB (255, 255, 255)) ;
    CBrush Wbrush (RGB (255, 255, 255)) ;
    dc.SelectObject (&Tpen) ;    // select pen and brush into dc
    dc.SelectObject (&Wbrush) ;  // context for highlight rectangle
    dc.Rectangle (nX + BALLRAD/3, nY - BALLRAD/3, nX + 2 + BALLRAD/3,
        nY - 2 - BALLRAD/3) ;

    dc.SelectObject (pOldPen) ;    // select original brush,pen into
    dc.SelectObject (pOldBrush) ;  // device context
}

void MovingBall::MoveBall ()     // move ball to new location
{
    CRect   WindowRect ;
    int     nXSize, nYSize ;

    if (!bBallOn)                // do nothing if ball is not to move
        return ;
```

```
pWindow->GetClientRect (&WindowRect) ;   // bounds of client area
nXSize = WindowRect.Width () ;
nYSize = WindowRect.Height () ;

nX += nVelX ;                    // move ball's location by velocity
nY += nVelY ;                    // units in both directions
                                 // check if user moved walls,
if (nY > nYSize)                 // covering up the ball
    nY = 2 * BALLRAD ;           // if so, put in a safe place
if (nX > nXSize)
    nX = 2 * BALLRAD ;
                 // reverse direction if within MINRAD of a wall
if (nY < MINRAD || nYSize - nY < MINRAD)
    nVelY *= -1 ;                // mutiplying by -1 reverses direction
if (nX < MINRAD || nXSize - nX < MINRAD)
    nVelX *= -1 ;
}
```

To make the ball look a bit more three-dimensional, a small white highlight is drawn at the upper right of the ball's surface. This requires deleting the thick pen used to draw the ball's outline, and creating a thin pen *Tpen* that is three pixels wide. This new pen is selected into the device context before **CDC::Rectangle()** is called to draw a small rectangle for the highlight. Finally, the pen and brush are deleted and the device context is released. Note that the old pen and brush are selected into the device context before the new pen and brush are deleted. This ensures that the new pen and brush are no longer

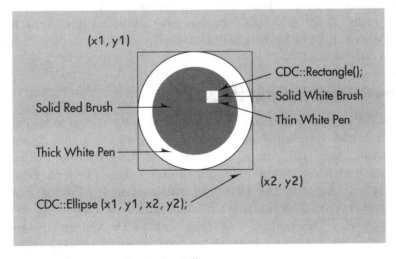

Figure 4-14 Drawing the Moving Ball

selected into the device context when they are deleted. Deleting objects that are selected into a device context will cause the application to crash randomly.

The **MovingBall::MoveBall()** function calculates the ball's next position. **MovingBall::MoveBall()** introduces a new function and MFC class. The **CWnd::GetClientRect()** function is used to obtain the dimensions of a window's client area. **MoveBall()** needs the window's dimensions in order to determine when to reverse the ball's direction so that the ball appears to bounce off the sides of the window. The variable *pWindow* (pointer to the window being painted) is used again, this time to call the **CWnd::GetClientRect()** function.

The **CWnd::GetClientRect()** function obtains the size of a window's client area and passes the data to a **CRect** object. **CRect** is another MFC class that operates on rectangles. Two of the **CRect** class functions are used to obtain the width and height of the client area rectangle after the rectangle is initialized by the **CWnd::GetClientRect()** function. The **CRect::Width()** and **CRect::Height()** functions return the rectangle's width and height, respectively. You may want to take a brief look at the **CRect** class description in the MFC documentation. Rectangles are such common objects in graphics programming that the **CRect** class ends up used in many other functions.

The actual movement of the ball is computed by adding the velocity values to the previous *X,Y* location of the ball. When the ball gets within MINRAD pixels of a wall (client area border), the velocity value in the direction of the collision is reversed. For example, if the ball hits the bottom wall, the *Y* velocity value is reversed in sign.

The BALL.CPP program provides the basic functions for drawing a ball on a window's client area, and for calculating the ball's next location. All we need to do to finish the GRAPHIC2 program is to repeatedly call the **MovingBall::MoveBall()** and **MovingBall::DrawBall()** functions during idle periods. This is done in the GRAPHIC2.CPP program, shown in the next section.

Using OnIdle() in GRAPHIC2.CPP

The animated graphics program file GRAPHIC2.CPP is shown in Listing 4-33. A pointer to a **MovingBall** object named *Ball* is stored as a global variable at the top of the listing. The pointer is initialized in the **CTheApp::InitInstance()** function, which creates the moving ball object. The reason for creating the moving ball object in the **CTheApp::Initinstance()** function is that the **MovingBall** constructor function needs a pointer to the main program window as a parameter. This pointer is available inside **CTheApp::InitInstance()** because the program's main window is created here with the line:

```
m_pMainWnd = new CMainWindow () ;
```

The *m_pMainWnd* variable is a public member of the **CWinApp** class and saves the pointer to the program's main window for the **CWinApp** functions to use. *m_pMainWnd* is also used to pass the pointer to the main window to the **MovingBall** constructor function:

```
Ball = new MovingBall (m_pMainWnd) ;
```

The **MovingBall** object *Ball* is then used to reposition and redraw the image of the ball in the window's client area when the **CTheApp::OnIdle()** function is executed. Note that the **MovingBall** object *Ball* could have been made a member of the **CTheApp** class instead of being declared a global variable. A global variable was used in GRAPHIC2.CPP for clarity, because it allows all of the initialization activities for the **MovingBall** object to be in the same source file.

Note that the **MovingBall** object *Ball* is deleted from memory during the processing of the WM_CLOSE message in the **CMainWindow::OnClose()** function. This assures that the memory occupied by **MovingBall** is freed before the program terminates. Listings 4-34 to 4-37 show the remaining source code files for GRAPHIC2. The program's icon is shown in Figure 4-15.

Listing 4-33 GRAPHIC2.CPP

```
// graphic2.cpp               demonstrate animated graphics

#include <afxwin.h>           // class library header file
#include "graphic2.h"         // header file for resource data
#include "graphic2.hpp"       // header file for this program
#include "ball.hpp"           // header file for moving ball routines

CTheApp theApp ;             // create one CTheApp object - runs program
MovingBall* pBall ;          // pointer to MovingBall object

BOOL CTheApp::InitInstance ()   // override default InitInstance()
{
    m_pMainWnd = new CMainWindow () ;        // create a main window
    m_pMainWnd->ShowWindow (m_nCmdShow) ;    // make it visible
    m_pMainWnd->UpdateWindow () ;            // paint center
    pBall = new MovingBall (m_pMainWnd) ;     // create one ball
object     return TRUE ;
}

BOOL CTheApp::OnIdle (LONG lCount)  // override idle time function
{
    if (lCount > 1000)         // if no activity for more than a second
    {
        pBall->MoveBall () ; // move and draw ball during idle time
        pBall->DrawBall () ; // neither function has impact if the
    }
    return TRUE ;
}
```

```
CMainWindow::CMainWindow ()          // constructor for window
{
    Create (NULL, "graphic2", WS_OVERLAPPEDWINDOW, rectDefault,
        NULL, "MyMenu") ;
}


BEGIN_MESSAGE_MAP (CMainWindow, CFrameWnd)
    ON_COMMAND (IDM_BALL, OnBall)
    ON_COMMAND (IDM_QUIT, OnExit)
    ON_WM_CLOSE ()
END_MESSAGE_MAP ()

void CMainWindow::OnBall ()          // respond to menu item "Ball On/Off"
{
    if (pBall->IsBallOn ())          // if now on
        pBall->BallOff () ;          // turn off
    else
        pBall->BallOn () ;           // otherwise turn on
}


void CMainWindow::OnExit ()          // respond to menu item "Quit"
{
    this->DestroyWindow () ;         // destroy main window,
}                                    // this ends application

void CMainWindow::OnClose ()         // process WM_CLOSE message - sent
{                                    // when program is about to terminate
    delete pBall ;                   // free ball object from memory
}
```

Listing 4-34 GRAPHIC2.HPP Header File

```
// graphic2.hpp    header file for graphic2.cpp
                                // derive a main window class
class CMainWindow : public CFrameWnd
{
public:
    CMainWindow () ;            // declare a constructor
private:
    void OnBall () ;           // turns ball on and off
    void OnExit () ;           // stop application function
    void OnClose () ;          // process WM_CLOSE messages

    DECLARE_MESSAGE_MAP()      // prepare for message processing
} ;


class CTheApp : public CWinApp    // derive an application class
{
public:
    BOOL InitInstance () ;        // override default InitInstance()
    BOOL OnIdle (LONG lCount) ;   // and override idle time function
} ;
```

Listing 4-35 GRAPHIC2.H Resource ID Header File

```
// graphic2.h  header file for resource ID numbers

#define IDM_BALL        1
#define IDM_QUIT        10
```

Listing 4-36 GRAPHIC2.RC Resource Script File

```
// graphic2.rc  resource script file

#include <afxres.h>
#include "graphic2.h"

AFX_IDI_STD_FRAME   ICON    graphic2.ico   // the program's icon

MyMenu MENU                                // define the menu
{
    MENUITEM "&Ball On/Off",    IDM_BALL
    MENUITEM "&Quit",           IDM_QUIT
}
```

Listing 4-37 GRAPHIC2.DEF Module Definition File

```
NAME            graphic2
DESCRIPTION     'graphic2 C++ program'
EXETYPE         WINDOWS
STUB            'WINSTUB.EXE'
CODE            PRELOAD MOVEABLE
DATA            PRELOAD MOVEABLE MULTIPLE
HEAPSIZE        1024
STACKSIZE       5120
```

Figure 4-15 GRAPHIC2.ICO Icon Image

Don't forget to add the BALL.CPP program to the GRAPHIC2 project file. The compiler will need to compile both BALL.CPP and GRAPHIC2.CPP to build the finished program.

When you get GRAPHIC2 running, you can experiment with moving and resizing the window. If you change the window's size, the ball will bounce off

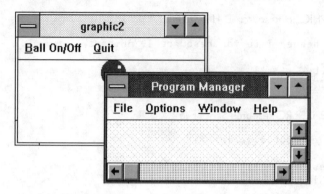

Figure 4-16 GRAPHIC2 Partially Covered by Program Manager

the walls in their new locations. An interesting case is where part of GRAPHIC2 is obscured by another program's window. In this case, the ball will continue to "bounce" underneath the hidden parts of the window, showing up again when it gets out from underneath. Figure 4-16 shows this effect, with the Program Manager window partially covering GRAPHIC2. The ball is bouncing out from under the corner of Program Manager's window. The calculation of which parts of the GRAPHIC2 window are covered up is all done by Windows. All GRAPHIC2 has to do is send the output to the device context. Windows takes care of figuring out which portions of the window are visible, and which are covered by other objects.

SUMMARY

Windows does all output to the video display in graphics mode. This means that everything, including text characters, is drawn one pixel at a time. Although slower than character mode output, graphics mode output is completely flexible. Windows can draw characters of any size or shape at any location on the screen. The designers of Windows took advantage of the graphics capability to create attractive buttons, window elements, and color combinations.

Windows uses the concept of a device context to insulate Windows applications from the computer's hardware. The application program sends graphics commands to the device context. Windows takes care of translating the device context data into the specific commands used by the hardware. As a software developer, you will not be concerned about the exact type of computer, video, or printer technology that the user may use. Properly written Windows programs will function on any hardware system that Windows supports.

A device context object must be created in order to output text or graphics to a window. The **CClientDC** class is used everywhere except when responding to a WM_PAINT message in an **OnPaint()** function. The **CPaintDC** class is used in **OnPaint()** functions. Both the **CClientDC** and **CPaintDC** classes are derived from the **CDC** class, which contains all of the output functions such as **CDC::TextOut()** and **CDC::Rectangle()**.

The WM_PAINT message is the method Windows uses to inform an application that some or all of the program window's client area needs to be repainted. This will occur when the window is changed in size or covered and uncovered by another window. WM_PAINT processing logic (the **OnPaint()** function) is the ideal place to put the program's graphics output functions so that the program's client area is repainted whenever necessary.

Graphics output for objects, such as rectangles and ellipses, take advantage of the currently selected pen and brush of the device context. When a device context is first created the default black pen and white brush are selected. An application can create new pens and brushes of any color and select them into the device context. The new pen and brush will then be used by any subsequent calls to **CDC::Ellipse()**, **CDC::Rectangle()**, **CDC::LineTo()**, and other drawing functions. New pens and brushes should be displaced from the device context before they are deleted. Selecting an old or stock pen or brush displaces the currently selected object from the device context so that it is safe to delete. Be sure to delete any pens or brushes you create, as otherwise they will continue to consume memory after the program has terminated. Stock pens and brushes are not deleted, as these objects are maintained at all times by Windows.

You can create programs with animated graphics that do not take over the entire Windows environment by defining a **CWinApp::OnIdle()** function. The **OnIdle()** function is called during periods when there are no other messages for Windows to process. You may find other uses for **CWinApp::OnIdle()** in advanced programs that need to perform tasks in the background when the system is not busy.

QUESTIONS

1. When using the **CDC::Rectangle()** function, the center of the rectangle is filled with the currently selected _____, and the border is drawn with the currently selected _____ of the device context.

2. To use a custom pen or a brush, you must first _____ the object and then select it into the _____.

3. The currently selected pen or brush cannot be deleted safely until it is selected out of the device context. (True/False)

4. How do you remove a pen or a brush from the device context?

5. To change the color of the characters output by **CDC::TextOut()**, use the _____ function. To change the background color of the characters, use the _____ function.

6. The _____ message is sent by Windows when some or all of the window's client area needs to be repainted.

7. The only time the **CPaintDC** class is used is to process a _____ message. In all other cases use the _____ class.

8. Stock pens and brushes can be safely deleted. (True/False)

EXERCISES

1. Modify TEXT1.C to create a graphics image using the **CDC::Rectangle()**, **CDC::MoveTo()**, and **CDC::LineTo()** functions. Fill the rectangle with a green brush, and draw the lines and the rectangle's border with a blue pen.

2. Convert the client area of GRAPHIC2 to a gray color. Modify the **DrawBall()** function appropriately so that the gray color is not disturbed by the ball's movement.

ANSWERS TO QUESTIONS

1. brush, pen.

2. create, device context.

3. True.

4. Selecting another pen or brush into the device context displaces the old object. This makes it safe to delete the old object.

5. **CDC::SetTextColor()**, **CDC::SetBkColor()**.

6. WM_PAINT.

7. WM_PAINT, **CClientDC**.

8. False. They are maintained by Windows.

SOLUTIONS TO EXERCISES

1. The only changes to TEXT1.CPP necessary are to the **CMainWindow::OnShowText()** function that responds to the "Show Text" menu item. Listing 4-38 shows an example solution. The full program is given under the name C4EXER1 on the source code disks.

2. The solution requires changes to both BALL.CPP and GRAPHIC2.CPP. Listing 4-39 shows the changes to the **MovingBall::DrawBall()** function in BALL.CPP. The pen used to draw the outline of the ball is created with a gray color using the RGB (200, 200, 200) value. Any RGB value with the red, green, and blue elements set to the same value will be gray.

   The other change is to paint the window's client area gray. This can be done by painting a gray rectangle over the client area. The **CDC::GetClientRect()** function is handy here to determine how big to draw the gray rectangle. Listing 4-40 shows the modifications to the GRAPHIC2.CPP program.

   The **CMainWindow::OnPaint()** function must also be declared in the program's header file. The complete solution is given under the file names C4EXER2 and BALL2 on the source code disks.

   (An interesting side effect of Windows painting logic is uncovered by this exercise. On most systems the gray color is created by dithering gray and white dots to approximate the RGB (200, 200, 200) color requested. The moving ball ends up painting over the dithered pattern with its thick border pen as the ball moves. This results in the white dots in the dithered gray brush pattern of the background being painted over as the ball moves over the screen, resulting in a "path" through the background. Figure 4-17 shows an example. This side effect can be avoided by selecting a gray color that exactly matches one of the system colors so that dithering is not used in painting the background color.

Listing 4-38 Modified OnShowText() Function

```
void CMainWindow::OnShowText ()  // respond to menu item "Message"
{
    CClientDC dc (this) ;   // construct client area device context
    CPen BluePen (PS_SOLID, 2, RGB (0, 0, 255)) ;
    CBrush GreenBrush (RGB (0, 255, 0)) ;
    CPen *pOldPen = dc.SelectObject (&BluePen) ;
    CBrush *pOldBrush = dc.SelectObject (&GreenBrush) ;
    dc.MoveTo (10, 10) ;
    dc.LineTo (100, 30) ;
    dc.Rectangle (50, 50, 150, 120) ;
    dc.SelectObject (pOldPen) ;
    dc.SelectObject (pOldBrush) ;
}
```

Listing 4-39 Modified DrawBall() Function

```
void MovingBall::DrawBall ()      // draw red ball2 at current nX,nY
{
    CPen*   OldPen ;
    CBrush* OldBrush ;

    if (!bBallOn)        // do nothing if ball2 is not to move
        return ;

    CClientDC dc(pWindow) ;      // get client area device context
                // construct a thick gray pen (covers old ball2 edge)
    CPen Wpen (PS_SOLID, VELOCITY + VELOCITY/2, RGB (200, 200, 200)) ;
    CBrush Rbrush (RGB (255, 0, 0)) ;    // red brush for interior
    OldPen = dc.SelectObject (&Wpen) ;  // red pen and solid brush
    OldBrush = dc.SelectObject (&Rbrush) ;  // into device context
                        // to draw ball2 using ellipse() function
    dc.Ellipse (nX - BALLRAD, nY - BALLRAD, nX + BALLRAD,
        nY + BALLRAD) ;

    // make thin pen and solid white brush for highlight mark on ball2
    CPen Tpen (PS_SOLID, 3, RGB (255, 255, 255)) ;
    CBrush Wbrush (RGB (255, 255, 255)) ;
    dc.SelectObject (&Tpen) ;   // select pen and brush into device
    dc.SelectObject (&Wbrush) ; // context to draw highlight rectangle
    dc.Rectangle (nX + BALLRAD/3, nY - BALLRAD/3, nX + 2 + BALLRAD/3,
        nY - 2 - BALLRAD/3) ;

    dc.SelectObject (OldPen) ;    // select original brush and pen into
    dc.SelectObject (OldBrush) ; // device context to restore state.
}
```

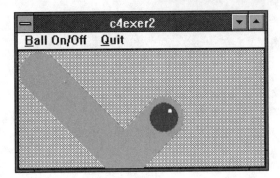

Figure 4-17 The C4EXER2 Program

Listing 4-40 Graying the GRAPHIC2 Window Client Area

```
BEGIN_MESSAGE_MAP (CMainWindow, CFrameWnd)
    ON_COMMAND (IDM_BALL, OnBall)             // turn ball on and off
    ON_COMMAND (IDM_QUIT, OnExit)             // exit function
    ON_WM_CLOSE ()                  // process WM_CLOSE
    ON_WM_PAINT ()                  // process WM_PAINT
END_MESSAGE_MAP ()

void CMainWindow::OnPaint ()     // process WM_PAINT message
{
    CPaintDC dc (this) ;
    CRect rect ;
    this->GetClientRect (&rect) ;
    CBrush GrayBrush (RGB (200, 200, 200)) ;
    CBrush *pOldBrush = dc.SelectObject (&GrayBrush) ;
    dc.Rectangle (&rect) ;
    dc.SelectObject (pOldBrush) ;
}
```

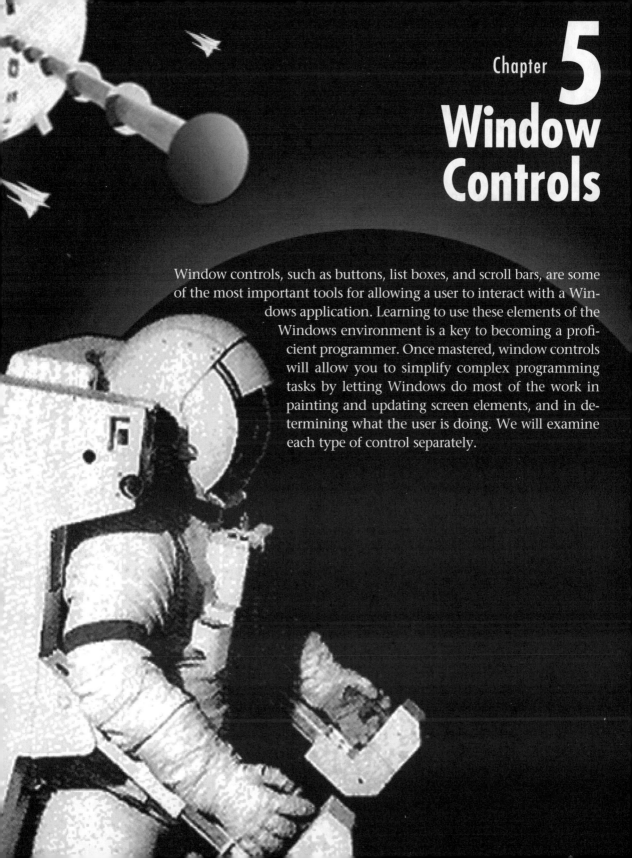

## Chapter 5

Window
Controls

Window controls, such as buttons, list boxes, and scroll bars, are some
of the most important tools for allowing a user to interact with a Windows application. Learning to use these elements of the
Windows environment is a key to becoming a profi-
cient programmer. Once mastered, window controls
will allow you to simplify complex programming
tasks by letting Windows do most of the work in
painting and updating screen elements, and in determining what the user is doing. We will examine
each type of control separately.

Concepts covered: Window controls, button styles, child and parent windows, control ID values, static text and icons, combo boxes, list boxes, scroll bars, edit controls, output streams.

Key words covered: All control styles (BS_PUSHBUTTON, etc.), WS_VSCROLL, WS_HSCROLL.

Functions covered: CWnd::SetWindowText(), CButton::SetCheck(), CButton::GetState(), CWnd::MessageBox(), CListBox::ResetContent(), CListBox::AddString(), CListBox::GetCurSel(), CListBox::GetText(), CScrollBar::GetScrollPos(), CScrollBar::GetScrollRange(), CScrollBar::Set-ScrollPos(), CScrollBar::SetScrollRange(), CWnd::Invalidate(), CEdit::Get-LineCount(), CEdit::LineIndex(), CEdit::LineLength().

Messages covered: WM_HSCROLL, WM_VSCROLL, WM_SIZE.

Classes covered: CStatic, CButton, CListBox, CComboBox, CScrollBar, CEdit, ostrstream.

WHAT IS A WINDOW?

The word "window" brings to mind the main window of a program. It turns out that the Windows environment uses the same low-level logic to create buttons, scroll bars, list boxes, combo boxes, edit controls, and the screen background. These objects have the following properties in common:

1. The object is rectangular.
2. To maintain the illusion of permanence, the area occupied by the object must be repainted when covered and uncovered by another object.
3. The object is a separate entity that can send and receive messages.

The Windows environment generalizes these characteristics into a common group of objects called "windows." The Windows environment manages windows for the program. Once created, the program communicates with the individual window elements by sending and receiving messages.

Using the windowing logic is much more powerful than simply drawing the shape using graphics commands. Once created, program windows and specialized window controls, such as buttons, are maintained by the Windows environment. This means that the Windows environment will repaint the object when needed, detect when it is selected with the mouse, and provide many ways for the programmer to change the appearance and functioning of the window object during the execution of a program.

Types of Window Controls

Windows uses the term "control" to describe predefined types of windows for common objects. Windows defines six different types of window controls, which are summarized in Table 5-1. Keep in mind that the appearance of each type of control can be modified by using different style parameters when calling the class **Create()** function. We will explore these options for each class of control during this chapter.

Object	Example Image	Description
Static Text	Static Text	Created from the **CStatic** class. Static controls are usually used for titles and other text that the user does not directly manipulate. Static controls can also be used to paint rectangular areas to improve the appearance of a screen.
Button	Button 1	Created from the **CButton** class. Button controls can have many shapes, including check boxes, radio buttons, group boxes, etc.
Edit Control	Try editing this text.	Created from the **CEdit** class. Edit controls can be a single line (as shown to the left), or multiline. Considerable word processing logic is built in.
List Box	isv.doc keycaps.doc	Created from the **CListBox** class. List boxes are used when the user needs to make a choice among selections, such as from a list of file names.
Combo Box	Second String First String Second String Inserted	Created from the **CComboBox** class. Combo boxes normally display only the top edit field. If the user clicks this area, a list box drops down underneath (as shown in the figure). Combo boxes are convenient if the user needs to be reminded which choice is in effect, but does not usually need to change the selection.
Scroll Bar		Created from the **CScrollBar** class. Scroll bars can be either separate controls, or attached to the edge of another window.

Table 5-1 Predefined Window Controls

There is an additional predefined window class, MDICLIENT. It is a programming convenience provided for complex applications like Excel and the Windows File Manager that use multiple child windows within the bounds of a single parent window. MDI stands for "Multiple Document Interface." MDI programs are not covered in this book. If you are interested, see Chapter 29 of *The Waite Group's Windows API Bible.*

Child and Parent Windows

Not all windows are created equal. If you create a program window that contains a number of controls, such as buttons and scroll bars, the buttons and scroll bars should all vanish when the main program window disappears. Otherwise you would end up with the controls hanging around on the screen like ghosts. To "attach" the controls to the parent window requires that the program tell the Windows environment which controls are attached to which main program window. This is done by establishing a "parent-child" relationship between the controls and the main window.

A parent window is any window that contains children. All of the child windows are "attached" to the parent by passing the parent window object as a parameter when the child window is created. We will see how this is done in a moment. The Windows environment maintains a list of which windows are children. When a parent window is covered up or destroyed, all of the child windows attached to the parent are also covered or destroyed. This all happens automatically, which is a great benefit of programming within the Windows environment.

Windows allows child windows to be parents of other "lower level" child windows. For example, you can create a child window button control, and attach other smaller buttons to this main button. This is not a good idea (few real buttons have other buttons attached to them), but it can be done. We will look at more reasonable uses for child windows of child windows in Chapter 8, *Child and Pop-Up Windows.* For now we will concentrate on attaching child window controls directly to the main program "parent" window.

MFC Classes for Controls

The MFC approach to window controls is to derive a separate class for each type of control. All of the control classes are derived from the **CWnd** class, which provides functions that are common to all types of windows, as shown in Figure 5-1. All of the functions in the **CWnd** base class are available to the control classes, plus the additional functions specific to each type of control.

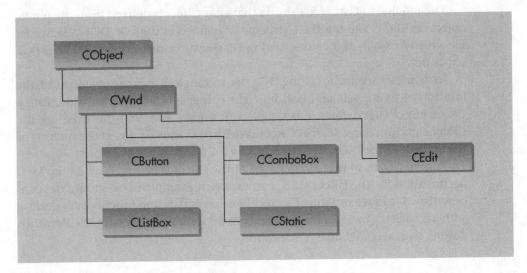

Figure 5-1 Derivation of MFC Control Classes

Another MFC class that is used with all of the control classes is **CRect**. **CRect** encapsulates the data and operations that apply to rectangles. Because all window controls are rectangular, the size and location of the control can be described in terms of a bounding rectangle. The **CRect** class is interesting in that it is not derived from the **CObject** class like most of the other MFC classes. Instead, the **CRect** class is derived from the **tagRECT** structure that is used in conventional C programming for Windows. If you look up the **CRect** class definition in AFXWIN.H, you will find the code shown in Listing 5-1.

Listing 5-1 CRect Class Definition in AFXWIN.H

```
class CRect : public tagRECT
{
public:

// Constructors
    CRect();
    CRect(int l, int t, int r, int b);
    CRect(const RECT& srcRect);
    CRect(LPRECT lpSrcRect);
    CRect(POINT point, SIZE size);

// Attributes (in addition to RECT members)
    int Width() const;
    int Height() const;
    CSize Size() const;
// etc...
}
```

The top line in Listing 5-1 shows that class **CRect** is derived from the public object **tagRECT**. The **tagRECT** structure is defined in the WINDOWS.H header file which AFXWIN.H includes. Listing 5-2 shows the definition of the **tagRECT** structure.

As you can see from Listing 5-2, the rectangle is defined in terms of the location of its top left and bottom right corners. Typically, you will create a **CRect** object that defines a rectangle with a fixed size. You can then use the **CRect** class functions, such as **CRect::Width()**, or directly access the integers of the embedded **tagRECT** structure. Listing 5-3 shows a few examples.

You may want to take a quick look at the **CRect** class functions in the MFC documentation. The **CRect** class is an excellent example of extending the concept of a C language structure to a complete set of data and functions for dealing with an object. The MFC classes also contain a similar class named **CPoint** for dealing with an individual *X,Y* location.

STATIC CONTROLS

The simplest of the six types of window controls are static controls. Static controls are used primarily for displaying text, although they can also display icon images and rectangles. The advantage of using a static control over painting on the window's client area is that the static control is automatically redrawn if it is covered by another window and then uncovered. This avoids having to process WM_PAINT messages to keep the window's client area up-to-date. Static controls are unique in that selecting one with the mouse cursor does not result in a message being sent. Static controls, therefore, cannot be used for user input.

Listing 5-2 tagRECT Structure Definition in WINDOWS.H

```
typedef struct tagRECT
{
    int left;
    int top;
    int right;
    int bottom;
} RECT;
```

Listing 5-3 Using the CRect Class

```
CRect MyRect (10, 20, 100, 70) ;        // create a CRect object
int wide = MyRect.Width () ;            // use the Width() function
int TopLeft = MyRect.left ;            // access tagRECT member
```

The MFC **CStatic** class is the basis for creating static controls. To create a **CStatic** object you simply use the constructor function:

```
CStatic StaticText ;
```

This creates a **CStatic** object named *StaticText*, but does not create a visible static window control. In other words, simply creating a **CStatic** object does not pass any information on to the Windows environment. To create a visible static control, you must also call the **CStatic::Create()** class function. The declaration of this function is shown below, with each of the parameter types explained in Table 5-2.

```
BOOL CStatic::Create (const char FAR* lpText, DWORD dwStyle,
    const RECT& rect, CWnd* pParentWnd, UINT nID) ;
```

Note that the *pParentWnd* parameter is used to pass a pointer to the parent window object to which the static control will be attached. This is how the parent-child relationship is established. Calling the **CStatic::Create()** function passes this data on to the Windows environment, which tracks which windows are child windows and to which parent they are attached.

The *dwStyle* parameter passed to **CStatic::Create()** can take a number of values, which are summarized in Table 5-3. The most common style is SS_LEFT, which is left-justified text. However, static controls can be used to shade and outline areas, using styles like SS_GRAYRECT and SS_BLACKFRAME. You can also display an icon image created with the Image Editor, using the SS_ICON style.

Parameter	Meaning
lpText	A pointer to a character string containing the text that will appear in the control.
dwStyle	A DWORD (four-byte) value containing a combination of style values that define the appearance of the static control. These styles are described in the following sections.
rect	A rectangle defining the size and location of the static control.
pParentWnd	A pointer to the parent window of the control. This is the window to which the static control will be attached. The static control will be visible only if the parent is visible.
nID	An integer value which will be the ID number for the control. This value is used when sending and receiving messages to or from a control.

Table 5-2 Parameters in CStatic::Create() Function

Style	Meaning
SS_BLACKFRAME	A static control with a black frame outline.
SS_BLACKRECT	A static control with the entire center filled with the color used to draw the window frame. This is black with the default Windows color scheme.
SS_CENTER	A static text control with the text centered.
SS_GRAYFRAME	A static control with the frame color equal to the Windows desktop background. This is gray with the default Windows color scheme.
SS_GRAYRECT	A static control with the entire center filled with the color used to draw the Windows desktop background. This is gray with the default Windows color scheme.
SS_ICON	A static control containing an icon. The *lpWindowName* parameter specifies the name of the icon to use.
SS_LEFT	A static text control with the text left aligned.
SS_LEFTNOWORDWRAP	A static text control. Text is flush left and truncated to the size of the control.
SS_NOPREFIX	A static control where it is desirable to display ampersands (&) in the text of the control. Normally, ampersands are used to cause the next character in the static control's text string to be underlined.
SS_RIGHT	A static text control with the text string right aligned.
SS_SIMPLE	A static text control consisting of only text.
SS_USERITEM	A user-defined static control.
SS_WHITEFRAME	A static text control with a frame matching the window's background color (default is white).
SS_WHITERECT	A static control with the entire center filled with the color used to draw the parent window's background. This is white with the default Windows color scheme.

Table 5-3 Static Control Styles

An Example Using Static Controls

Figure 5-2a shows the STATIC program, which is designed to demonstrate different types of static controls. Inside the client area you will see some text, an icon image, and a gray rectangle. Each of these is a static window control. The

a) At Startup

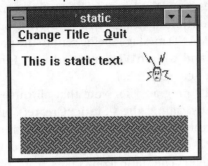

b) After Selecting "Change Title"

Figure 5-2 The STATIC Program

program also has two menu options. Selecting the "Change Title" menu item results in changing the text in the static text control, as shown in Figure 5-2b. This points out that static controls are not necessarily "static" all of the time. You can change the text in a static control any time you want. The "Quit" menu item simply terminates the program.

The STATIC program requires the usual collection of program files. Listing 5-4 shows the program's header file STATIC.HPP. Note that the **CMainWindow** class includes declarations of three **CStatic** objects. These declarations result in three separate calls to the **CStatic** class constructor function.

Listing 5-4 STATIC.HPP Header File

```
// static.hpp    header file for static.cpp

class CMainWindow : public CFrameWnd    // derive a main window class
{
public:
    CMainWindow () ;                // declare a constructor
private:
    CStatic StaticText ;            // static objects
    CStatic StaticIcon ;            // destroyed when CMainWindow goes
    CStatic StaticRect ;            // out of scope (is destroyed)
    void OnChange () ;              // respond to "Change" menu item
    void OnExit () ;                // stop application

    DECLARE_MESSAGE_MAP()          // prepare for message processing
} ;


class CTheApp : public CWinApp  // derive an application class
{
public:
    BOOL InitInstance () ;         // declare new InitInstance()
} ;
```

Note that the **CMainWindow** class definition includes the DECLARE_MES-SAGE_MAP() macro because messages from Windows will be processed. Because static controls themselves do not generate messages when selected, only the two menu items result in WM_COMMAND messages being sent to the program. The **CMainWindow::OnChange()** and **CMainWindow::OnExit()** functions are declared to respond to the menu item selections.

Listing 5-5 shows the STATIC.CPP program file. Note that all three of the static window controls are created by calling the **CStatic::Create()** function within the **CMainWindow** constructor. The **CRect** object *ControlRect* is used to specify the size and location of each of the controls. The static text item is passed a text string as its first parameter. The static icon is passed the name of the icon file in the program's resource script file. You will see the "MyIcon" definition in STATIC.RC in a moment. The gray rectangle does not need any additional data as the first parameter for the **CStatic::Create()** function, so a NULL value is passed.

Note the different combinations of style values for each of the controls are combined with the C++ language binary OR operator (|). All of the controls are child window controls, as specified with the WS_CHILD style. As child windows all of the static controls will be attached to the main parent window, and only visible if the parent window is visible. The WS_VISIBLE style makes the controls visible the moment they are created.

The last two parameters passed to the **CStatic::Create()** function are a pointer to the parent window object and the ID value for the control. The *this* pointer provides an easy way to get a handle to the **CMainWindow** object, as all three of the calls to **CStatic::Create()** are within a function member of the **CMainWindow** class (the constructor function in this case). The pointer is passed on to the Windows environment to establish the parent-child relationship.

The control ID numbers are the last parameter in the **CStatic::Create()** function calls. The ID values are defined in the STATIC.H header file which is shown in Listing 5-5.

The message map for STATIC.CPP is very simple. The only messages processed are the WM_COMMAND messages sent if either of the menu items is selected. The text string of the static control *StaticText* is changed in the **CMainWindow::OnChange()** function by calling the **CWnd::SetWindowText()** function. **SetWindowText()** is available to the static window control because the **CStatic** class is derived from **CWnd**, so all **CStatic** objects inherit the **CWnd** public functions and public data.

If the "Quit" menu item is selected, the message map executes the **CMainWindow::OnExit()** function. The **CWnd::DestroyWindow()** function

Listing 5-5 STATIC.CPP

```cpp
// static.cpp                    example using static window controls

#include <afxwin.h>     // class library header file
#include "static.h"     // header file for resource data
#include "static.hpp"    // header file for this program

CTheApp theApp ;          // create one CTheApp object - runs program

BOOL CTheApp::InitInstance ()    // override default InitInstance()
{
    m_pMainWnd = new CMainWindow () ;        // create a main window
    m_pMainWnd->ShowWindow (m_nCmdShow) ;    // make it visible
    m_pMainWnd->UpdateWindow () ;            // paint center
    return TRUE ;
}


CMainWindow::CMainWindow ()        // constructor for main window
{
    Create (NULL, "static", WS_OVERLAPPEDWINDOW, rectDefault,
        NULL, "MyMenu") ;
                            // create static child window controls
    CRect ControlRect (10, 10, 130, 60) ;   // rect for control size
    StaticText.Create ("This is static text.",
        SS_CENTER | WS_CHILD | WS_VISIBLE, ControlRect,
        this, ID_STEXT) ;               // "this" is parent window

    ControlRect.SetRect (150, 10, 0, 0) ;    // icon position
    StaticIcon.Create ("MyIcon", SS_ICON | WS_CHILD | WS_VISIBLE,
        ControlRect, this, ID_SICON) ;

    ControlRect.SetRect (10, 80, 200, 120) ; // static rectangle size
    StaticRect.Create (NULL, SS_GRAYRECT | WS_CHILD | WS_VISIBLE,
        ControlRect, this, ID_SRECT) ;
}

BEGIN_MESSAGE_MAP (CMainWindow, CFrameWnd)
    ON_COMMAND (IDM_CHANGE, OnChange)
    ON_COMMAND (IDM_QUIT, OnExit
END_MESSAGE_MAP ()

void CMainWindow::OnChange ()    // change static text using
{                                // SetWindowText() function
    StaticText.SetWindowText ("New Text Via SetWindowText().") ;
}


void CMainWindow::OnExit ()      // respond to menu item "Quit"
{
    this->DestroyWindow () ;     // destroy main window,
}                                // this stops application
```

is used to destroy the STATIC program's main window, which terminates the program. All three of the static control windows are automatically deleted from memory and the screen by Windows because they are child windows of the main program window.

Listing 5-6 shows the module definition file for the STATIC program.

The menu item and control ID numbers are defined in the STATIC.H header file (Listing 5-7). It is not necessary to give static controls ID numbers because they do not generate messages from Windows and the ID value is never used. If you omit the last (*nID*) parameter in the **CStatic::Create()** function call, the default ID value of 0xFFFF hexadecimal will be used.

Listing 5-8 shows the STATIC.RC resource script file. Note that the same icon file STATIC.ICO is included twice in the program's resources. This is not necessary, but serves to demonstrate that an icon can be named anything you want. The first inclusion of the icon data is assigned the identifier AFX_IDI_STD_FRAME, which is defined equal to the number two in the AFXRES.H file that is included by AFXWIN.H. The AFX_ID_STD_FRAME value is recognized by the MFC classes as the icon ID value for program icons, so this icon is automatically displayed when the STATIC program is minimized.

In addition, the STATIC.ICO icon is included in STATIC.RC with the name "MyIcon." This is the name that is used in STATIC.CPP to associate an icon with a static control. You could also use the AFX_IDI_STD_FRAME icon identifier when creating the static icon control. This would eliminate the need to include the same icon data twice in STATIC.RC.

Listing 5-6 STATIC.DEF Module Definition File

```
NAME            static
DESCRIPTION     'static C++ program'
EXETYPE         WINDOWS
STUB            'WINSTUB.EXE'
CODE            PRELOAD MOVEABLE
DATA            PRELOAD MOVEABLE MULTIPLE
HEAPSIZE        1024
STACKSIZE       5120
```

Listing 5-7 STATIC.H Resource ID Header File

```
// static.h  header file for resource ID numbers

#define IDM_CHANGE      1       // menu item ID numbers
#define IDM_QUIT        10

#define ID_STEXT        50      // control window ID numbers
#define ID_SICON        51
#define ID_SRECT        52
```

Listing 5-8 STATIC.RC Resource Script File

```
// static.rc  resource script file

#include <afxres.h>
#include "static.h"

AFX_IDI_STD_FRAME    ICON     static.ico    // the program's icon
MyIcon               ICON     static.ico    // second icon -
                                            // different icon name

MyMenu MENU                                 // define the menu
{
    MENUITEM "&Change Title",      IDM_CHANGE
    MENUITEM "&Quit",              IDM_QUIT
}
```

Figure 5-3 shows the STATIC program's icon image that was created with the Image Editor application.

Compile STATIC and get it running. Test the automatic repainting of the child window controls by covering STATIC with another program's window, and then uncovering it. The controls will be automatically redrawn. The redrawing will also occur if you resize the window, or minimize it and then restore it. The Windows environment takes care of keeping all of the windows current. This is a lot easier than having to process WM_PAINT messages for the text and icons.

It is not always possible or desirable to eliminate WM_PAINT message processing logic from your program. Although static controls are handy, they are limited to text, icons, and rectangles. Window controls also take up considerable processing time, as Windows must continually check each of the controls to see if it needs to be repainted, made invisible, deleted, and so on. If you want to have more elaborate colored images in the program's client area, you will need to process WM_PAINT messages, and repaint each time the WM_PAINT message is received. You can use a combination of static controls and direct painting logic in many applications. As long as the program's performance is acceptable (not too slow) use static controls whenever possible to simplify your program, and just paint the portions that demand the use of graphics functions.

Figure 5-3 STATIC.ICO Icon Image

BUTTON CONTROLS

Windows supports a variety of objects created from the **CButton** class, such as push buttons, radio buttons, check boxes, and group outlines. Our next example demonstrates most of these button styles. Along the way, you will learn how to use the handy **CWnd::MessageBox()** and output stream operators.

Creating a button control is similar to creating a static window control. First you create a **CButton** object:

```
CButton DoneButton ;
```

Second, you inform the Windows environment about the new button control by calling the **CButton::Create()** function. This function has exactly the same syntax as the **CStatic::Create()** function:

```
BOOL CButton::Create (const char FAR* lpText, DWORD dwStyle, const
RECT& rect, CWnd* pParentWnd, UINT nID) ;
```

Although the parameters passed to the **CButton::Create()** function are identical to those passed to **CStatic::Create()** (see Table 5-2 for the parameter meanings), the *dwStyle* parameter uses a different set of flags when creating a button control. The *dwStyle* parameter passed to **CreateWindow()** can have any of the values shown in Table 5-4. Some of these styles can be combined using the OR operator (|). For example, to create a check box control with the text on the left side (the default is the right side), use WS_CHILD | BS_CHECKBOX | BS_LEFTTEXT. Buttons are almost always child windows, so the WS_CHILD style will usually be part of the *dwStyle* definition.

The example program for this section is called BUTTON. When activated, the program's window appears as shown in Figure 5-4. BUTTON has two radio

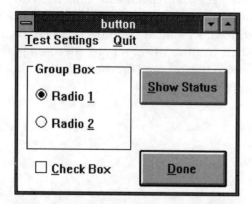

Figure 5-4 BUTTON Program in Operation

Style	Meaning
BS_AUTOCHECKBOX	Small rectangular button with text to the right. The rectangle can be either open or checked. This style toggles automatically between checked and open.
BS_AUTORADIOBUTTON	Small circular button with text to the right. The circle can be either filled or open. This style toggles automatically between checked and open.
BS_AUTO3STATE	Small rectangular button with text to the right. The button can be filled, grayed, or open. This style toggles automatically among checked, grayed, and open.
BS_CHECKBOX	Small rectangular button with text to the right. The rectangle can be either open or checked.
BS_DEFPUSHBUTTON	Button with text in the center and with a defined (dark) border. This style is used to indicate the button that is pressed when the user presses the (ENTER) key.
BS_GROUPBOX	A box outline with text at the upper left. Used to group other controls.
BS_LEFTTEXT	Causes text to be on the left side of the button. Use this with other button styles.
BS_OWNERDRAW	Designates a button that will be drawn by the program. Windows sends messages to request paint, invert, and disable. Use this style for custom button controls.
BS_PUSHBUTTON	A rectangular button with text in the center.
BS_RADIOBUTTON	Small circular button with text to the right. The circle can be either filled or open.
BS_3STATE	Small rectangular button with text to the right. The button can be filled, grayed, or open.

Table 5-4 Button Styles

buttons inside of a group box. Radio buttons and group boxes are forms of buttons. There is also a check box button at the bottom left. Two push buttons are on the right side of the window. All told, there are six buttons inside of the parent window's client area, counting the group box control.

The most obvious type of button is the push button. The BUTTON program has two of these on the right side. Push buttons initiate some action when selected. The other types of buttons allow the user to make selections. Radio buttons are used to make a single selection from a group of possibilities. In the BUTTON program, selecting radio button one automatically results in de-selecting radio button two, and vice-versa. This is typical of a situation where only one of a group of possibilities can be selected at any one time. It is common to put related radio buttons into groups, so that their relationship is clear. In BUTTON, the group box is sized to hold both radio buttons.

Check boxes are specialized buttons that are used to show an on/off status for a selection. Both check boxes and radio buttons have the ability to show three states: off, checked, and grayed. The grayed state fills in the selection area on the left with a gray color, rather than showing a solid radio button or an X for the check box. Graying the selection can be used to allow three different selection states, such as on/off/disabled. Generally, it is best to stick with just two states, off and checked, as users may confuse the grayed and checked states. The BUTTON program implements a three-state check box, so that you can experiment with this option.

An interesting characteristic of both radio and check box buttons is that the "button" includes both the small circle or square that gets checked and the text string to the side. Using the mouse to click any part of the control's text string or the circle or square area results in the control being selected. The combination of the text string and the circle or square make up a single rectangular window area.

Listing 5-9 shows the BUTTON.HPP header file. All of the **CButton** objects are declared in this header file. The push buttons, radio buttons, and check box all generate WM_COMMAND messages if they are selected by the user, so each of the controls has a matching response function such as **CMainWindow::OnRadio1()** for the *Radio1* control. WM_COMMAND messages are also generated for the two menu items, so two response functions named **CMainWindow::OnTest()** and **CMainWindow::OnExit()** are also declared. Finally, two integer values named *nRadioSelection* and *nCheckBoxState* are defined in the **CMainWindow** class. These variables will be used within the program logic to keep track of the current state of the radio button and check box selections.

The BUTTON.H header file is shown in Listing 5-10. Each of the controls is assigned a separate ID value. It is important that menu items and controls have different ID numbers because both generate WM_COMMAND messages.

BUTTON.CPP (Listing 5-11) shows many similarities to the STATIC.CPP program we just finished. All of the button controls are created using the **CButton::Create()** function. Each is a child window (WS_CHILD style). The second style parameter determines what type of button is created. The BS_GROUPBOX style creates the group box. This is an open rectangle with a

Listing 5-9 BUTTON.HPP Header File

```
// button.hpp    header file for button.cpp
                            // derive a main window class
class CMainWindow : public CFrameWnd
{
public:
    CMainWindow () ;              // declare a constructor
    void ShowButtonStates () ;   // displays the current status
private:
    void OnTest () ;             // "test settings" menu item
    void OnExit () ;             // "quit" menu item
    void OnRadio1 () ;           // respond to radio 1 button
    void OnRadio2 () ;           // radio 2
    void OnCheckBox () ;         // check box
    void OnShowButn () ;         // "Show Status" button
    void OnDoneButn () ;         // "Done" button
    CButton GroupBox ;           // button objects
    CButton Radio1 ;
    CButton Radio2 ;
    CButton CheckBox ;
    CButton ShowButton ;
    CButton DoneButton ;
    int nRadioSelection ;        // 0 for top, 1 for bottom
    int nCheckBoxState ;         // 0 off, 1 checked, 2 grayed

    DECLARE_MESSAGE_MAP()        // prepare for message processing
} ;

class CTheApp : public CWinApp  // derive an application class
{
public:
    BOOL InitInstance () ;       // declare new InitInstance()
} ;
```

Listing 5-10 BUTTON.H Resource ID Header File

```
// button.h  header file for resource ID numbers

#define IDM_TEST       1        // menu item ID numbers
#define IDM_QUIT       10

#define ID_RADIO1      50       // button control ID numbers
#define ID_RADIO2      51
#define ID_CHECKBOX    52
#define ID_SHOWBUTN    53
#define ID_DONEBUTN    54
```

title at the upper left corner. The BS_RADIOBUTTON style is used to create the two radio buttons. By default, the selection area (small circle) is on the left side, but you can move it to the right by adding the BS_LEFTTEXT style to the radio button or check box style.

Listing 5-11 BUTTON.CPP

```cpp
// button.cpp              example showing button controls

#include <afxwin.h>     // class library header file
#include <strstrea.h>   // class library for streams
#include "button.h"     // header file for resource data
#include "button.hpp"   // header file for this program

CTheApp theApp ;         // create one CTheApp object - runs program

BOOL CTheApp::InitInstance ()    // override default InitInstance()
{
    m_pMainWnd = new CMainWindow () ;        // create a main window
    m_pMainWnd->ShowWindow (m_nCmdShow) ;   // make it visible
    m_pMainWnd->UpdateWindow () ;           // paint center
    return TRUE ;
}


CMainWindow::CMainWindow ()       // constructor for main window
{
    Create (NULL, "button", WS_OVERLAPPEDWINDOW, rectDefault,
        NULL, "MyMenu") ;
                                // create button controls
    CRect ControlRect (10, 10, 130, 110) ;  // rect to hold size
    GroupBox.Create ("Group Box",           // first is group box
        BS_GROUPBOX | WS_CHILD | WS_VISIBLE, ControlRect,
        this, NULL) ;                       // "this" is parent window

    ControlRect.SetRect (20, 40, 100, 60) ; // radio button 1
    Radio1.Create ("Radio &1",
        BS_RADIOBUTTON | WS_CHILD | WS_VISIBLE, ControlRect,
        this, ID_RADIO1) ;
    Radio1.SetCheck (1) ;                    // initialize to checked

    ControlRect.SetRect (20, 70, 100, 90) ; // radio button 2
    Radio2.Create ("Radio &2",              // defaults unchecked
        BS_RADIOBUTTON | WS_CHILD | WS_VISIBLE, ControlRect,
        this, ID_RADIO2) ;

    ControlRect.SetRect (20, 120, 120, 140) ;    // check box
    CheckBox.Create ("&Check Box",
        BS_AUTO3STATE | WS_CHILD | WS_VISIBLE, ControlRect,
        this, ID_CHECKBOX) ;

    ControlRect.SetRect (140, 20, 240, 60) ;    // top push button
    ShowButton.Create ("&Show Status",
        BS_PUSHBUTTON | WS_CHILD | WS_VISIBLE, ControlRect,
        this, ID_SHOWBUTN) ;
```

```
        ControlRect.SetRect (140, 110, 240, 150) ;  // lower push button
        DoneButton.Create ("&Done",
            BS_DEFPUSHBUTTON | WS_CHILD | WS_VISIBLE, ControlRect,
            this, ID_DONEBUTN) ;
}


BEGIN_MESSAGE_MAP (CMainWindow, CFrameWnd)
    ON_COMMAND (IDM_TEST, OnTest)              // menu items
    ON_COMMAND (IDM_QUIT, OnExit)
    ON_COMMAND (ID_RADIO1, OnRadio1)           // controls
    ON_COMMAND (ID_RADIO2, OnRadio2)
    ON_COMMAND (ID_CHECKBOX, OnCheckBox)
    ON_COMMAND (ID_SHOWBUTN, OnShowButn)
    ON_COMMAND (ID_DONEBUTN, OnDoneButn)
END_MESSAGE_MAP ()


void CMainWindow::OnTest ()      // respond to "Show Status" menu item
{
    ShowButtonStates () ;
}


void CMainWindow::OnExit ()      // respond to menu item "Quit"
{
    this->DestroyWindow () ;     // destroy main window,
}                                // this stops application


void CMainWindow::OnShowButn()   // respond to "Show Status" button
{
    ShowButtonStates () ;
}


void CMainWindow::OnDoneButn ()  // respond to "Done" button
{
    this->DestroyWindow () ;     // also stops application
}


void CMainWindow::OnRadio1 ()
{
    Radio1.SetCheck (1) ;              // check radio 1
    Radio2.SetCheck (0) ;              // uncheck radio 2
    nRadioSelection = 0 ;              // save state
}


void CMainWindow::OnRadio2 ()
{
    Radio1.SetCheck (0) ;              // uncheck radio 1
    Radio2.SetCheck (1) ;              // check radio 2
    nRadioSelection = 1 ;              // save state
}
```

```
void CMainWindow::OnCheckBox ()       // respond to check box
{
    // do not need to set state, as this is an auto 3 state control
    nCheckBoxState = 0x03 & CheckBox.GetState () ;  // save state
}   //   0x03 mask selects only the bits used for check status

void CMainWindow::ShowButtonStates ()   // display message box
{                                       // showing current status
    char str [256] ;
                                // construct string object in memory
    ostrstream msgString (str, sizeof (str)) ;
    msgString << "Radio button selection = " <<
        nRadioSelection << ", Check box status = " <<
        nCheckBoxState << ends ;

    CMainWindow::MessageBox (str, "Message Box", MB_OK) ;
}
```

The check box uses the BS_AUTO3STATE style. "AUTO" means that the check box automatically cycles through the off, checked, and grayed states each time it is selected. "3STATE" means that the off, checked, and grayed states are all available. The BS_AUTOCHECKBOX is the equivalent style with only the off and checked states available. If you do not want the button's state to change automatically each time it is selected, use the BS_CHECKBOX (two states) or BS_3STATE (three states) styles.

The two push buttons are created with the BS_PUSHBUTTON and BS_DEFPUSHBUTTON styles. The only difference is that the BS_DEFPUSH-BUTTON style adds a dark outline to the button's outline. This is usually used to highlight the default action that will happen if the user presses the (ENTER) key. We have not covered keyboard input yet, so this feature is not implemented in BUTTON.CPP.

The message map in BUTTON.CPP routes execution to the correct function depending on which control or menu item is selected. For example, the menu item with the ID value IDM_TEST is mapped to the **CMainWindow::OnTest()** function while the control with the ID value ID_RADIO1 results in the **CMainWindow::OnRadio1()** function being called.

If one radio button control is selected, the other must be de-selected. This is done in the **CMainWindow::OnRadio1()** and **CMainWindow::OnRadio2()** functions that are called if one of the radio button controls is selected. Both **CMainWindow::OnRadio1()** and **CMainWindow::OnRadio2()** use the **CButton::SetCheck()** function to change the status of the radio buttons to reflect a selection. The current selection status is also saved in the *nRadioSelection* integer variable.

The check box control uses the BS_AUTO3STATE style, so it automatically changes from open to checked to grayed each time it is selected. There is no need to call the **CButton::SetCheck()** function for an automatic button style, although doing so does not cause an error. Instead, **CMainWindow::On-CheckBox()** just determines the current status of the check box using the **CButton::GetState()** function. The **CButton::GetState()** function returns the status of the button control in the lower two bits of the function's returned value. The higher value bits are used to code if the button control is highlighted or currently has the "input focus," meaning that the next keyboard input will be processed by the button. We do not need this esoteric data, so only the lowest two bits are evaluated. The code

```
nCheckBoxState = 0x03 & CheckBox.GetState () ;
```

masks off the bottom two bits and stores them in the *nCheckBoxState* variable. The *nCheckBoxState* variable will contain zero if the control is not checked, one if the control is checked, and two if the control (a three-state check box) is grayed. Normal radio buttons and check boxes that are not three-state controls will return only zero and one for unchecked and checked, respectively.

Selecting either the "Test Settings" menu item or the push button control labeled "Show Status" results in the current radio button and check box status being displayed in a small window by the **ShowButtonStates()** function. We will examine this function in a moment. Listing 5-12 shows the module definition file BUTTON.DEF.

Listing 5-13 shows the resource script file for BUTTON. Figure 5-5 shows the program's icon image.

Listing 5-12 BUTTON.DEF Module Definition File

```
NAME                button
DESCRIPTION         'button C++ program'
EXETYPE             WINDOWS
STUB                'WINSTUB.EXE'
CODE                PRELOAD MOVEABLE
DATA                PRELOAD MOVEABLE MULTIPLE
HEAPSIZE            1024
STACKSIZE           5120
```

Figure 5-5 BUTTON.ICO Icon Image

Listing 5-13 BUTTON.RC Resource Script File

```
// button.rc  resource script file

#include <afxres.h>
#include "button.h"

AFX_IDI_STD_FRAME  ICON    button.ico        // the program's icon

MyMenu MENU                                  // define the menu
{
    MENUITEM "&Test Settings",     IDM_TEST
    MENUITEM "&Quit",              IDM_QUIT
}
```

Displaying a Message Box

One of the more interesting parts of the BUTTON program is that it displays the current status of the radio and check box buttons in a small window if either the "Test Settings" menu item or the "Show Status" push button is selected. Figure 5-6 shows the small window which is called a "Message Box." The message box window remains on the screen until the user clicks the "OK" button.

Message boxes are easily created using the **CWnd::MessageBox()** function. In BUTTON.CPP, the message box is created within the **CMainWindow::ShowButtonStates()** function, which is shown again in Listing 5-14. The **CWnd::MessageBox()** function takes three parameters: a character string which is displayed within the message box, a character string which becomes the message box window caption, and a flag value which is created using predefined values such as MB_OK to display a button labeled "OK." You can also display "Cancel," "Retry," "Yes," and "No" buttons as well as stock icons like a question mark or a picture of a hand using other flag values. Take a look at the **CWnd::MessageBox()** documentation for additional flag values.

Note that the **CMainWindow** class is derived in BUTTON.HPP (Listing 5-10) from **CFrameWnd**, which in turn is derived from the **CWnd** class. This makes

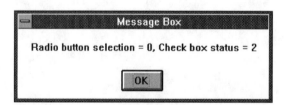

Figure 5-6 The Message Box from the BUTTON Program

Listing 5-14 Creating a Message Box

```
void CMainWindow::ShowButtonStates ()    // display message box
{                                        // showing current status
    char str [256] ;
                                // construct string object in memory
    ostrstream msgString (str, sizeof (str)) ;
    msgString << "Radio button selection = " <<
        nRadioSelection << ", Check box status = " <<
        nCheckBoxState << ends ;

    CMainWindow::MessageBox (str, "Message Box", MB_OK) ;
}
```

the **CWnd::MessageBox()** function directly available to the **CMainWindow** class. Most C++ programmers would use the *this* pointer in place of explicitly referencing the **CMainWindow** class as shown at the bottom of Listing 5-14. The equivalent function call using the *this* pointer would be:

```
this->MessageBox (str, "Message Box", MB_OK) ;
```

The remaining examples in this book use the *this* pointer technique.

Streams

As mentioned previously, the **CMainWindow::MessageBox()** function takes two character strings as parameters. In Listing 5-14, you can see that the message box caption string is always set to "Message Box." However, the character string that shows up within the message box client area is used to show the values of the two integers *nRadioSelection* and *nCheckBoxState* that track the radio and check box status. Displaying numeric values in a character string requires formatted output.

In a conventional C language program, you would use an output function, such as **printf()**, to produce formatted output containing both characters and digits. The C++ language includes a more elegant technique for formatting output using output streams. For example, in a DOS program you might use code like:

```
int nDays = 31 ;

cout << "January has " << nDays << " days" ;
```

This would cause the string "January has 31 days" to show up on the DOS output console. This simple approach cannot be applied in Windows because there is no standard output console in the Windows environment. The output must be routed to some sort of window function or client area output device.

The MFC libraries include an extensive collection of stream functions for both input and output of formatted data. These stream classes are defined in separate header files, such as the STRSTREA.H header file that is included at the top of BUTTON.CPP (Listing 5-11). The stream objects are not defined in the AFXWIN.H header file because streams are useful outside of Windows when creating DOS programs that have no use for the other classes defined in AFXWIN.H. In the course of this book, you will be exposed to a number of applications for the stream classes; but for now, we will concentrate on formatting a string for use in the **CWnd::MessageBox()** function.

The **ostrstream** class is used in the BUTTON.CPP program to format a character string for the message box. **ostrstream** is a compound name that stands for Output STRing STREAM. In other words, the **ostrstream** class is a specialized class for applying formatted output to character strings in memory buffers, rather than sending the output directly to a device like a DOS **cout** object. The **ostrstream** class is a derived class, as shown in Figure 5-7.

Applying the ostrstream class takes a few steps. First you will need to set aside a character buffer in memory. The following code establishes a 256-byte temporary buffer in the program's stack. This is ideal for a string that will not be of any value after the message box has been displayed, because the stack memory area is reused once the function declaring the buffer returns.

```
char str [256] ;
```

With the character buffer available, you can create an **ostrstream** object. The **ostrstream** constructor accepts a pointer to the character buffer and the size of the buffer as parameters. The result is that an **ostrstream** object is

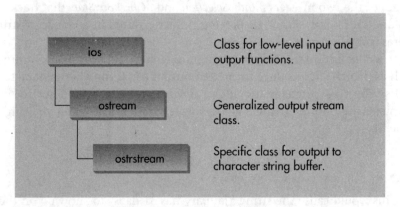

Figure 5-7 Derivation of the ostrstream Class

"wrapped around" the character buffer, directing all of the output stream functions towards the buffer memory area.

```
ostrstream msgString (str, sizeof (str)) ;
```

With the **ostrstream** object *msgString* defined, you can now use standard C++ output string syntax to create formatted output in the buffer. The *ends* "class manipulator" caps the end of the string with a terminating-null character.

```
msgString << "Radio button selection = " <<
    nRadioSelection << ", Check box status = " <<
    nCheckBoxState << ends ;
```

All that remains is to call the **CWnd::MessageBox()** function to make the character string visible in a small message box window.

```
CMainWindow::MessageBox (str, "Message Box", MB_OK) ;
```

If you are a long-time C programmer, output streams will take a little getting used to. However, after a few weeks you will probably never want to go back to the older approaches of using **printf()** and similar functions. The C++ stream approach is more flexible, and less prone to error.

LIST BOXES

List boxes and combo boxes are similar, as they both have a list of items that can be selected. The main difference is that the list box is always visible, and the combo box can be "shrunk" to show only the top edit line where selections can be entered. Combo boxes take up less space, and are a better choice if the user will not normally make a selection, but just needs to be reminded of the currently selected value. List boxes are more appropriate if the user will usually make a selection.

Creating a list box control is similar to creating a static window or button control. First you create a **CListBox** object:

```
CListBox AList ;
```

Second, you inform the Windows environment about the new list box control by calling the **CListBox::Create()** function. This function has syntax similar to the **CStatic::Create()** function, except that there is no text string to be passed to the list box because list boxes do not have a title. We will examine how to fill a list box with entries in a moment.

```
BOOL CListBox::Create (DWORD dwStyle, const RECT& rect,
    CWnd* pParentWnd, UINT nID) ;
```

The parameters passed to the **CListBox::Create()** function have the same meanings as those passed to **CStatic::Create()** (see Table 5-2 for the parameter meanings). However, the *dwStyle* parameter uses a different set of flags when creating a list box control. The *dwStyle* parameter can have any of the values shown in Table 5-5. Some of these styles can be combined using the OR operator (|). A typical set of style values would be WS_CHILD | LBS_NOTIFY | LBS_SORT | LBS_HASSTRINGS. The LBS_HASSTRINGS style tells Windows to store the list box contents in the application's local heap. Windows will delete the list box data when the list box is destroyed. LBS_NOTIFY tells Windows to send messages to the list box's parent window when items are selected in the list box. Otherwise, the application will have no way of determining if the list box has been selected. The LBS_NOTIFY style is included in the LBS_STANDARD style, which is the most common type of list box.

Owner-drawn list boxes are mentioned in Table 5-5, but are not used in this book. This is an advanced technique that allows list boxes to contain graphic images. See Chapter 9 of *The Waite Group's Windows API Bible* for an example of how to use owner-drawn controls.

A List Box Example

Figure 5-8 shows the LISTBOX example program. When the program is started, the list box is empty and shows up as a rectangle without the scroll bar at the right. If the user selects the "Fill Listbox" menu item, a series of strings is added to the list box. The strings are automatically sorted into ASCII order. If the user selects a string in the list box, the program displays a message box containing the selected string.

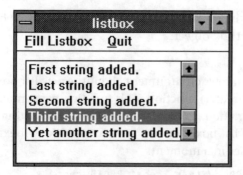

Figure 5-8 The LISTBOX Program

Style	Meaning
LBS_DISABLENOSCROLL	The list box control shows a disabled, vertical scroll bar when the list box does not contain enough items to fill the list box window. Without this style, the scroll bar disappears when there are not enough items to fill the list box.
LBS_EXTENDEDSEL	List box control where more than one item can be selected by using the mouse and the (SHIFT) key.
LBS_HASSTRINGS	List box control containing lists of strings.
LBS_MULTICOLUMN	List box with multiple columns. Can be scrolled horizontally and vertically.
LBS_MULTIPLESEL	Any number of strings can be selected within the list box. Selection by mouse clicking, de-selection by double-clicking.
LBS_NOINTEGRALHEIGHT	A list box of fixed size. The list box height is not scaled to match an even number of items (the default case).
LBS_NOREDRAW	A list box which is not automatically redrawn.
LBS_NOTIFY	A list box that sends the parent window messages when the user selects one or more items.
LBS_OWNERDRAWFIXED	A list box where the program is responsible for drawing all items. Items are of fixed vertical size.
LBS_OWNERDRAWVARIABLE	A list box where the program is responsible for drawing all items. Items can be of different vertical sizes.
LBS_SORT	A list box where the items are maintained in ASCII sort order.
LBS_STANDARD	A list box containing strings, automatically sorted, with messages sent to the parent window when selections are made.
LBS_USETABSTOPS	A list box that recognizes and expands tab characters. By default, tabs are every eight spaces. See the EM_SETTABSTOPS message to change this value.
LBS_WANTKEYBOARDINPUT	The parent window receives WM_VKEYTOITEM and WM_CHARTOITEM messages from the list box when it has the input focus and keys are pressed. Handy for setting up keyboard shortcut combinations. Keyboard input is discussed in Chapter 7, *Fonts and the Keyboard*.

Table 5-5 List Box Styles

The LISTBOX program only has one child window control, a list box. This makes the LISTBOX.HPP header file (Listing 5-15) reasonably short. A **CListBox** object named *MyListBox* is declared in the header file, along with several functions.

The ID values for the menu items and the list box control are defined in the LISTBOX.H header file, as shown in Listing 5-16.

Listing 5-17 shows the program file LISTBOX.CPP. The list box is created using the window style LBS_STANDARD | WS_CHILD | WS_VISIBLE. This makes the list box a visible child window, with standard list box attributes. The standard list box sorts the entries in ASCII sort order, and displays a vertical scroll bar on the right side of the list box if all of the entries cannot be seen. LBS_STANDARD also includes the LBS_NOTIFY style, so the list box will result in messages being sent to the parent window if an item in the list box is selected.

Listing 5-15 LISTBOX.HPP Header File

```
// listbox.hpp    header file for listbox.cpp

class CMainWindow : public CFrameWnd  // derive a main window class
{
public:
    CMainWindow () ;              // declare a constructor
private:
    void OnListSelect() ;        // list box item picked
    CListBox MyListBox ;         // listbox object
    void OnFill () ;             // respond to "fill" menu item
    void OnExit () ;             // stop application

    DECLARE_MESSAGE_MAP()        // prepare for message processing
} ;

class CTheApp : public CWinApp // derive an application class
{
public:
    BOOL InitInstance () ;       // declare new InitInstance()
} ;
```

Listing 5-16 LISTBOX.H Resource ID Header File

```
// listbox.h  header file for resource ID numbers

#define IDM_FILL        1       // menu item ID numbers
#define IDM_QUIT        10

#define ID_LISTBOX      100     // list box ID number
```

Listing 5-17 LISTBOX.CPP

```cpp
// listbox.cpp                example using a listbox control

#include <afxwin.h>      // class library header file
#include <strstrea.h>    // class library for streams
#include "listbox.h"     // header file for resource data
#include "listbox.hpp"   // header file for this program

CTheApp theApp ;          // create one CTheApp object - runs program

BOOL CTheApp::InitInstance ()    // override default InitInstance()
{
    m_pMainWnd = new CMainWindow () ;        // create a main window
    m_pMainWnd->ShowWindow (m_nCmdShow) ;    // make it visible
    m_pMainWnd->UpdateWindow () ;            // paint center
    return TRUE ;
}

CMainWindow::CMainWindow ()      // constructor for main window
{
    Create (NULL, "listbox", WS_OVERLAPPEDWINDOW, rectDefault,
        NULL, "MyMenu") ;
                                 // create listbox child window
    CRect ListRect (10, 10, 190, 90) ;       // rect to hold size
    MyListBox.Create (LBS_STANDARD | WS_CHILD | WS_VISIBLE,
        ListRect, this, ID_LISTBOX) ;
}

BEGIN_MESSAGE_MAP (CMainWindow, CFrameWnd)
    ON_COMMAND (IDM_FILL, OnFill)                // "fill" menu item
    ON_COMMAND (IDM_QUIT, OnExit)                // "quit" menu item
    ON_LBN_SELCHANGE (ID_LISTBOX, OnListSelect) // list box selection
END_MESSAGE_MAP ()

void CMainWindow::OnFill ()      // fill listbox text with strings
{
    MyListBox.ResetContent () ; // empty listbox, then add strings
    MyListBox.AddString ("First string added.") ;
    MyListBox.AddString ("Second string added.") ;
    MyListBox.AddString ("Third string added.") ;
    MyListBox.AddString ("Another string added.") ;
    MyListBox.AddString ("Yet another string added.") ;
    MyListBox.AddString ("Last string added.") ;
}

void CMainWindow::OnExit ()      // respond to menu item "Quit"
{
    this->DestroyWindow () ;     // destroy main window,
}                                // this stops application
```

```
void CMainWindow::OnListSelect ()    // item in list box was selected
{
    int     nCurSel ;
    char    str [256], seltext [128] ;
                                // construct string object in memory
    ostrstream msgString (str, sizeof (str)) ;

    nCurSel = MyListBox.GetCurSel () ;  // get # of current selection
    MyListBox.GetText (nCurSel, seltext) ;  // copy string to buffer
    msgString << "The selected item = " << seltext << ends ;
                                        // show in message box
    this->MessageBox (str, "Message Box", MB_OK) ;
}
```

Listings 5-18 and 5-19 show the LISTBOX.RC and LISTBOX.DEF files. There is nothing new here. The program's icon image is shown in Figure 5-9.

Listing 5-18 LISTBOX.RC Resource Script File

```
// listbox.rc  resource script file

#include <afxres.h>
#include "listbox.h"

AFX_IDI_STD_FRAME   ICON    listbox.ico      // the program's icon

MyMenu MENU                                  // define the menu
{
    MENUITEM "&Fill Listbox",        IDM_FILL
    MENUITEM "&Quit",                IDM_QUIT
}
```

Listing 5-19 LISTBOX.DEF Module Definition File

```
NAME            listbox
DESCRIPTION     'listbox C++ program'
EXETYPE         WINDOWS
STUB            'WINSTUB.EXE'
CODE            PRELOAD MOVEABLE
DATA            PRELOAD MOVEABLE MULTIPLE
HEAPSIZE        1024
STACKSIZE       5120
```

Figure 5-9 LISTBOX.ICO Icon Image

Using a List Box

The interesting parts of the LISTBOX program are filling of the list box with new entries and detecting when the user selects an item. The list box is filled when the user selects the "Fill Listbox" menu item, which has the menu ID value IDM_FILL. The LISTBOX.CPP message map calls the **CMainWindow::OnFill()** function when the IDM_FILL menu ID is received. The code to fill the list box is shown again in Listing 5-20.

The **CListBox::ResetContent()** function simply empties the list box. After that, **CListBox::AddString()** is called repeatedly to put new entries into the list box. The list box was created with the LBS_STANDARD style, so the strings are automatically sorted into alphabetical order as they are added.

With the list box created and filled with items, the only task left is to respond to the user making a selection. Because list boxes are child window controls, selecting a list box with the mouse results in a WM_COMMAND message being sent to the parent window, just as occurs with button controls. List boxes are a bit more complex than buttons because the user can select one of a number of items within a single list box. The MFC classes deal with this by defining several different message map entries for list boxes, in place of the simple ON_COMMAND() entry used for button controls and menu items. Table 5-6 shows a list of the message map entries that are possible for a list box control.

Most of the time you will use only the ON_LBN_SELCHANGE message map entry that provides notification that an item in a list box has been selected. Listing 5-21 shows the message map for LISTBOX.CPP, including the ON_LBN_SELCHANGE entry.

Note that the ON_LBN_SELCHANGE message map entry uses the ID number for the list box control. This is important because a parent window can have more than one list box control. The ID number is used to route the ON_LBN_SELCHANGE message to the correct message response function. In LISTBOX.CPP, there is only one list box that has an ID value of ID_LISTBOX.

Listing 5-20 Filling the List Box in LISTBOX.CPP

```
void CMainWindow::OnFill ()      // fill listbox text with strings
{
    MyListBox.ResetContent () ; // empty listbox, then add strings
    MyListBox.AddString ("First string added.") ;
    MyListBox.AddString ("Second string added.") ;
    MyListBox.AddString ("Third string added.") ;
    MyListBox.AddString ("Another string added.") ;
    MyListBox.AddString ("Yet another string added.") ;
    MyListBox.AddString ("Last string added.") ;
}
```

Message map	Meaning
ON_LBN_DBLCLK	Notification that the user double-clicked an item in a list box.
ON_LBN_ERRSPACE	Notification that the list box cannot allocate any more memory to store items.
ON_LBN_KILLFOCUS	Notification that a list box has lost the input focus.
ON_LBN_SELCHANGE	Notification that the user has selected or de-selected an item in a list box.
ON_LBN_SETFOCUS	Notification that a list box has received the input focus.

Table 5-6 List Box Message Map Entries

Listing 5-21 LISTBOX.CPP Message Map

```
BEGIN_MESSAGE_MAP (CMainWindow, CFrameWnd)
    ON_COMMAND (IDM_FILL, OnFill)                // "fill" menu item
    ON_COMMAND (IDM_QUIT, OnExit)                // "quit" menu item
    ON_LBN_SELCHANGE (ID_LISTBOX, OnListSelect) // list box selection
END_MESSAGE_MAP ()
```

The **CMainWindow::OnListSelect()** function, which is shown in Listing 5-22, is called if a selection is made from this list box. The **CListBox::Get-CurSel()** function is used to determine which item in the list box the user selected. The selection numbers start with zero for the top item, one for the second, and so on. By using the selection number, the program can fetch the character string from the list box contents using the **CListBox::GetText()** function. The character string is copied from the list box into the buffer *seltext[]*. The **ostrstream** class is then used to construct a formatted output string that is

Listing 5-22 OnListSelect() Function from LISTBOX.CPP

```
void CMainWindow::OnListSelect ()    // item in list box was selected
{
    int     nCurSel ;
    char    str [256], seltext [128] ;
                                // construct string object in memory
    ostrstream msgString (str, sizeof (str)) ;

    nCurSel = MyListBox.GetCurSel () ;  // get # of current selection
    MyListBox.GetText (nCurSel, seltext) ;  // copy string to buffer
    msgString << "The selected item = " << seltext << ends ;
                                    // show in message box
    this->MessageBox (str, "Message Box", MB_OK) ;
}
```

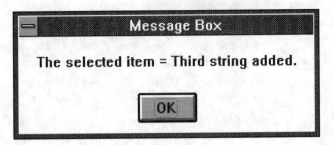

Figure 5-10 Message Box for Display of Selected Item in LISTBOX

passed to the **CWnd::MessageBox()** function to display the selected text. Figure 5-10 shows the appearance of the message box after the string "Third string added." was selected from the list box.

COMBO BOXES

Combo boxes are so similar to list boxes that you can switch between them in your program code quickly. The differences boil down to the following:

1. List boxes are created from the **CListBox** class, combo boxes are created from the **CComboBox** class.

2. Combo boxes have their own window style values that start with CBS_.

3. Combo box message map entries start with CBN_, rather than the LBN_ entries for list boxes.

4. Combo boxes have an extra object—an edit field at the top of the combo box. You normally will not deal with this edit field directly, although it is possible via functions defined in the **CComboBox** class.

The **CComboBox::Create()** function takes exactly the same parameters as **CListBox::Create()**:

```
BOOL CComboBox::Create (DWORD dwStyle, const RECT& rect,
    CWnd* pParentWnd, UINT nID) ;
```

Table 5-7 summarizes the *dwStyle* values available for combo boxes. Two of the styles apply to owner-drawn combo boxes, which allow you to put graphical images as items in the combo box. This advanced technique is not covered in this book. Refer to Chapter 9 of *The Waite Group's Windows API Bible* if you need to use owner-drawn combo box controls.

Style	Meaning
CBS_AUTOHSCROLL	Combo box control. This is a list box with an edit control at the top to display the current selection. With the CBS_AUTOHSCROLL style, the edit area at the top automatically scrolls when typing fills the edit box.
CBS_DISABLENOSCROLL	The list box of the combo box control shows a disabled vertical scroll bar when the list box does not contain enough items to fill the list box window. Without this style, the scroll bar disappears when there are not enough items.
CBS_DROPDOWN	Combo box control with a drop-down scroll area. This reduces the space taken by the combo box when the list is not needed.
CBS_DROPDOWNLIST	Combo box control with a drop-down scroll area. The edit area at top is a static text item that only displays the current selection in the list box.
CBS_HASSTRINGS	The combo box control maintains the list box strings in memory.
CBS_OEMCONVERT	Combo box edit text is converted to OEM character set and then back to ANSI. Useful for lists of file names.
CBS_OWNERDRAWFIXED	An owner-drawn combo box. The combo box items are of fixed height.
CBS_OWNERDRAWVARIABLE	An owner-drawn combo box. The combo box items can be of different heights.
CBS_SIMPLE	The combo box has a list box that is displayed at all times. This style just inhibits the normal action of reducing the combo box to the top edit control area when the combo box is not selected.
CBS_SORT	The combo box items are automatically sorted.

Table 5-7 Combo Box Styles

The COMBO Program

Figure 5-11 shows the COMBO program in operation. Only the edit control at the top of the combo box and the arrow button to the right are visible. The drop-down list box is not shown unless the arrow button is selected. Although the arrow button is slightly to the right of the edit control, it is logically part of the

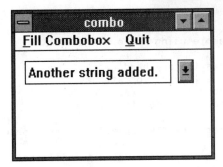

Figure 5-11 The COMBO Program

complete combo box control. Figure 5-12 shows the combo box after the arrow
button was selected, making the list box portion of the combo box visible.

Initially the combo box is created empty. Selecting the "Fill Combobox"
menu item results in six character strings being added to the combo box. The
selection "First string added" is initially visible in the edit control. Selecting an
item in the drop-down list box causes the selection to become visible in the edit
control. The selected string is also displayed in a message box, following the
previous examples for button and list box controls.

Listing 5-23 shows the COMBO.CPP program. COMBO.CPP is so similar to
LISTBOX.CPP that only a few highlights will be mentioned. The CBS_SORT
style is not included in the **CComboBox::Create()** function call, so the strings
are not sorted in alphabetical order within the list box. Another change is that
the first item in the list is selected when the combo box is filled by calling the
CComboBox::SetCurSel() function. Unless an item is initially selected, the
combo box edit control at the top will remain blank until the user makes a
selection. Selecting the top item (index number zero) is a typical default behavior for a combo box.

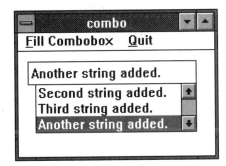

Figure 5-12 The COMBO Program After Selecting the Arrow Button

Listing 5-23 COMBO.CPP

```
// combo.cpp              example using combo box control

#include <afxwin.h>      // class library header file
#include <strstrea.h>    // class library for streams
#include "combo.h"        // header file for resource data
#include "combo.hpp"      // header file for this program

CTheApp theApp ;          // create one CTheApp object — runs program

BOOL CTheApp::InitInstance ()   // override default InitInstance()
{
    m_pMainWnd = new CMainWindow () ;        // create a main window
    m_pMainWnd->ShowWindow (m_nCmdShow) ;    // make it visible
    m_pMainWnd->UpdateWindow () ;            // paint center
    return TRUE ;
}


CMainWindow::CMainWindow ()      // constructor for main window
{
    Create (NULL, "combo", WS_OVERLAPPEDWINDOW, rectDefault,
        NULL, "MyMenu") ;
                                 // create combo child window
    CRect ComboRect (10, 10, 190, 90) ;     // rect to hold  size
    MyComboBox.Create (CBS_DROPDOWN | WS_CHILD | WS_VISIBLE,
        ComboRect, this, ID_COMBOBOX) ;
}

BEGIN_MESSAGE_MAP (CMainWindow, CFrameWnd)
    ON_COMMAND (IDM_FILL, OnFill)              // "fill" menu item
    ON_COMMAND (IDM_QUIT, OnExit)              // "quit" menu item
    ON_CBN_SELCHANGE (ID_COMBOBOX, OnSelect)   // combo box select
END_MESSAGE_MAP ()

void CMainWindow::OnFill ()           // fill combo box with strings
{
    MyComboBox.ResetContent () ;      // empty combo box
    MyComboBox.AddString ("First string added.") ;
    MyComboBox.AddString ("Second string added.") ;
    MyComboBox.AddString ("Third string added.") ;
    MyComboBox.AddString ("Another string added.") ;
    MyComboBox.AddString ("Yet another string added.") ;
    MyComboBox.AddString ("Last string added.") ;
    MyComboBox.SetCurSel (0) ;        // start with first item selected
}

void CMainWindow::OnSelect ()         //  item in  combo box selected
{
    int     nCurSel ;
    char    str [256], seltext [128] ;
                                      // construct string object
    ostrstream msgString (str, sizeof (str)) ;
```

```
     nCurSel = MyComboBox.GetCurSel () ;           // get # of selection
     MyComboBox.GetLBText (nCurSel, seltext) ;    // get sel. string
     msgString << "The selected item = " << seltext << ends ;
                                                // show selection in message box
     this->MessageBox (str, "Message Box", MB_OK) ;
}

void CMainWindow::OnExit ()              // respond to menu item "Quit"
{
     this->DestroyWindow () ;            // destroy main window,
}                                        // this stops application
```

The support files for the COMBO program are shown in Listings 5-24 to 5-27. Figure 5-13 shows the program's icon image.

Listing 5-24 COMBO.HPP Header File

```
// combo.hpp    header file for combo.cpp
                              // derive a main window class
class CMainWindow : public CFrameWnd
{
public:
     CMainWindow () ;               // declare a constructor
     void OnSelect() ;             // list box item picked
private:
     CComboBox MyComboBox ;        // combobox object
     void OnFill () ;              // respond to "fill" menu item
     void OnExit () ;              // stop application

     DECLARE_MESSAGE_MAP()         // prepare for message processing
} ;

class CTheApp : public CWinApp    // derive an application class
{
public:
     BOOL InitInstance () ;        // declare new InitInstance()
} ;
```

Listing 5-25 COMBO.H Resource ID Header File

```
// combo.h   header file for resource ID numbers

#define IDM_FILL       1        // menu item ID numbers
#define IDM_QUIT       10

#define ID_COMBOBOX    1000     // combo box ID number
```

Listing 5-26 COMBO.RC Resource Script File

```
// combo.rc   resource script file

#include <afxres.h>
#include "combo.h"

AFX_IDI_STD_FRAME    ICON     combo.ico      // the program's icon

MyMenu MENU                                   // define the menu
{
    MENUITEM "&Fill Combobox",      IDM_FILL
    MENUITEM "&Quit",               IDM_QUIT
}
```

Listing 5-27 COMBO.DEF Module Definition File

```
NAME            combo
DESCRIPTION     'combo C++ program'
EXETYPE         WINDOWS
STUB            'WINSTUB.EXE'
CODE            PRELOAD MOVEABLE
DATA            PRELOAD MOVEABLE MULTIPLE
HEAPSIZE        1024
STACKSIZE       5120
```

Figure 5-13 COMBO.ICO Icon Image

SCROLL BARS

There are two types of scroll bar controls in the Windows interface. The most common type is attached to the edge of a parent window. These scroll bars are used to scroll the image in the window's client area. The second type of scroll bar is a stand-alone control. They are child window controls, and are typically used to allow the user to enter an integer value by moving the scroll bar thumb (the thumb is the moveable central button on the scroll bar). We will look at two example programs, one for each type of scroll bar.

Scroll Bar Messages

Both types of scroll bars send messages to the scroll bar's parent window when the user moves the scroll bar thumb. The messages sent are WM_HSCROLL if a horizontal scroll bar is being used, and WM_VSCROLL if a vertical scroll bar is being used. For both messages, Windows passes additional data with the message reflecting what part of the scroll bar control was activated. Figure 5-14 summarizes the scroll bar codes that are transmitted with the WM_HSCROLL and WM_VSCROLL messages.

The WM_HSCROLL and WM_VSCROLL messages are the first messages introduced in this book that pass data to the message response function. To process either of these messages, you must include entries in the program's message map, as shown in Listing 5-28.

These message map entries are simple because the function that is called for the WM_VSCROLL message is always called **OnVScroll()**, and the function for the WM_HSCROLL message is always called **OnHScroll()**. These two functions are both passed three parameter values each time they are called. Listing 5-29 shows an **OnHScroll()** function outline.

The *nSBCode* parameter passed to **OnHScroll()** or **OnVScroll()** is the code number describing what part of the scroll bar was activated. These are the codes summarized in Figure 5-14. The *nPos* value gives the current scroll bar thumb

Listing 5-28 Message Map Entries for WM_HSCROLL and WM_VSCROLL

```
BEGIN_MESSAGE_MAP (CMainWindow, CFrameWnd)
    ON_WM_VSCROLL()                    // process WM_VSCROLL
    ON_WM_HSCROLL()                    // process WM_HSCROLL
END_MESSAGE_MAP ()
```

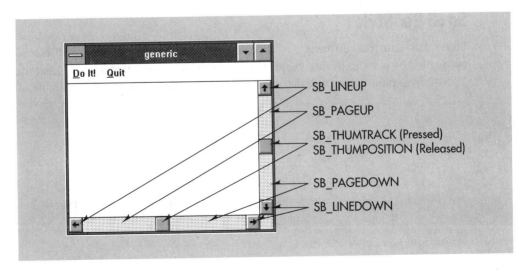

Figure 5-14 Scroll Bar Codes

Listing 5-29 OnHScroll() Function

```
void CMainWindow::OnHScroll (UINT nSBCode, UINT nPos,
    CScrollBar* pCntl)
{
    // logic to respond to scroll bar movement here
}
```

position. The *pCntl* parameter provides a pointer to the scroll bar object. This is useful in applications that have more than one vertical scroll bar or more than one horizontal scroll bar. The *pCntl* parameter can be used to determine which scroll bar generated the message. *pCntl* can also be used to access the **CScrollBar** class functions.

Scroll Bar Functions

The **CScrollBar** class provides four functions that are used to manipulate the scroll bar thumb position, as summarized in Table 5-8. When initially created, the scroll bar thumb position has a range of values from 0 to 10. You can change the range using the **CScrollBar::SetScrollRange()** function. The maximum range for a scroll bar is 32,768. You cannot reverse the direction of the scroll bar. Increasing values for the scroll bar always reflect lower thumb positions for vertical scroll bars, and positions to the right for horizontal scroll bars.

Scroll Bar Styles

Like static controls, buttons, and list boxes, the appearance of a scroll bar is controlled by a series of flag values that are used when the scroll bar is created. The *dwStyle* parameter passed to the **CScrollBar::Create()** function can have

Function	Purpose
GetScrollPos()	Retrieve the current position of the scroll bar's thumb.
GetScrollRange()	Retrieve the minimum and maximum value range of a scroll bar.
SetScrollPos()	Set the position of the scroll bar thumb.
SetScrollRange()	Set the minimum and maximum values of a scroll bar.

Table 5-8 CScrollBar Class Function Summary

any of the values shown in Table 5-9. If you are creating a stand-alone scroll bar control, you will only need the SBS_VERT or SBS_HORZ style to specify whether the scroll bar should be vertical or horizontal. The remaining styles apply to scroll bars that are attached to a parent window, which is usually the main program window.

Style	Meaning
SBS_BOTTOMALIGN	A horzontal scroll bar control, aligned with the bottom edge of the rectangle specified by the X, Y, nWidth, and nHeight parameters used in calling **Create()** for the parent window. The default scroll bar height is used.
SBS_HORZ	A horizontal scroll bar control.
SBS_LEFTALIGN	A vertical scroll bar control, aligned with the left edge of the rectangle specified by the X, Y, nWidth, and nHeight parameters used in calling **Create()** for the parent window. The default scroll bar width is used.
SBS_RIGHTALIGN	A horizontal scroll bar control, aligned with the right edge of the rectangle specified by the X, Y, nWidth, and nHeight parameters used in calling **Create()** for the parent window. The default scroll bar width is used.
SBS_SIZEBOX	A scroll bar size box control. This is a small box that allows sizing of a window from one location.
SBS_SIZEBOXBOTTOMRIGHTALIGN	Used with the SBS_SIZEBOX style. A size box control, aligned with the lower right edge of the rectangle specified by the X, Y, nWidth, and nHeight parameters used in calling **Create()** for the parent window. The default size box size is used.
SBS_SIZEBOXTOPLEFTALIGN	Used with the SBS_SIZEBOX style. A size box control, aligned with the top left edge of the rectangle specified by the X, Y, nWidth, and nHeight parameters used in calling **Create()** for the parent window. The default size box size is used.
SBS_TOPALIGN	Used with the SBS_HORZ style. Puts the horizontal scroll bar at the top of the parent window's client area.
SBS_VERT	A vertical scroll bar control.

Table 5-9 Scroll Bar Styles

If a scroll bar is to be attached to the edge of a parent window, the **CWnd::Create()** or **CFrameWnd::Create()** function call for the parent window will include the WS_HSCROLL and/or WS_VSCROLL styles. You will not need to separately create a scroll bar control if either of these two styles is specified when creating the parent window. The default alignment attaches this type of scroll bar to the right side and/or bottom of the parent window. The SBS_LEFTALIGN and SBS_TOPALIGN can be used with the SBS_VERT and SBS_HORZ styles to attach scroll bars to the top and left edges of a window if desired. For example, the combination SBS_LEFTALIGN | SBS_VERT would specify a vertical scroll bar on the left side of a window.

The SBS_SIZEBOX is seldom used. This is a small box with four arrows that the user can grab with the mouse to size an object. Windows uses thick borders for these operations, so the size box style has become obsolete.

The SCROLL1 Program

Let's create a program with a single scroll bar control in the center of the client area to show how the scroll bar styles, functions, and messages are used. The scroll bar control will allow the user to enter an integer value within a range of 0 to 50. Figure 5-15 shows the SCROLL1 program in operation. The integer value is displayed in a static control to the left of the scroll bar. The scroll bar is horizontal, and not attached to the window's frame. This is a stand-alone child window control.

Listing 5-30 shows the SCROLL1.HPP header file. Note that **CStatic** and **CScrollBar** objects are defined as elements of the **CMainWindow** class. The **CMainWindow** class also contains the **CMainWindow::OnHScroll()** function declaration and an integer named *nScrollPos* to keep track of the current position of the scroll bar control. Also note that the constant MAXSCROLL is defined in SCROLL1.HPP with a value of 50. This constant will be used to set the logical range the scroll bar represents.

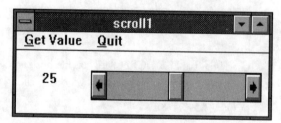

Figure 5-15 The SCROLL1 Program

The scroll bar and static control are given ID numbers in the SCROLL1.H header file (Listing 5-31).

Listing 5-32 shows the SCROLL1.CPP program file. The static text control and scroll bar **CScrollBar::Create()** functions are called within the **CMainWindow()** constructor function, just as we did in the examples for button controls and list boxes. Note that the scroll bar range is set from 0 to MAXSCROLL (50) using the **CScrollBar::SetScrollRange()** function, and the thumb is placed in the center using **CScrollBar::SetScrollPos()**. The static text control is started with an initial text string of "25" to reflect the starting position of the scroll bar thumb. This text string will be changed when the scroll bar thumb is moved through the logic in the **CMainWindow::OnHScroll()** function.

Listing 5-30 SCROLL1.HPP Header File

```
// scroll1.hpp     header file for scroll1.cpp

#define MAXSCROLL   50                     // scroll bar max value

class CMainWindow : public CFrameWnd     // derive a main window class
{
public:
    CMainWindow () ;                      // declare a constructor
private:
    CScrollBar MyScrollBar ;              // scroll bar object
    CStatic StaticCntl ;                  // static control object
    void OnExit () ;                      // stop application
    void OnGetValue () ;                  // respond to "get" menu item
    void OnHScroll (UINT nSBCode, UINT nPos,
        CScrollBar* pCntl) ;
    int nScrollPos ;                      // current scroll position

    DECLARE_MESSAGE_MAP()                 // prepare for message processing
} ;

class CTheApp : public CWinApp           // derive an application class
{
public:
    BOOL InitInstance () ;               // declare new InitInstance()
} ;
```

Listing 5-31 SCROLL1.H Resource ID Header File

```
// scroll1.h  header file for resource ID numbers

#define IDM_GET        1         // menu item ID numbers
#define IDM_QUIT       10

#define ID_SCROLL      1000      // scroll bar ID number
#define ID_STATIC      1001      // static control ID
```

Listing 5-32 SCROLL1.CPP

```cpp
// scroll1.cpp            example using scroll bar control

#include <afxwin.h>     // class library header file
#include <strstrea.h>   // class library for streams
#include "scroll1.h"    // header file for resource data
#include "scroll1.hpp"  // header file for this program

CTheApp theApp ;        // create one CTheApp object - runs program

BOOL CTheApp::InitInstance ()    // override default InitInstance()
{
    m_pMainWnd = new CMainWindow () ;        // create a main window
    m_pMainWnd->ShowWindow (m_nCmdShow) ;   // make it visible
    m_pMainWnd->UpdateWindow () ;           // paint center
    return TRUE ;
}


CMainWindow::CMainWindow ()         // constructor for main window
{
    Create (NULL, "scroll1", WS_OVERLAPPEDWINDOW, rectDefault,
        NULL, "MyMenu") ;
                            // create scroll bar child window
    CRect MyRect (80, 20, 260, 50) ;    // size of scroll bar
    MyScrollBar.Create (SBS_HORZ | WS_CHILD | WS_VISIBLE,
        MyRect, this, ID_SCROLL) ;
    MyScrollBar.SetScrollRange (0, MAXSCROLL) ; // set range
    MyScrollBar.SetScrollPos (MAXSCROLL/2) ;    // start in center

    MyRect.SetRect (10, 20, 60, 60) ;   // static text control
    StaticCntl.Create ("25", SS_CENTER | WS_CHILD | WS_VISIBLE,
        MyRect, this, ID_STATIC) ;

    nScrollPos = MAXSCROLL/2 ;              // initialize integer
}


BEGIN_MESSAGE_MAP (CMainWindow, CFrameWnd)
    ON_COMMAND (IDM_GET, OnGetValue)    // "Get Value" menu item
    ON_COMMAND (IDM_QUIT, OnExit)       // "Quit" menu item
    ON_WM_HSCROLL()                     // process WM_HSCROLL
END_MESSAGE_MAP ()

void CMainWindow::OnHScroll (UINT nSBCode, UINT nPos,
    CScrollBar* pCntl)
{
    switch (nSBCode)
    {
        case SB_THUMBPOSITION:  // user moved scroll thumb
            nScrollPos = nPos ;
            break ;
```

```
        case SB_LINEDOWN:        // user clicked right arrow
            nScrollPos++ ;
            break ;
        case SB_LINEUP:          // user clicked left arrow
            nScrollPos-- ;
            break ;
        case SB_PAGEDOWN:        // user clicked right gray area
            nScrollPos += 10 ;
            break ;
        case SB_PAGEUP:          // user clicked left gray area
            nScrollPos -= 10 ;
            break ;
    }
    nScrollPos = nScrollPos < 0 ? 0 : nScrollPos ;
    nScrollPos = nScrollPos > MAXSCROLL ? MAXSCROLL : nScrollPos ;
    MyScrollBar.SetScrollPos (nScrollPos) ;

    char    str [5] ;    // put value in static control as text
    ostrstream msgString (str, sizeof (str)) ;
    msgString << nScrollPos << ends ;
    StaticCntl.SetWindowText (str) ;
}

void CMainWindow::OnExit ()      // respond to menu item "Quit"
{
    this->DestroyWindow () ;     // destroy main window,
}                                // this stops application

void CMainWindow::OnGetValue () // respond to "Get Value" menu item
{                               // by showing value in message box
    char    str [256] ;
                                // construct string object
    ostrstream msgString (str, sizeof (str)) ;
    msgString << "The current value = " << nScrollPos << ends ;
    this->MessageBox (str, "Message Box", MB_OK) ;
}
```

The **CMainWindow::OnHScroll()** function is the heart of the SCROLL1 program. Windows sends a WM_HSCROLL message to the SCROLL1 main window any time the horizontal scroll bar is activated. This message is mapped to the **CMainWindow::OnHScroll()** function by the message map entry ON_WM_HSCROLL(). Because the **CMainWindow::OnHScroll()** function will be called regardless of what portion of the scroll bar the user selected, the program must use the *nSBCode* value to determine what action the user intended. This also gives the program logic an opportunity to determine how large a scroll bar thumb movement to make. In SCROLL1.CPP, selecting the left and right arrow buttons results in a movement of one unit (response to the SB_LINEUP and SB_LINEDOWN codes), and selecting the area between the thumb and an arrow button results in a movement of 10 units (SB_PAGEUP and SB_PAGEDOWN codes).

Note that the amount of thumb movement when the arrow buttons or body of the scroll bar control is selected is totally up to the program. The only case where the position of the scroll bar thumb is specified automatically by Windows is when the user drags the thumb to a new position with the mouse. In this case, the SB_THUMBPOSITION code is sent, and the new position of the thumb is passed with the *nPos* parameter in **CMainWindow::OnHScroll()**. The *nPos* parameter cannot be used with the SB_LINEDOWN, SB_LINEUP, SB_PAGEDOWN, and SB_PAGEUP codes, because Windows has no way of determining how much the thumb should be moved.

The C++ code that checks that the position of the scroll bar is within range takes advantage of the shorthand notation (? :) for an if, then, else, comparison. This is part of the normal C++ language, but this is the first example in this book that has taken advantage of this logic. The (? :) syntax is best used for simple comparisons that will fit all on one line, such as the two examples shown here:

```
nScrollPos = nScrollPos < 0 ? 0 : nScrollPos ;

nScrollPos = nScrollPos > MAXSCROLL ? MAXSCROLL : nScrollPos ;
```

At the bottom of the **CMainWindow::OnHScroll()** function is the logic for moving the scroll bar thumb and updating the number shown in the static control. The scroll bar thumb is repositioned using the **CScrollBar::Set-ScrollPos()** function after the position value is verified to be between 0 and MAXSCROLL. The text in the static control is changed using the **CWnd::SetWindowText()** function. The conversion of the integer value *nScrollPos* to a character string is done by creating an **ostrstream** object, just as was done to produce formatted output for the message boxes displayed in the previous examples. SCROLL1 also displays the current scroll bar position in a message box if the "Get Value" menu item is selected.

Listings 5-33 and 5-34 show the SCROLL1.RC and SCROLL1.DEF files. The program's icon image is shown in Figure 5-16.

SCROLL BARS ATTACHED TO A WINDOW

The most common use of scroll bar controls is to scroll the central area of a main program window. Word processing programs frequently use both horizontal and vertical scroll bars on the edges of the window. The vertical scroll bar is used to move to new locations in the text. The horizontal scroll bar is used to move the far right edge of the text area into view.

Listing 5-33 SCROLL1.RC Resource Script File

```
// scroll1.rc  resource script file

#include <afxres.h>
#include "scroll1.h"

AFX_IDI_STD_FRAME   ICON    scroll1.ico    // the program's icon

MyMenu MENU                                // define the menu
{
    MENUITEM "&Get Value",        IDM_GET
    MENUITEM "&Quit",             IDM_QUIT
}
```

Listing 5-34 SCROLL1.DEF Module Definition File

```
NAME            scroll1
DESCRIPTION     'scroll1 C++ program'
EXETYPE         WINDOWS
STUB            'WINSTUB.EXE'
CODE            PRELOAD MOVEABLE
DATA            PRELOAD MOVEABLE MULTIPLE
HEAPSIZE        1024
STACKSIZE       5120
```

Figure 5-16 SCROLL1.ICO Icon Image

The easy way to add scroll bars to the edge of a window is to add a scroll bar style to the window's style when creating the window. The WS_HSCROLL style adds a horizontal scroll bar, and the WS_VSCROLL style adds a vertical scroll bar. Listing 5-35 shows a typical main window constructor function, including the **Create()** function call which creates a main program window with both vertical and horizontal scroll bars attached to the edges.

You can add and subtract attached scroll bars from the window's edge while the program is running with the **CWnd::ShowScrollBar()** function. In most cases, the scroll bar will be attached at all times, so **CWnd::ShowScrollBar()** is not needed.

Listing 5-35 Creating a Program Window with Two Scroll Bars

```
CMainWindow::CMainWindow () // constructor for main window
{
    Create (NULL, "Caption",
        WS_OVERLAPPEDWINDOW | WS_VSCROLL | WS_HSCROLL,
        rectDefault, NULL, "MenuName") ;
// other code in main window constructor function here
}
```

The SCROLL2 Program

Figure 5-17 shows the SCROLL2 program window. SCROLL2 writes three lines of text on the window's client area. The window has a vertical scroll bar, allowing the client area to be scrolled up and down. Figure 5-17 shows the window after the window's client area has been scrolled down to the point that the third line of text is partially obscured.

Listing 5-36 shows SCROLL2.CPP. The listing is similar to the previous example SCROLL1.CPP using a scroll bar control. The differences boil down to:

.   The scroll bar is created by adding the WS_HSCROLL style to the **CFrameWnd::Create()** function call for the main program window, rather than by creating a separate child window scroll bar control.

.   The scroll bar's position is again stored in a static variable, *nScrollPos*. The value is used in positioning the text lines. The higher the *nScrollPos* value, the lower in the window's client area the text is painted. The painting logic is all in the WM_PAINT message processing section of SCROLL2.CPP.

Once the scroll bar is moved, the client area needs to be repainted so that the text lines show up in the new positions. To do this, SCROLL2 needs to convince

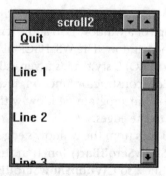

Figure 5-17 The SCROLL2 Program

Windows to send the program a WM_PAINT message for repainting the entire client area. This is done by calling the **CWnd::Invalidate()** function. Windows detects that the SCROLL2 client area is invalid, and sends a WM_PAINT message to the program. Windows also erases the client area, by painting it white. SCROLL2 gets the WM_PAINT message, and paints the text lines at the new locations from within the message response function **CMainWindow::OnPaint()**. The illusion is that the text lines moved down, but actually they are erased and redrawn in a new location.

Listing 5-36 SCROLL2.C

```
// scroll2.cpp          example using scroll bar attached to window

#include <afxwin.h>     // class library header file
#include <strstrea.h>   // class library for streams
#include "scroll2.h"    // header file for resource data
#include "scroll2.hpp"  // header file for this program

CTheApp theApp ;         // create one CTheApp object - runs program

BOOL CTheApp::InitInstance ()   // override default InitInstance()
{
    m_pMainWnd = new CMainWindow () ;       // create a main window
    m_pMainWnd->ShowWindow (m_nCmdShow) ;   // make it visible
    m_pMainWnd->UpdateWindow () ;           // paint center
    return TRUE ;
}


CMainWindow::CMainWindow ()      // constructor for main window
{                                // note addition of WS_VSCROLL style
    Create (NULL, "scroll2", WS_OVERLAPPEDWINDOW | WS_VSCROLL,
        rectDefault, NULL, "MyMenu") ;
                                 // set scroll range and position
    this->SetScrollRange (SB_VERT, 0, MAXSCROLL, FALSE) ;
    this->SetScrollPos (SB_VERT, 0, TRUE) ;
    nScrollPos = 0 ;             // initialize
}


BEGIN_MESSAGE_MAP (CMainWindow, CFrameWnd)
    ON_COMMAND (IDM_QUIT, OnExit)    // "Quit" menu item
    ON_WM_VSCROLL()                  // process WM_VSCROLL
    ON_WM_PAINT()                    // and WM_PAINT messages
END_MESSAGE_MAP ()

void CMainWindow::OnPaint ()         // repaint client area
{
    CPaintDC dc(this) ;              // get client area device context
                                     // locate based on scroll position
```

```
        dc.TextOut (0, nScrollPos, "Line 1", 6) ;
        dc.TextOut (0, nScrollPos + 50, "Line 2", 6) ;
        dc.TextOut (0, nScrollPos + 100, "Line 3", 6) ;
}

void CMainWindow::OnVScroll (UINT nSBCode, UINT nPos,
        CScrollBar* pCntl)
{
    switch (nSBCode)
        {
        case SB_THUMBPOSITION:      // user moved scroll thumb
            nScrollPos = nPos ;
            break ;
        case SB_LINEDOWN:           // user clicked down arrow
            nScrollPos++ ;
            break ;
        case SB_LINEUP:             // user clicked up arrow
            nScrollPos-- ;
            break ;
        case SB_PAGEDOWN:           // user clicked lower gray area
            nScrollPos += 10 ;
            break ;
        case SB_PAGEUP:             // user clicked upper gray area
            nScrollPos -= 10 ;
            break ;
        }                           // make sure within range
    nScrollPos = nScrollPos < 0 ? 0 : nScrollPos ;
    nScrollPos = nScrollPos > MAXSCROLL ? MAXSCROLL : nScrollPos ;
                                    // change scroll position
    this->SetScrollPos (SB_VERT, nScrollPos, TRUE) ;
    this->Invalidate (TRUE) ;// force paint client area
}

void CMainWindow::OnExit ()  // respond to menu item "Quit"
{
    this->DestroyWindow () ; // destroy main window,
}                            // this stops application
```

The support files for SCROLL2 are shown in Listings 5-37 to 5-40. No new concepts are introduced in these files. Figure 5-18 shows the icon image for SCROLL2. The alert reader may note that the scrolling of the client area in the SCROLL2 program is backwards from word processing conventions. You can reverse the signs of the adjustments to *nScrollPos* in the **CMainWindow::On-Scroll()** function to reverse the direction of scrolling.

Figure 5-18 SCROLL2.ICO Icon Image

Listing 5-37 SCROLL2.HPP Header File

```cpp
// scroll2.hpp    header file for scroll2.cpp

#define MAXSCROLL   100              // scroll bar max value

class CMainWindow : public CFrameWnd  // derive a main window class
{
public:
    CMainWindow () ;                 // declare a constructor
private:
    int nScrollPos ;                 // current scroll position
    void OnExit () ;                 // stop application
                                     // override OnHScroll()
    void OnVScroll (UINT nSBCode, UINT nPos, CScrollBar* pCntl) ;
    void OnPaint () ;                // override OnPaint()
    DECLARE_MESSAGE_MAP()            // prepare for message processing
} ;

class CTheApp : public CWinApp      // derive an application class
{
public:
    BOOL InitInstance () ;           // declare new InitInstance()
} ;
```

Listing 5-38 SCROLL2.H Resource ID Header File

```cpp
// scroll2.h  header file for resource ID numbers

#define IDM_QUIT        10      // menu item ID numbers
```

Listing 5-39 SCROLL2.RC Resource Script File

```
// scroll2.rc  resource script file

#include <afxres.h>
#include "scroll2.h"

AFX_IDI_STD_FRAME   ICON    scroll2.ico     // the program's icon

MyMenu MENU                                 // define the menu
{
    MENUITEM "&Quit",               IDM_QUIT
}
```

Listing 5-40 SCROLL2.DEF Module Definition File

```
NAME           scroll2
DESCRIPTION    'scroll2 C++ program'
EXETYPE        WINDOWS
STUB           'WINSTUB.EXE'
CODE           PRELOAD MOVEABLE
DATA           PRELOAD MOVEABLE MULTIPLE
HEAPSIZE       1024
STACKSIZE      5120
```

EDIT CONTROLS

The last window control style we have to examine is the edit control. Edit controls can range from a small rectangle for entering a single word or number, up to a window that occupies the parent window's entire client area. The MFC classes provide the **CEdit** class for creating and manipulating edit controls. Edit controls come with many word processing features built in. The key features are

. When you type text, the edit control automatically recognizes the (BACKSPACE) key to delete the previous character, the (DEL) key to delete the next character, and the arrow keys for movement inside the edit control. The current location in the edit control is marked by a small vertical line, called the "caret."

. Blocks of text can be marked for selection using the mouse or keyboard. Marked blocks of text can be deleted and/or copied to the Clipboard for pasting somewhere else, including pasting the text into another application. Cut-and-paste operations are explained in Chapter 17, *The Clipboard*.

. Simply adding the scroll bar styles (WS_HSCROLL and WS_VSCROLL) during the **CEdit::Create()** function call that creates the edit control will add the ability to scroll the text. You do not need to code the repainting logic as we did in the SCROLL2 example if all of the text is within an edit control.

This is enough functionality for most applications' text editing needs. Edit controls do not have the ability to format text with different fonts and character styles. Complete word processors generally create their own editing logic, painting the formatted text directly on the screen. Even if you are planning to add text formatting to your program, you may find that the edit control provides an excellent prototyping tool during the early stages of building a program.

Creating an edit control is just like creating a list box or combo box control. First you create a **CEdit** object:

```
CEdit AnEdit ;
```

Second, you inform the Windows environment about the new edit control by calling the **CEdit::Create()** function:

```
BOOL CEdit::Create (DWORD dwStyle, const RECT& rect,
    CWnd* pParentWnd, UINT nID ) ;
```

The *dwStyle* parameter passed to the **CEdit::Create()** function can have any of the values shown in Table 5-10. Unless the ES_MULTILINE style is included, the edit control will have only a single line of text. Multiline edit controls are usually combined with scroll bar controls, as we will see in the example.

Style	Meaning
ES_AUTOHSCROLL	Edit control with automatic horizontal scrolling if the text will not fit within the edit box.
ES_AUTOVSCROLL	Automatic vertical scrolling for an edit control. Used with ES_MULTILINE.
ES_CENTER	Text is centered within the edit control.
ES_LEFT	Text is left aligned within the edit control.
ES_LOWERCASE	All characters within the edit control are converted to lowercase as they are entered.
ES_MULTILINE	Allows multiple lines of input within an edit control. This type of control provides basic text processing functions.
ES_NOHIDESEL	Edit control where the text is left unchanged when the control loses the input focus.
ES_OEMCONVERT	Edit control text is converted to OEM character set and then back to ANSI. Useful for file names.
ES_PASSWORD	Displays letters as "*" characters when the letters are typed. The actual letters typed are stored by the edit control.
ES_READONLY	The edit text can be viewed, but not changed by the user.
ES_RIGHT	Right aligned letters within the edit control.
ES_UPPERCASE	All characters within the edit control are converted to uppercase as they are entered.

Table 5-10 Edit Control Styles

To explore edit controls, we will create a small example called EDIT1. Figure 5-19 shows EDIT1 in action, after the user has typed in a few lines of text. The edit control has a vertical scroll bar, but not a horizontal one. The text automatically wraps words to form new lines if the last word will not fit on a line. When the user selects the "Get Text" menu item, the text inside the edit control is extracted and displayed in the parent window's client area, below the edit control.

Listing 5-41 shows EDIT1.CPP. The attributes of the edit control are specified using window style flags in the **CEdit::Create()** function call. In the case of EDIT1.CPP, the edit control's style flags are:

```
WS_CHILD | WS_VISIBLE | WS_VSCROLL | ES_MULTILINE |
    ES_AUTOVSCROLL | WS_BORDER
```

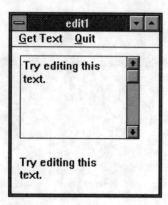

Figure 5-19 EDIT1 Program After Selecting "Get Text"

These flags add up to create a child window control, with multiple lines, with a vertical scroll bar attached to the right side, that is created visible, that automatically scrolls vertically when text exceeds the limits of the edit control's size, and with a visible border. Edit controls are initially created empty, but it is a simple matter to put text into the control using the **CWnd::SetWindowText()** function:

```
EditCntl.SetWindowText ("Try editing this text.") ;
```

Once the edit control is created, any text entered into the control is maintained by Windows in a separate memory block. All of the text in the control is stored as one long character string. If you type in a carriage return to end a line, the string will contain the CR LF character pair (0x0D, 0x0A hexadecimal). If the line wraps because the next word will not fit on the same line, the edit control will insert the characters CR CR LF (0x0D, 0x0D, 0x0A hexadecimal). You will not find a null character until the end of the last line's text.

The lack of null characters to mark the end of the lines makes getting the edit control's contents a bit tricky. The easiest way to get the complete text string is to extract each line separately. To do this, you will need to find the location and length of each line of text within the edit control's text buffer. The **CEdit::GetLineCount()** function returns the number of lines of text in the edit control. This is usually called first to determine how many lines there are to extract. For example, the following call will determine the number of lines of text within a **CEdit** object named *EditCntl.*:

```
int nLines = EditCntl.GetLineCount () ;
```

The **CEdit::LineIndex()** function is used to find the position of the start of a line in the text buffer.

```
int nCharIndex = EditCntl.LineIndex (1) ;
```

Note that the line numbers start with zero, so the second line has an index of one (not two). Use the **CEdit::LineLength()** function to find the length of a specific line of text in the edit control's buffer:

```
int nLineLong = EditCntl.LineLength (nCharIndex) ;
```

Figure 5-20 shows how the **CEdit::LineIndex()** and **CEdit::LineLength()** functions work together to find the location and length of lines of text in an edit control. The EDIT1.CPP program repeatedly calls **CEdit::LineIndex()** and **CEdit::LineLength()** to extract each line of text from the edit control, and then outputs the lines on the parent window's client area below the edit control.

Note in EDIT1.CPP that none of the program's code involves manipulating data in the edit control for editing operations. This is done entirely by the edit control logic that is built into Windows. The only task that was "hard coded" in the example is the **CMainWindow::OnGetText()** function that extracts each line of text from the edit control's memory buffer.

The support files for EDIT1 are shown in Listings 5-42 to 5-45. Figure 5-21 shows the program's icon image.

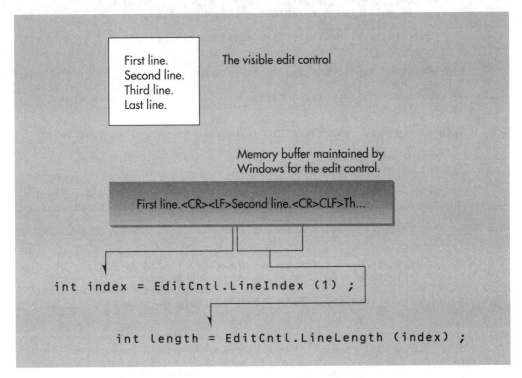

Figure 5-20 Extracting Text from an Edit Control's Text Buffer

Listing 5-41 EDIT1.CPP

```cpp
// edit1.cpp              using an edit control

#include <afxwin.h>      // class library header file
#include "edit1.h"       // header file for resource data
#include "edit1.hpp"      // header file for this program

CTheApp theApp ;         // create one CTheApp object - runs program

BOOL CTheApp::InitInstance ()   // override default InitInstance()
{
    m_pMainWnd = new CMainWindow () ;        // create a main window
    m_pMainWnd->ShowWindow (m_nCmdShow) ;    // make it visible
    m_pMainWnd->UpdateWindow () ;            // paint center
    return TRUE ;
}

CMainWindow::CMainWindow ()      // constructor for window
{                                // create main window
    Create (NULL, "edit1", WS_OVERLAPPEDWINDOW, rectDefault,
        NULL, "MyMenu") ;
                                 // then create edit control
    CRect ControlRect (10, 10, 160, 110) ;
    EditCntl.Create (WS_CHILD | WS_VISIBLE | WS_VSCROLL |
        ES_MULTILINE | ES_AUTOVSCROLL | WS_BORDER,
        ControlRect, this, NULL) ;
    EditCntl.SetWindowText ("Try editing this text.") ;
}

BEGIN_MESSAGE_MAP (CMainWindow, CFrameWnd)
    ON_COMMAND (IDM_GET, OnGetText)          // "Get Text" menu item
    ON_COMMAND (IDM_QUIT, OnExit)            // "Quit" menu item
END_MESSAGE_MAP ()

void CMainWindow::OnGetText ()  // respond to menu item "Get Text"
{
    char cBuf [128] ;
    int  nCharIndex, nLineLong ;

    CClientDC dc (this) ;   // construct client area device context
    int nLines = EditCntl.GetLineCount () ; // find no. lines of text

    for (int i = 0 ; i < nLines ; i++)
    {
        EditCntl.GetLine (i, cBuf, 128) ;        // get a line of text
        nCharIndex = EditCntl.LineIndex (i) ;    // find start of line
        nLineLong = EditCntl.LineLength (nCharIndex) ;  // length
                                        // show text under edit cntl
        dc.TextOut (10, 130 + (15 * i), cBuf, nLineLong) ;
    }
}

void CMainWindow::OnExit ()      // respond to menu item "Quit"
{
    this->DestroyWindow () ;     // destroy main window
}                                // this stops application
```

Listing 5-42 EDIT1.HPP Header File

```
// edit1.hpp      header file for edit1.cpp
                              // derive a main window class
class CMainWindow : public CFrameWnd
{
public:
    CMainWindow () ;            // declare a constructor
private:
    CEdit EditCntl ;           // create an edit object
    void OnGetText () ;        // display message box
    void OnExit () ;           // stop application

    DECLARE_MESSAGE_MAP()      // prepare for message processing
} ;

class CTheApp : public CWinApp  // derive an application class
{
public:
    BOOL InitInstance () ;      // declare new InitInstance()
} ;
```

Listing 5-43 EDIT1.H Resource ID Header File

```
// edit1.h  header file for resource ID numbers

#define IDM_GET        1      // menu item ID numbers
#define IDM_QUIT       10
```

Listing 5-44 EDIT1.RC Resource Script File

```
// edit1.rc  resource script file

#include <afxres.h>
#include "edit1.h"

AFX_IDI_STD_FRAME    ICON    edit1.ico   // the program's icon

MyMenu MENU                              // define the menu
{
    MENUITEM "&Get Text",   IDM_GET
    MENUITEM "&Quit",       IDM_QUIT
}
```

Listing 5-45 EDIT1.DEF Module Definition File

```
NAME             edit1
DESCRIPTION      'edit1 C++ program'
EXETYPE          WINDOWS
STUB             'WINSTUB.EXE'
CODE             PRELOAD MOVEABLE
DATA             PRELOAD MOVEABLE MULTIPLE
HEAPSIZE         1024
STACKSIZE        5120
```

Figure 5-21 EDIT1.ICO Icon Image

SUMMARY

Windows comes equipped with six predefined window classes for common objects: static controls, buttons, list boxes, combo boxes, scroll bars, and edit controls. These objects are called "window controls." The MFC classes support these controls by deriving separate classes for each type of control from the **CWnd** base class.

All six of the controls are types of windows. The Windows environment will automatically repaint the control if it is covered up and later uncovered. Controls are almost always created as child windows, using the WS_CHILD style when calling the class **Create()** function. Child windows are attached to their parent, and only visible if the parent window is visible on the screen. Child window controls always have an ID number, which is set when the control is created. The ID number is important, as your program will determine which control was activated by examining the ID values.

Static controls are used for displaying text, icons, and rectangles. Normally, static text is used for titles and fixed character data that does not change. However, the text in a static text control can be changed while the program runs by calling the **CWnd::SetWindowText()** function.

Button controls can take a variety of shapes, including push buttons, radio buttons, check boxes, and group boxes. List boxes and combo boxes are similar. Both display a list of items, allowing the user to make selections. Both list boxes and combo boxes send messages to their parent window if the user selects an item. The program logic can then determine which entry was selected using the **CListBox** or **CComboBox** class functions.

Scroll bar controls are unique in that they can be either stand-alone controls or can be attached to the parent window's border by creating the parent with the WS_VSCROLL and/or WS_HSCROLL style. Scroll bar controls generate either WM_VSCROLL or WM_HSCROLL messages, depending on whether the control is a vertical or horizontal scroll bar. The data passed with the WM_VSCROLL and WM_HSCROLL messages is sent on to the **OnVScroll()** and

OnHScroll() message response functions, and used to determine what action the user intended with the scroll bar control.

Edit controls are the most sophisticated of the control styles. Edit controls can be thought of as miniature word processor windows. All of the basic logic for entering and editing text is built into the control. Edit controls can be either a single line, or multiline, and can have scroll bars attached. Reading the text data inside of the control requires using **CEdit** class functions and is generally done by extracting each line of text separately.

QUESTIONS

1. Are the button, scroll bar, and edit controls created in the MFC classes, or are they an intrinsic part of Windows?

2. How is a button's text string specified?

3. Attaching a scroll bar to the program's main window will automatically allow scrolling of the program's window client area. (True/False)

4. In creating child window controls, the dimensions passed to the **Create()** function in the **CRect** data are relative to the upper left corner of the parent window, not relative to the upper left corner of the screen. (True/False)

5. If you click the left arrow on a horizontal scroll bar, which message is sent to the scroll bar's parent window?
   a. SB_LINEDOWN
   b. SB_LINEUP
   c. WM_HSCROLL
   d. None of the above

6. If there is more than one vertical scroll bar control, how would you determine which one resulted in a WM_VSCROLL message?

7. If the user will normally make a selection from a list, which type of control is preferable, a list box or a combo box?

8. What **CStatic** *dwStyle* value would you use to color a rectangular portion of the parent window's client area black? (Hint: More than one style must be combined.)

9. What **CButton** *dwStyle* would you use to create a radio button with the text on the right side?

EXERCISES

1. Modify the BUTTON1.CPP program so that the client area of the parent window is painted gray. What do you notice about the background color of the controls? Can you explain?

2. Modify the EDIT1.CPP program so that the edit control takes up the entire client area of the parent window. (Hint: You will need to process the WM_SIZE message, and use the **CWnd::MoveWindow()** function to resize the edit control every time the parent's size is changed.)

ANSWERS TO QUESTIONS

1. The controls are part of Windows. The MFC classes just combine a number of operations into a single convenient class.

2. A button's text string is specified either as the *lpCaption* parameter when the button control is created with **CButton::Create()**, or by calling the **CWnd::SetWindowText()** function after the control is created.

3. False. You must add the scrolling logic to the program.

4. True.

5. c. SB_LINEDOWN and SB_LINEUP are codes sent with the message, and are not message ID values.

6. A pointer to the **CScrollBar** object is passed to the **OnHScroll()** or **OnVScroll()** function when a message generated by the scroll bar is processed.

7. A list box is preferable, as the list is always visible. This saves the user the step of selecting the combo box to make the list box visible. A CBS_SIMPLE combo box is also a possibility, as the list box is always visible with this style.

8. WS_CHILD | SS_BLACKRECT.

9. WS_CHILD | BS_RADIOBUTTON.

SOLUTIONS TO EXERCISES

1. The simplest way to paint the parent window's client area gray is to process WM_PAINT messages, and use this opportunity to paint a gray rectangle covering the client area. Listing 5-46 shows the affected portions of BUTTON.CPP. You will also need to declare the **OnPaint()** function in the program's header file. Listing 5-46 takes the shortcut of using the **CDC::Rectangle()** function to paint a very large gray rectangle filling the client area. A more elegant technique would be to use the **CWnd::GetClientRect()** function to determine the exact size of the window's client area, and then dimension the gray rectangle to exactly fit.

The impact of these changes is shown in Figure 5-22. Note that the white background of the static control's client areas covers the gray background. This is because the automatic painting logic for the static controls includes repainting the control's client area with a white brush. The complete solution is given on the source code disks under the file name C5EXER1.

Listing 5-46 Changes to BUTTON.CPP

```
BEGIN_MESSAGE_MAP (CMainWindow, CFrameWnd)
    ON_WM_PAINT ()                      // process WM_PAINT
    ON_COMMAND (IDM_TEST, OnTest)           // menu items
    ON_COMMAND (IDM_QUIT, OnExit)
    ON_COMMAND (ID_RADIO1, OnRadio1)        // controls
    ON_COMMAND (ID_RADIO2, OnRadio2)
    ON_COMMAND (ID_CHECKBOX, OnCheckBox)
    ON_COMMAND (ID_SHOWBUTN, OnShowButn)
    ON_COMMAND (ID_DONEBUTN, OnDoneButn)
END_MESSAGE_MAP ()

void CMainWindow::OnPaint () // process WM_PAINT to paint gray rect
{
    CPaintDC dc (this) ;
    CBrush GBrush (RGB (192, 192, 192)) ;   // create a gray brush
    CBrush* pOldBrush = dc.SelectObject (&GBrush) ;
    dc.Rectangle (0, 0, 4000, 4000) ; // paint BIG gray rectangle
    dc.SelectObject (pOldBrush) ;    // select old brush to free
}                               // gray brush from the dc
```

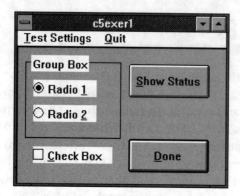

Figure 5-22 Modified BUTTON Program

The coding of this exercise could be improved by using the WM_SIZE message to determine the size of the main program window's client area before painting the client area gray. The next solution shows an example that processes WM_SIZE.

2. The key to having the edit control exactly fit into the center of the parent window's client area is to process the WM_SIZE message. Listing 5-47 shows the key changes to the EDIT1.CPP program. The **CWnd::Move-Window()** function takes care of resizing the edit control's client area to fit the parent window's new size. The complete solution is given on the source code disks under the file name C5EXER2.

The results of these changes are shown in Figure 5-23. The beauty of using the WM_SIZE message to resize the edit control is that it will be resized automatically anytime the parent window's size changes.

Listing 5-47 Processing WM_SIZE messages for EDIT1.CPP

```
BEGIN_MESSAGE_MAP (CMainWindow, CFrameWnd)
    ON_WM_SIZE ()                             // WM_SIZE message
    ON_COMMAND (IDM_GET, OnGetText)           // "Get Text" menu item
    ON_COMMAND (IDM_QUIT, OnExit)             // "Quit" menu item
END_MESSAGE_MAP ()

void CMainWindow::OnSize (UINT nType, int cx, int cy)
{
    EditCntl.MoveWindow (0, 0, cx, cy) ;      // resize edit cntl
}
```

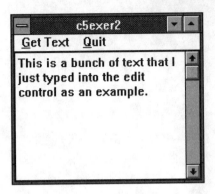

Figure 5-23 Solution to Exercise 5-2

An interesting side effect of this exercise can be noticed if you select the "Get Text" menu item. The program extracts the text from the edit control and displays it on the parent window's client area. The parent window's client area is now completely covered by the edit control. The text still ends up visible, as the edit control's client area is transparent. Text painted on the underlying client area ends up "showing through" the edit control.

## Chapter 6

Taming the Mouse

If you have been programming under MS-DOS or on a mainframe computer system, you may have gotten away with not supporting a mouse
in your programs. This is not possible under Windows. Although it is
possible to *use* Windows applications without the mouse, as a programmer you must support mouse operations when you create new Windows applications.

Every example program so far has used the mouse to some extent.
Even the lowly MINIMAL1 program introduced in Chapters 2 and 3
responded to the mouse cursor for resizing the program window and
accessing the system menu. All of the programs with menu items and
child window controls have responded to mouse selections. These re-
sponses are examples of Windows' built-in support for the
mouse. In most cases, you do not have to do anything
special to support the mouse as a pointing device.
Mouse support is included in many Windows
objects.

There are a few situations where your program will need to deal more directly with the mouse. Examples include painting programs where you will use the mouse to position lines and objects on the screen, and word processing programs that use the mouse to position the input point. In these situations, you will need to determine where the mouse cursor is located and when the user depresses and releases the mouse buttons. You may also find it useful to change the mouse cursor's shape from the normal arrow to something more appropriate for the task, such as a pen or brush.

Closely tied to the mouse cursor is the caret. Carets are normally thin vertical lines, used to show a position in an edit control or in the window's client area. Word processors use the caret to show the location at which the next character will appear. The last example in this chapter explores using the caret with an application that also changes the cursor shape.

Concepts covered: Mouse messages, client coordinates, screen coordinates, binary flags, focus window, cursor hot spot, nonclient mouse messages, stock cursors, pop-up menus.

Key words covered: CURSOR, POPUP, IDC_ARROW, IDC_CROSS.

Functions covered: CWnd::OnMouseMove(), CWnd::OnLButtonDown(), CWnd::OnLButtonUp(), CDC::MoveTo(), CDC::LineTo(), CPoint::Offset(), CWnd::SetCapture(),   ::ReleaseCapture(),   CWnd::ScreenToClient(), CWnd::ClientToScreen(), ostrstream.seekp(), CWinApp::LoadCursor(), CWinApp::LoadStandardCursor(), ::SetCursor(), CWnd::CreateSolidCaret(), ::DestroyCaret(), CWnd::SetCaretPos(), CWnd::ShowCaret(), ::GetSystemMetrics(), AfxGetApp().

Messages covered: WM_MOUSEMOVE, WM_LBUTTONDOWN, WM_RBUTTONDOWN, WM_SETFOCUS, WM_KILLFOCUS, WM_NCMOUSEMOVE, WM_SETCURSOR.

Classes covered: CPoint.

THE WM_MOUSEMOVE MESSAGE

When you use the mouse, Windows automatically moves the mouse cursor on the screen. The cursor position on the screen is updated by low-level logic within Windows, and you will not need to concern yourself with it when programming. To keep programs informed as to the location of the mouse cursor, Windows sends WM_MOUSEMOVE messages as the mouse moves. The WM_MOUSEMOVE messages are sent to the program whose window is under the mouse cursor, not to every running application at once. The data passed with each WM_MOUSEMOVE message contains the mouse cursor's position in the window's client area. Listing 6-1 shows a typical code fragment from an MFC C++ program that processes WM_MOUSEMOVE messages.

The message response function for WM_MOUSEMOVE messages must be named **OnMouseMove()** and must be a member of a class derived from the **CWnd** class, such as **CMainWindow** in Listing 6-1. (**CMainWindow** is derived from the **CFrameWnd** class which in turn is derived from **CWnd**, so **CMainWindow** is a derived class based on **CWnd**.) The **CWnd::On-MouseMove()** function passes two parameter values that reflect data that the Windows environment sends along with the WM_MOUSEMOVE message. The *nFlags* value gives the status of the mouse buttons and the (CONTROL) and (SHIFT) keys at the time the message was sent. These codes will be described in a moment. The position of the mouse cursor is sent as a **CPoint** object.

The **CPoint** class is an MFC object that simplifies working with *X, Y* locations on the screen. The **CPoint** class is similar to the **CRect** class that was used in the last chapter to define the size of window controls. In both cases, the MFC class is a generalization of a C structure that is defined in the WINDOWS.H header file. The definition of the **CPoint** class is in the AFXWIN.H file and is partially shown in Listing 6-2.

Listing 6-1 Processing WM_MOUSEMOVE Messages

```
BEGIN_MESSAGE_MAP (CMainWindow, CFrameWnd)
    ON_WM_MOUSEMOVE ()        // process WM_MOUSEMOVE messages
    // other message map entries here
END_MESSAGE_MAP ()

void CMainWindow::OnMouseMove (UINT nFlags, CPoint Point)
{
    int nXpos = Point.x ;
    int nYpos = Point.y ;
    // do some action relating to mouse movement
}
```

Listing 6-2 Definition of CPoint Class in AFXWIN.H

```
class CPoint : public tagPOINT
{
public:

// Constructors
    CPoint();
    CPoint(int initX, int initY);
    CPoint(POINT initPt);
[other program lines]
```

The **tagPOINT** structure is defined in WINDOWS.H, as shown in Listing 6-3. This is a classic C structure, combining the *X* and *Y* values that describe a single point into one structure.

Because the **CPoint** class is derived from the **tagPOINT** structure, you can directly access the *x* and *y* members. This is how the example in Listing 6-1 determines the location of the mouse from the data passed to the **CWnd::OnMouseMove()** function.

```
int nXpos = Point.x ;
```

Screen and Client Coordinates

Both the *X* and *Y* positions passed with the **CPoint** object to the **CWnd::On-MouseMove()** function use "client coordinates." These coordinates represent the position of the mouse relative to the upper left corner of the program window's client area. Client coordinates are different from screen coordinates, which are relative to the upper left corner of the screen. Figure 6-1 shows a

Listing 6-3 Definition of tagPoint Structure in WINDOWS.H

```
typedef struct tagPOINT
{
    int x;
    int y;
} POINT;
```

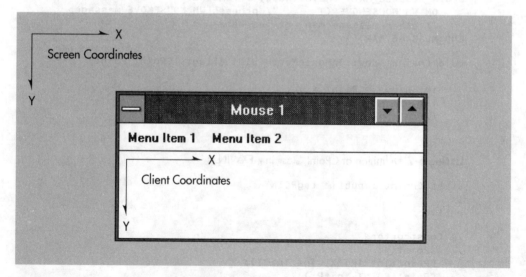

Figure 6-1 Client and Screen Coordinates

diagram of the two sets of units. Note that *Y* values increase downward in both systems of units.

Notification Codes with WM_MOUSEMOVE

The *nFlags* value that is passed to the **CWnd::OnMouseMove()** function (Listing 6-1) is used to indicate if one of the mouse buttons, the (SHIFT) key, or the (CONTROL) key was depressed when the WM_MOUSEMOVE message was sent. Some applications use combinations of the (SHIFT) or (CONTROL) key and the mouse to allow selections of multiple items, or to perform special drawing functions. You can determine which combination of keys and buttons was depressed by comparing the *nFlags* value sent to **CWnd::OnMouseMove()** to the mouse notification codes defined in Table 6-1.

A typical example that uses the *nFlags* data is shown in Listing 6-4.

Binary Flags

Note that the MK values shown in Table 6-1 are binary flags, so more than one of these values can be set at one time. You need to combine the *wParam* value with a flag using the C language binary AND operator (&) to find out if a

Listing 6-4 Processing the nFlags Sent to OnMouseMove()

```
void CMainWindow::OnMouseMove (UINT nFlags, CPoint Point)
{
    if (nFlags & MK_SHIFT)
        // do something because shift key was down
    else if (nFlags & MK_LBUTTON)
        // do something because the left mouse button was down
    // etc.
}
```

nFlags VALUE	Meaning
MK_CONTROL	The (CONTROL) key was down when the message was sent.
MK_LBUTTON	The left mouse button was down when the message was sent.
MK_MBUTTON	The center mouse button was down when the message was sent.
MK_RBUTTON	The right mouse button was down when the message was sent.
MK_SHIFT	The (SHIFT) key was down when the message was sent.

Table 6-1 Mouse Notification Codes Combined to Form wParam Value

Flag Name	Hexadecimal	Binary
MK_SHIFT	0x04	00000100
MK_CONTROL	0x08	00001000
Combined	0x0C	00001100

Table 6-2 Combining Binary Flags

particular flag was set. For example, if both the (SHIFT) key and (CONTROL) key were depressed at the time the WM_MOUSEMOVE message was sent, the *wParam* value would be as shown in Table 6-2.

Because the binary flags are combined to make the *nFlags* value, you cannot use simple code like:

```
if (nFlags == MK_SHIFT)    // WRONG !
```

This would only be true if the (SHIFT) key was depressed, not the (SHIFT) key plus another key or button. To find out if the (SHIFT) key was depressed, independent of any other key or button, combine the *nFlags* value with the flag value for the condition you are testing, using the AND operator (&). Here is an example:

```
if (nFlags & MK_SHIFT)     // Correct
```

Using a binary flag and the C++ language AND operator (&) is sometimes called using a "mask." This is because combining the *nFlags* value with a predefined flag eliminates any bits that do not match the flag. This is like using masking tape to cover up (mask) the areas that you do not want painted before turning on the paint sprayer. Table 6-3 shows an example of what happens at the binary level if the *nFlags* value sent to **CWnd::OnMouseMove()** reflects both the (SHIFT) and (CONTROL) keys being depressed, and the program compares the *nFlags* value with the MK_SHIFT flag.

In this case, (*nFlags* & MK_SHIFT) will be TRUE (nonzero), so the (SHIFT) key was depressed when the WM_MOUSEMOVE message was sent.

	Hexadecimal	Binary
nFlags value sent	0x0C	00001100
MK_SHIFT	0x04	00000100
Combined Using &	0x04	00000100

Table 6-3 Binary & Operator Example

MOUSE BUTTON MESSAGES

Although the *nFlags* values sent to the **CWnd::OnMouseMove()** function will be encoded if one of the mouse buttons was depressed, this information is normally not used. Windows sends additional specific messages when a mouse button is depressed or released. Table 6-4 shows the messages that the program will receive if a mouse button is depressed and released over the client area of a program. (Remember that the client area is the central portion of the program's window, excluding the borders, menu bar, and caption bar.) The mouse button messages also pass the client coordinates of the mouse cursor to the message response function, such as **CWnd::OnLButtonDown()**. These functions use the same *nFlags* binary flags listed in Table 6-4 to determine if one of the other mouse buttons, the (SHIFT) key, or the (CONTROL) key was depressed when the message was sent.

Windows does not provide a means of determining if the user is using a one, two, or three button mouse. Most programs assume the conservative case and only use the left mouse button. This means that you will usually only deal with two of the button messages, WM_LBUTTONDOWN and WM_LBUTTONUP, and their matching message response functions, **CWnd::OnLButtonDown()** and **CWnd::OnLButtonUp()**.

Windows sends additional messages if the mouse is double-clicked. Table 6-5 summarizes these messages. As it is impossible to double-click a mouse button without first single-clicking it, the double-click messages are always preceded by a single-click message. You will need to consider this if you are designing a program that will respond to double-click messages.

As with the other mouse messages, the mouse cursor location when the double-click message was sent is encoded in the **CPoint** value using client coordinates. The *nFlags* value encodes the binary flags shown in Table 6-1 for the combination of other mouse buttons, and (SHIFT) and (CONTROL) keys that were depressed when the message was sent.

	Button Depressed	Button Released
Left Mouse Button	WM_LBUTTONDOWN	WM_LBUTTONUP
Center Mouse Button	WM_MBUTTONDOWN	WM_MBUTTONUP
Right Mouse Button	WM_RBUTTONDOWN	WM_RBUTTONUP

Table 6-4 Client Area Mouse Button Messages

	Button Double-Clicked
Left Mouse Button	WM_LBUTTONDBLCLK
Center Mouse Button	WM_MBUTTONDBLCLK
Right Mouse Button	WM_RBUTTONDBLCLK

Table 6-5 Client Area Mouse Double-Click Messages

THE MOUSE1 PROGRAM

With the preliminaries out of the way, it's time to look at some working code. The MOUSE1 program is designed to give you a feel for how rapidly the WM_MOUSEMOVE messages are sent from Windows, and to practice using this and the button messages. Figure 6-2 shows MOUSE1 in action. If the "Show Mouse Tracks" menu item is selected, the mouse cursor will leave behind a small line on the window's client area every time a WM_MOUSEMOVE message is received. If the left mouse button is clicked, the letter "L" is painted. "R" is painted for the right button, and a "D" is painted if the left button is double-clicked. Notice in Figure 6-2 that the WM_MOUSEMOVE messages are *not* sent every time the cursor moves from one pixel to the next on the screen. If the cursor is moving rapidly (rapid mouse movement), the WM_MOUSEMOVE message will only be sent every 10 to 20 pixels. The exact distance between WM_MOUSEMOVE messages depends on the mouse speed, and on the speed of the computer running Windows.

Listing 6-5 shows MOUSE1.CPP. The mouse tracks are just horizontal lines drawn with the **CDC::MoveTo()** and **CDC::LineTo()** functions every time a WM_MOUSEMOVE message is received. The letters "L," "R," and "D" (for left,

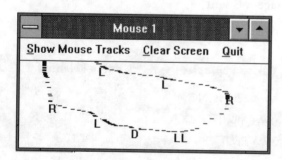

Figure 6-2 The MOUSE1 Program

Listing 6-5 MOUSE1.CPP

```cpp
// mouse1.cpp              shows mouse tracks on client area

#include <afxwin.h>     // class library header file
#include "mouse1.h"     // header file for resource data
#include "mouse1.hpp"   // header file for this program

CTheApp theApp ;         // create one CTheApp object - runs program

BOOL CTheApp::InitInstance ()   // override default InitInstance()
{
    m_pMainWnd = new CMainWindow () ;        // create a main window
    m_pMainWnd->ShowWindow (m_nCmdShow) ;   // make it visible
    m_pMainWnd->UpdateWindow () ;           // paint center
    return TRUE ;
}

CMainWindow::CMainWindow ()     // constructor for window
{
    Create (NULL, "Mouse 1", WS_OVERLAPPEDWINDOW, rectDefault,
        NULL, "MyMenu") ;
    bTracksOn = FALSE ;                     // initialize
}

BEGIN_MESSAGE_MAP (CMainWindow, CFrameWnd)
    ON_COMMAND (IDM_SHOW, OnShow)       // "Show Tracks" menu item
    ON_COMMAND (IDM_CLEAR, OnClear)     // "Clear" menu item
    ON_COMMAND (IDM_QUIT, OnExit)       // "Quit" menu item
    ON_WM_MOUSEMOVE ()                  // process mouse messages
    ON_WM_LBUTTONDOWN ()
    ON_WM_RBUTTONDOWN ()
    ON_WM_LBUTTONDBLCLK ()
END_MESSAGE_MAP ()

void CMainWindow::OnShow ()     // menu item "Show Mouse Tracks"
{
    bTracksOn = bTracksOn ? FALSE : TRUE ;  // toggle on/off
}

void CMainWindow::OnClear ()    // menu item "Clear"
{
    this->Invalidate (TRUE) ;   // force repainting of client area
}                               // erases old mouse tracks

void CMainWindow::OnExit ()     // menu item "Quit"
{
    this->DestroyWindow () ;    // destroy main window,
}                               // this stops application
```

```
void CMainWindow::OnLButtonDown (UINT nFlags, CPoint Point)
{
    if (!bTracksOn)
        return ;
    CClientDC dc (this) ;          // construct client area dc
    dc.TextOut (Point.x, Point.y, "L", 1) ;     // letter L
}

void CMainWindow::OnRButtonDown (UINT nFlags, CPoint Point)
{
    if (!bTracksOn)
        return ;
    CClientDC dc (this) ;          // construct client area dc
    dc.TextOut (Point.x, Point.y, "R", 1) ;     // letter R
}

void CMainWindow::OnLButtonDblClk (UINT nFlags, CPoint Point)
{
    if (!bTracksOn)
        return ;
    CClientDC dc (this) ;          // construct client area dc
    dc.TextOut (Point.x, Point.y, "D", 1) ;     // letter D
}
                                   // show mouse tracks (lines)
void CMainWindow::OnMouseMove (UINT nFlags, CPoint Point)
{
    if (!bTracksOn)
        return ;
    CClientDC dc (this) ;          // construct client area dc
    dc.MoveTo (Point) ;            // start at mouse location
    Point.Offset (4, 0) ;          // calc location 4 pixels right
    dc.LineTo (Point) ;            // draw line to new point
}
```

right, and double-click) are written on the screen using the **CDC::TextOut()** function. Note in Listing 6-5 that the processing of all of the mouse messages is similar. In each case, the mouse cursor location is extracted from the **CPoint** value passed with the mouse message. Like most Windows programs, MOUSE1 ignores the information passed in the *nFlags* parameter with each mouse message.

There is an interesting trick in MOUSE1.CPP to clear the program window's client area. The **CWnd::Invalidate()** function is called to do the erasing:

```
this->Invalidate (TRUE) ;
```

Invalidating the window's client area causes the client area to be repainted. WM_PAINT messages are not processed by MOUSE1.CPP, so the default action for a WM_PAINT message takes place when **CWnd::Invalidate()** is called. The default action is to repaint the client area with a white brush, which ends up erasing the client area.

Another item worth noting is the subtle method of calculating the location of the points in order to draw a line to mark the mouse location in the **CMainWindow::OnMouseMove()** function. The mouse position is passed as a **CPoint** object. The **CPoint** class includes a function called **CPoint::Offset()**, which allows a point to be offset in both the *X* and *Y* directions from a starting point. The **CMainWindow::OnMouseMove()** function takes advantage of this function to pick a point four pixels to the right of the mouse location as the destination point for the line:

```
Point.Offset (4, 0) ;
```

You may want to examine the **CPoint** class in the MFC documentation. A number of other useful functions and operators are provided for this class. Listings 6-6 to 6-9 show the support files for MOUSE1. The program's icon image is shown in Figure 6-3.

Listing 6-6 MOUSE1.HPP Header File

```
// mouse1.hpp    header file for mouse1.cpp

class CMainWindow : public CFrameWnd    // derive a main window class
{
public:
    CMainWindow () ;                     // declare a constructor
private:
    BOOL bTracksOn ;                     // TRUE if tracks visible
    void OnShow () ;                     // toggle mouse tracks on/off
    void OnClear () ;                    // clear client area
    void OnExit () ;                     // stop application
                                         // message processing functions
    void OnLButtonDown (UINT nFlags, CPoint pPoint) ;
    void OnRButtonDown (UINT nFlags, CPoint pPoint) ;
    void OnLButtonDblClk (UINT nFlags, CPoint pPoint) ;
    void OnMouseMove (UINT nFlags, CPoint pPoint) ;

    DECLARE_MESSAGE_MAP()                // prepare for message processing
} ;

class CTheApp : public CWinApp          // derive an application class
{
public:
    BOOL InitInstance () ;              // declare new InitInstance()
} ;
```

Listing 6-7 MOUSE1.H Resource ID Header File

```
// mouse1.h  header file for resource ID numbers

#define IDM_SHOW      1      // menu item ID numbers
#define IDM_CLEAR     2
#define IDM_QUIT      10
```

Listing 6-8 MOUSE1.RC Resource Script File

```
// mouse1.rc  resource script file

#include <afxres.h>
#include "mouse1.h"

AFX_IDI_STD_FRAME   ICON   mouse1.ico   // the program's icon

MyMenu MENU                             // define the menu
{
    MENUITEM "&Show Mouse Tracks",      IDM_SHOW
    MENUITEM "&Clear Screen",           IDM_CLEAR
    MENUITEM "&Quit",                   IDM_QUIT
}
```

Listing 6-9 MOUSE1.DEF Module Definition File

```
NAME            mouse1
DESCRIPTION     'mouse1 C++ program'
EXETYPE         WINDOWS
STUB            'WINSTUB.EXE'
CODE            PRELOAD MOVEABLE
DATA            PRELOAD MOVEABLE MULTIPLE
HEAPSIZE        1024
STACKSIZE       5120
```

Figure 6-3 MOUSE1.ICO Icon Image

THE INPUT FOCUS

An interesting experiment with MOUSE1 is to get two copies running at the same time. You can do this from the Windows File Manager window by double-clicking the MOUSE1.EXE file name, resizing the program window to make the

first copy smaller, and then double-clicking the MOUSE1.EXE file name again. Each of the running copies is called an "instance" of the program. With both instances of MOUSE1 visible, select the "Show Mouse Tracks" menu item in each copy. You will notice that the mouse tracks show up in both windows as you move the mouse cursor over their respective client areas. Figure 6-4 shows two instances of MOUSE1 overlapping, with a mouse track extending from one into the next.

One of the two instances of MOUSE1 will have a dark (highlighted) top caption line. The other instance will have a lighter colored caption. The exact color will depend on the selections you have made using the colors option in the Windows Control Panel application. The window with the highlighted caption is said to have the "input focus." This is the window that will receive any keyboard input.

You can prove to yourself that only the window with the input focus gets the keyboard input by trying the keyboard shortcut for the "Clear Screen" menu item. In MOUSE1.RC (Listing 6-8), we put an ampersand (&) in front of the first letter in the menu caption. This makes the "C" underlined in the MOUSE1 menu, and makes the (ALT)-(C) key combination a keyboard shortcut for that menu item. (ALT)-(C) activates the menu item, clearing the window's client area. Only the instance of MOUSE1 that has the input focus is affected. You can switch the focus to another running application by pressing a mouse key over any part of that program's window. Try switching the focus to the second copy of MOUSE1, and then using the (ALT)-(C) keyboard shortcut to clear that window's screen.

You can see from this discussion that having the input focus is significant for keyboard input, but not significant for mouse actions. The mouse tracks show up in the MOUSE1 client area even if that instance does not have the focus. It makes sense that mouse messages are processed by windows that do

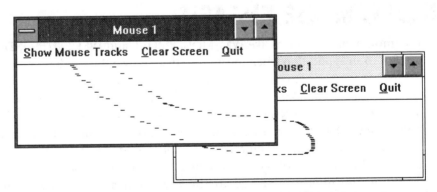

Figure 6-4 Two Instances of MOUSE1; the instance on the left has the input focus

not have the focus. After all, you will normally use the mouse to pick which window is active (has the focus). If mouse messages were ignored by inactive windows, the inactive windows would never be able to gain the input focus.

When a window gains the input focus, Windows sends a WM_SETFOCUS message. When the window loses the input focus, Windows sends a WM_KILLFOCUS message. Common actions are to highlight an edit area when the window has focus, or do some other action that is only necessary when the window may receive keyboard input. One of the exercises at the end of this chapter modifies MOUSE1 to change the window caption when the program gains or loses the input focus.

Normally, you will let the user use the mouse to pick which window has the input focus. You may want to explicitly give a window or a window control the focus. For example, you might want an edit control to have the input focus when the program's main window is first displayed. You may also want to allow the user to pick which child window control has the input focus by using the tab or arrow keys. The **CWnd::SetFocus()** function allows you to explicitly give a window or window control the input focus. A typical call to **CWnd::SetFocus()** would be:

```
Edit.SetFocus() ;
```

In this case, *Edit* is a **CEdit** object for an edit control. Different styles of windows respond differently to gaining the input focus. Windows with caption bars have their caption bar highlighted. Edit controls start showing a blinking vertical line (the caret) at the point where keyboard input will start. Button controls show a highlighted outline. List boxes show a highlighted selection item. Combo boxes will either display their list box, or highlight a list box item if the list box is already displayed.

NONCLIENT MOUSE MESSAGES

Common mouse messages like WM_MOUSEMOVE and WM_LBUTTONDOWN are sent to an application when the mouse cursor is over the window's client area. These messages are not sent when the mouse cursor is over the window's caption bar or menu. Instead, Windows sends nonclient mouse messages. The "nonclient area" of a window is everything except the client area. This includes the window's borders, menu bar, caption bar, system menu button in the upper left corner, and the minimize and maximize buttons in the upper right corner. Figure 6-5 shows a diagram of which parts of the window are in the nonclient portion.

When the mouse is moved in the nonclient area, Windows sends a WM_NCMOUSEMOVE message to the window. There are also nonclient

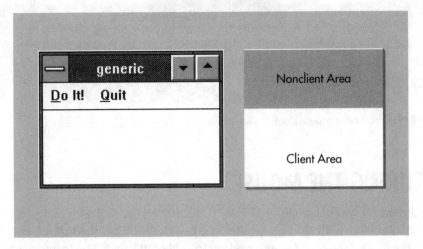

Figure 6-5 Nonclient Parts of a Program Window

equivalents for all of the mouse button click and double-click messages. These messages are summarized in Tables 6-6 and 6-7. With all of these messages, the **CPoint** data sent to the message response function contains the mouse position, while *nFlags* value contains the status of the buttons, (CONTROL) and (SHIFT) keys (summarized in Table 6-1). One difference between the client and nonclient messages is that the nonclient messages encode the mouse position using screen coordinates, not client coordinates.

It is unusual for a program to process the nonclient mouse messages. Normally, you will take advantage of Windows' built-in logic that converts low-level messages, such as WM_NCLBUTTONDOWN, over a menu item into a WM_COMMAND message encoding the menu item selected. It is much easier to figure out which menu item was picked by processing the WM_COMMAND message than by using the coordinates of the cursor sent with WM_NCLBUTTONDOWN.

	Button Depressed	**Button Released**
Left Mouse Button	WM_NCLBUTTONDOWN	WM_NCLBUTTONUP
Center Mouse Button	WM_NCMBUTTONDOWN	WM_NCMBUTTONUP
Right Mouse Button	WM_NCRBUTTONDOWN	WM_NCRBUTTONUP

Table 6-6 Nonclient Area Mouse Button Messages

	Button Double-Clicked
Left Mouse Button	WM_NCLBUTTONDBLCLK
Center Mouse Button	WM_NCMBUTTONDBLCLK
Right Mouse Button	WM_NCRBUTTONDBLCLK

Table 6-7 Nonclient Area Mouse Double-Click Messages

CAPTURING THE MOUSE

If you get two instances of MOUSE1 running, you can switch between them by clicking one with the mouse. The one you click will get the input focus, darken its caption bar, and start responding to keyboard input. The instance losing the focus will lighten its caption bar, and stop responding to keyboard input. This is the way most Windows programs operate. The mouse is used to select which of the running applications is to have the focus.

There are a few occasions where you will want to limit the mouse to interaction with only one program. This can be useful in screen capture programs and utility programs that replace the Program Manager application. An application that takes complete control of the mouse is said to have "captured" the mouse. The application that captures the mouse will be the only one that receives messages, such as WM_MOUSEMOVE and WM_LBUTTONDOWN.

The MOUSE2 program is designed to demonstrate capturing the mouse. The mouse is captured to demonstrate the difference between screen and client coordinates. When you first start MOUSE2, it will appear in the lower right corner of the screen, looking roughly like Figure 6-6. Initially, MOUSE2 only receives mouse messages if the mouse cursor is inside the window's client area. The mouse position is displayed using both screen and client coordinates.

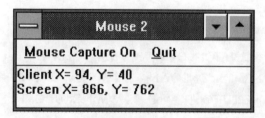

Figure 6-6 The MOUSE2 Program

When the "Mouse Capture On" menu item is selected, MOUSE2 captures the mouse. With the mouse captured, the screen and client coordinates are updated if the mouse cursor is moved anywhere on the screen. This is because only MOUSE2 is getting the mouse messages. Clicking the left mouse button over another program's window will not switch the focus to that application. MOUSE2 continues to hog the mouse until the right mouse button is clicked. At that point, MOUSE2 releases the mouse, and things go back to normal.

You can do an interesting experiment by getting both MOUSE1 and MOUSE2 running at the same time. Before the mouse is captured, MOUSE1 will show mouse tracks in its client area if its "Show Mouse Tracks" menu item has been selected. This is true whether or not MOUSE1 has the focus, as WM_MOUSEMOVE messages are received in either case. However, if MOUSE2 captures the mouse, mouse tracks will not be visible inside MOUSE1's client area as the mouse cursor moves over the MOUSE1 window. This is because only MOUSE2, the application that captured the mouse, is getting the mouse messages.

Listing 6-10 shows the MOUSE2.CPP program. Unlike the previous examples where the Windows environment decided where to place the program window, the MOUSE2 program's window is created with a location and size that fit exactly into the lower right corner of the screen. To do this, we need to know how big the screen is. This is not obvious, as Windows can be run on systems ranging from a CGA resolution monitor to high-end graphics workstations. We need to determine what resolution screen the system is running while MOUSE2 is running.

Windows provides the ::GetSystemMetrics() function to retrieve information about the system. When a C++ function name is preceded only by a double colon (a double colon is the C++ scope resolution operator) the function is a "global" function and not part of any class. The ::MessageBeep() function, which was introduced in Chapter 3, *First Programming Experiments*, is another global function. ::GetSystemMetrics() and ::MessageBeep() are not part of any MFC classes. As such, you will not find an explanation of these functions in the MFC documentation, although they are documented in the Microsoft *Windows Programming Reference*, and in *The Waite Group's Windows API Bible*. Although the MFC classes include almost everything you will need to create Windows applications, there are a few functions that have no reason to be included in a class.

In MOUSE2, ::GetSystemMetrics() is used to find the size of the screen and the height of a program's menu bar. The program's window is made five times the height of a menu bar to make room for the caption, menu bar, and two lines of text. MOUSE2's horizontal window size is made equal to one-fourth of the screen width. **CFrameWnd::Create()** is then called with the correct *X,Y* position for the window to fit exactly into the corner of the screen.

The actual capturing of the mouse boils down to just one function call: **CWnd::SetCapture()**. **CWnd::SetCapture()** is called if the "Mouse Capture On" menu item is selected. The window's caption is also changed to "R. Button Releases" at this point as a reminder of how to free the mouse. **CWnd::SetWindowText()** changes the MOUSE2 window's caption.

Once **CWnd::SetCapture()** is called, the mouse messages go to the application until **::ReleaseCapture()** is called (another global function). To make things simple, the WM_RBUTTONDOWN message (right mouse button depressed) is used in the MOUSE2 program as the point at which to call the **::ReleaseCapture()** function. When the user clicks the right mouse button, Windows sends the WM_RBUTTONDOWN message to MOUSE2, which calls **::ReleaseCapture()** to free the mouse. The WM_RBUTTONDOWN message is received whether or not MOUSE2 has captured the mouse. Calling **::ReleaseCapture()** when the mouse is not captured does no harm.

The display of the screen and client coordinates is handled by the **CMainWindow::OnMouseMove()** function in MOUSE2.CPP. This has the advantage of updating the values every time a WM_MOUSEMOVE message is processed. The **CMainWindow::OnMouseMove()** function introduces two new functions. The **ostrstream::seekp()** function is used to move to a new location in an **ostrstream** object. By moving to the first byte, the same **ostrstream** object can be used a second time, copying over any bytes previously stored. The **seekp()** function is actually a member of the **ostream** class. The **ostrstream** class is derived from **ostream** and, therefore, has access to public member functions in **ostream**, such as **seekp()**.

The second new function introduced in the **CMainWindow::OnMouseMove()** function of MOUSE2.CPP is **CWnd::ClientToScreen()**. **CWnd::ClientToScreen()** converts a **CPoint** object from client coordinates to screen coordinates. This is just what is needed in the **CMainWindow::OnMouseMove()** function because the **CPoint** data passed to **CMainWindow::OnMouseMove()** uses client coordinates. There is also a reciprocal function called **CWnd::ScreenToClient()**, which converts a **CPoint** object from screen to client coordinates.

Listings 6-11 to 6-14 show the support files for MOUSE2.CPP. The program's icon image is shown in Figure 6-7.

There are some interesting side effects to capturing the mouse. When MOUSE2 has captured the mouse, you will not be able to select a menu item in MOUSE2 with the left mouse button. This seems a bit odd, as it is MOUSE2 that

Listing 6-10 MOUSE2.CPP

```cpp
// mouse2.cpp              example that captures the mouse

#include <afxwin.h>        // class library header file
#include <strstrea.h>      // streams header file
#include "mouse2.h"        // header file for resource data
#include "mouse2.hpp"      // header file for this program

CTheApp theApp ;           // create one CTheApp object - runs program

BOOL CTheApp::InitInstance ()   // override default InitInstance()
{
    m_pMainWnd = new CMainWindow () ;        // create a main window
    m_pMainWnd->ShowWindow (m_nCmdShow) ;    // make it visible
    m_pMainWnd->UpdateWindow () ;            // paint center
    return TRUE ;
}

CMainWindow::CMainWindow ()        // constructor for window
{                                  // determine size of screen
    int nScreenX = ::GetSystemMetrics (SM_CXSCREEN) ;
    int nScreenY = ::GetSystemMetrics (SM_CYSCREEN) ;
                                   // and height of the menu bar
    int nMenuY = ::GetSystemMetrics (SM_CYMENU) ;
                                   // build rectangle for window
    CRect WinRect ((nScreenX * 3)/4, nScreenY - (5 * nMenuY),
        nScreenX, nScreenY) ;
    Create (NULL, "Mouse 2", WS_OVERLAPPEDWINDOW, WinRect,
        NULL, "MyMenu") ;
}

BEGIN_MESSAGE_MAP (CMainWindow, CFrameWnd)
    ON_COMMAND (IDM_CAPTURE, OnCapture)    // "Capture On" menu item
    ON_COMMAND (IDM_QUIT, OnExit)          // "Quit" menu item
    ON_WM_MOUSEMOVE ()                     // process mouse messages
    ON_WM_RBUTTONDOWN ()
END_MESSAGE_MAP ()

void CMainWindow::OnCapture ()     // menu item "Mouse Capture On"
{
    this->SetCapture () ;              // capture the mouse ;
    this->SetWindowText ("R. Button Releases") ;// change caption
}

void CMainWindow::OnExit ()        // menu item "Quit"
{
    this->DestroyWindow () ;        // destroy main window,
}                                  // this stops application
```

```
void CMainWindow::OnRButtonDown (UINT nFlags, CPoint Point)
{
    ::ReleaseCapture () ;                // release the mouse
    this->SetWindowText ("Mouse 2") ; // restore old caption
}

void CMainWindow::OnMouseMove (UINT nFlags, CPoint Point)
{
    CClientDC dc (this) ;        // construct client area dc
    char cBuf [128] ;            // pre-allocate char buffer on stack

    ostrstream myString (cBuf, sizeof (cBuf)) ;
                                 // first show client coordinates
    myString << "Client X= " << Point.x << ", Y="
        << Point.y << "        " ;
    dc.TextOut (0, 0, cBuf, myString.pcount ()) ;

    this->ClientToScreen (&Point) ; // convert to screen coordinates
    myString.seekp (0) ;            // move back to beginning of buffer
    myString << "Screen X= " << Point.x << ", Y="
        << Point.y << "        " ;
    dc.TextOut (0, 15, cBuf, myString.pcount ()) ;
}
```

Listing 6-11 MOUSE2.HPP Header File

```
// mouse2.hpp    header file for mouse2.cpp

class CMainWindow : public CFrameWnd    // derive a main window class
{
public:
    CMainWindow () ;                 // declare a constructor
private:
    void OnCapture () ;              // mouse capture on
    void OnExit () ;                 // stop application
                                     // message processing functions
    void OnRButtonDown (UINT nFlags, CPoint pPoint) ;
    void OnMouseMove (UINT nFlags, CPoint pPoint) ;

    DECLARE_MESSAGE_MAP()
} ;

class CTheApp : public CWinApp       // derive an application class
{
public:
    BOOL InitInstance () ;           // declare new InitInstance()
} ;
```

Listing 6-12 MOUSE2.H Resource ID Header File

```
// mouse2.h  header file for resource ID numbers

#define IDM_CAPTURE      1        // menu item ID numbers
#define IDM_QUIT        10
```

Listing 6-13 MOUSE2.RC Resource Script File

```
// mouse2.rc  resource script file

#include <afxres.h>
#include "mouse2.h"

AFX_IDI_STD_FRAME   ICON    mouse2.ico   // the program's icon

MyMenu MENU                              // define the menu
{
    MENUITEM "&Mouse Capture On",       IDM_CAPTURE
    MENUITEM "&Quit",                   IDM_QUIT
}
```

Listing 6-14 MOUSE2.DEF Module Definition File

```
NAME            mouse2
DESCRIPTION     'mouse2 C++ program'
EXETYPE         WINDOWS
STUB            'WINSTUB.EXE'
CODE            PRELOAD MOVEABLE
DATA            PRELOAD MOVEABLE MULTIPLE
HEAPSIZE        1024
STACKSIZE       5120
```

Figure 6-7 MOUSE2.ICO Icon Image

is getting the mouse messages. Why doesn't it respond to menu selections until the mouse is released?

The problem is that the menu bar is actually another small window. Menus are specialized window controls that have built-in logic for highlighting selections and generating WM_COMMAND messages when an item is selected. Windows will not switch the focus to the menu window (so that it can act like a menu) when MOUSE2 has the mouse captured. The result with the mouse captured is that the WM_MOUSEMOVE and WM_LBUTTONDOWN messages are sent to MOUSE2 when the menu bar is clicked, but the menu bar does not get the messages and generate the WM_COMMAND message that we expect from a menu item when it is selected. The result is that the menu does not function when the mouse is captured.

CHANGING THE MOUSE CURSOR SHAPE

For our last experiment on the mouse (sounds sinister doesn't it?), we will switch from the usual arrow cursor shape to some more interesting shapes. We will also try out a related Windows tool, the blinking caret. The easiest way to create new cursor shapes is to draw them with the Microsoft Image Editor application. Figure 6-8 shows two cursor shapes created for the MOUSE3 program. These shapes are actually small bitmap images. Each pixel can be black, white, transparent, or the inverse of the color under it.

When you create cursors, the editor programs allow you to select a "hot spot." This is the point on the cursor bitmap that is exactly at the cursor's *X,Y* position. The hot spot should be located at the "point" of the cursor, where the user can be expected to visualize the cursor to be "pointing." For MOUSE.ICO, this is at the upper left corner, right on the mouse's nose. For HAND.ICO, it is at the tip of the extended index finger.

After you have created the cursor files, you can add them to a program's resource data. The syntax is:

```
CursorName    CURSOR       FileName
```

CURSOR is a reserved word used in resource script files. The file name of the cursor image file is to the right of the word CURSOR. The name given to the resource data within the program is to the left of the word CURSOR. The cursor's name can be anything you want. Listing 6-15 shows two cursor files being added to a program's resource data. Inside of the program, the cursor data will be named "Mouse" and "Hand."

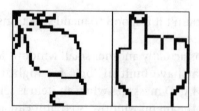

Figure 6-8 Mouse Cursor Shapes Created with Image Editor

Listing 6-15 Adding Cursor Data to a Resource Script File

```
Mouse    CURSOR  mouse.cur   // two cursor files
Hand     CURSOR  hand.cur
```

    With the cursor files referenced in the resource script file, the cursor data will be added to the finished program. In order to use the cursor while the program is operating, you will need to load the cursor data into memory and obtain the "handle" of the cursor data. Remember from Chapter 1, *How Windows Works*, that handles are used by Windows for tracking objects that can be moved in memory. The **CWinApp::LoadCursor()** function loads the cursor data from the program's resource data on disk into memory and returns the handle of the cursor data:

```
hCursor = theApp.LoadCursor ("Mouse") ;
```

    This example assumes that the **CWinApp** object is named *theApp*, as it is in all of the examples in this book. There is a clever alternative to this construction that avoids directly naming the **CWinApp** object. It is better to use a generic name for the program's application object so that the same code can be used in many programs without modification. The MFC classes provide the **AfxGetApp()** function, which returns a pointer to the **CWinApp** object of the program. This will work no matter what you call the **CWinApp** object that your program creates. The generalized means of calling the **CWinApp::LoadCursor()** function is

```
hCursor = AfxGetApp()->LoadCursor ("Mouse") ;
```

    This code accomplishes exactly the same result as using the **CWinApp** object name directly. The next example program uses the **AfxGetApp()** approach so that you can see this construction in context.

    The **CWinApp::LoadCursor()** function returns a handle to the cursor data. You will need to save this handle (usually as a class member) and use it when processing WM_SETCURSOR messages. In order to give the application a chance to change the cursor shape, the WM_SETCURSOR message is sent by Windows to an application when the cursor shape is about to be painted. To specify the cursor shape you loaded with **CWinApp::LoadCursor()**, you will need to call the **::SetCursor()** global function while processing the WM_SETCURSOR message. The MFC classes map the WM_SETCURSOR message to a function called **OnSetCursor()**, which typically looks like the example in Listing 6-16. You will also need to have an ON_WM_SETCURSOR() message map entry, and declare the **OnSetCursor()** function in the program's header file.

Listing 6-16 Setting the Cursor Shape

```
BOOL CMainWindow::OnSetCursor (CWnd *pWnd, UINT nHitTest,
    UINT nMessage)
{
    ::SetCursor (hCursor) ;
    return TRUE ;
}
```

Note in Listing 6-16 that the **CMainWindow::OnSetCursor()** function receives data from the Windows environment as three parameters. *pWnd* is a pointer to the window object that received the message. *nHitTest* is a mouse "hit test" code that specifies what part of the window the mouse is above. The hit test codes are listed in Appendix C, *Mouse Hit Test Codes*. The *nMessage* parameter just gives the message number. You probably will not use these parameters often when coding the **CWnd::OnSetCursor()** function.

Stock Cursors

You will not always need to add cursor data to your program's resources. Windows always has several *stock cursor* shapes available. You can retrieve the handle of a stock cursor using the **CWinApp::LoadStandardCursor()** function. For example, to load a cross hair shape:

```
hCursor = AfxGetApp()->LoadStandardCursor (IDC_CROSS) ;
```

You can use this handle just like the handle in the **CWnd::OnSetCursor()** function, as shown in Listing 6-16. Table 6-8 gives a list of the stock cursor shapes available at all times. Most programs do not have a **CWnd::OnSetCursor()** function and, therefore, end up with the default action of using the stock IDC_ARROW cursor all of the time. However, changing the cursor shape is an excellent way to improve an application in cases where the cursor is going to act on another object. Using a changing cursor shape to match the task at hand is sometimes called the "tool metaphor." The user visualizes the cursor as a "tool" in performing a task. Paint programs frequently change the cursor to a brush shape when painting and to an eraser when deleting.

The Caret

The caret is a small blinking line that is used in applications like word processors to mark a location on the screen. The caret marks the point where the next typed letter will show up. Carets appear automatically in edit controls for this purpose. The caret is interesting from a programming point of view because it is shared by all running application programs. There will never be more than one

Value	Meaning
IDC_ARROW	The standard arrow shape.
IDC_CROSS	A thin cross hair cursor.
IDC_IBEAM	An I-beam cursor. Used for positioning text.
IDC_ICON	An empty icon.
IDC_SIZE	A square with a smaller square in the lower right corner. Looks like a window being reduced in size.
IDC_SIZENESW	The double-headed arrow Windows uses when adjusting the upper right and lower left sizing borders. Points "NE by SW."
IDC_SIZENS	The double-headed arrow Windows uses when adjusting the top and bottom sizing borders. Points "North/South."
IDC_SIZENWSE	The double-headed arrow Windows uses when adjusting the upper left and lower right sizing borders. Points "NW by SE."
IDC_SIZEWE	The double-headed arrow Windows uses when adjusting the right or left sizing borders. Points "West/East."
IDC_UPARROW	An arrow pointing up.
IDC_WAIT	The hourglass cursor shape.

Table 6-8 Stock Cursor Shapes

caret visible on the screen at one time. This is logical, as otherwise the user would not be able to tell where the next typed letter will show up. The caret is closely tied to the concept of input focus. The caret should be visible when a window has the focus, and it should vanish when the window loses the focus.

The WM_SETFOCUS and WM_KILLFOCUS messages provide an ideal point to create and remove the caret. A typical source code excerpt is shown in Listing 6-17. The caret is created when the WM_SETFOCUS message is received by calling the **CWnd::CreateSolidCaret**() function. In Listing 6-17, a caret 3 pixels wide by 15 pixels high is created. The caret is positioned on the window's client area with the **CWnd::SetCaretPos**() function and is made visible by calling **CWnd::ShowCaret**(). There is also a **CWnd::HideCaret**() function to temporarily hide the caret shape. This function is not used in Listing 6-17. The caret continues to be visible on the window's client area until a WM_KILLFOCUS message is received. The global function **::DestroyCaret**() removes the caret from the screen. In Listing 6-17, the **CPoint** object *CaretPoint* is assumed to be defined in the **CMainWindow** class, or as a global variable.

Listing 6-17 Creating and Removing the Caret

```
BEGIN_MESSAGE_MAP (CMainWindow, CFrameWnd)
    ON_WM_SETFOCUS ()
    ON_WM_KILLFOCUS ()
    // other message map entries
END_MESSAGE_MAP ()

void CMainWindow::OnSetFocus (CWnd* pOldWnd)
{
    this->CreateSolidCaret (3, 15) ;     // make a new caret
    this->SetCaretPos (CaretPoint) ;     // specify X,Y location
    this->ShowCaret () ;                 // make it visible
}

void CMainWindow::OnKillFocus (CWnd* pNewWnd)
{
    ::DestroyCaret () ;         // destroy the caret
}
```

Once a caret has been created, it is positioned on the window's client area using the **CWnd::SetCaretPos()** function. **CWnd::SetCaretPos()** is often used in response to the left mouse button being depressed (WM_LBUTTONDOWN message) or after keyboard input to advance to the next letter in a character string. The MOUSE3 example in Listing 6-18 repositions the caret when the left mouse button is depressed. The next chapter, *Fonts and the Keyboard*, demonstrates moving the caret in response to keyboard input.

Experimenting with Cursor Shapes and the Caret

The last example program in this chapter is MOUSE3. MOUSE3 demonstrates changing the cursor's shape and positioning the caret in the window's client area. We will also learn how to create menus with drop-down (pop-up) menus attached. Listing 6-18 shows the resource script file for MOUSE3. Note that an icon file and two cursor files have been added to the resource data. The icon will be used for the main window's class icon, visible when the window is minimized. The cursor shapes will be used for alternatives to the usual arrow cursor.

Note that the menu definition in MOUSE3.RC includes a line titled "POPUP." This line starts the definition of a pop-up menu. The top menu bar will contain the selection choice "Cursor Shape." When this top item is selected, a pop-up menu will appear under the menu bar with four selections: Arrow, Cross, Hand, and Mouse. Figure 6-9 shows the appearance of the MOUSE3 window after the "Cursor Shape" menu item has been selected.

The pop-up menu allows the choice of one of four cursor shapes. Selecting an item in the pop-up menu results in a WM_COMMAND message being sent

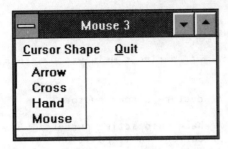

Figure 6-9 MOUSE3 Pop-Up Menu

Listing 6-18 MOUSE3.RC Resource Script File

```
// mouse3.rc   resource script file

#include <afxres.h>
#include "mouse3.h"

AFX_IDI_STD_FRAME    ICON     mouse3.ico      // the program's icon

Mouse                CURSOR   mouse.cur       // cursor image files
Hand                 CURSOR   hand.cur

MyMenu MENU                                   // define the menu
{
    POPUP "&Cursor Shape"                     // top level heading
    {
        MENUITEM "&Arrow",          IDM_ARROW
        MENUITEM "&Cross",          IDM_CROSS
        MENUITEM "&Hand",           IDM_HAND
        MENUITEM "&Mouse",          IDM_MOUSE
    }
    MENUITEM "&Quit",               IDM_QUIT
}
```

to the MOUSE3 program, using the menu item's ID number to determine which menu item was selected. Note in Listing 6-18 that the POPUP menu line with the string "Cursor Shape" does not have an ID number. Selecting the top element of a pop-up menu does not result in a WM_COMMAND message, so no ID number is needed. Only the items within the POPUP menu (MENUITEM's between the curly brackets following the POPUP statement) have ID values.

Listing 6-19 shows the MOUSE3.HPP header file. Note that the **CMainWindow** class definition contains the *hCursor* variable to keep track of the handle of the cursor shape that is currently being displayed. There is also a **CPoint** object *CaretPoint* to track the position of the caret.

Listing 6-19 MOUSE3.HPP Header File

```
// mouse3.hpp    header file for mouse3.cpp

class CMainWindow : public CFrameWnd     // derive a main window class
{
public:
    CMainWindow () ;                 // declare a constructor
private:
    HCURSOR hCursor ;                // handle to active cursor
    CPoint  CaretPoint ;             // current caret position

    void OnArrow () ;                 // functions handling menu
    void OnCross () ;                 // selections
    void OnHand () ;
    void OnMouse () ;
    void OnExit () ;

                                      // message processing functions
    void OnSetFocus (CWnd* pOldWnd) ;
    void OnKillFocus (CWnd* pNewWnd) ;
    void OnLButtonDown (UINT nFlags, CPoint point) ;
    BOOL OnSetCursor (CWnd *pWnd, UINT nHitTest, UINT nMessage) ;

    DECLARE_MESSAGE_MAP()            // prepare for message processing
} ;

class CTheApp : public CWinApp      // derive an application class
{
public:
    BOOL InitInstance () ;                  // declare new InitInstance()
} ;
```

Listing 6-20 shows the MOUSE3.CPP program file. The **CMainWindow** constructor initializes *hCursor* to the handle of the stock arrow cursor as the program is starting. This is necessary in MOUSE3.CPP because the program processes WM_SETCURSOR messages and changes the cursor shape to the cursor specified in the data pointed to by *hCursor*. Unless you initialize *hCursor*, the handle will not point to cursor data and the **::SetCursor()** function will fail, making the cursor invisible.

When the MOUSE3 program receives the input focus (WM_SETFOCUS message received), a new caret is created and displayed. When the input focus is lost (WM_KILLFOCUS message), the caret is destroyed. Creating and destroying the caret as it is needed is the "safe" way to avoid conflicts with other applications that may be creating and destroying the caret for their own purposes. Remember that the caret is a global resource, so only one caret is available on the system at any one time regardless of the number of applications that are running.

Listing 6-20 MOUSE3.CPP

```cpp
// mouse3.cpp                    example changing mouse cursor shape
//                              also demonstrates moving the caret

#include <afxwin.h>      // class library header file
#include <strstrea.h>    // streams header file
#include "mouse3.h"      // header file for resource data
#include "mouse3.hpp"    // header file for this program

CTheApp theApp ;         // create one CTheApp object - runs program

BOOL CTheApp::InitInstance ()    // override default InitInstance()
{
    m_pMainWnd = new CMainWindow () ;         // create a main window
    m_pMainWnd->ShowWindow (m_nCmdShow) ;     // make it visible
    m_pMainWnd->UpdateWindow () ;             // paint center
    return TRUE ;
}

CMainWindow::CMainWindow ()        // constructor for window
{
    Create (NULL, "Mouse 3", WS_OVERLAPPEDWINDOW, rectDefault,
        NULL, "MyMenu") ;
    hCursor = theApp.LoadStandardCursor (IDC_ARROW) ;
    ::SetCursor (hCursor) ;
    CaretPoint.x = 0 ;
    CaretPoint.y = 0 ;
}

BEGIN_MESSAGE_MAP (CMainWindow, CFrameWnd)
    ON_COMMAND (IDM_ARROW, OnArrow)              // menu item selections
    ON_COMMAND (IDM_CROSS, OnCross)
    ON_COMMAND (IDM_HAND, OnHand)
    ON_COMMAND (IDM_MOUSE, OnMouse)
    ON_COMMAND (IDM_QUIT, OnExit)
    ON_WM_SETFOCUS ()                            // message functions
    ON_WM_KILLFOCUS ()
    ON_WM_LBUTTONDOWN ()
    ON_WM_SETCURSOR ()
END_MESSAGE_MAP ()

void CMainWindow::OnArrow ()          // load the stock arrow cursor
{
    hCursor = AfxGetApp()->LoadStandardCursor (IDC_ARROW) ;
}

void CMainWindow::OnCross ()          // load the stock cross cursor
{
    hCursor = AfxGetApp()->LoadStandardCursor (IDC_CROSS) ;
}
```

```
void CMainWindow::OnHand ()            // load from resource data
{
    hCursor = AfxGetApp()->LoadCursor ("Hand") ;
}


void CMainWindow::OnMouse ()           // load from resource data
{
    hCursor = AfxGetApp()->LoadCursor ("Mouse") ;
}


void CMainWindow::OnExit ()            // respond to menu item "Quit"
{
    this->DestroyWindow () ;           // destroy main window,
}                                      // this stops application

void CMainWindow::OnSetFocus (CWnd* pOldWnd)
{
    this->CreateSolidCaret (3, 15) ;   // make a new caret
    this->SetCaretPos (CaretPoint) ;   // specify X,Y location
    this->ShowCaret () ;               // make it visible
}


void CMainWindow::OnKillFocus (CWnd* pNewWnd)
{
    ::DestroyCaret () ;        // destroy the caret
}


void CMainWindow::OnLButtonDown (UINT nFlags, CPoint point)
{                                      // move caret position
    this->SetCaretPos (point) ;        // to mouse location
    CaretPoint = point ;               // save new location
}


BOOL CMainWindow::OnSetCursor (CWnd *pWnd, UINT nHitTest,
    UINT nMessage)
{
    ::SetCursor (hCursor) ;
    return TRUE ;
}
```

The caret is repositioned in the MOUSE3 client area when the user depresses the left mouse button. The **CWnd::SetCaretPos()** function is called in response to the WM_LBUTTONDOWN message to reposition the caret. The new caret position is saved as the *CaretPoint* variable. Note that the **CPoint** class overloads the assignment operator (= operator), making it possible to use easy-to-read code to make one **CPoint** object equal to another:

```
CaretPoint = point ;
```

Listings 6-21 and 6-22 show the MOUSE3.H and MOUSE3.DEF files, respectively. The program's icon image is shown in Figure 6-10.

Listing 6-21 MOUSE3.H Resource ID Header File

```
// mouse3.h  header file for resource ID numbers

#define IDM_ARROW        1        // menu item ID numbers
#define IDM_CROSS        2
#define IDM_HAND         3
#define IDM_MOUSE        4
#define IDM_QUIT         10
```

Listing 6-22 MOUSE3.DEF Module Definition File

```
NAME           mouse3
DESCRIPTION    'mouse3 C++ program'
EXETYPE        WINDOWS
STUB           'WINSTUB.EXE'
CODE           PRELOAD MOVEABLE
DATA           PRELOAD MOVEABLE MULTIPLE
HEAPSIZE       1024
STACKSIZE      5120
```

Figure 6-10 MOUSE3.ICO Icon Image

The different cursor shapes loaded by menu selections in MOUSE3 remain in effect as long as the cursor is within the window's area. This includes both the client and nonclient parts of the window. As soon as the cursor is moved past the edge of MOUSE3's window, the cursor shape reverts to the default arrow. The cursor shape also reverts to the arrow shape if the MOUSE3 program is terminated.

SUMMARY

Windows lets your program know what the mouse is doing by sending messages. You can use the WM_MOUSEMOVE message to detect mouse movement and find the current mouse cursor position. Messages like WM_LBUT-TONDOWN are used to tell the program that one of the mouse buttons has been depressed. The client and nonclient areas of a window generate different sets of mouse messages. Normally, a program will process only client area mouse messages, and will let the Windows environment process the nonclient messages.

If more than one application is running, the user can use the mouse to select which window has the input focus. The window with the input focus will have its caption highlighted, and will be the window to receive any keyboard input. Windows sends a WM_SETFOCUS message to the window when it receives the input focus, and sends WM_KILLFOCUS when the focus is lost. Programs can capture the mouse by calling the **CWnd::SetCapture()** function. Once the mouse is captured, all mouse messages are sent to the program that captured the mouse, even if the mouse is not over any portion of the program's window. This continues until the mouse is freed with the **::ReleaseCapture()** function.

You can change cursor shapes by calling the **::SetCursor()** function, usually in response to a WM_SETCURSOR message from Windows. The cursor shape can be either a stock cursor or a custom cursor image that you create with the Image Editor application. Cursor data files are added to the program's resource data, and then accessed with the **CWinApp::LoadCursor()** function prior to calling **::SetCursor()**.

Some applications use a caret to mark a location in the client area where text will be inserted. Only one caret is visible on the screen at any one time. Carets are created when the window receives the input focus (WM_SETFOCUS message received), and destroyed when the window loses the input focus (WM_KILLFOCUS message received). The caret can be made temporarily visible or hidden by using **CWnd::ShowCaret()** or **CWnd::HideCaret()**.

QUESTIONS

1. If an edit control shows the caret, you know that the edit control has the
   _____ _____.

2. The same Windows message will be received if the left mouse button is depressed anywhere above a program window. (True/False)

3. If the right mouse button is depressed in the client area of a window, the window's message function will receive a _____ message. If the right mouse button is depressed in the nonclient area, the _____ message will be received.

4. If there are two edit controls in the client area of a window, both child windows of the parent, both of the edit controls can have the caret showing at the same time. (True/False)

5. Carets are created when processing the _____ message, and de-stroyed when processing the _____ message.

6. You can fetch the name of the **CWinApp** object using the MFC function _____ at any point in the code.

7. To use a custom cursor shape in a program, you must add the cursor to the program's _____ _____ file.

EXERCISES

1. Modify the MOUSE1 program so that the window's caption bar shows "I have the focus" when the program's window gets the input focus, and shows "I lost the focus" when the program's window loses the focus.

2. Get two copies of the modified MOUSE1 program running from exercise one. How do you get both of the windows to display the "I lost the focus" caption? How do you get both to display the "I have the focus" caption?

3. Create a program that displays a button control on the program's client area at the location that the user clicks the left mouse button. The button should be destroyed and re-created at the cursor location every time the left mouse button is clicked. Is it possible to get WM_COMMAND messages from this control?

ANSWERS TO QUESTIONS

1. Input focus.

2. False. Client area mouse messages are received over the window's client area, while nonclient area messages are received if the mouse cursor is over the menu, caption, border, or other nonclient areas of the window.

3. WM_RBUTTONDOWN, WM_NCRBUTTONDOWN.

4. False. Only one caret will ever be visible on the screen at any one time.

5. WM_SETFOCUS, WM_KILLFOCUS.

6. **AfxGetApp()**.

7. Resource script.

SOLUTIONS TO EXERCISES

1. The program will need to process WM_SETFOCUS and WM_KILLFOCUS messages, and use **CWnd::SetWindowText()** to change the caption string. Listing 6-23 shows the portion of MOUSE1.CPP that must be changed. The full program is called C6EXER1 on the source code disks.

2. You can get both instances of the modified MOUSE1 program to show "I lost the focus" by selecting some other program's window. It is not possible to have both instances display "I have the focus," as only one window can gain the focus at one time.

3. Listing 6-24 shows the portion of the modified MOUSE1.CPP program that repositions a button control every time the left mouse button is depressed over the program window's client area. The full program is called C6EXER3 on the source code disks.

   The button control is moved every time the WM_LBUTTONDOWN message is received. The control generates WM_COMMAND messages if the mouse is clicked inside the button control's client area. This is demonstrated in this example by calling the ::**MessageBeep()** function when the button is clicked.

Listing 6-23 Modifications to MOUSE1.CPP

```
BEGIN_MESSAGE_MAP (CMainWindow, CFrameWnd)
    ON_COMMAND (IDM_SHOW, OnShow)          // "Show Tracks" menu item
    ON_COMMAND (IDM_CLEAR, OnClear)        // "Clear" menu item
    ON_COMMAND (IDM_QUIT, OnExit)          // "Quit" menu item
    ON_WM_SETFOCUS ()                      // message functions
    ON_WM_KILLFOCUS ()
    ON_WM_MOUSEMOVE ()                     // process mouse messages
    ON_WM_LBUTTONDOWN ()
    ON_WM_RBUTTONDOWN ()
    ON_WM_LBUTTONDBLCLK ()
END_MESSAGE_MAP ()

void CMainWindow::OnSetFocus (CWnd* pOldWnd)
{
    this->SetWindowText ("I have the focus.") ;
}

void CMainWindow::OnKillFocus (CWnd* pNewWnd)
{
    this->SetWindowText ("I lost the focus.") ;
}
```

Listing 6-24 Repositioning a Button Control

```
BEGIN_MESSAGE_MAP (CMainWindow, CFrameWnd)
    ON_COMMAND (IDM_QUIT, OnExit)            // "Quit" menu item
    ON_COMMAND (IDM_SHOW, OnShow)            // "Show Button" menu item
    ON_COMMAND (ID_BUTTON, OnButton)         // button was selected
    ON_WM_LBUTTONDOWN ()
END_MESSAGE_MAP ()

void CMainWindow::OnShow ()        // make button visible
{
    CRect rect (20, 20, 170, 70) ;
    Button.Create ("I beep and move",
        BS_PUSHBUTTON | WS_CHILD | WS_VISIBLE,
        rect, this, ID_BUTTON) ;
}

void CMainWindow::OnButton ()      // respond to button being selected
{
    ::MessageBeep (0) ;            // just beep
}

void CMainWindow::OnExit ()        // respond to menu item "Quit"
{
    this->DestroyWindow () ;       // destroy main window,
}                                  // this also destroys button child

                                   // move button to mouse location
void CMainWindow::OnLButtonDown (UINT nFlags, CPoint Point)
{
    Button.MoveWindow (Point.x, Point.y, 150, 50) ;
}
```

## Chapter 7

Fonts and the Keyboard

Most people think of Windows as a mouse-driven environment. Certainly the mouse is important in Windows, and it is used more frequently than in most MS-DOS programs. But the keyboard can offer shortcuts (called "keyboard accelerators") that are alternatives to the mouse for menu selections and special functions. Touch typists frequently prefer using keyboard actions because they do not have to take one hand off the keyboard to use the mouse. The keyboard is also the primary means for the user to enter text and numbers.

Windows allows programs to display text and digits using character fonts with different styles, sizes, and colors. Several fonts are always available under Windows, and others can be added by installing fonts from the Windows Control Panel application. The MFC classes also provide the powerful **CFont** class, which allows you to create new font sizes and styles based on the currently installed fonts.

Windows does not use the same IBM PC character set that is used by MS-DOS. Instead, Windows uses the more international ANSI character set. This can be a bit tricky, as many C++ compiler runtime library functions assume that the IBM PC or ASCII character sets are in use. Windows has its own specialized functions for working with the ANSI character set, and for converting between ANSI and IBM PC character codes.

Although Windows tools, such as edit controls, take care of many of the nitty-gritty details of dealing with the keyboard for you, there are situations where you will need to work more directly with the keyboard hardware. For example, word processing programs make heavy use of the keyboard and cannot live with the limitations imposed by edit controls, such as using only one font. In these cases, you will need to process messages that Windows generates when keys are depressed and released. You can also take advantage of another time saver in Windows: keyboard accelerators. Accelerators provide a simple way to add keyboard shortcuts to your program. They are often used to provide alternatives to selecting menu items and clicking button controls.

Concepts covered: ANSI character set, keyboard messages, virtual keys, variable pitch fonts, logical fonts, keyboard accelerators.

Key words covered: HFONT, ACCELERATOR.

Functions covered: CString::GetLength(), CString::MakeUpper(), CString::MakeLower(), CString::Left(), ::AnsiLower(), ::AnsiUpper(), ::IsCharAlphaNumeric(), CWnd::OnKeyDown(), CWnd::OnKeyUp(), CWnd::OnChar(), CDC::SelectStockObject(), CFont::CreateFont(), CFrameWnd::LoadAccelTable(), CDC::GetTextMetrics(), CDC::GetTextExtent().

Messages covered: WM_KEYDOWN, WM_KEYUP, WM_CHAR, WM_SYSKEYDOWN, WM_SYSCHAR, WM_SYSKEYUP, WM_DEADCHAR.

Classes covered: CString, CFont, CSize.

THE ANSI CHARACTER SET

Computers store and transmit letters and digits using coding systems. Each character is given a number code. A collection of characters given number codes is called a "character set." Over time, the number of character sets has grown. The most common set is the ASCII character set, which uses code numbers between 0 and 127 to encode the letters, numbers, and common keyboard symbols. When the IBM PC was designed, the builders of the hardware and software added additional graphic and special symbol characters to the ASCII character set to come up with the IBM PC character set. This character set is shown in Figure 7-1, encoding all of the symbols with numbers between 0 and 255 (0x0 to 0xFF hexadecimal). Within Windows, the IBM PC character set is called the "OEM" character set, for Original Equipment Manufacturer.

The problem with the OEM character set is that it uses most of the character positions for graphic symbols, and does not have a complete collection of accented characters for other languages. The graphic symbols are of little value in an environment where the entire screen is drawn one pixel at a time. The designers of Windows decided to use a more international character coding system, the ANSI character set, which is shown in Figure 7-2. The ANSI set has fewer graphic symbols, but a more complete collection of accented characters and international symbols. Some of the characters in the ANSI character set are used for control commands like tabs and line feeds. These characters are shown as vertical lines in Figure 7-2.

Normally, you will not need to concern yourself with the exact coding of the characters. A letter "A" is a letter "A." There are a few situations where the differences are important. Windows programs are expected to work in any language, so care needs to be taken to ensure that accented characters are correctly processed. For example, the code in Listing 7-1 works correctly for the unaccented A-Z characters, but completely ignores accented characters.

	0	1	2	3	4	5	6	7	8	9	A	B	C	D	E	F
0		☺	☻	♥	♦	♣	♠	•	◘	○	◙	♂	♀	♪	♫	☼
10	►	◄	↕	‼	¶	§	▬	↨	↑	↓	→	←	∟	↔	▲	▼
20		!	"	#	$	%	&	'	(	)	*	+	,	-	.	/
30	0	1	2	3	4	5	6	7	8	9	:	;	<	=	>	?
40	@	A	B	C	D	E	F	G	H	I	J	K	L	M	N	O
50	P	Q	R	S	T	U	V	W	X	Y	Z	[	\	]	^	_
60	`	a	b	c	d	e	f	g	h	i	j	k	l	m	n	o
70	p	q	r	s	t	u	v	w	x	y	z	{	¦	}	~	⌂
80	Ç	ü	é	â	ä	à	å	ç	ê	ë	è	ï	î	ì	Ä	Å
90	É	æ	Æ	ô	ö	ò	û	ù	ÿ	Ö	Ü	¢	£	¥	₧	ƒ
A0	á	í	ó	ú	ñ	Ñ	ª	º	¿	⌐	¬	½	¼	¡	«	»
B0	░	▒	▓	│	┤	╡	╢	╖	╕	╣	║	╗	╝	╜	╛	┐
C0	└	┴	┬	├	─	┼	╞	╟	╚	╔	╩	╦	╠	═	╬	╧
D0	╨	╤	╥	╙	╘	╒	╓	╫	╪	┘	┌	█	▄	▌	▐	▀
E0	α	β	Γ	π	Σ	σ	µ	τ	Φ	Θ	Ω	δ	∞	ø	∈	∩
F0	≡	±	≥	≤	⌠	⌡	÷	≈	°	∙	·	√	ⁿ	²	■	

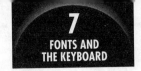

Add the hexadecimal numbers on the left column and top row to find the code number for a character.

Figure 7-1 OEM Character Set

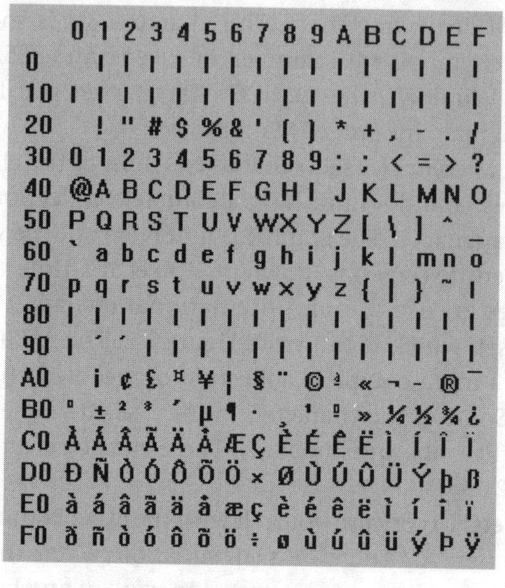

Figure 7-2 ANSI Character Set

Listing 7-1 Error in Character Classification

```
char c ;
if (c >= 'A' && c <= 'Z || c >= 'a' && c <= 'z') // wrong !!
        // do something assuming c is a character
```

More difficult to spot are hidden assumptions in standard C++ compiler library functions, such as **ischar()**, **toupper()**, **tolower()**, and so on. These functions assume the ASCII character set, and typically ignore accented characters completely. The problem will not show up until you give your program to a French person to test, and you hear "Il ne march pas!" (It does not work!). It is not possible to spell French, Spanish, German, or most other languages properly without accented characters.

THE CSTRING CLASS

The MFC classes provide the handy **CString** class for manipulating character strings. The **CString** class is different from the **ostrstream** class we used to format output to a character buffer. Instead of the C++ stream syntax (<< and >> operators), the **CString** class uses operators somewhat like the BASIC language string operations. For example, Listing 7-2 shows a short example that creates a **CString** object, adds (concatenates) a second string to the first, and then outputs the string

Listing 7-2 Using the CString Class

```
#include <strstrea.h>            // header file for strings/
streams
CString AString ;               // create a CString object
AString = "The full string " ;  // initialize string
AString += "is this long." ;    // add more characters to end
dc.TextOut (10, 10, AString, AString.GetLength ()) ;
```

to a device context named *dc*. The device context was presumably created at some earlier point using the **CPaintDC** or **CClientDC** classes.

The assignment operator (=) initializes a **CString** object to contain a given string. The **CString** object automatically allocates enough memory to hold the character data. The "+=" operator concatenates additional characters to the end of a **CString** object. The **CString** class also has several handy functions, like **CString::GetLength()** that returns the number of characters in the string. In Listing 7-2, the **CString::GetLength()** function is used to pass the length of the string to the **CDC::TextOut()** function. You should take a look at the **CString** documentation at this point to familiarize yourself with the functions and operators that are available.

You can easily convert from a **CString** object to a pointer to a normal character buffer. The **CString** class overloads the **(const char *)** operator to return a pointer to the character data in the **CString** object, as shown here:

```
char * pCharBuffer = (const char *) AString ;
```

Although the **CString** class is convenient, it suffers from a significant problem in Windows applications. The **CString** class is not Windows-specific and can be used in DOS programs by including the STRSTREA.H header file. The **CString** class assumes that the ASCII character set is being used, not the Windows ANSI character set. For example, the **CString::MakeLower()** and **CString::MakeUpper()** functions do *not* correctly process accented characters.

The **CString** class does provide the **CString::AnsiToOem()** and **CString::OemToAnsi()** functions that convert the characters within the **CString** object between the two character sets. In practice, these functions are not particularly useful, as the OEM character set is missing a number of the accented characters in the ANSI set, so converting between the two sets risks errors in some languages.

Global Character Functions

To get around these problems, Windows provides its own set of functions for doing character conversions using the ANSI character set. These are global functions, and not part of an MFC class. The functions all operate on normal C++ character data, rather than **CString** object data. Table 7-1 provides a summary of the character functions.

There are two reasons to use the Windows character functions in Table 7-1, rather than the compiler library functions or the **CString** functions like **CString::MakeUpper()**. One reason is that the Windows functions correctly deal with the ANSI character set, including accented characters. The other reason to use the global Windows functions is because they are part of Windows, not part of your program. If you use compiler library functions, the function's code is added to your program. If you use the Windows versions, the function

Function	Purpose
::AnsiLower()	Convert a null-terminated character string to lowercase.
::AnsiLowerBuff()	Convert a character string to lowercase. The string does not need to be null-terminated.
::AnsiNext()	Move to the next character in a string.
::AnsiPrev()	Move to the previous character in a string.
::AnsiToOem()	Convert a string from the ANSI character set to the OEM character set.
::AnsiToOemBuff()	Convert a character string from the ANSI to the OEM character set. The string does not need to be null-terminated.
::AnsiUpper()	Convert a null-terminated character string to uppercase.
::AnsiUpperBuff()	Convert a character string to uppercase. The string does not have to be null-terminated.
::IsCharAlpha()	Determine if an ANSI character is an alphabetical character.
::IsCharAlphaNumeric()	Determine if an ANSI character is an alphabetical or numeric character.
::IsCharLower()	Determine if an ANSI character is lowercase.
::IsCharUpper()	Determine if an ANSI character is uppercase.
::OemToAnsi()	Convert a character string from the OEM character set to the ANSI character set.
::OemToAnsiBuff()	Convert a character string from the OEM character set to the ANSI character set. The string does not have to be null-terminated.
::ToAscii()	Conversion from virtual key/scan code data to an ASCII character.

Table 7-1 Windows Global Character Set Functions

code remains part of Windows, so your program can be that much smaller. The corrected code for Listing 7-1 is shown in Listing 7-3, using the Windows function **::IsCharAlpha()**.

You will note in Table 7-1 that several of the functions allow conversion between the ANSI and OEM character sets. These functions are useful if the text is being exchanged between Windows programs and non-Windows (DOS) programs. Within the Windows environment, you will be using the ANSI character set for everything except disk file names. Windows uses MS-DOS to do file input and output, and DOS uses the OEM character set. We will see in Chapter 15, *Disk File Access*, that the file names are automatically converted by the **CFile::Open()** function. However, the file's contents may need to be converted if it is text written using the OEM character set.

While we are discussing Windows character functions, it is worth noting that Windows includes five functions for copying and comparing strings, which are shown in Table 7-2. Again, when you use these functions, the function's code remains part of Windows, not your program. These functions all start with the letter "l," reflecting that they all can handle both long (far) pointers to character strings, as well as near pointers. The functions are indifferent to the character set being used, and will process both ANSI and OEM character strings.

In general, you will probably find that the **CString** class is more convenient than using the functions in Table 7-2. Just keep in mind that the **CString** class does not assume the ANSI character set, so avoid the **CString::MakeUpper()** and **CString::MakeLower()** functions.

Listing 7-3 Correct Character Classification

```
char c ;
if (::IsCharAlpha (c))          // correct
     // do something assuming c is a character
```

Function	Meaning
::lstrcat()	Add one character string on to the end of another string.
::lstrcmp()	Compare two character strings.
::lstrcmpi()	Compare two character strings, ignoring the difference between uppercase and lowercase letters.
::lstrcpy()	Copy a character string to a memory buffer.
::lstrlen()	Determine the length of a character string.

Table 7-2 Windows Functions for Copying and Comparing Character Strings

Trying Out the Character Functions

The first example program in this chapter is called CHAR1. It demonstrates several of the global character functions, and also shows the effects of incorrectly using the **CString::MakeUpper()** function on an ANSI character string. Figure 7-3 shows CHAR1 as displayed on the screen. The first line of text in the client area is the original string. The last word is "Aîné," meaning "aged" in French. This word has two accented characters. The second line shows the effect of using **::AnsiUpperBuff()** to convert the string to the right of the function name to uppercase. Note that the accented characters are correctly converted. **::AnsiLowerBuff()** is then called to convert the string to entirely lowercase.

The last line in Figure 7-3 shows a programming error. In this case, the **CString::MakeUpper()** function is used to convert the string back to uppercase. Note that the two accented characters are not converted. **CString::MakeUpper()** assumes that the two accented characters must be graphic symbols, as their codes do not fall in the A-Z, a-z range. The bottom line is: Do not use the ASCII string conversion functions in a Windows program!

Listing 7-4 shows the CHAR1.CPP program file. All of the character conversion functions are used in the processing of WM_PAINT messages to repaint the screen. *cStart[]* contains the string "Accented chars here: "Aîné." The accented characters were input into the program file using the Windows Charmap application that comes with Windows 3.1. The output to the device context using **CDC::TextOut()**.

The character conversions to uppercase and lowercase are done using the **::AnsiUpperBuff()** and **::AnsiLowerBuff()** functions. Note that the Windows **::lstrlen()** function is used to determine the length of the string, so that the character conversion functions know how many characters to change. **::lstrlen()** works by finding the first null character (zero) in the string, so the strings must be null-terminated for **::lstrlen()** to work properly. The *cStart[]* string has an implied null character, as any string enclosed in double quotes will have a null character added to the end by the C++ compiler.

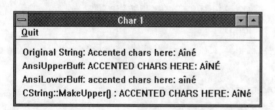

Figure 7-3 The CHAR1 Program Window

Listing 7-4 CHAR1.CPP

```cpp
// char1.cpp                 example of ANSI string conversions

#include <afxwin.h>       // class library header file
#include <strstrea.h>     // streams header file
#include "char1.h"        // header file for resource data
#include "char1.hpp"      // header file for this program

CTheApp theApp ;          // create one CTheApp object - runs program

BOOL CTheApp::InitInstance ()    // override default InitInstance()
{
    m_pMainWnd = new CMainWindow () ;         // create a main window
    m_pMainWnd->ShowWindow (m_nCmdShow) ;     // make it visible
    m_pMainWnd->UpdateWindow () ;             // paint center
    return TRUE ;
}

CMainWindow::CMainWindow ()       // constructor for window
{
    Create (NULL, "Char 1", WS_OVERLAPPEDWINDOW, rectDefault,
        NULL, "MyMenu") ;
}

BEGIN_MESSAGE_MAP (CMainWindow, CFrameWnd)
    ON_COMMAND (IDM_QUIT, OnExit)            // "Quit" menu item
    ON_WM_PAINT ()                           // process paint message
END_MESSAGE_MAP ()

void CMainWindow::OnExit ()               // respond to menu item "Quit"
{
    this->DestroyWindow () ;               // destroy main window,
}                                          // this stops application

void CMainWindow::OnPaint ()     // show string 4 times
{
    char cStart [] = "Accented chars here: Aine" ;
    char cBuf [128] ;          // 128 byte char buffer
    CPaintDC dc (this) ;       // construct client area dc
                // make cBuf an ostrstream object
    ostrstream bufStream (cBuf, sizeof (cBuf)) ;

                // make complete output string
    bufStream << "Original String: " << cStart; // copy to cBuf
    dc.TextOut (10, 10, cBuf, bufStream.pcount ()) ;// display

    ::AnsiUpperBuff (cStart, ::lstrlen (cStart)) ;  // uppercase
    bufStream.seekp (0) ;         // go back to beginning of bufStream
    bufStream << "AnsiUpperBuff: " << cStart ;
    dc.TextOut (10, 30, cBuf, bufStream.pcount ()) ;// display

    ::AnsiLowerBuff (cStart, ::lstrlen (cStart)) ;  // lowercase
    bufStream.seekp (0) ;         // go back to beginning of bufStream
    bufStream << "AnsiLowerBuff: " << cStart ;
    dc.TextOut (10, 50, cBuf, bufStream.pcount ()) ;// display
```

```
        // now do programming error, use MakeUpper() on ANSI string
CString csTest (cStart) ;     // make CString from char []
csTest.MakeUpper () ;         // convert uppercase
bufStream.seekp (0) ;         // go back to beginning of bufStream
bufStream << "CString::MakeUpper() : " << csTest ;
dc.TextOut (10, 70, cBuf, bufStream.pcount ()) ;// display
}
```

At the end of the **CMainWindow::OnPaint()** function, the *cStart* character buffer is converted into a **CString** object to demonstrate the problems with the **CString::MakeUpper()** function. The **CString** object *csTest* is created and initialized to contain *cStart* in a single line of code:

```
CString csTest (cStart) ;
```

This is a shorthand constructor function for creating a **CString** object, which accomplishes the same thing as the more explicit constructor followed by initialization:

```
CString csTest ;          // constructor
csTest = cStart ;         // initialize with character data
```

Once the **CString** object is created, the **CString::MakeUpper()** function can be used to convert its contents (incorrectly) to uppercase.

Listings 7-5 to 7-8 show the support files for CHAR1.CPP. The program's icon image is shown in Figure 7-4.

KEYBOARD MESSAGE PROCESSING

Now that you have seen the underlying ANSI character sets, we can turn our attention to how characters are generated in the first place. The most important source of character input is, of course, the keyboard. While pressing a key is a simple matter for the user, the process by which that keypress becomes character data recognized by a Windows application program is fairly complex. We will examine each step in the process.

Figure 7-4 CHAR1.ICO Icon Image

Listing 7-5 CHAR1.HPP Header File

```
// char1.hpp    header file for char1.cpp

class CMainWindow : public CFrameWnd    // derive a main window class
{
public:
    CMainWindow () ;                    // declare a constructor
private:
    void OnExit () ;                    // message processing functions
    void OnPaint () ;

    DECLARE_MESSAGE_MAP()               // prepare for message processing
} ;

class CTheApp : public CWinApp         // derive an application class
{
public:
    BOOL InitInstance () ;             // declare new InitInstance()
} ;
```

Listing 7-6 CHAR1.H Resource ID Header File

```
// char1.h  header file for resource ID numbers

#define IDM_QUIT        10       // menu item ID numbers
```

Listing 7-7 CHAR1.RC Resource Script File

```
// char1.rc  resource script file

#include <afxres.h>
#include "char1.h"

AFX_IDI_STD_FRAME   ICON    char1.ico   // the program's icon

MyMenu MENU                             // define the menu
{
    MENUITEM "&Quit",                   IDM_QUIT
}
```

Listing 7-8 CHAR1.DEF Module Definition File

```
NAME           char1
DESCRIPTION    'char1 C++ program'
EXETYPE        WINDOWS
STUB           'WINSTUB.EXE'
CODE           PRELOAD MOVEABLE
DATA           PRELOAD MOVEABLE MULTIPLE
HEAPSIZE       1024
STACKSIZE      5120
```

Windows was designed to support different types of keyboards for different languages, with different locations on the keyboard for normal and accented characters. When you install Windows, you pick a language. The Windows installation program then takes a keyboard translation table from the installation disks, and copies the data to your Windows subdirectory. Your program can find out which language was installed using the **::GetKBCodePage()** function.

When you depress a key, Windows sends a WM_KEYDOWN message to the window with the input focus. Recall that the main program window with the input focus is the window with the highlighted caption bar. When the key is released, Windows sends a WM_KEYUP message to the window. The **CWnd::OnKeyDown()** and **CWnd::OnKeyUp()** message response functions will receive the "virtual key code" for the key pressed and released as a parameter passed to the message. This key code is sent with the message data in order to encode which key was activated.

Virtual key codes are one of the ways Windows makes sure that a program written for one type of computer keyboard will function properly on another type. The idea is that no matter what type of hardware is being used, the virtual key code for the Ⓐ will have the same value. The virtual codes are all defined in WINDOWS.H, and summarized in Appendix B, *Virtual Key Codes*, of this book.

The virtual key codes for the letter keys and the numbers at the top of the keyboard have the same value as the ANSI character set. You can just use the letter code, such as 'A' or 'b,' for these virtual keys. The other keys have names like VK_F1 for the (F1) function key, VK_TAB for the (TAB) key, VK_CONTROL for the (CONTROL) key, and so on. The numeric keypad keys have virtual codes that differ from those of the corresponding number keys at the top of the keyboard. VK_NUMPAD0 is the code for the zero key on the numeric keypad key, while '0' is the code for the zero key at the top of the main keyboard group. The only key that does not have a virtual key code is (ALT). The status of the (ALT) key is passed with a parameter sent to the **CWnd::OnKeyDown()** and **CWnd::OnKeyUp()** message response functions.

Using the virtual key codes, you can figure out what the user is doing with the keyboard. Listing 7-9 shows a typical example that checks for the letter Ⓐ key, the (TAB) key, and the (SHIFT) key when a WM_KEYDOWN message is processed. The virtual key code for the key depressed is passed as the *nVKey* parameter to the **CWnd::OnKeyDown()** function. The **CWnd::OnKeyUp()** message response function (for the WM_KEYUP message) is passed the same parameters as **CWnd::OnKeyDown()**.

Listing 7-9 Processing WM_KEYDOWN Messages

```
void CMainWindow::OnKeyDown (UINT nVKey, UINT nRepCnt, UINT nFlags)
{
    switch (nVKey)
    {
        case ('A'):          // letter A key
            // do logic for A key
            break ;
        case (VK_TAB):       // tab key
            // do logic for tab key
            break ;
        case (VK_SHIFT):     // either shift key
            // do logic for shift key
            break ;
        // etc.
    }
}
```

The **CWnd::OnKeyDown()** and **CWnd::OnKeyUp()** message response functions provide two other parameters. The *nRepCnt* parameter encodes the number of times the keystroke was repeated due to the user holding down the key. Windows will store up a series of repeated keystrokes and send a single WM_KEYDOWN / WM_KEYUP message pair with the *nRepCnt* value encoding the number of repeated keystrokes. The *nFlags* parameter encodes additional information about the keyboard event as a coded block of bit values. Table 7-3 summarizes the data format. Normally, you will use the *nFlags* value to determine if the (ALT) key was depressed. You might also use *nFlags* to distinguish between the right and left (SHIFT) keys. The OEM scan code for the two keys is different, although Windows gives them both the same VK_SHIFT virtual key code. The standard OEM scan code for the left (SHIFT) key is 0x2A hexadecimal, and 0x36 hexadecimal for the right (SHIFT) key.

Bits	Meaning
0-7	The keyboard OEM scan code.
8	1 if an extended key, such as a function key or a key on the numeric keypad.
9-12	Reserved.
13	1 if the (ALT) key was held down when the key was pressed, 0 if not.
14	1 if the key was down before the message was sent, 0 if not.
15	1 if the key is being released, 0 if the key is being pressed.

Table 7-3 nFlags Data for CWnd::OnKeyDown() and CWnd::OnKeyUp()

The WM_CHAR Message

The WM_KEYDOWN and WM_KEYUP messages have a limitation. The virtual key code for the letter (A) key is the same whether the user is typing an upper-case or lowercase letter. You could figure out what the user is doing by tracking whether the (SHIFT) keys are depressed or not, but Windows provides an easier way. The **CWinApp** class includes built-in code that detects keyboard actions that translate to an ANSI character, and then generates a WM_CHAR message for the character. The first parameter sent to the **CWnd::OnChar()** response function is the ANSI character code for the key typed. This is handy, as the ANSI code is almost always what you will want to display. Function keys and other keys that do not have an ANSI character equivalent do not generate a WM_CHAR message. You will pick those up with the **CWnd::OnKeyDown()** and **CWnd::OnKeyUp()** message response functions using the virtual key code. **CWnd::OnChar()** uses the same coding for the *nRepCnt* and *nFlags* parameters (Table 7-3). You probably will not find *nFlags* very useful with this message.

If you monitor the messages being sent to an application when a key is pressed (you can do this with the SPY application) you will see the following sequence of messages:

WM_KEYDOWN	The key is depressed.
WM_CHAR	The ANSI character (if there is one).
WM_KEYUP	The key is released.

Most of the time you will ignore the WM_KEYUP messages. WM_KEYDOWN is processed for the function keys, the (CONTROL) key, and other virtual keys that do not have ANSI equivalents. WM_CHAR is used for the ANSI characters.

System Key Messages and Dead Characters

There are situations when a different series of messages is sent for keyboard actions. One occurs when the user has the (ALT) key down, or when no window on the system has the input focus. In this case, the system key messages are sent. They are just like the normal character messages, and use the same coding of the parameters sent to the message response functions. The sequence of messages is:

WM_SYSKEYDOWN	The key is depressed with (ALT) down.
WM_SYSCHAR	The ANSI character (if there is one).
WM_SYSKEYUP	The key is released.

With the (ALT) key down, the keystroke signals some special function. Usually, you will only use the WM_SYSKEYDOWN message to determine which virtual key is depressed, and ignore the WM_SYSCHAR and WM_SYSKEYUP messages. Note that the (CONTROL) key does *not* generate WM_SYSKEYDOWN and WM_SYSKEYUP messages.

One last message is worth noting: WM_DEADCHAR. If the user installed any language other than English, the keyboard logic will include special combinations to generate accent characters. For example, the French accent circumflex (^) is obtained by pressing (CONTROL)-(I), and then the letter key. This will only work if French was chosen as the default language when Windows was installed. Windows will then send the following series of messages:

WM_KEYDOWN	Depressed an accent key.
WM_DEADCHAR	The character message for the accent.
WM_KEYUP	Released the accent key.
WM_KEYDOWN	Depressed the letter key.
WM_CHAR	The character code for the accented letter.
WM_KEYUP	Released the letter key.

The phrase "dead character" brings all sorts of gruesome images to mind, but all it means is that the keystroke does not result in a visible character. The dead character just modifies the next character typed, to add an accent. You can usually ignore the WM_DEADCHAR message. The **CWinApp** class logic automatically picks the right ANSI character including the accent, and sends it with the WM_CHAR message. Impossible accents for the language, such as an accent circumflex over a consonant, do not have ANSI character codes. There is even a WM_SYSDEADCHAR message for accent keys depressed with the (ALT) key down.

Ignored Messages

You have probably noticed in the discussion on keyboard messages that most of the messages sent to the program are ignored. For example, if the user types the letter A, the program will process the WM_CHAR message, but it will probably ignore the WM_KEYDOWN and WM_KEYUP messages. If you move the mouse cursor across the program's client area, the program may receive fifty or more WM_MOUSEMOVE messages, but will probably ignore all of them (unless your program happens to be a paint program in a painting mode, or something similar). Why does Windows bother sending all of these messages?

The answer lies in the basic design philosophy behind Windows. Windows programs are expected to sit there and wait for messages. The vast majority of the messages sent to an application are "passed through" without any action. The Windows environment has no way of knowing which messages will be significant to any particular program at any particular time. Windows just sends all of the messages and lets the application program decide which ones are significant and which ones to ignore.

In an MFC-based application, the **CWinApp** class contains the logic that fetches messages from Windows. If you insert a message map entry, messages are routed to your message processing function. If there is no message map entry, **CWinApp** will either take care of the default action for a message (such as sizing the program window if the program's thick main window border is dragged to a new location) or **CWinApp** will ignore the message and return control back to Windows. As a Windows programmer, you will decide which messages to process, and you can safely ignore all of the other messages that will be "passed through" your application.

Implementing a Simple Keyboard Interface

Let's put our knowledge of keyboard messages to work with a simple program that allows you to type a line of text. Figure 7-5 shows the KEYBD1 program in action. When the user types at the keyboard, blue characters appear in the client area. The only editing feature is the (BACKSPACE) key. Pressing this key erases the last letter typed. The (ENTER) key is ignored, so typing produces a maximum of one line of text. We will improve on this program in the next two examples, but KEYBD1 provides the minimum logic for keyboard input.

The KEYBD1.HPP header file (Listing 7-10) declares a **CString** object named *cString*, which will store the characters that the user typed. The integer *nTypedChars* is declared to keep track of the number of characters typed. Note that KEYBD1 will be processing WM_CHAR, WM_KEYDOWN, and WM_PAINT messages, so the **OnChar()**, **OnKeyDown()**, and **OnPaint()** message response functions are all declared in the **CMainWindow** class definition.

Listing 7-11 shows the KEYBD1.CPP program. Typed input is detected using the WM_CHAR message from Windows, which ends up being mapped to the **CMainWindow::OnChar()** message processing function. The **::IsCharAlphaNumeric()** function and the **CMain::IsAnsiPunc()** functions are used to

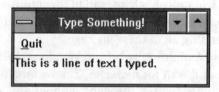

Figure 7-5 KEYBD1 Program Window

Listing 7-10 KEYBD1.HPP Header File

```
// keybd1.hpp    header file for keybd1.cpp

#define MAXCHARS    256

class CMainWindow : public CFrameWnd    // derive a main window class
{
public:
    CMainWindow () ;                     // declare a constructor
private:
    CString cString ;                    // char buffer to hold typing
    int nTypedChars ;                    // number of chars in buffer
    BOOL IsAnsiPunc (int nChar) ;        // helper function
    void OnExit () ;                     // message processing functions
    void OnPaint () ;
    void OnChar (UINT nChar, UINT nRepCnt, UINT nFlags) ;
    void OnKeyDown (UINT nVKey, UINT nRepCnt, UINT nFlags) ;

    DECLARE_MESSAGE_MAP()                // prepare for message processing
} ;

class CTheApp : public CWinApp          // derive an application class
{
public:
    BOOL InitInstance () ;              // declare new InitInstance()
} ;
```

verify that the character passed with the WM_CHAR message is printable, before adding it to *cString*. **::IsCharAlphaNumeric()** is one of the global Windows functions. **CMain::IsAnsiPunc()** is defined in KEYBD1.CPP at the end of the listing, and just checks whether the character is in the range of printable punctuation characters in the ANSI character set.

Note that the **CMainWindow::OnChar()** function in KEYBD1.CPP does not output characters to the window's client area. Instead, **CMainWindow::OnChar()** calls **CWnd::Invalidate()**, forcing Windows to send a WM_PAINT message to the program. This WM_PAINT message is processed in the **CMainWindow::OnPaint()** function, which outputs the *cString* character string to the client area device context. The advantage of this approach is that the client area is always repainted with the correct character string, including after the window is covered and uncovered, or repainted after the window is resized.

The only editing feature implemented in KEYBD1.CPP is the use of the (BACKSPACE) key to delete the last character in the string. The (BACKSPACE) key does not equate to an ANSI character, so a WM_CHAR message is not sent when the (BACKSPACE) key is depressed. KEYBD1.CPP processes the WM_KEYDOWN message to check if the (BACKSPACE) key has been used. The logic in the

Listing 7-11 KEYBD1.CPP

```cpp
// keybd1.cpp                example of ANSI string conversions

#include <afxwin.h>      // class library header file
#include <strstrea.h>    // streams header file
#include "keybd1.h"      // header file for resource data
#include "keybd1.hpp"    // header file for this program

CTheApp theApp ;          // create one CTheApp object - runs program

BOOL CTheApp::InitInstance ()    // override default InitInstance()
{
    m_pMainWnd = new CMainWindow () ;        // create a main window
    m_pMainWnd->ShowWindow (m_nCmdShow) ;    // make it visible
    m_pMainWnd->UpdateWindow () ;            // paint center
    return TRUE ;
}


CMainWindow::CMainWindow ()      // constructor for window
{
    Create (NULL, "Type Something!", WS_OVERLAPPEDWINDOW, rectDefault,
        NULL, "MyMenu") ;
    nTypedChars = 0 ;           // initialize
}

BEGIN_MESSAGE_MAP (CMainWindow, CFrameWnd)
    ON_COMMAND (IDM_QUIT, OnExit)           // "Quit" menu item
    ON_WM_PAINT ()                          // process paint message
    ON_WM_CHAR ()                           // char input
    ON_WM_KEYDOWN ()                        // and keyboard input
END_MESSAGE_MAP ()

void CMainWindow::OnExit ()               // respond to menu item "Quit"
{
    this->DestroyWindow () ;      // destroy main window,
}                                 // this stops application

void CMainWindow::OnChar (UINT nChar, UINT nRepCnt, UINT nFlags)
{
    if (nTypedChars == MAXCHARS - 1)// do not exceed max length
        return ;
    else if (IsCharAlphaNumeric (nChar) || IsAnsiPunc (nChar))
    {
        cString += (char) nChar ;    // add typed char to string
        nTypedChars++ ;
        this->Invalidate (TRUE) ;    // force repaint of client area
    }
}
```

```
void CMainWindow::OnKeyDown (UINT nVKey, UINT nRepCnt, UINT nFlags)
{
    if (nVKey == VK_BACK && nTypedChars > 0)      // backspace key
    {
        int nLong = cString.GetLength () ;        // find length
        cString = cString.Left (nLong - 1) ;      // drop last char
        nTypedChars-- ;
        this->Invalidate (TRUE) ;                 // force repaint
    }
}

void CMainWindow::OnPaint ()            // show string of typed chars
{
    CPaintDC dc (this) ;                     // construct client area dc
    dc.TextOut (0, 0, cString, nTypedChars) ; // display
}


    // returns TRUE if character is punctuation, FALSE otherwise
BOOL CMainWindow::IsAnsiPunc (int nChar)
{
    if ((nChar >= ' ' && nChar <= '@')
        || (nChar >= '[' && nChar <= ''')
        || (nChar >= '(' && nChar <='~')
        || (nChar >= 0xA0 && nChar <= 0xBF))  // ANSI symbols
        return TRUE ;
    else
        return FALSE ;
}
```

CMainWindow::OnKeyDown() function checks if the virtual key code of the latest keypress matches VK_BACK, and if there is at least one visible character to delete. If both conditions are met the string is shortened by one character using the **CString::Left()** function. **CString::Left()** returns a **CString** object containing characters from the start (left side) of another **CString** object. In KEYBD1.CPP, *cString* is shortened in place using the **CString::Left()** function and the assignment (=) statement:

```
cString = cString.Left (nLong - 1) ;
```

This statement copies the substring of *cString* back into *cString* itself. The result is that *cString* no longer contains the last character. The **CWnd::Invalidate()** function is again called to force a WM_PAINT message. When the **CMainWindow::OnPaint()** function repaints *cString* on the screen, the shortened string is displayed.

Listings 7-12 to 7-14 show the remaining support files for KEYBD1.CPP. The program's icon is shown in Figure 7-6.

Listing 7-12 KEYBD1.H Resource ID Header File

```
// keybd1.h  header file for resource ID numbers

#define IDM_QUIT        10      // menu item ID numbers
```

Listing 7-13 KEYBD1.RC Resource Script File

```
// keybd1.rc  resource script file

#include <afxres.h>
#include "keybd1.h"

AFX_IDI_STD_FRAME  ICON    keybd1.ico   // the program's icon

MyMenu MENU                             // define the menu
{
    MENUITEM "&Quit",              IDM_QUIT
}
```

Listing 7-14 KEYBD1.DEF Module Definition File

```
NAME            keybd1
DESCRIPTION     'keybd1 C++ program'
EXETYPE         WINDOWS
STUB            'WINSTUB.EXE'
CODE            PRELOAD MOVEABLE
DATA            PRELOAD MOVEABLE MULTIPLE
HEAPSIZE        1024
STACKSIZE       5120
```

Figure 7-6 KEYBD1.ICO Icon Image

SELECTING A STOCK FONT

KEYBD1.CPP provides a good outline for how a Windows program handles text input. We can build on this example to explore other aspects of processing text, including changing the character fonts and managing the caret to help guide editing. These improvements will be added in two steps. The next program, FONT1, will add new fonts to our KEYBD1 example. The chapter closes with FONT2, which adds control of the caret to the example.

There are two basic kinds of fonts that you can use in developing a Windows program. The simplest to use are the stock fonts, which are always available within Windows. The stock fonts are shown in Figure 7-7. Windows uses the SYSTEM_FONT as the default font when a device context is first created. The OEM_FIXED_FONT is sometimes useful because it uses the OEM character set, rather than the ANSI set. The OEM character set can be used to display file names from DOS, rather than converting the file names from the OEM to ANSI character sets before display. The ANSI_VAR_FONT is handy as a compact font if space is limited. The DEVICE_DEFAULT_FONT is most significant with printers, which may have a built-in font that is faster to output. Printing under Windows is described in Chapter 14, *Printing*.

Like stock pens and brushes, stock fonts are accessed with the **CDC::SelectStockObject()** function. In the KEYBD1 program, we did not select a font, so the default font SYSTEM_FONT was used for character output. This is a variable-pitch font, meaning that the characters are not all the same width. For example, with variable-pitch fonts the letter "I" takes up less room horizontally than the letter "M." Fixed-pitch fonts use the same spacing between characters regardless of the letter being output. Variable fonts are easier to read and take up less space. Fixed fonts are more appropriate for tables where numerals and characters need to be aligned.

Using Logical Fonts

Besides the stock fonts, Windows also comes with separate font files that define the characteristics of characters written in a number of different styles and sizes. You can find the font files in your Windows system directory, usually C:\WINDOWS\SYSTEM. Font files have the extension .FON, or .FOT for True-Type fonts introduced with Windows 3.1. These files contain detailed descriptions of each character. You can install new fonts using the Windows Control Panel application.

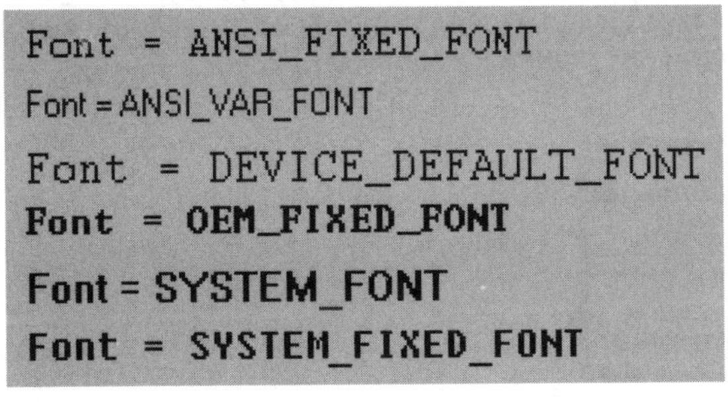

```
Font = ANSI_FIXED_FONT
Font = ANSI_VAR_FONT
Font = DEVICE_DEFAULT_FONT
Font = OEM_FIXED_FONT
Font = SYSTEM_FONT
Font = SYSTEM_FIXED_FONT
```

Figure 7-7 Windows Stock Fonts

The MFC classes provide the **CFont** class for creating and manipulating font objects. This class has few functions because its main purpose is to allow you to create fonts. The function you will use the most is **CFont::CreateFont()**, which creates a logical font of any size based on a long list of parameters passed to the function. Listing 7-15 shows a typical call to **CFont::CreateFont()**.

The font created by the **CFont::CreateFont()** function call in Listing 7-15 is shown in Figure 7-8. The characters are interpolated to a size of 36 pixels high based on the Roman font that is supplied with Windows. This results in a variable-pitched font, based on the ANSI character set.

The sizing of the characters for both height and width is in *logical units*. With the default units of a device context, logical units are equal to pixels (dots on the screen). We will see in Chapter 13, *The Device Context*, that other systems of units can be used. This will allow you to size fonts and other graphical objects in inches, millimeters, or printer's units. For now we will just use pixels. The vertical measurements of a font are shown in Figure 7-9.

Fourteen parameters are passed to the **CFont::CreateFont()** function. The example in Listing 7-15 is typical in that many of the options are set to default values, usually zero. You can go wild with **CFont::CreateFont()** and make fonts with characters lying on their sides, going upward on the device context instead of left-to-right, etc. These changes are done using the parameters passed to **CFont::CreateFont()**, which are described in Table 7-4.

Text Metrics

Because of the way the **CFont::CreateFont()** function generates a logical font using stored font data modified by the **CFont::CreateFont()** parameters, you

Listing 7-15 Creating a Font

```
CFont Roman36 ;
Roman36.CreateFont (36, 0, 0, 0, FW_NORMAL, 0, 0, 0, ANSI_CHARSET,
        OUT_DEFAULT_PRECIS, CLIP_DEFAULT_PRECIS, DEFAULT_QUALITY,
        VARIABLE_PITCH | FF_ROMAN, "Roman") ;
```

Figure 7-8 A Logical Roman Font

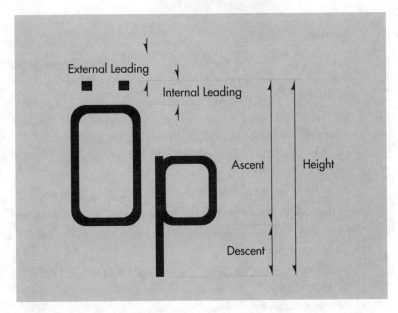

Figure 7-9 Font Measurements

BOOL **CFont::CreateFont** (int *nHeight*, int *nWidth*, int *nEscapement*, int *nOrientation*, int *nWeight*, BYTE *cItalic*, BYTE *cUnderline*, BYTE *cStrikeOut*, BYTE *cCharSet*, BYTE *cOutputPrecision*, BYTE *cClipPrecision*, BYTE *cQuality*, BYTE *cPitchAndFamily*, LPSTR *lpFacename*) ;

Parameter	Meaning
nHeight	int: The desired height of the characters, including internal leading, excluding external leading, in logical units. To set the ascent size, rather than the total height, make this value negative. The absolute value will then be used to set the ascent size.
nWidth	int: The desired width of the characters in logical units. Normally set to 0, which allows Windows to match the width to the height. Positive values force that width, changing the character's aspect ratio.
nEscapement	int: Specifies the orientation of the next character output relative to the previous one in tenths of a degree. Normally set to 0. Set to 900 to have all the characters go upward from the first character, 1800 to write backwards, or 2700 to write each character from the top down. See Figure 7-10.

Table 7-4 CFont::CreateFont() Parameters

continued on next page

continued from previous page

Parameter	Meaning
nOrientation	int: Specifies how much the character should be rotated when output in tenths of a degree. Set to 900 to have all the characters lying on their backs, 1800 for upside-down writing, etc. See Figure 7-10.
nWeight	int: Sets the thickness of each character. The units are arbitrary, with the values of FW_NORMAL (400) for normal characters and FW_BOLD (700) for boldface defined in WINDOWS.H. WINDOWS.H has eight other weights defined.
cItalic	BYTE: TRUE to specify italic characters, FALSE (zero) for normal.
cUnderline	BYTE: TRUE to specify underlined characters, FALSE (zero) for normal.
cStrikeOut	BYTE: TRUE to specify characters with a line through the center, FALSE (zero) for normal.
cCharSet	BYTE: The character set of the font. This can be ANSI_CHARSET, SYMBOL_CHARSET, OEM_CHARSET or (with Japanese versions of Windows) SHIFTJIS_CHARSET.
cOutputPrecision	BYTE: Set equal to OUT_DEFAULT_PRECIS (zero). This parameter does not do anything.
cClipPrecision	BYTE: Set equal to CLIP_DEFAULT_PRECIS.
cQuality	BYTE: Can be either DRAFT_QUALITY, PROOF_QUALITY, or DEFAULT_QUALITY (the most common choice). PROOF_QUALITY forces the closest match to the loaded font data, which may change the font size if the specified size is not available.
cPitchAndFamily	BYTE: Two values combined with the C language binary OR operator (I). The two low-order bits specify the font pitch. This can be either DEFAULT_PITCH, FIXED_PITCH or VARIABLE_PITCH. The four high-order bits specify the font family. This can be any of the following: FF_DECORATIVE, FF_DONTCARE, FF_MODERN, FF_ROMAN, FF_SCRIPT, or FF_SWISS. For example, use the combination DEFAULT_PITCH I FF_ROMAN to create a Roman typeface, using the character pitch of the nearest matching font installed on the system. This will be a variable-pitch font if the normal Windows Times Roman typeface is installed.
lpFacename	LPSTR: A pointer to a null-terminated string that specifies the name of the font data. The maximum length of the name is LF_FACESIZE, which is defined in WINDOWS.H as 32.

Table 7-4 CFont::CreateFont() Parameters

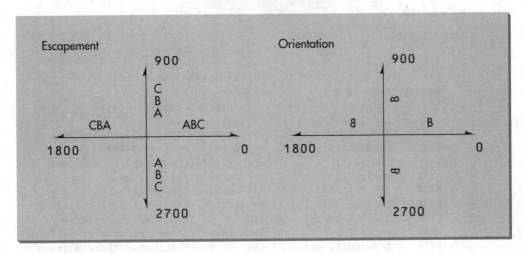

Figure 7-10 Character Orientation and Escapement

will not know all of the dimensions of a font after you create it. The MFC classes provide the **CDC::GetTextMetrics()** function to find out details about a font. **CDC::GetTextMetrics()** determines the characteristics of the font currently selected into the device context, and copies the data into a data structure called TEXTMETRIC. The TEXTMETRIC structure is defined in WINDOWS.H and shown in Listing 7-16.

That is probably more information about a font than you will ever need. The most common reason to call **CDC::GetTextMetrics()** is to find the height of the font's characters. The height can be used to set line spacing, size the caret, or proportion other objects, such as buttons. A typical call to **CDC::GetTextMetrics()** is shown in Listing 7-17. In this case, the spacing between lines is determined by adding the character height and the external leading height.

Putting Fonts to Work

Our next program, FONT1, improves on KEYBD1 by allowing a choice of three fonts for output of the text that the user types. Figure 7-11a shows output using the stock ANSI variable font. Figure 7-11b shows the same text string using a logical font based on the ROMAN.FON data.

The FONT1 program is similar to the KEYBD1 program we just examined, but adds logic for choosing and displaying text the user types using different fonts. Listing 7-18 shows the FONT1.HPP header file. Note that the **CFont** object *Roman36* is declared, along with the integer *nFontChoice*, which tracks which font was most recently selected.

Listing 7-16 The TEXTMETRIC Structure

```
typedef struct tagTEXTMETRIC
{
    int     tmHeight;              // character height
    int     tmAscent;             // ascent height
    int     tmDescent;            // descent height
    int     tmInternalLeading;    // internal leading height
    int     tmExternalLeading;    // external leading height
    int     tmAveCharWidth;       // average width of a character
    int     tmMaxCharWidth;       // widest character width
    int     tmWeight;             // weight (thickness) of the font
    BYTE    tmItalic;             // nonzero for italics
    BYTE    tmUnderlined;         // nonzero for underlined
    BYTE    tmStruckOut;        // nonzero for strike through characters
    BYTE    tmFirstChar;        // code value for first character defined
    BYTE    tmLastChar;         // code value for last character defined
    BYTE    tmDefaultChar;      // char to substitute for those missing
    BYTE    tmBreakChar;        // word break character - usually a space
    BYTE    tmPitchAndFamily;    // pitch and family code
    BYTE    tmCharSet;          // either ANSI_CHARSET, SYMBOL_CHARSET,
                                // SHIFTJIS_CHARSET or OEM_CHARSET
    int     tmOverhang;         // extra width allowed for bold, etc
    int     tmDigitizedAspectX; // ratio of the X and Y aspects
    int     tmDigitizedAspectY; // is the aspect ratio for which the
                                // font was originally designed
} TEXTMETRIC;
```

Listing 7-17 Using the GetTextMetrics() Function to Find Line Spacing

```
void CMainWindow::OnPaint ()          // show string of typed chars
{
    TEXTMETRIC  tm ;                  // structure to hold tm data
    CPaintDC dc (this) ;              // construct client area dc
    dc.GetTextMetrics (&tm) ;         // get text size data
    int nLineSpacing = tm.tmHeight + tm.tmExternalLeading ;
    // other program lines
}
```

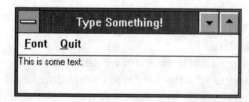

Figure 7-11a FONT1 Program with Stock
ANSI Variable Font

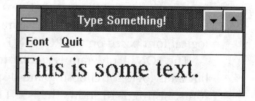

Figure 7-11b FONT1 Program with a Logical
36-Unit Roman Font

Listing 7-18 FONT1.HPP Header File

```
// font1.hpp     header file for font1.cpp

#define MAXCHARS    256

class CMainWindow : public CFrameWnd    // derive a main window class
{
public:
    CMainWindow () ;                    // declare a constructor
private:
    CFont Roman36 ;                     // roman logical font object
    int nFontChoice ;                   // track currently selected font
    CString cString ;                   // char buffer to hold typing
    int nTypedChars ;                   // number of chars in buffer
    BOOL IsAnsiPunc (int nChar) ;       // helper function

    void OnPaint () ;                   // message processing functions
    void OnChar (UINT nChar, UINT nRepCnt, UINT nFlags) ;
    void OnKeyDown (UINT nVKey, UINT nRepCnt, UINT nFlags) ;

    void OnExit () ;                    // menu items - define here
    void OnAnsi () ;
    void OnOem () ;
    void OnRoman () ;

    DECLARE_MESSAGE_MAP()               // prepare for message processing
} ;

class CTheApp : public CWinApp    // derive an application class
{
public:
    BOOL InitInstance () ;              // declare new InitInstance()
} ;
```

Listing 7-19 shows the FONT1.CPP program file. The **CFont::CreateFont()** function is called in the main window constructor function to create a 36-pixel high "Roman" font. This font is not displayed unless the user selects the "Roman Font" menu item, which is mapped to the **CMainWindow::OnRoman()** function. **CMainWindow::OnRoman()** sets the *nFontChoice* variable equal to IDM_ROMAN and then calls **CWnd::Invalidate()** to force repainting of the client area.

As in KEYBD1.CPP, all of the character display logic in FONT1.CPP is in the **CMainWindow::OnPaint()** function. The color of any text displayed is changed to blue using the **CDC::SetTextColor()** function before a font is selected. The text color will apply regardless of the font type selected. A font is then selected based on the *nFontChoice* value. The stock fonts

Listing 7-19 FONT1.CPP

```cpp
// font1.cpp                    example using a logical font

#include <afxwin.h>      // class library header file
#include <strstrea.h>    // streams header file
#include "font1.h"       // header file for resource data
#include "font1.hpp"     // header file for this program


CTheApp theApp ;            // create one CTheApp object - runs program

BOOL CTheApp::InitInstance ()    // override default InitInstance()
{
    m_pMainWnd = new CMainWindow () ;        // create a main window
    m_pMainWnd->ShowWindow (m_nCmdShow) ;    // make it visible
    m_pMainWnd->UpdateWindow () ;            // paint center
    return TRUE ;
}

CMainWindow::CMainWindow ()              // constructor for window
{
    Create (NULL, "Type Something!", WS_OVERLAPPEDWINDOW, rectDefault,
        NULL, "MyMenu") ;
    nTypedChars = 0 ;                // initialize private data
    nFontChoice = IDM_ANSI ;         // and font object
    Roman36.CreateFont (36, 0, 0, 0, FW_NORMAL, 0, 0, 0, ANSI_CHARSET,
        OUT_DEFAULT_PRECIS, CLIP_DEFAULT_PRECIS, DEFAULT_QUALITY,
        VARIABLE_PITCH | FF_ROMAN, "Roman") ;
}

BEGIN_MESSAGE_MAP (CMainWindow, CFrameWnd)
    ON_COMMAND (IDM_QUIT, OnExit)           // menu item response
    ON_COMMAND (IDM_ANSI, OnAnsi)
    ON_COMMAND (IDM_OEM, OnOem)
    ON_COMMAND (IDM_ROMAN, OnRoman)
    ON_WM_PAINT ()                          // process paint message
    ON_WM_CHAR ()                           // char input
    ON_WM_KEYDOWN ()                        // other keyboard input
END_MESSAGE_MAP ()

void CMainWindow::OnExit ()         // respond to menu item "Quit"
{
    this->DestroyWindow () ;        // destroy main window,
}                                   // this stops application

void CMainWindow::OnAnsi ()         // user selected ANSI font
{
    nFontChoice = IDM_ANSI ;
    this->Invalidate () ;           // force repaint
}
```

```
void CMainWindow::OnOem ()               // user selected OEM font
{
    nFontChoice = IDM_OEM ;
    this->Invalidate () ;                // force repaint
}

void CMainWindow::OnRoman ()             // user selected roman font
{
    nFontChoice = IDM_ROMAN ;
    this->Invalidate () ;                // force repaint
}

void CMainWindow::OnChar (UINT nChar, UINT nRepCnt, UINT nFlags)
{
    if (nTypedChars == MAXCHARS - 1)// do not overflow buffer
        return ;
    else if (IsCharAlphaNumeric (nChar) || IsAnsiPunc (nChar))
    {
        cString += (char) nChar ;    // add typed char to string
        nTypedChars++ ;
        this->Invalidate (TRUE) ;    // force repaint of client area
    }
}

void CMainWindow::OnKeyDown (UINT nVKey, UINT nRepCnt, UINT nFlags)
{
    if (nVKey == VK_BACK && nTypedChars > 0)     // backspace key
    {
        int nLong = cString.GetLength () ;       // find length
        cString = cString.Left (nLong - 1) ;     // drop last char
        nTypedChars-- ;
        this->Invalidate (TRUE) ;                // force repaint
    }
}

void CMainWindow::OnPaint ()             // show string of typed chars
{
    CPaintDC dc (this) ;                         // construct client area dc
    dc.SetTextColor (RGB (0, 0, 255)) ; // with blue text letters

    switch (nFontChoice)                 // select a font
    {
        case IDM_ANSI:
            dc.SelectStockObject (ANSI_VAR_FONT) ;
            break ;
        case IDM_OEM:
            dc.SelectStockObject (OEM_FIXED_FONT) ;
            break ;
        case IDM_ROMAN :
            dc.SelectObject (&Roman36) ;
            break ;
    }
```

```
    dc.TextOut (0, 0, cString, nTypedChars) ; // display using font
        // select default font to free selected font from dc
        // before the dc is deleted automatically (out of scope).
        // this is only needed for Roman36, but does no harm
        // for the stock fonts
    dc.SelectStockObject (SYSTEM_FONT) ;
}


    // returns TRUE if character is punctuation, FALSE otherwise
BOOL CMainWindow::IsAnsiPunc (int nChar)
{
    if ((nChar >= ' ' && nChar <= '@')
        || (nChar >= '[' && nChar <= '`')
        || (nChar >= '(' && nChar <='~')
        || (nChar >= 0xA0 && nChar <= 0xBF))
        return TRUE ;
    else
        return FALSE ;
}
```

ANSI_VAR_FONT and OEM_FIXED_FONT are selected (if chosen) using the
CDC::SelectStockObject() function. The *Roman32* font is not a stock object, so
it is selected with the **CDC::SelectObject()** function. Once a font is selected, any
output to the device context using **CDC::TextOut()** will use the currently selected font. At the end of the **CMainWindow::OnPaint()** function, the
SYSTEM_FONT is selected into the device context, displacing any previously
selected font. This makes sure that the *Roman36* font is not selected into the
device context prior to deletion.

The remaining support files for FONT1.CPP are shown in Listings 7-20 to
7-22. Figure 7-12 shows the icon image for the program.

Listing 7-20 FONT1.H Resource ID Header File

```
// font1.h  header file for resource ID numbers

#define IDM_ANSI      1        // menu item ID numbers
#define IDM_OEM       2
#define IDM_ROMAN     3
#define IDM_QUIT      10
```

Figure 7-12 FONT1.ICO Icon Image

Listing 7-21 FONT1.RC Resource Script File

```
// font1.rc  resource script file

#include <afxres.h>
#include "font1.h"

AFX_IDI_STD_FRAME   ICON     font1.ico    // the program's icon

MyMenu MENU                               // define the menu
{
    POPUP "&Font"
    {
        MENUITEM "ANSI Variable Font",   IDM_ANSI
        MENUITEM "OEM Fixed Font",       IDM_OEM
        MENUITEM "Roman Font",           IDM_ROMAN
    }
    MENUITEM "&Quit",                    IDM_QUIT
}
```

Listing 7-22 FONT1.DEF Module Definition File

```
NAME           font1
DESCRIPTION    'font1 C++ program'
EXETYPE        WINDOWS
STUB           'WINSTUB.EXE'
CODE           PRELOAD MOVEABLE
DATA           PRELOAD MOVEABLE MULTIPLE
HEAPSIZE       1024
STACKSIZE      5120
```

KEYBOARD ACCELERATORS

Keyboard alternatives to mouse actions are always a good idea, giving the user a choice as to the most convenient way to select an item in a menu. The simplest keyboard alternatives are provided by preceding the menu item's title string with an ampersand character in the program's resource script file. For example, the menu definition in Listing 7-23 will produce a menu that responds to (ALT)-(P) for Paint, (ALT)-(C) for Clear, and (ALT)-(Q) for Quit.

Listing 7-23 Ampersand Characters in Menu Definitions

```
MyMenu      MENU
{
    MENUITEM "&Paint",          IDM_PAINT
    MENUITEM "&Clear",          IDM_CLEAR
    MENUITEM "&Quit",           IDM_QUIT
}
```

The character following the ampersand ends up underlined in the menu bar. The ampersand character itself is not visible when the menu is displayed. Using the ampersand approach is fine for a single menu bar, but becomes cumbersome if there are pop-up menus. The user must select the (ALT)-(KEY) combination for the top menu item, and then select (ALT)-(KEY) for the item in the pop-up menu. A better keyboard shortcut would require only one keyboard combination to execute the command, no matter where it was in the menu structure.

You can create keyboard shortcuts by processing WM_KEYDOWN and WM_CHAR messages, and directing the program logic accordingly. However, Windows provides a much simpler alternative in the form of keyboard accelerators. The basic idea is that you define the key combinations in the resource script file. Each key combination that is defined ends up sending a WM_COMMAND message to the program. The WM_COMMAND messages imitate menu selections.

Listing 7-24 shows part of the resource script file for our next example program FONT2. The ACCELERATORS key word at the top starts the definition of the keyboard accelerators. Each line between the curly braces after the ACCELERATORS key word defines a keyboard combination. For example, (F1) corresponds to the virtual key code VK_F1. The accelerator table defines that this keyboard combination will send a WM_COMMAND message with the ID value set equal to IDM_ANSI. This is the same as the WM_COMMAND message sent if the user selects the menu item with the ID value IDM_ANSI, so the (F1) key will result in the same actions by the program as if the user had selected the menu item directly.

The syntax for an accelerator table is shown in Listing 7-25. The accelerator table is given a name, followed by the key word ACCELERATORS in uppercase letters. We will use the accelerator table name in a moment to load the accelerator data. The keystroke for each key combination is called the "event." There are three ways to specify a key. One is to put just the letter of the key in double quotes, such as "A" for the letter (A) key. The second way to specify the event is by putting an integer representing the ANSI code for the key. This works fine for the letters and digits at the top of the keyboard (not the numeric keypad). The third

Listing 7-24 The Accelerator Table from FONT2.RC

```
MyAccel       ACCELERATORS
{
    VK_F1,      IDM_ANSI,        VIRTKEY
    VK_F2,      IDM_OEM,         VIRTKEY, CONTROL
    VK_F3,      IDM_ROMAN,       VIRTKEY, ALT
    "A",        IDM_NOMENU,      VIRTKEY, ALT
}
```

Listing 7-25 Accelerator Table Syntax

```
TableName      ACCELERATORS
{
    event,     ID Value,     [VIRTKEY][NOINVERT][ALT][SHIFT][CONTROL]
}
```

way is to put the virtual key code for the key, like VK_TAB or VK_NUMPAD1. The virtual key codes for the letter and digit keys are the same as their ANSI equivalents, so you can just put the letter in double quotes for these events.

After the event is a comma, and then the ID value. This is the integer value that will be sent as the ID value with a WM_COMMAND message when the key combination is pressed. This should be the same ID value of the corresponding menu item that you want the keystoke to activate. Following the ID value is another comma, and then zero or more flags specifying the type of accelerator. If there are no flags, then the event must be a letter in double quotes. If the event type is labeled VIRTKEY, the event is interpreted as a virtual key code. You can also put the ALT, SHIFT, and CONTROL key words, separated by commas, in any combination. For example, if you want the (CONTROL)-(SHIFT)-(Z) key combination to send a WM_COMMAND message with the number 36 for the ID value, code the accelerator as shown in Listing 7-26.

One additional key word that can be used with an accelerator is NOINVERT. This stops the corresponding menu item (if any) from flashing when the accelerator is activated. Normally, the top menu bar selection corresponding to the accelerator is switched quickly to reverse video and back again to simulate a mouse click. NOINVERT stops this default action.

Adding an accelerator table to the program's resource script file does not immediately make the data available to the program when the program runs. To be used, the accelerator table must be loaded into memory and attached to the **CFrameWnd** class object for the program's main window. The **CFrameWnd::LoadAccelTable()** function loads the accelerator table into memory, ready for use.

```
LoadAccelTable ("TableName") ;
```

Listing 7-26 Accelerator Table Example

```
TableName      ACCELERATORS
{
    "Z",       36,       SHIFT,CONTROL
}
```

You can define more than one accelerator table in the resource script file, and then load different ones at different times using **CFrameWnd::Load-AccelTable()**. Most programs have just one accelerator table. Although accelerators are usually used to activate menu items, they can also be used to send WM_COMMAND messages that do not have menu equivalents. The WM_COMMAND message will be sent with the accelerator's ID value as the message ID value. Accelerators without menus are typically used to provide keyboard alternatives for selecting buttons or other controls. The next example program will demonstrate an example of an accelerator without a menu item equivalent.

The FONT2 Program

Our last example in this chapter is called FONT2. Figure 7-13 shows FONT2 in action, displaying some typed text. FONT2 uses a Swiss font, along with two stock fonts. The Swiss font is shown in the figure. FONT2 improves on our previous example, FONT1, in two ways:

1. Keyboard accelerators are provided as alternatives to menu selections.
2. The current editing point is marked by the blinking caret.

The accelerator table is defined in the FONT2.RC resource script file (Listing 7-27). The program has a pop-up menu, allowing selection of three different fonts. Note how the menu strings show the keyboard shortcut to the user when displayed. This is a good practice because it helps the user remember the accelerator key combinations. The accelerator table named "MyAccel" is defined at the bottom of FONT2.RC. This is the name we will pass to the **CFrameWnd::Load-AccelTable()** function. Note that two keyboard shortcuts are provided for the IDM_OEM shortcut. Both (F2) and (CONTROL)-(F2) will generate the same keyboard shortcut. You can have as many shortcuts for one action as you like, but one is usually enough.

The last accelerator defined in FONT2.RC is for the (ALT)-(A) combination. In this case, a WM_COMMAND message will be sent that does not correspond to any menu item. We will process this WM_COMMAND message in the message

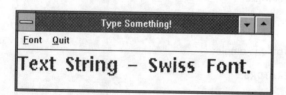

Figure 7-13 The FONT2 Program

Listing 7-27 FONT2.RC Resource Script File

```
// font2.rc  resource script file

#include <afxres.h>
#include <windows.h>              // for VK_ #defines
#include "font2.h"

AFX_IDI_STD_FRAME   ICON    font2.ico    // the program's icon

MyMenu MENU                        // define the menu
{
    POPUP "&Font"
    {
        MENUITEM "ANSI Variable Font (F1)",      IDM_ANSI
        MENUITEM "OEM Fixed Font (Cntl-F2)",     IDM_OEM
        MENUITEM "Swiss Font (Alt-F3)",          IDM_SWISS
    }
    MENUITEM "&Quit",                            IDM_QUIT
}


MyAccel ACCELERATORS               // define keyboard accelerators
{
    VK_F1,       IDM_ANSI,      VIRTKEY
    VK_F2,       IDM_OEM,       VIRTKEY, CONTROL
    VK_F2,       IDM_OEM,       VIRTKEY        // two accels for OEM
    VK_F3,       IDM_SWISS,     VIRTKEY, ALT
    "A",         IDM_NOMENU,    VIRTKEY, ALT   // accel without a
                                               // menu equivalent
}
```

mapping logic of FONT2.CPP as a demonstration of accelerators that do not have menu item equivalents.

Listing 7-28 shows the FONT2.HPP header file. Several new variables have been added to the **CMainWindow** class compared to the FONT1.HPP example. The *nCaretTall* and *nCaretWide* integers are used to store the size of the caret. The caret size will be adjusted to match the font in use. In addition, the **CPoint** object *CaretPoint* has been added to track the current location of the caret on the screen.

The FONT2.CPP program file is shown in Listing 7-29. Note that the **CFrameWnd::LoadAccelTable()** function is called in the **CMainWindow** constructor function to load the "MyAccel" data into memory. The constructor function is also used as a convenient place to initialize variables, including the creation of a 36-pixel high "Swiss" font.

The message map in FONT2.CPP incudes ON_COMMAND() entries for all of the menu items plus the IDM_NOMENU entry, which corresponds to the accelerator table item that does not have a menu item equivalent. Because menu item selections and accelerator key combinations both generate

Listing 7-28 FONT2.HPP Header File

```
// font2.hpp    header file for font2.cpp

#define MAXCHARS    256

class CMainWindow : public CFrameWnd    // derive a main window class
{
public:
    CMainWindow () ;                    // declare a constructor
private:
    CFont Swiss36 ;                     // swiss logical font object
    int nFontChoice ;                   // track currently selected font
    CString cString ;                   // char buffer to hold typing
    int nTypedChars ;                   // number of chars in buffer
    int nCaretTall ;                    // save caret dimensions
    int nCaretWide ;
    CPoint CaretPoint ;                 // current caret position

    BOOL IsAnsiPunc (int nChar) ;       // helper function

    void OnPaint () ;                   // message processing functions
    void OnChar (UINT nChar, UINT nRepCnt, UINT nFlags) ;
    void OnKeyDown (UINT nVKey, UINT nRepCnt, UINT nFlags) ;
    void OnSetFocus (CWnd* pOldWnd) ;
    void OnKillFocus (CWnd* pNewWnd) ;

    void OnExit () ;                    // menu items - define here
    void OnAnsi () ;
    void OnOem () ;
    void OnSwiss () ;
    void OnNoMenu () ;

    DECLARE_MESSAGE_MAP()               // prepare for message processing
} ;

class CTheApp : public CWinApp         // derive an application class
{
public:
    BOOL InitInstance () ;             // declare new InitInstance()
} ;
```

WM_COMMAND messages, the same message response function will be called for either the menu item selection or the accelerator. The only case in FONT2.CPP where the use of a keyboard accelerator requires additional program code is the IDM_NOMENU entry that does not have a menu item equivalent. A new message response function named **CMainWindow::OnNoMenu()** was added to FONT2.CPP to respond to this accelerator key combination. **CMainWindow::OnNoMenu()** simply displays a message box to prove that the accelerator WM_COMMAND message is correctly processed.

Listing 7-29 FONT2.CPP

```cpp
// font2.cpp                example using font and caret

#include <afxwin.h>      // class library header file
#include <strstrea.h>    // streams header file
#include "font2.h"       // header file for resource data
#include "font2.hpp"     // header file for this program

CTheApp theApp ;          // create one CTheApp object - runs program

BOOL CTheApp::InitInstance ()   // override default InitInstance()
{
    m_pMainWnd = new CMainWindow () ;        // create a main window
    m_pMainWnd->ShowWindow (m_nCmdShow) ;    // make it visible
    m_pMainWnd->UpdateWindow () ;            // paint center
    return TRUE ;
}

CMainWindow::CMainWindow ()             // constructor for window
{
    LoadAccelTable ("MyAccel") ;        // load keyboard accelerator table
    Create (NULL, "Type Something", WS_OVERLAPPEDWINDOW, rectDefault,
        NULL, "MyMenu") ;
    nTypedChars = 0 ;                   // initialize private data
    nFontChoice = IDM_ANSI ;            // and font object
    CaretPoint.x = 0 ;
    CaretPoint.y = 0 ;
    Swiss36.CreateFont (36, 0, 0, 0, FW_NORMAL, 0, 0, 0, ANSI_CHARSET,
        OUT_DEFAULT_PRECIS, CLIP_DEFAULT_PRECIS, DEFAULT_QUALITY,
        VARIABLE_PITCH | FF_SWISS, "Swiss") ;
}

BEGIN_MESSAGE_MAP (CMainWindow, CFrameWnd)
    ON_COMMAND (IDM_QUIT, OnExit)             // menu item response
    ON_COMMAND (IDM_ANSI, OnAnsi)
    ON_COMMAND (IDM_OEM, OnOem)
    ON_COMMAND (IDM_SWISS, OnSwiss)
    ON_COMMAND (IDM_NOMENU, OnNoMenu)         // from accel table only
    ON_WM_PAINT ()                            // process paint message
    ON_WM_CHAR ()                             // char input
    ON_WM_KEYDOWN ()                          // other keyboard input
    ON_WM_SETFOCUS ()
    ON_WM_KILLFOCUS ()
END_MESSAGE_MAP ()

void CMainWindow::OnExit ()          // respond to menu item "Quit"
{
    this->DestroyWindow () ;         // destroy main window,
}                                    // this stops application
```

```
void CMainWindow::OnAnsi ()              // user selected ANSI font
{
    nFontChoice = IDM_ANSI ;
    this->Invalidate () ;                // force repaint
}

void CMainWindow::OnOem ()               // user selected OEM font
{
    nFontChoice = IDM_OEM ;
    this->Invalidate () ;                // force repaint
}

void CMainWindow::OnSwiss ()             // user selected roman font
{
    nFontChoice = IDM_SWISS ;
    this->Invalidate () ;                // force repaint
}

void CMainWindow::OnNoMenu ()            // Alt-A key combination used
{
    CString string = "Got IDM_NOMENU WM_COMMAND message." ;
    CString title = "Accelerator Only"  ;
    CMainWindow::MessageBox (string, title, MB_OK) ;
}

void CMainWindow::OnChar (UINT nChar, UINT nRepCnt, UINT nFlags)
{
    if (nTypedChars == MAXCHARS - 1)// do not overflow buffer
        return ;
    else if (IsCharAlphaNumeric (nChar) || IsAnsiPunc (nChar))
    {
        cString += (char) nChar ;    // add typed char to string
        nTypedChars++ ;
        this->Invalidate (TRUE) ;    // force repaint of client area
    }
}

void CMainWindow::OnKeyDown (UINT nVKey, UINT nRepCnt, UINT nFlags)
{
    if (nVKey == VK_BACK && nTypedChars > 0)     // backspace key
    {
        int nLong = cString.GetLength () ;       // find length
        cString = cString.Left (nLong - 1) ;     // drop last char
        nTypedChars-- ;
        this->Invalidate (TRUE) ;                // force repaint
    }
}

void CMainWindow::OnPaint ()             // show string of typed chars
{
    TEXTMETRIC  tm ;                             // structure to hold tm data
    CPaintDC dc (this) ;                         // construct client area dc
    dc.SetTextColor (RGB (0, 0, 255)) ; // with blue text letters
```

```
    switch (nFontChoice)                     // select a font
    {
        case IDM_ANSI:
            dc.SelectStockObject (ANSI_VAR_FONT) ;
            break ;
        case IDM_OEM:
            dc.SelectStockObject (OEM_FIXED_FONT) ;
            break ;
        case IDM_SWISS :
            dc.SelectObject (&Swiss36) ;
            break ;
    }
    dc.GetTextMetrics (&tm) ;                // get text size data
        // make caret height equal to total font height
    nCaretTall = tm.tmHeight + tm.tmExternalLeading ;
        // make caret width two times the window border width
    nCaretWide = 2 * GetSystemMetrics (SM_CXBORDER) ;
    ::DestroyCaret () ;            // kill old caret
                                             // make new one
    this->CreateSolidCaret (nCaretWide, nCaretTall) ;
    CaretPoint.y = 0 ;                       // only using top text line
        // locate caret at end of the text line
        // GetTextExtent() returns a CSize pointer
    CSize SizeText =
        dc.GetTextExtent (cString, cString.GetLength ()) ;
    CaretPoint.x = SizeText.cx ;             // extract width from CSize
    this->SetCaretPos (CaretPoint) ;         // specify location
    this->ShowCaret () ;                     // make caret visible

    dc.TextOut (0, 0, cString, nTypedChars) ; // display using font
        // select default font to free selected font from dc
        // before the dc is deleted automatically (out of scope).
        // this is only needed for Swiss36, but does no harm
        // for the stock fonts
    dc.SelectStockObject (SYSTEM_FONT) ;
}

void CMainWindow::OnSetFocus (CWnd* pOldWnd)
{                                            // make a new caret
    this->CreateSolidCaret (nCaretWide, nCaretTall) ;
    this->SetCaretPos (CaretPoint) ;       // specify X,Y location
    this->ShowCaret () ;                     // make it visible
}

void CMainWindow::OnKillFocus (CWnd* pNewWnd)
{
    ::DestroyCaret () ;             // destroy the caret
}
```

```
     // returns TRUE if character is punctuation, FALSE otherwise
BOOL CMainWindow::IsAnsiPunc (int nChar)
{
    if ((nChar >= ' ' && nChar <= '@')
        || (nChar >= '[' && nChar <= '`')
        || (nChar >= '(' && nChar <='~'))
        || (nChar >= 0xA0 && nChar <= 0xBF))
        return TRUE ;
    else
        return FALSE ;
}
```

Sizing and Showing the Caret

The **CMainWindow::OnPaint()** function in FONT2.CPP includes logic for re-drawing the caret at the end of the string to mark the editing point. This is a rudimentary use of the caret, as a real text editor would include logic to reposition the caret using the arrow keys and the mouse, and to delete and insert characters at the caret position. The only editing features supported in FONT2 are the ability to add new characters by typing, and the use of the (BACKSPACE) key to delete the last character in the string. Both of these actions result in movement of the caret.

The caret needs to be the same size as the font's characters to look properly sized. **CDC::GetTextMetrics()** is used to determine the height of a character with whatever font is currently selected into the device context. The caret's height is set equal to the character height plus the external leading space. The caret's width is set equal to twice the thickness of a window border line, obtained by **::GetSystemMetrics()**. This assures that the caret will be a reasonable width, regardless of the video equipment in use. Using **CDC::GetTextMetrics()** and **::GetSystemMetrics()** to determine the size of objects while the program is running is a good programming practice, as the program is sure to look right regardless of what new equipment the manufacturers dream up in the future.

Positioning the caret at the end of the character string is a bit more complex than you might expect. The width of the characters in a variable-pitch font varies depending on the character. The letter "I" is much narrower than the letter "M." You cannot simply multiply the average character width by the length of the character string to find the string's length. The MFC classes provide the **CDC::GetTextExtent()** function to determine the size of a character string. The size of the string (height and width) will reflect the font currently selected into the device context.

CDC::GetTextExtent() returns a pointer to a **CSize** object. The **CSize** class is similar to **CPoint** in that it contains two-dimensional information. **CSize** is used to store and manipulate the size of rectangular objects. **CPoint** is used to store the *X,Y* location of an object. If you search through the AFXWIN.H header file, you will find that the **CSize** class is derived from the **tagSIZE** structure. A portion of AFXWIN.H is shown in Listing 7-30, including the declaration of the **CSize** class.

The *cx* and *cy* members of the **tagSize** structure are used to hold the width and height of an object. The caret is positioned at the end of the line of text shown in the FONT2 window with the code shown in Listing 7-31. The *Y* value for the caret position is always equal to zero in this simple example because only a single line of text at the top of the FONT2 client area is displayed.

CDC::GetTextExtent() is used frequently in programs that manipulate text. It is the only reliable way to determine how long a character string will be, even if the string is made up of digits. Ones are narrower than twos! Manipulating the caret also requires that the WM_SETFOCUS and WM_KILLFOCUS messages be processed from Windows. The caret must be created when the window gets the input focus, and destroyed when the window loses the focus. The message logic in FONT2.CPP is similar to the discussion of MOUSE3.CPP at the end of Chapter 6, *Taming the Mouse*.

Listings 7-32 to 7-33 show the remaining support files for FONT2.CPP. The program's icon image is shown in Figure 7-14.

Listing 7-30 CSize Class Declaration from AFXWIN.H

```
typedef struct tagSIZE
{
    int cx;
    int cy;
} SIZE;

class CSize : public tagSIZE
{
public:

// Constructors
    CSize();
    CSize(int initCX, int initCY);
// etc.
```

Listing 7-31 FONT2 Excerpt Showing Caret Positioning

```
CSize SizeText =
    dc.GetTextExtent (cString, cString.GetLength ()) ;
CaretPoint.x = SizeText.cx ;          // extract width from CSize
this->SetCaretPos (CaretPoint) ;      // specify location
this->ShowCaret () ;                  // make caret visible
```

Listing 7-32 FONT2.H Resource ID Header File

```
// font2.h  header file for resource ID numbers

#define IDM_ANSI      1        // menu item ID numbers
#define IDM_OEM       2
#define IDM_SWISS     3
#define IDM_NOMENU    4        // only has accelerator
#define IDM_QUIT      10
```

Listing 7-33 FONT2.DEF Module Definition File

```
NAME           font2
DESCRIPTION    'font2 C++ program'
EXETYPE        WINDOWS
STUB           'WINSTUB.EXE'
CODE           PRELOAD MOVEABLE
DATA           PRELOAD MOVEABLE MULTIPLE
HEAPSIZE       1024
STACKSIZE      5120
```

Figure 7-14 FONT2.ICO Icon Image

SUMMARY

Windows uses the ANSI character set to encode each letter, digit, and symbol. This character set is more suitable for international use than the OEM character set used by MS-DOS because it includes a more complete set of the accented characters used in many European languages. Not all functions work properly with the ANSI character set. For example, the **CString** class functions **CString::MakeUpper()** and **CString::MakeLower()** do not correctly process accented characters. Windows provides a number of global functions for manipulating character strings, and correctly processing accented characters. Always use the Windows functions, such as **::AnsiLower()** and **::AnsiUpper()**, rather than the **CString** or C++ compiler library functions so that your program will work properly regardless of the language used.

Although you will need to avoid the **CString::MakeUpper()** and **CString::MakeLower()** functions in Windows programs, the **CString** class is useful. The **CString** class allows strings to be manipulated using operators, such as the "+" and "=" operators, much like the syntax used in the BASIC language. The **CString** class automatically allocates additional room to hold character data as the string is lengthened.

Windows sends WM_KEYDOWN and WM_KEYUP messages when a key is depressed and released. The keys are coded using "virtual key" codes, defined in WINDOWS.H. The program window will also receive WM_CHAR messages when a printable character key is depressed. WM_CHAR messages encode the ANSI character code. WM_CHAR messages are used for the printable character keys, and WM_KEYDOWN is used for the nonprintable keys, such as function keys.

If the user has the (ALT) key depressed when another key is depressed, Windows will send WM_SYSKEYDOWN, WM_SYSCHAR, and WM_SYSKEYUP messages. If Windows is installed with a language other than English, accented characters will be defined. Windows will send WM_DEADCHAR when the user selects an accent key. The WM_CHAR message will transmit the ANSI code for the accented version of the letter.

Windows provides a quick way to add keyboard shortcuts to a program. Keyboard accelerators are defined in the program's resource script file, and loaded into memory using **CFrameWnd::LoadAccelTable()**. Once installed, accelerator combinations generate WM_COMMAND messages, just as if a menu item had been selected with the mouse.

You can change fonts in a program either by selecting one of the stock fonts or by using a logical font created with **CFont::CreateFont()**. Logical fonts are based on font data in font files. **CFont::CreateFont()** can approximate bold, italics, and other font sizes by interpolating from the existing font data. Once you have selected a new font into the device context, you can find out all of its characteristics (size, width, etc.) using the **CDC::GetTextMetrics()** function. You can find the height and width of a character string drawn with the selected font using the **CDC::GetTextExtent()** function.

QUESTIONS

1. The unaccented characters and digits in the OEM and ANSI character sets have the same code values. (True/False)

2. Use the _____ function to convert a character string to uppercase.

3. Both WM_KEYDOWN and WM_CHAR send the ANSI character code for the key depressed with the message. (True/False)

4. How would you detect the (TAB) key being depressed in a program?

5. The **CString** class properly handles ANSI character conversions. (True/False)

6. If the (ALT) key is down when another key is pressed, which messages will be sent to the window with the input focus?

7. To select a stock font into the device context, use the _____ function. To select a logical font into the device context, use the _____ function.

8. Once a font is selected into a device context, you can find out the dimensions and attributes of the font using the _____ function. Use the _____ function to determine the length of a character string.

9. The two steps needed to use keyboard accelerators in a program are: 1) Add an _____ table to the resource script file; 2) Use the _____ function to load the accelerator data into memory.

10. The line in an accelerator table (see Listing 7-34) will generate a WM_COMMAND message with an ID value equal to _____ when the _____-_____ key combination is selected.

Listing 734 Accelerator Table Syntax

```
TableName       ACCELERATORS
BEGIN
    VK_F10,     19,     VIRTKEY,CONTROL
END
```

EXERCISES

1. Modify the FONT2.C program to create a 36 logical-unit high font using the Modern style, based on the OEM character set. Set up the logical font so that the adjacent characters appear vertically downward. How do you determine the location of the end of the string when it is aligned vertically?

2. Modify the keyboard accelerators for FONT2 so that the three font selections can be made with the (ALT)-(1) (digit one, not function key one), (CONTROL)-(2), and (SHIFT)-(3) key combinations.

ANSWERS TO QUESTIONS

1. True.

2. **::AnsiUpper()** or **::AnsiUpperBuff()**.

3. False. WM_CHAR does send the ANSI character code. WM_KEYDOWN
   and WM_KEYUP send the virtual key code for the key. The virtual key
   code only equals the ANSI code for the uppercase letters and the digits.

4. Process WM_KEYDOWN messages and look for VK_TAB.

5. False. The **CString::MakeLower()** and **CString::MakeUpper()** functions
   assume the ASCII (not ANSI) character set and therefore do not properly
   convert accented characters.

6. WM_SYSKEYDOWN, WM_SYSCHAR, WM_SYSKEYUP.

7. **CDC::SelectStockObject(), CDC::SelectObject()**.

8. **CDC::GetTextMetrics(), CDC::GetTextExtent()**.

9. Accelerator table; **CFrameWnd::LoadAccelTable()**.

10. 19, (CONTROL)-(F10).

SOLUTIONS TO EXERCISES

1. The solution is under the file name C7EXER1 on the source code disks. To
   create a Modern font that aligns the characters vertically, the **CFont::Cre-
   ateFont()** function call is modified as follows:

```
Modern36.CreateFont (36, 0, 2700, 0, FW_NORMAL, 0, 0, 0,
    OEM_CHARSET, OUT_DEFAULT_PRECIS, CLIP_DEFAULT_PRECIS,
    DEFAULT_QUALITY, DEFAULT_PITCH | FF_MODERN, "Modern") ;
```

Setting the *nEscapement* parameter (third parameter) to 2700 causes the
characters to appear 270 degrees offset from the right. This is straight
down. Due to a minor bug in the **CreateFont()** function, the
OEM_CHARSET must be selected for this example to work.

   The **GetTextExtent()** function continues to provide the vertical and
horizontal size of a string output using the font, even if the font's characters are rotated or appear at an angle to the horizontal. You can position
the caret using both the *X* and *Y* values returned by **CDC::GetTextEx-
tent()** as follows:

```
CSize SizeText = dc.GetTextExtent (cString,
    cString.GetLength ()) ;
CaretPoint.x = SizeText.cx ;
CaretPoint.y = SizeText.cy - nCaretTall ;
this->SetCaretPos (CaretPoint) ;
```

The result of these changes is shown in Figure 7-15.

2. The solution is under the file name C7EXER2 on the source code disks. The resource script file should be modified as shown in Listing 7-35. Note that the menu strings have been changed to reflect the new accelerators.

Listing 7-35 C7EXER2.RC Resource Script File

```
// c7exer2.rc  resource script file

#include <afxres.h>
#include <windows.h>               // for VK_ #defines
#include "c7exer2.h"

AFX_IDI_STD_FRAME    ICON    c7exer2.ico    // the program's icon

MyMenu MENU                          // define the menu
{
    POPUP "&Font"
    {
        MENUITEM "ANSI Variable Font (Alt-1)",      IDM_ANSI
        MENUITEM "OEM Fixed Font (Cntl-2)",         IDM_OEM
        MENUITEM "Swiss Font (Shift-3)",            IDM_SWISS
    }
    MENUITEM "&Quit",                               IDM_QUIT
}

MyAccel ACCELERATORS                // define keyboard accelerators
{
    "1",       IDM_ANSI,        VIRTKEY, ALT
    "2",       IDM_OEM,         VIRTKEY, CONTROL
    "3",       IDM_SWISS,       VIRTKEY, SHIFT
}
```

Figure 7-15 Chapter 7, Exercise 1 Solution

Chapter **8**

Child and Pop-Up Windows

So far we have created main program windows and used predefined window controls, such as buttons and static text. Window controls are convenient if you can take advantage of the exact features provided. If you need other features, you will need to create your own specialized windows. The most common type of "custom" windows are child windows, which are attached to a parent window at all times. Child windows are visible only if they are within the client area of their parent. Child windows can be used to deal with a specific task, such as getting input from the user. Child windows are also useful as a programming tool to break up a large screen area into smaller portions, each with its own message processing logic.

Pop-up windows are another useful tool. Pop-ups are not physically attached to a parent window, and they can be positioned anywhere on the screen. However, pop-up windows disappear the instant their parent window is destroyed. Pop-ups are handy for items that the user may want to reposition on the screen (for example, tool bars). We will look at several examples in this chapter with both child windows and pop-up windows.

One of the confusing elements of creating child and pop-up windows is the use of the word "class." In the C++ language, a "class" is a collection of functions and data. The Windows programming API also uses the word "class" to describe a set of parameters that describe a type of window. The Windows API includes functions for registering new "classes" of windows with the Windows environment as your program operates. Keep in mind that both of these uses of the word "class" are independent, but both types of "class" are frequently used when creating child and pop-up windows using C++.

Child and pop-up windows typically process messages independently from their parent windows. Child and parent windows can communicate by sending each other messages. Windows allows you to define your own "user" messages, which can have any meaning desired. We will look at several examples of exchanging messages between windows in this chapter.

Concepts covered: Child windows, separate class definitions and window functions, stock icons, pop-up windows, registering a new class of windows, user messages sent between windows.

Key words covered: WS_CHILD, WS_POPUP, WS_MINIMIZEBOX, WS_BORDER, WS_VISIBLE, IDI_APPLICATION, WS_THICKFRAME, COLOR_BTNFACE, COLOR_WINDOW, CS_VREDRAW, CS_HREDRAW, CS_DBLCLKS.

Functions covered: CWnd::Create(), CWnd::SendMessage(), CWnd::GetParent(), CWnd::OnMessage(), ::AfxRegisterWndClass(), ::AfxGetApp(), CWinApp::LoadStandardCursor(), CWinApp::LoadStandardIcon(), CGdiObject::GetSafeHandle().

Messages covered: WM_USER.

CREATING A CHILD WINDOW

The first example program in this chapter creates a single child window that can be moved in the center of the parent's client area. Figure 8-1 shows the CHILD1 program in action. When the "Create" menu item is selected, a child window appears inside the main program window. The child window displays a gray

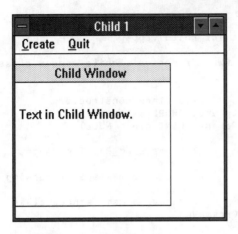

Figure 8-1 The CHILD1 Program

(inactive) caption bar and a white client area of its own. The child window's client area contains the string "Text in Child Window."

Because CHILD1's child window has a caption bar, the child window can be moved in the client area of the parent window by using the mouse. The child window is only visible within the bounds of the parent's client area. If you move it to an edge of the parent window's border, the child window is clipped. Figure 8-1 shows the left side of the child window being clipped by the parent window. The clipping of the child window is done automatically by the same built-in logic that the Windows environment uses to show portions of program windows on the screen when they overlap. The child window is visible only if the parent window is visible.

The CHILD1 program introduces separation of messages between the parent window and a child window. The result is that the child window becomes its own "little world." Messages from Windows to the child window are not intercepted by the parent window. The child window's message mapping logic and message response functions are completely independent of the parent. CHILD1.CPP does the following:

1. Creates the child window using the **CWnd::Create()** function.

2. Includes a separate message map for the child window and message processing functions for the child window.

Listing 8-1 shows the CHILD1.HPP header file. In addition to the **CMainWindow** and **CTheApp** classes that the previous example programs used, CHILD1.HPP declares a new class called **CChildWindow**. The **CChildWindow**

Listing 8-1 CHILD1.HPP Header File

```
// child1.hpp     header file for child1.cpp

class CChildWindow : public CWnd // derive a child window class
{
public:
    CChildWindow () ;            // declare constructor
    BOOL Create (char FAR* lpName, DWORD dwStyle,
        RECT& rect, CWnd* pParent, UINT nID = NULL) ;
private:
    void OnPaint () ;            // process WM_PAINT messages

    DECLARE_MESSAGE_MAP()        // separate message processing
} ;
                                 // derive a main window class
class CMainWindow : public CFrameWnd
{
public:
    CMainWindow () ;             // declare a constructor
private:
    BOOL bMadeChild ;            // track if child already made
    CChildWindow Child ;         // child window object
    void OnChildCreate () ;      // "Create" menu item
    void OnExit () ;             // "Quit" menu item

    DECLARE_MESSAGE_MAP()        // prepare for message processing
} ;

class CTheApp : public CWinApp  // derive an application class
{
public:
    BOOL InitInstance () ;       // declare new InitInstance()
} ;
```

class includes a constructor function, **Create()** function, and **OnPaint()** message response function. The class declares its own message map with the DECLARE_MESSAGE_MAP() macro, indicating that this window class will process its own messages.

One nicety in the **CChildWindow** class definition is the use of a default argument in the **CChildWindow::Create()** function. The parameter *nID* is used to give the child window an ID value. The ID value is not necessary in CHILD1 because the child window will have its own message processing logic and does not send WM_COMMAND messages to the parent window when the child is activated. The function declaration for the **CChildWindow::Create()** function includes a default argument for the *nID* value:

```
UINT nID = NULL ;
```

The default argument allows the *nID* parameter to be omitted when **CChildWindow::Create()** is called. If the *nID* value is not specified, NULL (zero) will be used for the window ID.

Listing 8-2 shows the CHILD1.CPP program. The child window is not created until the user selects the "Create" menu item. At this point the **CMainWindow::OnChildCreate()** message response function is called, which in turn calls **CChildWindow::Create()**. The secrets to creating a child window are to pass the WS_CHILD window style and a pointer to the parent window object (*this* pointer) to **CChildWindow::Create()**.

```
Child.Create ("Child Window",
        WS_CHILD | WS_BORDER | WS_CAPTION | WS_VISIBLE,
        ChildRect, this) ;
```

These window style values specify a child window (WS_CHILD) with a thin border (WS_BORDER), a caption bar so that the window will be moveable (WS_CAPTION), and that is initially visible (WS_VISIBLE). Without the WS_VISIBLE style, the window would be created, but would not be displayed until the **CWnd::ShowWindow()** function was used to make the window visible.

Separate Message Processing for Child Windows

An interesting aspect of the CHILD1.CPP program is that it has two message maps. The main program window has the normal message map for handling WM_COMMAND messages from the program's menu and other messages from Windows. However, these messages are not sent to the child window. The child window declares its own message map by including the DECLARE_MES-SAGE_MAP() macro in the child window class definition, and by including a message map in the CHILD1.CPP program specific to the child window class. Listing 8-3 shows the child window's message map, extracted from CHILD1.CPP.

This is a very simple message map with only the WM_PAINT message processed. The MFC class logic differentiates between the two message maps in CHILD1.CPP, based on the parameters passed to the BEGIN_MESSAGE_MAP() macro. The first parameter is the name of the window class for the window receiving the messages. The second parameter is the name of the MFC base class from which the window class was derived. These parameters allow the MFC logic to segregate the message maps for different windows. We will make more use of this separation in later example programs in this chapter.

Listing 8-2 CHILD1.CPP

```cpp
// child1.cpp                demonstrate independent child window

#include <afxwin.h>      // class library header file
#include "child1.h"      // header file for resource data
#include "child1.hpp"    // header file for this program

CTheApp theApp ;         // create one CTheApp object - runs program

BOOL CTheApp::InitInstance ()    // override default InitInstance()
{
    m_pMainWnd = new CMainWindow () ;         // create a main window
    m_pMainWnd->ShowWindow (m_nCmdShow) ;     // make it visible
    m_pMainWnd->UpdateWindow () ;             // paint center
    return TRUE ;
}

CMainWindow::CMainWindow ()      // constructor for main window
{
    Create (NULL, "Child 1", WS_OVERLAPPEDWINDOW, rectDefault,
        NULL, "MyMenu") ;
    bMadeChild = FALSE ;         // initialize variable
}


BEGIN_MESSAGE_MAP (CMainWindow, CFrameWnd)
    ON_COMMAND (IDM_CREATE, OnChildCreate)
    ON_COMMAND (IDM_QUIT, OnExit)
END_MESSAGE_MAP ()

void CMainWindow::OnExit ()      // respond to menu item "Quit"
{
    this->DestroyWindow () ;      // destroy main window,
}                                 // this stops application

void CMainWindow::OnChildCreate () // respond to "Create" menu item
{
    if (bMadeChild)                // only allow one child window
        return ;
    CRect ChildRect (10, 30, 210, 180) ;      // rect holds child size
    Child.Create ("Child Window",
        WS_CHILD | WS_BORDER | WS_CAPTION | WS_VISIBLE,
        ChildRect, this) ;
    bMadeChild = TRUE ;
}


//------------------- Child Window Section -------------------//

                            // new Create function
BOOL CChildWindow::Create (char FAR* lpName, DWORD dwStyle,
    RECT& rect, CWnd* pParent, UINT nID)
```

```
{                                          // calls CWnd::Create ()
    return CWnd::Create (NULL, lpName, dwStyle, rect,
        pParent, nID) ;
}

BEGIN_MESSAGE_MAP (CChildWindow, CWnd)  // messages for child
    ON_WM_PAINT ()
END_MESSAGE_MAP ()

void CChildWindow::OnPaint ()          // child window paint function
{
    CString string ("Text in Child Window.") ;
    CPaintDC dc (this) ;
    dc.TextOut (10, 25, string, string.GetLength () ) ;
}
```

Listing 8-3 Child Window Message Map

```
BEGIN_MESSAGE_MAP (CChildWindow, CWnd)  // messages for child
    ON_WM_PAINT ()
END_MESSAGE_MAP ()
```

Listings 8-4 to 8-6 show the remaining support files for CHILD1.CPP. The program's icon is shown in Figure 8-2.

Listing 8-4 CHILD1.DEF Module Definition File

```
NAME            child1
DESCRIPTION     'child1 C++ program'
EXETYPE         WINDOWS
STUB            'WINSTUB.EXE'
CODE            PRELOAD MOVEABLE
DATA            PRELOAD MOVEABLE MULTIPLE
HEAPSIZE        1024
STACKSIZE       5120
```

Figure 8-2 CHILD1.ICO Icon Image

Listing 8-5 CHILD1.H Resource ID Header File

```
// child1.h  header file for resource ID numbers

#define IDM_CREATE      1
#define IDM_QUIT        10
```

Listing 8-6 CHILD1.RC Resource Script File

```
// child1.rc  resource script file

#include <afxres.h>
#include "child1.h"

AFX_IDI_STD_FRAME   ICON    child1.ico    // the program's icon

MyMenu MENU                               // define the menu
{
    MENUITEM "&Create",     IDM_CREATE
    MENUITEM "&Quit",       IDM_QUIT
}
```

A BETTER CHILD WINDOW

CHILD1 has the virtue of simplicity, but the child window does not do much. The child window is also remarkably plain, with a white client area and simple caption bar. The next example creates a somewhat more complex child window. Figure 8-3 shows the CHILD2 program in action. The child window in the client area of CHILD2 has a caption bar, minimize button, and a thick frame that can be used to change the size of the child window. The client area of the child window is painted with a gray brush instead of the default white color. Inside the child window's client area is some text and a button control containing the text

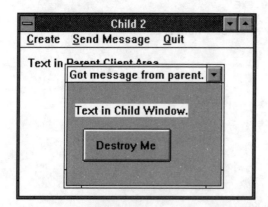

Figure 8-3 CHILD2 Program After Creating Child Window

"Destroy Me." Clicking this button destroys the child window, but does not affect CHILD2's parent window.

Creating the child window in the CHILD2 program will require that a new "class" of windows be registered with the Windows environment. So far, all of the example programs in this book have taken advantage of predefined types of windows. Registering a new class of windows allows CHILD2 to create a child window with a gray background color. We will go over the structure of the CHILD2 program first, and then explore registering new window classes in the next section.

The CHILD2 parent window has three menu items. The "Create" menu item creates the child window. The "Send Message" menu item sends a special message to the child window. When the child window in CHILD2 receives the message, its caption is changed to "Got message from parent," as shown in Figure 8-3. We will explore sending user messages in a moment.

Because the CHILD2 child window has a minimize button, the child window can be minimized. Clicking the child window's minimize button results in the child window being iconized at the bottom left of the parent window's client area. This is a built-in feature of the Windows environment. Minimized child windows are always constrained to the parent window's client area. Figure 8-4 shows the CHILD2 program after the child window has been minimized, displaying the Windows 3.1 default program icon. The minimized child window can be moved in the parent window's client area using the mouse, and it can be restored by double-clicking the icon box. The title string shown under the window icon will be the child window's caption string. This behavior for minimized windows is probably familiar, as this is how the Windows Program Manager and File Manager applications behave.

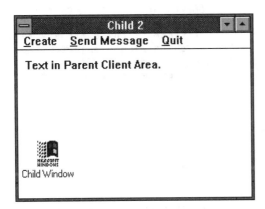

Figure 8-4 CHILD2 with Child Window Minimized

The CHILD2.HPP header file (Listing 8-7) has a few added items. The **CChildWindow** class now declares a constructor function, implying that CHILD2.CPP will no longer use the default constructor for the class. Note the addition of the **CString** and **CButton** objects in the **CChildWindow** definition. Two additional message response functions are also declared in the **CChildWindow** class: **CChildWindow::OnMessage()** and **CChildWindow::OnKillButton()**.

Listing 8-8 shows the CHILD2.CPP program. When the user selects the "Create" menu item the **CMainWindow::OnChildCreate()** message response

Listing 8-7 CHILD2.HPP Header File

```
// child2.hpp    header file for child2.cpp

class CChildWindow : public CWnd // derive a child window class
{
public:
    CChildWindow () ;               // declare constructor
    BOOL Create (char FAR* lpName, DWORD dwStyle,
        RECT& rect, CWnd* pParent, UINT nID = NULL) ;
private:
    CString ClassName ;             // name of new window class
    CButton ChildButton ;           // child window's own button
    void OnPaint () ;               // process WM_PAINT messages
    LONG OnMessage (UINT, LONG) ;// respond to msg. from parent
    void OnKillButton () ;          // respond to button selection
    DECLARE_MESSAGE_MAP()           // separate message processing
} ;
                                    // derive a main window class
class CMainWindow : public CFrameWnd
{
public:
    CMainWindow () ;                // declare a constructor
private:
    BOOL bMadeChild ;               // track if child already made
    CChildWindow Child ;            // child window object
    void OnChildCreate () ;         // "Create" menu item
    void OnSendMessage () ;         // "Send Message" menu item
    void OnExit () ;                // "Quit" menu item
    void OnPaint () ;

    DECLARE_MESSAGE_MAP()           // prepare for message processing
} ;

class CTheApp : public CWinApp // derive an application class
{
public:
    BOOL InitInstance () ;          // declare new InitInstance()
} ;
```

Listing 8-8 CHILD2.CPP

```cpp
// child2.cpp              demonstrate independent child window

#include <afxwin.h>     // class library header file
#include "child2.h"     // header file for resource data
#include "child2.hpp"   // header file for this program

CTheApp theApp ;        // create one CTheApp object - runs program

BOOL CTheApp::InitInstance ()   // override default InitInstance()
{
    m_pMainWnd = new CMainWindow () ;        // create a main window
    m_pMainWnd->ShowWindow (m_nCmdShow) ;    // make it visible
    m_pMainWnd->UpdateWindow () ;            // paint center
    return TRUE ;
}

CMainWindow::CMainWindow ()        // constructor for main window
{
    Create (NULL, "Child 2", WS_OVERLAPPEDWINDOW, rectDefault,
        NULL, "MyMenu") ;
    bMadeChild = FALSE ;           // initialize
}

BEGIN_MESSAGE_MAP (CMainWindow, CFrameWnd)
    ON_COMMAND (IDM_CREATE, OnChildCreate)
    ON_COMMAND (IDM_SEND, OnSendMessage)
    ON_COMMAND (IDM_QUIT, OnExit)
    ON_WM_PAINT ()
END_MESSAGE_MAP ()

void CMainWindow::OnExit ()         // respond to menu item "Quit"
{
    this->DestroyWindow () ;        // destroy main window,
}                                   // this stops application

void CMainWindow::OnChildCreate ()  // respond to "Create" menu item
{
    if (bMadeChild)                 // only make one child window
        return ;
    CRect ChildRect (10, 30, 210, 180) ;    // rect holds child size
    Child.Create ("Child Window",
        WS_CHILD | WS_THICKFRAME | WS_CAPTION |
            WS_VISIBLE | WS_MINIMIZEBOX,
        ChildRect, this, NULL) ;
    bMadeChild = TRUE ;
}

void CMainWindow::OnSendMessage ()  // "Send Message" menu item
{                                   // send WM_COMMAND to child window
    Child.SendMessage (WM_USER, 0, 0L) ;
}
```

```
void CMainWindow::OnPaint ()          // parent window paint function
{
    CString string ("Text in Parent Client Area.") ;
    CPaintDC dc (this) ;
    dc.TextOut (10, 10, string, string.GetLength () ) ;
}


//------------------ Child Window Section ----------------------//

CChildWindow::CChildWindow ()          // constructor for child window
{                                      // register new window class
    ClassName = AfxRegisterWndClass (CS_HREDRAW | CS_VREDRAW,
        AfxGetApp()->LoadStandardCursor (IDC_ARROW),
        COLOR_BTNFACE + 1,
        AfxGetApp()->LoadStandardIcon (IDI_APPLICATION) ) ;
}
                                       // new Create function
BOOL CChildWindow::Create (char FAR* lpName, DWORD dwStyle,
    RECT& rect, CWnd* pParent, UINT nID)
{                                          // create child window
    CWnd::Create (ClassName, lpName, dwStyle, rect, pParent, nID) ;
    CRect ButtonRect (20, 55, 130, 95) ;
    ChildButton.Create ("Destroy Me",       // create button control
        WS_CHILD | BS_PUSHBUTTON | WS_VISIBLE, ButtonRect,
        this, IDM_KILLBUTTON) ;
    return TRUE ;
}


BEGIN_MESSAGE_MAP (CChildWindow, CWnd)  // process messages for child
    ON_WM_PAINT ()
    ON_MESSAGE (WM_USER, OnMessage)              // message from parent
    ON_COMMAND (IDM_KILLBUTTON, OnKillButton)    // button selected
END_MESSAGE_MAP ()

void CChildWindow::OnPaint ()              // child window paint function
{
    CString string ("Text in Child Window.") ;
    CPaintDC dc (this) ;
    dc.TextOut (10, 25, string, string.GetLength () ) ;
}


LONG CChildWindow::OnMessage (UINT un, LONG ln) // message from parent
{
    this->SetWindowText ("Got message from parent.") ;
    return NULL ;
}


void CChildWindow::OnKillButton ()        // respond to button selection
{
    this->DestroyWindow () ;                // kill child window
}
```

function is called. This time the child window is created with the style combination:

```
WS_CHILD | WS_THICKFRAME | WS_CAPTION | WS_VISIBLE | WS_MINIMIZEBOX
```

The WS_THICKFRAME style gives the child window a thick border that can be sized. The WS_MINIMIZEBOX provides a minimize button at the child window's top right corner and makes it possible to minimize the window.

Listings 8-9 to 8-11 show the remaining support files for CHILD2.CPP. The program's icon is shown in Figure 8-5.

Listing 8-9 CHILD2.H Resource ID Header File

```
// child2.h   header file for resource ID numbers

#define IDM_CREATE      1           // menu item ID numbers
#define IDM_SEND        2
#define IDM_QUIT        10


#define IDM_CUSTOM      100
#define IDM_KILLBUTTON  101
```

Listing 8-10 CHILD2.RC Resource Script File

```
// child2.rc  resource script file

#include <afxres.h>
#include "child2.h"

AFX_IDI_STD_FRAME   ICON    child2.ico   // the program's icon

MyMenu MENU                                  // define the menu
{
    MENUITEM "&Create",        IDM_CREATE
    MENUITEM "&Send Message",   IDM_SEND
    MENUITEM "&Quit",          IDM_QUIT
}
```

Listing 8-11 CHILD2.DEF Module Definition File

```
NAME            child2
DESCRIPTION     'child2 C++ program'
EXETYPE         WINDOWS
STUB            'WINSTUB.EXE'
CODE            PRELOAD MOVEABLE
DATA            PRELOAD MOVEABLE MULTIPLE
HEAPSIZE        1024
STACKSIZE       5120
```

Figure 8-5 CHILD2.ICO Icon Image

Registering a New Window Class

One of the improvements in CHILD2 compared with CHILD1 is that the child window is filled with a gray brush instead of the standard white interior. It turns out that accomplishing this requires a fairly subtle operation within

const char* **::AfxRegisterWndClass** (UINT *nClassStyle*, HCURSOR *hCursor*, HBRUSH *hbrBackground*, HICON *hIcon*) ;

Parameter	Meaning
nClassStyle	The style values for the window class. This is a series of zero or more binary flag values, such as CS_VREDRAW. The complete set of class style flags is shown in Table 8-2.
hCursor	The handle of the cursor that will be displayed when the mouse cursor is over the window. This is normally fetched with either the **CWinApp::LoadStandardCursor()** or **CWinApp::LoadCursor()** functions.
hbrBackground	The handle of the brush to use in painting the window's client area. This can either be a brush created with the **CBrush** class, or one of the standard brushes that Windows uses. The standard brushes are all given names in the WINDOWS.H file, such as COLOR_WINDOW for the window center. Add one to the COLOR_ value to use a standard Windows color in the new window class. Note that the user can change the standard colors using the Windows Control Panel application. These changes will affect colors displayed in the new window class. (With Windows NT you must create a **CBrush** object or load a stock brush.)
hIcon	A handle to the icon to use when a window created from the class is minimized. This can either be a stock icon loaded with **CWinApp::LoadStandardIcon()**, or an icon in the program's resource data loaded with **CWinApp::LoadIcon()**. Set this value to NULL if the windows created from the class will never be minimized.

Table 8-1 Parameters Passed to ::AfxRegisterWndClass()

Windows. This operation is called "registering a new window class." The idea is that the Windows environment keeps a small set of basic values that define a "class" of windows. This has nothing to do with C++ classes and is specific to the Windows environment. Windows within a class share a few common characteristics, such as displaying the same icon when minimized, displaying the same cursor shape when the mouse is over the window, and using the same color brush to fill the interior of the window. Any number of windows can be created from a single class once it is registered with the Windows environment.

The **CChildWindow** class (C++ class) in CHILD2.CPP includes a constructor function that is called when an object of the **CChildWindow** (C++) class is created. The only activity in the constructor function is to register a new class (Windows class) of windows using the global **::AfxRegisterWndClass()** function. This function takes four parameters, which are summarized in Table 8-1.

The class style values passed to **::AfxRegisterWndClass()** can be any combination of the binary flags listed in Table 8-2. The most common case is the

Style	Meaning
CS_BYTEALIGNCLIENT	Aligns a window's client area on the byte boundaries horizontally. This makes a small savings in memory consumed by windows.
CS_BYTEALIGNWINDOW	Aligns a window on the byte boundaries horizontally.
CS_CLASSDC	Gives the window class its own device context. Every window created from this class will share the DC.
CS_DBLCLKS	Mouse double-click messages are sent to the window.
CS_GLOBALCLASS	Makes an application global class. Available to all applications while the program that created the class is running.
CS_HREDRAW	Redraws the window if the horizontal size changes.
CS_NOCLOSE	Stops the close option on the system menu.
CS_OWNDC	Gives each window instance its own device context. Note that each device context requires 800 bytes of memory.
CS_PARENTDC	The window class uses the parent window's device context.
CS_SAVEBITS	Instructs window to save the bitmap of parts of the window that may be obscured by overlapping windows.
CS_VREDRAW	Redraws the window when the vertical size changes.

Table 8-2 Window Class Style Flags

combination of the CS_HREDRAW | CS_VREDRAW flags. Windows created from the new class will not receive mouse double-click messages unless the CS_DBLCLKS style is added.

You can think of registering a new window class as providing the Windows environment with the minimum outline of what windows created from the class will look like. The class definition does not specify the size of the window, its caption string, or its parent window (if any). All of these values are specified when an individual window is created from the new class. The class name returned by **::AfxRegisterWndClass()** is used in the **CWnd::Create()** function to tell Windows which window class to use when creating a new window. In CHILD2.CPP, the **CWnd::Create()** function call for the child window uses the *ClassName* **CString** object to store the name of the window class:

```
CWnd::Create (ClassName, lpName, dwStyle, rect, pParent, nID) ;
```

You may be wondering why the applications up to now have not needed to register a window class for either the parent window or the window controls. The answer is that the classes are already registered. The **CFrameWnd** class takes care of registering a window class for you automatically, and provides default values for all of the **::AfxRegisterWndClass()** parameters. For example, the icon for a main program window created from the **CFrameWnd** class is assumed to have the ID value AFX_IDI_STD_FRAME. That is why we have used this ID for all of the program icons in the example programs. Controls, such as buttons and list boxes, do not require calling **::AfxRegister-WndClass()** because these window classes are always available as part of the Windows environment.

It was not strictly necessary to register a new window class prior to creating the child window in CHILD2.CPP. The **CWnd** class allows NULL to be passed for the class name, which results in a default class being used as we did in CHILD1.CPP. However, to get the interior of the child window automatically painted with a gray brush required that a new class be registered with this characteristic.

Children of Child Windows

Another interesting aspect of the CHILD2.CPP program is that the child window contains a button. You may recall from Chapter 5, *Window Controls*, that a button control is a form of child window. The button control is a child window of the main child window. You can think of this relationship as a genealogical chain, as shown in Figure 8-6. (Child windows spawn from a single parent, so perhaps the analogy should be to asexual reproduction....)

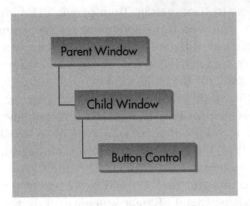

Figure 8-6 Child Window Hierarchy in CHILD2

Figure 8-6 may remind you of the class relationships shown for several derived MFC classes. Both C++ classes and window objects are forms of object oriented programming. C++ classes abstract and hide programming functions and data. Window objects abstract the process of writing to certain areas of the screen. Both types of objects make your job as a programmer much easier.

The parent-child relationship is established when the child window and button control are created in the **CChildWindow::Create()** function. The button control is passed a pointer to the **CChildWindow** object (a *this* pointer) as the parent window. The button control is, therefore, made a child of the larger child window. The WS_CHILD window style must also be included to make the button control a child window.

```
ChildButton.Create ("Destroy Me",        // create button control
       WS_CHILD | BS_PUSHBUTTON | WS_VISIBLE, ButtonRect,
       this, IDM_KILLBUTTON) ;
```

When the button control is selected with the mouse, a WM_COMMAND message is sent to its parent, which is the gray child window that contains the button, not to the main program window. The button control has the ID value IDM_KILLBUTTON, so the WM_COMMAND message passing this ID is mapped to the **CChildWindow::OnKillButton()** function. When the WM_COMMAND message is received, the **CWnd::DestroyWindow()** function is called to destroy the child window.

Sending a Message to a Window

The CHILD2 program has one more trick that you will want to understand. When the menu item "Send Message" is clicked on the parent window, the child window's caption changes to "Got message from parent." This probably does not seem too spectacular until you think about what is happening. The parent window and child window are different Windows objects, are defined in different C++ classes, and have completely separate message processing logic. How does the parent window "talk to" the child window?

The answer lies in the ability of different windows to exchange messages. You can send predefined messages like WM_COMMAND to a window or invent your own messages, as was done in CHILD2.CPP. The WINDOWS.H header file defines a constant WM_USER, which is the lowest message number you can use to define a custom message. In CHILD2.CPP, the **CWnd::Send-Message()** function is used to transmit the WM_USER message to the child window when the user selects the "Send Message" menu item on the main program window.

```
Child.SendMessage (WM_USER, 0, 0L) ;
```

If an application uses a series of custom messages, the usual practice is to define new constants that better represent the meaning of the message. For example:

```
#define WM_CHANGETITLE    WM_USER
#define WM_BEEPCHILD      WM_USER + 1
```

CHILD2.CPP takes a shortcut and uses the WM_USER value directly. The child window's message map includes an entry to route the WM_USER message to a message response function:

```
ON_MESSAGE (WM_USER, OnMessage)
```

The ON_MESSAGE message map entry is a special one, in that it allows *any* message to be mapped. The only restriction is that the message processing function must have the form:

```
LONG CWndClass::FunctionName (UINT, LONG) ;
```

In CHILD2.CPP, the message processing function for the WM_USER message is called **CChildWindow::OnMessage()**. All the function does is change the child window's title to "Got message from parent."

Although CHILD2.CPP only makes limited use of transmitting messages, the concept is extremely powerful. Experienced Windows programmers take advantage of WM_USER messages to provide communication links between different parts of the program. You may also find it useful to simulate the selection of a menu item or the depression of a key by sending a "fake" WM_COMMAND or WM_KEYDOWN message to the main program window. The program will behave just as if the user took the action. This is a general approach to providing macro capabilities for any Windows application.

THE WM_SIZE MESSAGE

Any window that has a thick border (such as all of the program windows created from the **CFrameWnd** MFC class) can be resized by the user. Normally, the window's size is changed by using the mouse to drag one of the window's borders to a new location. Windows also change size when they are minimized, maximized, or restored.

If the user changes the size of a window, Windows will send the program window a WM_SIZE message. Included with the WM_SIZE message are data containing the new size of the window's client area. Determining the size of the client area is frequently useful as a prelude to painting operations. To process WM_SIZE messages, you must add an entry to the program's message map and add an **OnSize()** message response function to process the message. Listing 8-13 shows a typical example.

The Windows environment sends three values with the WM_SIZE message, which end up as parameters passed to the **OnSize()** message response function. The *cx* and *cy* values provide the new width and height of the window's client area measured in pixels. The *nType* parameter passes the type of resizing that is occurring. Table 8-3 lists the possible values for *nType*.

As you can see from this example, Windows has the ability to send a considerable amount of information along with a message. This provides for efficient processing of the message data, an important point in an environment that supports many programs running at the same time. The next example will use the WM_SIZE message to determine the size of the main program window client area so that two child windows can be exactly sized to cover the client area completely.

Listing 8-13 Processing WM_SIZE Messages

```
BEGIN_MESSAGE_MAP (CMainWindow, CFrameWnd)
    ON_WM_SIZE ()                       // message map entry for WM_SIZE
    // other message map entries here
END_MESSAGE_MAP ()
            // message response function must be called OnSize()
void CMainWindow::OnSize (UINT nType, int cx, int cy)
{
    int ClientWide = cx ;
    int ClientHigh = cy ;
    if (nType == SIZE_MINIMIZED)
        // do something
}
```

Value	Meaning
SIZE_MAXIMIZED	The window has been maximized.
SIZE_MINIMIZED	The window has been minimized.
SIZE_RESTORED	The window has been resized, but not minimized or maximized. This usually means that the user has dragged one of the thick borders of the window to change its size.
SIZE_MAXHIDE	Another window has been maximized. This message is sent to all pop-up windows when some other window is maximized.
SIZE_MAXSHOW	Another window which was maximized has been restored to its former size. This message is sent to all pop-up windows when another window is restored.

Table 8-3 nType values passed to OnSize()

FIXED CHILD WINDOWS

In the CHILD1 and CHILD2 examples, the child windows had caption bars. This allowed the child windows to be moved on the parent window's client area. Sometimes it is useful to have fixed child windows that cannot be moved. Button controls are a classic example of a small, fixed child window designed for a special purpose. The usual reason for creating larger fixed child windows is to use child windows to break up a larger window into manageable pieces. Our next example, called FIXCHILD, demonstrates fixed child windows by dividing the parent window's client area into two halves. Figure 8-7 shows FIXCHILD in action. The left half of the parent window's client area is covered with a red child window, while the right half is covered by a blue child window. The result

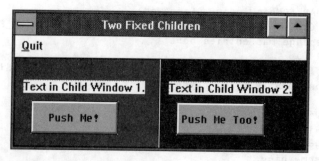

Figure 8-7 The FIXCHILD Program

is that the child windows completely cover the parent window's client area, so the child windows end up getting the Windows messages.

The FIXCHILD.HPP header file is shown in Listing 8-12. The left and right child windows that will cover the parent window's client area are each given a separate C++ class. The **LChild** and **RChild** class definitions are essentially identical, and could be combined into a single more general class with a bit of work. These classes were deliberately kept separate in the FIXCHILD example to illustrate the general case of having multiple child windows and multiple message maps within a single program.

The **Create()** functions for the two child window classes have been expanded to include a new parameter named *dwColor*. This parameter is used to specify the color of the child window's client area when painted. Otherwise, the **LChild** and **RChild** class definitions are very similar to the child window class in the CHILD2.HPP file. Note that the **CMainWindow** class now declares **LChild** and **RChild** objects named *RightSide* and *LeftSide* in the class definition.

Listing 8-13 shows the FIXCHILD.CPP program. The two child windows are created in the **CMainWindow** constructor function. The child windows are sized to exactly fit the main program window's client area. The **CWnd::GetClientRect()** function comes in handy here to determine the initial size of the client area rectangle. Note that the child windows are created with the WS_CHILD | WS_BORDER | WS_VISIBLE style flags. Because there is no caption bar with this style combination, the child windows will not be moveable. This is ideal for our purpose of covering the parent window's client area at all times.

The parent window can be resized at any time, so the child windows must also be resized any time the parent window receives a WM_SIZE message. The **CMainWindow::OnSize()** function in FIXCHILD.CPP resizes both child windows with the **CWnd::MoveWindow()** function.

The **Create()** functions for the two child windows register new window classes in order to specify the color of the brushes used to paint their client areas. There is no need to load an icon as part of these window classes because neither of the child windows can be minimized to an icon. Therefore, NULL is passed for the icon handle in the calls to the **::AfxRegisterWndClass()** function. Each of the child windows creates its own button controls, which again become child window controls of other child windows.

The child windows both process WM_PAINT messages and display text strings in their client areas. More interesting is the processing of the WM_COMMAND message generated by the button controls in each child window. Selecting the buttons changes the caption string for the main program window. This is done in a rather indirect way by taking advantage of the

Listing 8-12 FIXCHILD.HPP Header File

```
// fixchild.hpp    header file for fixchild.cpp

class LChild : public CWnd        // derive left child window
{                                 // uses default constructor
public:
    BOOL Create (char FAR* lpName, DWORD dwStyle,
        RECT& rect, CWnd* pParent, UINT nID = NULL,
        DWORD dwColor = OL) ;
private:
    CString ClassName ;           // name of new window class
    CButton ChildButton ;         // child window's own button
    void OnPaint () ;             // process WM_PAINT messages
    void OnButton () ;            // respond to button selection

    DECLARE_MESSAGE_MAP()         // separate message processing
} ;


class RChild : public CWnd        // derive right child window
{                                 // uses default constructor
public:
    BOOL Create (char FAR* lpName, DWORD dwStyle,
        RECT& rect, CWnd* pParent, UINT nID = NULL,
        DWORD dwColor = OL) ;
private:
    CString ClassName ;           // name of new window class
    CButton ChildButton ;         // child window's own button
    void OnPaint () ;             // process WM_PAINT messages
    void OnButton () ;            // respond to button selection

    DECLARE_MESSAGE_MAP()         // separate message processing
} ;

                                  // derive a main window class
class CMainWindow : public CFrameWnd
{
public:
    CMainWindow () ;              // declare a constructor
private:
    RChild RightSide ;
    LChild LeftSide ;
    void OnExit () ;             // "Quit" menu item
    void OnSize (UINT nType, int cx, int cy) ;

    DECLARE_MESSAGE_MAP()         // prepare for message processing
} ;

class CTheApp : public CWinApp // derive an application class
{
public:
    BOOL InitInstance () ;       // declare new InitInstance()
} ;
```

Listing 8-13 FIXCHILD.CPP

```cpp
// fixchild.cpp                    demonstrate independent child window

#include <afxwin.h>          // class library header file
#include "fixchild.h"        // header file for resource data
#include "fixchild.hpp"      // header file for this program

CTheApp theApp ;             // create one CTheApp object - runs program

BOOL CTheApp::InitInstance ()    // override default InitInstance()
{
    m_pMainWnd = new CMainWindow () ;       // create a main window
    m_pMainWnd->ShowWindow (m_nCmdShow) ;   // make it visible
    m_pMainWnd->UpdateWindow () ;           // paint center
    return TRUE ;
}

CMainWindow::CMainWindow ()      // constructor for main window
{
    Create (NULL, "Two Fixed Children", WS_OVERLAPPEDWINDOW,
        rectDefault, NULL, "MyMenu") ;

    CRect ClientRect ;
    this->GetClientRect (ClientRect) ;      // get client area size
    int nWidth = ClientRect.Width () ;
    ClientRect.right -= nWidth / 2 ;        // cut in half
    LeftSide.Create ("", WS_CHILD | WS_BORDER | WS_VISIBLE,
        ClientRect, this, NULL, RGB (255, 0, 0)) ;

    ClientRect.left++ ;                     // reduce width by one
    ClientRect.OffsetRect (nWidth / 2, 0) ; // move to right side
    RightSide.Create ("", WS_CHILD | WS_BORDER | WS_VISIBLE,
        ClientRect, this, NULL, RGB (0, 0, 255)) ;
}

BEGIN_MESSAGE_MAP (CMainWindow, CFrameWnd)
    ON_COMMAND (IDM_QUIT, OnExit)    // "Quit" menu item
    ON_WM_SIZE ()                    // parent window size changed
END_MESSAGE_MAP ()

void CMainWindow::OnExit ()          // respond to menu item "Quit"
{
    this->DestroyWindow () ;         // destroy main window,
}                                    // this stops application

void CMainWindow::OnSize (UINT nType, int cx, int cy)
{                                    // resize child windows to fit
    LeftSide.MoveWindow (0, 0, cx/2, cy, TRUE) ;
    RightSide.MoveWindow (1 + (cx/2), 0, cx, cy, TRUE) ;
}
```

```
//--------------- Left child window section ---------------------//

BOOL LChild::Create (char FAR* lpName, DWORD dwStyle,
    RECT& rect, CWnd* pParent, UINT nID, DWORD dwColor)
{
    CBrush brush (dwColor) ;
                                            // create child window
    ClassName = AfxRegisterWndClass (CS_HREDRAW | CS_VREDRAW,
        AfxGetApp()->LoadStandardCursor (IDC_ARROW),
        brush.GetSafeHandle (), NULL ) ;
    CWnd::Create (ClassName, lpName, dwStyle, rect,
        pParent, nID) ;
    CRect ButtonRect (20, 50, 130, 90) ;
    ChildButton.Create ("Push Me!",
        WS_CHILD | BS_PUSHBUTTON | WS_VISIBLE, ButtonRect,
        this, IDM_LEFTBUTTON) ;
    return TRUE ;
}

BEGIN_MESSAGE_MAP (LChild, CWnd)  // process messages for child
    ON_WM_PAINT ()
    ON_COMMAND (IDM_LEFTBUTTON, OnButton)
END_MESSAGE_MAP ()

void LChild::OnPaint ()          // child window paint function
{
    CString string ("Text in Child Window 1.") ;
    CPaintDC dc (this) ;
    dc.TextOut (10, 25, string, string.GetLength () ) ;
}

void LChild::OnButton ()          // respond to button selection
{
    (this->GetParent ())->SetWindowText ("Child 1 Button") ;
}

//--------------- Right child window section ---------------------//

BOOL RChild::Create (char FAR* lpName, DWORD dwStyle,
    RECT& rect, CWnd* pParent, UINT nID, DWORD dwColor)
{                                         // create child window
    CBrush brush (dwColor) ;
                                            // create child window
    ClassName = AfxRegisterWndClass (CS_HREDRAW | CS_VREDRAW,
        AfxGetApp()->LoadStandardCursor (IDC_ARROW),
        brush.GetSafeHandle (), NULL ) ;
    CWnd::Create (ClassName, lpName, dwStyle, rect,
        pParent, nID) ;
    CRect ButtonRect (20, 50, 130, 90) ;
```

```
    ChildButton.Create ("Push Me Too!",
        WS_CHILD | BS_PUSHBUTTON | WS_VISIBLE, ButtonRect,
        this, IDM_RIGHTBUTTON) ;
    return TRUE ;
}

BEGIN_MESSAGE_MAP (RChild, CWnd)          // process messages for child
    ON_WM_PAINT ()
    ON_COMMAND (IDM_RIGHTBUTTON, OnButton)
END_MESSAGE_MAP ()

void RChild::OnPaint ()                   // child window paint function
{
    CString string ("Text in Child Window 2.") ;
    CPaintDC dc (this) ;
    dc.TextOut (10, 25, string, string.GetLength () ) ;
}

void RChild::OnButton ()                  // respond to button selection
{
    (this->GetParent ())->SetWindowText ("Child 2 Button") ;
}
```

CWnd::GetParent() function. **CWnd::GetParent()** returns a pointer to any child window's immediate parent. The construction:

```
(this->GetParent ())->SetWindowText ("Child 2 Button") ;
```

in the **RChild::OnButton()** and **LChild::OnButton()** functions results in the parent window's caption being changed. Let's break this down into understandable pieces using the **RChild** class as an example,. Within a member function of the **RChild** class, such as **RChild::OnButton()**, the *this* pointer points to the right child window object. Therefore, *this->GetParent()* retrieves the parent window for the right child, which is the FIXCHILD main program window. The main program window pointer is then used to call the **SetWindowText()** function, which is the full expression shown earlier.

The **CWnd::GetParent()** function is useful in cases where you want to write a generic program for a child window that may be used for a number of different parent windows in different programs. By using **CWnd::GetParent()** instead of "hard coding" the parent window name, the same program will work fine with its child window attached to any parent window.

You may be wondering if Windows allows you to find out the child windows of a parent, doing the opposite of the **CWnd::GetParent()** function. This is certainly possible, but the MFC classes do not include these functions because there is seldom a need to find child windows. Normally, a parent window creates all of its child windows and, therefore, knows their names. If you really need to find the children of a parent, take a look at the **EnumChildWindows()** example in *The Waite Group's Windows API Bible*.

Listings 8-14 to 8-16 show the remaining support files for FIXCHILD.CPP. The program's icon image is shown in Figure 8-8.

Listing 8-14 FIXCHILD.H Resource ID Header File

```
// fixchild.h  header file for resource ID numbers

#define IDM_QUIT            10        // menu item ID

#define IDM_LEFTBUTTON      100       // button control IDs
#define IDM_RIGHTBUTTON     101
```

Listing 8-15 FIXCHILD.RC Resource Script File

```
// fixchild.rc  resource script file

#include <afxres.h>
#include "fixchild.h"

AFX_IDI_STD_FRAME   ICON    fixchild.ico   // the program's icon

MyMenu MENU                                // define the menu
{
    MENUITEM "&Quit",           IDM_QUIT
}
```

Listing 8-16 FIXCHILD.DEF Module Definition File

```
NAME            fixchild
DESCRIPTION     'fixchild C++ program'
EXETYPE         WINDOWS
STUB            'WINSTUB.EXE'
CODE            PRELOAD MOVEABLE
DATA            PRELOAD MOVEABLE MULTIPLE
HEAPSIZE        1024
STACKSIZE       5120
```

Figure 8-8 FIXCHILD.ICO Icon Image

Although the FIXCHILD program does not do a lot of processing for each child window, you can imagine that this approach would work well for applications with complex displays. By splitting the parent window into different child windows, the problem can be broken down into manageable pieces. Microsoft Project is an excellent example of a program that uses this approach to simplify coding and to improve the user interface.

POP-UP WINDOWS

The last type of window we will explore in this chapter is the pop-up window. Pop-ups are similar to child windows, in that they are related to a parent window. However, pop-up windows are not restricted to the parent window's client area. Pop-ups can appear anywhere on the screen and can cover up portions of the parent window and other program windows. One interesting aspect of pop-up windows is that they can never be covered by their parent window. Both the pop-up and its parent can be covered by other windows and uncovered, but the parent window will always be "under" the pop-up window. This is true even if the parent window gains the input focus (has a dark caption bar).

Figure 8-9 shows our next example program in action. The POPUP program creates a pop-up window when the "Create" menu item is selected. The pop-up window has a caption bar, so it can be moved on the screen. In Figure 8-9, the pop-up window is partially covering the parent window. Note that the pop-up window extends well beyond the bounds of the parent window and can be completely separated from the parent on the screen. This makes pop-up windows handy for small utility windows, such as windows that show the current cursor *X,Y* position in painting programs.

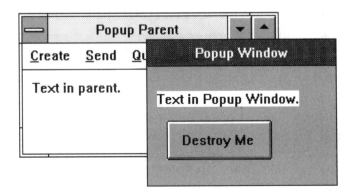

Figure 8-9 The POPUP Program

If the parent window is minimized, the pop-up window automatically disappears from the screen. When the parent is restored, the pop-up automatically reappears at its previous screen location. You can think of a pop-up window as an obedient dog. It is always around its master (the main program window), but not always in the master's lap.

Creating pop-up windows is just like creating child windows, except the WS_POPUP window style is used in place of WS_CHILD when calling **CWnd::Create()**. You cannot use the WS_CHILD and WS_POPUP styles at the same time to create a window because the two styles are mutually exclusive. Another difference between child and pop-up windows is that the coordinates passed to **CWnd::Create()** are interpreted as screen coordinates for pop-up windows, not as client coordinates of the parent window. This makes sense, as pop-up windows can be located anywhere on the screen, while child windows are restricted to the parent window's client area.

Listing 8-17 shows the POPUP.CPP program. The pop-up window is created when the user selects the "Create" menu item that is mapped to the **CMainWindow::OnCreatePopup()** function. The combination of the WS_POPUP | WS_BORDER | WS_VISIBLE | WS_CAPTION window styles is used for the pop-up window. You can also add minimize and maximize boxes to pop-up windows with the WS_MINIMIZEBOX and WS_MAXIMIZEBOX styles.

Like the previous CHILD2 and FIXCHILD examples, POPUP.CPP registers a new class of windows in the **CPopup::Create()** function. The new window class uses a custom brush for the background color, which is created using a **CBrush** object. You cannot use the **CBrush** object directly because the **AfxRegisterWndClass()** function expects to get the handle of the brush used to paint the background color as the fourth parameter. The handle of the **CBrush** object can be extracted using the **CGdiObject::GetSafeHandle()** function (the **CBrush** class is derived from the **CGdiObject** class). The handle provides Windows with the information about where to find the brush color data in memory.

```
CBrush brush (dwColor) ;
ClassName = AfxRegisterWndClass (CS_HREDRAW | CS_VREDRAW,
    AfxGetApp()->LoadStandardCursor (IDC_ARROW),
    brush.GetSafeHandle (), NULL ) ;
```

CPopup::Create() also creates the button control labeled "Destroy Me," which is a child window of the pop-up window. The pop-up window has its own message map, and processes WM_PAINT, WM_COMMAND and user messages. The user messages are discussed below.

If you compare the POPUP.CPP and CHILD2.CPP listings, you will note that there are remarkably few differences. You can easily change from pop-up to child windows and back if the structure of the window is an independent entity.

Listing 8-17 POPUP.CPP

```cpp
// popup.cpp                 demonstrate an independent pop-up window

#include <afxwin.h>     // class library header file
#include "popup.h"      // header file for resource data
#include "popup.hpp"    // header file for this program

CTheApp theApp ;        // create one CTheApp object - runs program

BOOL CTheApp::InitInstance ()   // override default InitInstance()
{
    m_pMainWnd = new CMainWindow () ;        // create a main window
    m_pMainWnd->ShowWindow (m_nCmdShow) ;    // make it visible
    m_pMainWnd->UpdateWindow () ;            // paint center
    return TRUE ;
}

CMainWindow::CMainWindow ()      // constructor for main window
{
    Create (NULL, "Popup Parent", WS_OVERLAPPEDWINDOW, rectDefault,
        NULL, "MyMenu") ;
    bPopupExists = FALSE ;       // initialize
}

BEGIN_MESSAGE_MAP (CMainWindow, CFrameWnd)
    ON_COMMAND (IDM_SEND, OnSend)
    ON_COMMAND (IDM_QUIT, OnExit)
    ON_COMMAND (IDM_CREATE, OnCreatePopup)
    ON_MESSAGE (WM_POPUPMESSAGE, OnPopupMessage)
END_MESSAGE_MAP ()

void CMainWindow::OnExit ()         // respond to menu item "Quit"
{
    this->DestroyWindow () ;        // destroy main window,
}                                   // this stops application

void CMainWindow::OnCreatePopup ()  // create pop-up window
{
    if (bPopupExists)               // only make one at a time
        return ;
    CRect PopupRect (10, 50, 210, 200) ;
    Popup.Create ("Pop-up Window",
        WS_POPUP | WS_BORDER | WS_VISIBLE | WS_CAPTION,
        PopupRect, this, NULL, RGB (194, 194, 194)) ;
    bPopupExists = TRUE ;
}

void CMainWindow::OnSend ()         // send a message to pop-up
{
    if (bPopupExists)
        Popup.SendMessage (WM_CUSTOM, 0, 0L) ;
}
```

```
LONG CMainWindow::OnPopupMessage (UINT, LONG) // message from pop-up
{
    bPopupExists = FALSE ;            // remember pop-up destroyed
    return NULL ;
}


//---------------- Pop-up window section --------------------//

BOOL CPopup::Create (char FAR* lpName, DWORD dwStyle,
    RECT& rect, CWnd* pParent, UINT nID, DWORD dwColor)
{                                         // create pop-up window
    CBrush brush (dwColor) ;

    ClassName = AfxRegisterWndClass (CS_HREDRAW | CS_VREDRAW,
        AfxGetApp()->LoadStandardCursor (IDC_ARROW),
        brush.GetSafeHandle (), NULL ) ;
    CWnd::Create (ClassName, lpName, dwStyle, rect,
        pParent, nID) ;
    CRect ButtonRect (20, 50, 130, 90) ;
    ChildButton.Create ("Destroy Me",
        WS_CHILD | BS_PUSHBUTTON | WS_VISIBLE, ButtonRect,
        this, IDM_POPUPBUTTON) ;
    return TRUE ;
}


BEGIN_MESSAGE_MAP (CPopup, CWnd)     // process messages for pop-up
    ON_WM_PAINT ()
    ON_COMMAND (IDM_POPUPBUTTON, OnButton)  // button pressed
    ON_MESSAGE (WM_CUSTOM, OnMessage)      // message from parent
END_MESSAGE_MAP ()

void CPopup::OnPaint ()              // Pop-up window paint function
{
    CString string ("Text in Popup Window.") ;
    CPaintDC dc (this) ;
    dc.TextOut (10, 25, string, string.GetLength () ) ;
}

void CPopup::OnButton ()            // respond to button selection
{                                   // tell parent pop-up is exiting
    (this->GetParent ())->SendMessage (WM_POPUPMESSAGE, 0, OL) ;
    this->DestroyWindow () ;        // remove pop-up window
}

LONG CPopup::OnMessage (UINT, LONG) // respond to message from parent
{
    this->SetWindowText ("Got message!") ;  // change pop-up caption
    return NULL ;
}
```

It would not make sense to use fixed POPUP windows to partition the parent window's client area as we did in the FIXCHILD.CPP example. Pop-ups are almost always moveable.

The POPUP program takes advantage of user messages to send messages from the parent to the pop-up window, and from the pop-up window to the child. Selecting the "Send" menu item in the parent window menu results in the **CMainWindow::OnSend()** function being called. This function uses the **CWnd::SendMessage()** function to send the user message WM_CUSTOM to the pop-up window. WM_CUSTOM is defined later in POPUP.H (Listing 8-19) as WM_USER + 2, making it a safe value to use for a user message. The WM_CUSTOM message is mapped to the **CPopup::OnMessage()** function in the pop-up's program logic, which simply changes the pop-up window's caption to "Got message!"

A second user message is used for a more pragmatic purpose. The POPUP program is designed so that only one pop-up window is created at a time. However, if the user selects the "Destroy Me" button on the pop-up window, the pop-up window is destroyed and the main program window should be free to create a new pop-up window if the "Create" menu item is selected again. The problem is that the pop-up window destroys itself without any involvement from the parent. The parent window has no immediate way of knowing when the pop-up is destroyed.

To get around this problem, the pop-up window sends the WM_POPUP-MESSAGE user message (defined equal to WM_USER + 1 in POPUP.H) to its parent window right before the pop-up destroys itself (like a suicide note). The user message is sent in the **CPopup::OnButton()** function, which uses the **CWnd::GetParent()** function to retrieve a pointer to the parent window. The parent window logic maps the WM_POPUPMESSAGE to the **CMainWindow::OnPopupMessage()** message processing function, which records the fact that the pop-up has been destroyed by changing the value of the Boolean variable *bPopupExists*. The main program window is now free to create another pop-up window.

User Messages Between Windows

For small amounts of data, sending user messages between windows is preferable to using global variables to track information shared by more than one window object. By using messages, the data used by each window object can be kept separate and made a part of the C++ classes that support each

continued on next page

---

continued from previous page

window. You can think of each window as being a seprate business with its own file system. User messages are analogous to using mail or a FAX machine to transmit data between the two businesses. This type of organization is much easier to manage in the long term compared to getting the two separate businesses to share the same file system (two windows sharing the same global data).

If the amount of data shared between the separate window objects is large, the message approach will be too slow. In these cases, you may want to use advanced C++ techniques, such as virtual functions and "friend" relataionships between classes, to manage the data. See the Bibliography for references on advanced C++ programming techniques.

Listings 8-18 to 8-21 show the support files for POPUP.CPP. The program's icon is shown in Figure 8-10.

The user messages in the POPUP.CPP program are simple notifications and do not pass any data. You have the option of sending both an integer (UINT) and a LONG value along with the message. For example, the parent might send the pop-up window a WM_CUSTOM message with the values 27 and 3478 as parameters:

```
Popup.SendMessage (WM_CUSTOM, 27, 3478) ;
```

The message processing function for this custom message would have the following form:

```
LONG CPopup::OnMessage (UINT nIntValue, LONG lLongValue) { }
```

The **CPopup::OnMessage()** function would receive the value of 27 as *nIntValue* and the value of 3478 as *lLongValue*. An integer and a LONG value probably do not sound like a lot of data to transmit with a message. However, as you will see in Chapter 12, *Managing Memory*, Windows allows you to safely pass a handle to a memory block as a 16-bit value. You can send another window the

Figure 8-10 POPUP.ICO Icon Image

Listing 8-18 POPUP.HPP Header File

```cpp
// popup.hpp    header file for pop-up.cpp

class CPopup : public CWnd          // derive pop-up window class
{                                   // uses default constructor
public:
    BOOL Create (char FAR* lpName, DWORD dwStyle,
        RECT& rect, CWnd* pParent, UINT nID = NULL,
        DWORD dwColor = OL) ;
private:
    CString ClassName ;             // name of new window class
    CButton ChildButton ;           // pop-up window's own button
    void OnPaint () ;               // process WM_PAINT messages
    void OnButton () ;              // respond to button selection
    LONG OnMessage (UINT, LONG) ;// respond to custom message

    DECLARE_MESSAGE_MAP()           // separate message processing
} ;

                                    // derive a main window class
class CMainWindow : public CFrameWnd
{
public:
    CMainWindow () ;                // declare a constructor
private:
    CPopup Popup ;                  // pop-up object
    BOOL bPopupExists ;             // track if pop-up window exists
    void OnExit () ;                // "Quit" menu item
    void OnCreatePopup () ;         // "Create" menu item
    void OnSend () ;                // "Send" menu item
    LONG OnPopupMessage (UINT, LONG) ;// message from pop-up

    DECLARE_MESSAGE_MAP()           // prepare for message processing
} ;

class CTheApp : public CWinApp  // derive an application class
{
public:
    BOOL InitInstance () ;          // declare new InitInstance()
} ;
```

Listing 8-19 POPUP.H Resource ID Header File

```cpp
// popup.h  header file for resource ID numbers

#define IDM_CREATE          1       // menu item ID
#define IDM_SEND            2
#define IDM_QUIT           10

#define IDM_POPUPBUTTON    100      // button control IDs

#define WM_POPUPMESSAGE    WM_USER + 1 // custom messages
#define WM_CUSTOM          WM_USER + 2
```

Listing 8-20 POPUP.RC Resource Script File

```
// popup.rc   resource script file

#include <afxres.h>
#include "popup.h"

AFX_IDI_STD_FRAME   ICON     popup.ico    // the program's icon

MyMenu MENU                                // define the menu
{
    MENUITEM "&Create",        IDM_CREATE
    MENUITEM "&Send",          IDM_SEND
    MENUITEM "&Quit",          IDM_QUIT
}
```

Listing 8-21 POPUP.DEF Module Definition File

```
NAME            popup
DESCRIPTION     'popup C++ program'
EXETYPE         WINDOWS
STUB            'WINSTUB.EXE'
CODE            PRELOAD MOVEABLE
DATA            PRELOAD MOVEABLE MULTIPLE
HEAPSIZE        1024
STACKSIZE       5120
```

handle for a block of data in memory, and let the receiving window's logic read the data from the block. This is the foundation behind the Windows Dynamic Data Exchange (DDE) mechanism that allows separate programs to exchange data in memory while they are running. DDE is an advanced topic, and not covered in this book. See Chapter 30 of *The Waite Group's Windows API Bible* if you need to learn the basics of DDE.

THE BIG PICTURE

You may have noticed the similarity between the way child and pop-up windows behave and the way program windows behave on the Windows desktop (the background screen on which all of the program windows appear). This is not an accident. The Windows desktop is just another window, admittedly a slightly odd one, as it lacks a caption bar and border. All of the running program main windows behave like children of the desktop window. When you minimize a main program window, it shrinks to an icon on the desktop, just like our child window in CHILD2 shrinks to an icon in the corner of its parent window's client area.

When you write a program with one or more moveable child windows (like CHILD2), you end up creating a miniature "little world" in your program's client area. Your program's client area behaves very much like the full Windows desktop. Windows uses the same built-in logic for handling a wide variety of windowing situations, such as minimizing and maximizing windows, and moving child windows within a limited area. Using the same code for both main program windows and child windows keeps the size of the Windows system down, and gives the environment consistent behavior in a wide variety of situations.

SUMMARY

Child windows are created by using the **CWnd::Create()** function with the WS_CHILD style. Child windows are restricted to the bounds of the parent window's client area. Child windows normally use a separate message map and message processing functions. Messages to the child window are processed by the child window's message functions, not by the parent window. Child windows can be either moveable (if they have a caption bar) or fixed at a location in the parent window's client area. Fixed child windows are useful for breaking up the program logic for complex screens into manageable chunks.

It is frequently useful to register a new class of windows prior to creating a child window. A window class provides some basic data about window objects that will be created from the class, such as the color of the window client area, the icon to use when the window is minimized, and the cursor shape to display when the cursor is above the window. Window classes are an element of the Microsoft Windows environment and have nothing to do with C++ classes. The MFC classes (which are C++ classes) provide the **AfxRegisterWndClass()** function to create new window classes. The **CWnd::Create()** function takes the class name as a parameter when creating new windows. Any number of windows can be created from a window class.

Pop-up windows are like child windows, except that they are free to be located anywhere on the screen. Pop-up windows are usually based on a separate window class and use a separate message processing function. Pop-up windows are ideal for applications that have multiple independent sections, such as a communications program that supports a number of simultaneous terminal sessions in different pop-up windows.

User messages are used to communicate between windows with separate message processing functions. Windows defines WM_USER as the first ID value that is above any of the predefined Windows messages. You can use WM_USER and above to define messages for any type of activity. Experienced Windows programmers use user messages and separate message processing functions to break complex programming problems into manageable pieces.

QUESTIONS

1. To create a child window, use the _____ window style when calling **CWnd::Create**(). To create a pop-up window, use the _____ window style.

2. You must register a new window class in order to create a child or pop-up window. (True/False)

3. The function type and parameters for the message processing functions for parent windows, child windows, and pop-up windows are the same. (True/False)

4. To process messages separately from the parent window, the child window class definition must include the _____ macro.

5. The location of a pop-up window is relative to the upper left corner of the _____.

6. In order for a child or pop-up window to be moveable, it must be created with the _____ style (or another style that contains the same binary flag.)

7. Child and pop-up windows with the WS_MINIMIZEBOX style automatically have the ability to be minimized without any other programming effort. (True/False)

8. The lowest message number that is safe to use for a user message is defined in WINDOWS.H as _____.

9. The message map entry for a user message is _____.

10. The message processing function for a user message can have any desired list of parameters. (True/False)

EXERCISES

1. Modify the POPUP1.CPP program so that a white rectangle is painted in the pop-up window's client area in place of the text string. Also change the message response function logic so that the pop-up window responds to

the WM_CUSTOM user message by beeping the computer's speaker. The result should look roughly like Figure 8-11.

2. Modify the CHILD2.CPP program so that selection of a menu item on the parent window results in the child window being enlarged by 20 units in each direction. (Hint: You may find the **CWnd::GetWindowRect()** function useful to find the current size and location of the child window.)

ANSWERS TO QUESTIONS

1. WS_CHILD, WS_POPUP.

2. False. The **CWnd::Create()** function will accept NULL for the window class name parameter. This results in the default window class being used. See the CHILD1.CPP program for an example.

3. True.

4. DECLARE_MESSAGE_MAP().

5. screen.

6. WS_CAPTION.

7. True.

8. WM_USER.

9. ON_MESSAGE().

10. False. The message processing function must have the form:

```
LONG Class::FunctionName (UINT, LONG)
```

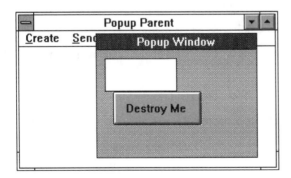

Figure 8-11 Solution to Exercise 8-1

SOLUTIONS TO EXERCISES

1. The full listings are under the file name C8EXER1 on the source code disks. Listing 8-22 shows the changes to the **CPopup::OnPaint()** and **CPopup::OnMessage()** functions.

2. The only changes necessary to CHILD2.CPP are to the **CChildWindow::OnMessage()** function, which responds to the child window receiving a user message from the parent. Listing 8-23 shows the modified function. The full solution is given under the file name C8EXER2 on the source code disks.

   Getting the child window to enlarge its own size at the same location on the screen is a bit tricky. The **CWnd::GetWindowRect()** function fetches the current location of the child window, but uses screen coordinates when filling in the **CRect** parameter data. They must be converted to client coordinates *of the parent window* before passing the rectangle back to **CWnd::MoveWindow()** to resize the child window. To convert the child window screen coordinates to parent window client coordinates requires the interesting construction:

   ```
   (this->GetParent ())->ScreenToClient (&rect) ;
   ```

   Listing 8-23 takes advantage of a **CRect** class function **CRect::InflateRect()** to increase the size of the child window rectangle by 20 units in both directions with a single function call. The **CRect** class has a number of useful functions and overloaded operators. Finally, the **CWnd::MoveWindow()** function is used to resize and repaint the child window based on the inflated rectangle. The result is that the child window appears to grow "in place."

Listing 8-22 Solution to Exercise 8-1

```
void CPopup::OnPaint ()                 // Pop-up window paint function
{
    CPaintDC dc (this) ;
    dc.Rectangle (10, 10, 100, 50) ;
}
LONG CPopup::OnMessage (UINT, LONG) // respond to message from parent
{
    ::MessageBeep (0) ;                 // just beep
    return NULL ;
}
```

Listing 8-23 Changes to CHILD2.CPP for C8EXER2.CPP

```
LONG CChildWindow::OnMessage (UINT un, LONG ln) // message from parent
{                                               // increase child wind. size
    CRect rect ;
    this->GetWindowRect (&rect) ;           // get current size/location
    (this->GetParent ())->ScreenToClient (&rect) ;
    rect.InflateRect (20, 20) ;             // enlarge by 20 each way
    this->MoveWindow (&rect, TRUE) ;        // repaint with new size
    return NULL ;
}
```

## Chapter 9

Menus

This chapter begins the first of a series of three chapters devoted to resources. The most common types of resources are data defining menus, dialog boxes, and small images (icons and bitmaps). Chapter 7, *Fonts and the Keyboard*, also introduced keyboard accelerators, which are stored as resource data. This chapter will examine menus, including menus containing graphic objects. Dialog boxes are the subject of Chapter 10, and Chapter 11 covers miscellaneous types of data that can be stored in resources.

Up to now the examples in this book have used simple menus, defined as part of the program's resource data. Windows provides tremendous built-in support for more complex menus, including pop-up menus that appear under the main menu bar, and menu items containing graphic images. Windows also allows a program's menu to be altered as the program operates. This is useful if you want to support beginner and advanced versions of the menus or have a program that operates in more than one state, such as a spreadsheet program that can switch to a graphics mode with a different menu.

The MFC classes combine most of the menu operations into a single **CMenu** class. The **CMenu** class is used in conjunction with the program's resource data to define and use menus. This chapter examines a variety of menu types, including complex menus with several levels of submenus, menus that change as the program runs, and menus that include bitmap images. We will also look at how you can use an application's system menu, using a simple program that continually moves its icon around the screen. The system menu example also introduces the Windows timer, which can be used to start actions at fixed time intervals.

Concepts covered: Main menus, pop-up menus, discardable resource data, graying and checking menu items, creating menus as the program operates, the system menu, Windows timers.

Key words covered: MENU, LOADONCALL, MOVEABLE, FIXED, DISCARDABLE, POPUP, BEGIN, END, CHECKED, GRAYED, HELP, INACTIVE, MENUBARBREAK, MENUBREAK , MF_BYCOMMAND, MF_BYPOSITION, MF_ENABLED, MF_GRAYED, MF_DISABLED, SC_CLOSE, SC_MAXIMIZE, SC_MINIMIZE, SC_MOVE, SC_RESTORE, SC_SIZE, SC_TASKLIST.

Functions covered: CMenu::CreateMenu(), CMenu::LoadMenu(), CMenu::EnableMenuItem(), CMenu::CheckMenuItem(), CMenu::AppendMenu(), CMenu::CreatePopupMenu(), CMenu::DeleteMenu(), CMenu::InsertMenu(), CMenu::Detach(), CWnd::SetMenu(), CWnd::GetMenu(), CWnd::GetSystemMenu(), CWnd::DrawMenuBar(), CWnd::SetTimer(), CWnd::KillTimer().

Messages covered: WM_SYSCOMMAND, WM_TIMER.

Classes covered: CMenu, CBitmap.

CREATING MENUS

Most programs have a menu that consists only of key words (not graphics), and which does not change as the program operates. Creating this type of menu is almost trivial. You define the menu structure as part of the program's resource script file (.RC file), compile all the resources with the resource compiler, and let Windows take care all of the details of positioning each item, highlighting items when selected, and sending WM_COMMAND messages when items are selected.

The MINIMAL3 program in Chapter 3, *First Programming Experiments*, provides a good example of a simple menu. Listing 9-1 shows the MINIMAL3.RC resource script file, including the menu definition. MINIMAL3.RC also includes an icon file in the program's resources.

When you compile your program, the resource compiler (RC.EXE) reads the entire .RC file and converts it into the .RES resource data format that Windows can read directly. The .RES data is added on to the end of the program's code to make a finished Windows program. Figure 9-1 shows the sequence of events that end up with a complete Windows program, containing both the program's instructions and the resource data. For the finished MINIMAL3.EXE program, the resource data will contain the icon data and the menu definition in the compiled format Windows uses internally.

"MENU" is a key word that the resource compiler recognizes. Listing 9-2 shows the complete syntax of the MENU statement.

MenuName is a character string that you use to find the menu data in the program's resources. Even the simple MINIMAL3.RC resource script file has two types of resources, an icon and a menu. More complex programs can have several icons, more than one menu, and all sorts of other data in the resource file. To keep track of all the resources, the resource data is organized by name. Each resource gets a name, which is saved as part of the resource data. When you load resource data into memory to use it, Windows finds the part of the resource data you have requested using the resource name. Figure 9-2 shows how the resource data is organized in a finished Windows program.

Listing 9-1 MINIMAL3.RC Resource Script File

```
// minimal3.rc  resource script file

#include <afxres.h>
#include "minimal3.h"

AFX_IDI_STD_FRAME   ICON    minimal3.ico    // the program's icon

MyMenu MENU                                 // define the menu
{
    MENUITEM "&Beep",       IDM_BEEP
    MENUITEM "&Quit",       IDM_QUIT
}
```

Listing 9-2 MENU Statement Syntax

```
MenuName    MENU    [load option] [memory option]
BEGIN
        // menu definition goes here
END
```

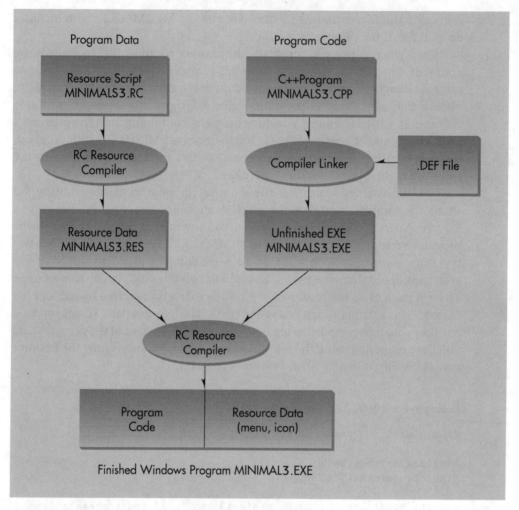

Figure 9-1 How Resource Data Is Added to a Windows Program

Menu Loading and Memory Options

There are two load options for menus (and all other types of resources), PRELOAD and LOADONCALL. PRELOAD tells Windows to load the menu data into memory as soon as the program starts running. LOADONCALL tells Windows to wait until the program needs the data to load it into memory. If you do not specify either option, the default value is LOADONCALL. The load option does not make much difference with main program menus, as they are usually needed to create the program's main window when the program starts running.

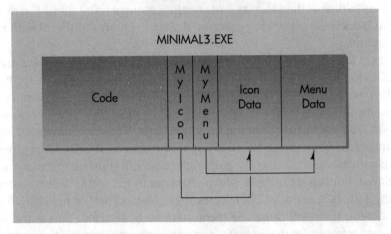

MINIMAL3.EXE

Figure 9-2 How Resource Names Are Used to Locate Resource Data

Once a menu is loaded into memory, it can have different memory options based on the key words FIXED, MOVEABLE, and DISCARDABLE. FIXED means that the data cannot be moved in memory. This is the least desirable option, and using it for a menu would be silly because there is no reason to fix the menu data at one address in memory. MOVEABLE means that the resource data can be moved in memory. DISCARDABLE tells Windows that the data can be temporarily removed from memory if the system runs low on memory room. Windows will reload the menu data when it is needed again. The DISCARDABLE statement is always used with MOVEABLE, and the combination of DISCARDABLE plus MOVEABLE is the default case for resources. The menu in MINIMAL3.RC could have been declared LOADONCALL, MOVEABLE, and DISCARDABLE, as shown in Listing 9-3, to explicitly show the default load and memory options. Normally, you can forget about all of these options and just use the defaults.

Menu Items

An open curly bracket ({) follows the MENU statement in the program's resource script file. Everything between the brackets ({and}) is part of the menu definition. You can also use the BEGIN and END statements in place of the curly

Listing 9-3 Specifying Load and Memory Options

```
MyMenu        MENU        LOADONCALL MOVEABLE DISCARDABLE
{
    MENUITEM "&Beep"              IDM_BEEP
    MENUITEM "&Quit",             IDM_QUIT
}
```

brackets (which is the older style of creating resource script files). The examples in this book use curly brackets because their use is more consistent with normal C++ syntax.

There are only two kinds of statements that can be placed between the curly brackets following MENU: MENUITEM and POPUP. We will get to POPUP menus in the next section. MENUITEM statements are used to define individual menu elements, including their character string and ID numbers. Listing 9-3 shows two MENUITEM statements, defining the "Beep" and "Quit" menu items. Note that the menu characters are enclosed in double quotes, and the first letter is preceded by an ampersand character. The ampersand does not show up in the menu when displayed, but is used to mark which character in the menu item is underlined. Holding the (ALT) key down and depressing the letter key that matches an underlined menu item will cause the menu item to be selected. This is the built-in keyboard interface for menu items. If you want an ampersand in the menu string, put two ampersands together. For example, "&Me&&You" in the menu definition will be displayed "Me&You" on the menu bar.

You can underline any letter in the menu item's string. For example, you might define the menu items "O&n" and "O&ff." (ALT)-(N) would then activate the "On" menu item, and (ALT)-(F) would activate the "Off" menu item. The keyboard shortcuts for the menu will be more obvious to the user if you always use the first letter of the menu item's string, so you might choose alternative words like "&Start" and "&Cancel" to avoid having two menu items that begin with the same letter.

The menu item's string is followed by a comma and then the menu item ID number. These ID numbers are important, as they become the ID value passed with the WM_COMMAND message when a menu item is selected. The WM_COMMAND message will be identical whether the mouse or keyboard shortcut is used to select a menu item. Normally, menu item ID numbers are defined in the program's resource ID header file to give each item a readable name. It is convenient to use numbers between 0 and 99 for the menu item IDs, as the dialog box editor starts automatic numbering of dialog box controls at 100 (the next chapter discusses dialog boxes). If you are using a number of child windows with menus, the menu item ID numbers can overlap, as a window will receive WM_COMMAND messages only when it is the active window, and will never get them from another window's menu bar.

Pop-Up Menus

The main menu bar will hold only a few menu items. If you put in more menu items than will fit on a single line, Windows will automatically wrap the menu, creating a two line menu bar. Two line menus are awkward and take up valuable space from the window's client area. It is much better to use pop-up menus if you need to provide more options. Pop-up menus (sometimes called "drop-down" or "pull-down" menus) are used to give user access to more selections, without requiring additional space on the top menu bar. Figure 9-3 shows a typical pop-up menu, used by the Windows Notepad application. When the user selects "File," a pop-up menu appears with another group of options. Notepad is typical of most Windows applications, having both a main menu bar and pop-up menus that drop down from the main menu. You can have pop-ups from pop-ups, with up to eight levels of nesting. The MENU1 example program in this chapter has a menu with a second level pop-up menu defined in another pop-up. Generally, you are better off using dialog boxes in place of many levels of pop-up menus, because complex menus can be confusing for the user. Dialog boxes are the subject of the next chapter.

Pop-up menus are defined inside the menu definition, between the curly brackets (or BEGIN and END menu statements). Figure 9-4 shows a typical example, with two levels of pop-up menus. The key word "POPUP" is followed by the title (character string) that will head the pop-up menu. Note that there is no ID number following the pop-up's string. This is because pop-up titles cannot be selected by themselves, and they do not generate WM_COMMAND messages. Pop-up titles are used to allow the user to select a pop-up menu, which will contain the menu items that can be selected. Only the menu items have ID values and generate WM_COMMAND messages.

Figure 9-4 shows an example with two levels of pop-up menus. Everything between the curly brackets that follow the POPUP key word is part of

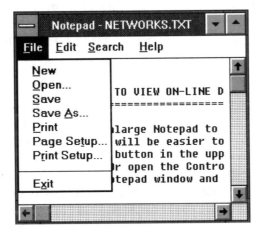

Figure 9-3 The Notepad Application's File Menu

```
Menu1    MENU
{
  POPUP "&First Pop-up"
  {
    MENUITEM "Sel &1", 10
    MENUITEM "Sel &2", 20
    POPUP "&Second Level pop-up"
    {
      MENUITEM "&High", 30
      MENUITEM "&Low", 40
    }
  }
  MENUITEM "&Quit", 50
  MENUITEM "&Help", 60
}
```

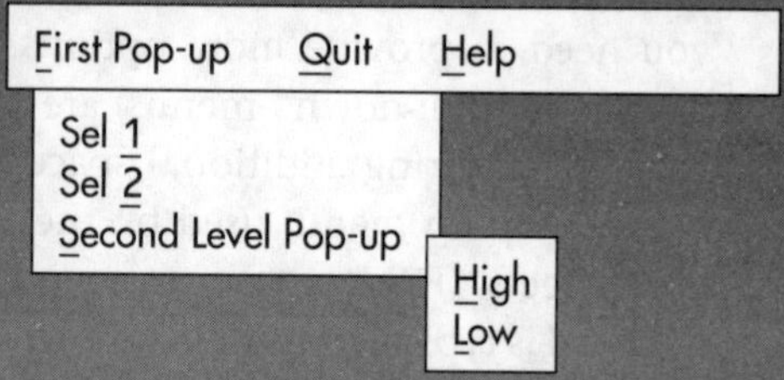

Figure 9-4 Defining Pop-Up Menus

the pop-up, and will be at a lower level in the menu structure than the pop-up's title string. Note how the listing on the left side of Figure 9-4 uses indents to make the different levels of pop-up menus clear. The indents are not necessary, and they do not affect the resource compiler's conversion of the menu statements into the .RES format, but they definitely help make the resource script file more readable.

Another way to look at the menu definition is to realize that the only two statements that can be put between the curly brackets for a menu are MENUITEM and POPUP. POPUP is followed by its own set of curly brackets. The only thing that can go between *those* curly brackets are MENUITEM and POPUP.

Menu Item Options

Sometimes you will want to make a menu item inoperative during part of a program's operation. For example, the user should not be able to select a "Paste" menu item if there is nothing to paste. Menu items can be written in gray characters to show that they are inactive. "Grayed" menu items cannot be selected and do not generate WM_COMMAND messages. Another handy option is to be able to put a check mark next to the left side of a menu item. This is ideal for situations where there are a few options that are either on or off. If there are more than about four options, menus with check marks become a bit overwhelming, and you are better off using a dialog box with radio buttons for the selection.

You can start a menu with menu items in either a grayed or checked state. This is done by following the menu item's ID number with a menu option key word. Table 9-1 summarizes the various menu item options. You will probably not want to use the INACTIVE key word, as this makes the menu item inactive without graying the menu item's text characters, which is a confusing combination for the user.

The MENUBARBREAK and MENUBREAK options are used to create multiline menus. Although this can be done for the main menu bar, these key words are almost always used with pop-up menus to form horizontal menus, instead of the default vertical alignment. These options should be used with discretion, as they differ from the usual vertical menu arrangement and can confuse the user. The MENU1 example program in this chapter has a horizontal pop-up menu to demonstrate this capability.

One additional feature that can be added to menu definitions is having items separated by lines, which helps break menus into logical groupings. The MENUITEM SEPARATOR statement is used to insert a horizontal line between two menu items. The line does not have an ID value and cannot be selected. Listing 9-4 shows a typical example that uses the MENUITEM SEPARATOR line in the first pop-up menu. Figure 9-5 shows the result of this example with the separator line visible between menu items "Selection 1" and "Selection 2." Also note

Option	Meaning
CHECKED	The item has a check mark next to it.
GRAYED	The item's text is inactive and appears in gray letters.
INACTIVE	The item name is displayed, but cannot be selected. No WM_COMMAND messages are sent from this item until it is enabled. Normally, programs use the GRAYED option in place of INACTIVE to make the inactive status obvious to the user.
MENUBARBREAK	For menus, places the item on a new line, creating a multiline menu. For pop-ups, places the new item on a new column, creating a multicolumn (rectangular) pop-up menu. A line is used to separate this item from the previous one.
MENUBREAK	Same as MENUBARBREAK, except when used with pop-up menus. For menus, places the item on a new line, creating a multiline menu. For pop-ups, places the new item on a new column, creating a multicolumn (rectangular) pop-up menu without a dividing line.

Table 9-1 Menu Item Options—Used to the Right of the Menu Item ID Number

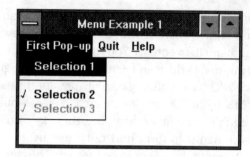

Figure 9-5 Menu Appearance from Listing 9-4

Listing 9-4 Menu Definition Using MENUITEM SEPARATOR

```
ExampleMenu        MENU
{
    POPUP "&First Pop-up"
    {
        MENUITEM "Selection &1",   IDM_SEL1
        MENUITEM SEPARATOR
        MENUITEM "Selection &2",   IDM_SEL2, CHECKED
        MENUITEM "Selection &3",   IDM_SEL3, GRAYED, CHECKED
    }
    MENUITEM "&Quit",              IDM_QUIT
    MENUITEM "&Help",              IDM_HELP
}
```

the combination of the GRAYED and CHECKED options for the "Selection 3"
menu items.

A COMPLEX MENU EXAMPLE

The first example program in this chapter is called MENU1, and it demonstrates
a number of the menu features. Figure 9-6 shows MENU1 in action, with one of
the menu items being selected. MENU1 has two levels of pop-up menus. The
first level of pop-up menu contains four items, Selection 1 through 3, and the
title of the second level pop-up. The second level pop-up is interesting in that its
two items are arranged horizontally. MENU1 also demonstrates a checked and a
grayed menu item.

The MENU1 menu is defined in the program's resource script file, as shown
in Listing 9-5. The menu is named "BigMenu," and it uses most of the possible
menu features that can be defined in a resource script file. "Selection 2" is set to
CHECKED, and "Selection 3" is set to GRAYED. The GRAYED status means that
"Selection 3" will not be active (cannot be selected) when the menu first

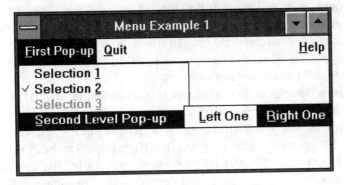

Figure 9-6 The MENU1 Program

Listing 9-5 MENU1.RC Resource Script File

```
// menu1.rc   resource script file

#include <afxres.h>
#include "menu1.h"

AFX_IDI_STD_FRAME   ICON    menu1.ico   // the program's icon

BigMenu        MENU
{                                       // define the menu
    POPUP "&First Pop-up"
    {
        MENUITEM "Selection &1",        IDM_SEL1
        MENUITEM "Selection &2",        IDM_SEL2, CHECKED
        MENUITEM "Selection &3",        IDM_SEL3, GRAYED
        POPUP "&Second level pop-up"
        {
            MENUITEM "&Left One",       IDM_LEFT
            MENUITEM "&Right One",      IDM_RIGHT, MENUBARBREAK
        }
    }
    MENUITEM "&Quit",                   IDM_QUIT
    MENUITEM "\a&Help",                 IDM_HELP
}
```

appears. The status of that item will be changed as the program runs, as we will see in a moment.

The secret to the second level pop-up menu appearing in the horizontal format is the MENUBARBREAK statement. This key word instructs Windows to put a vertical line in front of the item and to split the menu at that point. If the menu is horizontal (the main menu bar), the menu is split into two lines. If the menu is vertical (any pop-up menu), the menu is split into two side-by-side halves at that point.

The last menu item in Listing 9-5 is the "Help" selection. Help items are often placed at the far right side of the menu (see Figure 9-6). This is accomplished by putting the special code "\a" in the help item's text string ("a" for align). Having the "Help" menu item on the right side of the menu bar is now considered "old fashioned" and not often used.

MENU1 defines the menu item ID numbers in a header file, MENU1.H, which is shown in Listing 9-6. Note again that the title strings for pop-up menus do not have ID numbers. Only MENUITEMs have ID numbers, and they send WM_COMMAND messages to the program. The ID numbers can be in any order.

Listing 9-7 shows the MENU1.HPP program header file. The key item to note is the declaration of a **CMenu** object named *Menu*. This object will be the

Listing 9-6 MENU1.H Resource ID Header File

```
// menu1.h   header file for resource ID numbers

#define IDM_SEL1    1       // menu item ID
#define IDM_SEL2    2
#define IDM_SEL3    3
#define IDM_LEFT    4
#define IDM_RIGHT   5
#define IDM_QUIT    6
#define IDM_HELP    10
```

Listing 9-7 MENU1.HPP Header File

```
// menu1.hpp    header file for menu1.cpp
                              // derive a main window class
class CMainWindow : public CFrameWnd
{
public:
    CMainWindow () ;          // declare a constructor
private:
    BOOL bCheckOnOff ;        // track if checkmark is on
    CMenu Menu ;              // pointer to menu object
    void OnSel1 () ;          // respond to menu items
    void OnSel2 () ;
    void OnSel3 () ;
    void OnRight () ;
    void OnLeft () ;
    void OnHelp () ;
    void OnQuit () ;

    DECLARE_MESSAGE_MAP()     // prepare for message processing
} ;

class CTheApp : public CWinApp // derive an application class
{
public:
    BOOL InitInstance () ;     // declare new InitInstance()
} ;
```

foundation for the manipulation of the menu as the program operates. Note that a number of message response functions are declared to handle the ON_COMMAND messages generated by the menu items.

The MENU1.CPP program file is shown in Listing 9-8. Unlike the previous example programs, the menu is not attached in the **CMainWindow** constructor function's call to **CFrameWnd::Create()**. Instead the menu is explicitly loaded by calling the **CMenu::LoadMenu()** function. **CMenu::LoadMenu()** loads the menu data out of the program's resources into memory. The **CWnd::SetMenu()** function is then called to attach the menu to the program's main window:

```
Menu.LoadMenu ("BigMenu") ; // loads menu data into memory
this->SetMenu (&Menu) ;     // attaches the menu to main window
```

This is a bit more work than just putting the menu name in the **CFrame-Wnd::Create()** function's parameter list. The payoff is that the **CMenu** object

Listing 9-8 MENU1.CPP

```
// menu1.cpp              example with two levels of pop-up menus

#include <afxwin.h>    // class library header file
#include "menu1.h"     // header file for resource data
#include "menu1.hpp"    // header file for this program

CTheApp theApp ;         // create one CTheApp object - runs program

BOOL CTheApp::InitInstance ()   // override default InitInstance()
{
    m_pMainWnd = new CMainWindow () ;       // create a main window
    m_pMainWnd->ShowWindow (m_nCmdShow) ;   // make it visible
    m_pMainWnd->UpdateWindow () ;           // paint center
    return TRUE ;
}

CMainWindow::CMainWindow ()       // constructor for main window
{
    Create (NULL, "Menu Example 1", WS_OVERLAPPEDWINDOW, rectDefault,
        NULL, NULL) ;             // do not load menu in Create()
    Menu.LoadMenu ("BigMenu") ; // instead, load it explicitly
    this->SetMenu (&Menu) ;     // attach menu to window
    bCheckOnOff = FALSE ;        // initialize variable
}

BEGIN_MESSAGE_MAP (CMainWindow, CFrameWnd)
    ON_COMMAND (IDM_SEL1, OnSel1)          // respond to menu selections
    ON_COMMAND (IDM_SEL2, OnSel2)
```

```
    ON_COMMAND (IDM_SEL3, OnSel3)
    ON_COMMAND (IDM_LEFT, OnLeft)
    ON_COMMAND (IDM_RIGHT, OnRight)
    ON_COMMAND (IDM_HELP, OnHelp)
    ON_COMMAND (IDM_QUIT, OnQuit)
END_MESSAGE_MAP ()

void CMainWindow::OnSel1 ()                  // menu item "Selection 1"
{
    this->MessageBox ("Selection 1 enables Selection 3",
        "Surprise!", MB_OK) ;
    Menu.EnableMenuItem (IDM_SEL3, MF_BYCOMMAND | MF_ENABLED) ;
}


void CMainWindow::OnSel2 ()                  // menu item "Selection 2"
{
    bCheckOnOff = bCheckOnOff ? FALSE : TRUE ;  // toggle on/off
    if (bCheckOnOff)
        Menu.CheckMenuItem (IDM_SEL2, MF_BYCOMMAND | MF_CHECKED) ;
    else
        Menu.CheckMenuItem (IDM_SEL2, MF_BYCOMMAND | MF_UNCHECKED) ;
}


void CMainWindow::OnSel3 ()                  // menu item "Selection 3"
{
    this->MessageBox ("Selection 3 now enabled.", "So what?", MB_OK) ;
}

void CMainWindow::OnLeft ()                  // menu item "Left One"
{
    this->MessageBox ("Left side just beeps.", "", MB_OK) ;
    MessageBeep (0) ;
}

void CMainWindow::OnRight ()                 // menu item "Right One"
{
    this->MessageBox ("Right side disables Selection 3.",
        "Surprise!", MB_OK) ;
    Menu.EnableMenuItem (IDM_SEL3, MF_BYCOMMAND | MF_GRAYED) ;
}


void CMainWindow::OnHelp ()                  // menu item "Help"
{
    this->MessageBox ("Try selecting any menu item.",
        "Not much help.", MB_OK) ;
}


void CMainWindow::OnQuit ()                  // menu item "Quit"
{
    this->DestroyWindow () ;                 // destroy main window,
}                                            // this stops application
```

named *Menu* is now initialized and ready to be used for access to a variety of **CMenu** member functions.

Once the menu is loaded and attached to the program window it behaves just like any other menu. Selecting a menu item results in a WM_COMMAND message being sent to the program, which transmits the menu item ID number. The MENU1.CPP message map routes theses messages to the appropriate message processing functions.

Listing 9-9 shows the MENU1.DEF module definition file. The program's icon is shown in Figure 9-7.

Menu Functions

The message processing functions in MENU1 are designed to demonstrate several of the common member functions of the **CMenu** class. When the MENU1 program first starts, the third menu item titled "Selection 3" is grayed and cannot be selected. This is because the GRAYED style was specified in MENU1.RC for this item. Selecting the first menu item labeled "Selection 1" results in the **CMainWindow::OnSel1()** function being called (via the program's message map). A message box containing the string "Selection 1 enables Selection 3" is displayed, and then the IDM_SEL3 menu item is enabled. Enabling the menu item is done using the **CMenu::EnableMenuItem()** function:

```
Menu.EnableMenuItem (IDM_SEL3, MF_BYCOMMAND | MF_ENABLED) ;
```

Listing 9-9 MENU1.DEF Module Definition File

```
NAME            menu1
DESCRIPTION     'menu1 C++ program'
EXETYPE         WINDOWS
STUB            'WINSTUB.EXE'
CODE            PRELOAD MOVEABLE
DATA            PRELOAD MOVEABLE MULTIPLE
HEAPSIZE        1024
STACKSIZE       5120
```

Figure 9-7 MENU1.ICO Icon Image

The **CMenu::EnableMenuItem()** function must be told which of the menu items to enable or disable. There are two ways to specify the menu item, by the menu item ID number or by the position of the menu item in the menu. WINDOWS.H has two binary flags defined to specify the selection option: MF_BYCOMMAND and MF_BYPOSITION. The following two **CMenu::EnableMenuItem()** function calls are equivalent:

```
Menu.EnableMenuItem (IDM_SEL3, MF_BYCOMMAND | MF_ENABLED) ;
Menu.EnableMenuItem (2, MF_BYPOSITION | MF_ENABLED) ;
```

The menu item position is relative to the top-most, left-most item that has the position number zero. It is more difficult to keep track of the position of a menu item than the ID number, so the MF_BYPOSITION option is almost never used. The MF_BYCOMMAND option is used in all of the examples in this book.

Having specified the menu item, you must also tell **CMenu::EnableMenuItem()** whether to make the menu item enabled, disabled, or grayed. These possibilities are specified with three additional binary flag values defined in WINDOWS.H: MF_ENABLED, MF_DISABLED, and MF_GRAYED. You will probably never use MF_DISABLED, as this disables the menu item without graying the menu item's text string. MF_GRAYED both disables and grays the menu item, and is a much better choice. MF_ENABLED both enables and removes graying from a menu item.

The second menu item in the pop-up has the ID value IDM_SEL2. This item is defined as CHECKED in the MENU1.RC file. The program logic in MENU1.CPP switches the check mark on and off each time the menu IDM_SEL2 item is selected. MENU1.CPP uses a BOOL variable *bCheckOnOff* to keep track of whether the IDM_SEL2 item is checked or unchecked. The **CMenu::CheckMenuItem()** function is used to check or remove a check from a menu item. The syntax is very similar to the **CMenu::EnableMenuItem()** function:

```
Menu.CheckMenuItem (IDM_SEL2, MF_BYCOMMAND | MF_CHECKED) ;
```

Again you have the choice between the MF_BYCOMMAND and MF_BYPOSITION flags. For check marks, there are only two choices: MF_CHECKED and MF_UNCHECKED.

Determining Menu Item Status

Normally, your program logic will control the menu item status as checked or grayed, and you can track the status of any item using static variables (such as *bCheckOnOff* in MENU1.CPP). However, Windows provides an alternative: you can determine the status of a menu item as the program runs using the **CMenu::GetMenuState()** function. **CMenu::GetMenuState()** returns a UNIT value that encodes the status of a menu item as a combination of MF_CHECKED, MF_DISABLED, MF_ENABLED, MF_GRAYED, or MF_UNCHECKED. Here is a typical example that determines if the menu item IDM_MENUID is currently checked:

```
if (Menu.GetMenuState (IDM_MENUID, MF_BYCOMMAND) & MF_CHECKED)
```

You can also determine the character string of a menu item at runtime using the **CMenu::GetMenuString()** function. This is useful in cases where the program allows the user to add new menu items, such as user-defined macros. Here is a simple example using **CMenu::GetMenuString()**, which copies the menu item IDM_MENUID's string into the **CString** object *String*:

```
Menu.GetMenuString (IDM_MENUID, String, 100, MF_BYCOMMAND) ;
```

The third parameter passed to **CMenu::GetMenuString()** is the maximum number of characters to copy to the string buffer. In this case, the menu string was limited to 100 characters. The fourth parameter is set to either MF_BYCOMMAND or MF_BYPOSITION to specify whether the first parameter is interpreted as a menu item ID number or as the relative position of the menu item in the menu. MF_BYCOMMAND is almost always used.

CREATING A MENU AS THE PROGRAM RUNS

Most programs have a fixed menu structure defined in the resource script file, and they use that menu as long as the program is operating. There are two situations where you will want to create and destroy menus and/or menu items as the program operates:

1. When certain operations are not always possible and you want to delete the menu items when the action is not possible, rather than just graying the item.

2. When you want to use a bitmap graphical image in place of text for one or more pop-up menu items. This is particularly useful for tool selections, such as picking a brush image for painting. Graphical menu items cannot be defined in the resource script file, but they can be created as the program runs.

The **CMenu** class provides several member functions that allow you to create and destroy menu items, as summarized in Table 9-2.

In addition, you will be using **CWnd** class member functions that deal with a window's menu. Table 9-3 summarizes these functions. You have already seen the **CWnd::SetMenu()** function used in the MENU1.CPP example.

Function	Purpose
AppendMenu()	Adds a new menu item or pop-up to the end of a menu.
CreateMenu()	Creates a new menu, ready to add items.
CreatePopupMenu()	Creates a new pop-up menu, ready to add items.
DeleteMenu()	Removes a menu item from a menu or pop-up menu.
DestroyMenu()	Deletes an entire menu, removing it from memory. This is necessary only if the menu has been loaded and is not attached to a window. Menus attached to windows are automatically removed from memory when the window is destroyed.
InsertMenu()	Inserts a new menu item or pop-up into a menu or pop-up menu.
LoadMenu()	Loads a menu from the program's resource data, ready to be attached to a window with **SetMenu()**. You can define more than one menu in the resource data, and switch between menus as the program operates. **LoadMenu()** will load only one copy of each menu into memory, no matter how often the function is called.
ModifyMenu()	Changes a menu item in place. This function is handy for changing the wording of a menu item.
RemoveMenu()	Deletes a menu item including any attached pop-up menus.

Table 9-2 CMenu Class Member Functions for Creating Menus

The basic sequence of creating a new menu is to:

1. Use **CMenu::CreateMenu()** to create a new, empty menu.

2. Use **CMenu::AppendMenu()** and/or **CMenu::InsertMenu()** to add menu items as needed.

3. Use **CWnd::SetMenu()** to attach the menu to a window, so that it can be used.

Function	Purpose
DrawMenuBar()	Draws the menu bar (the main menu line, right below the window's caption), making any recent changes visible.
SetMenu()	Attaches a menu to a window. This is frequently used with **LoadMenu()** to switch between two or more menus used by the program.

Table 9-3 CWnd Class Member Functions Used with Menus

If the main menu contains pop-up menus, the pop-ups are created separately, and then attached to the menu as follows:

1. Use **CMenu::CreatePopupMenu()** to create a new, empty pop-up menu.

2. Use **CMenu::AppendMenu()** and/or **CMenu::InsertMenu()** to add menu items to the pop-up as needed.

3. Use **CMenu::AppendMenu()** and/or **CMenu::InsertMenu()** to add the finished pop-up menu to the main menu.

If the menu, including all pop-ups, is attached to the window when the window is destroyed, the menu will automatically be removed from memory. If the menu is not attached to a window, it must be explicitly destroyed using the **CMenu::DestroyMenu()** function. Otherwise, the menu data will remain in memory for the duration of the Windows session.

You can also insert and delete menu items as the program operates, using the **CMenu::InsertMenu()** and **CMenu::DeleteMenu()** functions. This is frequently simpler than creating an entire menu from scratch each time a change to the menu is needed, and more flexible than defining multiple menus in the program's resource script file and switching between them with **CMenu::LoadMenu()** and **CWnd::SetMenu()**.

As mentioned above, menus can be created at runtime in order to include graphics images as menu items. The graphics images are bitmaps that are created with the Image Editor application and stored in .BMP files. With the MFC classes, bitmaps are manipulated with the **CBitmap** class, which contains a number of useful member functions. We will only make limited use of the **CBitmap** class in this chapter. Chapter 16, *Bitmaps*, provides a more complete discussion.

The steps needed to create a menu including bitmap images are:

1. Create the image as a bitmap using the Image Editor. A 32 by 32 pixel 16-color bitmap is a standard size and color resolution, while 64 by 64 pixel bitmaps provide a larger image.

2. Include the bitmaps in the program's resource data. We will see an example of this in the next program, MENU2.

3. Load the bitmap data into memory while the program is running. The **CBitmap::LoadBitmap()** function does this, and it returns a handle to the bitmap in memory.

4. Use **CMenu::AppendMenu()** and/or **CMenu::InsertMenu()** to add the bitmap to the menu as a menu item.

The next example program, MENU2, will illustrate these menu operations by creating two graphic menu items, and by allowing a whole section of the menu to be deleted and restored as the program operates.

The MENU2 Program

The MENU2 program does not have a menu defined in its resource script file. Instead, the program's main menu is created as the program starts operation. Figure 9-8 shows the MENU2 program in operation, with its initial pop-up menu item displayed. The pop-up menu item consists of two bitmap images that were created as .BMP files using the Image Editor application.

Listing 9-10 shows the MENU2.RC resource script file, which includes an icon file, two bitmaps, and two cursor files. Selecting either of the bitmap menu items in MENU2 causes the cursor shape to change. The cursor files are needed for the cursor shapes, because bitmaps have a different file format and cannot be used as cursors.

Listing 9-10 MENU2.RC Resource Script File

```
// menu2.rc   resource script file

#include <afxres.h>
#include "menu2.h"

AFX_IDI_STD_FRAME   ICON    menu2.ico    // the program's icon

CutBmp       BITMAP   scissor.bmp        // bitmap files
PasteBmp     BITMAP   glue.bmp

CutCur       CURSOR   scissor.cur        // cursor files
GlueCur      CURSOR   glue.cur
```

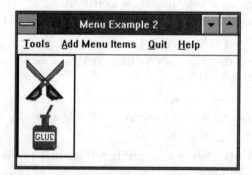

Figure 9-8 The MENU2 Program's Graphic Pop-Up Menu

Listing 9-11 shows the MENU2.HPP header file. Note that three **CMenu** objects are declared as part of the **CMainWindow** class, as well as two **CBitmap** objects. All of these objects will be put to work to create the complete menu. The MENU2 program changes the cursor shape when a graphic menu item is selected, so the **CWnd::OnSetCursor()** message processing function is declared in MENU2.HPP, along with all of the functions for responding to menu selections. Review Chapter 6, *Taming the Mouse*, if you have forgotten about the WM_SETCURSOR message and **CWnd::OnSetCursor()** function.

The MENU2.CPP program is shown in Listing 9-12. The program's menu is created in the **CMainWindow** constructor function. The program's window is initially created without an attached menu (NULL passed in place of the menu name when calling the **CFrameWnd::Create()** function). Instead, the

Listing 9-11 MENU2.HPP Header File

```
// menu2.hpp     header file for menu2.cpp
                                 // derive a main window class
class CMainWindow : public CFrameWnd
{
public:
    CMainWindow () ;              // declare a constructor
private:
    CMenu Menu ;                 // menu objects
    CMenu Popup ;
    CMenu AddedPopup ;
    CBitmap CutBmp ;             // bitmap objects
    CBitmap PasteBmp ;
    HANDLE  hCursor ;            // cursor handle
    BOOL bAddItems ;             // track if menu items added

    void OnCut () ;             // respond to menu items
    void OnPaste () ;
    void OnAdd () ;
    void OnHelp () ;
    void OnQuit () ;
    void OnRemove () ;
    BOOL OnSetCursor (CWnd *pWnd, UINT nHitTest,
        UINT nMessage) ;

    DECLARE_MESSAGE_MAP()        // prepare for message processing
} ;

class CTheApp : public CWinApp  // derive an application class
{
public:
    BOOL InitInstance () ;       // declare new InitInstance()
} ;
```

CMenu::CreateMenu() function is called to create an empty menu object, ready to have menu items added.

```
Menu.CreateMenu () ;          // create a new, empty menu
```

The MENU2 top menu bar starts with the menu caption "Tools," which has two graphic bitmap menu items as a pop-up menu below it (see Figure 9-8). The first step in creating this pop-up menu is to call the **CMenu::CreatePopupMenu()** function to initialize an empty pop-up menu, ready for menu items.

```
Popup.CreatePopupMenu () ;  // create a pop-up menu
```

The bitmap data must be loaded into memory from the program's resources before the bitmap data can be passed to the pop-up menu. The **CBitmap::LoadBitmap()** function does this for both the "CutBmp" and "PasteBmp" bitmaps, which are included in the MENU2.RC resources (Listing 9-10).

```
CutBmp.LoadBitmap ("CutBmp") ;  // load from resource data
PasteBmp.LoadBitmap ("PasteBmp") ;
```

Next the bitmaps are added as menu items to the pop-up menu using the **CMenu::AppendMenu()** function. The **CMenu::AppendMenu()** function establishes the initial state of the menu item (MF_ENABLED, MF_DISABLED, or MF_CHECKED) and the menu item's ID number. A pointer to the loaded bitmap data in memory is also passed to **CMenu::AppendMenu()** when the menu is a bitmap.

```
Popup.AppendMenu (MF_ENABLED, IDM_CUT, &CutBmp) ;
Popup.AppendMenu (MF_ENABLED, IDM_PASTE, &PasteBmp) ;
```

At this point, the pop-up menu is complete, but not attached to the main menu. The **CMenu::AppendMenu()** function is again used to attach the pop-up menu to the main menu named *Menu*. This is a bit tricky, as the **CMenu::AppendMenu()** function must be passed an internal Windows handle that tracks the location of the pop-up menu's data in memory. The easiest way to do this is to use the **CMenu::m_hMenu** public data member, which is the handle of the memory block containing the menu definition. The menu handle is then passed to the **CMenu::AppendMenu()** function, which appends the completed pop-up menu data to the main menu.

```
Menu.AppendMenu (MF_POPUP, (UINT) Popup.m_hMenu, "&Tools") ;
```

The MENU2.CPP menu is completed by appending three more menu items to the main menu using **CMenu::AppendMenu()**. Once the menu is complete, it must be attached to the program window using the **CWnd::SetMenu()** function.

```
this->SetMenu (&Menu) ;       // attach menu to window
```

Listing 9-12 MENU2.CPP

```cpp
// menu2.cpp                 example with bitmap menu items

#include <afxwin.h>    // class library header file
#include "menu2.h"     // header file for resource data
#include "menu2.hpp"   // header file for this program

CTheApp theApp ;        // create one CTheApp object - runs program

BOOL CTheApp::InitInstance ()   // override default InitInstance()
{
    m_pMainWnd = new CMainWindow () ;        // create a main window
    m_pMainWnd->ShowWindow (m_nCmdShow) ;    // make it visible
    m_pMainWnd->UpdateWindow () ;            // paint center
    return TRUE ;
}


CMainWindow::CMainWindow ()      // constructor for main window
{
    Create (NULL, "Menu Example 2", WS_OVERLAPPEDWINDOW, rectDefault,
        NULL, NULL) ;               // do not load menu in Create()
    Menu.CreateMenu () ;            // create a new, empty menu
    Popup.CreatePopupMenu () ;   // create a pop-up menu too

    CutBmp.LoadBitmap ("CutBmp") ;  // load from resource data
    PasteBmp.LoadBitmap ("PasteBmp") ;
                                // add bitmaps as menu items
    Popup.AppendMenu (MF_ENABLED, IDM_CUT, &CutBmp) ;
    Popup.AppendMenu (MF_ENABLED, IDM_PASTE, &PasteBmp) ;
                                // attach pop-up to main menu
    Menu.AppendMenu (MF_POPUP, (UINT) Popup.m_hMenu, "&Tools") ;
                                // add other text menu items
    Menu.AppendMenu (MF_ENABLED, IDM_ADD, "&Add Menu Items") ;
    Menu.AppendMenu (MF_ENABLED, IDM_QUIT, "&Quit") ;
    Menu.AppendMenu (MF_ENABLED, IDM_HELP, "&Help") ;

    this->SetMenu (&Menu) ;       // attach menu to window
            // this is a convenient place to initialize the
            // second pop-up, even if not yet added to main menu
    AddedPopup.CreatePopupMenu () ;
    AddedPopup.AppendMenu (MF_ENABLED, IDM_REMOVE, "&Remove Popup") ;

    bAddItems = FALSE ;           // initialize
    hCursor = AfxGetApp()->LoadStandardCursor (IDC_ARROW) ;
}


BEGIN_MESSAGE_MAP (CMainWindow, CFrameWnd)
    ON_COMMAND (IDM_CUT, OnCut)              // respond to menu selections
    ON_COMMAND (IDM_PASTE, OnPaste)
    ON_COMMAND (IDM_ADD, OnAdd)
```

```
    ON_COMMAND (IDM_HELP, OnHelp)
    ON_COMMAND (IDM_QUIT, OnQuit)
    ON_COMMAND (IDM_REMOVE, OnRemove)
    ON_WM_SETCURSOR ()
END_MESSAGE_MAP ()

void CMainWindow::OnCut ()              // scissors menu item
{
    hCursor = AfxGetApp()->LoadCursor ("CutCur") ;
}

void CMainWindow::OnPaste ()            // glue pot menu item
{
    hCursor = AfxGetApp()->LoadCursor ("GlueCur") ;
}

void CMainWindow::OnAdd ()              // menu item "Add Menu Items"
{
    if (bAddItems)                      // only add to menu 1 time
        return ;
    Menu.InsertMenu (IDM_ADD, MF_POPUP, (UINT)* AddedPopup.m_hMenu,
        "&New Popup") ;
    this->DrawMenuBar () ;              // make changes visible
    bAddItems = TRUE ;
}

void CMainWindow::OnHelp ()            // menu item "Help"
{
    this->MessageBox ("Try selecting any menu item.",
        "Not much help.", MB_OK) ;
}

void CMainWindow::OnQuit ()            // menu item "Quit"
{
    this->DestroyWindow () ;           // destroy main window,
}                                      // this stops application

void CMainWindow::OnRemove ()          // "Remove" menu item
{
    if (!bAddItems)                    // can't delete if not there
        return ;
    Menu.RemoveMenu (1, MF_BYPOSITION) ;
    bAddItems = FALSE ;
    this->DrawMenuBar () ;             // make changes visible
}

BOOL CMainWindow::OnSetCursor (CWnd *pWnd, UINT nHitTest,
    UINT nMessage)
{
    ::SetCursor (hCursor) ;
    return TRUE ;
}
```

At the bottom of the **CMainWindow** constructor function, another pop-up menu object named **AddedPopup** is initialized with a single menu item. This is just preparation, as this pop-up menu is alternately added and removed from the main menu as the program operates. The *hCursor* handle for a cursor is also initialized with the **CWinApp::LoadStandardCursor()** function, loading the stock IDC_ARROW cursor shape. This is the initial cursor shape displayed over the MENU2 program window when the program starts running.

The selection of the bitmap menu items showing a pair of scissors and a glue pot are mapped to the **CMainWindow::OnCut()** and **CMainWindow::OnPaste()** message processing functions, respectively. In both cases, the functions call **CWinApp::LoadCursor()** to load cursor data into memory from the program's resources. The handle returned by **CWinApp::LoadCursor()** is saved as *hCursor*, which is used in processing the WM_SETCURSOR message. The **CMainWindow::OnSetCursor()** function changes the cursor shape to the image stored in the *hCursor* memory block by calling the *::SetCursor()* global function.

```
::SetCursor (hCursor) ;
```

The **CMainWindow::OnAdd()** function is called when the user selects the "Add Menu Items" menu item. **CMainWindow::OnAdd()** adds a new pop-up menu to the main menu bar using the **CMenu::InsertMenu()** function. **CMenu::InsertMenu()** is like **CMenu::AppendMenu()** except that menu items can be added anywhere with **InsertMenu()**, while **AppendMenu()** only adds to the end of a menu. To insert a pop-up menu as a menu item, you must pass the handle to the pop-up menu in memory to the **CMenu::InsertMenu()** function:

```
Menu.InsertMenu (IDM_ADD, MF_POPUP, AddedPopup.m_hMenu,
    "&New Popup") ;
```

Listings 9-13 and 9-14 show the remaining support files for MENU2.CPP. Figure 9-9 shows several icon, cursor, and bitmap images that are needed as resource data. All of these images were created using the Image Editor application.

Listing 9-13 MENU2.H Resource ID Header File

```
// menu2.h  header file for resource ID numbers

#define IDM_CUT      1      /* menu item ID numbers */
#define IDM_PASTE    2
#define IDM_ADD      3
#define IDM_QUIT     4
#define IDM_REMOVE   5
#define IDM_ARROW    6
#define IDM_HELP     10
```

a) MENU2.ICO
Icon Image

b) GLUE.CUR
Cursor

c) SCISSOR.CUR
Cursor

d) GLUE.BMP
Bitmap

e) SCISSOR.BMP
Bitmap

Figure 9-9 MENU2 Icon, Cursor, and Bitmap Images

Listing 9-14 MENU2.DEF Module Definition File

```
NAME          menu2
DESCRIPTION   'menu2 C++ program'
EXETYPE       WINDOWS
STUB          'WINSTUB.EXE'
CODE          PRELOAD MOVEABLE
DATA          PRELOAD MOVEABLE MULTIPLE
HEAPSIZE      1024
STACKSIZE     5120
```

CHANGING AN EXISTING MENU

The MENU2.CPP program creates a menu from scratch using the **CMenu** class functions. You can also take advantage of the **CMenu** class to manipulate an existing menu. Listing 9-15 shows a typical example of a **CMainWindow** constructor function that creates a main program window with a menu named "MyMenu" (defined in the program's resource script file). The **CWnd::GetMenu()** function returns a pointer to the window's menu. The pointer (a pointer to a **CMenu** object) can then be used to add and subtract menu items, enable, disable, check, and uncheck items, and so on. Listing 9-15 shows the **CMenu::CheckMenuItem()** function being applied to start the menu with one item checked and a second one unchecked.

In general, it is best to define all of the menu items that are character strings in the program's resource script file. You can then add bitmap items and change menu items as the program runs by using the **CWnd::GetMenu()** function to obtain a pointer to the **CMenu** object.

THE SYSTEM MENU

The system menu is an important built-in feature of Windows. Main program windows have a system menu box at their upper left corner. Clicking this box

Listing 9-15 Modifying an Existing Menu

```
CMainWindow::CMainWindow ()        // constructor for window
{
    CString title ;
    title.LoadString (S_PROGRAMCAPTION) ;

    Create (NULL, title, WS_OVERLAPPEDWINDOW | WS_VSCROLL,
        rectDefault, NULL, "MyMenu") ;

    CMenu * pMenu = this->GetMenu () ;
    pMenu->CheckMenuItem (IDM_MONON, MF_BYCOMMAND | MF_UNCHECKED) ;
    pMenu->CheckMenuItem (IDM_MONOFF, MF_BYCOMMAND | MF_CHECKED) ;
}
```

once displays the system menu, or you can use the (ALT)-(SPACEBAR) key combination to activate the system menu for the window that has the input focus. Figure 9-10a shows the system menu for the Notepad application. Notepad uses the default system menu, which is used by most applications. The primary purpose of the system menu is to provide a keyboard alternative for actions such as moving the window or minimizing the program to an icon.

The system menu is also displayed if the program is minimized to an icon and the icon is clicked once with the mouse. This is shown in Figure 9-10b, again for the Notepad application. This brings up a reason that you might want to use the system menu. If the program is never allowed to be any bigger than

a) Displayed While Program Is Active

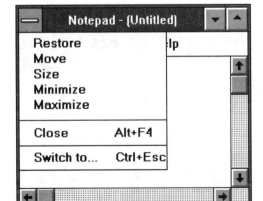

b) Displayed While Program Is Minimized

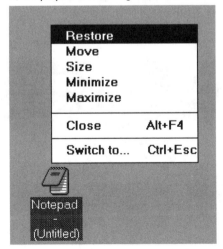

Figure 9-10 The Notepad Application's System Menu

an icon, the system menu is the only menu that will ever be visible. Adding to and modifying the system menu is an ideal way to add functionality to a miniature program.

System menus are attached to the program window by including the WS_SYSMENU window style when calling **CWnd::Create()**. WS_SYSMENU is part of the WS_OVERLAPPEDWINDOW style which is the default style for the **CFrameWnd::Create()** function used to create most main program windows. You can explicitly add the WS_SYSMENU style to child and pop-up windows.

The key to working with the system menu is the **CWnd::GetSystemMenu()** function. **CWnd::GetSystemMenu()** returns a pointer to a **CMenu** object for a window's system menu. You can then operate on the system menu, as you would any other menu, adding items with **CMenu::AppendMenu()**, graying them with **CMenu::EnableMenuItem()**, and so on. If you want to modify the default system menu items, you will need to know their menu item ID values. These values are all defined in WINDOWS.H, and summarized in Table 9-4.

When the user selects an item in the system menu, Windows sends WM_SYSCOMMAND messages, not WM_COMMAND messages (which are sent for program menu items). The WM_SYSCOMMAND message is mapped to the **CWnd::OnSysCommand()** message processing function, which has the following form:

```
void CMainWindow::OnSysCommand (UINT nID, LONG lParam) ;
```

The *nID* parameter passes the system menu item ID number (Table 9-4) to identify the user's selection. *lParam* contains the mouse location if the system menu item was chosen with the mouse. These mouse coordinate values are of little value.

ID Value	Displayed in System Menu as
SC_CLOSE	Close
SC_MAXIMIZE (or SC_ZOOM)	Maximize
SC_MINIMIZE (or SC_ICON)	Minimize
SC_MOVE	Move
SC_RESTORE	Restore
SC_SIZE	Size
SC_TASKLIST	Switch To...

Table 9-4 System Menu Item ID Values

Changing the System Menu

The last example in this chapter is named SYSMENU. This program is a bit of fun, as it creates an icon-sized space ship that appears to "fly" around on the screen. When the space ship hits the edge of the screen, it changes course and keeps going. The space ship icon goes over inactive windows, and under active ones as it travels around the screen area. The program's image never gets bigger than an icon, and it can only be controlled via the program's system menu. Figure 9-11 shows what the SYSMENU icon looks like on the screen with the program's system menu displayed. Note that several of the default system menu entries ("Restore," "Size," and "Maximize") have been removed, and two new entries ("Start" and "Stop") have been added at the bottom. If the "Start" menu item is selected, the icon begins moving, and "Stop" stops the movement.

SYSMENU employs a couple of tricks to keep the program window from being enlarged from the icon size. The normal "Restore," "Size," and "Maximize" system menu items are deleted, as this removes several of the ways the user might try to resize the program window. In addition, if the WM_SIZE message is received, meaning that the program window has been resized (perhaps by the user double-clicking the icon), the **CWnd::ShowWindow()** function is executed to reduce the window back to an icon. This is a brute force way of keeping a program iconized, but it works.

Setting a Timer

The movement of the program icon on the screen is done with the **CWnd::Move-Window()** function, which was introduced in Chapter 8, *Child and Pop-Up*

Figure 9-11 The SYSMENU Program with Its System Menu Displayed

Windows. In order to make the SYSMENU icon move at a steady rate, the program must call **CWnd::MoveWindow()** at a fixed time interval. This is done by using the timer functions, **CWnd::SetTimer()** and **CWnd::KillTimer()**. **CWnd::SetTimer()** allows up to sixteen timers to be set at one time. The limit of sixteen applies to the sum of all the timers set by every application running on the system, not just to one program. Once a program calls **CWnd::SetTimer()**, the program begins receiving WM_TIMER messages at a fixed time interval.

To start a timer that will send the program WM_TIMER messages once per second, use the code in Listing 9-16. **CWnd::SetTimer()** takes three parameters. The first parameter is the timer's ID number. This value will end up as the timer ID value passed to the program with each WM_TIMER message. The ID value allows you to set more than one timer in an application, perhaps for separate activities that take place at different times. You can distinguish which timer caused the WM_TIMER message by checking the ID value. The second parameter is the number of milliseconds Windows should wait between WM_TIMER messages. A value of 1000 is a one-second time interval. The third parameter for the **CWnd::SetTimer()** function is usually set to NULL. (You can put the address of a separate function that will receive the WM_TIMER messages as the third parameter of **CWnd::SetTimer()**. We will not be using that technique in this book.)

CWnd::SetTimer() will return zero if all 16 timers have been used. This is a distinct possibility, so be sure to check whether the timer was set, and alert the user if the system has used all 16 timers. Normally, the user will be able to close at least one application, such as a clock, and then have access to another timer. WM_TIMER messages are mapped to the **CWnd::OnTimer()** function, which has the following format:

```
void CWnd::OnTimer (UINT nIDEvent) ;
```

The *nIDEvent* is the ID value for the timer which was passed with the WM_TIMER messages. Check this value to find out which timer generated the WM_TIMER message if your program uses more than one timer. If the program only uses one timer, the message must be from that timer, so there is no need to check the *nIDEvent* value. Timers are specific to one window object, so there is no way your program will get a stray WM_TIMER message from another application.

Listing 9-16 Starting a Timer

```
int nTimer ;
nTimer = CWindowName::SetTimer (1, 1000, NULL) ;
if (nTimer == NULL)
   CWindowName::MessageBox ("No timers left.", "Message", MB_OK) ;
```

When the timer is no longer needed, remove it from memory with the **CWnd::KillTimer()** function. This must be done explicitly, as terminating the program will not automatically remove the timer. Listing 9-17 shows a typical **CWnd::KillTimer()** function call.

Timers have all sorts of uses. You will probably find that you use timers more often in Windows than in DOS programming, as timers are a convenient way to make sure some activity happens, without having a program take over the system. The maximum accuracy for a timer is about 1/18 of a second with the standard version of Windows. (Timer accuracy down to 1 millisecond is possible using the Multimedia extensions to Windows, but this requires special attention so as not to bog down the system with the overhead of processing the timer calls.) Windows will not put more than one WM_TIMER message in a program's message queue, so there is no danger of having WM_TIMER messages "pile up" waiting to be processed. Nevertheless, it is always better to use a long time interval, if possible, to minimize the effect of the timer on the overall performance of the system.

SYSMENU Program Files

Listing 9-18 shows the SYSMENU.HPP header file. The **CMainWindow** class contains a number of integer parameters that are used to keep track of the current position of the program icon as it "flies" around on the screen (x,y), the dimensions of the screen (*ScnWide, ScnTall*), the number of pixels in the X and Y direction the icon will move when a WM_TIMER message is received (*Xvel, Yvel*), and the size of the icon itself (*IconWide, IconTall*). The *bMoveOn* value tracks whether the icon is moving. *nTimer* is the timer number. *pSysMenu* is a pointer to a **CMenu** object that is used to manipulate the system menu using **CMenu** member functions.

Listing 9-19 shows the SYSMENU.CPP program. Note in **CTheApp::InitInstance()** that the value SW_SHOWMINIMIZED is passed to the **CWnd::ShowWindow()** function. This displays the program window initially minimized, rather than the usual SW_SHOWNORMAL value.

The **CMainWindow** constructor function does all of the modifications to the system menu. The **CWnd::GetSystemMenu()** function is used to obtain a pointer to the system menu, which is stored as *pSysMenu*. A separator bar and two menu items labeled "Stop" and "Start" are added to the bottom of the system menu

Listing 9-17 Killing a Timer

```
if (nTimer)
 CWindowName::KillTimer (nTimer) ;
```

Listing 9-18 SYSMENU.HPP Header File

```
// sysmenu.hpp     header file for sysmenu.cpp

class CMainWindow : public CFrameWnd    // derive a main window class
{
public:
    CMainWindow () ;                    // declare a constructor
private:
    int x, y ;                          // save window position
    int ScnWide, ScnTall ;              // screen size ;
    int Xvel, Yvel ;                    // velocity values
    int IconWide, IconTall ;            // icon size
    BOOL bMoveOn ;                      // TRUE if moving
    UINT nTimer ;                       // timer number
    CMenu* pSysMenu ;                   // pointer to system menu

    void OnSysCommand (UINT nID, LONG lParam) ;
    void OnMove (int x, int y) ;
    void OnSize (UINT nType, int cx, int cy) ;
    void OnTimer (UINT nIDEvent) ;
    void OnDestroy () ;

    DECLARE_MESSAGE_MAP()               // prepare for message processing
} ;

class CTheApp : public CWinApp     // derive an application class
{
public:
    BOOL InitInstance () ;         // declare new InitInstance()
} ;
```

using the **CMenu::AppendMenu()** function. Four of the normal system menu items are deleted using the **CMenu::DeleteMenu()** function so that the user is not tempted to change the size of the iconized SYSMENU program using the default system menu choices, such as "Maximize" and "Restore."

The last activity in the **CMainWindow** constructor function is to initialize the values that store the screen and icon size. The **::GetSystemMetrics()** global function is used to fetch the size of the screen and icon at the time the program starts running. This assures that the values will be correct regardless of the type of video equipment on which the program is running.

The **CWnd::OnSysCommand()** message processing function handles all WM_SYSCOMMAND messages. This is a bit different from WM_COMMAND messages that are mapped to different message processing functions based on the ID value. With WM_SYSCOMMAND, the ID value is passed to the **CWnd::OnSysCommand()** function as the *nID* parameter, and it is up to the function to decide which menu item has been selected. In SYSMENU.CPP, only

Listing 9-19 SYSMENU.CPP

```cpp
// sysmenu.cpp              example that uses the system menu
                           // flies its icon around screen !
#include <afxwin.h>        // class library header file
#include "sysmenu.h"       // header file for resource data
#include "sysmenu.hpp"     // header file for this program


CTheApp theApp ;           // create one CTheApp object - runs program

BOOL CTheApp::InitInstance ()    // override default InitInstance()
{
    m_pMainWnd = new CMainWindow () ;        // create a main window
    m_pMainWnd->ShowWindow (SW_SHOWMINIMIZED) ; // make it visible
    return TRUE ;
}


CMainWindow::CMainWindow ()       // constructor for window
{
    Create (NULL, "SysMenu") ;   // use default parameters
    pSysMenu = this->GetSystemMenu (FALSE) ;// get sys menu pointer
                               // add new menu items to sys menu
    pSysMenu->AppendMenu (MF_SEPARATOR) ;
    pSysMenu->AppendMenu (MF_ENABLED, IDM_STOP, "Sto&p") ;
    pSysMenu->AppendMenu (MF_ENABLED, IDM_START, "Sta&rt") ;
                               // delete unneeded sys menu items
    pSysMenu->DeleteMenu (SC_MAXIMIZE, MF_BYCOMMAND) ;
    pSysMenu->DeleteMenu (SC_MINIMIZE, MF_BYCOMMAND) ;
    pSysMenu->DeleteMenu (SC_RESTORE, MF_BYCOMMAND) ;
    pSysMenu->DeleteMenu (SC_SIZE, MF_BYCOMMAND) ;

    bMoveOn = FALSE ;                // initialize data
    IconWide = ::GetSystemMetrics (SM_CXICON) ;
    IconTall = ::GetSystemMetrics (SM_CYICON) ;
    ScnWide = ::GetSystemMetrics (SM_CXSCREEN) ;
    ScnTall = ::GetSystemMetrics (SM_CYSCREEN) ;
    Xvel = Yvel = 1 ;
}

BEGIN_MESSAGE_MAP (CMainWindow, CFrameWnd)
    ON_WM_SYSCOMMAND ()
    ON_WM_MOVE ()
    ON_WM_SIZE ()
    ON_WM_TIMER ()
    ON_WM_DESTROY ()
END_MESSAGE_MAP ()

void CMainWindow::OnSysCommand (UINT nID, LONG lParam)
{
    switch (nID)
```

```
        {
            case IDM_START:                 // start timer
                nTimer = this->SetTimer (1, 100, NULL) ;
                if (nTimer == NULL)
                    this->MessageBox ("No timers left.",
                        "Message", MB_OK) ;
                else
                    bMoveOn = TRUE ;
                break ;
            case IDM_STOP:                  // stop timer
                this->KillTimer (nTimer) ;
                bMoveOn = FALSE ;
                break ;
            default:                        // pass others on
                CWnd::OnSysCommand (nID, lParam) ;
        }
    }

void CMainWindow::OnMove (int wx, int wy)
{
    x = wx ;        // OnMove parameters give the x,y position of the
    y = wy ;        // upper left corner of the window in screen coord.
}

void CMainWindow::OnSize (UINT nType, int cx, int cy)
{
    this->ShowWindow (SW_SHOWMINIMIZED) ;   // always minimized
}

void CMainWindow::OnTimer (UINT nIDEvent)   // timer event received
{                                           // move program icon
    x += Xvel ;                             // move location
    y += Yvel ;
    if (x <= 0 || x >= ScnWide - IconWide)
        Xvel *= -1 ;                        // reverse direction
    if (y <= 0 || y >= ScnTall - IconTall)
        Yvel *= -1 ;
    this->MoveWindow (x, y, 0, 0, TRUE) ;   // move icon
            // height and width == 0, as icon determines size
}

void CMainWindow::OnDestroy ()  // function executed just before
{                               // the application terminates
    if (bMoveOn)
        this->KillTimer (nTimer) ;
}
```

the IDM_START and IDM_STOP menu items are processed. Any other system
menu choices are passed on to the **CWnd::OnSysCommand()** function for
default actions. The form of this function call is critical. You must call the
CWnd::OnSysCommand() function as a **CWnd** class member as shown in
SYSMENU.CPP, *not* by using the derived **CMainWindow** class *this* pointer.

```
this->OnSysCommand (nID, lParam) ; // wrong !!
CWnd::OnSysCommand (nID, lParam) ; // right
```

The **CWnd::OnSysCommand()** function call makes sure that the built-in logic in Windows for handling system messages is not bypassed. Calling **CWnd::OnSysCommand()** results in immediate execution of the program code in the Windows environment for handling system messages.

The IDM_START system menu item starts the icon moving by calling the **CWnd::SetTimer()** function. Timer 1 is set to generate a WM_TIMER message every 10th of a second (100 milliseconds) with the following code:

```
nTimer = this->SetTimer (1, 100, NULL) ;
```

Similarly, the timer is stopped if the IDM_STOP system menu item is selected by calling the **CWnd::KillTimer()** function:

```
this->KillTimer (nTimer) ;
```

The movement of the program's icon is done when the WM_TIMER message is processed. The **CMainWindow::OnTimer()** function checks to make sure that the icon has not reached one of the edges of the screen before moving the icon. If an edge is reached, the direction of movement is reversed. This is the same type of logic that was used for the GRAPHIC2 program in Chapter 4, *Text and Graphics Output*. The **CWnd::MoveWindow()** function does the actual movement of the icon.

You may be surprised to see that the WM_MOVE message is processed by SYSMENU.CPP. This is not necessary for the normal movement of the icon on the screen as the program can track the icon's position as it is moved. However, the user can also move the icon using the mouse. The current *X,Y* position of the icon is recorded each time a WM_MOVE message is received to make sure that the current location is known at all times. The user may also try to resize the icon by double-clicking the icon with the mouse. Any attempt to resize the window is stopped by processing the WM_SIZE message in the **CWnd::OnSize()** function and again minimizing the window using **CWnd::ShowWindow()**.

One last detail worth noting is that the SYSMENU.CPP **CMainWindow::OnDestroy()** function checks whether the timer is set before exiting. The timer is killed using **CWnd::KillTimer()** if it is running. Otherwise, the timer would continue to operate after the program was terminated and would not be available for other applications.

The remaining files for the SYSMENU program are pretty simple. There are only two menu item ID numbers, used for the two added items in the system menu. Listing 9-20 shows the SYSMENU.H header file that provides the menu item ID numbers. If you look in WINDOWS.H, you will find that the ID numbers for the default system menu items are above 0xF000 hexadecimal, so normal numbering of menu items between 0 and 100 will not overlap the default system menu item ID values.

Because SYSMENU does not have a menu, the only resource data included is the icon's image. Listing 9-21 shows the SYSMENU.RC resource script file. Listing 9-22 shows the module definition file. The program's icon image is shown in Figure 9-12.

Listing 9-20 SYSMENU.H Header File

```
// sysmenu.h  header file for resource ID numbers

#define IDM_START      1
#define IDM_STOP       2
```

Listing 9-21 SYSMENU.RC Resource Script File

```
// sysmenu.rc  resource script file

#include <afxres.h>

AFX_IDI_STD_FRAME  ICON    sysmenu.ico   // the program's icon
```

Listing 9-22 SYSMENU.DEF Module Definition File

```
NAME            sysmenu
DESCRIPTION     'sysmenu C++ program'
EXETYPE         WINDOWS
STUB            'WINSTUB.EXE'
CODE            PRELOAD MOVEABLE
DATA            PRELOAD MOVEABLE MULTIPLE
HEAPSIZE        1024
STACKSIZE       5120
```

Figure 9-12 The SYSMENU.ICO Icon Image

SUMMARY

The MFC classes allow menus to be created and used with a combination of the **CMenu** class and menu definition data in the program's resource script file. By default, menu data in the program's resources is loaded into memory when needed (LOADONCALL) and moved and discarded from memory if Windows needs to make room for other programs or data (MOVEABLE, DISCARDABLE). You can override these default memory options, but there is seldom any reason to do so.

The two basic building blocks of menus are menu items and pop-up menus. Menu items are the only objects that can be selected, and that generate WM_COMMAND messages. Pop-up menus are used to create "drop-down" menus, containing additional menu items. You can create pop-ups within pop-ups in pop-ups, down to eight levels, but this tends to be confusing for the user. Normally, only one level of pop-up menus is used.

Individual menu items can be either enabled (can be selected), checked or unchecked, grayed or disabled. Graying is used to stop a menu item from being active, when a menu operation is not possible or appropriate. The **CMenu::EnableMenuItem()** function allows menu items to be switched between enabled, grayed, and disabled as the program runs. **CMenu::CheckMenuItem()** allows the program to change a menu item from checked to unchecked. Checking a menu item is used to show if a particular option is currently selected.

Menus can also be created and destroyed as the program operates. The **CMenu::CreateMenu()** and **CMenu::CreatePopupMenu()** functions create empty main and pop-up menus, respectively. New menu items can be appended to the end of the menu, or inserted, using **CMenu::AppendMenu()** and **CMenu::InsertMenu()**. Menus are attached to a window with the **CMenu::SetMenu()** function. Once a menu is attached to a window, the menu data will be removed from memory when the program terminates. Otherwise, the **CMenu::DestroyMenu()** function must be used to remove a menu from memory once it has been loaded or created. One of the advantages of adding menu items while the program operates is that bitmap images can be used as menu items, in place of text strings.

Main program windows, child windows, and pop-up windows can also have a system menu. The system menu is activated by clicking the system menu box at the top left corner of the window's caption area, by selecting a program icon with a single mouse click, or by using the (ALT)-(SPACEBAR) key combination. A handle to the system menu can be obtained using **CWnd::GetSystemMenu()**. The normal menu functions (**CMenu::EnableMenuItem()**, **CMenu::DeleteMenu()**, **CMenu::AppendMenu()**) can then be used to modify the program's system menu.

Windows provides a handy feature of allowing a program to set timers. Up to sixteen timers can be active on the system at one time. Timers result in WM_TIMER messages being sent to the program at fixed intervals. The **CWnd::SetTimer()** function starts a timer, and **CWnd::KillTimer()** removes the timer.

QUESTIONS

1. The default load option for a menu defined in a program's resource script file is _____. The default memory options are _____ and _____.

2. The only two types of statements that can be placed between the curly brackets following the key word MENU in a resource script file are _____ and _____.

3. The CHECKED and DISABLED menu item options cannot be used together because CHECKED items are always ENABLED. (True/False)

4. To insert a line between two items in a pop-up menu, use a MENUITEM _____ menu item.

5. To break a pop-up menu horizontally, use the
   a. MENUBARBREAK
   b. MENUBREAK
   c. a and b
   d. neither

6. The _____ function obtains a handle to a window's main menu. The _____ function obtains a handle to a window's system menu.

7. Main menus generate _____ messages when a menu item is selected. System menus generate _____ messages.

8. Timers are created with the _____ function, and destroyed with the _____ function. When a timer is operating, it generates _____ messages.

9. Only one timer can be started in a program at any one time. (True/False)

10. If changes are made to a main program menu as the program is running, the _____ function must be called to make the changes visible.

11. The _____ function deletes a menu item. The _____ function removes the entire menu from memory.

12. Unprocessed WM_SYSCOMMAND messages must be passed on to the _____ function to avoid disabling many default program actions.

EXERCISES

1. Modify the MENU2 program so that there is a third menu item in the pop-up containing the two bitmaps. The new menu item should have the ID value IDM_ARROW, and should contain the text "Default <u>A</u>rrow." Selecting this menu item should cause the cursor to switch back to the normal arrow shape.

2. Modify the MENU2 program again to make the new third menu item a bitmap image of the default arrow shape.

ANSWERS TO QUESTIONS

1. LOADONCALL, MOVEABLE, DISCARDABLE.

2. MENUITEM, POPUP.

3. False. Checked items are not always enabled. It is up the program logic to determine the implications of checking a menu item.

4. SEPARATOR.

5. c.

6. **CWnd::GetMenu(), CWnd::GetSystemMenu().**

7. WM_COMMAND, WM_SYSCOMMAND.

8. **CWnd::SetTimer(), CWnd::KillTimer(), WM_TIMER.**

9. False. You can have up to 16 timers in use at one time. However, there is a limit of 16 timers maximum among all running applications on the system.

10. **CWnd::DrawMenuBar().**

11. **CMenu::DeleteMenu(), CMenu::DestroyMenu().**

12. **CWnd::OnSysCommand().**

SOLUTIONS TO EXERCISES

1. No changes to the MENU2 program's resource script file are required because the menu is created entirely within the **CMainWindow** constructor function. Listing 9-23 shows the addition of the new menu item.

In addition, you will need to add a new message map entry and message processing function to handle WM_COMMAND messages from the added menu item. Listing 9-24 shows the additions to MENU2.CPP.

The **CMainWindow::OnArrow()** function must also be declared in the **CMainWindow** class definition in the program's header file. The complete solution is under the file name C09EXER1 on the source code disks.

2. First you will need to create a bitmap image of an arrow. Use the Microsoft Image Editor to create a file ARROW.BMP. A 64 by 64 pixel 16-color bitmap will match the other two items. Figure 9-13 shows the new bitmap. Add this file to the data in the program's resource file as shown in Listing 9-25.

Listing 9-23 Added Menu Item for Arrow Cursor Selection

```
CMainWindow::CMainWindow ()          // constructor for main window
{
    Create (NULL, "Menu Example 2", WS_OVERLAPPEDWINDOW, rectDefault,
        NULL, NULL) ;                // do not load menu in Create()
    Menu.CreateMenu () ;             // create a new, empty menu
    Popup.CreatePopupMenu () ;  // create a pop-up menu too

    CutBmp.LoadBitmap ("CutBmp") ;   // load from resource data
    PasteBmp.LoadBitmap ("PasteBmp") ;
                                     // add bitmaps as menu items
    Popup.AppendMenu (MF_ENABLED, IDM_CUT, &CutBmp) ;
    Popup.AppendMenu (MF_ENABLED, IDM_PASTE, &PasteBmp) ;
    Popup.AppendMenu (MF_ENABLED, IDM_ARROW, "Default &Arrow") ;
[Other program lines]
```

Listing 9-24 Added Message Processing Function

```
BEGIN_MESSAGE_MAP (CMainWindow, CFrameWnd)
    ON_COMMAND (IDM_CUT, OnCut)
    ON_COMMAND (IDM_PASTE, OnPaste)
    ON_COMMAND (IDM_ARROW, OnArrow)        // added function
    ON_COMMAND (IDM_ADD, OnAdd)
    ON_COMMAND (IDM_HELP, OnHelp)
    ON_COMMAND (IDM_QUIT, OnQuit)
    ON_COMMAND (IDM_REMOVE, OnRemove)
    ON_WM_SETCURSOR ()
END_MESSAGE_MAP ()

void CMainWindow::OnArrow ()                // "Default Arrow" item
{
    hCursor = AfxGetApp()->LoadStandardCursor (IDC_ARROW) ;
}
```

Figure 9-13 Arrow Bitmap

Listing 9-25 Adding a New Bitmap to MENU2.RC

```
// c9exer2.rc   resource script file

#include <afxres.h>
#include "c9exer2.h"

AFX_IDI_STD_FRAME   ICON    c9exer2.ico    // the program's icon

CutBmp       BITMAP   scissor.bmp      // bitmap files
PasteBmp     BITMAP   glue.bmp
ArrowBmp     BITMAP   arrow.bmp

CutCur       CURSOR   scissor.cur      // cursor files
GlueCur      CURSOR   glue.cur
```

The new bitmap must be loaded into memory and attached to the program's menu as it is created in the **CMainWindow** constructor function. Listing 9-26 shows the additions. The menu map and message processing functions are identical to those added for Exercise 1. The complete solution is under the file name C09EXER2 on the source code disks.

Listing 9-26 Adding a Third Bitmap Menu Item

```
CMainWindow::CMainWindow ()       // constructor for main window
{
    Create (NULL, "Menu Example 1", WS_OVERLAPPEDWINDOW, rectDefault,
        NULL, NULL) ;           // do not load menu in Create()
    Menu.CreateMenu () ;        // create a new, empty menu
    Popup.CreatePopupMenu () ;  // create a pop-up menu too

    CutBmp.LoadBitmap ("CutBmp") ;   // load from resource data
    PasteBmp.LoadBitmap ("PasteBmp") ;
    ArrowBmp.LoadBitmap ("ArrowBmp") ;
                                // add bitmaps as menu items
    Popup.AppendMenu (MF_ENABLED, IDM_CUT, &CutBmp) ;
    Popup.AppendMenu (MF_ENABLED, IDM_PASTE, &PasteBmp) ;
    Popup.AppendMenu (MF_ENABLED, IDM_ARROW, &ArrowBmp) ;
[Other Program Lines]
```

## Chapter 10

Dialog Boxes

In Chapter 8, *Child and Pop-Up Windows*, we created a program with a pop-up window. Pop-up windows are most commonly used to prompt the user for specific information. Examples include pop-up windows that allow the user to select a subdirectory or file, prompt for input of a string at the start of a search operation, and configure a program using groups of selection buttons. In these cases, the pop-up window can be constructed entirely of child window controls, such as list boxes, buttons, and edit controls.

Adding pop-up windows to an application is such a common task that Windows provides a shortcut called a "dialog box." Dialog boxes can be designed using a dialog box editor. The editor is a Windows program that allows you to quickly position child window controls on the dialog box and save the final positions as a dialog box template. The resource compiler reads the template file and creates a dialog box definition that is added to the finished program as resource data. Using a dialog box editor is much faster than designing a pop-up window by hand.

Although the dialog box editor speeds up designing dialog boxes, you must still code the program logic that responds to the user's actions when the dialog box is visible. The MFC classes provide some automation of dialog box operations via the **CDialog** and **CModalDialog** classes. We will explore both of these classes in this chapter, and test them with examples ranging from simple message boxes to complex dialog boxes containing several types of window controls.

Concepts covered: Using the dialog box editor, dialog base units, initializing the dialog box, passing data to a dialog box, string lists, C++ language casts, modal dialog boxes, system modal dialog boxes, modeless dialog boxes.

Key words covered: DIALOG, DS_SYSMODAL, WS_DLGFRAME, BEGIN, END.

Functions covered: CModalDialog::OnInitDialog(), CDialog::EndDialog(), CStringList::AddHead(), CStringList::FindIndex(), CStringList::GetAt(), CStringList::GetCount(), CStringList::GetHeadPosition(), CStringList::Get-Next(), CWnd::GetDlgItem(), CWnd::CheckRadioButton().

Messages covered: WM_CLOSE.

Classes covered: CDialog, CModalDialog, CStringList.

WHAT IS A DIALOG BOX?

Dialog boxes are nothing more than pop-up windows. Any time you need a small window to appear for user information or input, you can use a pop-up window (as was demonstrated in Chapter 8, *Child and Pop-Up Windows*) or you can use a dialog box. The advantage of using a dialog box is that it can be constructed quickly using a dialog box editor program. Microsoft C++ includes the Microsoft Dialog Editor (MSDE) application for this purpose. The only restriction when using a dialog box editor is that the dialog box must be constructed entirely of child window controls. There is no facility for painting designs on the dialog box window using the editors, although painting can be done by including WM_PAINT message processing logic. Normally, dialog boxes are constructed entirely with child window controls, such as buttons, list boxes, static text, and icons.

The MFC classes provide the **CDialog** and **CModalDialog** classes for manipulating dialog boxes. Figure 10-1 shows the derivation of these two classes. It should not be too surprising that dialog boxes are derived from the **CWnd** class, as dialog boxes are just forms of windows. The **CDialog** class is the more general

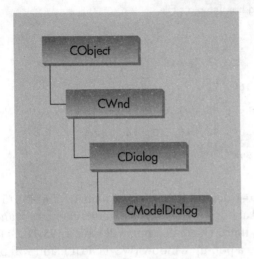

Figure 10-1 Derivation of the CDialog and CModalDialog Classes

class containing most of the dialog box functions. The **CModalDialog** class provides an additional derived class for "modal" dialog boxes. Modal dialog boxes take over control from their parent window until the dialog box disappears. This contrasts to "modeless" dialog boxes, which can stay on the screen for extended periods of time, gaining and losing the input focus just like a pop-up window. We will examine both types of dialog boxes in this chapter.

Creating Dialog Boxes

The first step in creating a dialog box is to design the dialog box window using the Microsoft Dialog Editor (MSDE) application. Your design is saved as a text file called a "dialog box template," usually with the extension ".DLG." The template file consists of a series of command lines that define the dialog box window and each of its controls. Listing 10-1 shows an example dialog box template. Normally, you will not need to examine these template files directly, as the MSDE takes care of all the editing chores. However, templates are fairly simple to read once you are familiar with the format.

The first four lines of code in DIALG1.DLG instruct the resource compiler to save the name of the header file containing the control ID numbers with the dialog box data. This makes it easy for the MSDE to determine the name of the header file and automatically open it during subsequent editing sessions. In this case, the header file name is "DIALG1.H." Following the four lines that include the header file name is the actual dialog box template data.

Listing 10-1 DIALG1.DLG Dialog Box Template File

```
DLGINCLUDE RCDATA
BEGIN
    "DIALG1.H\0"
END

FIRSTDIALOG DIALOG 6, 9, 160, 72
FONT 8, "MS Sans Serif"
STYLE WS_POPUP | WS_VISIBLE | WS_DLGFRAME
BEGIN
    DEFPUSHBUTTON "OK", IDOK, 92, 46, 40, 14
    ICON "DIALG1", -1, 8, 21, 16, 16
    LTEXT "Simple Dialog Box", -1, 53, 7, 78, 15
END
```

The template in Listing 10-1 defines a dialog box named "FIRSTDIALOG." The dialog box will be located at position 6, 9 on its parent's client area, and will be 160 units wide by 72 units high. The dialog box will have a WS_DLGFRAME frame (thick blue line), will be a pop-up window (WS_POPUP), and will be created initially visible on the screen (WS_VISIBLE). All text will be shown using an eight point "sans serif" font (FONT statement). Inside the dialog box will be three controls: a DEFPUSHBUTTON labeled "OK" (default push button that is activated if the user presses the (ENTER) key), a static icon named "dialg1," and a static text control containing the string "Simple Dialog Box."

Each of the controls in the dialog box is defined between the BEGIN and END key words. BEGIN and END are equivalent to the { and } characters that we have been using in the resource script files for other types of resource data, such as menus and string tables. You can use either curly brackets or the BEGIN and END key words if you are creating a dialog box template file "by hand" with a text editor. The author prefers the curly brackets to the BEGIN and END key words because the brackets are more consistent with C++ syntax. The MSDE continues to use the older BEGIN and END key words, so the dialog box templates in this chapter are shown exactly as created by the MSDE.

Dialog Base Units

One of the peculiarities of dialog box templates is the system of units used to size the dialog box and all of the child window controls. Dialog box templates use "dialog base units." Vertical sizes are measured in 1/8 of the height of a character. Horizontal heights are 1/4 of the width of a character. Using the character size makes the dialog box automatically proportion itself when displayed on monitors with different resolutions. A side effect is that you can change the size of the entire dialog box and every control just by changing the font being used. The dialog box editor will allow you to change the font, although normally the default system font is fine.

Compiling a Dialog Box

To make the dialog box template usable by Windows, it must be compiled using the resource compiler. The compiled dialog box definition data becomes part of the program's resource data and is added to the finished program (.EXE file). When the program needs to display the dialog box, the dialog box data is loaded into memory. Windows decodes the resource data and creates the dialog box and all of the child window controls from the information in the resource data. Figure 10-2 shows the chain of events leading to a dialog box showing up on the screen.

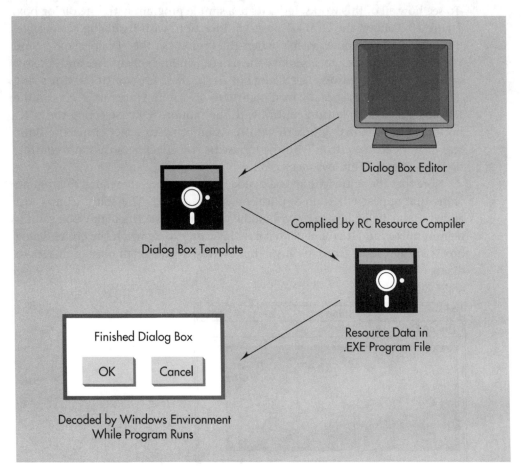

Figure 10-2 Creation of a Dialog Box

This probably sounds like a roundabout way to create a pop-up window. The advantage to the programmer is that the dialog box editor makes designing a dialog box very simple. Also, the dialog box definition gets added to the program's resource data and (by default) only gets brought into memory if the dialog box needs to be displayed. This makes dialog boxes memory efficient. If you need to have the dialog box preloaded into memory, you can override the default behavior by changing settings within the dialog box editor. 99% of all dialog boxes use the default settings, and are only loaded into memory when needed.

Designing a Dialog Box

To see how all of this works, let's create a simple program with one dialog box. Figure 10-3 shows the DIALG1 program in action, with its dialog box visible. The dialog box becomes visible when the user clicks the "Dialog Box" menu item. The dialog box appears above the parent window's client area and consists of three window controls. The dialog box uses a static text control for the string "Simple Dialog Box," a static icon control to display the program's icon on the left side, and a push button control with the caption "OK." Selecting the "OK" button causes the dialog box to vanish. Attempting to select either the static text or static icon controls with the mouse has no effect because static controls do not generate Windows messages.

Note that the static icon in the dialog box is not directly related to program icons that appear when an application is minimized. The static icon is just added to the dialog box to provide some visual interest. The dialog box cannot be minimized, and it will never display this icon except when the entire dialog box is visible. Static icons are just a handy way to add small bitmap images to dialog boxes.

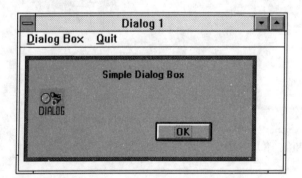

Figure 10-3 The DIALG1 Program's Dialog Box

Using the Dialog Box Editor

The Microsoft dialog box editor (MSDE) is a self-contained application that automates designing dialog boxes. It is easier to use the MSDE if you prepare a small header file before starting the MSDE session. The header file defines the ID numbers for the controls in the dialog box. You can edit the header file from within the MSDE to create or change ID numbers as needed. This same header file can be included in your C++ program, so that the compiler gets the same definitions for all the dialog box ID numbers. For the DIALG1 program, create a header file named DIALG1.H, as shown in Listing 10-2. (The header file is not strictly necessary in DIALG1.H because WINDOWS.H includes definitions of the common IDOK and IDCANCEL constants.)

When you first start the MSDE, you will be presented with a blank work area containing the tool menu. Select the "File/New" menu item to create an empty dialog box as a starting point. To let the MSDE know about the header file, select the "File/Set Include" menu item and load the DIALG1.H file. You will see the header file name at the top of the MSDE screen. You are now ready to create a dialog box using the graphical tools.

The MSDE default style for the dialog box frame has a caption bar and system menu button. This will be shown on the empty "target" dialog box in the MSDE edit area. Before adding controls, the dialog box style needs to be changed to match our needs. The default combination of caption bar and system menu button is a good style for many dialog boxes, but not for our DIALG1 example. DIALG1 needs a simple dialog box frame without a caption bar or system menu. Double-click the target dialog box to cause the MSDE to display the options for a dialog box. The MSDE will display the "Dialog Styles" box, as shown in Figure 10-4. Turn off the "Caption" and "System Menu" styles, and select the "Dialog" frame style. Click the "OK" button to save the style information, and return to the MSDE main window. Note that the position of the target dialog box in the editor screen will determine where the dialog box shows up when it appears "above" the parent window's client area when the dialog box is displayed. You can move the target dialog box by dragging it with the mouse.

Listing 10-2 DIALG1.H Resource ID Header File

```
// dialg1.h  header file for resource ID numbers

#define IDM_DIALOG     1
#define IDM_QUIT       10
#define ID_OK          1      // or use IDOK in Windows.H
#define ID_ICON        2
```

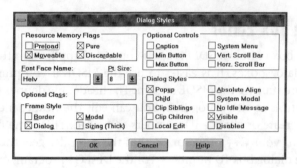

Figure 10-4 Specifying the Dialog Box Style Using the MSDE

One of the automatic features of the MSDE is the generation of ID numbers for objects like controls and the target dialog box. This is not always helpful. The target dialog box will be automatically assigned the ID number of 100. Every control added will receive a default ID number one greater than the last (100, 101, 102...). This incorrect ID number assignment shows up in the upper right portion of Figure 10-5, just below the menu. The easiest way to get around this type of problem is to invent a new ID number, and assign it to the target dialog box. Unfortunately, this has the effect of making the ID *number* the name of the dialog box, rather than the character string name. Unless you want your dialog box to have a name like "100," the Dialog Symbol needs to be changed to a character string that does *not* have a numeric definition in the header file.

To name the dialog box "FIRSTDIALOG," the "Dlg. Sym." (dialog symbol) item in the extended menu area must be changed to "FIRSTDIALOG," and the number to the right of it must be erased. The white rectangles to the right of "Dlg. Sym." in the info bar are actually edit controls, so you can select them

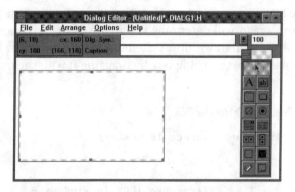

Figure 10-5 MSDE Showing an Initial Assignment of ID 100 to the Target Dialog Box

10
DIALOG BOXES

with the mouse, and edit their contents. The info bar should be as shown in Figure 10-6 when you correctly specify the dialog box name as "FIRSTDIALOG."

Now you can go ahead and add all of the controls to the dialog box. Select the button from the tool menu, and place it in the lower center of the dialog box. The button does not appear until you click the left mouse button. If you double-click the new button control, the "Push Button Styles" dialog box will appear. Selecting the "Default" push button style gives the button a highlighted border. Select the "OK" button to go back to the main MSDE window. The button's text and ID numbers are specified in the gray info bar area, below the editor's menu. Change the first button's ID number to ID_OK, with a text field of "OK." Only one button can have the "Default" push button style, as the default button is usually the one that is activated when the user presses the (RETURN) key, and it would not be logical for two buttons to be activated if the user pressed (ENTER).

The icon tool looks like a small pencil at the bottom left of the MSDE tool menu. To continue with our example, you should select the icon tool from the tool bar with the mouse, and place the icon on the left side of the target dialog box by moving and clicking the mouse cursor. Once you have positioned the icon, select the icon control by clicking it again with the mouse. The upper menu area of the MSDE changes wording, reflecting that an icon is currently selected. In the gray info bar area, you will want to make the "Symbol" field equal to ID_ICON, and "IconSym." equal to DIALG1, the name of the icon in the program's resource script file. Finally, add a static text field containing the text "Simple Dialog Box" to the top center of the target dialog box. You can select the "(Unused)" symbol name for the static text field, as this ID value is not

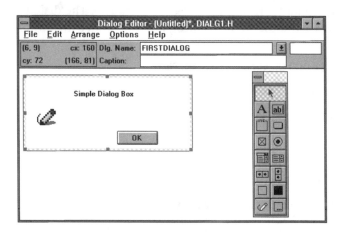

Figure 10-6 MSDE with the FIRSTDIALOG Dialog Box Defined

important. "Unused" gets translated to an ID value of –1. With all of the controls in place, your MSDE screen will look approximately like Figure 10-6.

When you have added all the controls, you can save the dialog box definition and any changes to the header file. Select the "File/Save As" menu item. Two dialog boxes will appear in sequence, the first one captioned "Save Include File." Clicking the "OK" button will save any changes to DIALG1.H. The second dialog box will then appear, captioned "Save Resource File," and allow you to save the dialog box definition in either compiled (.RES) form or as a dialog box definition. Change the file name to "DIALG1.RES." The MSDE will save the dialog box data as both the compiled DIALG1.RES and the resource script format DIALG1.DLG automatically. Listing 10-3 shows the output of the MSDE for the example dialog box.

As mentioned previously, the top four lines add the dialog box header file name to the program's resource data. This wastes a little space, but allows the MSDE to find the header file from the compiled version of the dialog box definition, by reading the header file name out of the resource data. We will examine other uses for including raw data in a program's resources in the next chapter. For now, you can ignore these lines in the .DLG file. The MSDE also defaults to adding a FONT statement to the dialog box definition, selecting an eight point Helvitica font. Because dialog base units are fractions of the font size, selecting a small font, such as Helvitica 8, reduces the size of the dialog box on the screen. Helvetica 8 is used by all of the Microsoft applications supplied with Windows.

USING THE DIALOG BOX

All we have done so far is create the dialog box template. The dialog box definition created with the dialog box editor must be added to the program's

Listing 10-3 DIALG1.DLG Dialog Box Definition File

```
DLGINCLUDE RCDATA
BEGIN
    "DIALG1.H\0"
END

FIRSTDIALOG DIALOG 6, 9, 160, 72
FONT 8, "MS Sans Serif"
STYLE WS_POPUP | WS_VISIBLE | WS_DLGFRAME
BEGIN
    DEFPUSHBUTTON "OK", ID_OK, 92, 46, 40, 14
    ICON "DIALG1", ID_ICON, 8, 21, 16, 16
    LTEXT "Simple Dialog Box", -1, 53, 7, 78, 15
END
```

resources. Listing 10-4 shows a simple way to do this. The dialog box template file DIALG1.DLG is added using the *#include* directive. Note that the DIALG1.H header file is included *before* the dialog box template, because the resource compiler needs the ID values from DIALG1.H to make sense out of the dialog box template. Also note that the icon data DIALG1.ICO is included twice. The name AFX_IDI_STD_FRAME is used to assign the icon for the main program window. The name DIALG1 is used within the dialog box template to specify the icon that is visible inside the dialog box. The same name could have been used for both the program icon and the dialog box icon. You could also load two different icons, assigning each a different name.

That is all there is to defining a dialog box as part of the program's resources. This still leaves the problem of displaying the dialog box window. It turns out that if a dialog box contains nothing more than static controls and one or two buttons, the **CModalDialog** class can almost completely automate the display of a dialog box control. The **CModalDialog** class has built-in message processing logic for these simple dialog boxes, so there will be no need to define a separate message map for the dialog box window. (We will use a message map in the next example program, DIALG2.) Listing 10-5 shows the DIALG1.HPP program header file. The only message processing functions are the **CMainWindow::OnDialog()** and **CMainWindow::OnQuit()** functions for responding to the two main program window menu items.

Listing 10-6 shows the DIALG1.CPP program. This program is very similar to the MINIMAL3.CPP program introduced in Chapter 3, *First Programming Experiments*. The only difference is that one of the menu items (labeled "Dialog Box") is mapped to the **CMainWindow::OnDialog()** message processing function. This function creates and displays a modal dialog box based on the dialog box defini-

Listing 10-4 DIALG1.RC Resource Script File

```
// dialg1.rc  resource script file

#include <windows.h>
#include <afxres.h>
#include "dialg1.h"              // ID values
#include "dialg1.dlg"            // the dialog box definition

AFX_IDI_STD_FRAME    ICON    dialg1.ico // the program's icon
DIALG1               ICON    dialg1.ico // rename for dlg box

MyMenu MENU                          // define the menu
{
    MENUITEM "&Dialog Box", IDM_DIALOG
    MENUITEM "&Quit",       IDM_QUIT
}
```

Listing 10-5 DIALG1.HPP Header file

```
// dialg1.hpp     header file for dialg1.cpp

class CMainWindow : public CFrameWnd    // derive a main window class
{
public:
    CMainWindow () ;                    // declare a constructor
private:
    void OnDialog () ;                  // runs dialog box
    void OnQuit () ;                    // stop application

    DECLARE_MESSAGE_MAP()               // prepare for message processing
} ;

class CTheApp : public CWinApp         // derive an application class
{
public:
    BOOL InitInstance () ;                  // declare new InitInstance()
} ;
```

tion in the DIALG1.DLG dialog box template. A **CModalDialog** object named *FirstDialog* is created using the **CModalDialog** class constructor function:

```
CModalDialog FirstDialog ("FIRSTDIALOG", this) ;
```

Note that a pointer to the parent window object (a *this* pointer) is passed to the **CModalDialog** constructor function. The constructor is also passed the name of the dialog box data in the program's resources, "FIRSTDIALOG." The constructor function results in the dialog box data being loaded into memory from the program's resources. Note that because the **CModalDialog** object is declared within the body of the **CMainWindow::OnDialog()** function, the object is stored on the application's stack as an automatic variable. This means that the *FirstDialog* object will automatically be destroyed when the **CMainWindow::OnDialog()** function returns. This is ideal for a temporary dialog box that displays a message and then immediately vanishes.

The only step left is to display the dialog box on the screen and wait for the user to select the "OK" button. This is done by calling the **CModalDialog::DoModal()** function:

```
FirstDialog.DoModal () ;
```

This single function call takes care of displaying the dialog box, and makes the dialog box window the active window until the "OK" button is displayed. All message processing is handled by the dialog box until it vanishes from the screen. You can switch to another application while the dialog box is visible, but you cannot select the main program window or switch the input focus to any part of DIALG1 that is not in the modal dialog box. This behavior is ideal for displaying critical messages, which is the most common use for modal dialog boxes.

When the user selects the "OK" button, the **CModalDialog::DoModal()** function returns. The dialog box vanishes from the screen and control passes back to the parent window, the main program window for DIALG1.

Listing 10-7 shows the module definition file for DIALG1. The program's icon image is shown in Figure 10-7.

Listing 10-6 DIALG1.CPP

```
// dialg1.cpp                 example of a simple modal dialog box

#include <afxwin.h>      // class library header file
#include "dialg1.h"      // header file for resource data
#include "dialg1.hpp"    // header file for this program

CTheApp theApp ;         // create one CTheApp object - runs program

BOOL CTheApp::InitInstance ()   // override default InitInstance()
{
    m_pMainWnd = new CMainWindow () ;         // create a main window
    m_pMainWnd->ShowWindow (m_nCmdShow) ;     // make it visible
    m_pMainWnd->UpdateWindow () ;             // paint center
    return TRUE ;
}


CMainWindow::CMainWindow ()      // constructor for window
{
    Create (NULL, "Dialog 1", WS_OVERLAPPEDWINDOW, rectDefault,
        NULL, "MyMenu") ;
}


BEGIN_MESSAGE_MAP (CMainWindow, CFrameWnd)
    ON_COMMAND (IDM_DIALOG, OnDialog)
    ON_COMMAND (IDM_QUIT, OnQuit)
END_MESSAGE_MAP ()

void CMainWindow::OnDialog ()    // respond to menu item "Dialog Box"
{
    CModalDialog FirstDialog ("FIRSTDIALOG", this) ;
    FirstDialog.DoModal () ;
}


void CMainWindow::OnQuit ()      // respond to menu item "Quit"
{
    this->DestroyWindow () ;     // destroy main window,
}                                // this stops application
```

Figure 10-7 DIALG1.ICO Icon Image

Listing 10-7 DIALG1.DEF Module Definition File

```
NAME            dialg1
DESCRIPTION     'dialg1 C++ program'
EXETYPE         WINDOWS
STUB            'WINSTUB.EXE'
CODE            PRELOAD MOVEABLE
DATA            PRELOAD MOVEABLE MULTIPLE
HEAPSIZE        1024
STACKSIZE       5120
```

The first time you use a dialog box function, it seems like an incredible amount of work. After you have created a few dialog boxes, the steps become almost automatic. The dialog box editor comes in very handy when you need to update a dialog box you worked on months ago, and you no longer remember the ID numbers for the controls. The dialog box in DIALG1.CPP is an ideal starting point for any dialog box. Our next example will add radio buttons and a check box to the dialog box template.

A MORE COMPLEX DIALOG BOX

The next example, DIALG2, is designed to illustrate using a dialog box to obtain input from the user. Figure 10-8 shows the program running, with the dialog box visible. This dialog box has a caption bar, with a system menu button on the upper left corner. The caption bar allows the dialog box to be moved on the screen. This is a handy feature if the user may need to see what is under the dialog box to fill in the dialog box data. The dialog box allows the user to make two choices. The first is a selection between one of two radio button controls labeled "Choice 1" and "Choice 2." The two radio buttons are surrounded in a group box control to indicate that the radio buttons are related. Group boxes are rectangular outlines, with a title at the top left corner. The radio buttons within the group box are set up so that if one is selected, the other radio button is automatically de-selected.

Below the group box is a check box control. Check boxes are typically used for options that are either on or off, although a three-state check box (on, off, grayed) is possible. In this case, the check box has the text string "Check On/Off." The dialog box also has two button controls, "OK" and "Cancel." The DIALG2 program's main window (see Figure 10-8) displays the most recent selections from the radio buttons, check box, and whether the user last killed the dialog box with the "OK" or "Cancel" buttons. Selecting the "OK" button results in the dialog box returning a value of one as the dialog box vanishes. Selecting the "Cancel" button results in a value of zero being returned. Using the system menu button also cancels the dialog box, returning two. We will see how these values are passed to the main program window logic in a moment.

Creating the DIALG2 Dialog Box

The first step in creating the DIALG2 program is to design the dialog box. This time, the step-by-step instructions for operating the dialog box editor will not be given. However, here is an outline of the steps you should take to create the dialog box template:

1. Create a header file defining the ID numbers for the dialog box controls in advance. The header is called DIALG2.H and is shown in Listing 10-8.

2. Use the MSDE to define a dialog box named PICKDIALOG with the appearance shown in Figure 10-8. You will need to specify the "Caption" and "System Menu" styles for the dialog box window. The group box control can have an ID value of –1, as this control is never selected. The other controls

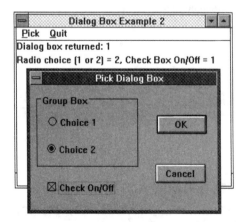

Figure 10-8 The DIALG2 Program's Dialog Box

Listing 10-8 DIALG2.H Resource ID Header File

```
// dialg2.h  header file for resource ID numbers

#define IDM_DIALOG    1        // menu item ID numbers
#define IDM_QUIT      2

#define DLI_CHECKBOX  104      // dialog box control IDs
#define DLI_RADIO2    103
#define DLI_RADIO1    102      // (can be in any order)
#define DLI_CANCEL    101
#define DLI_OK        100
```

should use the ID values defined in the DIALG2.H header file. The output of the dialog box editor should be similar to DIALG2.DLG in Listing 10-9. The exact dimensions and placement of each control are not critical, so the numbers at the end of each definition line in DIALG2.DLG for your version will be slightly different.

Creating the DIALG2 Program

The dialog box displayed by the DIALG2 program is more complex than can be handled by using the **CModalDialog** class directly as was done for the DIALG1 example. To extend the **CModalDialog** class requires deriving a new class. Listing 10-10 shows the DIALG2.HPP header file, which derives the **CMyDialog** class from the **CModalDialog** MFC class. The **CMyDialog** class contains both public and private functions, and takes advantage of C++ inline functions.

Listing 10-9 DIALG2.DLG Dialog Box Definition File

```
DLGINCLUDE RCDATA DISCARDABLE
BEGIN
    "DIALG2.H\0"
END

PICKDIALOG DIALOG 10, 40, 142, 92
STYLE DS_MODALFRAME | WS_POPUP | WS_CAPTION | WS_SYSMENU
CAPTION "Pick Dialog Box"
BEGIN
    DEFPUSHBUTTON   "OK", DLI_OK, 96, 22, 38, 14
    PUSHBUTTON      "Cancel", DLI_CANCEL, 95, 58, 38, 14
    RADIOBUTTON     "Choice 1", DLI_RADIO1, 14, 21, 54, 12,
        WS_TABSTOP
    RADIOBUTTON     "Choice 2", DLI_RADIO2, 13, 41, 61, 12,
        WS_TABSTOP
    CHECKBOX        "Check On/Off", DLI_CHECKBOX, 13, 69, 68, 12
    GROUPBOX        "Group Box", -1, 5, 6, 77, 54
END
```

The first inline function is the constructor function for the new class of dialog boxes. This function is defined inline as being a direct call to the **CModalDialog** constructor function. The result is that constructing a **CMyDialog** object creates a modal dialog box based on the resource data named "PickDialog" and with a parent window *pParent*.

```
CMyDialog (CWnd* pParent) : CModalDialog ("PickDialog",
    pParent) {}
```

One of the predefined functions in the **CModalDialog** class is the **CModalDialog::OnInitDialog()** function, which is called when the dialog box is first

Listing 10-10 DIALG2.HPP Header File

```
// dialg2.hpp    header file for dialg2.cpp

class CMyDialog : public CModalDialog
{
public:
    CMyDialog (CWnd* pParent) :      // constructor
        CModalDialog ("PickDialog", pParent) {}
    BOOL OnInitDialog () ;           // override default
    int GetChoice () {return nChoice ; }
    int GetCheckStatus () {return nCheckStatus ; }
private:
    int nChoice ;
    int nCheckStatus ;
    void OnChoiceOne () ;
    void OnChoiceTwo () ;
    void OnCheck () ;
    void OnOkBtn () {this->EndDialog (TRUE) ; }
    void OnCancelBtn () {this->EndDialog (FALSE) ; }

    DECLARE_MESSAGE_MAP ()           // message map for dialog
} ;

class CMainWindow : public CFrameWnd    // derive a main window class
{
public:
    CMainWindow () ;                 // declare a constructor
private:
    void OnDialog () ;               // runs dialog box
    void OnQuit () ;                 // stop application

    DECLARE_MESSAGE_MAP()            // prepare for message processing
} ;

class CTheApp : public CWinApp     // derive an application class
{
public:
    BOOL InitInstance () ;            // declare new InitInstance()
} ;
```

created. By writing an **OnInitDialog()** function as part of the **CMyDialog** class, the new **OnInitDialog()** function will override the default function (defined as a virtual function in the **CModalDialog** class). The **OnInitDialog()** function provides a perfect place to put initialization code that should be executed right before the dialog box is made visible on the screen. We will examine the coding of the **CMyDialog::OnInitDialog()** function in a moment.

The **CMyDialog** class includes two private data items, *nChoice* and *nCheckStatus,* which are used to store the current status of the radio button selection and the check box status. Private items cannot be accessed from outside of the class, so two access functions named **CMyDialog::GetChoice()** and **CMyDialog::GetCheckStatus()** are provided so that the status of the radio buttons and check box can be determined from outside of the class definition. The access functions are also defined inline within the class definition because they are so short.

```
int GetChoice () {return nChoice ; }
int GetCheckStatus () {return nCheckStatus ; }
```

The remaining functions in the **CMyDialog** class definition are message processing functions for the dialog box. The DECLARE_MESSAGE_MAP() macro is also included at the bottom of the class definition so that the dialog box can have its own message map. Two of the message processing functions respond to the selection of the push button controls. They are also defined inline and return either TRUE or FALSE to the calling program depending on whether the "OK" or "Cancel" button was selected. The **CDialog::EndDialog()** function destroys the dialog box and returns an integer value to the calling program. Note that the *this* pointer to the **CMyDialog** object works just fine within the class definition as a pointer to the dialog box window object.

```
void OnOkBtn () {this->EndDialog (TRUE) ; }
void OnCancelBtn () {this->EndDialog (FALSE) ; }
```

The **CMainWindow** and **CTheApp** classes are also defined in the DIALOG2.HPP header file. The **CMainWindow** class also uses the DECLARE_MESSAGE_MAP() macro, so you can expect to see two message maps in the DIALG2.CPP program file.

Listing 10-11 shows the DIALG2.CPP program file. When the user selects the "Pick" menu item, the WM_COMMAND message is routed to the **CMainWindow::OnDialog()** function. The code in **CMainWindow::OnDialog()** creates a **CMyDialog** object named *PickDialog* and runs it by calling the **CModalDialog::DoModal()** function.

```
CMyDialog PickDialog (this) ; // create a CMyDialog object
int nRetVal = PickDialog.DoModal () ; // run the dialog box
```

Listing 10-11 DIALG2.CPP Program File

```cpp
// dialg2.cpp              // example of a dialog box with controls

#include <afxwin.h>        // class library header file
#include <strstrea.h>      // for stream functions
#include "dialg2.h"        // header file for resource data
#include "dialg2.hpp"      // header file for this program

CTheApp theApp ;           // create one CTheApp object - runs program

BOOL CTheApp::InitInstance ()   // override default InitInstance()
{
    m_pMainWnd = new CMainWindow () ;       // create a main window
    m_pMainWnd->ShowWindow (m_nCmdShow) ;   // make it visible
    m_pMainWnd->UpdateWindow () ;           // paint center
    return TRUE ;
}

CMainWindow::CMainWindow ()     // constructor for window
{
    Create (NULL, "Dialog Box Example 2", WS_OVERLAPPEDWINDOW,
        rectDefault, NULL, "MyMenu") ;
}


BEGIN_MESSAGE_MAP (CMainWindow, CFrameWnd)
    ON_COMMAND (IDM_DIALOG, OnDialog)
    ON_COMMAND (IDM_QUIT, OnQuit)
END_MESSAGE_MAP ()

void CMainWindow::OnDialog ()   // respond to menu item "Pick"
{                               // run dialog box
    CMyDialog PickDialog (this) ;         // create a CMyDialog object
    int nRetVal = PickDialog.DoModal () ; // run the dialog box

    CClientDC dc (this) ;       // show selections in client area
    char cBuf [128] ;
    ostrstream myStream (cBuf, sizeof (cBuf)) ;

    myStream << "Dialog box returned: " << nRetVal ;
    dc.TextOut (0, 0, cBuf, myStream.pcount ()) ;

    myStream.seekp (0) ;        // put pointer to start
    myStream << "Radio choice (1 or 2) = "
        << PickDialog.GetChoice () << ", Check Box On/Off = "
        << PickDialog.GetCheckStatus () ;
    dc.TextOut (0, 20, cBuf, myStream.pcount ()) ;
}

void CMainWindow::OnQuit ()     // respond to menu item "Quit"
{
    this->DestroyWindow () ;    // destroy main window,
}                               // this stops application
```

```
//--------------------- Dialog box section ----------------------//

BOOL CMyDialog::OnInitDialog () // function called just before dialog
{                               // box becomes visible
    nChoice = 1 ;
    nCheckStatus = 0 ;
    this->CheckDlgButton (DLI_RADIO1, 1) ;
    this->CheckDlgButton (DLI_RADIO2, 0) ;
    this->CheckDlgButton (DLI_CHECKBOX, 0) ;
    return TRUE ;
}                               // note no message map required for
                                // OnInitDialog() function

BEGIN_MESSAGE_MAP (CMyDialog, CModalDialog)
    ON_COMMAND (DLI_RADIO1, OnChoiceOne)
    ON_COMMAND (DLI_RADIO2, OnChoiceTwo)
    ON_COMMAND (DLI_CHECKBOX, OnCheck)
    ON_COMMAND (DLI_CANCEL, OnCancelBtn)
    ON_COMMAND (DLI_OK, OnOkBtn)
END_MESSAGE_MAP ()

void CMyDialog::OnChoiceOne ()
{
    nChoice = 1 ;
    this->CheckDlgButton (DLI_RADIO1, 1) ;
    this->CheckDlgButton (DLI_RADIO2, 0) ;
}

void CMyDialog::OnChoiceTwo ()
{
    nChoice = 2 ;
    this->CheckDlgButton (DLI_RADIO1, 0) ;
    this->CheckDlgButton (DLI_RADIO2, 1) ;
}

void CMyDialog::OnCheck ()
{
    if (nCheckStatus)
    {
        this->CheckDlgButton (DLI_CHECKBOX, 0) ;
        nCheckStatus = 0 ;
    }
    else
    {
        this->CheckDlgButton (DLI_CHECKBOX, 1) ;
        nCheckStatus = 1 ;
    }
}
```

At this point, execution passes to the dialog box program logic. The **CMyDialog::OnInitDialog()** function is executed before the dialog box is made visible. This function initializes the *nChoice* and *nCheckStatus* variables and sets the radio buttons and the check box controls to their startup states. The dialog box window is then made visible and takes control from the parent window.

The user cannot select any portion of the main program window while the dialog box is active.

When the dialog box is destroyed, the **CDialog::EndDialog()** function returns either TRUE or FALSE depending on which button was selected. This value is captured as the *nRetVal* integer, which makes it easy for the calling program to determine if the "OK" or "Cancel" button was selected. In DIALG2.CPP, the returned value is just displayed in the parent window's client area. The selection status of the radio buttons and the check box is also displayed after fetching these values using **CMyDialog::GetChoice()** and **CMyDialog::GetCheckStatus()** access functions.

You might be surprised that the access functions **CMyDialog::GetChoice()** and **CMyDialog::GetCheckStatus()** can still be used after the dialog box disappears from the screen. Keep in mind that the **CMyDialog** object is created by the constructor function as an automatic or stack object. The object continues to exist on the program's stack until the **CMainWindow::OnDialog()** function returns. The dialog box window is visible only between the time the **CModalDialog::DoModal()** function is called and when it returns. Destroying the dialog box window does not destroy the **CMyDialog** class object.

All messages pass to the dialog box message map when the dialog box is visible. Note that the message map for the dialog box includes entries for the two push button controls with ID values DLI_CANCEL and DLI_OK. These message map entries are required even though the message processing functions are declared inline in the DIALG2.HPP header file. The message processing logic for the radio buttons and check box control in DIALG2.CPP is similar to that demonstrated in the button control example BUTTON.CPP in Chapter 5, *Window Controls*. The main difference is that the button controls in DIALG2.CPP are part of a separate window (the dialog box window) and not attached directly to the main program window as in BUTTON.CPP.

Listing 10-12 shows the DIALG2.RC resource script file. Note that the DIALG2.DLG dialog box template is included. Listing 10-13 shows the DIALG2.DEF module definition file. The program's icon is shown in Figure 10-9.

Figure 10-9 DIALG2.ICO Icon Image

Listing 10-12 DIALG2.RC Resource Script File

```
// dialg2.rc  resource script file

#include <windows.h>
#include <afxres.h>
#include "dialg2.h"
#include "dialg2.dlg"              // the dialog box definition

AFX_IDI_STD_FRAME   ICON   dialg2.ico // the program's icon

MyMenu MENU                          // define the menu
{
    MENUITEM "&Pick",       IDM_DIALOG
    MENUITEM "&Quit",       IDM_QUIT
}
```

Listing 10-13 DIALG2.DEF Module Definition File

```
NAME            dialg2
DESCRIPTION     'dialg2 C++ program'
EXETYPE         WINDOWS
STUB            'WINSTUB.EXE'
CODE            PRELOAD MOVEABLE
DATA            PRELOAD MOVEABLE MULTIPLE
HEAPSIZE        1024
STACKSIZE       5120
```

PASSING DATA TO A DIALOG BOX

Sometimes you will want to pass data to the dialog box. For example, Figure 10-10 shows an example program named DIALG3 that displays a list of food items inside of a list box control. The most direct way to create a dialog box like the one shown in Figure 10-10 would be to code the list of items right into the dialog box logic. However, selecting an item from a list is such a common task that it would be much better to write the dialog box logic so that it would work with any list. That way the same dialog box could be reused for many programming projects. It also makes it easier when a new item such as "Grilled Tofu Burger" needs to be added to the selection list.

The key to making the dialog box reusable is to allow the program calling the dialog box to pass the list of items to be displayed in the dialog box before the dialog box becomes visible. That way, the program using the dialog box can pass any list of items without modifying the dialog box logic. This brings up a second problem. The list can contain any number of items. How do you pass a list of items to the dialog box if you do not know in advance how many items there will be?

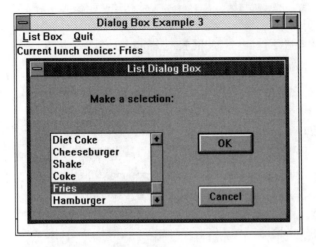

Figure 10-10 The DIALG3 Program

The CStringList Class

The MFC classes provide three generic list objects that can be used to encapsulate lists of items. The **CObList** class is for lists of other class objects, the **CPtrList** class is for lists of pointers to objects, and the **CStringList** class is for lists of strings. The **CStringList** is ideal for containing a list of strings (such as the names of the food items in Figure 10-10). The list classes are declared in a separate header file named AFXCOLL.H. The **CStringList** class is the only list object used in this book, although the other two list classes are very similar. AFXCOLL.H also declares three array classes named **CObArray**, **CPtrArray**, and **CStringArray** that are useful if the data elements need to be randomly accessed. The array classes are not used in this book.

Table 10-1 shows a list of the member functions of the **CStringList** class. The technical name for this type of list is a "doubly linked list" because you can move both forward and backward through the list using functions like **CStringList::GetNext()** and **CStringList::GetPrev()**. You will find that the member functions are described under the **CObList** description in the MFC documentation because the **CObList**, **CPtrList**, and **CStringList** classes have essentially identical member functions.

Creating and using a **CStringList** object is simple. For example, to create a list containing two strings:

```
CStringList AList ;       // construct a CStringList object
AList.AddHead ("First Item") ;    // add items to the list
AList.AddHead ("Second Item") ;   // etc.
```

Function	Purpose
AddHead()	Adds an element to the head of the list.
AddTail()	Adds an element to the tail (end) of the list.
CStringList()	Constructor function.
~CStringList()	Destructor function.
Find()	Finds the position of a string in the list.
FindIndex()	Finds the position in the list of an element based on an index.
GetAt()	Retrieves an element at a given position.
GetCount()	Determines the number of elements in the list.
GetHeadPosition()	Returns the position of the head element in the list.
GetNext()	Gets the next element in the list.
GetPrev()	Gets the previous element in the list.
GetTailPosition()	Returns the position of the tail (end) element in the list.
InsertBefore()	Inserts a new element before a given position.
InsertAfter()	Inserts a new element after a given position.
IsEmpty()	Determines if the list has zero elements.
RemoveAll()	Empties the list.
RemoveAt()	Deletes a specific element of the list.
RemoveHead()	Deletes the first element of the list.
RemoveTail()	Deletes the last element of the list.
SetAt()	Changes an element's contents at a given position.

Table 10-1 CStringList Member Functions

The **CStringList::AddHead()** function adds each new item to the top of the list, causing all of the existing list items to be "bumped" to new positions. You can also use **CStringList::AddTail()** to add new items to the end of the list, which leaves all of the existing list items in their current positions.

Once the list is complete you can find the position of an item in the list using the **CStringList::FindIndex()** function. Note that this position value may *not* equal the logical index of an item in the list (zero for the first item, one for the second, etc.), so you must determine the position of an item before retrieving its contents. The AFXCOLL.H header file defines a variable type of POSITION to hold the position of an item in a list. Once you have the position, you can retrieve the contents of the item using **CStringList::GetAt()**, which returns a pointer to the character string contained by the element of the list. The following code finds the position value of the second item in the list and then displays the string stored at that location to a device context named *dc*.

```
POSITION MyChoice = AList.FindIndex (1) ; // get second item.
dc.TextOut (10, 10, AList.GetAt (MyChoice),  // output text
    lstrlen (AList.GetAt (MyChoice)) ;       // to dev. context
```

Besides providing a convenient group of functions for manipulating lists, a pointer to a **CStringList** object can be passed to another function. This is a simple way to pass a list of any length from one function to another.

Using the CStringList Class in a Dialog Box

The DIALG3 example program uses the **CStringList** to pass a list of restaurant menu items (not a very good restaurant) to a dialog box function. The code for the dialog box is stored in separate program files with the name LISTDLG so that the dialog box can be reused in other programming projects. We will examine the dialog box definition and code before looking at the DIALG3 program, which uses the dialog box to display the junk food menu (as shown in Figure 10-10).

Listing 10-14 shows the "ListDialog" dialog box template. This dialog box was created with the MSDE and contains the list box control, two push buttons, and a static text control. The dialog box controls are given ID numbers in the LISTDLG.H header file (Listing 10-15).

Note that the list box control in Listing 10-14 contains the style values LBS_HASSTRINGS and WS_VSCROLL. The LBS_HASSTRINGS style tells Windows to store the character string data for each list item in the application's

Listing 10-14 LISTDLG.DLG Dialog Box Template

```
DLGINCLUDE RCDATA DISCARDABLE
BEGIN
    "LISTDLG.H\0"
END

LISTDIALOG DIALOG 9, 21, 174, 95
STYLE DS_MODALFRAME | WS_POPUP | WS_CAPTION | WS_SYSMENU
CAPTION "List Dialog Box"
BEGIN
    LISTBOX         DLI_LISTBOX, 14, 38, 76, 53,
        LBS_HASSTRINGS | WS_VSCROLL
    DEFPUSHBUTTON   "OK", DLI_OK, 114, 38, 38, 14
    PUSHBUTTON      "Cancel", DLI_CANCEL, 114, 73, 38, 14
    LTEXT           "Make a selection:", -1, 41, 11, 78, 20
END
```

local data segment. The WS_VSCROLL style places a vertical scroll bar on the right side of the list box if there are more items in the list than can be displayed at one time. The combination of LBS_HASSTRINGS | WS_VSCROLL is the most common style for a list box, and it is the default style created by the MSDE.

Listing 10-16 shows the LISTDLG.HPP header file for the dialog box program logic. Note the extension of the constructor function for the new **CListDialog** class. The constructor function now takes two arguments, a pointer to the parent window object and a pointer to a **CStringList** object. The pointer to the **CStringList** object is stored as the *pList* member of the class. This allows the **CListDialog** box object to have access to a list of character strings the moment the dialog box object is created. The constructor function also invokes the **CModalDialog** constructor and passes the name of the dialog box template "ListDialog" and the pointer to the parent window. This is identical to the last example program (DIALG2.HPP).

Note that selecting the "OK" button on the dialog box results in the **CListDialog::OnOkBtn()** function being executed (the message map that does this is shown later in LISTDLG.CPP). The value of the *nChoice* variable is

Listing 10-15 LISTDLG.H Resource ID Header File

```
// listdlg.h   header file for listdlg.cpp

#define DLI_LISTBOX     102     // dialog box control ID's
#define DLI_CANCEL      101
#define DLI_OK          100
```

Listing 10-16 LISTDLG.HPP Header File

```
// listdlg.hpp    header file for generic list choice dialog box

class CListDialog : public CModalDialog
{
public:                                 // constructor
    CListDialog (CWnd* pParent, CStringList* inList) :
        CModalDialog ("ListDialog", pParent) {pList = inList ; }
private:
    int nChoice ;                       // current selection no.
    CStringList* pList ;                // pointer to string list
    CListBox* pListBox ;                // pointer to list box control
    BOOL OnInitDialog () ;              // override default
    void OnListBoxSel () ;
    void OnOkBtn () {EndDialog (nChoice) ; }
    void OnCancelBtn () {EndDialog (-1) ; }

    DECLARE_MESSAGE_MAP ()              // message map for dialog
} ;
```

returned by the **CDialog::EndDialog()** function. *nChoice* gives the index number of the current selection in the list box starting with an index of zero for the first item. If the "Cancel" button is selected, the **CListDialog::OnCancelBtn()** function is called, returning a value of –1. If the system menu is used to exit the dialog box, the value IDCANCEL (2) is returned automatically by the built-in dialog box logic.

The program file for the dialog box (LISTDLG.CPP in Listing 10-17) introduces several new functions. The **CListDialog::OnInitDialog()** function is called before the dialog box is made visible. This is an ideal place to fill the list box with the character strings stored in the **CStringList** object. In order to use

Listing 10-17 LISTDLG.CPP

```
// listdlg.cpp     source code for generic list dialog box

#include <afxwin.h>      // class library header file
#include <afxcoll.h>     // library for list objects
#include "listdlg.h"
#include "listdlg.hpp"

BOOL CListDialog::OnInitDialog ()    // function called just before
{                                    // dialog box becomes visible
    nChoice = -1 ;                   // -1 means no choice made
    int nItems = pList->GetCount(); // get number of list items
    if (nItems > 0)
    {                                // get the list box control
        pListBox = (CListBox*) this->GetDlgItem (DLI_LISTBOX);
        pListBox->ResetContent();    // empty list box contents
                                     // move to top of string list
        POSITION pos = pList->GetHeadPosition();
        for (int i = 0; i < nItems; i++)
        {                                // copy list item to list box
            CString Str = pList->GetNext(pos);
            pListBox->AddString(Str);
        }
    }
    return TRUE ;
}


BEGIN_MESSAGE_MAP (CListDialog, CModalDialog)
    ON_COMMAND (DLI_CANCEL, OnCancelBtn)     // defined in .hpp
    ON_COMMAND (DLI_OK, OnOkBtn)             // defined in .hpp
    ON_LBN_SELCHANGE (DLI_LISTBOX, OnListBoxSel)// defined below
END_MESSAGE_MAP ()

void CListDialog::OnListBoxSel ()    // user made selection
{
    nChoice = pListBox->GetCurSel () ;  // save selection no.
}
```

the **CListBox** class member functions (introduced in Chapter 5, *Window Controls*), you must obtain a pointer to the list box object. The list box is not immediately available as a separate C++ object because the list box object is created by the Windows environment based on the dialog box definition in the program's resource data. Fortunately, the MFC classes provide the handy **CWnd::GetDlgItem()** function, which retrieves a pointer to a window control in a dialog box based on the ID number of the control. **CWnd::GetDlgItem()** is used in **CListDialog::OnInitDialog()** to fetch a pointer to the list box object:

```
pListBox = (CListBox*) this->GetDlgItem (DLI_LISTBOX);
```

The **CWnd::GetDlgItem()** function returns a pointer to a **CWnd** object. This must be cast to a pointer to a list box object (**CListBox ***) to correctly initialize the *pListBox* pointer. This is one of the few times the C++ language casting operator is needed to convert one type of pointer to another type when using the MFC classes. The (**CListBox ***) cast is necessary in this case because the **CWnd::GetDlgItem()** function can return a pointer to any type of window control in a dialog box including **CButton** objects, **CStatic** objects, and so on.

Once you have the pointer to the list box object, you are free to use all of the **CListBox** class member functions. For example, the list box is initially emptied by calling the **CListBox::ResetContent()** function. (**CListBox::ResetContent()** is not strictly necessary at this point because the list box will be created empty.)

```
pListBox->ResetContent();
```

Each character string from the **CStringList** object is then added to the list box using the **CListBox::AddString()** function. The **CStringList::GetNext()** function is used to fetch each character string in the list. Sequentially accessing each member of a list is sometimes called "iterating the list," which is the terminology that you will find if you review the MFC documentation for list objects.

The only other function of interest is the **CListDialog::OnListBoxSel()** function, which is called if the user selects an item in the list box. The current list box selection is fetched with the **CListBox::GetCurSel()** function and stored as the *nChoice* variable. *nChoice* is the value returned if the user selects the "OK" button in the dialog box.

Using the List/Dialog Box

To put the LISTDLG.CPP program to work, you must create a program that uses the generic dialog box to display a list of items. Listing 10-18 shows the DIALG3.RC resource script file that includes both LISTDLG.H and LISTDLG.DLG. This is how the dialog box template is added to the DIALG3 program's resources.

The DIALG3.H header file (Listing 10-19) contains the ID values for the DIALG3 menu items.

The DIALG3.HPP program header file (Listing 10-20) is very simple. There are only two message processing functions declared, **CMainWindow::OnDialog()** and **CMainWindow::OnQuit()**. These functions are called in response to the user selecting either of the two program menu items.

Listing 10-21 shows the DIALG3.CPP program file. The program includes a total of six different header files. The AFXCOLL.H header is needed for the **CStringList** class, and STRSTREA.H is needed to use output streams. Note that LISTDLG.H is not included because the ID values of the controls in the dialog box are only useful to the LISTDLG.CPP program and are not directly accessed by the DIALG3.CPP program, which uses the dialog box as a self-contained "black box." LISTDLG.H was created strictly for use within LISTDLG.CPP and LISTDLG.RC.

When the user selects the "List Box" menu item, the DIALG3.CPP function **CMainWindow::OnDialog()** is called. Before the dialog box is displayed, a **CStringList** object named **MenuList** is created and initialized with a list of food items. The list is then passed to the dialog box constructor function when the dialog box object is created:

```
CListDialog ListDialog (this, &MenuList) ;
```

Listing 10-18 DIALG3.RC Resource Script File

```
// dialg3.rc   resource script file

#include <windows.h>
#include <afxres.h>
#include "dialg3.h"
#include "listdlg.h"        // header file for generic list box
#include "listdlg.dlg"      // generic list dialog box definition

AFX_IDI_STD_FRAME   ICON    dialg3.ico  // the program's icon

MyMenu MENU                     // define the menu
{
    MENUITEM "&List Box",       IDM_DIALOG
    MENUITEM "&Quit",           IDM_QUIT
}
```

Listing 10-19 DIALG3.H Resource ID Header File

```
// dialg3.h  header file for resource ID numbers

#define IDM_DIALOG     1       // menu item ID numbers
#define IDM_QUIT       2
```

Listing 10-20 DIALG3.HPP Header File

```
// dialg3.hpp    header file for dialg3.cpp

class CMainWindow : public CFrameWnd    // derive a main window class
{
public:
    CMainWindow () ;                     // declare a constructor
private:
    void OnDialog () ;                   // runs dialog box
    void OnQuit () ;                     // stop application

    DECLARE_MESSAGE_MAP()                // prepare for message processing
} ;

class CTheApp : public CWinApp    // derive an application class
{
public:
    BOOL InitInstance () ;               // declare new InitInstance()
} ;
```

At this point the dialog box object has been created, but the dialog box is not visible on the screen. The **CModalDialog::DoModal()** function makes the dialog box appear. This is the point at which the **CListDialog::OnInitDialog()** function in the LISTDLG.CPP program is called (Listing 10-17), filling the list box with the **CStringList** data.

```
int nRetVal = ListDialog.DoModal () ;
```

When the user selects the "OK" or "Cancel" button on the dialog box, the **CDialog::EndDialog()** function is called within the LISTDLG logic, returning either –1 if "Cancel" was selected or the index of the selection if an item was chosen. –1 is also returned if the "OK" button was selected prior to the user selecting an item from the list.

The selection is displayed in the DIALG3 main program window client area after the dialog box vanishes (after the **CModalDialog::DoModal()** function

Listing 10-21 DIALG3.CPP

```
// dialg3.cpp            using a list dialog box

#include <afxwin.h>      // class library header file
#include <afxcoll.h>     // for list objects
#include <strstrea.h>    // for stream functions
#include "dialg3.h"      // header file for resource data
#include "dialg3.hpp"    // header file for this program
#include "listdlg.hpp"   // header file for listdlg.cpp
```

```
CTheApp theApp ;          // create one CTheApp object - runs program

BOOL CTheApp::InitInstance ()    // override default InitInstance()
{
    m_pMainWnd = new CMainWindow () ;        // create a main window
    m_pMainWnd->ShowWindow (m_nCmdShow) ;    // make it visible
    m_pMainWnd->UpdateWindow () ;            // paint center
    return TRUE ;
}


CMainWindow::CMainWindow ()     // constructor for window
{
    Create (NULL, "Dialog Box Example 3", WS_OVERLAPPEDWINDOW,
        rectDefault, NULL, "MyMenu") ;
}


BEGIN_MESSAGE_MAP (CMainWindow, CFrameWnd)
    ON_COMMAND (IDM_DIALOG, OnDialog)
    ON_COMMAND (IDM_QUIT, OnQuit)
END_MESSAGE_MAP ()

void CMainWindow::OnDialog ()     // menu item "List Box"
{                                 // run dialog box
    CStringList MenuList ;        // create a list of strings
    MenuList.AddHead ("Hamburger") ;
    MenuList.AddHead ("Fries") ;
    MenuList.AddHead ("Coke") ;
    MenuList.AddHead ("Shake") ;
    MenuList.AddHead ("Cheeseburger") ;
    MenuList.AddHead ("Diet Coke") ;
    MenuList.AddHead ("Onion rings") ;

    CListDialog ListDialog (this, &MenuList) ;
    int nRetVal = ListDialog.DoModal () ;        // run dialog box
                    // convert selection number to a POSITION
    POSITION Pos = MenuList.FindIndex (nRetVal) ;
                    // display the choice
    CClientDC dc (this) ;
    char cBuf [128] ;
    ostrstream myStream (cBuf, sizeof (cBuf)) ;
    myStream << "Current lunch choice: " <<
        MenuList.GetAt (Pos) << "                    " ;
    dc.TextOut (0, 0, cBuf, myStream.pcount ()) ;
}


void CMainWindow::OnQuit ()     // respond to menu item "Quit"
{
    this->DestroyWindow () ;     // destroy main window,
}                                // this stops application
```

returns). The character string is extracted from the **CStringList** using the **CStringList::GetAt()** function with the index of the selected item in the list. An index value of –1 results in the **CStringList::GetAt()** function returning a NULL value, which just displays a blank (null string) for the selection. The output string is formatted using the **ostrstream** stream operators.

Listing 10-22 shows the DIALG3.DEF module definition file for DIALG3. The program's icon is shown in Figure 10-11.

The DIALG3 and LISTDLG programs provide a general outline of how to pass data from a calling program to a dialog box. There is no limit to the amount of data that can be exchanged. One of the exercises at the end of this chapter improves the LISTDLG logic by allowing the calling program to pass a title string to the dialog box.

MODELESS AND SYSTEM MODAL DIALOG BOXES

The dialog boxes created in the previous three examples are technically known as "modal" dialog boxes. A modal dialog box takes control from the application while it is visible. The user can switch to other running applications, but cannot switch to another window in the same application that created the dialog box. Modal dialog boxes are ideal for prompting the user to make a selection, or enter a small amount of data, before continuing to use the rest of the program.

In a few rare cases you will want to prohibit the user from switching to another program or program window. "System modal" dialog boxes take over the

Listing 10-22 DIALG3.DEF Module Definition File

```
NAME            dialg3
DESCRIPTION     'dialg3 C++ program'
EXETYPE         WINDOWS
STUB            'WINSTUB.EXE'
CODE            PRELOAD MOVEABLE
DATA            PRELOAD MOVEABLE MULTIPLE
HEAPSIZE        1024
STACKSIZE       5120
```

Figure 10-11 DIALG3.ICO Icon Image

entire Windows environment and do not allow any other application to receive messages or gain the input focus until the system modal dialog box disappears. System modal dialog boxes should only be used for serious error messages, because taking over the system violates the basic principle that Windows programs should cooperate and allow other applications to run.

You can create a system modal dialog box by selecting the "System Modal" style for the dialog box window when you are using the dialog box editor. The MSDE has this selection in the editor's "dialog style" dialog box that appears when you click the dialog box you are editing within the MSDE edit area. Selecting "system modal" results in the DS_SYSMODAL style being added to the dialog box template, as shown in Listing 10-23. When Windows creates the dialog box, this style information is recognized by Windows, and only the system modal dialog box receives messages while it is visible.

The other extreme in dialog boxes is the "modeless" dialog box. It is basically a pop-up window that remains on the screen for extended periods of time. Modeless dialog boxes allow the user to switch to other applications, and to other windows in the application that created the dialog box. Modeless dialog boxes are frequently used for small "tool" windows, that can be moved on the screen. Modeless dialog boxes are defined in the dialog box template exactly the same as regular modal dialog boxes—there is no special style that defines a modeless dialog box. Instead, you derive the dialog box class directly from the **CDialog** class instead of **CModalDialog**. The **CDialog** class defaults to creating a modeless dialog box, which is the style most similar to a normal pop-up window.

It is up to you to decide between a pop-up window and a modeless dialog box, as both accomplish the same thing. Generally, modeless dialog boxes are easier to use if the dialog box is created entirely from child window controls that the dialog box editor can manipulate. Pop-up windows are better if you will be painting or otherwise modifying the client area of the pop-up window.

Creating a Modeless Dialog Box

The last example in this chapter creates a modeless dialog box that displays three cursor shapes. The user can select a cursor shape from this list, which

Listing 10-23 A System Modal Dialog Box Template

```
SYSMODALEXAMPLE DIALOG 6, 18, 160, 100
STYLE DS_SYSMODAL | DS_MODALFRAME | WS_POPUP | WS_VISIBLE
FONT 8, "Helv"
BEGIN
        // controls defined here
END
```

results in the new cursor being used within the program's window. Figure 10-12 shows the MDIALG program in action, with the modeless dialog box overlapping the program's main window. The modeless dialog box acts like a pop-up window. It can be moved on the screen, always appears to be "above" the parent's main program window, and can be covered up by other program's windows. The modeless dialog box disappears when its parent window is minimized or destroyed, and reappears when the parent is restored.

Defining the Modeless Dialog Box

Before you can create the modeless dialog box template, you will need to create three icon images that will be used to show graphical images of the cursor shapes within the dialog box. Use the Image Editor application to create the icons. The example icons provided with the source code disks use the default 32 by 32 pixel, 16-color format, and are shown in Figure 10-13 a–c. The program's icon is shown in Figure 10-13d. Although you can display icons as pictures of cursors within a dialog box, you cannot use "cursor" data as a means of displaying static images. Icons are used to display the cursor images in MDIALG. The arrow and cross cursors are stock cursors, always available within Windows. The hand cursor image must be created twice, once as an icon file, and once as a cursor file, with both files added to the program's resources. Review Chapter 6, *Taming the Mouse*, if you are not familiar with defining a new cursor shape. The hand cursor should look like the hand icon in Figure 10-13c.

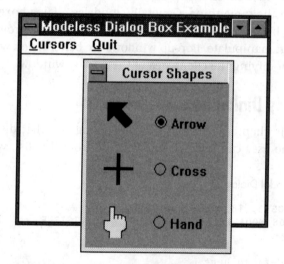

Figure 10-12 The MDIALG Program

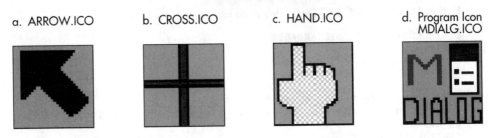

a. ARROW.ICO   b. CROSS.ICO   c. HAND.ICO   d. Program Icon
                                                     MDIALG.ICO

Figure 10-13 Icon Images for MDIALG

The ID numbers for the dialog box controls are stored in a separate file, MDIALG.H, shown in Listing 10-24. Note that the user message WM_DLG-CLOSE is defined as equal to WM_USER + 1. This message will be used to communicate between the dialog box and the main program window.

The modeless dialog box is defined using the MSDE. Listing 10-25 shows the MDIALG.DLG dialog template. As mentioned previously, the MDIALG.DLG modeless dialog box definition is identical to what the definition would be if a normal modal dialog box were being defined. No special style values are added for a modeless dialog box. (The difference between modal and modeless dialog boxes is specified when the dialog box is created in the C++ program file, which will be explained in a moment.) The dialog box definition includes six controls, the three icons and three radio buttons. The dialog box window itself has both a caption and system menu box included. These are important for modeless dialog boxes, because the user will need to move the dialog box on the screen.

The dialog box template is included in the program's resource script file, along with the header files, icon, and cursor data. Listing 10-26 shows the MDIALG.RC file, including the definition of the program's menu. Note that the names given to the icons match the names in the MDIALG.DLG file for the

Listing 10-24 MDIALG.H Header File

```
// mdialg.h  header file for resource ID numbers

#define DLI_ARROW              100      // dialog box ID numbers
#define DLI_HAND               101
#define DLI_CROSS              102

#define IDM_CREATE             1        // main menu ID values
#define IDM_DESTROY            2
#define IDM_QUIT               10

#define WM_DLGCLOSE                     WM_USER + 1 // user message
```

Listing 10-25 MDIALG.DLG Dialog Template File

```
DLGINCLUDE RCDATA DISCARDABLE
BEGIN
    "MDIALG.H\0"
END

ModeLessExample DIALOG 6, 18, 75, 84
STYLE DS_MODALFRAME | WS_POPUP | WS_VISIBLE | WS_CAPTION |
WS_SYSMENU
CAPTION "Cursor Shapes"
FONT 10, "System"
BEGIN
    ICON        "ArrowIcon", -1, 9, 9, 16, 16
    ICON        "CrossIcon", -1, 9, 36, 16, 16
    ICON        "HandIcon", -1, 9, 63, 16, 16
    CONTROL     "Arrow", DLI_ARROW, "Button", BS_AUTORADIOBUTTON,
        36, 15, 39, 10
    CONTROL     "Cross", DLI_CROSS, "Button", BS_AUTORADIOBUTTON,
        36, 39, 39, 10
    CONTROL     "Hand", DLI_HAND, "Button", BS_AUTORADIOBUTTON,
        36, 66, 39, 10
END
```

Listing 10-26 MDIALG.RC Resource Script File

```
// mdialg.rc  resource script file

#include <windows.h>
#include <afxres.h>
#include "mdialg.h"
#include "mdialg.dlg"              // the dialog box definition

AFX_IDI_STD_FRAME   ICON    mdialg.ico  // the program's icon

ArrowIcon   ICON    arrow.ico
CrossIcon   ICON    cross.ico
HandIcon    ICON    hand.ico
HandCursor  CURSOR  hand.cur

MyMenu MENU
{
    POPUP   "&Cursors"
    {
        MENUITEM "&Create Modeless Dlg Box",    IDM_CREATE
        MENUITEM "&Destroy Modeless Dlg Box",   IDM_DESTROY
    }
    MENUITEM "&Quit",       IDM_QUIT
}
```

three static icon controls. The dialog box display logic within Windows will find the icon data in the program's resources using these names when it is time to display the dialog box.

Calling the Modeless Dialog Box

Listing 10-27 shows the MDIALG.HPP header file. The **CModeLess** class is derived from the **CDialog** class (not from the **CModalDialog** class used in the previous examples), which results in creating a modeless dialog class. The **CModeLess** class declares a message map because the modeless dialog will be a separate window object and will receive messages directly from the Windows environment. For example, the **CModeLess** class declares a **CWnd::OnSetCursor()** function so that

Listing 10-27 MDIALG.HPP Header File

```
// mdialg.hpp    header file for mdialg.cpp

class CModeLess : public CDialog         // derive dialog class
{
public:
    CModeLess (HANDLE *phCursor) ;        // constructor
private:
    HANDLE *pCursor ;                // pointer to parent cursor handle
    void OnArrow () ;                // cursor button selections
    void OnCross () ;
    void OnHand () ;
    void OnClose () ;                // process WM_CLOSE
    BOOL OnSetCursor (CWnd *pWnd, UINT nHitTest, UINT nMessage) ;

    DECLARE_MESSAGE_MAP ()           // message map for dialog
} ;

class CMainWindow : public CFrameWnd    // derive a main window class
{
public:
    CMainWindow () ;                 // declare a constructor
private:
    CModeLess* pModeLess ;           // pointer to dialog box
    HANDLE hCursor ;                 // cursor handle
    void OnCreate () ;               // runs dialog box
    void OnDestroy () ;              // removes dialog box
    void OnQuit () ;                 // stop application
    LONG OnDlgClose (UINT, LONG) ;   // message from dialog box
    BOOL OnSetCursor (CWnd *pWnd, UINT nHitTest, UINT nMessage) ;

    DECLARE_MESSAGE_MAP()            // prepare for message processing
} ;

class CTheApp : public CWinApp      // derive an application class
{
public:
    BOOL InitInstance () ;                  // declare new InitInstance()
} ;
```

the cursor shape can be changed while the cursor is above the modeless dialog box. The **CMainWindow** class also declares a **CWnd::OnSetCursor()** function to change the cursor shape above the MDIALG main program window. Both **CWnd::OnSetCursor()** functions are necessary because the dialog box window and main program window are independent entities and will receive WM_SETCURSOR messages from Windows when the cursor is above their respective client areas.

The **CModeLess** class includes a private data item named *pCursor*. This variable is used to store a pointer to the handle of the currently selected cursor in the main program window. This variable is the key to the dialog box being able to display the same cursor shape that is displayed over the main program window. You can get a clue to how the dialog box finds out about the parent window's cursor handle by looking at the **CModeLess** constructor function declaration. A pointer to the parent window's cursor is passed to the **CModeLess** object when the modeless dialog box is created.

Note in MDIALG.HPP (Listing 10-27) that the **CMainWindow** class includes two private data members. *pModeLess* is a pointer to the modeless dialog box object. *hCursor* contains the handle to the currently selected cursor shape that is displayed above the main program window. These variables are both initialized by code in the **CMainWindow** constructor function when the program first starts.

```
pModeLess = NULL ;
hCursor = AfxGetApp()->LoadStandardCursor (IDC_ARROW) ;
```

The *pModeLess* variable is initially set to NULL because the modeless dialog box is not created until the user selects the "Cursors/Create Modeless Dlg Box" menu item. The modeless dialog box is then created by creating a new **CModeLess** object. A pointer to the *hCursor* data is passed as a parameter to the **CModeLess** constructor function. This is how the **CModeLess** class gets around the fact that *hCursor* is a private data member of the **CMainWindow** class, and not directly accessible (out of scope) for member functions of the **CModeLess** class.

```
if (pModeLess == NULL)        // only create one dialog box
    pModeLess = new CModeLess (&hCursor) ;
```

A critical difference between creating a modeless dialog box and a regular modal dialog box is the way in which the constructor function is called. Modeless dialog boxes are expected to remain on the screen for extended periods of time. You cannot make a modeless dialog box object an automatic variable stored on the program's stack. If you did, the dialog box data would be erased immediately after the function creating the dialog box returns. Instead, the modeless dialog box object is stored in the program's data heap by using the C++ language *new* operator. The data defining the **CModeLess** object will remain safely in the program's heap while the program operates. The only special requirement is that the object must eventually be deleted from memory when it is no longer needed. The C++ *delete* operator takes care of this important chore.

```
delete pModeLess ;        // remove object from memory
```

The *new* and *delete* operators are discussed in more detail in Chapter 12, *Managing Memory*, along with specialized memory management functions that Windows provides. Listing 10-28 shows the complete MDIALG.CPP file.

The dialog box is physically created on the screen by calling the **CDialog::Create()** function within the **CModeLess** constructor function. **CDialog::Create()** can be passed either one or two parameters. The first parameter is always a character string containing the name of the dialog box template in the program's resource data. In MDIALOG, the dialog box template has the name "ModeLessExample."

```
this->Create ("ModeLessExample") ;  // parent = main window
```

With only one parameter, **CDialog::Create()** defaults to assuming that the parent window is the main program window. This is almost always the case. Once in a while you may want to have a modeless dialog box that has a child window as a parent. In this case, you can pass a pointer to the parent window as the second parameter passed to **CDialog::Create()**. For example, if *pChildWnd* is a pointer to a **CWnd** object, then a dialog box can be created with *pChildWnd* as the parent window:

```
this->Create ("ModeLessExample", pChildWnd) ;
```

Once the modeless dialog box is created, it behaves much like a pop-up window. Messages sent to the modeless dialog box are routed by a separate message map to the message processing functions. Most of the functions in the MDIALG.CPP program simply process WM_COMMAND messages from the controls in the dialog box. If the user selects one of the radio button controls, the control is checked (center darkened) with the handy **CWnd::CheckRadioButton()** function. This function checks one member of a group of radio buttons, and unchecks all the others. The only restriction is that the radio buttons must all be numbered in sequence. For example, to check the DLI_ARROW radio button while unchecking other radio controls in the sequence between DLI_ARROW and DLI_HAND:

```
this->CheckRadioButton (DLI_ARROW, DLI_HAND, DLI_ARROW) ;
```

The first two parameters passed to **CWnd::CheckRadioButton()** pass the range of radio buttons in the group. The third parameter passes the number of

Listing 10-28 MDIALG.CPP

```cpp
// mdialg.cpp                      modeless dialog box example

#include <afxwin.h>         // class library header file
#include "mdialg.h"         // header file for resource data
#include "mdialg.hpp"       // header file for this program

CTheApp theApp ;           // create one CTheApp object - runs program

BOOL CTheApp::InitInstance ()   // override default InitInstance()
{
    m_pMainWnd = new CMainWindow () ;         // create a main window
    m_pMainWnd->ShowWindow (m_nCmdShow) ;     // make it visible
    m_pMainWnd->UpdateWindow () ;             // paint center
    return TRUE ;
}


CMainWindow::CMainWindow ()        // constructor for window
{
    Create (NULL, "Modeless Dialog Box Example",
        WS_OVERLAPPEDWINDOW, rectDefault, NULL, "MyMenu") ;
    pModeLess = NULL ;             // initialize
    hCursor = AfxGetApp()->LoadStandardCursor (IDC_ARROW) ;
}


BEGIN_MESSAGE_MAP (CMainWindow, CFrameWnd)
    ON_COMMAND (IDM_CREATE, OnCreate)          // menu item messages
    ON_COMMAND (IDM_DESTROY, OnDestroy)
    ON_COMMAND (IDM_QUIT, OnQuit)
    ON_MESSAGE (WM_DLGCLOSE, OnDlgClose)
    ON_WM_SETCURSOR ()
END_MESSAGE_MAP ()

void CMainWindow::OnCreate ()    // menu item "Create Modeless..."
{                                // runs dialog box
    if (pModeLess == NULL)       // only create one dialog box
        pModeLess = new CModeLess (&hCursor) ;
}


void CMainWindow::OnDestroy ()   // menu item "Destroy Modeless..."
{                                // removes dialog box
    if (pModeLess)
    {
        delete pModeLess ;       // delete pModeLess object
        pModeLess = NULL ;       // set pointer to NULL
    }
}


void CMainWindow::OnQuit ()      // respond to menu item "Quit"
{
    this->DestroyWindow () ;     // destroy main window,
}                                // this stops application
```

```
LONG CMainWindow::OnDlgClose (UINT un, LONG ln)
{                                   // user message from dialog box
    pModeLess = NULL ;              // so pModeLess set to NULL
    return NULL ;
}


BOOL CMainWindow::OnSetCursor (CWnd *pWnd, UINT nHitTest,
    UINT nMessage)
{
    ::SetCursor (hCursor) ;         // change the cursor shape
    return TRUE ;
}


//-------------------- Dialog box section ----------------------//

CModeLess::CModeLess (HANDLE *phCursor) // constructor
{
    this->Create ("ModeLessExample") ;  // parent = main window
    pCursor = phCursor ;
    this->CheckRadioButton (DLI_ARROW, DLI_HAND, DLI_ARROW) ;
    *pCursor = AfxGetApp()->LoadStandardCursor (IDC_ARROW) ;
}


BEGIN_MESSAGE_MAP (CModeLess, CDialog)
    ON_WM_CLOSE ()                      // WM_CLOSE message
    ON_WM_SETCURSOR ()                  // WM_SETCURSOR
    ON_COMMAND (DLI_ARROW, OnArrow)     // menu items
    ON_COMMAND (DLI_CROSS, OnCross)
    ON_COMMAND (DLI_HAND, OnHand)
END_MESSAGE_MAP ()

void CModeLess::OnClose ()          // process WM_CLOSE message
{                                   // tell parent dialog is closing
    (this->GetParent ())->SendMessage (WM_DLGCLOSE, O, OL) ;
    delete this ;                   // destroys window and object
}

void CModeLess::OnArrow ()          // user selected arrow cursor
{
    this->CheckRadioButton (DLI_ARROW, DLI_HAND, DLI_ARROW) ;
    *pCursor = AfxGetApp()->LoadStandardCursor (IDC_ARROW) ;
}

void CModeLess::OnCross ()          // user selected cross cursor
{
    this->CheckRadioButton (DLI_ARROW, DLI_HAND, DLI_CROSS) ;
    *pCursor = AfxGetApp()->LoadStandardCursor (IDC_CROSS) ;
}
```

```
void CModeLess::OnHand ()          // user selected hand cursor
{
    this->CheckRadioButton (DLI_ARROW, DLI_HAND, DLI_HAND) ;
    *pCursor = AfxGetApp()->LoadCursor ("HandCursor") ;
}


BOOL CModeLess::OnSetCursor (CWnd *pWnd, UINT nHitTest,
    UINT nMessage)
{
    ::SetCursor (*pCursor) ;
    return TRUE ;
}
```

the one radio button that should be checked. After the button is checked, the cursor handle used by both the main program window and modeless dialog box window is changed to the appropriate cursor shape.

```
*pCursor = AfxGetApp()->LoadStandardCursor (IDC_ARROW) ;
```

Both the main program window and modeless dialog box classes process WM_SETCURSOR messages to change the cursor shape to the currently loaded cursor. The global function **::SetCursor()** physically changes the cursor shape.

One last complication in the MDIALG.CPP program arises from the fact that the modeless dialog box has a system menu button. Dialog box system menus only contain two items, "Move" and "Close." Selecting the "Close" menu item results in the dialog box being sent a WM_CLOSE message and being destroyed. The trouble with this is that the main program window will not immediately be aware of the dialog box being destroyed.

To get around this problem, the modeless dialog box logic in MDIALG.CPP processes the WM_CLOSE message in the **CWnd::OnClose()** function. When the WM_CLOSE message is received, the dialog box sends its parent window a user message with the ID value WM_DLGCLOSE (defined as WM_USER + 1 in MDIALG.H, Listing 10-24). The WM_DLGCLOSE user message is mapped to the **CMainWindow::OnDlgClose()** function by the **CMainWindow** message map. **CMainWindow::OnDlgClose()** simply sets the *pModeLess* value to NULL, so that the **CMainWindow** program logic tracks that the dialog box is now deleted.

One last detail worth noting is how the modeless dialog box is deleted. You can use the **CWnd::DestroyWindow()** function to simply remove the dialog box from the screen. This does not delete the **CDialog** object's data in the local heap. To free the memory tied up with the **CDialog** object, you must use the C++ *delete* operator. For example, in MDIALG.CPP the **CMainWindow::OnDestroy()** function is called when the user selects the "Cursors/Destroy Modeless

Dlg Box" menu item. The dialog box is removed from memory (and from the screen) by the line:

```
delete pModeLess ;
```

Within a member function of the modeless dialog box class, you can delete the dialog box using the *this* pointer. This shortcut is used in MDIALG.CPP when the user selects the "Close" system menu item, which is mapped to the **CModeLess::OnClose()** function.

```
delete this ;
```

Every call to the C++ *new* operator must have a matching call to *delete* in order to free the object from memory when it is no longer needed. In MDIALG.CPP, there are two ways the dialog box can be deleted (the dialog box system menu, or one of the main program window's menu items), so there are two calls to *delete*.

Listing 10-29 shows the only remaining program file for the MDIALG program, the MDIALG.DEF module definition file.

SUMMARY

Dialog boxes are defined in a dialog box template file, usually saved with the file extension ".DLG." These files are created using a dialog box editor (MSDE), which speeds the process of creating and positioning child window controls. The dialog box template data is compiled by the resource compiler, and added to the finished Windows program as resource data. Windows creates the dialog box from the resource data, and displays it on the screen. Although the MSDE automates the process of designing the dialog box, the message processing logic for each dialog box must be written by the programmer.

Simple dialog boxes can be created directly from the **CModalDialog** class if the dialog box has only one or two controls. The controls must be buttons with the resource ID numbers of IDOK and/or IDCANCEL. Such simple dialog boxes

Listing 10-29 MDIALG.DEF Module Definition File

```
NAME            mdialg
DESCRIPTION     'mdialg C++ program'
EXETYPE         WINDOWS
STUB            'WINSTUB.EXE'
CODE            PRELOAD MOVEABLE
DATA            PRELOAD MOVEABLE MULTIPLE
HEAPSIZE        1024
STACKSIZE       5120
```

are of little value because the **CWnd::MessageBox()** function accomplishes roughly the same thing with much less effort. You will normally need to derive a new class from the **CModalDialg** class to create a useful dialog box. The dialog box will have its own message map and message processing functions. The program logic for the dialog box should call the **CDialog::EndDialog()** function to destroy the dialog box, returning control to the parent window.

There are actually three kinds of dialog boxes. The normal type of dialog box created by deriving a class from the **CModalDialog** class is called a "modal" dialog box. While a modal dialog box is visible, the user cannot switch the input focus to any other portion of the program, although another program can be selected. If the DS_SYSMODAL style is added to the dialog box definition, the dialog box becomes "system modal." System modal dialog boxes take over the entire system, and do not allow any other window or application to receive messages or gain the input focus. System modal dialog boxes should be used only for critical error messages.

The third type of dialog box is the "modeless" dialog box. Modeless dialog boxes are similar to pop-up windows, in that they remain on the screen for extended periods of time, and can gain and lose the input focus based on the user's actions. Modeless dialog boxes are frequently used to display small tool bars, and other utility windows. Modeless dialog boxes are created by deriving a class from the **CDialog** class. Modeless dialog boxes also have their own message map and process messages independently from the parent window.

QUESTIONS

1. To allow a dialog box to be moved on the screen, include a _____ in the dialog box style.
2. Only modeless dialog boxes can be moved on the screen. (True/False)
3. System modal dialog boxes are:
    a. Derived from the **CModalDialog** class
    b. Have the DS_SYSMODAL style added to the dialog box definition
    c. Take over the entire screen until destroyed
    d. All of the above
4. The dialog box template is converted into instructions Windows can read by the _____ _____.
5. When a child window control in a dialog box is activated, Windows sends a _____ message to the dialog box.

6. Modeless dialog box objects are created by deriving a new class from the _____ MFC class.

7. The _____ function is called before a dialog box is first made visible and is an ideal place to initialize data the dialog box will use.

8. Modeless dialog boxes should be created using the C++ *new* operator so that the object remains in memory until deleted. (True/False)

9. Objects created with the C++ *new* operator must be freed from memory with the _____ operator.

EXERCISES

1. Improve the appearance of the dialog box in the DIALG2.CPP program by painting a white rectangle around the group box in the program's dialog box as shown in Figure 10-14. Use the **CDC::Rectangle()** function to draw the white rectangle. Is the rectangle output using dialog base units or client coordinates?

2. Improve the DIALG3 example by making the caption of the dialog box a parameter that can be specified before the dialog box is displayed. Make the title "Select some junk food."

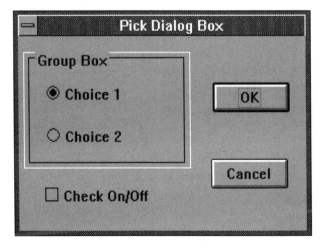

Figure 10-14 White Rectangle in a Dialog Box

ANSWERS TO QUESTIONS

1. caption or WS_CAPTION.
2. False. All types of dialog boxes can be moved if they are created with a caption bar.
3. d.
4. resource compiler.
5. WM_COMMAND.
6. **CDialog.**
7. **CDialog::OnInitDialog().**
8. True.
9. delete.

SOLUTIONS TO EXERCISES

1. The only change necessary is to add the WM_PAINT logic to the dialog box logic. Listing 10-30 shows the changes to the DIALG2.CPP program. Note that the stock NULL_BRUSH is used for the rectangle so that the interior of the rectangle is transparent. This makes it easy to draw the rectangle's outline using the **CDC::Rectangle()** function.

Listing 10-30 Adding WM_PAINT Logic to DIALG2.CPP

```
BEGIN_MESSAGE_MAP (CMyDialog, CModalDialog)
    ON_COMMAND (DLI_RADIO1, OnChoiceOne)
    ON_COMMAND (DLI_RADIO2, OnChoiceTwo)
    ON_COMMAND (DLI_CHECKBOX, OnCheck)
    ON_COMMAND (DLI_CANCEL, OnCancelBtn)
    ON_COMMAND (DLI_OK, OnOkBtn)
    ON_WM_PAINT ()
END_MESSAGE_MAP ()

void CMyDialog::OnPaint ()  // paint in dlg box
{
    CPaintDC dc (this) ;
    dc.SelectStockObject (NULL_BRUSH) ;
    dc.SelectStockObject (WHITE_PEN) ;
    dc.Rectangle (5, 15, 170, 125) ;
}
```

The rectangle is output using normal client coordinates (pixels from the upper left corner). Dialog box units are only used by the dialog box editor, and in the dialog box template. Once the dialog box window is created, it is a window like any other window. The complete solution is under the file name C10EXER1 on the source code disks.

2. Passing a string to the dialog box can be done by simply adding another parameter to the constructor function for the dialog box. The title can be passed as a **CString** object. Listing 10-31 shows the modified declaration of the **CListDialog** class, which now passes both the **CStringList** and **CString** objects to the dialog box for the list box items and dialog box caption, respectively.

The **CDialog::OnInitDialog()** function is a good place to change the dialog box window's caption to the string passed to the dialog box. Listing 10-32 shows the changes to the initialization function for the dialog box. The remaining logic that fills the list box with the items passed in the **CStringList** object is not affected.

Finally, the dialog box must be created by passing the title as a **CString** object. Listing 10-33 shows the creation of the dialog box passing the title string "Select some junk food."

The complete solution is given under the file name C10EXER2 on the source code disks.

Listing 10-31 Modified CListDialog Class Definition

```
class CListDialog : public CModalDialog
{
public:                                    // constructor
    CListDialog (CWnd* pParent, CStringList* inList, CString* title) :
        CModalDialog ("ListDialog", pParent)
    {
        pList = inList ;
        pTitle = title ;
    }
private:
    int nChoice ;                          // current selection no.
    CStringList* pList ;                   // pointer to string list
    CListBox* pListBox ;                   // pointer to list box control
    CString* pTitle ;
    BOOL OnInitDialog () ;                 // override default
    void OnListBoxSel () ;
    void OnOkBtn () {EndDialog (nChoice) ; }
    void OnCancelBtn () {EndDialog (-1) ; }

    DECLARE_MESSAGE_MAP ()                 // message map for dialog
} ;
```

Listing 10-32 Changing the Dialog Box Caption

```
BOOL CListDialog::OnInitDialog ()    // function called just before
{                                    // dialog box becomes visible
    nChoice = -1 ;                   // -1 means no choice made
    this->SetWindowText (*pTitle) ; // ** change window title **
    int nItems = pList->GetCount(); // get number of list items
    if (nItems > 0)
    {                                    // get the list box control
        pListBox = (CListBox*) GetDlgItem(DLI_LISTBOX);
        pListBox->ResetContent();    // empty list box contents
                                     // move to top of string list
        POSITION pos = pList->GetHeadPosition();
        for (int i = 0; i < nItems; i++)
        {                                // copy list item to list box
            CString Str = pList->GetNext(pos);
            pListBox->AddString(Str);
        }
    }
    return TRUE ;
}
```

Listing 10-33 Creating the Dialog Box

```
void CMainWindow::OnDialog ()    // respond to menu item "Pick"
{                                // run dialog box
    CStringList MenuList ;       // create a list of strings
    MenuList.AddHead ("Hamburger") ;
    MenuList.AddHead ("Fries") ;
    MenuList.AddHead ("Coke") ;
    MenuList.AddHead ("Shake") ;
    MenuList.AddHead ("Cheeseburger") ;
    MenuList.AddHead ("Diet Coke") ;
    MenuList.AddHead ("Onion rings") ;

    CString Title ("Select some junk food") ;

    CListDialog ListDialog (this, &MenuList, &Title) ;
    int nRetVal = ListDialog.DoModal () ;    // run dialog box
[other program lines]
```

## Chapter 11

Other Resources

This is the last of the chapters on resources. So far the focus has been on the most common types of resources: menus, dialog boxes, and icons. These common resource types are usually created interactively, using editing tools like the Image Editor and the Microsoft Dialog Editor. Resource files can contain more than these predefined types of resources. Essentially, any type of static data (data that does not change as the program runs) can be stored as part of the program's resources.

There are several advantages to storing static data in resources, compared with storing the data as part of the program's code. Resource data makes full use of the memory optimization functions in Windows to load and unload the data from memory to make room for other objects. Resources are also convenient for the programmer because they group all of the static data in a single location, which makes

updating the program more straightforward. You can even have different versions of the resource data for different languages (French, Spanish, etc.), without any changes to the C++ language portion of the program.

This chapter's examples cover several uses for resource data, including grouping all of the program's text in a string table, adding a raw text file to the resource script file, and storing numeric data as resources. This chapter introduces managing objects in memory and managing resource data, which leads into Chapter 12's broader discussion of allocating and manipulating memory blocks for all types of data.

Concepts covered: String tables, conditional compilation, user-defined resources, resources in separate files, "back-words" storage format of numbers in memory, overloading operators, formatting hexadecimal output, creating new classes.

Key words covered: STRINGTABLE, RCDATA, #ifdef, #else, #endif, DT_EX-PANDTABS, DT_LEFT , DT_WORDBREAK.

Functions covered: CDC::DrawText(), CString::LoadString(), ::FindResource(), ::LoadResource(), ::LockResource(), ::GlobalUnlock()::, AfxGetResource-Handle(), ios::flags(), ios::width().

Classes covered: StringResource, RcdataResource (developed in this chapter).

STRING TABLES

Up to this point, the example programs have put character strings directly into the C++ program source code with statements like:

```
static char   szMessage [ ] =
    "This string will become static data." ;
```

The C++ language "static" key word is included only for clarity, because the character string will become static data without explicitly declaring *szMessage[]* as a static variable. In a Windows program, static variables are stored in the program's local heap. (Refer to Chapter 1, *How Windows Works*, if you need to review the way Windows uses the local heap.) Windows maintains the local heap in memory as long as the program is running, so this character string will use up memory space whether or not it is about to be displayed. Programs with extensive text and other static data hog a lot of memory if all of the data is stored as static variables.

Another problem with putting character strings in the C++ program source code is that it is difficult to maintain. Imagine that your company decides to

market the program in France and Canada and wants all of the text that the user will see translated into French. The text strings will be scattered throughout the program, intermixed with program comments that you probably do not want translated. Worse, if you have the static text strings translated, you will end up with a different C++ program for English than for French. Every time you want to make a change in the program, you need to make the change in two different files, and compile twice. Wait until the boss asks for a German version....

Defining String Tables

Fortunately, Windows includes an easy-to-use method of storing text strings with the resource data, separate from the program's code. String tables are just what they sound like, tables or lists of strings. The syntax for defining a string table in the resource script file is shown in Listing 11-1. Each string table entry is on a separate line and has a unique ID number. All of the string table entries fall between the curly brackets that follow the STRINGTABLE statement. You can use the BEGIN and END key words in place of the curly brackets that enclose the string table entries if you prefer. The examples in this book use curly brackets.

There can be only one string table in a resource script file, so it is not given a title other than the "STRINGTABLE" key word. As with all resources, the string table can use either PRELOAD or LOADONCALL as the load options, and MOVEABLE, DISCARDABLE, or FIXED as memory options. The defaults are LOADONCALL, MOVEABLE, and DISCARDABLE, which are almost always what you will want with a string table, so you can just leave the load and memory options blank. Each line between the curly brackets defines a string. The string's ID number is defined first, followed by a comma and the text string in double quotes.

Conditional Compilation of Resources

Although you can put only one string table in a program's resources, you can include more than one string table definition in the program's resource script statement by taking advantage of conditional compilation. This is done using

Listing 11-1 String Table Syntax

```
STRINGTABLE [load option] [memory option]
{
    idNumber1, "Text string 1 here"
    idNumber2, "Text string 2 here"
    ...
}
```

the resource compiler key words #ifdef, #else, and #endif. The idea is that if a constant is defined, one portion of the resource script file is compiled. If the constant is not defined, the alternative portion of the file is compiled. This is ideal for cases where you want to have more than one language in the same resource script file for menus, string tables, dialog boxes, and so on.

Listing 11-2 shows a short resource file including a string table, with three character strings defined. In this case, there are two alternative string tables, one for a French version of the program, and a second for an English version. Remember that the resource compiler can compile only one string table in a resource script file. Only one of these two string tables will be used, as they are surrounded in the #ifdef, #else, and #endif conditional statements. With the second line defining the constant FRENCH, the French language portion of the resource script file is compiled. If the constant FRENCH is not defined, the lower (English) string table will be added to the program's resources.

Note in Listing 11-2 that the same ID numbers are used for both the English and French versions, so no change to the program's code will be needed, regardless of which language is being used. The ID numbers are defined in the program's header file, as shown in Listing 11-3.

You can also use conditional compilation in C++ programs for similar purposes. A common use is to surround debugging portions of the program with #ifdef DEBUG and #endif statements. Unless the constant DEBUG is defined, the debug code gets left out of the program.

Listing 11-2 Example String Tables

```
// example.rc    resource script file using two languages

#define  FRENCH        // define the constant FRENCH
#include "example.h"   // include the header file

#ifdef FRENCH          // compile section if FRENCH is defined
STRINGTABLE
{
    S_HELP ,           "Utiliser F1 pour l'assistance."
    S_PROGRAMCAPTION,  "Programme Fou"
    S_SERIOUSTEXT,     "Trouvais une probleme serieux"
}
#else                  // otherwise compile this section
STRINGTABLE
{
    S_HELP ,           "Hit the F1 key for help"
    S_PROGRAMCAPTION,  "Silly Program"
    S_SERIOUSTEXT,     "Encountered a serious error"
}
#endif
```

Listing 11-3 Header File Containing String Table ID Numbers

```
/* example.h  header file */

#define S_HELP              1
#define S_PROGRAMCAPTION    2
#define S_SERIOUSTEXT       3
```

Using the String Data

Within the body of the program, you will use the **CString::LoadString()** function to load a string table into memory. **CString::LoadString()** is passed the ID
number of the string so that the string can be located in the program's resource
data. The string is loaded from the program's resource data and copied into a
CString object. For example, to load the string table entry S_GENERAL into a
CString object named *string*:

```
CString string ;
string.LoadString (S_GENERAL) ;
```

   CString::LoadString() returns TRUE if the string was loaded, or FALSE if the
string was not found. Note that if this declaration of the **CString** object occurs
within the body of a function, the string is copied to an automatic variable
string that is stored on the program's stack. Automatic variables are ideal for
temporarily storing strings because the stack gets reused (deleting the string) as
soon as execution passes to another function in the program. Loading all of the
strings from the string table into a group of static objects would be a complete
waste because the data would still end up occupying space in the local heap
(static data is stored in an application's local heap).

A String Table Example

The first example program in this chapter is called STRTAB. STRTAB demonstrates using string tables for three purposes: setting the program's title, displaying text in the program's client area, and specifying text for a message box.
Figure 11-1 shows STRTAB in action, with the message box and client area
strings visible.

   Every word of text visible in Figure 11-1, including the menu and the
program's caption, is defined in the STRTAB.RC resource script file, shown in
Listing 11-4. The first string in the string table demonstrates how to embed
unprintable characters into the string in a string table. The resource compiler
recognizes three digits preceded by a "\" character as an octal constant. Unlike
hexadecimal numbers (such as 0x4A26), octal constants can be embedded in a
string and are interpreted as a number by the resource compiler, rather than as

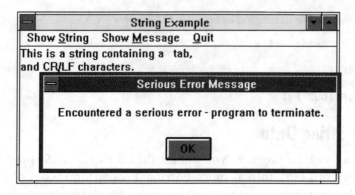

Figure 11-1 The STRTAB Program

just character data. Octal numbers use base eight and were once commonly used by computer programmers, but are no longer much in use. The only three characters you are likely to need are the tab character (\011 octal) and the carriage return, line feed combination to start a new line (\012\015 octal). You can see the effect of these unprintable characters on the text in the main window's client area in Figure 11-1.

Listing 11-4 STRTAB.RC Resource Script File

```
// strtab.rc  resource script file

#include <afxres.h>
#include "strtab.h"

AFX_IDI_STD_FRAME   ICON    strtab.ico   // icon

MyMenu      MENU
{
    MENUITEM "Show &String",     IDM_SHOW
    MENUITEM "Show &Message",    IDM_MESSAGE
    MENUITEM "&Quit",            IDM_QUIT
}


STRINGTABLE
{
    S_GENERAL, "This is a string containing a \011tab,
\012\015 and CR/LF characters."
    S_SERIOUSTITLE, "Serious Error Message"
    S_SERIOUSTEXT, "Encountered a serious error -
program to terminate."
    S_PROGRAMCAPTION, "String Example"
}
```

STRTAB also needs a header file to define the menu item and string table ID numbers. Listing 11-5 shows the STRTAB.H file. The program header file STRTAB.HPP (Listing 11-6) is straightforward. The only message processing functions declared correspond to the program's three menu items.

Listing 11-7 shows STRTAB.CPP, with the program lines specific to string tables boldfaced. The first use of a string table entry is for the program's caption. The string S_PROGRAMCAPTION is loaded in the **CMainWindow** constructor function to pass the program title.

The S_GENERAL string, containing the embedded tab and CR/LF characters, is output when the user selects the "Show String" menu item. The normal **CDC::TextOut()** function will not expand tabs or show multiple lines, so it is not used here. The **CDC::TabbedTextOut()** function will expand tabs, but it is

Listing 11-5 STRTAB.H Resource ID Header File

```
// strtab.h   header file

#define IDM_QUIT         1        // menu item id number
#define IDM_SHOW         2
#define IDM_MESSAGE      3

#define S_GENERAL        1        // string table ID numbers
#define S_SERIOUSTITLE   2
#define S_SERIOUSTEXT    3
#define S_PROGRAMCAPTION 4
```

Listing 11-6 STRTAB.HPP Header File

```
// strtab.hpp    header file for strtab.cpp
                              // derive a main window class
class CMainWindow : public CFrameWnd
{
public:
    CMainWindow () ;           // declare a constructor
private:
    void OnShow () ;           // menu item responses
    void OnMessage () ;
    void OnExit () ;

    DECLARE_MESSAGE_MAP()      // prepare for message processing
} ;

class CTheApp : public CWinApp // derive an application class
{
public:
    BOOL InitInstance () ;     // declare new InitInstance()
} ;
```

Listing 11-7 STRTAB.CPP

```cpp
// strtab.cpp              example using resource string tables

#include <afxwin.h>      // class library header file
#include "strtab.h"      // header file for resource data
#include "strtab.hpp"    // header file for this program

CTheApp theApp ;         // create one CTheApp object - runs program

BOOL CTheApp::InitInstance ()    // override default InitInstance()
{
    m_pMainWnd = new CMainWindow () ;        // create a main window
    m_pMainWnd->ShowWindow (m_nCmdShow) ;    // make it visible
    m_pMainWnd->UpdateWindow () ;            // paint center
    return TRUE ;
}


CMainWindow::CMainWindow ()        // constructor for window
{
    CString title ;      // get program caption from resource data
    title.LoadString (S_PROGRAMCAPTION) ;
    Create (NULL, title, WS_OVERLAPPEDWINDOW, rectDefault,
        NULL, "MyMenu") ;
}


BEGIN_MESSAGE_MAP (CMainWindow, CFrameWnd)
    ON_COMMAND (IDM_SHOW, OnShow)
    ON_COMMAND (IDM_MESSAGE, OnMessage)
    ON_COMMAND (IDM_QUIT, OnExit)
END_MESSAGE_MAP ()

void CMainWindow::OnShow ()      // "Show String" menu item
{
    CString string ;
    string.LoadString (S_GENERAL) ; // load string
    CClientDC dc (this) ;           // get client dc
    CRect rect (0, 0, 400, 100) ;   // text fits into rect

    dc.DrawText (string, string.GetLength (), &rect,
        DT_EXPANDTABS | DT_LEFT) ;  // output text
}

void CMainWindow::OnMessage ()   // "Show Message" menu item
{
    CString string ;
    string.LoadString (S_SERIOUSTEXT) ;
    CString title ;
    title.LoadString (S_SERIOUSTITLE) ;
    this->MessageBox (string, title, MB_OK) ;
}

void CMainWindow::OnExit ()      // "Quit" menu item
{
    this->DestroyWindow () ;      // destroy main window,
}                                 // this stops application
```

restricted to one line of output. To show the complete S_GENERAL text string, a more sophisticated text output function is used: **CDC::DrawText()**. **CDC::DrawText()** outputs text within the bounds of a rectangle, expands tabs, starts new lines after CR/LF pairs, and will add extra CR/LF pairs as needed to fit the text into a rectangle.

The **CDC::DrawText()** function requires a pointer to a **CRect** object to pass the dimensions of the rectangle that will contain the text. Review Chapter 4, *Text and Graphics Output*, if you have forgotten about the **CRect** class. **CDC::DrawText()** also accepts a combination of binary flag values for the fourth parameter that specify formatting options. In STRTAB.CPP, the DT_EXPANDTABS | DT_LEFT flag combination is used to specify left-justified text where tab characters are expanded to spaces. Other flag values (such as DT_BOTTOM, DT_CENTER, DT_RIGHT, and DT_LEFT) are described in the MFC documentation.

When the user selects the "Show Message" menu item, the STRTAB program displays a message box. Both the message box caption string and the internal contents of the message box are loaded from string table entries with the ID values S_SERIOUSTEXT and S_SERIOUSTITLE. You can see the appearance of the message box in Figure 11-1.

Listing 11-8 shows the STRTAB.DEF module definition file. The program's icon is shown in Figure 11-2.

Listing 11-8 STRTAB.DEF Module Definition File

```
NAME            strtab
DESCRIPTION     'strtab C++ program'
EXETYPE         WINDOWS
STUB            'WINSTUB.EXE'
CODE            PRELOAD MOVEABLE
DATA            PRELOAD MOVEABLE MULTIPLE
HEAPSIZE        1024
STACKSIZE       5120
```

Figure 11-2 STRTAB.ICO Icon Image

USER-DEFINED RESOURCES

String tables are ideal for single line text entries, but run out of steam when you need to include a larger block of text. Windows does not include any other predefined way to store blocks of text, but it does allow you to define your own resource types. The next example does this, creating the new resource type called "TEXT."

As an example, imagine that you need to display one or more paragraphs of text in a part of a program, perhaps as instructions for the user. There are several ways to go about doing this. One is to add the block of data right into the program's code as static text. The introduction to string tables earlier in this chapter explained why this approach is not such a good idea. You could also keep the text in a separate file, and read the file from disk when it is needed. This gets messy if you have a lot of little files that need to be available for your program to work, and it complicates program maintenance and installation.

An almost ideal solution is to add the text data to the program's resources. This makes the text part of the program, so the end user does not end up with a lot of little files on his or her hard disk. Resources can be set to be LOADONCALL and MOVEABLE plus DISCARDABLE (the default values), so they do not have the memory consumption problems of static text strings.

Resource Data in a Separate File

The next example program, named RESOR1, includes a block of text that is added to the program as resource data. During program development, the text is stored in a separate file, although it ends up added to the finished program during the compilation phase. The initial TESTTEXT.TXT file (shown in Listing 11-9) is a standard text file, which can be created with the Notepad application.

The text data can be easily added to a program's resource file. Listing 11-10 shows the RESOR1.RC resource script file. The TESTTEXT.TXT file is assigned the resource type "TEXT" and given the resource name "paragraph." "TEXT" is not a standard resource type like MENU, ICON, or STRINGTABLE, so RESOR1.RC invents this new resource type by simply using it as shown in Listing 11-10. The

Listing 11-9 TESTTEXT.TXT Text File

```
This is a bunch of text created with the notepad
application. Each line ends in a CR/LF pair.
This data is arbitrary, but allows the program
RESOR1 to demonstrate loading special resource
data that is not of a predefined resource type.
The end of the file is marked with null char.
```

Listing 11-10 RESOR1.RC Resource Script File

```
// resor1.rc  resource file

#include <afxres.h>
#include

AFX_IDI_STD_FRAME    ICON     resor1.ico      // standard resource type

paragraph            TEXT     testtext.txt    // custom resource

MyMenu     MENU
{
    MENUITEM "&Quit",         IDM_QUIT
}

STRINGTABLE
{
    S_PROGRAMCAPTION, "Custom Resource Example"
}
```

effect is that the text file is inserted into the program's resource data and assigned the name "paragraph" and the resource type "TEXT." The "paragraph" and "TEXT" words defined in the resource script file will be used to find and load this data into memory.

The rest of the RESOR1.RC program is pretty standard, with a simple menu and string table defined, along with the program's icon. Notice the parallel between the inclusion of the icon data and the text data. ICON happens to be a predefined key word that the resource compiler recognizes. The data from the icon file RESOR1.ICO gets added to the program's resources and assigned the name "MyIcon" and the resource type "ICON." The only difference between the icon data and text data is that the MFC classes do not have a special loading function like **CWinApp::LoadOEMIcon()** for the text data, because TEXT is not a standard resource type. The TEXT data will need to be loaded into memory using lower-level functions.

The RESOR1 program requires a short header file to define ID numbers for the menu item and string table entries. Listing 11-11 shows the RESOR1.H header file. Note that the custom TEXT resource does not require an ID number. We will access that resource based on the resource name "paragraph" rather than an ID number.

Listing 11-11 RESOR1.H Resource ID Header File

```
// resor1.h  header file

#define IDM_QUIT                1       // menu item id number
#define S_PROGRAMCAPTION        2       // string table id value
```

Loading a Custom Resource

The MFC classes do not include a general purpose class for loading custom character data (other than STRINGTABLE entries) from a program's resources. To load the data you will need to take advantage of several global Windows functions. Loading custom character data is a common enough task to make it worthwhile to create a new class for this purpose so that the program code can be reused in other projects. This section develops the STRRES.CPP and STRRES.HPP files defining a new class **StringResource**. When we are done creating these files, we will go back and finish the RESOR1 program, which puts the **StringResource** class to work.

To use custom resource data, we use four global Windows functions for dealing with resources: **::FindResource()**, **::LoadResource()**, **::LockResource()**, and **::GlobalUnlock()**. These functions take the place of the specialized resource functions, such as **CBitmap::LoadBitmap()** and **CString::LoadString()**, which work for the predefined resource types, but which will not handle user-defined resources like the TEXT resource type created in RESOR1.RC. You will also need to obtain the program's instance handle in order to call **::FindResource()** and **::LoadResource()**. The MFC class global function **AfxGetResourceHandle()** provides this handle. The handle is used by Windows to locate the program's data in memory.

The basic sequence for loading a user-defined resource into memory is:

1. Use **AfxGetResourceHandle()** to obtain the program's instance handle. This handle is used by both the **::FindResource()** and **::LoadResource()** functions.

2. Use the **::FindResource()** function to locate the specific resource in the program's resource data. **::FindResource()** returns a handle to the relative location of the resource in the resource data. This is not a handle to the resource in memory.

3. Use **::LoadResource()** to load the resource data into memory. **::LoadResource()** returns a handle to the data in memory.

4. Use **::LockResource()** to lock the data in memory before it is accessed. Otherwise, the resource data could be moved by Windows. **::LockResource()** returns a pointer to the data in memory.

5. Read the data in memory. Like all resource data, the data is read-only and cannot be changed. If you need to alter the data, copy it into a memory block and make any changes to the copy.

6. Use **::GlobalUnlock()** to free the resource data as soon as possible, so that it does not inhibit Windows' memory optimization.

7. Use the **::FreeResource()** function if you want to deliberately purge a resource from memory. Windows automatically frees all resource data associated with a program instance when the program terminates, so you do not have to call **::FreeResource()**.

By default, resources are both moveable and discardable and do not get in the way of Windows' memory optimization efforts, except for the brief period of time from when you call **::LockResource()** to access the data until you call **::GlobalUnlock()** to make the data moveable (and discardable) again. You will want **::LockResource()** and **::GlobalUnlock()** to be as close together in your program's code as possible to minimize the amount of time that the resource is fixed in memory.

Listing 11-12 shows a typical program fragment that accesses a custom resource of the type "TEXT" named "paragraph," and outputs the first 25 characters to the device context named *dc* (which is assumed to have been created earlier in the program).

For clarity, Listing 11-12 shows the **::FindResource()** function returning the *hResTemp* handle to the resource data, and this handle is then passed on to **::LoadResource()** to load the data into memory. The *hResTemp* variable does not accomplish anything, so most programmers uses a shorthand notation by combining the **::FindResource()** and **::LoadResource()** function calls into one program phrase:

```
HANDLE hTextResource = LoadResource (hInstance,
    FindResource (hInstance, "OneLine", "TEXT")) ;
```

One basic rule that must be obeyed is that resource data, even resource data locked in memory, is read-only. You cannot modify resource data. If you want to do anything other than read the data, copy the resource data into a local memory buffer, and then make the changes.

Listing 11-12 Loading and Accessing a Custom Resource

```
HANDLE hAppRes = AfxGetResourceHandle () ;
HANDLE hResTemp = ::FindResource (hAppRes, "paragraph", "TEXT") ;
HANDLE hTextResource = ::LoadResource (hAppRes, hResTemp) ;
if (hTextResource)      // if found resource data
{                       // lock resource in memory
    LPSTR lpResData = ::LockResource (hTextResource) ;
        // lpResData now points to locked data in memory
    dc.TextOut (0, 0, lpResData, 25) ;
    ::GlobalUnlock (hTextResource) ;// unlock resource in memory
    ::FreeResource (hTextResource) ;// explicit purge from memory
}
[Other program lines...]
```

Creating a StringResource Class

Although you can call the global resource functions (such as **::FindResource()**) in the body of your C++ program, it is better to "hide" these functions in a specialized class. The internal workings of the class can take care of the low-level details of manipulating the resource data and provide a more abstract interface for the rest of the program. A well-designed class will also provide some protection against the programmer forgetting to unlock locked resources and other possible errors.

The STRRES program was designed to abstract the process of loading a custom resource containing character data. Listing 11-13 shows the STRRES.HPP header file. The **StringResource** class declares four functions: a constructor, a destructor, a **GetLength()** function that returns the length of a character string, and a **GetString()** function that returns a pointer to a character string loaded from resource data. The **StringResource** class also has two private data members, *hResource*, which stores the handle of the resource data, and the **CString** object *StringData*, which stores the character string itself.

Listing 11-14 shows the STRRES.CPP program. The constructor function receives two parameters. The *ResourceName* parameter passes the name of the specific resource in the program's resource script file. The second parameter passes the resource type. For example, if the resource script file contains the line:

```
ABigLine     SPECIAL     textfile.txt
```

then *ABigLine* is the name of the resource and SPECIAL is the resource type. Given these two strings, the constructor function can load the resource data into memory using a combination of the **::FindResource()** and **::LoadResource()** functions. The handle returned by **::LoadResource()** is saved as the *hResource* private variable for use by the other member functions.

Listing 11-13 STRRES.HPP Header File

```
// strres.hpp   header file for strres.cpp

class StringResource : public CObject   // create new class
{
public:
    StringResource (const char far* ResourceName,
        const char far* ResourceType) ; // constructor
    ~StringResource () ;                 // destructor
    int GetLength () ;                   // return length of string
    const char *GetString () ;           // return string itself
private:
    HANDLE hResource ;                   // resource data's handle
    CString StringData ;                 // character data
} ;
```

Listing 11-14 STRRES.CPP

```cpp
// strres.cpp    string resource functions
// loads arbitrary resource data containing character strings
// into a string object.  The resource data must be null terminated.

#include <afxwin.h>
#include "strres.hpp"
                                        // constructor
StringResource::StringResource (const char far* ResourceName,
    const char far* ResourceType)
{                               // loads resource data into memory
    HANDLE AppRes = AfxGetResourceHandle () ;
    hResource = ::LoadResource (AppRes,
        ::FindResource (AppRes, ResourceName, ResourceType)) ;
}


StringResource::~StringResource ()   // destructor
{                                    // frees resource data from memory
    if (hResource)
        ::FreeResource (hResource) ;
}

int StringResource::GetLength ()     // returns length of string
{                                    // returns -1 on error
    if (hResource)
    {                                // lock resource data in memory
        LPSTR lpString = (LPSTR) ::LockResource (hResource) ;
        int i = 0 ;
        while (*lpString++)          // count until find null char
            i++ ;
        ::GlobalUnlock (hResource) ;// unlock resource data
        return i ;                   // return number of chars
    }
    else
        return -1 ;
}

const char* StringResource::GetString ()// returns string itself
{
    if (hResource)
    {                                   // lock resource data in memory
        LPSTR lpString = (LPSTR) ::LockResource (hResource) ;
        StringData = lpString ;     // copy to CString object
        ::GlobalUnlock (hResource) ;    // unlock resource data
    }
    else
        StringData = "" ;
    return (const char*) StringData ;   // return char string
}
```

The destructor function simply frees the resource data from memory. This provides for a symmetry between the constructor and destructor functions. Creating a **StringResource** object loads the resource into memory while deleting the resource object frees the resource data from memory.

The **StringResource::GetLength()** function returns the length of the character string. The resource data must be locked in memory with the **::LockResource()** function before the data can be accessed. **::LockResource()** returns a far pointer to the data in memory. **StringResource::GetLength()** simply counts characters until it finds a NULL character marking the end of the file. This obviously requires that the end of the file be marked with a NULL, which is the case with text saved by the Notepad application.

The **StringResource::GetString()** function is a bit more subtle. The most obvious way to return a pointer to the character string is to simply return the pointer provided by the **::LockResource()** function. This approach has the disadvantage of requiring that the resource data remain locked in memory. Another problem is that resource data is always read-only. If the user of the **StringResource** class attempted to modify the contents of the resource data, Windows would detect memory protection violation and terminate the program.

To avoid these problems, the **StringResource::GetString()** function copies the character string from the resource data into a **CString** object and then immediately unlocks the resource data with **::GlobalUnlock()**. **CString** objects have the advantage of automatically expanding to accommodate any length of string, and they provide a "safe" string that can be manipulated by the calling program. A pointer to the **CString** object's character data is provided by taking advantage of the **CString** class overloaded **(const char *)** operator. The **CString** class recognizes the cast **(const char *)** and returns a pointer to the character string stored in the **CString** object.

```
LPSTR lpString = (const char*) StringData ;
```

Using the **CString** class to contain the string data avoids the problem of read-only data. However, the **CString** object remains stored in memory until the **StringResource** object is deleted. This is not a problem for the RESOR1 program, which only uses the **StringResource** object for a short time and then deletes it. However, you might want to use a different approach to the **StringResource** class if the objective is to minimize memory consumption for objects that will exist for long periods of time.

The RESOR1 Program

Now that we have created the **StringResource** class in STRRES.CPP, we can complete the RESOR1 program. RESOR1 puts the **StringResource** class to work to load the paragraph of TEXT data defined in the RESOR1.RC resource script file, and it displays the text on the screen as shown in Figure 11-3.

Listing 11-15 shows the RESOR1.HPP header file. Only two message processing functions are declared. The **CMainWindow::OnPaint()** function is declared to process WM_PAINT messages, and **CMainWindow::OnExit()** is defined to respond to the single menu item "Quit."

The RESOR1.CPP program is shown in Listing 11-16. Note that the STRRES.HPP header file is included at the top of RESOR1.CPP so that the **StringResource** class is available to the program. The interesting part of the RESOR1.CPP is in the **CMainWindow::OnPaint()** function. The custom resource type TEXT is accessed by simply creating a **StringResource** object.

```
StringResource StrRes ("paragraph", "TEXT") ;
```

Listing 11-15 RESOR1.HPP Header File

```
// resor1.hpp    header file for resor1.cpp

class CMainWindow : public CFrameWnd    // derive a main window class
{
public:
    CMainWindow () ;                     // declare a constructor
private:
    void OnPaint () ;
    void OnExit () ;

    DECLARE_MESSAGE_MAP()                // prepare for message processing
} ;

class CTheApp : public CWinApp     // derive an application class
{
public:
    BOOL InitInstance () ;          // declare new InitInstance()
} ;
```

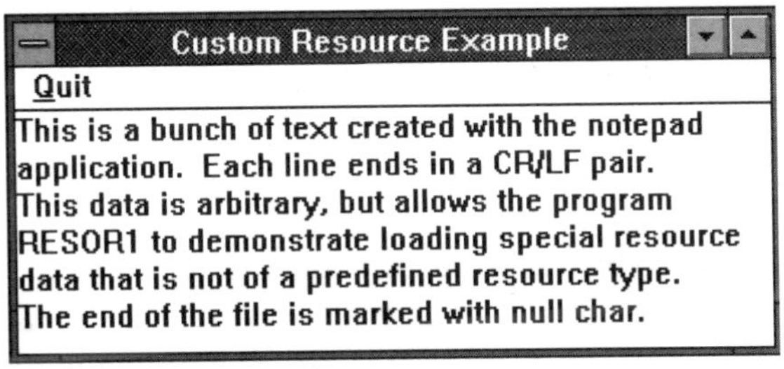

Figure 11-3 The RESOR1 Program

Listing 11-16 RESOR1.CPP

```cpp
// resor1.cpp          // example loading a custom resource

#include <afxwin.h>    // class library header file
#include "resor1.h"    // header file for resource data
#include "resor1.hpp"  // header file for this program
#include "strres.hpp"  // header file for string resource functions

CTheApp theApp ;       // create one CTheApp object - runs program

BOOL CTheApp::InitInstance ()   // override default InitInstance()
{
    m_pMainWnd = new CMainWindow () ;       // create a main window
    m_pMainWnd->ShowWindow (m_nCmdShow) ;   // make it visible
    m_pMainWnd->UpdateWindow () ;           // paint center
    return TRUE ;
}

CMainWindow::CMainWindow () // constructor for window
{
    CString title ;        // get program caption from resource data
    title.LoadString (S_PROGRAMCAPTION) ;
    Create (NULL, title, WS_OVERLAPPEDWINDOW, rectDefault,
        NULL, "MyMenu") ;
}

BEGIN_MESSAGE_MAP (CMainWindow, CFrameWnd)
    ON_WM_PAINT ()
    ON_COMMAND (IDM_QUIT, OnExit)
END_MESSAGE_MAP ()

void CMainWindow::OnPaint ()      // paint client area
{                                 // first create string res. object
    StringResource StrRes ("paragraph", "TEXT") ;
    CPaintDC dc (this) ;          // get client device context
    CRect rect ;                  // rectangle holds client area size
    this->GetClientRect (&rect) ; // get client area rectangle

    dc.DrawText (StrRes.GetString(), StrRes.GetLength (), &rect,
        DT_EXPANDTABS | DT_LEFT | DT_WORDBREAK) ;
}

void CMainWindow::OnExit ()       // respond to "Quit" menu item
{
    this->DestroyWindow () ;      // destroy main window,
}                                 // this stops application
```

The **CWnd::GetClientRect()** function is used to obtain the size of the RESOR1 window's client area as a **CRect** object. This is in preparation for calling the **CDC::DrawText()** function that outputs the text string within the rectangle's dimensions. **CDC::DrawText()** obtains a pointer to the string data loaded from

the custom resource using **StringResource::GetString()** and also uses the
StringResource::GetLength() function to obtain the length of the string.

```
CRect rect ;                     // rectangle holds client area size
this->GetClientRect (&rect) ;    // get client area rectangle
dc.DrawText (StrRes.GetString(), StrRes.GetLength (), &rect,
    DT_EXPANDTABS | DT_LEFT | DT_WORDBREAK) ;
```

CDC::DrawText() is also passed the combination of three binary flags
(DT_EXPANDTABS | DT_LEFT | DT_WORDBREAK) to specify formatting op-
tions. The DT_WORDBREAK flag tells **CDC::DrawText()** to break lines between
words if the lines will not fit within the bounds of the output rectangle. We will
look at the output of **CDC::DrawText()** in a moment.

The RESOR1 program also requires a module definition file and a program
icon, which are shown in Listing 11-17 and Figure 11-4, respectively. Don't
forget to include both the RESOR1.CPP and STRRES.CPP files in the project file
for the RESOR1 program when you compile the program.

Note how the **StringResource** class greatly simplified the process of loading
custom resource data for the RESOR1.CPP program. All of the low-level functions (such as **::FindResource()**) are hidden away in the **StringResource** class
definition. The declaration of the **StringResource** object within the body of the
CMainWindow::OnPaint() function makes the **StringResource** object an automatic variable stored on the RESOR1 program's stack. The **StringResource**
object is automatically destroyed when the **CMainWindow::OnPaint()** function returns. Destruction of the object results in a call to the object's destructor

Listing 11-17 RESOR1.DEF Module Definition File

```
NAME           resor1
DESCRIPTION    'resor1 C++ program'
EXETYPE        WINDOWS
STUB           'WINSTUB.EXE'
CODE           PRELOAD MOVEABLE
DATA           PRELOAD MOVEABLE MULTIPLE
HEAPSIZE       1024
STACKSIZE      5120
```

Figure 11-4 RESOR1.ICO Icon Image

function, which for the **StringResource** class results in freeing the resource data from memory. All of these clean-up activities happen automatically from the point of view of the RESOR1.CPP program.

Using CDC::DrawText()

One interesting aspect of the RESOR1 program is its ability to fit the paragraph of text into the window's client area. This is done by passing the size of the client area to the **CDC::DrawText()** function. If the client area is larger than the area occupied by the block of text, **CDC::DrawText()** respects the CR/LF hard carriage return characters in the resource data and breaks each line at those positions. However, if the client area is narrower than the text lines, **CDC::DrawText()** inserts additional CR/LF pairs to make the text fit the space available. Figure 11-5 shows an example illustrating the RESOR1 window sized with a narrow width. You can use the power of the **CDC::DrawText()** function to format long character strings that do not have embedded CR/LF pairs.

THE RCDATA STATEMENT

The RESOR1 program demonstrated how to include user-defined resources that are located in separate files into the program's resource data. This is frequently the most convenient way to add text and tables of numbers to a program's resources, but there is a drawback. Because the user-defined data (the paragraph

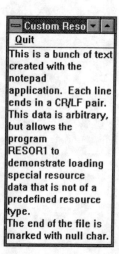

Figure 11-5 The RESOR1 Program with a Narrow Client Area

of text) was kept in a separate file, the programmer will need to keep track of this file during future program updates. If there are many such files included in the program's resources, updates can be complicated, as each of the files must be updated separately. (Putting resource data in separate files is not a problem to the end user of the program, as the data is ultimately included in the program's resources and becomes part of the finished program's .EXE file.)

Windows provides the alternative method of including user-defined data directly in the resource script file. The RCDATA statement can be used in the program's resource script file to include any collection of numeric and/or character data desired. The complete syntax of the RCDATA statement is as shown in Listing 11-18.

As always, you can specify a load option of either PRELOAD or LOAD-ONCALL, and a memory option of FIXED, MOVEABLE, or DISCARDABLE. The defaults are LOADONCALL, MOVEABLE, and DISCARDABLE. The actual data between the curly brackets (or BEGIN and END statements) is limited to integers and characters, which are the only two types of entries the resource compiler understands. You cannot put floating point (decimal) numbers directly into the resource data because any digits after the decimal will be ignored. Each entry in the resource data is separated from the previous one with a comma. Character strings are surrounded in double quotes. Integers can by shown in decimal notation (1234), hexadecimal (0x24b7), and octal preceded by a "\" character (\015).

Our next example program uses the RCDATA statement to include three integer values and a character string as a single block of resource data. Listing 11-19 shows the RCDATA.RC resource script file, which includes the RCDATA statement at the end of the listing. In this case, the resource data is given the name "Arbitrary" and specifically assigned the memory options PRELOAD and MOVEABLE. As the DISCARDABLE memory option was not selected, the "Arbitrary" data will be moveable in memory, but it will not be discarded if Windows runs short on memory space. PRELOAD and MOVEABLE were selected purely for demonstration purposes. Normally, you will use the default LOADONCALL, MOVEABLE, and DISCARDABLE options.

The RCDATA.RC file requires a matching header file to define the ID numbers for the menu items and string table entries. Listing 11-20 shows the

Listing 11-18 RCDATA Statement Syntax

```
ResName RCDATA   [load option] [memory option]
{
    // the data goes here */
}
```

Listing 11-19 RCDATA.RC Resource Script File

```
// rcdata.rc   resource file

#include <afxres.h>
#include "rcdata.h"

AFX_IDI_STD_FRAME   ICON    rcdata.ico      // standard resource ICON

MyMenu      MENU
{
    MENUITEM "&Show Data",      IDM_SHOW
    MENUITEM "&Quit",           IDM_QUIT
}


STRINGTABLE
{
    S_PROGRAMCAPTION, "RCDATA Example"
    S_DATAHEADING, "Here is the RCDATA in hexadecimal and ASCII:"
}


Arbitrary   RCDATA    PRELOAD MOVEABLE
{
    5, 11056, 0x2d,             /* three integers */
    "A String\0"                /* null-terminated string */
}
```

Listing 11-20 RCDATA.H Resource ID Header File

```
// rcdata.h   header file

#define IDM_QUIT            1       // menu item id numbers
#define IDM_SHOW            2

#define S_PROGRAMCAPTION    1       // string table id numbers
#define S_DATAHEADING       2
```

RCDATA.H header file. Note again that the RCDATA portion of the program's resources does not require an ID number because the name of the RCDATA member "Arbitrary" is used to find the resource data. You can have as many RCDATA objects in the program's resource script file as you like. Each must have a different name.

Figure 11-6 shows the RCDATA program in operation, after the user has selected the "Show Data" menu item. The upper line of data shows every byte from the resource in hexadecimal notation. The lower line shows each byte interpreted as a character. Neither representation is appropriate for all of the data, as the data consists of both numbers and characters. One thing you may notice in looking at the hexadecimal representation of the numbers is that they

RCDATA Example

Show Data   Quit

Here is the RCDATA in hexadecimal and ASCII:

5 0 30 2b 2d 0 41 20 53 74 72 69 6e 67 0

♣ 0 + − A S t r i n g

Figure 11-6 The RCDATA Program

are stored in reverse order. The least significant byte (word) is stored before the most significant byte. This "back-words" storage format for integer data in resources matches the way that integers are stored in memory for computers with the 80x86 CPU chips that Windows runs on. The resource data can be used without changing the order of the bytes.

Figure 11-7 shows the "back-words" storage format breakdown for the first two integers stored in the resource data, 5 and 11056 decimal. You can match the "in memory" representation with the output of the RCDATA program in Figure 11-7. The first six characters shown below the hexadecimal numbers in Figure 11-7 are the characters that happen to be defined for these byte values in the ANSI_FIXED_FONT character set used in the example. These characters are only meaningful for the character data "A String" defined at the end of the resource data.

The important point to understand from the RCDATA example is that the resource data ends up as a block of bytes. There is no internal structure to the data, other than the order you specify in the RCDATA statement in the

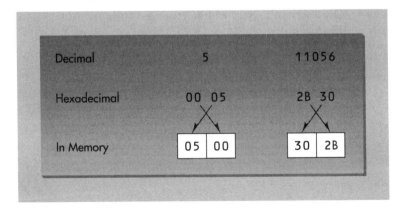

Figure 11-7 How Integers Are Stored in Memory and in Resource Data

program's resource script file. The program must interpret each byte of data as either character or numeric data when the resource data is read into memory.

Loading RCDATA

Loading RCDATA from a resource script file is another activity that you are likely to do in many programs, so it is best to make a specialized class to handle the low-level details. The RCDRES.CPP and RCDRES.HPP files define the **RcdataResource** class for this purpose. We will look at these two files first and then return to RCDATA.CPP, the program that puts the new class to work.

The logic for loading RCDATA resource data is almost identical for data stored as user-defined resources stored in a separate file. The sequence of function calls to load the RCDATA is as follows:

1. Use **AfxGetResourceHandle()** to obtain the program's instance handle. This handle is used by both the **::FindResource()** and **::LoadResource()** functions.

2. **::FindResource()** is used to locate the data in the program's resources. WINDOWS.H defines the special flag RT_RCDATA, which is used as the last parameter when calling **::FindResource()**.

3. **::LoadResource()** is used to load the resource data into memory.

4. **::LockResource()** is used to fix the resource data in memory and return a pointer (the address) of the data in memory.

5. The data is read, but cannot be written to.

6. **::GlobalUnlock()** is used to allow Windows to move the resource data in memory, and discard the data if the resource is discardable.

7. **::FreeResource()** can be used to explicitly remove the resource data from memory. Otherwise, the data will be removed from memory when the program terminates.

Listing 11-21 shows the RCDRES.HPP header file, which declares the **RcdataResource** class. This class is a bit more sophisticated than the **StringResource** class defined for the last example because we cannot assume that the RCDATA contains only character strings. Any type of data can be stored as RCDATA, so the data will be treated as an arbitrary collection of bytes. Note that the **RcdataResource** class overloads the [ ] operator with the function declaration:

```
BYTE far& operator [] (int i) ;
```

Overloading the [ ] operator will allow us to access any byte in the resource data just as if the data element were part of an array of bytes.

Listing 11-21 RCDRES.HPP Header File

```
// rcdres.hpp    header file for rcdres.cpp

class RcdataResource : public CObject        // create new class
{
public:
    RcdataResource (LPSTR ResourceName, int nBytes) ; // constructor
    ~RcdataResource () ;                       // destructor
    int GetLength () {return nDataLong ; }    // return length of string
    LPBYTE GetData () {return pData ; }        // return data
    BYTE far& operator [] (int i) ;           // overload operator [ ]
private:
    int nDataLong ;                           // number of bytes of data
    LPBYTE pData ;                            // pointer to the data
} ;
```

Note in RCDRES.HPP that two private data members are declared. The *nDataLong* variable is used to keep track of the number of bytes of data stored. *pData* is a pointer to the data itself. Windows will detect a memory protection error if the program using the RCDATA attempts to change the data in memory because resource data is always read-only. To avoid this problem, the resource data is copied into a memory buffer by the **RcdataResource** constructor function. Listing 11-22 shows the RCDRES.CPP program file with the constructor function at the top of the listing. The **::FindResource()** function is called with the special RT_RCDATA flag indicating that the resource data type is RCDATA.

```
HANDLE hResource = ::LoadResource (AppRes,
    ::FindResource (AppRes, ResourceName, RT_RCDATA)) ;
```

Once the resource data is loaded and locked into memory, it is copied into a memory buffer created with the C++ *new* operator. The address of this data buffer is stored as the *pData* private data member and is copied to a temporary pointer named *pv*, which is used in the data copying operations.

```
LPBYTE pv = pData = new (BYTE [nDataLong]) ;
```

The RCDATA is copied to the *pData* buffer, and then the resource data is unlocked and freed from memory. After all, there is no point in keeping both the original resource data and the copy in memory at the same time. The copy of the data is saved in memory until the **RcdataResource** object is destroyed. The destructor function takes care of freeing the memory block right before the **RcdataResource** object is deleted. The C++ *delete* operator deletes objects created with the *new* operator.

```
delete pData ;
```

Listing 11-22 RCDRES.CPP

```cpp
// rcdres.cpp   RCDATA resource data access functions

#include <afxwin.h>
#include "rcdres.hpp"
                                    // constructor
RcdataResource::RcdataResource (LPSTR ResourceName, int nBytes)
{                                   // loads resource data into memory
    HANDLE AppRes = AfxGetResourceHandle () ;
    HANDLE hResource = ::LoadResource (AppRes,
        ::FindResource (AppRes, ResourceName, RT_RCDATA)) ;
    nDataLong = nBytes ;
    pData = NULL ;
    if (hResource)
    {                                   // allocate a buffer to hold data
        LPBYTE pv = pData =  new (BYTE [nDataLong]) ;
        LPBYTE pResData = (LPBYTE) ::LockResource (hResource) ;
        for (int i = 0 ; i < nDataLong ; i++)
            *pv++ = *pResData++ ;    // copy resource data to buffer
        ::GlobalUnlock (hResource) ;
        ::FreeResource (hResource) ;// no need for resource data too
    }
}


RcdataResource::~RcdataResource ()  // destructor
{
    if (pData)
        delete pData ;              // get rid of buffer
}

BYTE far& RcdataResource::operator [ ] (int i) // overload [] operator
{
    static BYTE bError = 0 ;

    if (pData && i >= 0 && i < nDataLong)
        return pData [i] ;
    else
        return bError ;
}
```

One other item of interest in RCDRES.CPP is the declaration of the function that overloads the [ ] operator. C++ uses a somewhat obscure syntax for overloading operators. The return type BYTE far& declares that the operator will return a BYTE (defined equal to **unsigned char** in WINDOWS.H). One parameter (*int i*) is passed to the operator. The result is that you can access any single byte in the data block using array notation:

```cpp
BYTE b = RcdataObject [25] ;
```

One shortcoming of the RCDRES.CPP program is that it does not handle errors in a useful way. For example, if an attempt is made to read a byte that is past the end of the data block, the operator [ ] function simply returns zero. An improvement would be to save an error status as a private integer and provide a **GetErrorCode()** function to retrieve the error status. You may want to add this and other functionality to the RCDRES.CPP program if you use it in commercial applications.

The RCDATA Example Program

Continuing with the example, Listing 11-23 shows the RCDATA.HPP header file. The only two message processing functions respond to the "Show Data" and "Quit" menu items.

Listing 11-24 shows the RCDATA.CPP program file. When the user selects the "Show Data" menu item, the **CMainWindow::OnShow()** function is executed. The RCDATA is loaded by creating a **RcdataResource** object named *RcdRes* and passing the resource name "Arbitrary" and a data size of 15 bytes.

```
RcdataResource RcdRes ("Arbitrary", 15) ;
```

Two **ostrstream** objects are then created to allow formatted output of the data with both character and hexadecimal representation. Formatting hexadecimal output requires using several functions from the **ios** class, which is the base class from which most of the stream classes are derived. The **ios::flags()** function is used to specify that numbers for a stream should be shown in

Listing 11-23 RCDATA.HPP Header File

```
// rcdata.hpp     header file for rcdata.cpp

class CMainWindow : public CFrameWnd     // derive a main window class
{
public:
    CMainWindow () ;                      // declare a constructor
private:
    void OnShow () ;
    void OnExit () ;

    DECLARE_MESSAGE_MAP()                 // prepare for message processing
} ;

class CTheApp : public CWinApp     // derive an application class
{
public:
    BOOL InitInstance () ;                // declare new InitInstance()
} ;
```

Listing 11-24 RCDATA.CPP

```
// rcdata.cpp              example loading RCDATA resources

#include <afxwin.h>     // class library header file
#include <strstrea.h>   // streams header file
#include "rcdata.h"     // header file for resource data
#include "rcdata.hpp"   // header file for this program
#include "rcdres.hpp"   // header file for RCDATA resource functions

CTheApp theApp ;         // create one CTheApp object - runs program

BOOL CTheApp::InitInstance ()    // override default InitInstance()
{
    m_pMainWnd = new CMainWindow () ;        // create a main window
    m_pMainWnd->ShowWindow (m_nCmdShow) ;    // make it visible
    m_pMainWnd->UpdateWindow () ;            // paint center
    return TRUE ;
}

CMainWindow::CMainWindow ()       // constructor for window
{
    CString title ;     // get program caption from resource data
    title.LoadString (S_PROGRAMCAPTION) ;
    Create (NULL, title, WS_OVERLAPPEDWINDOW, rectDefault,
        NULL, "MyMenu") ;
}

BEGIN_MESSAGE_MAP (CMainWindow, CFrameWnd)
    ON_COMMAND (IDM_SHOW, OnShow)
    ON_COMMAND (IDM_QUIT, OnExit)
END_MESSAGE_MAP ()

void CMainWindow::OnShow ()            // display RCDATA in client area
{
    CString heading ;                  // get line of text from resources
    heading.LoadString (S_DATAHEADING) ;
                                       // create RCDATA resource object
    RcdataResource RcdRes ("Arbitrary", 15) ;

    CClientDC dc (this) ;              // get client area device context
    dc.SelectStockObject (OEM_FIXED_FONT) ; // ASCII fixed pitch font
                                       // display heading at top of dc
    dc.TextOut (0, 0, heading, heading.GetLength ()) ;
    int nBytes = RcdRes.GetLength () ;

    char HexBuf [64], CharBuf [64] ;    // create 2 buffered streams
    ostrstream HexStream (HexBuf, sizeof (HexBuf)) ;
    HexStream.flags (ios::hex) ;           // format numbers in hex
    HexStream.width (2) ;                  // showing only two digits
    ostrstream CharStream (CharBuf, sizeof (CharBuf)) ;
```

```
    for (int i = 0 ; i < nBytes ; i++)  // for each byte of RCDATA
    {                                   // add hex version in HexStream
        HexStream << (int) RcdRes [i] << " " ;
                                        // and char version in CharStream
        CharStream << RcdRes [i] << "  " ;
    }                                   // now output to dc
    dc.TextOut (0, 30, HexBuf, HexStream.pcount ()) ;
    dc.TextOut (0, 50, CharBuf, CharStream.pcount ()) ;
}

void CMainWindow::OnExit ()             // respond to "Quit" menu item
{
    this->DestroyWindow () ;            // destroy main window,
}                                       // this stops application
```

hexadecimal. The **ios::width()** function is used to specify the number of characters that are output for a field such as a number. This is used to space the hexadecimal characters evenly.

```
HexStream.flags (ios::hex) ;    // format numbers in hex
HexStream.width (2) ;           // showing only two digits
```

Data bytes are added to the two **ostrstream** objects by taking advantage of the overloaded [ ] operator in **RcdataResource** class. For example, the bytes are added to the *HexStream* object as follows:

```
HexStream << (int) RcdRes [i] << " " ;
```

The result is that each byte is formatted to a hexadecimal number consisting of two characters and added to the *HexStream* object. A single-space character is added after each hexadecimal number. The character representation is sent to the *CharStream* object in a similar fashion:

```
CharStream << RcdRes [i] << " " ;
```

In this case, the character will take up only one space. Two spaces are added after each byte to maintain the same spacing as the hexadecimal numbers. The completed **ostrstream** objects are output to the client area device context using the **CDC::TextOut()** function.

Listing 11-25 shows the RCDATA.DEF module definition file. The program's icon is shown in Figure 11-8.

The RCDATA.CPP program is one of the few examples in this book that uses formatted output of character data. The example only uses a fraction of the functions available through the stream classes. The reader should take a look at the **ios** class documentation at this point to get an idea of the wide range of formatting features available.

Figure 11-8 RCDATA.ICO Icon Image

Listing 11-25 RCDATA.DEF Module Definition File

```
NAME            rcdata
DESCRIPTION     'rcdata C++ program'
EXETYPE         WINDOWS
STUB            'WINSTUB.EXE'
CODE            PRELOAD MOVEABLE
DATA            PRELOAD MOVEABLE MULTIPLE
HEAPSIZE        1024
STACKSIZE       5120
```

SUMMARY

Windows' design encourages programmers to separate the program's code and static data. Resource data is used to store data for Windows programs, in place of static data defined in the body of the C++ program. Using resources improves Windows' ability to optimize memory and also makes the program easier to maintain. Essentially, any type of data can be stored as resources, including predefined resource types such as menus, icons, accelerators, bitmaps, cursors, and string tables, as well as data in any arbitrary format using either the RCDATA statement or by using a special user-defined resource type created by the program.

The resource compiler coverts the raw .RC resource script file into the .RES format and attaches the .RES data to the program. The resource compiler has the ability to conditionally compile only portions of a resource script file by using the #ifdef, #else, and #endif conditional statements within the body of the resource script file.

String tables provide a convenient way to put all of the character strings used by a program into the resource script file. Larger blocks of data can be included in the resource data either by writing the data using an RCDATA block, or by including a separate file in the resource data as a user-defined data type. User-defined resources and RCDATA must be loaded using the **::FindResource()**, **::LoadResource()**, **::LockResource()** function sequence, as specialized functions like **CWinApp::LoadOEMIcon()** and **CMenu::LoadMenu()** only exist for the predefined resource types.

By default, resource data is stored as moveable and discardable blocks of data in memory and is only loaded into memory when needed. These default memory options should be used whenever possible to make the best possible use of available memory while the program is running. User-defined data and RCDATA resource data must be locked in memory before it is read, and then immediately unlocked. Resource data can be read from memory after it is locked, but the locked memory block cannot be changed. The **::GlobalUnlock()** function is used to unlock resource data in memory, so that Windows can move and possibly discard the data after it has been used. **::FreeResource()** is used to explicitly remove a resource from memory, although Windows will do this automatically when the program terminates.

QUESTIONS

1. Static variables, such as static text, are stored in the program's:
   a. stack
   b. local heap
   c. resources
   d. none of the above

2. The default load and memory option for resources is:
   a. LOADONCALL
   b. MOVEABLE
   c. DISCARDABLE
   d. all of the above

3. You must load a string from a string table into a local memory buffer using **CString::LoadString()** before modifying the string data. (True/False)

4. The following line in a program's resource script file:

   ```
   SomeData    NUMB    datatab.txt
   ```

   would load the data file _____ as a user-defined resource of type _____.

5. The handle returned by the **::FindResource()** function is passed on to **::LoadResource()** to load the resource data into memory. (True/False)

6. There is no reason to lock discardable resource data in memory before reading the data. (True/False)

7. The RCDATA statement in a resource script file allows you to put user-defined data into the block between the curly brackets (or BEGIN and END statements) following RCDATA. This data can consist of:
   a. integers
   b. character strings
   c. floating point numbers
   d. a and b
   e. a,b, and c

8. The **ostrstream** class is derived from the _____ class, which is in turn derived from the _____ class.

9. Use the _____ function to format all integers to hexadecimal in an output stream.

EXERCISES

1. Change the resource data in the RESOR1 example program so that rather than being loaded from a separate text file, the resource data is included in the program's .RC file as RCDATA.

2. Add the integers 45, 33, 88, 982, and –12 to a program's RCDATA resources. Read the data into an array of integers, and then display each of the integer values in the program's client area. You can modify the RCDATA program for this example.

ANSWERS TO QUESTIONS

1. b.
2. d.
3. True.
4. DATATAB.TXT, NUMB.
5. True.
6. False. The block must be locked to avoid having Windows move or discard the block, resulting in a memory protection violation when the program attempts to access it.
7. d. Floating point numbers are not correctly parsed by the resource compiler.

8. **ostream**, **ios**.

9. **ios::flags()**.

SOLUTIONS TO EXERCISES

1. The program's resource script file will need to be modified as shown in Listing 11-26. Each line of text must be surrounded in quotes, and the terminating CR/LF pairs added with octal constants to produce the same stored data as the separate text file. The end of the text is also marked with a null byte (\000 octal).

   The only other change is to modify creation of the StringResource object so that data of type RCDATA is being located, not a user-defined resource type.

   ```
   StringResource StrRes ("paragraph", RT_RCDATA) ;
   ```

   Otherwise, the program is not changed. The complete solution is stored on the source code disks as C11EXER1.

Listing 11-26 Resource Script File for Exercise 1

```
// c11exer1.rc  resource file
#include <afxres.h>
#include "c11exer1.h"

MyIcon      ICON    c11exer1.ico

paragraph   RCDATA                      // put paragraph in as RCDATA
{
    "This is a bunch of text created with the notepad\012\015"
    "application.  Each line ends in a CR/LF pair.\012\015"
    "This data is arbitrary, but allows the program\012\015"
    "RESOR1 to demonstrate loading special resource\012\015"
    "data that is not of a predefined resource type.\012\015"
    "The end of the file is marked with NULL character.\000"
}

MyMenu      MENU
{
    MENUITEM "&Quit",        IDM_QUIT
}

STRINGTABLE
{
    S_PROGRAMCAPTION, "c11exer1"
}
```

2. The five integer values can be defined in the program's resource script file, as shown in Listing 11-27.

Listing 11-28 shows the **CMainWindow::OnShow()** function of the modified RCDATA.CPP program, which displays the RCDATA. The trick to this problem is to overcome the "back-words" storage format of the raw RCDATA in memory. An integer consists of two successive bytes that are stored in reverse order in the resource data. The following line reconstructs the integer value:

```
int n = (RcdRes [i + 1] << 8) + RcdRes [i] ;
```

The complete solution is under the file name C11EXER2 on the source code disks.

Listing 11-27 Integers as RCDATA in a .RC File

```
Arbitrary RCDATA
{
    45, 33, 88, 982, -12
}
```

Listing 11-28 Modified RCDATA.CPP Program

```
void CMainWindow::OnShow ()            // display RCDATA in client area
{
    CString heading ;                  // get line of text from resources
    heading.LoadString (S_DATAHEADING) ;
                                       // create RCDATA resource object
    RcdataResource RcdRes ("Arbitrary", 5 * sizeof (int)) ;

    CClientDC dc (this) ;              // get client area device context
    dc.SelectStockObject (OEM_FIXED_FONT) ; // ASCII fixed pitch font
                                       // display heading at top of dc
    dc.TextOut (0, 0, heading, heading.GetLength ()) ;

    char IntBuf [64] ;                 // buffered stream
    ostrstream IntStream (IntBuf, sizeof (IntBuf)) ;

    for (int i = 0 ; i < 10 ; i += 2)// for each two bytes of RCDATA
    {                                  // make an int from two bytes ;
        int n = (RcdRes [i + 1] << 8) + RcdRes [i] ;
                                       // build string for output
        IntStream << n << " " ;
    }                                  // now output to dc
    dc.TextOut (0, 30, IntBuf, IntStream.pcount ()) ;
}
```

Chapter 12

Managing Memory

Programs perform work by manipulating data in memory, so managing the computer's memory is fundamental to writing efficient programs. Windows provides the programmer with advanced memory management functions, which manage both memory local to the program and global memory blocks. Although the graphical and windowing functions are more visible to the user, the memory management functions give Windows its ability to efficiently run multiple programs.

The first release of the MFC classes does not provide classes for memory management. However, the C++ language *new* and *delete* operators can be used in Windows programs for basic memory allocation. In some situations, you will need to work directly with the Windows memory management functions to get more complete control over memory blocks. This chapter builds classes for managing local and global memory blocks in several stages so you can understand the Windows memory management functions, and follow the process of designing a new C++ class. In several of the example programs later in this book, the finished classes will be used without further modification to manage memory blocks.

Because Windows moves objects in memory, the memory management functions under Windows are a bit more complex to use than those of a DOS program, where memory blocks remain fixed in one location. The Windows approach to memory management revolves around the use of handles to memory blocks, rather than the absolute addresses in memory. This chapter will give you a number of examples using handles and the related functions that provide direct access to the full power of Windows' memory management capabilities.

Windows NT provides additional memory management features that are not available in Windows 3.1, such as transferring data blocks between applications using "pipes" and "file maps," and creating more than one local heap. This chapter covers only the memory management functions that are common to both Windows 3.1 and Windows NT. This is consistent with the design goal of the MFC classes to support both environments.

Concepts covered: Local and global memory, *new* and *delete* operators, locking memory blocks, lock count, discardable memory, memory handles, fixed memory blocks, passing handles to other functions, changing the size of a memory block, system resources.

Key words covered: LMEM_MOVEABLE, LMEM_DISCARDABLE, LMEM_FIXED, GMEM_MOVEABLE, GMEM_DISCARDABLE, GMEM_FIXED, LHND, LPTR, GHND, GPTR.

Functions covered: ::LocalAlloc(), ::LocalReAlloc(), ::LocalFree(), ::LocalLock(), ::LocalUnlock(), ::LocalCompact(), ::LocalFlags(), ::GlobalAlloc(), ::GlobalReAlloc(), ::GlobalFree(), ::GlobalLock(), ::GlobalUnlock(), ::GlobalCompact(), ::GlobalFlags().

Classes covered: CLocalBlock, CGlobalBlock (developed in this chapter).

LOCAL VERSUS GLOBAL MEMORY

Under Windows, programs can allocate blocks of memory for their own use in two locations, the program's own local heap and the global heap. The local heap is a portion of the program's private data segment, an area in memory limited to a maximum of 64K that the program uses for its stack, static data, and local heap. The global heap is all the free memory in the system, outside of any

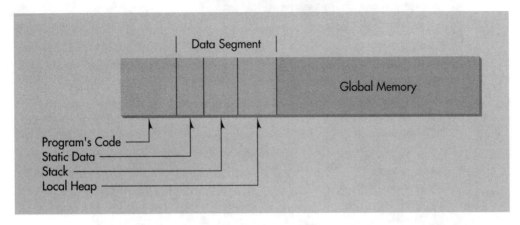

Data Segment

Global Memory

Program's Code
Static Data
Stack
Local Heap

Figure 12-1 Memory Available to a Windows Program

program's code or local data segment. Figure 12-1 shows a simplified diagram of what memory looks like to a single running program, ignoring other programs and parts of the Windows system that may occupy other areas of memory.

All of the data on the stack (automatic variables), static data, and data in the local heap, resides within a single segment. If you remember the discussion on segments and offsets from Chapter 2, *Using the MFC Classes*, you will recall that data in a single segment requires only the offset to specify an address. Using the C++ compiler conventions, addresses in the program's local data segment are "near" addresses, and they use *near* pointers. Addresses in the global memory area will have different segments and offsets and must, therefore, use the full segment/offset address. These are "far" addresses, requiring *far* pointers to memory. The advantage of using the local data segment is that access to a memory location is faster, because only the offset must be specified. The advantage of the global memory area is that it is limited only by the available memory space, not by the 64K limit to a program's local data segment.

In general, you will use the local data segment for small chunks of memory, something like a scratch pad, or sticky note. Access is fast, but the amount of room is limited. The global memory area is for big objects, and objects that will stay in memory for a while. Global memory blocks are like a full notebook for your program to write on. Figure 12-2 summarizes the differences. (Windows NT also supports the distinction between local and global memory. However, the local data segment is not limited to 64K under NT, and can have any size.)

In this chapter, local memory functions will be explored thoroughly before global memory allocation is discussed. The functions that operate on global memory blocks are similar to the ones for local memory, so the programming

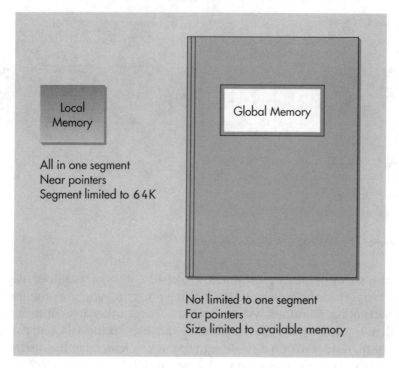

Local Memory

All in one segment
Near pointers
Segment limited to 64K

Global Memory

Not limited to one segment
Far pointers
Size limited to available memory

Figure 12-2 Local Versus Global Memory

techniques used to create, enlarge, and destroy memory blocks apply to both types of memory.

Windows Pointer Conventions

Windows programmers use a couple of handy shortcuts when defining variables that are pointers to memory locations. The normal C++ language declaration for a pointer to a character string is

```
char * pCharString ;     // a near pointer to a character string
```

This is a "near" pointer if the compiler's small memory model is being used, meaning that only the offset value is saved, not the segment. *Near* pointers are used with memory blocks in a single data segment, such as a memory block allocated in the local heap. You can be more explicit in the declaration, and use the "near" compiler key word to show that it is a *near* pointer ("near"

continued on next page

continued from previous page

is the default case for the small memory model, so most programmers leave out the "near" key word when declaring *near* pointers).

```
char near * pCharString ;     // same effect, but uses explicit
                              // "near" declaration
```

Pointers to characters are so common that WINDOWS.H includes a short-hand notation for this variable type. If you look in WINDOWS.H near the beginning of the file, you will see the definitions:

```
typedef unsigned char    BYTE;
typedef unsigned int     WORD;
typedef unsigned long    DWORD;
typedef char near        *PSTR;
typedef char near        *NPSTR;
typedef char far         *LPSTR;
typedef BYTE near         *PBYTE;
typedef BYTE far          *LPBYTE;
typedef int near          *PINT;
typedef int far           *LPINT;
typedef WORD near         *PWORD;
typedef WORD far          *LPWORD;
typedef long near         *PLONG;
typedef long far          *LPLONG;
typedef DWORD near        *PDWORD;
typedef DWORD far         *LPDWORD;
typedef void far          *LPVOID;
```

With WINDOWS.H included by using AFXWIN.H in your C++ program file, you can use these handy definitions to shorten variable declarations. For example, a *near* pointer to a character can be declared:

```
PSTR pChar ;
```

The PSTR declaration takes care of the "char near *" all in one short word. You could also use NPSTR (*near* pointer to a character string) which has exactly the same meaning. Similarly, if you are working with global memory blocks, you will need to declare *far* pointers to memory. The following two declarations are equivalent:

```
LPSTR     lpChar ;   // normal Windows convention
char far *lpChar ;   // spelled out - does the same thing
```

The "L" in LPSTR stands for "long." In other words, an LPSTR is a "long pointer to a character string." It would probably be clearer if the first Windows programmers had used FPSTR for a "far pointer to a character string," but the convention of using LPSTR is too well established to change. Almost

continued on next page

---

continued from previous page

all Windows programmers take advantage of the definitions in the WINDOWS.H file to make their declarations shorter and clearer.

Because Windows NT is a 32-bit operating system, all pointers are 32 bits long. The declarations NEAR and FAR have no meaning to the 32-bit compiler used to create Windows NT applications and are simply ignored. Having NEAR and FAR ignored by the 32-bit compiler is ideal because it means you can use these declarations in a Windows 3.1 program, and then re-compile the same application for Windows NT without editing out the NEAR and FAR declarations.

USING *NEW* AND *DELETE*

Unlike C++, the C language does not include memory allocation functions. Instead, C relies on library functions (such as **malloc()**) to manipulate memory blocks. One of the improvements in the C++ language was to build memory allocation operators into the core C++ language. The C++ *new* and *delete* operators are used to create and destroy memory blocks as the program runs.

There are two basic approaches to using the *new* operator to allocate memory space for a program to use while the program runs. The most direct way is to use *new* to set aside a block of a certain number of bytes of memory. Listing 12-1 shows a typical example where *new* is used to allocate a block of 128 bytes for use by the program. In this case, the uppercase alphabet is copied to the allocated block of memory and then output using **CDC::TextOut()**. The block is freed from memory using *delete* when it is no longer needed. A block of memory used in this fashion is often called a "buffer."

Note in Listing 12-1 that the *new* operator returns a pointer to the beginning of the allocated memory block. You will need to store this value because the *delete* operator uses this pointer to free the block.

Listing 12-1 Allocating a Memory Block

```
CClientDC dc (this) ;            // get client device context
char *pCharBuf = new char [128] ;   // allocate a buffer
if (pCharBuf)
{
    char *pchar = pCharBuf ;
    for (int i = 0 ; i < 26 ; i++)  // put alphabet in buf
        *pchar++ = 'A' + i ;        // and null terminate
    *pchar = 0 ;
    dc.TextOut (0, 0, pCharBuf, lstrlen (pCharBuf)) ;
    delete pCharBuf ;               // delete the buffer
}
```

A more subtle way of using the *new* and *delete* operators is to allocate space for an object rather than a simple block of bytes. Listing 12-2 shows a similar example, except this time room for a **CString** object is allocated with *new*. In this case, *new* returns a pointer to the **CString** object in memory. This pointer is then used to manipulate the **CString** object rather than working directly with the memory buffer. By using the **CString** approach, you get access to all of the **CString** member functions. For example, the += operator is used to add (concatenate) lowercase letters to the end of the existing string in Listing 12-2. The += operator is part of the **CString** class definition (review Chapter 4, *Text and Graphics Output*, if you have forgotten about the **CString** class).

The examples in Listings 12-1 and 12-2 take the precaution of verifying that the *new* operator was able to allocate space. *new* will return a NULL value if an error, such as no memory space being available, occurred. You will want to check to make sure that the pointer returned by *new* is not equal to NULL (zero) before using the pointer.

How new and delete Work

Under Windows, the *new* and *delete* operators create and delete memory blocks that have fixed addresses. Fixed addresses are required because the *delete* operator uses the pointer returned by *new* to determine which block to delete. If the block were moved in memory, the *delete* operator would not be able to find the memory block to delete.

Back in the Windows 2.0 days, using fixed memory blocks under Windows was taboo. Windows 2.0 had to fit everything in the lowest 640K of memory and did not have the advanced memory management features available in the Windows 3.0 and 3.1 enhanced mode. Things changed with the release of Windows 3.0. When running on 80386 or better computers, Windows implements

Listing 12-2 Allocating Room for an Object

```
CClientDC dc (this) ;        // get client device context
CString *pString = new CString ; // create CString object
if (pString)
{
    char c [2] ;             // make a two-byte char buffer
    c [1] = 0 ;              // to allow null term. string
    for (int i = 0 ; i < 26 ; i++)
    {
        c [0] = 'a' + i ;    // put alphabet in string
        *pString += c ;      // use CString += operator
    }
    dc.TextOut (0, 0, *pString, pString->GetLength ()) ;
    delete pString ;         // delete CString object
}
```

virtual memory management whenever Windows is running in enhanced mode. (You can verify that your system is running in enhanced mode by viewing the "About" box from the Windows Program Manager application.) Virtual memory management means that Windows will write blocks of memory to your hard disk if Windows runs low on "real" memory. That fixed memory address returned by the *new* operator remains valid even if the block is temporarily copied to the hard disk to make room. If your program later accesses the block, Windows will move the data back into "real" memory prior to use.

The result of Windows' virtual memory management is that Windows programmers no longer need to be as concerned about fixed memory blocks taking up valuable room. You can use the *new* and *delete* operators for most of your memory management needs. However, *new* and *delete* cannot be used in situations where you need to pass a handle to a block of memory to Windows or to another application. This situation occurs most frequently when working with the Windows Clipboard (discussed in Chapter 17, *The Clipboard*) and when passing handles to memory blocks with Windows messages. In these cases, you will need to use the Windows memory management functions (such as **::GlobalAlloc()** and **::GlobalFree()**) to allocate and free memory blocks.

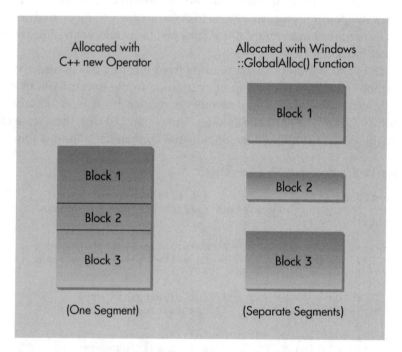

Figure 12-3 Memory Differences Between new and ::GlobalAlloc()

new and *delete* cannot be used all of the time because of the way *new* allocates memory blocks. If you allocate a series of small memory blocks using *new*, the blocks will end up positioned in the same segment in memory. This is called "subsegment allocation." This is different from the Windows global memory allocation functions that allocate each memory block as a separate segment (see Figure 12-3). By using fixed addresses, the *new* operator can allocate memory more efficiently by combining a number of memory blocks in the same segment. However, the drawback is that there is no way to obtain a unique Windows handle for a memory block allocated with *new*. If you need to use the handle of a memory block (for example to pass a memory block to Windows for the Clipboard), you will need to use Windows' memory management functions, such as **::GlobalAlloc()**.

Remember to Use the *delete* Operator

A very easy error to make is to allocate memory with the *new* operator, but forget to free it with *delete*. The result is that the memory block is never removed from memory. If *new* is called many times in the program, you may end up using all of the available memory, crashing the program. A good technique to protect yourself from this error is to use the *new* operator within the class constructor function, and use *delete* within the class destructor. That way any memory consumed by a class object will be freed automatically when the object goes out of scope. The memory classes developed in this chapter follow this principle.

Compiler Memory Models

One other thing to keep in mind when using the *new* and *delete* operators is that the location and maximum size of allocated memory blocks will depend on the compiler memory model you use when compiling a program for Windows 3.1. Table 12-1 shows the relationship between the memory model and memory allocation limitations. All of the examples in this book use the small memory model except for those in Chapter 18, *Dynamic Link Libraries*. This means that the *new* operator is allocating memory in the program's local data segment, and that the combination of the program's stack, local heap (for static variables), and allocated blocks must be less than 64K. 64K is the maximum size of a single segment under Windows.

Another implication of the compiler memory model is the type of pointer returned by the *new* operator. With the small and medium memory models, the *new* operator is allocating all blocks within a single segment, so the pointers

Memory Model	Space Available	Where Allocated
Small	64K total	Program's local data segment
Medium	64K total	Program's local data segment
Compact	no limit	Global memory area
Large	no limit	Global memory area

Table 12-1 Impact of Compiler Memory Model on the C++ new Operator (Windows 3.1)

returned by *new* are *near* pointers (16 bits containing only the offset value). *Near* pointers just contain the offset of the block within a single segment. With the compact and large memory models, the *new* operator allocates memory in segments outside of the program's local data segment and, therefore, must use *far* pointers (32 bits containing the segment and offset values) to encode both the segment and offset of the block's address.

 Under Windows NT, there is no such thing as a "compiler memory model" because all pointers are 32-bit quantities. *new* and *delete* always return 32-bit addresses under Windows NT, which makes life much simpler if you are writing an application strictly for Windows NT. Local memory blocks are not limited to 64K under Windows NT, and they behave just like global memory blocks.

WINDOWS MEMORY ALLOCATION FUNCTIONS

The Windows API includes two sets of memory allocation functions. One group allocates memory blocks in a program's local data segment. These functions have names like **::LocalAlloc()** and **::LocalFree()**. The other group of functions allocate memory outside of the program's local data segment in what is known as the "global heap." The global heap is all of the memory outside of that occupied by running programs. The global memory functions have names like **::GlobalAlloc()** and **::GlobalFree()**.

Unlike the *new* and *delete* operators, the Windows memory allocation functions are not affected by the compiler memory model. You can allocate and use global memory blocks from within a small memory model program, or allocate local memory blocks from within a large memory model program. Think of the Windows memory management functions as using the built-in power of the

Windows environment, rather than using compiler-generated code as with *new* and *delete*.

Although you can allocate fixed memory blocks using the Windows functions, programmers normally take advantage of moveable memory blocks when using the Windows functions. By using moveable memory blocks, a program gives Windows the maximum flexibility to optimize memory use while the program operates. Moveable blocks can be allocated in the local data segment or in the global heap. The Windows functions that allocate local memory are very similar to those used to allocate global memory. We will explore the local memory allocation functions first and then look at the global functions.

Local and Global Blocks–Terminology

One potentially confusing aspect of discussing local and global memory allocation functions is the two uses of the words "local" and "global." Windows uses these terms to describe whether the memory block is allocated in the program's local data segment or in the global heap. Unfortunately, the terms "local" and "global" are also used in the C++ language to describe the scope of a function, whether the function is local to a specific class or globally available. In this chapter, the terms "local" and "global" will refer to the memory location unless otherwise noted. Keep in mind that all of the Windows memory management functions are not defined in a C++ class and are, therefore, "global" from a C++ point of view. This will be indicated by preceding the function names with the double colon scope resolution operator. For example, **::LocalAlloc()** clearly allocates memory in the local heap, but it is a "global" function from the C++ standpoint (not a member of a class).

The primary reason for using local blocks in a Windows 3.1 application is that access is somewhat faster than for a global block because a pointer to a local address requires only the 16-bit (*NEAR*) offset, not the full 32-bit segment/offset used for *FAR* pointers to global memory blocks. Under Windows NT, this distinction disappears because all pointers are 32-bit values. There is little difference in Windows NT between a local memory block and a global one. Nevertheless, Windows NT supports both local and global blocks to make it easy to port a Windows 3.1 application to Windows NT.

LOCAL MEMORY BLOCKS

Because Windows frequently moves things around in memory, the address of an object is only meaningful while the object is locked in place. This leaves the problem of how to keep track of a memory block as it moves in memory. Windows solves this problem by using handles to identify each memory block regardless of where the block is located in memory. The handle of a memory block remains the same, even though the physical location (address) of the block may change many times. If you have been programming under MS-DOS or a similar operating system, you will need to get used to using the handle of a memory block to track it rather than a physical address.

Let's imagine that you need to store the character string "ABCDEFG" at some point in a program. This is a small piece of data, so a local memory block is ideal. The **::LocalAlloc()** function is used to request a memory block in the program's local data segment. **::LocalAlloc()** returns the handle of the memory block. **::LocalAlloc()** allows you to specify whether you want the memory block to be fixed in memory, moveable in memory (the normal case), or moveable and discardable, meaning that Windows can purge the data from memory if Windows needs more room. These options are specified with **::LocalAlloc()** flags (such as LMEM_MOVEABLE and LMEM_ZEROINIT, which are defined in WINDOWS.H and summarized in Table 12-2). Listing 12-3 shows an example that allocates a block of 10 bytes, and specifies that the block will be moveable in memory, and initially filled with *null* bytes (zeros).

::LocalAlloc() will return zero (NULL) if it cannot allocate the memory block, meaning that there is no more room in the program's local data segment. This is certainly possible because the combination of the program's stack, static data, and any allocated local memory blocks must fit within the 64K limit of a single segment under Windows 3.1. Be sure to check that a valid handle (any value not equal to zero) was returned before attempting to use the block.

Note that the handle returned by **::LocalAlloc()** is stored in a static variable. Normally, you will save the handles of memory blocks as member variables of a class that uses the memory block. Alternatively, you can use static or global variables to store the handle so that the value of the handle is not "forgotten" by the program as would happen if the handle were stored as an automatic variable. The memory block's handle is used to reference this block later in the program when you need to access the memory space.

Listing 12-3 Allocating 10 Bytes in the Local Data Segment

```
static HANDLE hMem ;    // handle of memory block as a static variable

hMem = ::LocalAlloc (LMEM_MOVEABLE | LMEM_ZEROINIT, 10) ;
if (hMem == NULL)    // check that allocation was successful
    this->MessageBox ("No more room in the local heap!",
        "Warning", MB_OK) ;
```

Value	Meaning
LMEM_DISCARDABLE	Allocates memory that can be discarded if Windows needs to make room. Used only with LMEM_MOVEABLE.
LMEM_FIXED	Allocates fixed memory. Do not use this unless necessary. Fixed memory limits Windows' ability to optimize memory use.
LMEM_MOVEABLE	Allocates moveable memory.
LMEM_NOCOMPACT	Allocates memory in the local heap that is not moved to make room for a new memory block.
LMEM_NODISCARD	Allocates nondiscardable memory in the local heap.
LMEM_ZEROINIT	Initializes the newly allocated memory block's contents to zero.

Table 12-2 Common ::LocalAlloc() Flags

Locking a Memory Block

In order to read or write data in the block, the block must be fixed in memory. Otherwise, the block might be moved during a reading or writing operation, causing the program to attempt to read or write to an old memory location that no longer belongs to the program. Windows will detect this and terminate the offending program to protect any other programs from being written over. (This is what is happening when you see a message box on the screen describing an "Application Error" and the program or all of Windows terminates.) To avoid this problem, the block is locked with ::**LocalLock**(), accessed, and then unlocked (allowed to move) using ::**LocalUnlock**(). Listing 12-4 shows an example.

The ::**lstrcpy**() Windows function copies the character string "ABCDEFG" into the memory location of the block. During the brief period when the block is locked, it is in a fixed memory location and can be accessed using normal C++ language pointer operations, and functions like ::**lstrcpy**(). The block is then unlocked, allowing Windows to move it if necessary. As soon as ::**LocalUnlock**() is called, the value of the pointer *pStr* becomes unreliable because

Listing 12-4 Locking and Unlocking a Memory Block

```
PSTR  pStr ;    // a near pointer to a character string

pStr = (PSTR) ::LocalLock (hMem) ;  // lock the block in memory
::lstrcpy (pStr, "ABCDEFG") ;  // copy the string to the block
::LocalUnlock (hMem) ;          // allow the block to be moveable again
```

Windows may move the block to a new location. If Windows moves the memory block, the data in the block will be copied to the new location. This means that the string "ABCDEFG" will continue to be in the memory block regardless of where the block is located.

When the program no longer needs the memory block, it can be freed from the system. The **::LocalFree()** function releases the memory block, so Windows can use the space for other local storage needs.

```
::LocalFree(hMem) ;  // free the block.  hMem now has no meaning
```

If you forget to call **::LocalFree()**, the block will remain in the application's local heap until the program terminates. This is a particularly severe error under Windows 3.1, which has a 64K limit to the size of the local heap. Once the local heap is filled, your program will not be able to allocate additional space and will almost certainly fail. The design of the **CLocalBlock** class in the following sections of this chapter reduces the chances of forgetting to free a local memory block by putting the **::LocalFree()** function in the class destructor function. This results in the **::LocalFree()** function being called automatically any time a **CLocalBlock** object goes out of scope. More on this subject in a moment.

Leave Blocks Unlocked

To give Windows the maximum ability to optimize memory, memory blocks allocated using the Windows memory management functions should be allocated as moveable whenever possible. Moveable blocks should only be locked during the brief periods of time when the data is being accessed. Always unlock the block as soon as possible after use.

The Lock Count

If more than one part of a program accesses the same memory block, it is likely that **::LocalLock()** will be called several times in sequence, without a call to **::LocalUnlock()**. This is not a problem, because Windows keeps track of each call to **::LocalLock()** as the block's "lock count." Every time **::LocalLock()** is called, the lock count is increased by one. Every time **::LocalUnlock()** is called, the lock count is reduced by one. When the lock count is zero, the block is unlocked. As long as every call to **::LocalLock()** has a matching call to **::LocalUnlock()** following it, Windows will keep the block locked until the "last" **::LocalUnlock()** function is called.

Storing Other Types of Data

The examples so far have stored character data, but any type of data can be put in a memory block. For example, to store the integers from 1 to 25 in a local memory block, use code similar to that shown in Listing 12-5. **sizeof()** comes in handy when calculating the amount of space to set aside.

This example again demonstrates that during the brief period when the memory block is locked, the block can be dealt with like any other address, using pointer operations as shown here, or functions that access a memory location (such as **::lstrcpy()** in the string examples).

Using Fixed Memory Blocks

Although you will normally use the C++ *new* operator to allocate fixed memory blocks, you can use the Windows memory functions. The advantage of a fixed block is that you save the time of locking and unlocking the block before and after use. Fixed blocks are always locked and always at the same address. One of the interesting side effects of using a fixed, local memory block is that the block's handle value equals the address of the block. This allows you to skip calling **::LocalLock()** to just get the address of a fixed memory block, as you can use the value returned by **::LocalAlloc()** as an address. The example in Listing 12-6 shows how a fixed block can be used for a "quickie" way to store the 26 letters of the alphabet, output them to a device context named *dc*, and then immediately free the block.

Note that the handle value returned by **::LocalAlloc()** is cast to a PSTR to use as a pointer, and then cast back to a HANDLE to call **::LocalFree()**. The pointer *pStr1* will remain valid until the block is freed with **::LocalFree()**. If the block

Listing 12-5 Storing Integer Data

```
static HANDLE   hMem ;
int             *pInt ;

hMem = ::LocalAlloc (LMEM_MOVEABLE, 25 * sizeof (int)) ;
if (hMem == NULL)
    // output an error message
else
{
    pInt = (PINT) ::LocalLock (hMem) ;
    for (i = 1 ; i <= 25 ; i++)
        *pInt++ = i ;     // copy integers 1 to 25 to memory block
    ::LocalUnlock (hMem) ;
}
```

Listing 12-6 Allocating a Fixed Memory Block

```
PSTR pStr1 = (PSTR) ::LocalAlloc (LMEM_FIXED | LMEM_ZEROINIT, 27) ;
PSTR pStr2 = pStr1 ;

for (int i = 0 ; i < 26 ; i++)
  *pStr2++ = 'A' + i ;
dc.TextOut (0, 0, pStr1, lstrlen (pStr1)) ;
::LocalFree ((HANDLE) pStr1) ;
```

were to be used for a longer period of time, *pStr1* would be saved and used to access the block elsewhere in the program. There is no reason to call **::LocalLock()** to access a fixed memory block—it is already locked!

Another trick here is to use the LMEM_ZEROINIT flag, which fills the block with null characters, saving you the trouble of filling in the terminal null for a character string. The combination of LMEM_FIXED and LMEM_ZEROINIT is so common that WINDOWS.H has a shortcut definition LPTR for "local pointer." This allows you to shorten the call to **::LocalAlloc()** shown above down to just:

```
PSTR pStr1 = (PSTR) LocalAlloc (LPTR, 27) ;
```

There are four of these memory combinations defined in WINDOWS.H. The definitions cover the most common cases of moveable and fixed blocks in local and global memory, all initialized to zero.

```
#define LHND        (LMEM_MOVEABLE | LMEM_ZEROINIT)
#define LPTR        (LMEM_FIXED | LMEM_ZEROINIT)
#define GHND        (GMEM_MOVEABLE | GMEM_ZEROINIT)
#define GPTR        (GMEM_FIXED | GMEM_ZEROINIT)
```

An Example Allocating Local Memory

The first full example in this chapter is the MEM1 program. Figure 12-4 shows MEM1 in action, displaying the lowercase alphabet. Selecting the "Change" menu item causes MEM1 to display the uppercase alphabet. The 26 letters of the

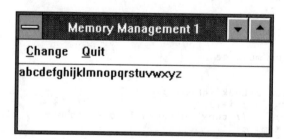

Figure 12-4 The MEM1 Program

alphabet are stored in a local memory block. Initially, the memory block contains the lowercase letters, but they are written over with the uppercase letters when the "Change" menu item is selected. This demonstrates allocating a memory block, and both reading and writing data as the program operates.

Allocating and manipulating memory blocks is clearly a candidate for a new C++ class so that we can reuse the logic in future programs. Building these classes is one of the objectives of the examples in this chapter. We will start with a simple class and then add functions over the course of the chapter. A minimal class named **CLocalBlock** is defined in the WINMEM1.HPP and WINMEM1.CPP files for use by the MEM1 example program. Listing 12-7 shows the WINMEM1.HPP header file. The class contains a constructor, destructor, and two functions named **CLocalBlock::lock()** and **CLocalBlock::unlock()**. There is one private data member that is the handle of the memory block named *hMem*.

A handy aspect of the **CLocalBlock** constructor function is that it provides a default argument for the second parameter passed to the constructor. If no value is specified for the *flags* parameter, the value LMEM_MOVEABLE | LMEM_ZEROINIT is used. This allows you to skip the second parameter when creating a **CLocalBlock** object if the default flag values are acceptable. For example, the following two lines of code are equivalent:

```
CLocalBlock lBlock1 (500, LMEM_ZEROINIT | LMEM_MOVEABLE) ;
CLocalBlock lBlock2 (500) ;  // default arguments for param. two
```

C++ allows you to have more than one default argument in a member function. However, the default arguments must be the last one or more parameters passed to the function. If default arguments were allowed before the end of the parameter list passed to a function, the C++ compiler would not be able to figure out the meaning of the remaining values passed to the function.

Listing 12-8 shows the WINMEM1.CPP program file. The memory block is allocated in the class constructor function and freed from memory in the

Listing 12-7 WINMEM1.HPP Header File

```
// winmem1.hpp           header file for winmem1.cpp (for mem1.cpp)

class CLocalBlock     // class for allocating local memory blocks
{
public:         // flags defaults to moveable & zero initialized
    CLocalBlock (WORD size,
        WORD flags = LMEM_MOVEABLE | LMEM_ZEROINIT) ;
    ~CLocalBlock () ;
    void near* lock () ;
    void unlock () ;
private:
    HANDLE hMem ;         // handle of the memory block
} ;
```

Listing 12-8 WINMEM1.CPP

```
// winmem1.cpp    memory allocation functions for mem1.cpp

#include <afxwin.h>     // class library header file
#include "winmem1.hpp"  // header file for this program

CLocalBlock::CLocalBlock (WORD size, WORD flags)// constructor
{
    hMem = ::LocalAlloc (flags, size) ;
}

CLocalBlock::~CLocalBlock ()                // destructor
{
    ::LocalFree (hMem) ;                    // deletes block from
}                                           // memory

void near* CLocalBlock::lock ()             // lock in memory
{
    return (void near *) ::LocalLock (hMem) ; // returns pointer to
}                                           // data in memory

void CLocalBlock::unlock ()                 // unlock block
{                                           // but do not delete
    ::LocalUnlock (hMem) ;
}
```

destructor function. The only other two operations are the **CLocalBlock::lock()** function, which locks the memory block, and **CLocalBlock::unlock()**, which unlocks the block. The block's handle is always stored as the *hMem* private data member for access by all of the functions.

Note that the **CLocalBlock::lock()** function casts its return value to (void near *). The reason for this is that the class can be used to store any type of data. Because there is no way of knowing in advance what type of data is being stored, the pointer is set to a void value, meaning that it can be applied to any type of data. The pointer is a *near* memory pointer because the local memory functions return memory blocks in the program's local data heap.

The MEM1 program puts the **CLocalBlock** class to work. Listing 12-9 shows the MEM1.HPP header file. Note that the **CMainWindow** class includes a private data member *string* that is a **CString** object. This is the character string data that will be displayed in the MEM1 program's client area when processing WM_PAINT messages.

The MEM1.CPP program is shown in Listing 12-10. A **CLocalBlock** object named *lBlock* is created in the **CMainWindow** constructor function to allocate a 27-byte local memory buffer. The buffer is used to construct a character string containing the lowercase alphabet. This string is then copied to the private

Listing 12-9 MEM1.HPP Header File

```cpp
// mem1.hpp     header file for mem1.cpp

class CMainWindow : public CFrameWnd     // derive a main window class
{
public:
    CMainWindow () ;                    // declare a constructor
private:
    CString string ;                    // string to hold output
    void OnPaint () ;                   // process WM_PAINT
    void OnChange () ;                  // menu items
    void OnExit () ;

    DECLARE_MESSAGE_MAP()               // prepare for message processing
} ;

class CTheApp : public CWinApp          // derive an application class
{
public:
    BOOL InitInstance () ;              // declare new InitInstance()
} ;
```

Listing 12-10 MEM1.CPP

```cpp
// mem1.cpp                   allocating and using local memory blocks

#include <afxwin.h>      // class library header file
#include "mem1.h"        // header file for resource data
#include "mem1.hpp"      // header file for this program
#include "winmem1.hpp"   // header file for Windows memory functions

CTheApp theApp ;         // create one CTheApp object - runs program

BOOL CTheApp::InitInstance ()    // override default InitInstance()
{
    m_pMainWnd = new CMainWindow () ;          // create a main window
    m_pMainWnd->ShowWindow (m_nCmdShow) ;      // make it visible
    m_pMainWnd->UpdateWindow () ;              // paint center
    return TRUE ;
}

CMainWindow::CMainWindow ()       // constructor for window
{
    CString title ;      // get program caption from resource data
    title.LoadString (S_PROGRAMCAPTION) ;
    Create (NULL, title, WS_OVERLAPPEDWINDOW, rectDefault,
        NULL, "MyMenu") ;
                                  // initialize string
```

```
        char *pStr, *ps ;
        CLocalBlock lBlock (27) ;    // allocate a 27 byte  block
                                     // lock in memory, get address
        pStr = ps = (char *) lBlock.lock () ;
        for (int i = 0 ; i < 26 ; i++)
            *ps++ = 'a' + i ;        // put 26 letters in block
        *ps = 0 ;                    // add terminating null
        string = pStr ;             // copy block to string object
        lBlock.unlock () ;          // unlock block
    }                               // lBlock destructor called here

BEGIN_MESSAGE_MAP (CMainWindow, CFrameWnd)
    ON_WM_PAINT ()
    ON_COMMAND (IDM_CHANGE, OnChange)
    ON_COMMAND (IDM_QUIT, OnExit)
END_MESSAGE_MAP ()

void CMainWindow::OnPaint ()     // window painting function
{
    CPaintDC dc(this) ;              // get client device context
    dc.TextOut (0, 0, string, string.GetLength ()) ;
}


void CMainWindow::OnChange ()    // menu item "Change"
{                                // puts 26 characters in CString object
    char *pStr, *ps ;
    CLocalBlock lBlock (27) ;    // allocate a 27 byte memory block
                                 // lock in memory, get address
    pStr = ps = (char *) lBlock.lock () ;
    for (int i = 0 ; i < 26 ; i++)
        *ps++ = 'A' + i ;        // put 26 uppercase letters in block
    *ps = 0 ;                    // add terminating null character
    string = pStr ;             // copy block to string object
    lBlock.unlock () ;          // unlock block
    this->Invalidate () ;       // force repainting - shows string
    }                           // block automatically deleted here

void CMainWindow::OnExit ()      // menu item "Quit"
{
    this->DestroyWindow () ;     // destroy main window,
    }                            // this stops application
```

CString object *string* for use in the **CWnd::OnPaint()** function to display the characters. Note that the value returned by the **CLocalBlock::lock()** function is cast to (char *), which is equivalent to (char near *) if you compile with the small memory model. This cast overcomes the default (void near *) cast of the **CLocalBlock::lock()** function so that the *ps* and *pStr* pointers are recognized by the C++ compiler as pointers to character data.

One subtle operation you might miss in the **CMainWindow** constructor function is the destruction of the **CLocalBlock** object. Because the **CLocalBlock** object is created within the body of a function, the object (not the memory block it allocates) is an automatic variable stored on the program's stack. Automatic variables are automatically destroyed when the function returns, so the **CLocalBlock** destructor is called at the end of the **CMainWindow** constructor function. Looking back at WINMEM1.CPP (Listing 12-8), you can see that the **CLocalBlock** destructor function frees the memory block, which is exactly what needs to be done to avoid tying up memory.

Another **CLocalBlock** object is created in the **CMainWindow::OnChange()** function. This block is not related in any way to the block created in the **CMainWindow** constructor function. However, the new block is used the same way in **CMainWindow::OnChange()** to provide a temporary memory block to hold the uppercase alphabet. The character data is again copied into the private **CString** object *string*. The **CWnd::Invalidate()** function is called to force repainting of the program's client area, which causes the new uppercase alphabet to be displayed.

There are certainly easier ways to create a temporary buffer to store the alphabet than using the **CLocalBlock** class. You could just declare a char [27] automatic variable or use the *new* operator. The only reason to use the **CLocalBlock** class in this example is to demonstrate how the class is used.

Listings 12-11 to 12-13 show the remaining files for the MEM1 program. The program's icon is shown in Figure 12-5. Don't forget to include both the MEM1.CPP and WINMEM1.CPP files in the project list when compiling MEM1.

Listing 12-11 MEM1.RC Resource Script File

```
// mem1.rc  resource script file

#include <afxres.h>
#include "mem1.h"

AFX_IDI_STD_FRAME   ICON    mem1.ico   // the program's icon

MyMenu MENU                            // define the menu
{
    MENUITEM "&Change",     IDM_CHANGE
    MENUITEM "&Quit",       IDM_QUIT
}

STRINGTABLE
{
    S_PROGRAMCAPTION    "Memory Management 1"
}
```

Figure 12-5 MEM1.ICO Icon Image

Listing 12-12 MEM1.H Resource ID Header File

```
// mem1.h  header file for resource ID numbers

#define IDM_CHANGE        1        // menu item ID's
#define IDM_QUIT          2

#define S_PROGRAMCAPTION  1        // string table ID
```

Listing 12-13 MEM1.DEF Module Definition File

```
NAME            mem1
DESCRIPTION     'mem1 C++ program'
EXETYPE         WINDOWS
STUB            'WINSTUB.EXE'
CODE            PRELOAD MOVEABLE
DATA            PRELOAD MOVEABLE MULTIPLE
HEAPSIZE        1024
STACKSIZE       5120
```

CHANGING MEMORY BLOCK SIZE

In many cases, you will need to change the size of a memory block after it has been created. For example, a memory block containing the text for a word processor will need to be increased in size as more text is entered. Windows makes this easy to do by providing the **::LocalReAlloc()** function. **::LocalReAlloc()** can either increase or decrease the size of a memory block after the block has been created with the **::LocalAlloc()** function. If the block is increased in size, the data in the "old" part of the block is not changed. If the block is decreased in size, the data at the end of the block is lost as the block is reduced in size. Figure 12-6 shows the effect of increasing and decreasing the size of a small memory block containing the letters of the alphabet.

A typical code sequence that creates a memory block and later increases it in size is shown in Listing 12-14. In this case, the memory block is initially allocated with a size of 512 bytes, but later reallocated to 1,024 bytes.

Both **::LocalAlloc()** and **::LocalReAlloc()** can be used to allocate a memory block with a size of zero bytes. This sounds silly at first because the block cannot

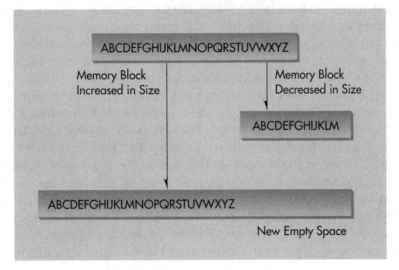

Figure 12-6 ::LocalReAlloc() Effects

Listing 12-14 Changing Memory Block Size

```
static HANDLE hMem ;

hMem = ::LocalAlloc (LMEM_MOVEABLE, 512) ;
[Other program lines...]
hMem = ::LocalReAlloc (hMem, 1024, LMEM_MOVEABLE) ;
```

be used to store any data. However, the handle to the block remains a valid handle even when the block has a size of zero. The usual reason for allocating zero length memory buffers is that it is convenient to allocate the blocks before their size is known. The blocks can be allocated with an initial size of zero, and then reallocated as needed when data becomes available. The next example uses this approach to store a data block that is gradually enlarged.

::LocalReAlloc() will not reliably change the memory options of a block during reallocation (from LMEM_FIXED to LMEM_MOVEABLE, etc.). If you need to change the memory options, you should allocate a new memory block with the desired memory flags, copy the contents of the old block to the new one, and then delete the old block. This technique is used for the **CLocalBlock** class in the last example in this chapter.

An Example Using ::LocalReAlloc()

The next example, MEM2, demonstrates using ::**LocalReAlloc()** to both enlarge and shrink a memory block. The memory block is used to hold a character string, containing the digit characters. Initially, the memory block is allocated with zero bytes. Each time the user clicks the "Add" menu item, the memory block is enlarged by ten bytes, and the added space is filled with digit characters using each digit in sequence. Figure 12-7 shows the MEM2 program after the user has selected the "Add" menu item three times. Selecting the "Delete" menu item reallocates the memory block back to zero bytes, eliminating all of the added digits.

As with the previous example, MEM2 uses memory allocation functions stored in separate files named WINMEM2.HPP and WINMEM2.CPP. These files contain improvements to the basic WINMEM1 files used in the last example. Listing 12-15 shows the WINMEM2.HPP header file. Three new functions are declared. The first is a default constructor function that takes no arguments. This will be used in MEM2 to initially create a **CLocalBlock** object containing zero bytes. Declaring multiple constructor functions is a common practice with C++ classes. The compiler determines which constructor function to call based on the number and type of arguments passed to the constructor function.

Listing 12-15 WINMEM2.HPP Header File

```
// winmem2.hpp           header file for winmem2.cpp (for mem2.cpp)

class CLocalBlock       // class for allocating local memory blocks
{
public:
    CLocalBlock (WORD size,
        WORD flags = LMEM_MOVEABLE | LMEM_ZEROINIT) ;
    CLocalBlock () ;           // new default constructor
    ~CLocalBlock () ;
    void near* lock () ;
    void unlock () ;           // new function to resize block
    WORD resize (WORD size, WORD flags = LMEM_MOVEABLE) ;
    WORD getsize () {return BlockSize ; } // new - return block size
private:
    HANDLE  hMem ;             // handle of the memory block
    WORD    BlockSize ;        // current size allocated
} ;
```

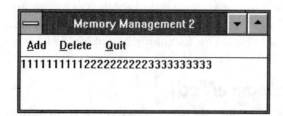

Figure 12-7 MEM2 Program After Selecting "Add" Three Times

WINMEM2.HPP also declares the **CLocalBlock::resize()** function for changing the size of the memory block, and **CLocalBlock::getsize()** to determine the current size of the block. The private integer member *BlockSize* is used to track the current size of the block.

Listing 12-16 shows the WINMEM2.CPP program file with the changes boldfaced. The default constructor function (which takes no arguments) initially allocates a moveable memory block containing zero bytes. Despite the zero-byte size **::LocalAlloc()** returns a valid handle to the memory block, but the block cannot initially be used to store anything. The new **CLocalBlock::resize()** function is provided to change the size of a block. For example, **CLocalBlock::resize()** can be used to increase the size of a block initially allocated with zero bytes so that it can be used to store data. **CLocalBlock::resize()** can also be used to reduce the size of a block.

Note throughout WINMEM2.CPP that the private data member *BlockSize* is used to keep track of the number of bytes in the local memory block. The **CLocalBlock::getsize()** function (declared inline in WINMEM2.HPP) simply returns this value.

The MEM2 program takes advantage of the new functions in WINMEM2. Listing 12-17 shows the MEM2.HPP header file. The most significant item is the declaration of a **CLocalBlock** object named **lBlock** as part of the **CMainWindow** class private data. The **CLocalBlock** declaration takes advantage of the new constructor function in WINMEM2 to create a local memory block

Listing 12-16 WINMEM2.CPP

```
// winmem2.cpp    windows memory allocation functions for mem2.cpp

#include <afxwin.h>      // class library header file
#include "winmem2.hpp"  // header file for this program

CLocalBlock::CLocalBlock (WORD size, WORD flags)// normal constructor
{
    hMem = ::LocalAlloc (flags, size) ;
    if (hMem)
        BlockSize = size ;
    else
        BlockSize = 0 ;
}

CLocalBlock::CLocalBlock ()                    // default constructor
{                                              // starts block with 0 bytes
    hMem = ::LocalAlloc (0, LMEM_MOVEABLE) ;
    BlockSize = 0 ;
}
```

```
CLocalBlock::~CLocalBlock ()                       // destructor
{
    ::LocalFree (hMem) ;                           // deletes block
from
}                                                  // memory

void near* CLocalBlock::lock ()                    // lock in memory
{
    return (void near *)::LocalLock (hMem) ;       // returns pointer to
}                                                  // data in memory

void CLocalBlock::unlock ()                        // unlock block
{                                                  // but do not delete
    ::LocalUnlock (hMem) ;
}

WORD CLocalBlock::resize (WORD size, WORD flags)// resize block
{                                                  // or change flags
    if (size > 0)
        hMem = ::LocalReAlloc (hMem, size, flags) ;
    else
    {                                              // if requesting 0 bytes
        ::LocalFree (hMem) ;                       // dispose of old block
        hMem = ::LocalAlloc (flags, 0) ;           // allocate new one
    }
    if (hMem)                                      // if no error
        BlockSize = size ;                         // return size
    else
        BlockSize = 0 ;                            // otherwise return zero
    return BlockSize ;
}
```

Listing 12-17 MEM2.HPP Header File

```
// mem2.hpp     header file for mem2.cpp

class CMainWindow : public CFrameWnd    // derive a main window class
{
public:
    CMainWindow () ;                    // declare a constructor
private:
    CLocalBlock lBlock ;                // local memory block
    void OnPaint () ;                   // process WM_PAINT
    void OnAdd () ;                     // menu items
    void OnDelete () ;
    void OnExit () ;

    DECLARE_MESSAGE_MAP()               // prepare for message processing
} ;

class CTheApp : public CWinApp     // derive an application class
{
public:
    BOOL InitInstance () ;              // declare new InitInstance()
} ;
```

containing zero bytes. The block can then be used in all of the **CMainWindow** class member functions for data storage.

Listing 12-18 shows the MEM2.CPP program file. MEM2.CPP uses the **CLocalBlock** object **lBlock** defined in the **CMainWindow** class definition to share the same data among several functions. When the user selects the "Add" menu item, the **CMainWindow::OnAdd()** function is executed. First, the current size of the *lBlock* memory block is determined by calling the **CLocalBlock::getsize()** function. If the program has just started, the block will contain zero bytes.

```
int nBlockSize = lBlock.getsize () ;    // get block size
```

One little complexity in working with character data is that you must make room for the terminal null character at the end of the string. To hold 10 characters, the block must initially be allocated with a size of eleven bytes so that the last byte will contain a null. Selecting the "Add" menu item increases the size of the block by 10 bytes each time "Add" is selected, so the number of bytes in the local memory block increases in the sequence 11, 21, 31, 41...

```
if (nBlockSize < 10)
    nNewSize = lBlock.resize (11) ;
else
    nNewSize = lBlock.resize (nBlockSize + 10) ;
```

MEM2.CPP checks to make sure that the block was resized properly, and it displays a message box if an error occurred. Otherwise, ten digit characters are copied to the end of the memory block taking care to preserve the terminal null character. The current contents of the memory block are displayed by forcing a WM_PAINT message to be sent to the main program window by calling **CWnd::Invalidate()**.

The **CWnd::OnPaint()** function displays the current contents of the local memory block. The block is first locked in memory using **CLocalBlock::lock()**, which returns a pointer to the character data. The data is copied into a temporary **CString** object that is used in the **CDC::TextOut()** function to display the contents of the memory block on the window's client area.

If the user selects the "Delete" menu item, the **CMainWindow::OnDelete()** function is called. This function simply resizes the local memory block to zero bytes, effectively deleting all of the data.

```
lBlock.resize (0) ;             // resize to zero bytes
```

Because the **CLocalBlock** object is a member of the **CMainWindow** class, it is destroyed when the program terminates and the **CMainWindow** object is destroyed. The **CLocalBlock** destructor function is automatically called at this point, which frees the local memory block before the MEM2 program terminates.

Listing 12-18 MEM2.CPP

```cpp
// mem2.cpp                    allocating and using local memory blocks

#include <afxwin.h>      // class library header file
#include "winmem2.hpp"   // header file for Windows memory functions
#include "mem2.h"        // header file for resource data
#include "mem2.hpp"      // header file for this program

CTheApp theApp ;         // create one CTheApp object - runs program

BOOL CTheApp::InitInstance ()    // override default InitInstance()
{
    m_pMainWnd = new CMainWindow () ;        // create a main window
    m_pMainWnd->ShowWindow (m_nCmdShow) ;    // make it visible
    m_pMainWnd->UpdateWindow () ;            // paint center
    return TRUE ;
}


CMainWindow::CMainWindow ()         // constructor for window
{
    CString title ;      // get program caption from resource data
    title.LoadString (S_PROGRAMCAPTION) ;
    Create (NULL, title, WS_OVERLAPPEDWINDOW, rectDefault,
        NULL, "MyMenu") ;
}

BEGIN_MESSAGE_MAP (CMainWindow, CFrameWnd)
    ON_WM_PAINT ()
    ON_COMMAND (IDM_ADD, OnAdd)                // menu items
    ON_COMMAND (IDM_DELETE, OnDelete)
    ON_COMMAND (IDM_QUIT, OnExit)
END_MESSAGE_MAP ()

void CMainWindow::OnPaint ()     // window painting function
{
    CPaintDC dc(this) ;          // get client device context
    CString string ;
    if (lBlock.getsize () > 0)
    {                       // get pointer to block in memory
        char* pStr = (char *) lBlock.lock () ;
        string = pStr ;          // copy block to string object
        lBlock.unlock () ;       // unlock block
    }
    dc.TextOut (0, 0, string, string.GetLength ()) ;
}


void CMainWindow::OnAdd ()       // "Add" menu item
{                                // makes block 10 bytes longer
    int nBlockSize = lBlock.getsize () ;    // get block size
    int nNewSize ;
```

```
    if (nBlockSize < 10)
        nNewSize = lBlock.resize (11) ;
    else
        nNewSize = lBlock.resize (nBlockSize + 10) ;

    if (nNewSize == 0)          // if resizing did not work
    {
        CString Caption ;
        Caption.LoadString (S_MEMERRORCAPTION) ;
        CString ErrorText ;
        ErrorText.LoadString (S_LREALLOCERROR) ;
        this->MessageBox (ErrorText, Caption, MB_OK) ;
        return ;
    }
    char* ps = (char *) lBlock.lock () ;// get pointer to block
    ps += nNewSize - 11 ;       // ps points to end of old text
    for (int i = 0 ; i < 10 ; i++)
        *ps++ = '1' + nBlockSize/10 ;   // put 10 digit chars in
    *ps = 0 ;                   // add terminating null character
    lBlock.unlock () ;          // unlock block
    this->Invalidate () ;       // force repainting - shows string
}                               // block automatically deleted here

void CMainWindow::OnDelete ()   // "Delete" menu item
{
    lBlock.resize (0) ;         // resize to zero bytes
    this->Invalidate () ;       // force repainting
}

void CMainWindow::OnExit ()     // respond to menu item "Quit"
{
    this->DestroyWindow () ;    // destroy main window,
}                               // this stops application
```

The remaining support files for MEM2 are shown in Listings 12-19 to 12-21. Figure 12-8 shows the program's icon. Don't forget to include WINMEM2.CPP in the project file when compiling MEM2.CPP.

Figure 12-8 MEM2.ICO Icon Image

Listing 12-19 MEM2.RC Resource Script File

```
// mem2.rc  resource script file

#include <afxres.h>
#include "mem2.h"

AFX_IDI_STD_FRAME   ICON    mem2.ico    // the program's icon

MyMenu MENU                             // define the menu
{
    MENUITEM "&Add",        IDM_ADD
    MENUITEM "&Delete",     IDM_DELETE
    MENUITEM "&Quit",       IDM_QUIT
}

STRINGTABLE
{
    S_PROGRAMCAPTION    "Memory Management 2"
    S_MEMERRORCAPTION   "Memory Error"
    S_LREALLOCERROR     "Error in resizing a local memory block."
}
```

Listing 12-20 MEM2.H Resource ID Header File

```
// mem2.h  header file for resource ID numbers

#define IDM_ADD             1       // menu item IDs
#define IDM_DELETE          2
#define IDM_QUIT            3

#define S_PROGRAMCAPTION    1       // string table IDs
#define S_MEMERRORCAPTION   2
#define S_LREALLOCERROR     3
```

Listing 12-21 MEM2.DEF Module Definition File

```
NAME            mem2
DESCRIPTION     'mem2 C++ program'
EXETYPE         WINDOWS
STUB            'WINSTUB.EXE'
CODE            PRELOAD MOVEABLE
DATA            PRELOAD MOVEABLE MULTIPLE
HEAPSIZE        1024
STACKSIZE       5120
```

DISCARDABLE MEMORY BLOCKS

Discardable blocks are the least memory-consuming of all of the memory options. If Windows needs to find room for another program or data, it follows this procedure:

1. Windows scans the available memory and looks for a block of sufficient size. If Windows finds one, this space is allocated and no other blocks are moved or discarded.

2. If a block of sufficient size is not available, Windows attempts to make room by relocating moveable code and data to make room. If a big enough space can be created by moving objects, no discardable data is removed.

3. If there still is not enough room in memory, Windows makes room by discarding discardable objects. The most recently accessed objects are the last to be discarded.

4. If there is still not enough room in memory after discarding every discardable block, **::LocalAlloc()** will return zero, indicating that there is not enough room to allocate the requested size block. Most programs display a message box at this point, telling the user that the system is out of memory and that other applications should be terminated before trying again.

When a data block is discarded, the data is no longer available in memory, but the handle to the data block remains valid. The handle points to a data block containing zero bytes. **::LocalReAlloc()** can be used to restore the block to its former size when it is needed again.

Discardable blocks are best suited to data that can be loaded again from disk if needed or that can be re-created in memory on demand. Resources are almost always discardable, as the data is always defined in the program's disk file. Discardable blocks are also useful for temporary files and for saving portions of large databases in memory, where the database can be large enough to exceed available memory.

The Importance of Discardable Memory Blocks
The importance of discardable memory blocks has diminished with the introduction of the virtual memory management features of Windows 3.0, 3.1, and Windows NT. When running in enhanced mode, Windows automatically will copy blocks of memory off to disk if Windows cannot find enough memory to allocate the next block. This is roughly equivalent to discarding a memory block, except virtual memory functions can copy *any* block of your program off to disk. The advantage of explicitly allocating discardable blocks is that you tell Windows which blocks should be discarded first. This can improve the performance of an otherwise slow program that may be constantly copying data to disk and reloading it.

Using Discardable Blocks

Discardable blocks are always moveable, so the **::LocalAlloc()** function call to create a discardable block combines the LMEM_MOVEABLE and LMEM_DISCARDABLE flags. To allocate a block of 100 bytes and copy some characters to the beginning of the block, use the code shown in Listing 12-22.

When you need to access a discardable data block, it is important to make sure that the data is still there and has not been discarded. The **::LocalFlags()** function does this, returning a WORD value that contains both the lock count for the block in the low-order byte, and the LMEM_DISCARDED and/or LMEM_DISCARDABLE flags as the high-order byte. Be sure to check that the data has not been discarded before attempting to read from a discardable block, as shown in Listing 12-23.

When **::LocalUnlock()** is called for a discardable block, the block is made both moveable and discardable again. When the program is done with the discardable block, use **::LocalFree()** to permanently remove it from memory. **::LocalFree()** makes the handle to the block invalid, so the block cannot be restored with **::LocalReAlloc()** again. If another discardable block is needed, it

Listing 12-22 Allocating a Discardable Memory Block

```
HANDLE hMem ;

hMem = ::LocalAlloc (LMEM_MOVEABLE | LMEM_DISCARDABLE, 100) ;
if (hMem)
{
    PSTR pStr = (PSTR) ::LocalLock (hMem) ;
    ::lstrcpy (pStr, "abcdefg") ;
    ::LocalUnlock (hMem) ;
}
```

Listing 12-23 Checking Whether a Block Was Discarded

```
if (LMEM_DISCARDED & ::LocalFlags (hMem))// block been discarded?
{                                        // if so, reallocate block
    hMem = ::LocalReAlloc (hMem, 100,
        LMEM_MOVEABLE | LMEM_DISCARDABLE)
    // reload or recreate the data here
}
else                                     // if block was not discarded
{                                        // can read data from block
    PSTR pStr = (PSTR) ::LocalLock (hMem) ;
    ::lstrcpy (cBuf, pStr) ;
    ::LocalUnlock (hMem) ;
}
```

must be created from scratch with **::LocalAlloc()**. You can also deliberately discard a discardable block without invalidating the block's handle by calling the **::LocalDiscard()** function. Normally, you will let Windows decide when memory is full, and not bother with **::LocalDiscard()**.

An Example Using Discardable Blocks

The next example is designed to illustrate both discardable and moveable memory blocks in more detail. The MEM3 program allocates four blocks of 512 bytes in the local heap, and displays the addresses, and discardable status for each block in the window's client area. Figure 12-9 shows the MEM3 program right after it was started. Note that blocks 0 and 2 are discardable, and blocks 1 and 3 are only moveable. Block 0 is allocated first and ends up at the highest address in memory. Blocks 1 and 3 are not discardable, and are put at the low end of the local heap.

The addresses output by the MEM3 program are in decimal, not hexadecimal. If you do a little arithmetic on the block 0 and 2 address values, you will note that one of the blocks actually contains 520 bytes (12306–11786 = 520), not the exact 512 bytes requested for each block. The extra bytes are taken up by a small header that Windows uses to keep track of the size and status of each local memory block. This is all internal to Windows, and does not affect our considering each block to contain 512 bytes of usable storage. As usual, Windows is doing a number of "low-level" tasks automatically, leaving the programmer to concentrate on the more important issues.

If the user selects the "Squish Memory" menu item, MEM3 compacts the local heap by calling the **::LocalCompact()** function. **::LocalCompact()** discards all discardable blocks in the local heap, and moves all moveable blocks to the high end of the local heap. This makes the maximum amount of room available in the local heap for allocating a new memory block, but discards every discardable block in the process. Figure 12-10 shows the MEM3 program

```
┌─────────────────────────────────────────────┬───┬───┐
│ ─        Memory Management 3                 │ ▼ │ ▲ │
├─────────────────────────────────────────────┴───┴───┤
│ Squish Memory   Restore Memory   Quit                │
├──────────────────────────────────────────────────────┤
│ Block 0's address = 12306, flags = Discardable       │
│ Block 1's address = 9908, flags = Not discardable    │
│ Block 2's address = 11786, flags = Discardable       │
│ Block 3's address = 10424, flags = Not discardable   │
└──────────────────────────────────────────────────────┘
```

Figure 12-9 The MEM3 Program, Immediately After Startup

489

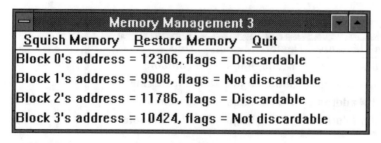

```
┌─────────────────────────────────────────────────────────┐
│ ─        Memory Management 3                  ▼  ▲        │
├─────────────────────────────────────────────────────────┤
│  Squish Memory   Restore Memory   Quit                   │
├─────────────────────────────────────────────────────────┤
│ Block 0's address = 0, flags = Discardable & Discarded   │
│ Block 1's address = 9908, flags = Not discardable        │
│ Block 2's address = 0, flags = Discardable & Discarded   │
│ Block 3's address = 10424, flags = Not discardable       │
└─────────────────────────────────────────────────────────┘
```

Figure 12-10 The MEM3 Program After "Squish Memory" Was Selected

after the "Squish Memory" menu item was selected. Blocks 0 and 2 are discarded, which results in their address being zero (NULL).

The "Restore Memory" menu item in MEM3 reallocates the two discardable blocks, restoring them to their 512-byte size. Figure 12-11 shows the MEM3 program after "Restore Memory" was selected. The discardable blocks end up restored to their original locations in memory.

Figure 12-12 shows a diagram of what Windows did with each of the memory blocks allocated by MEM3. Windows allocated discardable blocks at the high end of the local heap, and nondiscardable blocks at the low (address) end. Blocks 1 and 3 remain at the bottom of the heap when **::LocalCompact()** is called to compress the heap. When **::LocalReAlloc()** is called to restore the two discardable blocks, Windows puts them right back at their original locations at the high end of the heap. Note that these memory locations are specific to Windows 3.1. Windows 3.0 used a different allocation scheme.

Throughout all of these memory movements, the handles of the memory blocks remained the same. Even the discardable memory blocks that were purged from memory and then re-created at new locations retained valid memory handles. As a programmer, you will not normally be concerned with

```
┌─────────────────────────────────────────────────────────┐
│ ─        Memory Management 3                  ▼  ▲        │
├─────────────────────────────────────────────────────────┤
│  Squish Memory   Restore Memory   Quit                   │
├─────────────────────────────────────────────────────────┤
│ Block 0's address = 12306, flags = Discardable           │
│ Block 1's address = 9908, flags = Not discardable        │
│ Block 2's address = 11786, flags = Discardable           │
│ Block 3's address = 10424, flags = Not discardable       │
└─────────────────────────────────────────────────────────┘
```

Figure 12-11 The MEM3 Program After "Restore Memory" Was Selected

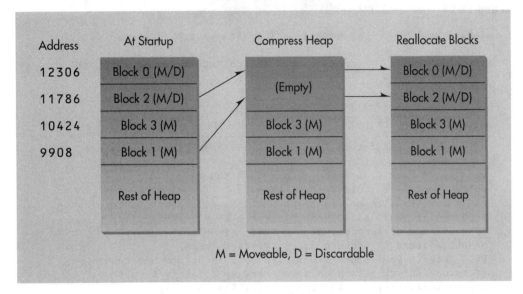

Figure 12-12 Local Heap Organization of MEM3 (Windows 3.1)

the physical address of a memory block. Keeping track of the memory handle is enough to assure access to the block regardless of where it is located.

The MEM3 Program

Listing 12-24 shows the WINMEM3.HPP header file. One of the changes to WINMEM3.HPP is to define as many of the functions inline as possible. This saves space in the WINMEM3.CPP program. There are also several new functions. **CLocalBlock::discard()** discards a memory block by calling **::LocalDiscard()**. **CLocalBlock::getactualsize()** returns the actual size of the allocated block of memory, not the requested size. The actual size may be slightly larger than the requested size returned by **CLocalBlock::getsize()** because Windows allocates local memory in even increments.

The new **CLocalBlock::getflags()** function returns the status of the block. This will be used to determine whether a discardable block has been discarded. **CLocalBlock::getspace()** returns the amount of free space available in the local memory heap by calling **::LocalCompact()**. Note also that the private member *LastFlags* has been added to the **CLocalBlock** class, which is used to store the memory options that are currently in force for the block (such as LMEM_FIXED, etc.). The *LastFlags* value is used within WINMEM3.CPP to determine if a reallocation request is also requesting a new set of memory options.

Listing 12-24 WINMEM3.HPP Header File

```
// winmem3.hpp            header file for winmem3.cpp (for mem3.cpp)

class CLocalBlock        // class for allocating local memory blocks
{
public:
    CLocalBlock (WORD size, WORD flags =
        LMEM_MOVEABLE | LMEM_ZEROINIT) ;
    CLocalBlock () ;            // default constructor - starts 0 bytes
    ~CLocalBlock () {::LocalFree (hMem) ; }    // dispose of block
    // lock block - returns current address
    void near* lock () {return ::LocalLock (hMem) ; }
    void unlock () {::LocalUnlock (hMem) ; }   // unlock block
    // change the size or flags for a block, can resize to zero bytes
    WORD resize (WORD size, WORD flags = LMEM_MOVEABLE) ;
    // discard a discardable block - returns NULL if done
    HANDLE discard () {return ::LocalDiscard (hMem) ; }
    WORD getsize () {return BlockSize ; }   // return block size
    // return actual allocated size - may be slightly larger
    WORD getactualsize () {return ::LocalSize (hMem) ; }
    // get block flags: LMEM_DISCARDED or LMEM_DISCARDABLE in high-
    // order byte, and lock count in low-order byte
    WORD getflags () {return ::LocalFlags (hMem) ; }
    // determine if ReqBytes of room is available in local heap
    // if ReqBytes == 0, returns total available space
    WORD getspace (WORD ReqBytes) {return ::LocalCompact (ReqBytes) ; }
private:
    HANDLE  hMem ;          // handle of the memory block
    WORD    BlockSize ;     // current size allocated
    WORD    LastFlags ;     // remember last flags
} ;
```

Listing 12-25 shows the WINMEM3.CPP program. The biggest change from WINMEM2.CPP is a more substantial **CLocalBlock::resize()** function. **::LocalReAlloc()** will not reliably change the status of a block from one state to another (discardable to moveable, etc.), so it is safer to create a new block if the flag status is changed. The *LastFlags* private data member is used to keep track of the last flag values. If the call to **CLocalBlock::resize()** changes the flags, a new memory block is created using the requested flag settings. The data in the "old" memory block is copied into the new one and then the "old" block is deleted. The result is that the "new" block completely replaces the old one, and has the correct flag settings.

Listing 12-26 shows the MEM3.HPP header file. This time an array of four **CLocalBlock** objects is created as part of the **CMainWindow** class. They all start out with zero bytes of room and with the LMEM_MOVEABLE flag setting.

Listing 12-25 WINMEM3.CPP

```cpp
// winmem3.cpp   Windows memory allocation functions for mem3.cpp

#include <afxwin.h>      // class library header file
#include "winmem3.hpp"   // header file for this program

CLocalBlock::CLocalBlock (WORD size, WORD flags)// normal constructor
{
    LastFlags = flags ;
    hMem = ::LocalAlloc (flags, size) ;
    if (hMem)
        BlockSize = size ;
    else
        BlockSize = 0 ;
}


CLocalBlock::CLocalBlock ()                 // default constructor
{                                           // starts block with 0 bytes
    hMem = ::LocalAlloc (0, LMEM_MOVEABLE) ;
    LastFlags = LMEM_MOVEABLE ;
    BlockSize = 0 ;
}


WORD CLocalBlock::resize (WORD size, WORD flags)// resize block
{                                               // or change flags
    if (flags == LastFlags) // true even if default flags used
    {
        if (size > 0)
            hMem = ::LocalReAlloc (hMem, size, flags) ;
        else
        {                                       // if requesting 0 bytes
            ::LocalFree (hMem) ;                // dispose of old block
            hMem = ::LocalAlloc (flags, 0) ;// allocate new one
        }
    }
    else    // changing flag status - safest to allocate a new block
    {       // and copy data to it, then delete old one.
        HANDLE hNewMem = ::LocalAlloc (flags, size) ;
        if (hNewMem)
        {
            PSTR pDest = (PSTR) ::LocalLock (hNewMem) ;// lock both
            PSTR pSource = (PSTR) ::LocalLock (hMem) ;
                // if sizes differ, copy smaller of two # of bytes
            int nToCopy = (size > BlockSize ? BlockSize : size) ;
            for (int i = 0 ; i < nToCopy ; i++)
                *pDest++ = *pSource++ ;
            ::LocalFree (hMem) ;                // get rid of old block
            ::LocalUnlock (hNewMem) ;
            hMem = hNewMem ;                    // new block now used
            LastFlags = flags ;
        }
    }
```

```
    if (hMem)                          // if no error
        BlockSize = size ;             // return size
    else
        BlockSize = 0 ;                // otherwise return zero
    return BlockSize ;
}
```

Listing 12-26 MEM3.HPP Header File

```
// mem3.hpp     header file for mem3.cpp

class CMainWindow : public CFrameWnd     // derive a main window class
{
public:
    CMainWindow () ;                  // declare a constructor
private:
    CLocalBlock lBlock [4] ;          // array of local memory blocks
    void OnPaint () ;                 // process WM_PAINT
    void OnSquish () ;                // menu items
    void OnRestore () ;
    void OnExit () ;

    DECLARE_MESSAGE_MAP()             // prepare for message processing
} ;

class CTheApp : public CWinApp       // derive an application class
{
public:
    BOOL InitInstance () ;           // declare new InitInstance()
} ;
```

Listing 12-27 shows the MEM3.CPP program file. The array of four **CLocalBlock** objects is initialized in the **CMainWindow** constructor function. All four blocks are set to contain 512 bytes. The first and third blocks are set with LMEM_MOVEABLE | LMEM_DISCARDABLE flags. This takes advantage of the improved **CLocalBlock::resize()** function in WINMEM3.CPP to change flag settings for a block. The second and fourth blocks are set to LMEM_MOVEABLE, which is the default value, so no change in flag settings occurs for these blocks when they are resized to hold 512 bytes.

The address and flag status of each block is displayed by the **CWnd::OnPaint()** logic. The address of a block is known only when it is locked, so **CLocalBlock::lock()** is called to find the address. The flag status of each block is obtained with **CLocalBlock::getflags()**. The combined output string is formatted using the **ostrstream** class and output using **CDC::TextOut()**.

When the user selects the "Squish" menu item, the **CMainWindow::OnSquish()** function is called. Compacting the local memory heap requires two

Listing 12-27 MEM3.CPP

```cpp
// mem3.cpp                       using discardable local memory blocks

#include <afxwin.h>      // class library header file
#include <strstrea.h>    // streams header file
#include "winmem3.hpp"   // header file for Windows memory functions
#include "mem3.h"        // header file for resource data
#include "mem3.hpp"      // header file for this program

CTheApp theApp ;          // create one CTheApp object - runs program

BOOL CTheApp::InitInstance ()    // override default InitInstance()
{
    m_pMainWnd = new CMainWindow () ;        // create a main window
    m_pMainWnd->ShowWindow (m_nCmdShow) ;    // make it visible
    m_pMainWnd->UpdateWindow () ;            // paint center
    return TRUE ;
}

CMainWindow::CMainWindow ()       // constructor for window
{
    CString title ;          // get program caption from resource data
    title.LoadString (S_PROGRAMCAPTION) ;
    Create (NULL, title, WS_OVERLAPPEDWINDOW, rectDefault,
        NULL, "MyMenu") ;
        // initialize the size and flags for the four blocks
    lBlock [0].resize (512, LMEM_MOVEABLE | LMEM_DISCARDABLE) ;
    lBlock [1].resize (512, LMEM_MOVEABLE) ;
    lBlock [2].resize (512, LMEM_MOVEABLE | LMEM_DISCARDABLE) ;
    lBlock [3].resize (512, LMEM_MOVEABLE) ;
}

BEGIN_MESSAGE_MAP (CMainWindow, CFrameWnd)
    ON_WM_PAINT ()
    ON_COMMAND (IDM_SQUISH, OnSquish)   // menu items
    ON_COMMAND (IDM_RESTORE, OnRestore)
    ON_COMMAND (IDM_QUIT, OnExit)
END_MESSAGE_MAP ()

void CMainWindow::OnPaint ()     // window painting function
{
    CPaintDC dc(this) ;          // get client device context
    char cBuf [128] ;            // pre-allocate char buffer on stack
    ostrstream myStream (cBuf, sizeof (cBuf)) ; // ostrstream object

    for (int i = 0 ; i < 4 ; i++)                  // for each block
    {
        myStream << "Block " << i << "'s address = " ;
        PSTR pStr = (PSTR) lBlock [i].lock () ; // lock to get address
        myStream << (WORD) pStr << ", flags = " ;
```

```
            lBlock [i].unlock () ;                   // unlock asap
            WORD wFlags = lBlock [i].getflags () ;   // get flag value
            if (wFlags & LMEM_DISCARDABLE)
                myStream << "Discardable " ;
            if (wFlags & LMEM_DISCARDED)
                myStream << "& Discarded" ;
            if (!(wFlags & (LMEM_DISCARDABLE | LMEM_DISCARDED)))
                myStream << "Not discardable" ;
            dc.TextOut (0, 20 * i, cBuf, myStream.pcount ()) ;
            myStream.seekp (0) ;     // move back to beginning of buffer
        }
    }

    void CMainWindow::OnSquish ()    // respond to "Squish" menu item
    {
        WORD FreeSpace = lBlock [0].getspace (0) ;  // get current space
        lBlock [0].getspace (FreeSpace + 500) ;     // force compacting
        this->Invalidate () ;
    }

    void CMainWindow::OnRestore ()   // respond to "Restore" menu item
    {
        lBlock [0].resize (512, LMEM_MOVEABLE | LMEM_DISCARDABLE) ;
        lBlock [2].resize (512, LMEM_MOVEABLE | LMEM_DISCARDABLE) ;
        this->Invalidate () ;        // force repainting
    }

    void CMainWindow::OnExit ()      // respond to menu item "Quit"
    {
        this->DestroyWindow () ;     // destroy main window,
    }                                // this stops application
```

calls to **CLocalBlock::getspace()**. The first time, a value of zero is passed to the function, causing **CLocalBlock::getspace()** to return the total amount of free memory in the local heap. The second call to **CLocalBlock::getspace()** requests 500 bytes more than the room available. This causes Windows to discard memory blocks in an effort to make more room available. The result is that the two discardable blocks are discarded.

When the "Restore" menu item is selected, the two discardable memory blocks are resized back to 512 bytes with no change in flag status. This gets all four of the blocks back to the startup condition of holding 512 bytes each. Note in all of these changes that the handles of all four memory blocks remained the same. The handles remained constant as the blocks were moved, discarded, and restored.

Listings 12-28 to 12-30 show the remaining files for MEM3. The program's icon is shown in Figure 12-13. Note that the HEAPSIZE value in MEM3.DEF (Listing 12-30) has been set to 4096 bytes to allow plenty of room for the four blocks. Be sure to include WINMEM3.CPP in the project file when compiling MEM3.CPP.

Listing 12-28 MEM3.RC Resource Script File

```
// mem3.rc   resource script file

#include <afxres.h>
#include "mem3.h"

AFX_IDI_STD_FRAME   ICON    mem3.ico    // the program's icon

MyMenu MENU                             // define the menu
{
    MENUITEM "&Squish Memory",  IDM_SQUISH
    MENUITEM "&Restore Memory", IDM_RESTORE
    MENUITEM "&Quit",           IDM_QUIT
}

STRINGTABLE
{
    S_PROGRAMCAPTION    "Memory Management 3"
}
```

Listing 12-29 MEM3.H Resource ID Header File

```
// mem3.h   header file for resource ID numbers

#define IDM_SQUISH          1       // menu item IDs
#define IDM_RESTORE         2
#define IDM_QUIT            3

#define S_PROGRAMCAPTION    1       // string table ID
```

Note that the HEAPSIZE entry in MEM3.DEF (Listing 12-30) has been increased to 4096 bytes to make room for the local memory blocks. One of

Listing 12-30 MEM3.DEF Module Definition File

```
NAME            mem3
DESCRIPTION     'mem3 C++ program'
EXETYPE         WINDOWS
STUB            'WINSTUB.EXE'
CODE            PRELOAD MOVEABLE
DATA            PRELOAD MOVEABLE MULTIPLE
HEAPSIZE        4096
STACKSIZE       5120
```

Figure 12-13 MEM3.ICO Icon Image

the exercises at the end of this chapter experiments with decreasing the HEAPSIZE value.

GLOBAL MEMORY ALLOCATION

So far we have been looking only at allocation of memory blocks in the local heap. It may be a pleasant surprise to find out that allocating blocks in the global memory area is done in exactly the same way. Windows has a parallel set of functions for global memory allocation that have the function names changed from "Local" to "Global." Table 12-3 summarizes the key memory allocation functions.

One of the global memory functions should look a bit familiar, because the ::**GlobalUnlock**() function was used in Chapter 11, *Other Resources*, to unlock resource data. Resource data is stored in the global memory area and resources have similar functions for loading and locking memory blocks (for example, ::**LoadResource**() and ::**LockResource**(), which are used for custom resource data).

The main difference you will need to remember between local and global memory blocks is that global memory blocks are not all in the same data segment and, therefore, must use *far* pointers to memory. A typical program excerpt is shown in Listing 12-31 that allocates 64 bytes of global memory and copies character data to it.

Local Block	Global Block	Purpose
::LocalAlloc()	::GlobalAlloc()	Allocate a memory block.
::LocalLock()	::GlobalLock()	Lock a memory block, return its address.
::LocalUnlock()	::GlobalUnlock()	Unlock a memory block.
::LocalFree()	::GlobalFree()	Free a memory block, return space to system.
::LocalFlags()	::GlobalFlags()	Determine if a block is discardable, or already discarded.
::LocalReAlloc()	::GlobalReAlloc()	Change the size of a memory block.
::LocalDiscard()	::GlobalDiscard()	Discard a discardable memory block.
::LocalCompact()	::GlobalCompact()	Determine the amount of memory space available, optionally moving and discarding memory blocks to make room.

Table 12-3 Memory Allocation Functions

Listing 12-31 Allocating a Global Memory Block

```
HANDLE hgMem = ::GlobalAlloc (GMEM_MOVEABLE, 64) ;
if (hgMem)
{
    LPSTR lpStr = (LPSTR) ::GlobalLock (hgMem) ;
    ::lstrcpy (lpStr, "Some data here.") ;
    ::GlobalUnlock (hgMem) ;
}
```

Global memory blocks are tracked using handles just as with local memory blocks. There is no obvious difference between a handle for a local block and a handle for a global one, so it is a good idea to use a variable name for global handles that contains a "g" or some other marker that makes it obvious to what type of object the handle refers. Also note that the pointer to the character data is a *far* pointer (LPSTR == "char far *" in WINDOWS.H), because the **::GlobalLock()** function returns a pointer to far memory. One final difference between local and global memory allocation is that the **::GlobalAlloc()** function's memory flags start with "GMEM" instead of the "LMEM" flags used by **::LocalAlloc()**. Table 12-4 summarizes the most common global memory flags.

When the program needs to access the data in the memory block, the block is locked with **::GlobalLock()**, which returns the address of the locked data. Listing 12-32 shows an example.

Flag	Meaning
GMEM_DISCARDABLE	Allocates memory that can be discarded if Windows needs to make room. Used only with GMEM_MOVEABLE.
GMEM_FIXED	Allocates fixed memory. Do not use this unless absolutely necessary. Fixed memory limits Windows' ability to optimize memory use.
GMEM_MOVEABLE	Allocates moveable memory.
GMEM_NOCOMPACT	Allocates memory in the global heap that is not moved to make room for new memory blocks.
GMEM_NODISCARD	Allocates nondiscardable memory in the global heap.
GMEM_ZEROINIT	Initialize the new allocated memory block contents to zero.

Table 12-4 Global Memory Flags

Listing 12-32 Accessing a Global Block

```
char        cBuf [64] ;

LPSTR lpStr = (LPSTR) ::GlobalLock (hgMem) ;
::lstrcpy (cBuf, lpStr) ;
::GlobalUnlock (hgMem) ;
```

You can change the size of a global memory block using the **::GlobalRe-Alloc()** function as the program operates. For example, to increase the size of the global block to 128 bytes, you would use the following code:

```
::GlobalReAlloc (hgMem, 128, GMEM_MOVEABLE) ;
```

Increasing the size of a global memory block does not affect the data already stored in the block. Decreasing the size of the block causes any data in the end of the block to be lost, but does not affect the data in the portion of the block that remains after resizing. When the memory block is no longer needed, **::Global-Free()** is used to remove it from memory, freeing Windows to use the block for other purposes. The handle becomes invalid after **::GlobalFree()** is called.

```
::GlobalFree (hMem) ;
```

Global memory blocks can also be allocated with the GMEM_DISCARDABLE flag set, which allows Windows to discard the block if it cannot make enough room in the global memory area for a new program or data by simply moving global objects. This option is demonstrated in the next program example.

A Global Memory Class

The Windows global memory functions are so similar to the local memory functions that we can essentially duplicate the **CLocalBlock** class developed in the previous examples. The final versions of these functions are in the files WINMEM.HPP and WINMEM.CPP, and will be used in the remaining chapters in this book when memory allocation is required. Besides adding a set of global memory block functions, WINMEM.CPP includes a number of overloaded operators that make it easy to do common activities such as copying data into the block.

Listing 12-33 shows the WINMEM.HPP header file, which is by far the longest header file in this book. The first thing you may notice is the interesting line: #ifndef WINMEM_H. The #ifndef directive means "if not defined" to the C++ compiler. The purpose of this line is to avoid having the compiler read the same header file more than once. This is a possibility with a general-purpose header file like WINMEM.HPP, which might be included in a number of program files used to build one large application. The #ifndef WINMEM_H line instructs the

Listing 12-33 WINMEM.HPP Header File

```
// winmem.hpp              Windows memory allocation functions

#ifndef WINMEM_H          // don't allow file to be included more
#define WINMEM_H          // than one time in a compilation

class CLocalBlock   // class for allocating local memory blocks
{
public:                   // flags defaults to moveable & zero initialized
    CLocalBlock (WORD size,
        WORD flags = LMEM_MOVEABLE | LMEM_ZEROINIT,
        BOOL IsPermanent = FALSE) ;
    CLocalBlock () ;          // default constructor - starts 0 bytes
    ~CLocalBlock ()  ;        // destructor to dispose of block
    // lock block - returns current address
    void near * lock () {return ::LocalLock (hMem) ; }
    void unlock () {::LocalUnlock (hMem) ; }     // unlock block
    // change the size or flags for a block, can resize to zero bytes
    WORD resize (WORD size, WORD flags = LMEM_MOVEABLE,
        BOOL IsPermanent = FALSE) ;
    // discard a discardable block - returns NULL if done
    HANDLE discard () {return ::LocalDiscard (hMem) ; }
    WORD getsize () {return BlockSize ; }   // return block size
    // return actual allocated size - may be slightly larger
    WORD getactualsize () {return ::LocalSize (hMem) ; }
    // get block flags: LMEM_DISCARDED or LMEM_DISCARDABLE in high-
    // order byte, and lock count in low-order byte
    WORD getflags () {return ::LocalFlags (hMem) ; }
    // get flags block was created or resized with (LMEM_MOVEABLE...)
    WORD getstartflags () {return LastFlags ; }
    // determine if ReqBytes of room is available in local heap
    // if ReqBytes == 0, returns total available space
    WORD getspace (WORD ReqBytes)
        {return ::LocalCompact (ReqBytes) ; }
    HANDLE gethandle () {return hMem ; }     // return block's handle
    void sethandle (HANDLE hLmem, BOOL IsPermanent = FALSE) ;
    void free () ;                           // free the memory block
    // copy block contents to buffer pointed to by lpStr
    WORD BlockToBuf (PSTR pStr, WORD Bytes) ;
    // overload = operator to copy beteen memory areas
    CLocalBlock& operator = (CLocalBlock&) ;    // between two blocks
    CLocalBlock& operator = (PSTR) ;         // from a pointer address
    CLocalBlock& operator = (CString) ;      // from CString to block
    // overload << operator to append to a memory block
    CLocalBlock& operator << (CLocalBlock&) ;   // between two blocks
    CLocalBlock& operator << (PSTR) ;        // from pointer address
    CLocalBlock& operator << (CString) ;     // from CStTring to block
protected:
    HANDLE   hMem ;           // handle of the memory block
    WORD     BlockSize ;      // current size allocated
    WORD     LastFlags ;      // remember last flags
```

```
        BOOL    Permanence ;      // true if handle should remain valid
    } ;                           // after CLocalBlock object is destroyed

    class CGlobalBlock        // class for allocating global memory blocks
    {
    public:                   // flags defaults to moveable & zero initialized
        CGlobalBlock (DWORD size,
            WORD flags = GMEM_MOVEABLE | GMEM_ZEROINIT,
            BOOL IsPermanent = FALSE) ;
        CGlobalBlock () ;         // default constructor - starts 0 bytes
        ~CGlobalBlock () ;        // destructor to dispose of block
        // lock block - returns current address
        void far * lock () {return ::GlobalLock (hMem) ; }
        void unlock () {::GlobalUnlock (hMem) ; }// unlock block
        // change the size or flags for a block, can resize to zero bytes
        DWORD resize (DWORD size, WORD flags = GMEM_MOVEABLE,
            BOOL IsPermanent = FALSE) ;
        // discard a discardable block - returns NULL if done
        HANDLE discard () {return ::GlobalDiscard (hMem) ; }
        DWORD getsize () {return BlockSize ; }    // return block size
        // return actual allocated size - may be slightly larger
        DWORD getactualsize () {return ::GlobalSize (hMem) ; }
        // get block flags: GMEM_DISCARDED or GMEM_DISCARDABLE in high-
        // order byte, and lock count in low-order byte
        WORD getflags () {return ::GlobalFlags (hMem) ; }
        // get flags block was created or resized with (LMEM_MOVEABLE...)
        WORD getstartflags () {return LastFlags ; }
        // determine if ReqBytes of room is available in local heap
        // if ReqBytes == 0, returns total available space
        DWORD getspace (DWORD ReqBytes)
            {return ::GlobalCompact (ReqBytes) ; }
        HANDLE gethandle () {return hMem ; }    // return block's handle
        // attach an existing global block handle to a CGlobalBlock object
        void sethandle (HANDLE hGmem, BOOL IsPermanent = FALSE) ;
        void free () ;                          // free the block ;
        // copy block contents to buffer pointed to by lpStr
        DWORD BlockToBuf (LPSTR lpStr, DWORD Bytes) ;
        // overload = operator to copy beteen memory areas
        CGlobalBlock& operator = (CGlobalBlock&) ;  // between two blocks
        CGlobalBlock& operator = (LPSTR) ;          // from a pointer address
        CGlobalBlock& operator = (CString) ;        // from CString to block
        // overload << operator to append to a memory block
        CGlobalBlock& operator << (CGlobalBlock&) ; // between two blocks
        CGlobalBlock& operator << (LPSTR) ;         // from pointer address
        CGlobalBlock& operator << (CString) ;       // from CString to block
    protected:
        HANDLE  hMem ;            // handle of the memory block
        DWORD   BlockSize ;       // current size allocated
        WORD    LastFlags ;       // remember last flags
        BOOL    Permanence ;//  TRUE if global handle should remain valid
    } ;                           // after CGlobalBlock has been destroyed

    #endif // WINMEM_H
```

compiler to proceed with reading the section up to the #endif line at the bottom of WINMEM.HPP *only* if the constant WINMEM_H is not defined. The next line immediately defines the WINMEM_H constant, so WINMEM_H is known to the compiler after the first time WINMEM.HPP is read. Any subsequent attempts to include WINMEM.HPP will not slow the compiler down or cause errors because the entire body of the file will be skipped when the compiler encounters the next #ifndef WINMEM_H line. Including conditional instructions is a common practice for all C++ header files.

The **CLocalBlock** and **CGlobalBlock** class definitions are essentially identical. The differences boil down to a few simple things (for example, global functions use *far* pointers, while the local functions use *near* pointers). We will focus on the **CGlobalBlock** class to describe the changes to the class definition, but all of the comments apply to the **CLocalBlock** class.

One important change is that the **CGlobalBlock** constructor function now includes a third parameter named *IsPermanent*. The reason for this parameter is that there are situations where you do not want the memory block to be destroyed when the **CGlobalBlock** object is destroyed. We will run into situations where we need to create permanent memory blocks to pass data to the Windows Clipboard and to edit controls. Normally, you will want the block to be removed from memory when the **CGlobalBlock** object is destroyed, so you can take advantage of the default value of FALSE for the *IsPermanent* parameter. All together there are four ways to create a **CGlobalBlock** object:

```
CGlobalBlock gBlock() ;      // default to 0 bytes, moveable
CGlobalBlock gBlock (100) ; // defaults to moveable/zero init
CGlobalBlock gBlock (100, GMEM_FIXED) ; // specify size & fixed

    // specify a 100 byte moveable block that is "permanent"
CGlobalBlock gBlock (100, GMEM_MOVEABLE, TRUE) ;
```

If you look at the bottom of WINMEM.HPP, you will see that a BOOL variable named *Permanence* has been added to track whether or not the block should remain in memory after the **CGlobalBlock** is destroyed.

The **CLocalBlock** and **CGlobalBlock** classes provide a number of functions and overloaded operators for copying and appending data to a block in memory. The assignment operator (=) is overloaded to copy data from another block, a character buffer, or a **CString** object into a memory block. The following three lines demonstrate uses of the assignment operator. The memory block is automatically resized to hold the new data when the new data is copied into the block. Any existing contents of the block are destroyed.

```
Block1 = Block2 ;  // Block2 contents are copied into Block 1
Block1 = "This is data" ;  // character data copied into block
Block1 = StringObject ;     // CString contents copied into block
```

Similarly, the **CLocalBlock** and **CGlobalBlock** classes overload the left shift operator (<<) to provide a simple way to copy data onto the end of the existing data stored in a memory block (concatenation). In the case of character data, the existing data in the block is assumed to contain a terminal null character, which is overwritten by the first character of the added data. This keeps the character data in the combined block null terminated, without having a null character stuck in the middle of the data.

```
Block1 << Block2 ;  // Block2 contents appended on Block 1
Block1 << "This is data" ;  // character data appended
Block1 << StringObject ;    // CString contents appended
```

Another useful function in both the **CLocalBlock** and **CGlobalBlock** functions is **BlockToBuf()**. **BlockToBuf()** copies a specified number of bytes from the memory block to an address specified by a pointer. This is not as elegant as the overloaded assignment and left shift operators, but can come in handy. Unlike the overloaded operators, there is no protection in **BlockToBuf()** from possibly copying more bytes from the memory block than the destination buffer will contain.

Listing 12-34 shows the WINMEM.CPP program. Many of these functions are copied directly from the WINMEM3.CPP program earlier in the chapter (Listing 12-25). The *Permanence* flag has been added to a number of functions to keep track of blocks where the memory block should not be deleted when the **CLocalBlock** or **CGlobalBlock** object is deleted.

The most interesting functions to review are the overloaded assignment and left shift operators. The assignment operator (=) is used to copy data into a block, with an analogy to using the assignment operator to copy a predefined type, such as an integer variable. The left shift operator (<<) is used to add new data to the end of a block, with an analogy to C++ stream operations. You could also use the addition operator (+) for adding data to the end of a block if that seems more intuitive. The overloaded operators do not use any new Windows memory management functions, but do exercise the C++ language. Note that all of the overloaded operators return "themselves." That is, you will find the line

```
return *this ;
```

as the termination of each of the overloaded operators. A particularly subtle example of this occurs in the two assignment operators that copy from a **CString** object into a memory buffer. This operation is done with a single line of code:

```
return *this = (PSTR) (const char *) string ;
```

Breaking this up into pieces, the (const char *) cast is defined in the **CString** class and causes the **CString** object to return a pointer to the string's character data. This pointer is then cast to a PSTR, a *near* pointer to a character string.

Listing 12-34 WINMEM.CPP

```cpp
// winmem.cpp    Windows memory allocation functions

#include <afxwin.h>     // class library header file
#include "winmem.hpp"   // header file for this program

                        // normal constructor
CLocalBlock::CLocalBlock (WORD size, WORD flags, BOOL IsPermanent)
{
    LastFlags = flags ;
    Permanence = IsPermanent ;
    hMem = ::LocalAlloc (flags, size) ;
    if (hMem)
        BlockSize = size ;
    else
        BlockSize = 0 ;
}


CLocalBlock::CLocalBlock ()             // default constructor
{                                       // starts block with 0 bytes
    hMem = ::LocalAlloc (0, LMEM_MOVEABLE) ;
    LastFlags = LMEM_MOVEABLE ;         // default is a moveable
    BlockSize = 0 ;                     // block that cleans up
    Permanence = FALSE ;                // memory when the object is
}                                       // deleted (not permanent)


CLocalBlock::~CLocalBlock ()            // destructor
{
    if (!Permanence)                    // if permanence flag FALSE
        ::LocalFree (hMem) ;            // free the block when the
}                                       // object goes out of scope

WORD CLocalBlock::resize (WORD size, WORD flags, BOOL IsPermanent)
{
    if (flags == LastFlags || flags & LMEM_FIXED)
    {
        if (size > 0)
            hMem = ::LocalReAlloc (hMem, size, flags) ;
        else
        {                                       // if requesting 0 bytes
            ::LocalFree (hMem) ;        // dispose of old block
            hMem = ::LocalAlloc (flags, 0) ;  // allocate new one
        }
    }
    else    // changing flag status - safest to allocate new block
    {       // and copy data to it, then delete old one.
        HANDLE hNewMem = ::LocalAlloc (flags, size) ;
        if (hNewMem)
        {
            PSTR pDest = (PSTR) ::LocalLock (hNewMem) ;// lock both
```

```
            PSTR pSource = (PSTR) ::LocalLock (hMem) ;
                // if sizes differ, copy smaller of two # of bytes
            int nToCopy = (size > BlockSize ? BlockSize : size) ;
            for (int i = 0 ; i < nToCopy ; i++)
                *pDest++ = *pSource++ ;
            ::LocalFree (hMem) ;          // get rid of old block
            ::LocalUnlock (hNewMem) ;
            hMem = hNewMem ;              // new block now used
            LastFlags = flags ;
        }
    }
    if (hMem)                            // if no error
    {
        Permanence = IsPermanent ;
        BlockSize = size ;               // return size
    }
    else
        BlockSize = 0 ;                  // otherwise return zero
    return BlockSize ;
}


    // attach an existing local block handle to a CLocalBlock object
void CLocalBlock::sethandle (HANDLE hLmem, BOOL IsPermanent)
{
    if (!hLmem)
        return ;
    if (!Permanence)
        ::LocalFree (hMem) ;             // get rid of old block
    hMem = hLmem ;                       // set hMem = new block
    BlockSize = ::LocalSize (hMem) ;     // initialize values
    LastFlags = ::LocalFlags (hMem) ;
    Permanence = IsPermanent ;
}


void CLocalBlock::free ()                // free the memory block
{
    ::LocalFree (hMem) ;
    hMem = ::LocalAlloc (0, LMEM_MOVEABLE) ;// create new 0 byte long
    LastFlags = LMEM_MOVEABLE ;          // block to retain integrity
    BlockSize = 0 ;                      // of the object
}
            // copy block contents to buffer pointed to by lpStr
WORD CLocalBlock::BlockToBuf (PSTR pStr, WORD Bytes)
{           // can't copy more bytes than are in block, so check
    WORD ToCopy = (Bytes > BlockSize ? BlockSize : Bytes) ;
    PSTR pSource = (PSTR) ::LocalLock (hMem) ;
    for (WORD i = 0 ; i < ToCopy ; i++)
        *pStr++ = *pSource++ ;
    ::LocalUnlock (hMem) ;
    return ToCopy ;
}
```

```
                   // overload = operator, copying one block to another
CLocalBlock& CLocalBlock::operator = (CLocalBlock& Source)
{
    int Size = Source.getsize () ;              // get source size
    WORD Flags = Source.getstartflags () ;   // and source mem flags
    this->resize (Size, Flags, Permanence) ;// make dest block match
    int i = 0 ;
    PSTR pDest = (PSTR) this->lock () ;
    PSTR pSource = (PSTR) Source.lock () ;   // copy bytes to dest
    if (pDest == NULL || pSource == NULL)
        return *this ;
    while (i++ < Size)
        *pDest++ = *pSource++ ;
    this->unlock () ;                            // decrement lock counts
    Source.unlock () ;
    return *this ;
}
        // overload = operator, copy string from address to block
CLocalBlock& CLocalBlock::operator = (PSTR pSource)
{
    WORD Size = lstrlen (pSource) ;        // find source length
    this->resize (Size + 1, LastFlags, Permanence) ;// resize block
    PSTR pDest = (PSTR) this->lock () ; // lock block
    if (pDest == NULL || pSource == NULL)   // return on error
        return *this ;
    lstrcpy (pDest, pSource) ;               // copy bytes
    *(pDest + Size) = 0 ;                    // null terminate
    this->unlock () ;                        // decrement lock count
    return *this ;
}
        // overload = operator, copy CString to a block
CLocalBlock& CLocalBlock::operator = (CString string)
{
    return *this = (PSTR) (const char *) string ;
}
        // overload << operator, append one block to end of another
CLocalBlock& CLocalBlock::operator << (CLocalBlock& Source)
{
    int SSize = Source.getsize () ;       // resize dest to hold sum
    int DSize = this->getsize () ;        // of source and dest
    this->resize (SSize + DSize, LastFlags, Permanence) ;
    int i = 0 ;
    PSTR pSource = (PSTR) Source.lock () ;   // lock both blocks
    PSTR pDest = (PSTR) this->lock () ;
    if (pDest == NULL || pSource == NULL)    // return on error
        return *this ;
    pDest += DSize ;                             // move to end of block
    while (i++ < SSize)
        *pDest++ = *pSource++ ;                  // copy bytes
    Source.unlock () ;                           // decrement lock counts
    this->unlock () ;
    return *this ;
}
```

```
                   // overload << operator, append string to end of a block
CLocalBlock& CLocalBlock::operator << (PSTR pSource)
{
    int SSize = lstrlen (pSource) ;        // resize dest to hold sum
    int DSize = this->getsize () ;         // of source and dest
    this->resize (SSize + DSize, LastFlags, Permanence) ;
    int i = 0 ;
    PSTR pDest = (PSTR) this->lock () ; // lock destination block
    if (pDest == NULL)                     // return on error
        return *this ;
    pDest += DSize - 1 ;                   // move to end of block
    while (i++ < SSize)                    // (-1 to write over null)
        *pDest++ = *pSource++ ;            // copy bytes
    *pDest = 0 ;                           // add terminal null
    this->unlock () ;
    return *this ;
}
                   // overload << operator, append CString to end of a block
CLocalBlock& CLocalBlock::operator << (CString string)
{
    return *this << (PSTR) (const char *) string ;
}

// ----------------- Global block section ------------------- //

                                            // normal constructor
CGlobalBlock::CGlobalBlock (DWORD size, WORD flags,
    BOOL IsPermanent)
{
    LastFlags = flags ;
    Permanence = IsPermanent ;
    hMem = ::GlobalAlloc (flags, size) ;
    if (hMem)
        BlockSize = size ;
    else
        BlockSize = 0 ;
}

CGlobalBlock::CGlobalBlock ()              // default constructor
{                                          // starts block with 0 bytes
    hMem = ::GlobalAlloc (0, LMEM_MOVEABLE) ;
    LastFlags = LMEM_MOVEABLE ;            // default is moveable
    BlockSize = 0 ;                        // block that cleans up
    Permanence = FALSE ;                   // memory when object is
}                                          // deleted (not permanent)

CGlobalBlock::~CGlobalBlock ()             // destructor
{
    if (!Permanence)                       // if permanence flag FALSE
        ::GlobalFree (hMem) ;              // free the block when the
}                                          // object goes out of scope
```

```cpp
DWORD CGlobalBlock::resize (DWORD size, WORD flags,
    BOOL IsPermanent)
{
    if (flags == LastFlags || flags & GMEM_FIXED)
    {
        if (size > 0)
            hMem = ::GlobalReAlloc (hMem, size, flags) ;
        else
        {                                   // if requesting 0 byte
            ::GlobalFree (hMem) ;           // dispose of old block
            hMem = ::GlobalAlloc (flags, 0) ; // allocate new one
        }
    }
    else    // changing flag status - safest to allocate a new block
    {       // and copy data to it, then delete old one.
        HANDLE hNewMem = ::GlobalAlloc (flags, size) ;
        if (hNewMem)
        {                                   // lock both
            LPSTR pDest = (LPSTR) ::GlobalLock (hNewMem) ;
            LPSTR pSource = (LPSTR) ::GlobalLock (hMem) ;
                // if sizes differ, copy smaller of two # of bytes
            DWORD ToCopy = (size > BlockSize ? BlockSize : size) ;
            for (DWORD i = 0 ; i < ToCopy ; i++)
                *pDest++ = *pSource++ ;
            ::GlobalFree (hMem) ;           // get rid of old block
            ::GlobalUnlock (hNewMem) ;
            hMem = hNewMem ;                // new block now used
            LastFlags = flags ;
        }
    }
    if (hMem)                               // if no error
    {
        Permanence = IsPermanent ;
        BlockSize = size ;                  // return size
    }
    else
        BlockSize = 0 ;                     // otherwise return zero
    return BlockSize ;
}

void CGlobalBlock::free ()                  // free the memory block
{
    ::GlobalFree (hMem) ;                   // frees even if "permenent"
    hMem = ::GlobalAlloc (0, GMEM_MOVEABLE) ; // create new 0 byte
    LastFlags = GMEM_MOVEABLE ;             // block to retain integrity
    BlockSize = 0 ;                         // of the object
    Permanence = FALSE ;
}

// attach an existing global block handle to a CGlobalBlock object
void CGlobalBlock::sethandle (HANDLE hGmem, BOOL IsPermanent)
```

```
{
    if (!hGmem)
        return ;
    if (!Permanence)
        ::GlobalFree (hMem) ;                // get rid of old block
    hMem = hGmem ;
    BlockSize = ::GlobalSize (hMem) ;
    LastFlags = ::GlobalFlags (hMem) ;
    Permanence = IsPermanent ;
}
                // copy block contents to buffer pointed to by lpStr
DWORD CGlobalBlock::BlockToBuf (LPSTR lpStr, DWORD Bytes)
{               // can't copy more bytes than are in block, so check
    DWORD dwToCopy = (Bytes > BlockSize ? BlockSize : Bytes) ;
    LPSTR lpSource = (LPSTR) ::GlobalLock (hMem) ;
    for (DWORD i = 0 ; i < dwToCopy ; i++)
        *lpStr++ = *lpSource++ ;
    ::GlobalUnlock (hMem) ;
    return dwToCopy ;
}

        // overload = operator, copying one block to another
CGlobalBlock& CGlobalBlock::operator = (CGlobalBlock& Source)
{
    DWORD Size = Source.getsize () ;        // get source size
    WORD Flags = Source.getstartflags () ;  // and source mem flags
    this->resize (Size, Flags, Permanence) ;// make dest block match
    DWORD dw = 0 ;
    LPSTR lpDest = (LPSTR) this->lock () ;
    LPSTR lpSource = (LPSTR) Source.lock () ;
    while (dw++ < Size)
        *lpDest++ = *lpSource++ ;            // copy bytes to dest
    this->unlock () ;                        // decrement lock counts
    Source.unlock () ;
    return *this ;
}

        // overload = operator, copy from pointer address to block
CGlobalBlock& CGlobalBlock::operator = (LPSTR lpSource)
{
    DWORD Size = lstrlen (lpSource) ;    // find source length
    this->resize (Size + 1, LastFlags, Permanence) ;// resize block
    LPSTR lpDest = (LPSTR) this->lock () ; // lock block
    lstrcpy (lpDest, lpSource) ;           // copy bytes
    *(lpDest + Size) = 0 ;                 // null terminate
    this->unlock () ;                      // decrement lock count
    return *this ;
}

        // overload = operator, copy from CString to block
CGlobalBlock& CGlobalBlock::operator = (CString string)
{
    return *this = (LPSTR) (const char *) string ;
}
```

```
        // overload << operator, append one block to end of another
CGlobalBlock& CGlobalBlock::operator << (CGlobalBlock& Source)
{
    DWORD SSize = Source.getsize () ;    // resize dest to hold sum
    DWORD DSize = this->getsize () ;     // of source and dest
    this->resize (SSize + DSize, LastFlags, Permanence) ;
    DWORD i = 0 ;
    LPSTR pSource = (LPSTR) Source.lock () ;// lock both blocks
    LPSTR pDest = (LPSTR) this->lock () ;
    if (pDest == NULL || pSource == NULL)   // return on error
        return *this ;
    pDest += DSize ;                        // move to end of block
    while (i++ < SSize)
        *pDest++ = *pSource++ ;             // copy bytes
    Source.unlock () ;                      // decrement lock counts
    this->unlock () ;
    return *this ;
}

        // overload << operator, append string to end of a block
CGlobalBlock& CGlobalBlock::operator << (LPSTR pSource)
{
    DWORD SSize = lstrlen (pSource) ;    // resize dest to hold sum
    DWORD DSize = this->getsize () ;     // of source and dest
    this->resize (SSize + DSize, LastFlags, Permanence) ;
    DWORD i = 0 ;
    LPSTR pDest = (LPSTR) this->lock () // lock destination block
    if (pDest == NULL)                  // return on error
        return *this ;
    pDest += DSize - 1 ;                // move to end of block
    while (i++ < SSize)                 // (-1 to write over null)
        *pDest++ = *pSource++ ;         // copy bytes
    *pDest = 0 ;                        // add terminal null
    this->unlock () ;
    return *this ;
}
        // overload << operator, append CString to end of block
CGlobalBlock& CGlobalBlock::operator << (CString string)
{
    return *this << (LPSTR) (const char *) string ;
}
```

The portion *this = takes advantage of the fact that the assignment operator for copying string data into a memory buffer is already defined as part of the **CGlobalBlock** class. In other words, the line of code is just calling another member function of the class.

We will not use all of the functions in the **CGlobalBlock** and **CLocalBlock** classes in this chapter. However, the WINMEM files will be included in a number of example programs throughout the remainder of the book to take care of the low-level details of managing blocks of memory.

An Example Allocating Global Memory Blocks

The last example program in this chapter, GMEM1, demonstrates a number of global memory options. GMEM1 is identical to the previous example program (MEM3) except that GMEM1 exclusively uses global memory blocks created with the **CGlobalBlock** class in WINMEM.CPP. This provides an interesting contrast between the address values used for local and global memory. Figure 12-14 shows the GMEM1 program in action, having allocated four global memory blocks each 1,024 bytes long. The first thing you may notice is the size of the address values. They are far address values, shown here in decimal notation (not hexadecimal). If you take the time to convert these addresses to hexadecimal, you will find that each address points to the beginning of a separate segment. For example, the block 0 address in hexadecimal is 0x24CF0000. Global memory blocks are always allocated as individual segments in memory.

If the user selects the "Squish Memory" menu item, GMEM1 uses the **CGlobalBlock::getspace()** function (which calls the Windows **::GlobalCompact()** function) to compact the global heap. This takes a second or more, depending on the amount of memory in the system and the speed of the computer. Figure 12-15 shows the result, with blocks 0 and 2 discarded.

Selecting the "Restore Memory" menu item causes the two discarded memory blocks to be restored, using the **CGlobalBlock::resize()** function to pump blocks 0 and 2 back up to 1,024 bytes of room. Figure 12-16 shows the result. Windows takes a shortcut, and reallocates the 1,024 bytes for

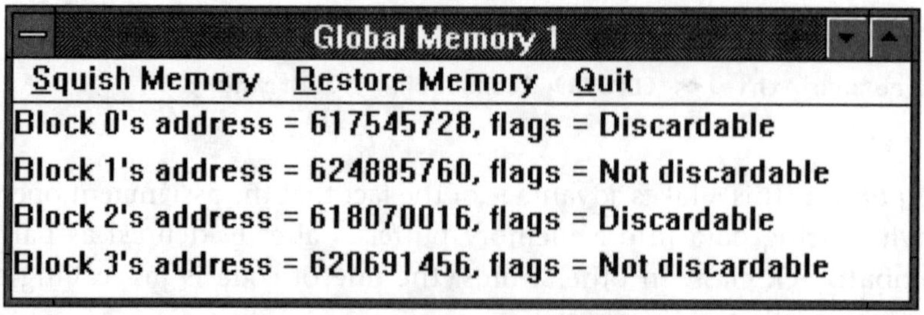

```
┌─────────────────────────────────────────────────┐
│ ─            Global Memory 1              ▼  ▲  │
├─────────────────────────────────────────────────┤
│ Squish Memory   Restore Memory   Quit           │
├─────────────────────────────────────────────────┤
│ Block 0's address = 617545728, flags = Discardable      │
│ Block 1's address = 624885760, flags = Not discardable  │
│ Block 2's address = 618070016, flags = Discardable      │
│ Block 3's address = 620691456, flags = Not discardable  │
└─────────────────────────────────────────────────┘
```

Figure 12-14 The GMEM1 Program at Startup

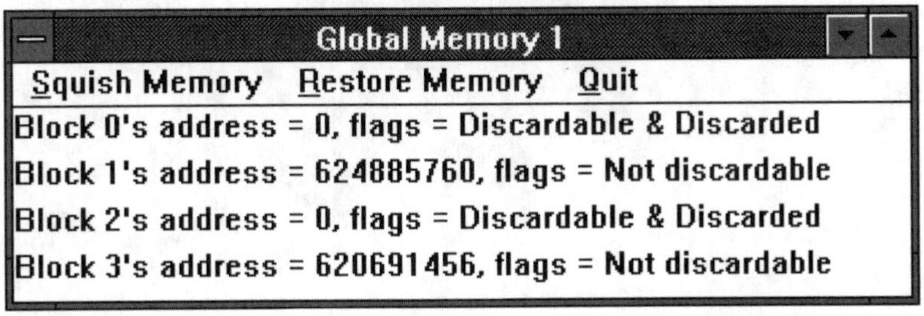

Global Memory 1

Squish Memory   Restore Memory   Quit

Block 0's address = 0, flags = Discardable & Discarded

Block 1's address = 624885760, flags = Not discardable

Block 2's address = 0, flags = Discardable & Discarded

Block 3's address = 620691456, flags = Not discardable

Figure 12-15 The GMEM1 Program After Selecting "Squish Memory"

blocks 0 and 2 back at their old memory locations. They happen to be free in the example, because compressing the global heap moved other objects lower in memory, leaving the old positions of blocks 0 and 2 still available in memory. If another program, or more data, were loaded into memory before the "Restore Memory" menu item was selected, Windows would have needed to find a new address for one or both of the two reallocated blocks.

Figure 12-17 shows a rough impression of what is happening to the global heap as GMEM1 compresses the global memory space, and then re-creates the two discardable memory blocks. Compressing the global heap results in all discardable objects being discarded, which will include all of the resources that programs have loaded, in addition to the two discardable blocks that GMEM1 allocates. When the two discardable blocks are reallocated, they are simply put back at their old locations in memory. Windows can move them later if needed to make a large space available, or Windows can discard them if moving objects does not free up enough space. Other programs will reload their menus, icons, and so forth when these resources are needed.

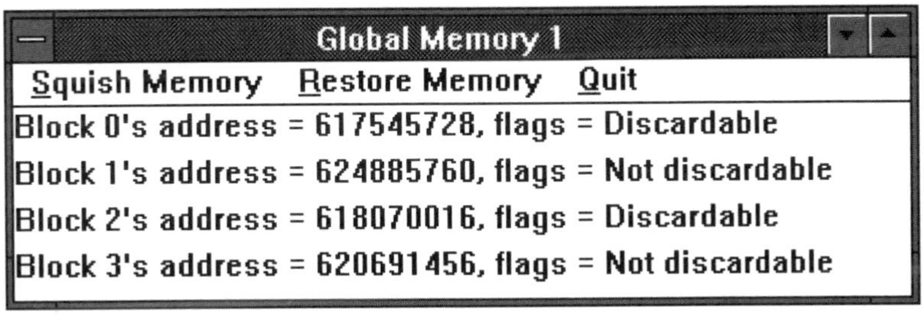

Global Memory 1

Squish Memory   Restore Memory   Quit

Block 0's address = 617545728, flags = Discardable

Block 1's address = 624885760, flags = Not discardable

Block 2's address = 618070016, flags = Discardable

Block 3's address = 620691456, flags = Not discardable

Figure 12-16 The GMEM1 Program After Selecting "Restore Memory"

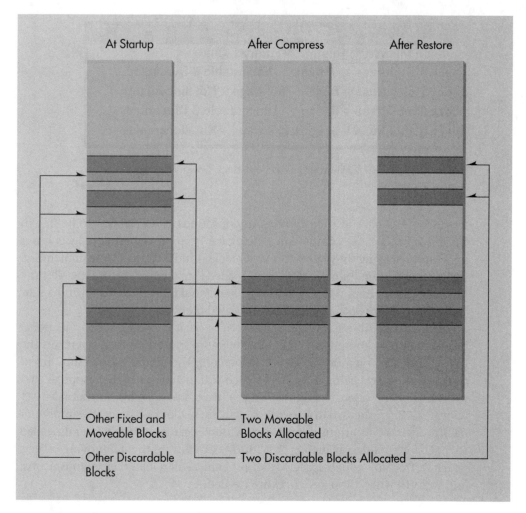

Figure 12-17 The Global Memory Heap While GMEM1 Runs

The GMEM1 Program

Listings 12-35 and 12-36 show GMEM1.HPP and GMEM1.CPP. They should look familiar because they are copied directly from the MEM3.HPP and MEM3.CPP. The only differences are to convert the **CLocalBlock** objects into **CGlobalBlock** objects, use *far* pointers in place of *near* pointers, and use DWORD values to hold the size of global memory blocks. Otherwise, the program logic is completely unchanged.

Listing 12-35 GMEM1.HPP Header File

```
// gmem1.hpp     header file for gmem1.cpp

class CMainWindow : public CFrameWnd    // derive a main window class
{
public:
    CMainWindow () ;                     // declare a constructor
private:
    CGlobalBlock gBlock [4] ;           // array of global memory blocks
    void OnPaint () ;                   // process WM_PAINT
    void OnSquish () ;                  // menu items
    void OnRestore () ;
    void OnExit () ;

    DECLARE_MESSAGE_MAP()               // prepare for message processing
} ;

class CTheApp : public CWinApp      // derive an application class
{
public:
    BOOL InitInstance () ;              // declare new InitInstance()
} ;
```

Listing 12-36 GMEM1.CPP

```
// gmem1.cpp                allocating and using global memory blocks

#include <afxwin.h>      // class library header file
#include <strstrea.h>    // streams header file
#include "winmem.hpp"    // header file for Windows memory functions
#include "gmem1.h"       // header file for resource data
#include "gmem1.hpp"     // header file for this program

CTheApp theApp ;         // create one CTheApp object - runs program

BOOL CTheApp::InitInstance ()    // override default InitInstance()
{
    m_pMainWnd = new CMainWindow () ;        // create a main window
    m_pMainWnd->ShowWindow (m_nCmdShow) ;    // make it visible
    m_pMainWnd->UpdateWindow () ;            // paint center
    return TRUE ;
}

CMainWindow::CMainWindow ()      // constructor for window
{
    CString title ;          // get program caption from resource data
    title.LoadString (S_PROGRAMCAPTION) ;
    Create (NULL, title, WS_OVERLAPPEDWINDOW, rectDefault,
        NULL, "MyMenu") ;
```

```
            // initialize the size and flags for the four blocks
        gBlock [0].resize (1024, GMEM_MOVEABLE | GMEM_DISCARDABLE) ;
        gBlock [1].resize (1024, GMEM_MOVEABLE) ;
        gBlock [2].resize (1024, GMEM_MOVEABLE | GMEM_DISCARDABLE) ;
        gBlock [3].resize (1024, GMEM_MOVEABLE) ;
    }

BEGIN_MESSAGE_MAP (CMainWindow, CFrameWnd)
    ON_WM_PAINT ()
    ON_COMMAND (IDM_SQUISH, OnSquish)    // menu items
    ON_COMMAND (IDM_RESTORE, OnRestore)
    ON_COMMAND (IDM_QUIT, OnExit)
END_MESSAGE_MAP ()

void CMainWindow::OnPaint ()      // window painting function
{
    CPaintDC dc(this) ;           // get client device context
    char cBuf [128] ;             // pre-allocate char buffer on stack
    ostrstream myStream (cBuf, sizeof (cBuf)) ; // ostrstream object

    for (int i = 0 ; i < 4 ; i++)                // for each block
    {
        myStream << "Block " << i << "'s address = " ;
        LPSTR pStr = (LPSTR) gBlock [i].lock () ; // lock for address
        myStream << (DWORD) pStr << ", flags = " ;
        gBlock [i].unlock () ;                    // unlock asap
        WORD wFlags = gBlock [i].getflags () ;  // get flag value
        if (wFlags & GMEM_DISCARDABLE)
            myStream << "Discardable " ;
        if (wFlags & GMEM_DISCARDED)
            myStream << "& Discarded" ;
        if (!(wFlags & (GMEM_DISCARDABLE | GMEM_DISCARDED)))
            myStream << "Not discardable" ;
        dc.TextOut (0, 20 * i, cBuf, myStream.pcount ()) ;
        myStream.seekp (0) ;     // move back to beginning of buffer
    }
}

void CMainWindow::OnSquish ()    // respond to "Squish" menu item
{
    DWORD FreeSpace = gBlock [0].getspace (0) ; // get current space
    gBlock [0].getspace (FreeSpace + 500) ;     // force compacting
    this->Invalidate () ;
}

void CMainWindow::OnRestore ()  // respond to "Restore" menu item
{
    gBlock [0].resize (1024, GMEM_MOVEABLE | GMEM_DISCARDABLE) ;
    gBlock [2].resize (1024, GMEM_MOVEABLE | GMEM_DISCARDABLE) ;
    this->Invalidate () ;        // force repainting
}

void CMainWindow::OnExit ()      // respond to menu item "Quit"
{
    this->DestroyWindow () ;   // destroy main window,
}                              // this stops application
```

 **12**

MANAGING MEMORY

Note the remarkable brevity of the GMEM1.CPP program, considering that a number of fairly complex memory management functions are taking place. All of that is hidden away in the WINMEM files and encapsulated in the **CGlobalBlock** objects. For simplicity, GMEM1.CPP does not bother copying data into the memory blocks after they are created. This could be easily added using the overloaded assignment operator (=) functions in the **CGlobalBlock** class.

Listings 12-37 to 12-39 show the remaining support files for GMEM1.CPP. Figure 12-18 shows the program icon. Don't forget to include WINMEM.CPP in the project file when you compile GMEM1.CPP.

Listing 12-37 GMEM1.RC Resource Script File

```
// gmem1.rc  resource script file

#include <afxres.h>
#include "gmem1.h"

AFX_IDI_STD_FRAME   ICON    gmem1.ico    // the program's icon

MyMenu MENU                              // define the menu
{
    MENUITEM "&Squish Memory",  IDM_SQUISH
    MENUITEM "&Restore Memory", IDM_RESTORE
    MENUITEM "&Quit",           IDM_QUIT
}

STRINGTABLE
{
    S_PROGRAMCAPTION    "Global Memory 1"
}
```

Listing 12-38 GMEM1.H Resource ID Header File

```
// gmem1.h  header file for resource ID numbers

#define IDM_SQUISH         1       // menu item IDs
#define IDM_RESTORE        2
#define IDM_QUIT           3

#define S_PROGRAMCAPTION   1       // string table ID
```

Figure 12-18 GMEM1.ICO Icon Image

Listing 12-39 GMEM1.DEF Module Definition File

```
NAME            gmem1
DESCRIPTION     'gmem1 C++ program'
EXETYPE         WINDOWS
STUB            'WINSTUB.EXE'
CODE            PRELOAD MOVEABLE
DATA            PRELOAD MOVEABLE MULTIPLE
HEAPSIZE        1024
STACKSIZE       5120
```

WHAT WINDOWS ACTUALLY DOES WITH MEMORY

This chapter has focused on the mechanics of creating and using memory blocks in the local and global heaps. The techniques discussed are all that you will need for the vast majority of Windows applications. However, there are a few situations that you might run into that require a deeper understanding of what Windows is really doing when you allocate and lock memory blocks. As a primer, this book cannot cover every possibility you may encounter, but at least you will be aware of situations that will require a bit more work.

When you call the **::LocalLock()** or **::GlobalLock()** functions, the value returned is an address. You have probably assumed that the returned value is the actual numeric location of a place in memory. Back in the Windows 2.0 days (and with the Windows 3.0 "real mode"), the returned address *was* the actual location of the block of data in memory. With Windows 3.0, 3.1, and Windows NT, things are not so simple. Windows now uses what is called "protected mode" memory addressing, so that Windows programs can access the entire computer's memory, not just the 640K of memory that Windows 2.0 used. When running on an 80386 computer or better, Windows can now run in "Enhanced" mode, meaning that free disk space can be used as "virtual memory," allowing Windows programs to behave as if there were much more memory than is actually installed in the system.

Deep down inside Windows, there is a lot of logic that handles the complexity of virtual memory and protected mode addressing. As a Windows programmer, you get all of that sophistication without doing any extra work. We can treat the address value returned by **::LocalLock()** and **::GlobalLock()** just as if it were a "real" address in memory. The fact that Windows is doing all sorts of things to figure out if the block is physically located in memory, or has been temporarily stored on the computer's hard disk, is transparent to the programmer and to the user.

The only times you will need to be aware of the low-level realities of Windows memory management operations is if you need to directly access the computer's hardware, or if you need to have a Windows program respond to a

non-Windows application, such as a device driver for a hardware data acquisition package. In these rare cases, you cannot make the assumption that an address returned by **::GlobalLock()** is the "real" address in memory. You must work with the physical address locations that the hardware works with.

The designers of Windows deliberately did not put access functions for "real" address locations into the standard Windows Software Development Kit (SDK). The low-level functions needed for this type of project are separately documented by Microsoft in the *Windows Device Drivers Development Kit* (DDDK). If you get involved in a hardware intensive Windows project, be sure to get a copy of the DDDK. This book, and most other books on Windows, do not cover these advanced subjects.

System Memory and System Resources

While on the subject of the inner workings of Windows, you may be curious about a couple of numbers that show up in the Windows Program Manager "About box." Figure 12-19 shows a typical group of settings in the About box, in this case for Windows 3.1. The figure shows that over 31 megabytes of memory are available. The system running Windows at this time had 16 megabytes of RAM memory, not the 31 megabytes of memory indicated in the About box. The memory value shown in the About box includes disk space that Windows can take advantage of as virtual memory. The "Memory" value represents the amount of room available to store memory objects, including disk space that Windows will automatically use if it is in 386 enhanced mode. 80286 computers do not use virtual memory management under Windows, and they will show the true amount of RAM memory available.

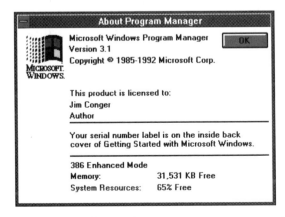

Figure 12-19 The Windows 3.1 Program Manager "About Box"

The other interesting entry is the "System Resources" percent free. This is the amount of room left in the local memory heaps of two parts of Windows, the USER and GDI portions. USER and GDI are just Windows programs (actually dynamic link libraries) that contain many of the functions we have been using, such as **CBrush::CreateSolidBrush()** and **CDC::Rectangle()**. When you create a brush, the data for the brush is stored in the local heap of the GDI module. Similarly, menus, window classes, and many other basic pieces of data that Windows needs are stored in the local heap of the USER module. If you create too many pens, brushes, window classes, etc., you can use up the local memory space of the USER and GDI modules of Windows. After all, like all other Windows programs, USER and GDI are each limited to 64K for their respective local heaps.

The point of this discussion is that Windows does not have unlimited room to store vast numbers of objects. Most Windows applications create only a few objects, and delete them as soon as possible. Check the system resources entry before and after your program is run, and make sure that it is not using up big chunks of these limited areas. A classic error is to create more than one menu, but then forget that only the menus attached to a window are deleted when the window is destroyed. The extra menus will remain stored in the USER module's heap, taking up space until the Windows session is ended. Similar problems occur if you forget to destroy pens and brushes. Errors like this are easy to spot, as the system resources value will not return to its previous value when the program is terminated.

 One of the subtle improvements in Windows NT is that the operating system no longer is constrained by the 64K segment limit and can, therefore, store a much larger number of GDI objects, menus, and so on. Nevertheless, good programming practices dictate that you tie up as little memory as possible to maximize the performance of your application.

SUMMARY

In most situations, applications can use the *new* and *delete* C++ operators to allocate and free blocks of memory as the application runs. *new* and *delete* operate on fixed blocks of memory. Windows provides more advanced memory allocation functions that allow you to create moveable and discardable blocks of memory in either the local heap or global heap. Windows memory management functions provide unique handles for each block allocated, while *new* and *delete* only provide the address of the fixed block, not a unique handle. Windows memory management functions must be used when you need to pass a handle to a memory block as a parameter (such as when working with the Clipboard or passing a memory block to an edit control).

Because Windows can move objects in memory, the address of a moveable block may change. Windows programs keep track of memory blocks using the block's handle, not the address. When the program needs to read or write to the block, the block is first fixed in memory with either **::LocalLock()** or **::GlobalLock()** and then accessed. The locking functions return the current address of the memory block, so that normal memory operations can be performed. Once the data has been used, the block is unlocked using **::LocalUnlock()** or **::GlobalUnlock()**, and again freed to move in memory. When the block is no longer needed, it can be freed with **::LocalFree()** or **::GlobalFree()**.

The size of a block can be changed as the program runs using **::LocalReAlloc()** or **::GlobalReAlloc()**. If the block is enlarged, the existing data in the block is not affected by reallocating additional room. Of course, shrinking the block truncates any data in the far end of the block as it is reduced in size. Discardable blocks must be reallocated if Windows has discarded the data. The handle to a discardable block remains valid even if the data has been discarded. Use **::LocalFlags()** or **::GlobalFlags()** to determine if a discardable block still contains data or has been discarded.

Local memory blocks are all within one data segment and use *near* pointers for addresses. Global memory blocks are outside of the program's data segment and must use *far* pointers. The WINDOWS.H file provides handy abbreviations for common pointers (such as PSTR for a *near* pointer to a character string, and LPSTR for a *far* pointer to a character string).

QUESTIONS

1. If a program has a 5K stack and no static data, what is the largest memory block that can be allocated in the program's local data segment?
   a. 5K
   b. 16K
   c. 64K
   d. about 59K

2. Write the full declaration for the following data types defined in WINDOWS.H. BYTE = _____, PSTR = _____, PBYTE = _____, LPINT = _____.

3. Call the _____ function to determine the address of a moveable memory block in the local heap.

4. Handles cannot be passed to other functions because the data may move in memory. (True/False)

5. Because memory is allocated in units of bytes, only byte-sized data, such as characters, can be stored in allocated memory. (True/False)

6. The handle returned by ::**LocalAlloc**() is equal to the allocated block's address if a fixed memory block is allocated (True/False)

7. Use the _____ function to determine if a discardable global memory block has been discarded.

8. Use the _____ function to change the size of a global memory block that has already been allocated.

9. Successively allocated memory blocks will always start out next to each other in memory. (True/False)

10. *Near* pointers can be used for addresses in a small global memory block, as long as the block fits into one segment (less than 64K). (True/False)

EXERCISES

1. Modify the MEM3 program so that the program starts with a heap size of 1,024 bytes. Are all four of the memory blocks still allocated when the program starts? Can you still restore and discard the two discardable blocks using the menu commands?

2. Modify the MEM1 program so that the program stores 50 integers in a local memory block. Initially set the integers to be the sequence from 0 to 49. When the "Change" menu item is selected, change the values to range from 100 to 149. Modify the WM_PAINT message processing logic to display the integers in the window's client area.

ANSWERS TO QUESTIONS

1. d.

2. BYTE = unsigned char; PSTR = char near *; PBYTE = unsigned char near *; LPINT = int far *.

3. ::LocalLock().

4. False. The handle remains valid regardless of where Windows locates the block in memory, so handles can be passed as valid parameters to functions.

5. False. Memory blocks are allocated in units of bytes, but any type of data can be stored in the memory block after the block is allocated.

6. True.

7. ::GlobalFlags().

8. ::GlobalReAlloc().

9. False. Windows may place successively allocated blocks next to each other, or separated if there is not enough continuous room in memory for the next block.

10. False. *Near* pointers can be used if the address is within the program's local heap (local memory). A small block allocated outside of the program's heap would require a *far* pointer.

SOLUTIONS TO EXERCISES

1. The only change needed to MEM3 is to edit the program's module definition file, and change the HEAPSIZE statement to show 1,024 bytes. Listing 12-40 shows the modified file, listed under the file name C12EXER1.DEF on the source code disks.

    The result of changing the heap size is that Windows discards the two discardable blocks on startup in an effort to fit the two moveable, but not discardable, blocks into the limited heap space. Selecting the "Restore Memory" menu item forces Windows to reallocate the two moveable blocks. Windows expands the heap at this point, making room for all four blocks in memory. Figure 12-20 shows the C12EXER1 program on startup,

Listing 12-40 C12EXER1.DEF

```
NAME            c12exer1
DESCRIPTION     'exercise 1 chapter 12'
EXETYPE         WINDOWS
STUB            'WINSTUB.EXE'
CODE            PRELOAD MOVEABLE DISCARDABLE
DATA            PRELOAD MOVEABLE MULTIPLE
HEAPSIZE        1024
STACKSIZE       5120
```

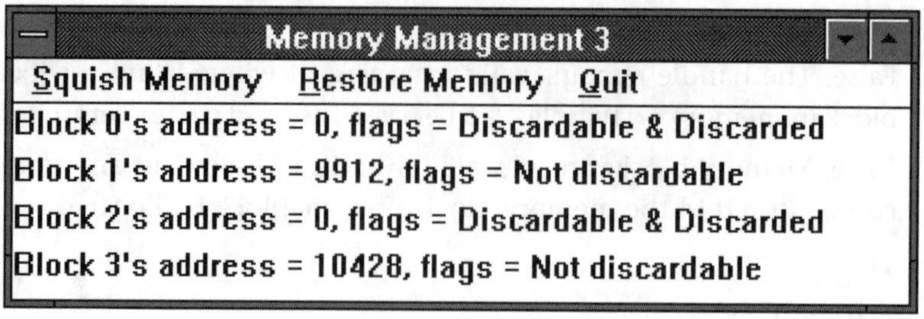

```
┌─────────────────────────────────────────────────────┬───┬───┐
│ ─          Memory Management 3                       │ ▼ │ ▲ │
├─────────────────────────────────────────────────────┴───┴───┤
│ Squish Memory   Restore Memory   Quit                        │
├──────────────────────────────────────────────────────────────┤
│ Block 0's address = 0, flags = Discardable & Discarded       │
│ Block 1's address = 9912, flags = Not discardable            │
│ Block 2's address = 0, flags = Discardable & Discarded       │
│ Block 3's address = 10428, flags = Not discardable           │
└──────────────────────────────────────────────────────────────┘
```

Figure 12-20 The C12EXER1 Program on Startup

which you can compare to Figure 12-9 for the MEM3 program that starts with a larger heap size defined in the program's .DEF file.

Note that during startup, when the blocks are first allocated, each of the discardable blocks is allocated before a moveable block is allocated. The discardable blocks are briefly allocated in memory, but then immediately discarded as Windows attempts to allocate another block in the small local heap, and finds a discardable block that can be discarded to make room.

2. The main change is to allocate room for 50 integers, and then fill the memory block with integer data. Listing 12-41 shows the modifications to the MEM1.CPP file. No changes to the other program files are needed. The full solution is under the file name C12EXER2 on the source code disks. Note that the pointer to the memory block returned by **CLocalBlock::lock()** is cast to a *near* pointer to an integer.

When started, the solution to Exercise 2 appears as shown in Figure 12-21. The solution shown takes advantage of the **CDC::DrawText()** function to fit the numbers within the main window client area.

```
┌────────────────────────────────────┬───┬───┐
│ ─    Chapter 12, Exercise 2         │ ▼ │ ▲ │
├────────────────────────────────────┴───┴───┤
│ Change   Quit                               │
├─────────────────────────────────────────────┤
│ 0  1  2  3  4  5  6  7  8  9  10  11  12     │
│ 13 14 15 16 17 18 19 20 21 22               │
│ 23 24 25 26 27 28 29 30 31 32               │
│ 33 34 35 36 37 38 39 40 41 42               │
│ 43 44 45 46 47 48 49                        │
│                                             │
└─────────────────────────────────────────────┘
```

Figure 12-21 C12EXER2 Program on Startup

Listing 12-41 Solution to Exercise 2, C12EXER2.CPP

```cpp
// c12exer2.cpp            solution to chapter 12, exercise 2

#include <afxwin.h>      // class library header file
#include <strstrea.h>    // streams header file
#include "winmem.hpp"    // header file for Windows memory functions
#include "c12exer2.h"    // header file for resource data
#include "c12exer2.hpp"  // header file for this program

CTheApp theApp ;         // create one CTheApp object - runs program

BOOL CTheApp::InitInstance ()    // override default InitInstance()
{
    m_pMainWnd = new CMainWindow () ;          // create a main window
    m_pMainWnd->ShowWindow (m_nCmdShow) ;      // make it visible
    m_pMainWnd->UpdateWindow () ;              // paint center
    return TRUE ;
}

CMainWindow::CMainWindow ()      // constructor for window
{
    CString title ;      // get program caption from resource data
    title.LoadString (S_PROGRAMCAPTION) ;
    Create (NULL, title, WS_OVERLAPPEDWINDOW, rectDefault,
        NULL, "MyMenu") ;

    lBlock.resize (50 * sizeof (int)) ; // resize memory block
    int* pi = (int *) lBlock.lock () ;  // initialize local block
    for (int i = 0 ; i < 50 ; i++)
        *pi++ = i ;                      // put 50 ints in block
    lBlock.unlock () ;                   // unlock block
}

BEGIN_MESSAGE_MAP (CMainWindow, CFrameWnd)
    ON_WM_PAINT ()
    ON_COMMAND (IDM_CHANGE, OnChange)
    ON_COMMAND (IDM_QUIT, OnExit)
END_MESSAGE_MAP ()

void CMainWindow::OnPaint ()     // window painting function
{
    CPaintDC dc(this) ;          // get client device context
    char cBuf [512] ;            // pre-allocate char buffer on stack
    ostrstream myString (cBuf, sizeof (cBuf)) ;

    int* pi = (int *) lBlock.lock () ;  // get address of block
    for (int i = 0 ; i < 50 ; i++)
        myString << *pi++ << "  " ;      // build string
    lBlock.unlock () ;                   // unlock block
```

```
        CRect rect ;
        this->GetClientRect (&rect) ;          // get client rectangle
        dc.DrawText (cBuf, myString.pcount (), &rect,
            DT_WORDBREAK | DT_LEFT) ;          // output string
    }


void CMainWindow::OnChange ()      // respond to menu item "change"
{                                  // puts 50 int's in CString object
                                   // lock in memory, get address
        int* pi = (int *) lBlock.lock () ;
        for (int i = 0 ; i < 50 ; i++)
            *pi++ =  i + 100 ;         // put different 50 int's in block
        lBlock.unlock () ;            // unlock block
        this->Invalidate () ;        // force repainting - shows string
    }


void CMainWindow::OnExit ()        // respond to menu item "Quit"
{
        this->DestroyWindow () ;    // destroy main window,
    }                              // this stops application
```

## Chapter 13

The Device Context

Device contexts and the **CDC** MFC class were introduced in Chapter 4, *Text and Graphics Output*. The video screen is the most common, but not the only, use of a device context because Windows programs are expected to output text and graphics to a wide range of printers, plotters, and video equipment.

The concept of a device context is used to provide the connection between Windows' graphics functions and the "real world" of computer hardware. Windows programs can use the same functions, such as **CDC::TextOut()** and **CDC::Rect-angle()**, to output to any device context. Windows translates the function calls into commands that a printer, plotter, or video board will understand. A handy feature of Windows' device context logic is the ability to describe the output surface (screen, printer page, etc.) with different sets of units. You can specify a location using inches, millimeters, printer's units (twips), or pixels (dots). You can even create your own arbitrary system of units. Windows also allows the origin of the device context to be relocated, which is a simple way to move an image without changing the graphics function calls.

One other subject discussed in this chapter is the technique of saving a set of device context settings with a window's private data. This allows you to save the current set of pens, brushes, and units with the window's data rather than having to re-create the settings each time a painting operation is done. Saving the device context data uses up memory, but speeds up output.

Concepts covered: A window's private device context, device units, logical units, mapping modes, moving the origin, text alignment, scaleable mapping modes.

Key words covered: CS_OWNDC, CS_CLASSDC, CS_PARENTDC, MM_ANISO-TROPIC, MM_HIENGLISH, MM_HIMETRIC, MM_ISOTROPIC, MM_LOENG-LISH, MM_LOMETRIC, MM_TEXT, MM_TWIPS.

Functions covered: CDC::SetMapMode(), CDC::SetWindowOrg(), CDC::Set-ViewportOrg(), CDC::SetWindowExt(), CDC::SetViewportExt().

PRIVATE DEVICE CONTEXTS

In all of the examples so far in this book, we have created a device context each time the program needed to output to its window's client area. The **CPaintDC** class is used when processing WM_PAINT messages, and the **CClientDC** class is used everywhere else in the program to retrieve a handle to the window's device context. Both **CPaintDC** and **CClientDC** are derived from the **CDC** class that contains most of the graphics output functions. Listing 13-1 shows a typical example of a sequence of function calls used to output an ellipse to the window's client area while processing a WM_PAINT message.

Windows sets aside a memory area for the device context data and initializes it with the default settings for the video equipment in use when the **CPaintDC** constructor function is called. The **CPen** and **CBrush** constructors set up additional memory areas to store the data for the pen and brush. Selecting the pen and brush into the device context modifies the data in the device context memory block, providing the device context with pointers to the pen and brush data in memory. The data is used when the **CDC::Ellipse()** function is called. The pen, brush, and **CPaintDC** objects are all deleted when the **CMainWindow::OnPaint()** function returns because the objects are all automatic variables. Prior to deleting the **CPaintDC** object, the pen and brush are displaced

Listing 13-1 Output of an Ellipse

```
void CMainWindow::OnPaint ()        // process WM_PAINT messages
{
    CPaintDC dc (this) ;            // get client area device context
    CPen Rpen (PS_SOLID, 3, RGB (255, 0, 0)) ; // red pen 3 wide
    CBrush Sbrush (RGB (0, 128, 128)) ;        // solid turq. brush
    CPen* pOldPen = dc.SelectObject (&Rpen) ;
    CBrush* pOldBrush = dc.SelectObject (&Sbrush) ;
    dc.Ellipse (100, 30, 180, 90) ;           // draw ellipse
// select old pen and brush into dc to free new ones before deletion
    dc.SelectObject (pOldPen) ;
    dc.SelectObject (pOldBrush) ;
}                                   // automatic variables deleted here
```

from the device context by selecting the "old" pen and brush. This makes it safe
to delete the device context.

This type of logic is fine for simple graphical output, but becomes cumbersome if you change many device context settings. Of the eight lines of code in
Listing 13-1, only one line outputs graphics data. All of the other lines are involved with setting up and freeing the device context. The approach shown in
Listing 13-1 is also slow because Windows must set up the device context each
time graphics output is needed.

To speed things up, you can create a private device context for the window
that will store all device context settings while the window exists. This also
means that you can save a set of pens, brushes, fonts, etc. with the device context, rather than having to re-create them each time they are needed. The trade-
off in using a private device context is an increase in memory use. Saving a
device context requires about 800 bytes of memory, plus the memory consumed by the pens, brushes, and other objects. This memory room comes out of
the local data heap maintained by the KERNEL and USER portions of Windows,
and shows up as a reduction in the amount of free "system resources" when you
check the "About" box on the Windows Program Manager. The Windows environment can definitely run out of system resource space, so use private device
contexts with discretion.

You will probably find that a private device context is most appropriate
when the application requires many changes to the default settings of the device context before it is used. Private device contexts are also convenient if your
application uses a number of child windows created from the same window
class. Each child window ends up with the same background brush, pen, font,
system of units, and so on, which gives every child window created from the
window class a consistent appearance.

Creating a Private Device Context

To create a window with its own private device context, you must register a new window class that uses the CS_OWNDC window style. Remember that window classes have nothing to do with C++ classes. A window class is just a collection of data that describes the background color, cursor shape, and so forth for a group of window objects.

The **AfxRegisterWndClass()** function is used to register a window class. This is a global function (not tied to a C++ class) that passes data directly to the Windows environment. Listing 13-2 shows a typical call to **AfxRegisterWnd-Class()** followed by the creation of a window based on the new class. The class name returned by **AfxRegisterWndClass()** is used as the first parameter (class name) when creating a new window.

The CS_OWNDC style instructs Windows to set aside a memory area large enough to hold the device context settings for each window created from this class. If you will be creating a number of similar windows that can share the same device context, use the CS_CLASSDC style in place of CS_OWNDC. CS_CLASSDC tells Windows to reserve only one memory area for a common device context, and let every window from the class share that group of device context settings. One last option is CS_PARENTDC, which can be used for child windows. Child windows created from a class using the CS_PARENTDC style use their parent's device context. This presumes the parent was created with either the CS_OWNDC or CS_CLASSDC style, so that the child has data to read.

Using a Private Device Context

With a private device context created, the program can save all sorts of settings into the device context, and then use the modified device context as desired. The device context data will continue to exist in memory until the window is destroyed. For example, the device context for the parent window can be initialized when the program first starts, as shown in Listing 13-3.

Listing 13-2 Registering a New Window Class

```
CString ClassName ;      // name of window class with CS_OWNDC
ClassName = AfxRegisterWndClass (
    CS_HREDRAW | CS_VREDRAW | CS_OWNDC,
    AfxGetApp()->LoadStandardCursor (IDC_ARROW),
    COLOR_APPWORKSPACE + 1,   // use default color (usually white)
    AfxGetApp()->LoadIcon (AFX_IDI_STD_FRAME) ) ;
                          // now create window based on new class
Create (ClassName, "New Window", WS_OVERLAPPEDWINDOW, rectDefault,
    NULL, "MenuName") ;
```

Listing 13-3 Initializing a Device Context

```
CMainWindow::CMainWindow () // constructor for main program window
{
    CString title ;          // get program caption from resource data
    title.LoadString (S_PROGRAMCAPTION) ;
    CString ClassName ;      // name of window class with CS_OWNDC
    ClassName = AfxRegisterWndClass (
        CS_HREDRAW | CS_VREDRAW | CS_OWNDC,
        AfxGetApp()->LoadStandardCursor (IDC_ARROW),
        COLOR_APPWORKSPACE + 1,
        AfxGetApp()->LoadIcon (AFX_IDI_STD_FRAME) ) ;
                             // now create window based on new class
    Create (ClassName, title, WS_OVERLAPPEDWINDOW, rectDefault,
        NULL, "MyMenu") ;
                             // put initial values in dc
    CClientDC dc (this) ;    // get dc handle
                             // create new pen and brush in memory
    pPen = new CPen (PS_SOLID, 3, RGB (255, 0, 0)) ;
    pBrush = new CBrush (RGB (255, 200, 0)) ;
    dc.SelectObject (pPen) ;            // select objects into dc
    dc.SelectObject (pBrush) ;
    dc.SelectStockObject (ANSI_VAR_FONT) ;  // select a small font
    dc.SetTextColor (RGB (0, 0, 255)) ; // set text color blue
    dc.SetBkMode (TRANSPARENT) ;        // set background draw mode
}
```

After the window object is created using the new window class (that has the CS_OWNDC style), the device context can be initialized with all sorts of settings. In Listing 13-3, a new pen and brush are created and selected into the device context. Note that the pen and brush are created using the C++ *new* operator so that the objects are stored in the program's local heap. If the pen and brush were created on the stack as automatic variables, they would be destroyed automatically as the **CMainWindow** constructor function returns. The *new* operator returns a pointer to the objects in memory. The pointers are saved as the *pPen* and *pBrush* pointers that are part of the **CMainWindow** class. The ANSI_VAR_FONT is also selected, with a text color of blue and a background painting mode of TRANSPARENT. All of these settings are "remembered" by the window's device context because of the CS_OWNDC style.

At some other point in the program's operation, the device context can be used to output text and graphics. If output is in the course of processing a WM_PAINT message, the **CWnd::OnPaint()** function will do the work. Listing 13-4 shows a typical **CWnd::OnPaint()** function that outputs an ellipse and some text. Note that no initialization activities, such as creating pens and brushes, are required. The WM_PAINT logic ends up simpler and will execute faster than if all of the device context settings are initialized each time a WM_PAINT message is processed.

Listing 13-4 Using the Device Context

```
void CMainWindow::OnPaint ()           // window painting function
{
    CPaintDC dc(this) ;                // get client device context
    dc.Ellipse (10, 10, 160, 110) ;    // draw ellipse
    CString string ;                   // load string from resources
    string.LoadString (S_CENTERTEXT) ;
    dc.TextOut (50, 50, string, string.GetLength ()) ;
}
```

The private device context will be destroyed automatically when the window that owns it is destroyed. Don't forget to delete any pens, brushes, or fonts before the program terminates. Otherwise, these objects will stay in memory after the program is gone, taking up valuable system memory space. Pens and brushes are just like any other object allocated using the *new* operator—there must be a matching call to *delete* the object from memory. A good place to do this is in processing the WM_DESTROY message, which is sent to the application right before it is terminated. Listing 13-5 shows a typical example.

An Example with a Private Device Context

The first example program in this chapter, OWNDC, demonstrates a program window with its own private device context. Figure 13-1 shows OWNDC in operation. Initially, the program window displays an ellipse filled with a yellow brush, outlined with a red pen, and containing small blue text characters. Selecting the "Change Colors" menu item changes the text font and causes the ellipse to be filled with a turquoise brush surrounded by a green pen. The color changes are not obvious in Figure 13-1, but the change to the text font shows up clearly.

The interesting thing about the graphics in Figure 13-1 is that both images are drawn with the same WM_PAINT logic. The changes to the colors and fonts are made by changing the settings in the program window's private device context. That device context's settings are used to paint the window's client area, so any change to the DC shows up when graphics functions are used.

Listing 13-6 shows the OWNDC.HPP header file. Note that pointers to the pen and brush objects are stored as private members of the **CMainWindow**

Listing 13-5 Deleting Pens and Brushes

```
void CMainWindow::OnDestroy ()    // main window about to be destroyed
{
    delete pPen ;                 // remove pen and brush from memory
    delete pBrush ;
}
```

a) On Startup

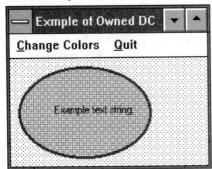

b) After Selecting "Change Colors"

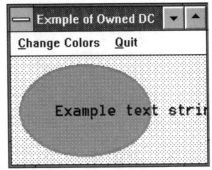

Figure 13-1 The OWNDC Program

class. The reason for this is so OWNDC.CPP will be able to delete the objects from memory right before the program terminates. The private device context keeps track of the pen and brush at all other times.

The OWNDC.CPP program is shown in Listing 13-7. The program logic follows the discussion in the previous section exactly. One point of interest is the **CMainWindow::OnChange()** function, which is executed if the user selects the "Change Colors" menu item. The **OnChange()** function deletes the previ-

Listing 13-6 OWNDC.HPP Header File

```
// owndc.hpp    header file for owndc.cpp

class CMainWindow : public CFrameWnd  // derive a main window class
{
public:
    CMainWindow () ;                 // declare a constructor
private:
    CPen* pPen ;                     // current brush and pen
    CBrush* pBrush ;
    void OnPaint () ;                // window painting function
    void OnDestroy () ;             // window about to be destroyed
    void OnChange () ;              // display message box
    void OnExit () ;                // stop application

    DECLARE_MESSAGE_MAP()           // prepare for message processing
} ;

class CTheApp : public CWinApp   // derive an application class
{
public:
    BOOL InitInstance () ;          // declare new InitInstance()
} ;
```

Listing 13-7 OWNDC.CPP

```cpp
// owndc.cpp                example with own dc for main window

#include <afxwin.h>      // class library header file
#include "owndc.h"       // header file for resource data
#include "owndc.hpp"     // header file for this program


CTheApp theApp ;     // create one CTheApp object - runs program

BOOL CTheApp::InitInstance ()    // override default InitInstance()
{
    m_pMainWnd = new CMainWindow () ;         // create a main window
    m_pMainWnd->ShowWindow (m_nCmdShow) ;    // make it visible
    m_pMainWnd->UpdateWindow () ;            // paint center
    return TRUE ;
}


CMainWindow::CMainWindow () // constructor for main program window
{
    CString title ;          // get program caption from resource data
    title.LoadString (S_PROGRAMCAPTION) ;
    CString ClassName ;      // name of window class with CS_OWNDC
    ClassName = AfxRegisterWndClass (
        CS_HREDRAW | CS_VREDRAW | CS_OWNDC,
        AfxGetApp()->LoadStandardCursor (IDC_ARROW),
        COLOR_APPWORKSPACE + 1,
        AfxGetApp()->LoadIcon (AFX_IDI_STD_FRAME) ) ;
                            // now create window based on new class
    Create (ClassName, title, WS_OVERLAPPEDWINDOW, rectDefault,
        NULL, "MyMenu") ;
                            // put initial values in dc
    CClientDC dc (this) ;   // get dc handle
                            // create new pen and brush in memory
    pPen = new CPen (PS_SOLID, 3, RGB (255, 0, 0)) ;
    pBrush = new CBrush (RGB (255, 200, 0)) ;
    dc.SelectObject (pPen) ;           // select objects into dc
    dc.SelectObject (pBrush) ;
    dc.SelectStockObject (ANSI_VAR_FONT) ;  // select a small font
    dc.SetTextColor (RGB (0, 0, 255)) ; // set text color blue
    dc.SetBkMode (TRANSPARENT) ;        // set background draw mode
}

BEGIN_MESSAGE_MAP (CMainWindow, CFrameWnd)
    ON_WM_PAINT ()                      // WM_PAINT messages
    ON_WM_DESTROY ()                    // and WM_DESTROY
    ON_COMMAND (IDM_CHANGE, OnChange)   // menu items
    ON_COMMAND (IDM_QUIT, OnExit)
END_MESSAGE_MAP ()
```

```
void CMainWindow::OnPaint ()          // window painting function
{
    CPaintDC dc(this) ;               // get client device context
    dc.Ellipse (10, 10, 160, 110) ;   // draw ellipse
    CString string ;                  // load string from resources
    string.LoadString (S_CENTERTEXT) ;
    dc.TextOut (50, 50, string, string.GetLength ()) ;
}

void CMainWindow::OnDestroy ()   // main window about to be destroyed
{
    delete pPen ;                     // remove pen and brush from memory
    delete pBrush ;
}

void CMainWindow::OnChange ()    // menu item "Change Colors"
{
    CClientDC dc (this) ;                     // get dc handle
    dc.SelectStockObject (OEM_FIXED_FONT) ;   // new font for text
    dc.SelectStockObject (BLACK_PEN) ;   // select stock pen and brush
    dc.SelectStockObject (WHITE_BRUSH) ;//    to displace current ones
    delete pPen ;                        // delete old pen and brush
    delete pBrush ;                      //    from memory
    pPen = new CPen (PS_SOLID, 3, RGB (0, 255, 0)) ;// create new
    pBrush = new CBrush (RGB (0, 200, 200)) ;  // pen and brush
    dc.SelectObject (pPen) ;                   // select objects into dc
    dc.SelectObject (pBrush) ;
    this->Invalidate () ;                      // force repainting
}

void CMainWindow::OnExit ()      // menu item "Quit"
{
    this->DestroyWindow () ;      // destroy main window,
}                                 // this stops application
```

ous pen and brush (after displacing them from the device context) and then selects a new pen and brush into the device context. Any subsequent painting operations use the new pen and brush because they are "remembered" by the window's private device context.

The remaining support files for OWNDC.CPP are shown in Listings 13-8 to 13-10. The program's icon is shown in Figure 13-2.

Figure 13-2 OWNDC.ICO Icon Image

Listing 13-8 OWNDC.H Resource ID Header File

```
// owndc.h   header file for resource ID numbers

#define IDM_CHANGE          1    // menu item ID numbers
#define IDM_QUIT            2

#define S_PROGRAMCAPTION    1    // string table ID numbers
#define S_CENTERTEXT        2
```

Listing 13-9 OWNDC.RC Resource Script File

```
// owndc.rc   resource script file

#include <afxres.h>
#include "owndc.h"

AFX_IDI_STD_FRAME   ICON    owndc.ico    // the program's icon

MyMenu MENU                              // define the menu
{
    MENUITEM "&Change Colors",     IDM_CHANGE
    MENUITEM "&Quit",              IDM_QUIT
}


STRINGTABLE
{
    S_PROGRAMCAPTION,       "Example of Owned DC"
    S_CENTERTEXT,           "Example text string."
}
```

Listing 13-10 OWNDC.DEF Module Definition File

```
NAME            owndc
DESCRIPTION     'owndc C++ program'
EXETYPE         WINDOWS
STUB            'WINSTUB.EXE'
CODE            PRELOAD MOVEABLE
DATA            PRELOAD MOVEABLE MULTIPLE
HEAPSIZE        1024
STACKSIZE       5120
```

MAPPING MODES

Graphics and text output functions (such as **CDC::Rectangle()** and
CDC::TextOut()) must be passed coordinates in the device context to specify
where the object should be painted. So far, we have been using the default system of units called "device units." Using a video screen as an example, device

units are the number of pixels measured from the upper left corner of a window area. For a printer, device units are the number of printer dots measured from the upper left corner of a printed page.

The problem with device units is that not all pixels and dots are the same size. If you create a nice looking picture on the screen and then try to output the same picture to a high-resolution laser printer, the whole picture will end up about the size of a postage stamp. That is because the printer's dots are a lot closer together than a video screen's pixels. You could go to all sorts of trouble to figure out how much bigger to draw every object on the printer, but fortunately Windows provides a more elegant solution—mapping modes.

Mapping modes allow you to create a logical system of units for use in text and graphics functions, and then let Windows figure out how to "map" the output to any real device. When you use a mapping mode, function calls such as **CDC::Rectangle()** and **CDC::TextOut()** will use "logical units." "Logical units" is a fancy way to say that Windows does not know exactly how big your video screen is. If you specify a logical location 100 millimeters to the left, Windows will make an intelligent guess as to how big a millimeter is on an average screen, and plot the point there. This will not be exactly 100 millimeters to the left on your screen, but it will be close. For printers, the location will be very close to 100 millimeters, because Windows can determine the spacing of the printer's dots by requesting information from the printer driver (printer drivers are explained in the next chapter).

Table 13-1 summarizes the most common mapping modes available in Windows. The default mapping mode is called MM_TEXT. The MM_TEXT mode is

Mapping Mode	Meaning
MM_HIENGLISH	Each logical unit is 0.001 inch. *X* increases to the right. *Y* increases upward.
MM_HIMETRIC	Each logical unit is 0.01 millimeter. *X* increases to the right. *Y* increases upward.
MM_LOENGLISH	Each logical unit is 0.01 inch. *X* increases to the right. *Y* increases upward.
MM_LOMETRIC	Each logical unit is 0.1 millimeter. *X* increases to the right. *Y* increases upward.
MM_TEXT	This is the default mapping mode. Each unit equals one pixel. *X* increases to the right. *Y* increases downward.
MM_TWIPS	Each logical unit is 1/20 point, or 1/1440 of an inch. *X* increases to the right. *Y* increases upward. This is typically used with text fonts.

Table 13-1 Fixed-Size Mapping Modes

the only mode that moves locations downward as the *Y* values increase. That is because text lines are typically numbered from top to bottom. All of the other modes move the location upward as the *Y* values increase, which is typical of mathematical coordinate systems. The MM_LOMETRIC and MM_LOENGLISH modes are the most commonly used. The "LO" prefix stands for "low resolution," while "HI" stands for "high resolution." MM_TWIPS uses printer's units and is most appropriate if you are primarily working with text.

Figure 13-3 shows how logical units are interpreted for several mapping modes. Any graphics or text output function that specifies a location will interpret the location using the current mapping mode for the device context. For example, in Figure 13-3 the **CDC::MoveTo(50, 90)** function call is interpreted as a location in pixels in the MM_TEXT mapping mode, a location in tenths of a millimeter in the MM_LOMETRIC mapping mode, and a location in hundredths of an inch in the MM_LOENGLISH mapping mode. Note that only the MM_TEXT mapping mode has *Y* values increasing downward.

The **CDC::SetMapMode()** function changes the mapping mode of a device context. A typical sequence of function calls to set the MM_LOMETRIC mapping mode is shown in Listing 13-11. In this case, the mapping mode is changed

Listing 13-11 Calling CDC::SetMapMode()

```
CClientDC dc (this) ;
dc.SetMapMode (MM_LOMETRIC) ;
dc.Rectangle (200, -200, 500, -800) ;
// other program lines
```

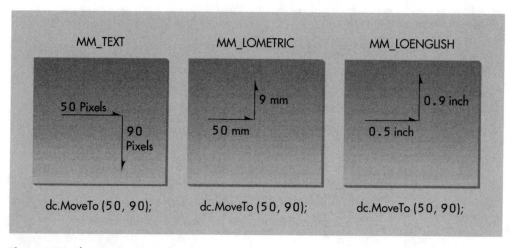

Figure 13-3 Three Mapping Modes

before the **CDC::Rectangle()** function is called, so the parameters passed to the **Rectangle()** function will be interpreted as sizing the rectangle in tenths of a millimeter, not in pixels. If the window has its own private device context, the mapping mode will be saved along with all of the other data stored with the DC.

Text and Mapping Modes

One thing to be aware of in setting mapping modes is that text is handled slightly differently than graphical objects. If you change the mapping mode, the location where the text will be placed will be interpreted using the logical coordinate system. For example, if you set the MM_LOMETRIC mapping mode and then call **CDC::TextOut(10, 20,...)**, the position that the text string will start on will be interpreted as $X = 1$ mm and $Y = 2$ mm. However, the size of the text will be determined by the font in use. Changing the mapping mode changes the location of the text, but not its size. Create and select a different font if you want to change the sizing of the characters.

MOVING THE ORIGIN

A default value for a device context that can lead to a lot of confusion is the location of the origin for the mapping modes. All of the modes start with the origin (0,0 point) at the upper left corner of the screen, or the upper left corner of the page for a printer or plotter. This works fine for the default MM_TEXT mapping mode, but means that positive X,Y locations for the other mapping modes are not visible, because they appear above the top of the screen or page. You can spend hours trying to figure out what happened to your output if you forget about this simple fact. Figure 13-4 illustrates the result of attempting to draw a rectangle at location 100, 100 using the different mapping modes. Only the MM_TEXT mapping mode will produce a visible result. The rectangle is drawn in both cases with a call to the **CDC::Rectangle()** function.

```
CDC::Rectangle (100, 100, 200, 150) ;
```

The most obvious way to get around the problem of the location of the origin for the mapping modes, such as MM_LOMETRIC, is to use negative Y values. Painting the rectangle starting at location 100, –100 would make the rectangle appear in the client area. A more elegant solution is to just move the origin of the logical coordinate system. Windows provides two functions for doing this, **CDC::SetWindowOrg()** and **CDC::SetViewportOrg()**. The reason for having two functions to do the same task is that **CDC::SetViewportOrg()** moves the origin using device units (pixels), while **CDC::SetWindowOrg()** uses

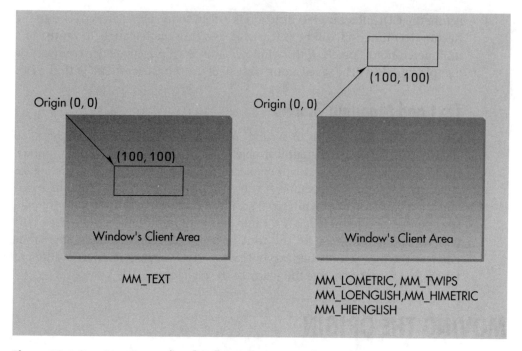

Figure 13-4 Drawing a Rectangle with Different Mapping Modes

whatever logical units are currently selected into the device context. The window origin is an offset from the viewport origin, as shown in Figure 13-5. "Viewport" is just a made-up word that describes the logical coordinate system of a device context.

It is common to use **CDC::SetWindowOrg()** to move the logical origin on the screen to the bottom left corner of the window's client area, and then use **CDC::SetViewportOrg()** to move the origin using the logical units, such as millimeters. The **CWnd::GetClientRect()** function is used to determine the size of a window's client area, prior to moving the origin. Listing 13-12 shows a typical sequence of function calls, setting the mapping mode to MM_LOENGLISH, and moving the origin to the bottom left corner of the client area.

Listing 13-12 Moving the Origin to the Bottom Left Corner

```
CClientDC dc (this) ;
CRect rect ;
this->GetClientRect (&rect) ;
dc.SetViewportOrg (0, rect.bottom) ;
dc.SetMapMode (MM_LOENGLISH) ;
dc.TextOut (100, 100, "Text string.", 12) ;
```

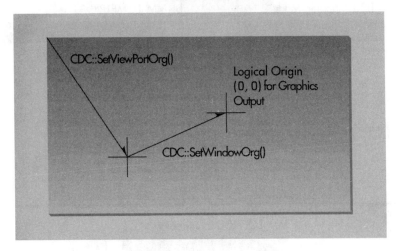

Figure 13-5 The Window and Viewport Origins

Once the origin is moved, all painting operations are relative to the new origin. You can move an image on the screen simply by moving the origin and repainting. Moving the origin and repainting is a simple way to scroll the client area.

An Example Program That Changes the Origin and Mapping Mode

The next example program, MAPMODE, demonstrates three of the mapping modes and moving the origin. Figure 13-6 shows MAPMODE displaying a rectangle and a line of text, each drawn at the same logical coordinates, but using three different mapping modes. The logical origin is also drawn with a cross in each mapping mode.

One difference between the three examples shown in Figure 13-6 is that in the text mapping mode, the text and rectangle end up below the origin, while in the MM_LOMETRIC and MM_LOENGLISH mapping modes, the text and rectangle end up above the origin. The reason for this difference is that the MM_TEXT mapping mode is the only case where Y values increase downward. In the other mapping modes, Y values increase upward. The text and rectangle both start at logical location 50,50, which will be below the origin in the MM_TEXT mapping mode, but above the origin in the other modes.

The physical size of the rectangle and its location are also different in the three mapping modes. In each case, the rectangle is created with the function call:

```
dc.Rectangle (50, 50, 200, 100) ;
```

a) MM_TEXT Mapping Mode

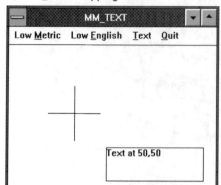

b) MM_LOMETRIC

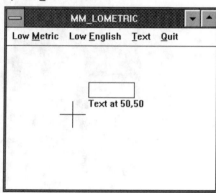

c) MM_LOENGLISH Mapping Mode

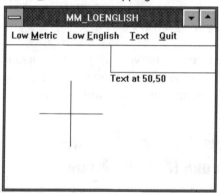

Figure 13-6 The MAPMODE Program

In the MM_TEXT mapping mode, this results in a rectangle that is 150 pixels wide (200 – 50) by 50 pixels tall (100 – 50). In the MM_LOMETRIC mapping mode, the rectangle is 150 * 0.1 = 15 logical millimeters wide by 50 * 0.1 = 5 logical millimeters tall. (The sizes are approximate. Remember that Windows does not know the exact size of your video screen.) In the MM_LOENGLISH mapping mode, the rectangle is 1.5 logical inches wide by 0.5 logical inch tall.

Another difference between the examples in Figure 13-6 is that the text falls inside the rectangle in the MM_TEXT mapping mode, but below the rectangle in the MM_LOMETRIC and MM_LOENGLISH modes. This is because the default basis for text alignment for a device context is the upper left corner of the first letter in a string. Figure 13-7 shows how the text and rectangle are positioned in two of the mapping modes. In both cases, the text extends downward from the logical location 50,50 on the device context. In the MM_TEXT mapping mode,

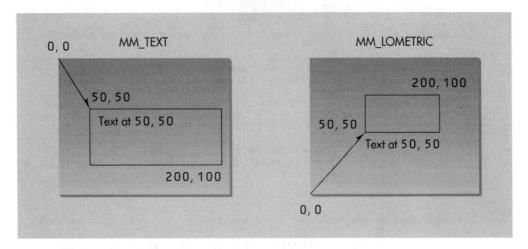

Figure 13-7 Text Alignment

the rectangle also extends downward, as *Y* values increase downward. In the other mapping modes, the rectangle extends upward, so the text ends up below the rectangle.

By the way, Windows allows you to change the text alignment for the device context. The **CDC::SetTextAlign()** function will change the basis for the vertical alignment of the first character to the top, middle, or bottom, and the horizontal alignment to left, center, or right. Usually, the default alignment at the upper left corner works fine, but you need to remember this position if you are combining text and graphics. The text alignment is yet another device context setting that can be saved if a window has its own private device context.

MAPMODE Program Listings

Listing 13-13 shows the MAPMODE.CPP program. MAPMODE does not use a private device context for the main program window, so the device context must be initialized every time output is performed. All of the output logic is done in processing WM_PAINT messages. Besides setting the mapping mode with **CDC::SetMapMode()**, the WM_PAINT logic moves the origin using **CDC::SetViewportOrg()**. The new origin is located at 100,100 relative to the top left corner of the client area. The origin is marked with a cross, formed by two lines drawn with the **CDC::MoveTo()** and **CDC::LineTo()** functions. Finally, the rectangle and text are output, starting at location 50,50 with the new mapping mode and origin.

Listing 13-13 MAPMODE.CPP

```
// mapmode.cpp              example that changes dc mapping modes

#include <afxwin.h>      // class library header file
#include "mapmode.h"     // header file for resource data
#include "mapmode.hpp"   // header file for this program

CTheApp theApp ;         // create one CTheApp object - runs program

BOOL CTheApp::InitInstance ()   // override default InitInstance()
{
    m_pMainWnd = new CMainWindow () ;       // create a main window
    m_pMainWnd->ShowWindow (m_nCmdShow) ;   // make it visible
    m_pMainWnd->UpdateWindow () ;           // paint center
    return TRUE ;
}

CMainWindow::CMainWindow ()      // constructor for main program window
{
    CString title ;     // get program caption from resource data
    title.LoadString (S_PROGRAMCAPTION) ;
    Create (NULL, title, WS_OVERLAPPEDWINDOW, rectDefault,
        NULL, "MyMenu") ;
    nMapMode = IDM_TEXT ;        // start with text mapping mode
}

BEGIN_MESSAGE_MAP (CMainWindow, CFrameWnd)
    ON_WM_PAINT ()                          // process WM_PAINT messages
    ON_COMMAND (IDM_LOMETRIC, OnLoMetric)   // menu items
    ON_COMMAND (IDM_LOENGLISH, OnLoEnglish)
    ON_COMMAND (IDM_TEXT, OnText)
    ON_COMMAND (IDM_QUIT, OnExit)
END_MESSAGE_MAP ()

void CMainWindow::OnPaint ()            // window painting function
{
    CPaintDC dc(this) ;              // get client device context
    switch (nMapMode)                // set mapping mode for dc
    {
        case IDM_LOMETRIC:
            dc.SetMapMode (MM_LOMETRIC) ;
            break ;
        case IDM_LOENGLISH:
            dc.SetMapMode (MM_LOENGLISH) ;
            break ;
        case IDM_TEXT:
            dc.SetMapMode (MM_TEXT) ;
            break ;
    }

    dc.SetBkMode (TRANSPARENT) ;    // set background painting mode
    dc.SetViewportOrg (100, 100) ;  // move origin to 100, 100
    dc.MoveTo (0, -40) ;            // paint cross to mark origin
    dc.LineTo (0, 40) ;
    dc.MoveTo (-40, 0) ;
    dc.LineTo (40, 0) ;
```

```
    dc.Rectangle (50, 50, 200, 100) ;    // paint rnctangle
    CString string ;                     // load string from resources
    string.LoadString (S_OUTTEXT) ; //    and display at 50, 50
    dc.TextOut (50, 50, string, string.GetLength ()) ;
}

void CMainWindow::OnLoMetric ()     // menu item "Low Metric"
{
    nMapMode = IDM_LOMETRIC ;       // change mapping mode
    CString string ;
    string.LoadString (S_LOMETRIC) ;
    this->SetWindowText (string) ; // change caption
    this->Invalidate () ;          // force repainting
}

void CMainWindow::OnLoEnglish ()    // menu item "Low English"
{
    nMapMode = IDM_LOENGLISH ;      // change mapping mode
    CString string ;
    string.LoadString (S_LOENGLISH) ;
    this->SetWindowText (string) ; // change caption
    this->Invalidate () ;          // force repainting
}

void CMainWindow::OnText ()         // menu item "Text"
{
    nMapMode = IDM_TEXT ;           // change mapping mode
    CString string ;
    string.LoadString (S_TEXT) ;
    this->SetWindowText (string) ;// change caption
    this->Invalidate () ;          // force repainting
}

void CMainWindow::OnExit ()         // menu item "Quit"
{
    this->DestroyWindow () ;        // destroy main window,
}                                   // this stops application
```

One nice touch in MAPMODE.CPP is that the program's caption is changed to reflect the current mapping mode. The **CWnd::SetWindowText()** function changes the window's caption. Each of the caption strings is stored in the program's resource script file in the string table. Listings 13-14 to 13-17 show the support files for MAPMODE.CPP. The program's icon is shown in Figure 13-8.

Figure 13-8 MAPMODE.ICO Icon Image

Listing 13-14 MAPMODE.HPP Header File

```
// mapmode.hpp    header file for mapmode.cpp

class CMainWindow : public CFrameWnd  // derive a main window class
{
public:
    CMainWindow () ;              // declare a constructor
private:
    int nMapMode ;               // current mapping mode
    void OnPaint () ;            // window painting function
    void OnLoMetric () ;        // menu item responses
    void OnLoEnglish () ;
    void OnText () ;
    void OnExit () ;            // stop application

    DECLARE_MESSAGE_MAP()       // prepare for message processing
} ;

class CTheApp : public CWinApp  // derive an application class
{
public:
    BOOL InitInstance () ;      // declare new InitInstance()
} ;
```

Listing 13-15 MAPMODE.H Resource ID Header File

```
// mapmode.h  header file for resource ID numbers

#define IDM_LOMETRIC         1       // menu item ID numbers
#define IDM_LOENGLISH        2
#define IDM_TEXT             3
#define IDM_QUIT             4

#define S_PROGRAMCAPTION     1       // string table ID numbers
#define S_OUTTEXT            2
#define S_TEXT               3
#define S_LOMETRIC           4
#define S_LOENGLISH          5
```

SCALABLE MAPPING MODES

There are two additional mapping modes that you may find useful. The MM_ISOTROPIC and MM_ANISOTROPIC mapping modes allow the axes to have any desired scaling or orientation. They are summarized in Table 13-2. Think of these two modes as ways to stretch or compress the coordinate system. The basic difference is that the MM_ISOTROPIC mapping mode maintains the same proportion for both the vertical and horizontal directions. MM_ANISO-TROPIC allows either axis to be set with any arbitrary scaling.

Listing 13-16 MAPMODE.RC Resource Script File

```
// mapmode.rc  resource script file

#include <afxres.h>
#include "mapmode.h"

AFX_IDI_STD_FRAME   ICON     mapmode.ico    // the program's icon

MyMenu MENU                                  // define the menu
{
    MENUITEM "Low &Metric",     IDM_LOMETRIC
    MENUITEM "Low &English",    IDM_LOENGLISH
    MENUITEM "&Text",           IDM_TEXT
    MENUITEM "&Quit",           IDM_QUIT

}

STRINGTABLE
{
    S_PROGRAMCAPTION     "Mapping Mode Example"
    S_TEXT               "MM_TEXT"
    S_LOMETRIC           "MM_LOMETRIC"
    S_LOENGLISH          "MM_LOENGLISH"
    S_OUTTEXT            "Text at 50,50"
}
```

Listing 13-17 MAPMODE.DEF Module Definition File

```
NAME             mapmode
DESCRIPTION      'mapmode C++ program'
EXETYPE          WINDOWS
STUB             'WINSTUB.EXE'
CODE             PRELOAD MOVEABLE
DATA             PRELOAD MOVEABLE MULTIPLE
HEAPSIZE         1024
STACKSIZE        5120
```

Mapping Mode	Meaning
MM_ISOTROPIC	Arbitrary scaling of the axes, but the X and Y scaling must be the same.
MM_ANISOTROPIC	This is the most flexible system of units. Either axis can have any scaling factor.

Table 13-2 Mapping Modes That Can Be Scaled

Windows uses the **CDC::SetWindowExt()** and **CDC::SetViewportExt()** functions together to set the scaling of the device context coordinate system when either the MM_ISOTROPIC or MM_ANISOTROPIC mapping mode is in effect. For example, to create a coordinate system where each logical unit is two pixels (twice the default device unit coordinates), use the code in Listing 13-18.

The reason for using two sets of X,Y values to set the scaling of the device context is that the ratio of the integer values passed for **CDC::SetWindowExt()** and **CDC::SetViewportExt()** is used to set the scaling factors. This could have been done using single, floating point values rather than integers. However, Windows does not use floating point values for any function parameters, but uses the ratios of the integers to pass the scaling factors. For example, a 50% scaling would require a 1 to 2 ratio, while a 66% scaling would require a 2 to 3 scaling. Fortunately, you do not need to use the factored form of the ratios, so a 20 to 30 scaling is identical to a 2 to 3 scaling.

You can reverse the orientation of the axes in the MM_ANISOTROPIC and MM_ISOTROPIC mapping modes by changing the sign of one of the scaling integers. For example, to create a coordinate system where one logical unit is one-fourth of a pixel and Y values increase upward, use the code in Listing 13-19. It does not matter whether **CDC::SetViewportExt()** or **CDC::SetWindowExt()** is called first. Only the ratio of the parameters is used to scale the device context.

With the MM_ANISOTROPIC mapping mode, you can have different scalings for the horizontal and vertical axes. The most common use of this mode is to create a coordinate system where the window's client area always has the same logical height and width. For example, to create a coordinate system where the client area is always 1,000 logical units high and wide and where Y values increase upward, use the code in Listing 13-20.

You can also move the origin using **CDC::SetWindowOrg()** and **CDC::Set-ViewportOrg()** functions with the MM_ISOTROPIC and MM_ANISOTROPIC

Listing 13-18 Using MM_ISOTROPIC

```
CClientDC dc (this) ;
dc.SetMapMode (MM_ISOTROPIC) ;
dc.SetViewportExt (2, 2) ;
dc.SetWindowExt (1, 1) ;
```

Listing 13-19 Reversing the Vertical Orientation

```
CClientDC dc (this) ;
dc.SetMapMode (MM_ISOTROPIC) ;
dc.SetViewportExt (1, 1) ;
dc.SetWindowExt (4, -4) ;
```

Listing 13-20 Reversing the Vertical Orientation

```
CClientDC dc (this) ;
CRect rect ;
this->GetClientRect (&rect) ;
dc.SetMapMode (MM_ANISOTROPIC) ;
dc.SetViewportExt (rect.right, rect.bottom) ;
dc.SetWindowExt (1000, -1000) ;
```

mapping modes. Just remember that **CDC::SetViewportOrg()** uses device units regardless of the mapping mode, and **CDC::SetWindowOrg()** uses logical units, which will change depending on the mapping mode in effect.

Text and Scalable Mapping Modes

As with the fixed-size mapping modes, text character sizing is not scaled as you change the device context mapping mode with the MM_ANISOTROPIC and MM_ISOTROPIC modes. The location where the text string starts *will* use the logical coordinate system, but the sizing of the text characters is determined by the font selected into the device context, not the scaling of the mapping mode. This is normally just what you want, but it can cause problems if you expect an image consisting of both text and graphics to be smoothly scaled as the mapping mode is changed. You can come close by creating different font sizes with **CFont::CreateFont()** as needed to scale the text. Review Chapter 4, *Text and Graphics Output*, if you have forgotten how to use the **CFont::CreateFont()** function.

An MM_ANISOTROPIC Example

The last example program in this chapter is called ANISO. Figure 13-9 shows the ANISO program in operation, with two different sizings of the main program window. The rectangle and the ellipse are always sized to fit the client area. The interesting thing about ANISO is that the **CDC::Ellipse()** and **CDC::Rectangle()** function calls that draw these figures are always drawn with the same dimensions specified:

```
dc.Ellipse (0, 0, 100, 100) ;        // paint ellipse
dc.Rectangle (20, 20, 80, 80) ;      // paint rectangle
```

The ellipse is always drawn from logical location 0,0 to 100,100, and the rectangle from location 20,20 to 80,80. The reason that the ellipse and rectangle continue to fit the window's client area exactly is that the logical coordinate system for the client area is always scaled to be a 100 by 100 logical unit square. Any output to this device context uses the logical units in place and, therefore, is deformed to fit.

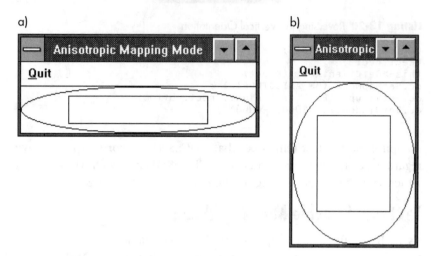

Figure 13-9 The ANISO Program with Two Window Sizes

Listing 13-21 shows the ANISO.HPP header file. Note that the private members *nClientX* and *nClientY* are declared as part of the **CMainWindow** class. These integers will be used to hold the size of the current client area.

Listing 13-22 shows ANISO.CPP. The actual code to accomplish the scaling is remarkably short. The size of the window's client area is saved in *nClientX* and *nClientY* when processing the WM_SIZE message in the **CWnd::OnSize()**

Listing 13-21 ANISO.HPP Header File

```
// aniso.hpp      header file for aniso.cpp

class CMainWindow : public CFrameWnd    // derive a main window class
{
public:
    CMainWindow () ;                // declare a constructor
private:
    int nClientX, nClientY ;        // current client area size
    void OnPaint () ;               // window painting function
    void OnSize (UINT nType, int cx, int cy) ;
    void OnExit () ;                // stop application

    DECLARE_MESSAGE_MAP()           // prepare for message processing
} ;

class CTheApp : public CWinApp    // derive an application class
{
public:
    BOOL InitInstance () ;          // declare new InitInstance()
} ;
```

Listing 13-22 ANISO.CPP

```
// aniso.cpp                 example using anisotropic mapping mode

#include <afxwin.h>      // class library header file
#include "aniso.h"       // header file for resource data
#include "aniso.hpp"     // header file for this program

CTheApp theApp ;         // create one CTheApp object - runs program

BOOL CTheApp::InitInstance ()   // override default InitInstance()
{
    m_pMainWnd = new CMainWindow () ;        // create a main window
    m_pMainWnd->ShowWindow (m_nCmdShow) ;    // make it visible
    m_pMainWnd->UpdateWindow () ;            // paint center
    return TRUE ;
}


CMainWindow::CMainWindow () // constructor for main program window
{
    CString title ;      // get program caption from resource data
    title.LoadString (S_PROGRAMCAPTION) ;
    Create (NULL, title, WS_OVERLAPPEDWINDOW, rectDefault,
        NULL, "MyMenu") ;
}

BEGIN_MESSAGE_MAP (CMainWindow, CFrameWnd)
    ON_WM_PAINT ()                      // process WM_PAINT messages
    ON_WM_SIZE ()                       // and WM_SIZE messages
    ON_COMMAND (IDM_QUIT, OnExit)       // only one menu item - Quit
END_MESSAGE_MAP ()

void CMainWindow::OnPaint ()            // window painting function
{
    CPaintDC dc(this) ;                 // get client device context
    dc.SetMapMode (MM_ANISOTROPIC) ;    // sent anisotropic map mode
    dc.SetViewportExt (nClientX, nClientY) ;    // scale to window
    dc.SetWindowExt (100, 100) ;        // logical size 100 x 100
    dc.Ellipse (0, 0, 100, 100) ;       // paint ellipse
    dc.Rectangle (20, 20, 80, 80) ;     // paint rectangle
}

void CMainWindow::OnSize (UINT nType, int cx, int cy)
{                               // process WM_SIZE messages
    nClientX = cx ;             //   which are sent when the window
    nClientY = cy ;             //   size is changed.  Save size.
}

void CMainWindow::OnExit ()         // menu item "Quit"
{
    this->DestroyWindow () ;        // destroy main window,
}                                   // this stops application
```

message processing function. WM_SIZE message is sent any time the window's size is changed, including when the program's window is first created. The WM_PAINT logic sets the mapping mode as MM_ANISOTROPIC, and then scales the viewport extent to map 100 by 100 logical units. This requires a call to both **CDC::SetViewportExt()** and **CDC::SetWindowExt()**. The **CDC::Ellipse()** and **CDC::Rectangle()** function calls occur after the device context mapping mode and scaling have been set and, therefore, use the new, logical coordinate system. Note in ANISO.CPP that the sign of the *Y* axis was not reversed, so the logical coordinate system continues to have *Y* values increase downward.

The remaining support files for ANISO.CPP are shown in Listings 13-23 to 13-25. The program's icon is shown in Figure 13-10.

Listing 13-23 ANISO.H Resource ID Header File

```
// aniso.h  header file for resource ID numbers

#define IDM_QUIT            1        // menu item ID numbers

#define S_PROGRAMCAPTION    1        // string table ID number
```

Listing 13-24 ANISO.RC Resource Script File

```
// aniso.rc  resource script file

#include <afxres.h>
#include "aniso.h"

AFX_IDI_STD_FRAME   ICON    aniso.ico      // the program's icon

MyMenu MENU                                // define the menu
{
    MENUITEM "&Quit",            IDM_QUIT
}

STRINGTABLE
{
    S_PROGRAMCAPTION     "Anisotropic Mapping Mode"
}
```

Listing 13-25 ANISO.DEF Module Definition File

```
NAME            aniso
DESCRIPTION     'aniso C++ program'
EXETYPE         WINDOWS
STUB            'WINSTUB.EXE'
CODE            PRELOAD MOVEABLE
DATA            PRELOAD MOVEABLE MULTIPLE
HEAPSIZE        1024
STACKSIZE       5120
```

Figure 13-10 ANISO.ICO Icon Image

SUMMARY

Windows uses the data in a device context to translate calls to functions, such as **CDC::TextOut()** and **CDC::Rectangle()**, into commands that an output device, such as a video board or a printer, will understand. Device contexts can be scaled to use different systems of coordinates by changing the mapping mode in effect. The MM_TEXT mapping mode is the default mode for a device context, but has the disadvantage of displaying different sized images depending on the resolution of the output device (how big the pixels are on the output surface). The fixed scaling mapping modes, such as MM_LOMETRIC and MM_LOENGLISH, are very useful because they will produce images that are almost the same size on any output device. All of the mapping modes except MM_TEXT use increasing values for Y to reference locations higher on the output surface, the normal convention for measurement in mathematics.

The MM_ANISOTROPIC and MM_ISOTROPIC mapping modes are interesting in that you can create your own system of units with any arbitrary scaling. This is a convenient way to stretch or expand graphics images. MM_ISOTROPIC always keeps the X and Y axes in proportion, while MM_ANISOTROPIC allows arbitrary scaling of both axes. The **CDC::SetWindowExt()** and **CDC::SetViewportExt()** functions are used with these two mapping modes to scale the device context.

Besides changing the scaling of the device context, you can also move the origin. **CDC::SetWindowOrg()** and **CDC::SetViewportOrg()** are used for this purpose. **CDC::SetViewportOrg()** uses device units (pixels), while **CDC::SetWindowOrg()** uses the logical coordinate system based on the current mapping mode. Moving the origin causes any subsequent graphics output to be based on the new location of the origin.

If a number of changes are made to a device context, it is desirable to save the settings so that they do not need to be re-created each time output occurs. You can create a private device context for a window or class of windows by changing the class definition for the window, and adding the CS_CLASSDC, CS_OWNDC, or CS_PARENTDC class style before calling **AfxRegisterWndClass()**. Private device contexts take up about 800 bytes of memory, but save time during graphics output. Private device contexts are usually used in programs that make many changes to the device context settings.

QUESTIONS

1. Every window created from a window class using the CS_OWNDC class style will have the same shared device context. (True/False)

2. The MFC classes abstract the concept of a device context into the _____ C++ class.

3. If a window has a private device context, you do not need to call the **CClientDC** or **CPaintDC** constructor function because the device context is not destroyed. (True/False)

4. If you want to save a new pen with the device context data for a window with a private device context, you will need to:
   a. Create the pen object
   b. Select it into the device context with **CDC::SelectObject()**
   c. Not destroy the pen until the window is destroyed
   d. a, b, and c

5. Objects should be displaced out of the device context by selecting another object of the same type before the object is deleted. (True/False)

6. The default mapping mode for a device context is _____.

7. Text character sizes change when you change the mapping mode of a device context. (True/False)

8. If the mapping mode is changed, locations on the device context are measured in _____ units. These are the same as _____ units in the MM_TEXT mapping mode.

9. If you move the origin of the device context for a window's client area, and do not redraw the image, the image will not move on the screen. (True/False)

10. In the MM_LOMETRIC mapping mode, a location $X = 100$, $Y = 300$ will be _____ mm to the right and _____ mm above the logical origin of the device context.

11. With the MM_ANISOTROPIC and MM_ISOTROPIC mapping modes, you use both the _____ and _____ functions to set the scaling of the device context.

12. Only the _____ mapping mode allows both the horizontal and vertical axes to be scaled independently.

EXERCISES

1. Change the mapping mode in the ANISO.CPP program to the MM_ISOTROPIC mapping mode. What happens to the image as the window's sizing is changed?

2. Change the MAPMODE program to use the CS_CLASSDC style, for a private device context. Change the program logic to take advantage of the private device context.

ANSWERS TO QUESTIONS

1. False. The CS_CLASSDC class style value allows all the windows created from a single window class to share the same device context data. CS_OWNDC provides each window with its own device context.

2. CDC. **CClientDC** and **CPaintDC** are also correct answers as these two classes are derived from **CDC**.

3. False. You must call the **CClientDC** or **CPaintDC** constructor functions to do any output to a device context.

4. d.

5. True.

6. MM_TEXT.

7. False. Select a different font size to change the text character size.

8. Logical, device.

9. True.

10. 10, 30.

11. **CDC::SetWindowExt(), CDC::SetViewportExt()**.

12. MM_ANISOTROPIC.

SOLUTIONS TO EXERCISES

1. The only change in the program's code is to change the mapping mode specified in the **CDC::SetMapMode()** function call as follows:

```
dc.SetMapMode (MM_ISOTROPIC) ;
```

The result of this change is that the image will always be displayed in proportion, regardless of the relative sizing of the window's horizontal and vertical extents. Figure 13-11 shows the program with the MM_ISOTROPIC mapping mode in effect. The complete solution is given under the C13EXER1 file name on the source code disks.

2. Listing 13-26 shows the modified MAPMODE.CPP program with the changes highlighted. Because the device context is saved, the device context can be altered outside of the WM_PAINT logic. The initialization of the device context is done in **CMainWindow** constructor function. The mapping mode is changed directly by calling **CDC::SetMapMode()** when the menu items are selected. The complete solution is under the file name C13EXER2 on the source code disks.

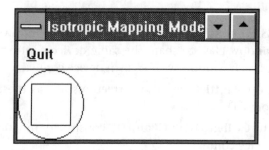

Figure 13-11 Solution to Exercise 1, Chapter 13

Listing 13-26 Solution to Exercise 2

```
// c13exer2.cpp              solution to chapter 13, exercise 2

#include <afxwin.h>     // class library header file
#include "c13exer2.h"   // header file for resource data
#include "c13exer2.hpp" // header file for this program

CTheApp theApp ;        // create one CTheApp object - runs program
```

```
BOOL CTheApp::InitInstance ()    // override default InitInstance()
{
    m_pMainWnd = new CMainWindow () ;        // create a main window
    m_pMainWnd->ShowWindow (m_nCmdShow) ;    // make it visible
    m_pMainWnd->UpdateWindow () ;            // paint center
    return TRUE ;
}

CMainWindow::CMainWindow () // constructor for main program window
{
    CString title ;            // get program caption from resource data
    title.LoadString (S_PROGRAMCAPTION) ;
    CString ClassName ;        // name of new window class with CS_OWNDC
    ClassName = AfxRegisterWndClass (
        CS_HREDRAW | CS_VREDRAW | CS_CLASSDC,
        AfxGetApp()->LoadStandardCursor (IDC_ARROW),
        COLOR_APPWORKSPACE + 1,
        AfxGetApp()->LoadIcon (AFX_IDI_STD_FRAME) ) ;
                                // now create window based on new class
    Create (ClassName, title, WS_OVERLAPPEDWINDOW, rectDefault,
        NULL, "MyMenu") ;
}

BEGIN_MESSAGE_MAP (CMainWindow, CFrameWnd)
    ON_WM_PAINT ()                           // process WM_PAINT messages
    ON_COMMAND (IDM_LOMETRIC, OnLoMetric)    // menu items
    ON_COMMAND (IDM_LOENGLISH, OnLoEnglish)
    ON_COMMAND (IDM_TEXT, OnText)
    ON_COMMAND (IDM_QUIT, OnExit)
END_MESSAGE_MAP ()

void CMainWindow::OnPaint ()        // window painting function
{
    CPaintDC dc(this) ;                // get client device context
    dc.SetBkMode (TRANSPARENT) ;       // set background painting mode
    dc.SetViewportOrg (100, 100) ;     // move origin to 100, 100
    dc.MoveTo (0, -40) ;               // paint cross to mark origin
    dc.LineTo (0, 40) ;
    dc.MoveTo (-40, 0) ;
    dc.LineTo (40, 0) ;
    dc.Rectangle (50, 50, 200, 100) ;   // paint rectangle
    CString string ;                    // load string from resources
    string.LoadString (S_OUTTEXT) ; //   and display at 50, 50
    dc.TextOut (50, 50, string, string.GetLength ()) ;
}

void CMainWindow::OnLoMetric ()        // menu item "Low Metric"
{
    CPaintDC dc(this) ;                // get client device context
    dc.SetMapMode (MM_LOMETRIC) ;      // change mapping mode
    this->Invalidate () ;              // force repainting
}
```

```
void CMainWindow::OnLoEnglish ()      // menu item "Low English"
{
    CPaintDC dc(this) ;               // get client device context
    dc.SetMapMode (MM_LOENGLISH) ;    // change mapping mode
    this->Invalidate () ;             // force repainting
}

void CMainWindow::OnText ()           // menu item "Text"
{
    CPaintDC dc(this) ;               // get client device context
    dc.SetMapMode (MM_TEXT) ;         // change mapping mode
    this->Invalidate () ;             // force repainting
}

void CMainWindow::OnExit ()           // menu item "Quit"
{
    this->DestroyWindow () ;          // destroy main window,
}                                     // this stops application
```

Chapter 14
Printing

Under MS-DOS, programs interact with the printer by sending commands directly to the printer hardware. Each type of printer has its own set of commands for setting tab stops, drawing graphic symbols, ejecting a page, and so on. DOS programs need to have all of these commands "hard wired" into the program logic, or in separate printer driver files that are copied to your hard disk when you install the program. Each DOS program has its own set of printer drivers to support the most common types of printers.

The situation is different under Windows. The Windows environment supports the printer, not Windows application programs. The user chooses one or more printers when Windows is first installed, or when the user selects a new printer using the Windows Control Panel application. From that point on, the installation of a printer applies to all of the Windows applications in the system, not to just one program. This frees you (the programmer) to concentrate on what the output should look like, not the specifics of a printer's commands. When you want a program to output text or graphics to a printer, your program obtains a device context handle for the printer, and then uses standard output functions like **CDC::TextOut()** and **CDC::Rectangle()** to output to the device.

Even though Windows takes care of all of the printer logic for you, there are differences between sending output to a printer or plotter and sending output to the screen. You may need to find out the paper sizes that the printer supports, and if it supports color output. You will probably also want to allow the user to quit in the middle of a printing job if the paper jams, or some other problem occurs. These operations are all possible under Windows, without ever needing to know the specifics of a printer's internal commands.

Concepts covered: Printer drivers, WIN.INI file, printer device context, abort procedures, accessing data stored in the device context, determining output device physical characteristics, using common dialogs, calling functions in the printer device driver.

Key words covered: DC_DRIVER, DC_PAPERS, DC_PAPERSIZE, DM_PROMPT.

Functions covered: CDC::CreateDC(), CDC::DeleteDC(), ::GetProfileString(), ::strtok(), CWnd::EnableWindow(), ::GetDeviceCaps(), ::DeviceCapabilities(), ::GetWindowsDirectory(), ::GetSystemDirectory(), ::PeekMessage(), ::IsDialogMessage(), ::TranslateMessage(), ::DispatchMessage().

Classes covered: CDC, CPrintDialog, CPrintAbort (developed in this chapter).

HOW WINDOWS SUPPORTS PRINTERS

Windows supports printers and other output devices by using special Windows programs called "drivers." These programs (which are actually dynamic link libraries) are stored in the Windows system directory, which by default will have the directory name "C:\WINDOWS\SYSTEM." In this directory, you will find a number of files with the extension ".DRV." If you install a printer, a new .DRV file will be copied to the system directory, such as PSCRIPT.DRV for a PostScript printer. The driver file contains all of the program logic that converts from the Windows graphics commands to the specific printer instructions that a printer understands. If you have more than one type of printer installed on your system, there will be more than one driver file. Figure 14-1 shows how the driver file is used in the Windows environment.

If you look in your Windows system directory, you will notice a number of other driver files, such as MOUSE.DRV for the mouse driver and VGA.DRV if

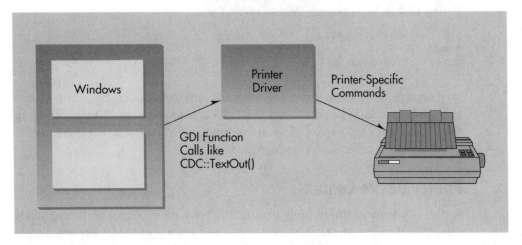

Figure 14-1 Windows Printer Drivers

you have a normal 16-color VGA display. Driver files are a general approach that Windows uses for supporting hardware. When new hardware comes along, only a driver file needs to be written, without any modification to the core logic of Windows. Microsoft encourages hardware manufacturers to write Windows drivers by supplying the documentation and tools for writing device drivers (called the "Device Driver Development Kit" or "DDDK") at a reasonable cost.

The other impact of installing a printer is that the WIN.INI file is modified. WIN.INI is a special file that Windows reads when it first starts to find out what type of equipment is installed, and startup values for various programs. The key line that determines what type of printer is installed is in a section labeled "[windows]," which is usually at the top of WIN.INI. The important lines for a printer look something like Listing 14-1.

This data informs Windows that a device with the name "HP LaserJet IIP PostScript" is installed, which uses the driver file PSCRIPT.DRV, and outputs to the serial port LPT1. This is how Windows knows which driver file to run when printer output is requested. You may also find some other information relating to the printer later in the WIN.INI file. For example, the lines in Listing 14-2 are in the author's WIN.INI file.

Listing 14-1 WIN.INI Excerpt—[Windows] Section

```
[windows]
...                    ; any number of other lines here
device=HP LaserJet IIP PostScript,pscript,LPT1:
```

Listing 14-2 WIN.INI Excerpt—Printer-Specific Data

```
[HP LaserJet IIP,LPT1]
Memory=2243
Number of Cartridges=0
```

This type of data is written into WIN.INI when you access the printer setup options from within the Windows Control Panel application. When you set up the printer, the choices you make are written into WIN.INI so they will be "remembered" in subsequent Windows sessions.

Printer Device Contexts

So far, all of the example programs in this book have output to the program window's device context. The device context for a window is obtained with either the **CClientDC** or **CPaintDC** MFC classes. To output to a printer, you will need to create a device context for the printer using the **CDC** class and the **CDC::CreateDC()** function. The syntax of the **CDC::CreateDC()** function is shown in Table 14-1.

As you may have noticed from the descriptions of the parameters for the **CDC::CreateDC()** function, all of the character strings needed to call **CDC::CreateDC()** are available from the "device=" line of the WIN.INI file. Windows provides the convenient global function **::GetProfileString()** to read lines from WIN.INI. To use **::GetProfileString()**, you specify the heading string (the

BOOL **CDC::CreateDC** (LPSTR *lpDriverName*, LPSTR *lpDeviceName*, LPSTR *lpOutput*,
LPDEVMODE *lpInitData*) ;

Parameter	Meaning
lpDriverName	A pointer to a character string containing the printer driver name, such as "PSCRIPT."
lpDeviceName	A pointer to a character string containing the device name, such as "HP LaserJet IIP PostScript."
lpOutput	A pointer to a character string containing the output device name, such as "LPT1."
lpInitData	A pointer to printer initialization data in a DEVMODE structure. This is seldom used. Normally, this parameter is just set to NULL.

Table 14-1 CDC::CreateDC Parameters

string, such as "windows," that appears in square brackets in WIN.INI) and the key word, such as "device," that starts the line. Here is a typical call to **::GetProfileString()**, obtaining the string following "device" in the "[windows]" section of WIN.INI:

```
char    szPrinter [64]
::GetProfileString ("windows", "device", "", szPrinter, 64) ;
```

The result is that up to 64 characters of the string following the characters "device=" are copied to the character buffer *szPrinter[]*. The third parameter in **::GetProfileString()** allows you to specify a default string, if no matching value is found in the WIN.INI file. This is just set to the null string ("") in the example.

Windows NT Configuration Database

In Windows 3.1, WIN.INI is a simple text file that you can edit with a text editor. Windows NT replaces the WIN.INI text file with a database that organizes the same type initialization of information in a more robust structure that is easier for LAN system administrators to update. Fortunately, the **::GetProfileString()** and **::WriteProfileString()** functions operate on the database with exactly the same syntax that Windows 3.1 uses to read and write to WIN.INI. Your program will work identically under both Windows 3.1 and Windows NT as long as you stick with the **::GetProfileString()** and **::WriteProfileString()** functions rather than attempting to edit WIN.INI as a text file.

Reading WIN.INI was easy, but there remains the problem of breaking up the string into the specific device name, driver name, and output device name strings needed by **CDC::CreateDC()**. Fortunately, each element of the "device=" line in WIN.INI is separated from the previous element by a comma.

```
device=HP LaserJet IIP PostScript,pscript,LPT1:
```

You can either write your own string parsing function or take advantage of the C++ library function **::strtok()**. The **::strtok()** function parses a string, advancing until it finds a specific character such as a comma, and returns a pointer to that position in the string. By using NULL as the first parameter for every call to the **::strtock()** function after the first one, you can call **::strtok()** several times on the same string to find the location of each comma. **::strtok()** recognizes NULL to mean "continue searching for the token from the last location searched." **::strtok()** is not part of Windows, so you will need to include the compiler library STRING.H if you use this function. Listing 14-3 shows the complete sequence

Listing 14-3 Creating a Printer Device Context

```
char szPrinter [64], *szDriver, *szDevice, *szOutput ;
::GetProfileString ("windows", "device", "", szPrinter, 64) ;
    // parse string to find device, driver, and output strings
szDevice = ::strtok (szPrinter, ",") ;// commas separate fields
szDriver = ::strtok (NULL, ",") ;
szOutput = ::strtok (NULL, ",") ;
CDC PrintDC ;                        // create a printer dc
PrintDC.CreateDC (szDriver, szDevice, szOutput, NULL) ;
```

of function calls that creates a printer device context based on the device data
in WIN.INI.

Note that the string is not copied into separate smaller strings for the driver
name, device name, and so on. The pointers to each portion of the string
(*szDriver, szDevice,* and *szOutput*) all point to locations in the *szPrinter[]* character buffer. **CDC::CreateDC()** is then passed these three pointers to create the
printer device context and return its handle. **CDC::CreateDC()** will return
NULL (zero) if the printer device context could not be created.

Once the printer's device context is created, you can output to the printer
using standard functions like **CDC::TextOut()** and **CDC::Rectangle()**. This will
be demonstrated in a moment in the first example program. When the output is
completed, the device context object should be deleted. The **CDC** destructor
function releases memory associated with the printer device context.

Sending Special Commands to a Printer

Although the normal Windows output functions like **CDC::TextOut()** and
CDC::Rectangle() work fine for any device context, there are a few commands
that you will need to send to a printer that do not have an equivalent on a video
device. For example, printers need to eject pages when a page break is reached.
The **CDC** class provides functions, which are summarized in Table 14-2, to take
care of common tasks relating to printers. You may hear these functions referred
to as "escape functions" because many printers respond to command sequences
starting with the (ESC) character to do special functions such as ejecting a page. We
will put these functions to work in the example programs in this chapter.

A Simple Printing Example

The first example program in this chapter is called PRINT1. PRINT1 demonstrates the minimum support that is necessary to output a line of text and a
rectangle to the printer. When operating, PRINT1 appears as shown in Figure
14-2, displaying the output text and rectangle in the window's client area.

Function	Meaning
CDC::StartDoc()	Starts a printing job.
CDC::StartPage()	Prepares the printer driver to receive data.
CDC::EndPage()	Ends a printing job.
CDC::EndDoc()	Ends a print job and instructs the printer driver to send all data to the printer.
CDC::AbortDoc()	Aborts a printer job, and erases all pending data from memory.
CDC::SetAbortProc()	Sets a function that will receive messages during a printing job, so that printing can be stopped in the middle of a print job. This function call will be demonstrated later in the chapter.

Table 14-2 Common CDC Function Calls for Printer Device Contexts

When the "Print" menu item is selected, the same text string and rectangle are output to the printer.

Listing 14-4 shows the full PRINT1.CPP program. PRINT1.CPP closely follows the previous discussion of parsing the WIN.INI file to obtain the device names, creating the printer device context, and using the special printer member functions of the **CDC** class. One interesting aspect of PRINT1.CPP is that the same function does the output of the text and rectangle for both the window's client area and the printer. At the bottom of the listing, you will see the **CMainWindow::OutputStuff()** function that receives a pointer to a **CDC** object as its only parameter. **CMainWindow::OutputStuff()** does not care whether it is outputting to a window or printer because the **CDC::TextOut()** and **CDC::Rectangle** function calls are the same in either case.

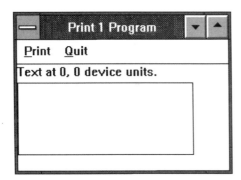

Figure 14-2 The PRINT1 Program

Listing 14-4 PRINT1.CPP

```cpp
// print1.cpp              minimal example that prints output

#include <afxwin.h>      // class library header file
#include <string.h>      // for strtok() function
#include "print1.h"      // header file for resource data
#include "print1.hpp"    // header file for this program

CTheApp theApp ;         // create one CTheApp object - runs program

BOOL CTheApp::InitInstance ()   // override default InitInstance()
{
    m_pMainWnd = new CMainWindow () ;        // create a main window
    m_pMainWnd->ShowWindow (m_nCmdShow) ;    // make it visible
    m_pMainWnd->UpdateWindow () ;            // paint center
    return TRUE ;
}

CMainWindow::CMainWindow () // constructor for main program window
{
    CString title ;      // get program caption from resource data
    title.LoadString (S_PROGRAMCAPTION) ;
    Create (NULL, title, WS_OVERLAPPEDWINDOW, rectDefault,
        NULL, "MyMenu") ;
}

BEGIN_MESSAGE_MAP (CMainWindow, CFrameWnd)
    ON_WM_PAINT ()                     // process WM_PAINT messages
    ON_COMMAND (IDM_PRINT, OnPrint) // menu items
    ON_COMMAND (IDM_QUIT, OnExit)
END_MESSAGE_MAP ()

void CMainWindow::OnPaint ()           // window painting function
{
    CPaintDC dc(this) ;                    // get client device context
    OutputStuff (&dc) ;                    // send ouput to client area
}

void CMainWindow::OnPrint ()               // menu item "Print"
{
    char szPrinter [64], *szDriver, *szDevice, *szOutput ;
        // read WIN.INI file section [windows], line "device=..."
    ::GetProfileString ("windows", "device", "", szPrinter, 64) ;
        // parse string to find device, driver, and output strings
    szDevice = ::strtok (szPrinter, ",") ;// commas separate fields
    szDriver = ::strtok (NULL, ",") ;
    szOutput = ::strtok (NULL, ",") ;
    CDC PrintDC ;                          // create a printer dc
    if (PrintDC.CreateDC (szDriver, szDevice, szOutput, NULL))
    {
```

```
            DOCINFO DocInfo ;   // initialize DOCINFO structure
            DocInfo.cbSize = sizeof (DOCINFO) ; // always
            DocInfo.lpszDocName = "Test" ;  // print job name
            DocInfo.lpszOutput = NULL ;     // not output to file
            if (PrintDC.StartDoc (&DocInfo) != -1)
            {
                PrintDC.StartPage () ;      // start a new page
                OutputStuff (&PrintDC) ;    // output to printer dc
                PrintDC.EndPage () ;        // eject a page
                PrintDC.EndDoc () ;         // end printing job
            }
        }
}

void CMainWindow::OnExit ()                 // menu item "Quit"
{
    this->DestroyWindow () ;                // destroy main window,
}                                           // this stops application

void CMainWindow::OutputStuff (CDC* pdc)// function to output to dc
{                                       // works for screen and printer
    CString string ;                    // outputs a string and rectangle
    string.LoadString (S_OUTTEXT) ;
    pdc->TextOut (0, 0, string, string.GetLength ()) ;
    pdc->Rectangle (0, 20, 200, 100) ;
}
```

Although PRINT1.CPP does not look too complex, there are a number of automatic features being accessed as the program processes its print job. If the "Use Print Manager" option was selected in the Windows Control Panel application (this is the default), the Print Manager will be loaded automatically when PRINT1 starts output to the printer. The Print Manager application will handle the printing job, along with any other printing jobs that are already in progress. If the Print Manager is not selected, the printer commands will be sent directly to the printer via the printer driver.

If the printer is off-line or busy when the PRINT1 program first attempts to print, a warning message box will appear after about 30 seconds. This warning message is generated automatically by the printer driver, without any intervention by the PRINT1 program. Not bad for so simple a program!

The basic sequence of events in PRINT1.CPP is typical of any printing job:

1. Start a new page.
2. Output to the page.
3. Eject the page and end printing.
4. Return control to Windows.

These operations occur in the **CMainWindow::OnPrint()** function. The actual output to the printer device context is handled by the **CMainWindow::OutputStuff()** function. Notice that the **CDC::StartDoc()** function takes a pointer to a DOCINFO structure to pass the name of the print job to the print manager. The MFC documentation shows an obsolete form of **CDC::StartDoc()** where a pointer to a character string containing the print job name is the only parameter passed to the function. With Windows 3.1 (and Windows NT), a DOCINFO structure is passed to **CDC::StartDoc()**, which provides the ability to have the printer output routed to a file. For example, if you specify a file name for the *lpszOutput* member of the DOCINFO structure, the output from the printer driver will be routed to that file.

```
DocInfo.lpszOutput = "OUTFILE.TXT" ;     // send output to file
if (PrintDC.StartDoc (&DocInfo) != -1)   // etc.
```

Normally, *lpszOutput* is just set to NULL as shown in Listing 14-4, meaning that the printer output should be sent to the printer. Listings 14-5 to 14-8 show the support files for PRINT1.CPP. The program's icon is shown in Figure 14-3.

Listing 14-5 PRINT1.HPP Header File

```
// print1.hpp    header file for print1.cpp

class CMainWindow : public CFrameWnd    // derive a main window class
{
public:
    CMainWindow () ;                     // declare a constructor
private:
    void OnPaint () ;                    // window painting function
    void OnPrint () ;                    // menu items
    void OnExit () ;
    void OutputStuff (CDC* pdc) ;        // output function
    DECLARE_MESSAGE_MAP()                // prepare for message processing
} ;

class CTheApp : public CWinApp          // derive an application class
{
public:
    BOOL InitInstance () ;              // declare new InitInstance()
} ;
```

Listing 14-6 PRINT1.H Resource ID Header File

```
// print1.h   header file for resource ID numbers

#define IDM_QUIT            1           // menu item ID numbers
#define IDM_PRINT           2

#define S_PROGRAMCAPTION    1           // string table ID numbers
#define S_OUTTEXT           2
```

Figure 14-3 PRINT1.ICO Icon Image

Listing 14-7 PRINT1.RC Resource Script File

```
// print1.rc  resource script file

#include <afxres.h>
#include "print1.h"

AFX_IDI_STD_FRAME   ICON    print1.ico        // the program's icon

MyMenu MENU                                   // define the menu
{
    MENUITEM "&Print",           IDM_PRINT
    MENUITEM "&Quit",            IDM_QUIT
}

STRINGTABLE
{
    S_PROGRAMCAPTION     "Print 1 Program"
    S_OUTTEXT            "Text at 0, 0 device units."
}
```

Listing 14-8 PRINT1.DEF Module Definition File

```
NAME                print1
DESCRIPTION         'print1 C++ program'
EXETYPE             WINDOWS
STUB                'WINSTUB.EXE'
CODE                PRELOAD MOVEABLE
DATA                PRELOAD MOVEABLE MULTIPLE
HEAPSIZE            1024
STACKSIZE           5120
```

Problems with PRINT1

If you go ahead and print using the PRINT1 program, the output will appear
roughly as shown in Figure 14-4. Although both the text and the rectangle are
displayed, their relative size and location do not look like the display on the
PRINT1 window's client area. This seems odd, as exactly the same calls to the
CDC::Rectangle() and **CDC::TextOut()** functions are made to draw on the client area and printer device contexts. What happened?

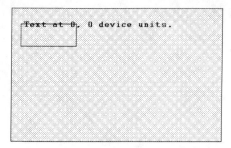

Figure 14-4 Printed Output from PRINT1

The reason the output looks different on the screen and printed page has to do with the interpretation of the default device context units. Remember from the last chapter that when a device context is first created, the default MM_TEXT mapping mode is used. With the MM_TEXT mapping mode distances are measured in units of pixels. A pixel on a laser printer is a lot smaller than a pixel on a video screen, so the rectangle ends up smaller and moved closer to the default origin at the upper left corner of the paper.

Another reason for the change in appearance is that text output is not scaled by the mapping mode in place. Instead, text characters are scaled based on the text font selected into the device context. Windows is smart enough to keep the default system font about the same point size on both the screen and the printer. This means that the text does not end up reduced in size due to the smaller pixel size on the printer.

The solution to these problems is to change the mapping mode of the device contexts for both the printer and video to a mode that uses physical units, such as inches or millimeters. The text size must also be treated as a variable, determined using the **CDC::GetTextExtent()** function and based on the device context in use. These techniques are demonstrated in the next example program, PRINT2.

SCALING THE PRINTER OUTPUT

The key to getting reasonably sized output on a printer is to select one of the five mapping modes that have fixed sizing. They are the MM_LOMETRIC, MM_LO-ENGLISH, MM_HIMETRIC, MM_HIENGLISH, and MM_TWIPS mapping modes that were discussed in the last chapter. The next example program, PRINT2, modifies the previous example by specifying the MM_LOMETRIC mapping mode. Figure 14-5 shows PRINT2 in action, displaying a text string, a rectangle that exactly surrounds the text string, and a blue circle. In this case, the printed output will be very close to the image in Figure 14-5. There may be a difference

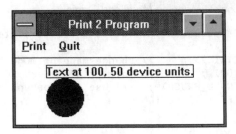

Figure 14-5 The PRINT2 Program

in the relative length of the text string because this is based on the font size, not a physical distance. However, the rectangle will exactly fit the size of the string, and the text, rectangle, and circle will be properly positioned. Figure 14-6 shows a typical printed output.

The PRINT2 Program

PRINT2.CPP is very close to PRINT1.CPP, except for changing the mapping mode and the different graphics and text string output. Because both the printer device context and window client area device context use the same settings, the mapping mode is set in a separate function called **CMainWindow::SetDC()** at the end of PRINT2.CPP, and shown here in Listing 14-9.

The **CMainWindow::SetDC()** function changes the mapping mode of a device context to MM_LOMETRIC, moves the origin to 20,100, selects the stock NULL_BRUSH (transparent brush) for the rectangle, and sets the text alignment to be based on the bottom left corner of the first letter in a string. **CMainWindow::SetDC()** is passed a pointer to the device context object as a parameter, so the function can be used to modify the device context for either a printer or a window's client area DC.

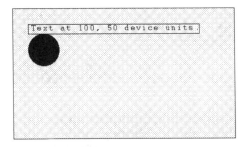

Figure 14-6 PRINT2 Printed Output

Listing 14-9 Changing the Device Context Mapping Mode and Origin

```
void CMainWindow::SetDC (CDC* pdc)  // initialize a device context
{
    pdc->SetMapMode (MM_LOMETRIC) ;      // change mapping mode
    pdc->SetWindowOrg (20, 100) ;        // move origin to 20,100
    pdc->SelectStockObject (NULL_BRUSH) ;   // use transparent brush
    pdc->SetTextAlign (TA_LEFT | TA_BOTTOM) ;
}
```

The actual output of the text and graphics is also done in a separate function, **CMainWindow::OutputStuff()**, which is shown in Listing 14-10. The function is used for output to both the printer and the client area DC. One of the tricks used in **CMainWindow::OutputStuff()** is to use the **CDC::GetTextExtent()** function to determine the size of the text string on the current device context. This allows the **CMainWindow::OutputStuff()** function to size the rectangle so as to exactly surround the text string. **CDC::GetTextExtent()** returns the size of the text string using logical units, which is exactly what is needed to call the **CDC::Rectangle()** function. **CMainWindow::OutputStuff()** also temporarily creates a blue brush to paint the circle (using the **CDC::Ellipse()** function), but then restores the old brush and deletes the new brush. This leaves the default NULL_BRUSH installed in the device context when **CMainWindow::OutputStuff()** returns.

The remainder of the PRINT2.CPP program (Listing 14-11) should look familiar. The same use of the WIN.INI file is made to get the names of the printer device, etc. for calling **CDC::CreateDC()**.

Listings 14-12 to 14-15 show the support files for PRINT2.CPP. The program's icon is shown in Figure 14-7.

Listing 14-10 Output to the Screen or Printer in PRINT2.CPP

```
void CMainWindow::OutputStuff (CDC* pdc)// function to output to dc
{                                        // works for screen and printer
    CString string ;
    string.LoadString (S_OUTTEXT) ;
    pdc->TextOut (100, 50, string, string.GetLength ()) ;
        // determine the height and width of string output in dc
    CSize TextSize = pdc->GetTextExtent (string,
        string.GetLength ()) ;
        // draw rectangle exactly surrounding text string
    pdc->Rectangle (100, 50, 100 + TextSize.cx, 50 + TextSize.cy) ;
        // create a blue brush to fill a circle
    CBrush BlueBrush (RGB (0, 0, 255)) ;
    CBrush* pOldBrush = pdc->SelectObject (&BlueBrush) ;
    pdc->Ellipse (100, 50, 200, -50) ;  // draw the blue circle
    pdc->SelectObject (pOldBrush) ;     // reselect old brush
}
```

Listing 14-11 PRINT2.CPP

```cpp
// print2.cpp              printing, including initialized dc

#include <afxwin.h>      // class library header file
#include <string.h>      // for strtok() function
#include "print2.h"      // header file for resource data
#include "print2.hpp"    // header file for this program

CTheApp theApp ;         // create one CTheApp object - runs program

BOOL CTheApp::InitInstance ()    // override default InitInstance()
{
    m_pMainWnd = new CMainWindow () ;        // create a main window
    m_pMainWnd->ShowWindow (m_nCmdShow) ;    // make it visible
    m_pMainWnd->UpdateWindow () ;            // paint center
    return TRUE ;
}

CMainWindow::CMainWindow () // constructor for main program window
{
    CString title ;          // get program caption from resource data
    title.LoadString (S_PROGRAMCAPTION) ;
    Create (NULL, title, WS_OVERLAPPEDWINDOW, rectDefault,
        NULL, "MyMenu") ;
}

BEGIN_MESSAGE_MAP (CMainWindow, CFrameWnd)
    ON_WM_PAINT ()                          // process WM_PAINT messages
    ON_COMMAND (IDM_PRINT, OnPrint)         // menu items
    ON_COMMAND (IDM_QUIT, OnExit)
END_MESSAGE_MAP ()

void CMainWindow::OnPaint ()                // window painting function
{
    CPaintDC dc(this) ;          // get client device context
    SetDC (&dc) ;                // initialize dc settings
    OutputStuff (&dc) ;          // send ouput to client area
}

void CMainWindow::OnPrint ()                // menu item "Print"
{
    char szPrinter [64], *szDriver, *szDevice, *szOutput ;
        // read WIN.INI file section [windows], line "device=..."
    GetProfileString ("windows", "device", "", szPrinter, 64) ;
        // parse string to find device, driver, and output strings
    szDevice = strtok (szPrinter, ",") ;    // commas separate fields
    szDriver = strtok (NULL, ",") ;
    szOutput = strtok (NULL, ",") ;

    CDC PrintDC ;                           // create a printer dc
    if (PrintDC.CreateDC (szDriver, szDevice, szOutput, NULL))
```

```
        {
            DOCINFO DocInfo ;    // initialize DOCINFO structure
            DocInfo.cbSize = sizeof (DOCINFO) ; // always
            DocInfo.lpszDocName = "Test" ;  // print job name
            DocInfo.lpszOutput = NULL ;     // not output to file
            if (PrintDC.StartDoc (&DocInfo) != -1)
            {
                PrintDC.StartPage () ;  // start a new page
                SetDC (&PrintDC) ;      // initialize the dc
                OutputStuff (&PrintDC) ;// output to printer dc
                PrintDC.EndPage () ;    // eject a page
                PrintDC.EndDoc () ;     // end printing job
            }
        }
}


void CMainWindow::OnExit ()         // menu item "Quit"
{
    this->DestroyWindow () ;         // destroy main window,
}                                    // this stops application


void CMainWindow::SetDC (CDC* pdc)  // initialize a device context
{
    pdc->SetMapMode (MM_LOMETRIC) ;     // change mapping mode
    pdc->SetWindowOrg (20, 100) ;       // move origin to 20,100
    pdc->SelectStockObject (NULL_BRUSH) ;   // use transparent brush
    pdc->SetTextAlign (TA_LEFT | TA_BOTTOM) ;
}


void CMainWindow::OutputStuff (CDC* pdc)// function to output to dc
{                                   // works for screen and printer
    CString string ;
    string.LoadString (S_OUTTEXT) ;
    pdc->TextOut (100, 50, string, string.GetLength ()) ;
        // determine the height and width of string output in dc
    CSize TextSize = pdc->GetTextExtent (string,
        string.GetLength ()) ;
        // draw rectangle exactly surrounding text string
    pdc->Rectangle (100, 50, 100 + TextSize.cx, 50 + TextSize.cy) ;
        // create a blue brush to fill a circle
    CBrush BlueBrush (RGB (0, 0, 255)) ;
    CBrush* pOldBrush = pdc->SelectObject (&BlueBrush) ;
    pdc->Ellipse (100, 50, 200, -50) ;  // draw the blue circle
    pdc->SelectObject (pOldBrush) ;     // reselect old brush
}
```

Figure 14-7 PRINT2.ICO Icon Image

Listing 14-12 PRINT2.HPP Header File

```
// print2.hpp    header file for print2.cpp

class CMainWindow : public CFrameWnd    // derive a main window class
{
public:
    CMainWindow () ;                     // declare a constructor
private:
    void OnPaint () ;                    // window painting function
    void OnPrint () ;                    // menu items
    void OnExit () ;
    void SetDC (CDC* pdc) ;              // function to initialize a dc
    void OutputStuff (CDC* pdc) ;        // output function
    DECLARE_MESSAGE_MAP()                // prepare for message processing
} ;

class CTheApp : public CWinApp          // derive an application class
{
public:
    BOOL InitInstance () ;               // declare new InitInstance()
} ;
```

Listing 14-13 PRINT2.H Resource ID Header File

```
// print2.h  header file for resource ID numbers

#define IDM_QUIT            1           // menu item ID numbers
#define IDM_PRINT           2

#define S_PROGRAMCAPTION    1           // string table ID numbers
#define S_OUTTEXT           2
```

Listing 14-14 PRINT2.RC Resource Script File

```
// print2.rc  resource script file

#include <afxres.h>
#include "print2.h"

AFX_IDI_STD_FRAME    ICON    print2.ico      // the program's icon

MyMenu MENU                                  // define the menu
{
    MENUITEM "&Print",          IDM_PRINT
    MENUITEM "&Quit",           IDM_QUIT
}

STRINGTABLE
{
    S_PROGRAMCAPTION     "Print 2 Program"
    S_OUTTEXT            "Text at 100, 50 device units."
}
```

Listing 14-15 PRINT2.DEF Module Definition File

```
NAME            print2
DESCRIPTION     'print2 C++ program'
EXETYPE         WINDOWS
STUB            'WINSTUB.EXE'
CODE            PRELOAD MOVEABLE
DATA            PRELOAD MOVEABLE MULTIPLE
HEAPSIZE        1024
STACKSIZE       5120
```

PRINT JOB INTERRUPTION

The PRINT2 program is a good template for a program that has a small amount of printing to do. For larger amounts of printing, it is a good idea to allow the user to cancel the print job while the program is printing. Otherwise, there will be no way for the user to stop a printing job until the program has completed output. Writing a program that allows a print job to be interrupted requires some fairly sophisticated Windows programming. This section goes through the steps and logic involved, and then demonstrates the techniques with another example program.

The starting point for allowing a printing job to be interrupted is the **CDC::SetAbortProc()** function, which passes the address of an "abort" function to the printer driver. The printer driver then periodically allows messages to be sent to this abort function instead of the program's normal message loop. The abort function is designed so it can stop the printing process if necessary. A typical sequence of commands to alert the printer driver about the abort function is shown in Listing 14-16. The **CDC::SetAbortProc()** function is called after the printer device context has been created, but before printing is started. In this case, a function named **AbortProc()** will be the abort function that will receive messages from Windows while the printer is active.

The actual abort function is one of the most unusual examples of C++ programming in this book. The MFC classes do not provide any encapsulation of

Listing 14-16 Setting a Printer Abort Procedure

```
CDC *pPrintDC = new CDC ;                    // create a printer dc
if (pPrintDC->CreateDC (szDriver, szDevice, szOutput, NULL))
{
    pPrintDC->SetAbortProc (AbortProc) ;
    // printer output logic goes here
}
delete pPrintDC ;
```

the low-level details of aborting printing, so you must do it yourself. As you will see in the next example, the code provided with this book provides a simple way to implement an abort procedure without needing to code a low-level abort procedure every time. Nevertheless, looking at an abort procedure will give you an idea of how messages are actually processed within the logic that we have been obtaining automatically as part of the MFC classes.

Listing 14-17 shows a typical abort procedure. The function consists of a loop that continually calls the **::PeekMessage()** function. **::PeekMessage()** is a Windows function that will fetch message data from the Windows environment and put the data into an MSG data structure. If there is no message data to process, the loop just continues. If a message has been sent to the program, the message is passed on either to a dialog box (the **::IsDialogMessage()** function checks if the message is for a dialog box) or is sent on to the program's message processing logic by the combination of the **::TranslateMessage()** and **::DispatchMessage()** functions. This type of loop is familiar to C programmers, who must code a similar loop into every Windows program they write. The same logic is encapsulated in the **CWinApp** class, so all of the examples in this book contain similar code that is automatically included in your program when you created a **CWinApp** object.

As you may have gathered from the description of the message loop, the abort procedure does not do anything except check for messages and pass them on if they are received. The abort procedure provides an opportunity to redirect the program's execution while the printer is running. Another key to the printer

Listing 14-17 A Printer Abort Procedure

```
                            // declare two global variables:
BOOL _bPrintContinue ;      // TRUE if printing should continue
HWND _hDlg ;                // dialog box window handle

BOOL FAR PASCAL EXPORT AbortProc(HDC hDC, int nCode)
{
    MSG msg;    // message structure
            // loop checks bPrintContinue every time a message is sent
    while (_bPrintContinue &&
            ::PeekMessage(&msg, NULL, 0, 0, PM_REMOVE))
    {
        if (_hDlg && !::IsDialogMessage (_hDlg, &msg))
        {
            ::TranslateMessage (&msg);   // send message on to whatever
            ::DispatchMessage (&msg);    // application is active
        }
    }
    return _bPrintContinue ;                // returns when bPrintContinue
}
```

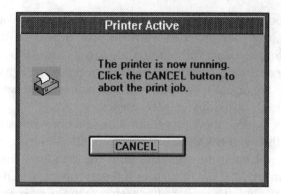

Figure 14-8 The Print Abort Dialog Box from PRINT3

abort function is that it checks a global variable, _bPrintContinue, each time the message loop is accessed. If _bPrintContinue is TRUE, the looping just continues. However, if _bPrintContinue is FALSE, the abort function returns. This is the point at which the print job will be terminated using the **CDC::AbortDoc()** function.

That leaves us with just one more challenge: how to allow the user to change the value of the global variable _bPrintContinue while the printing job is in progress. This is typically done by putting a small dialog box on the screen while the printer job is active. The dialog box contains a "Cancel" button. Selecting the "Cancel" button causes the _bPrintContinue global variable to be changed from TRUE to FALSE, which means that the abort function will return the next time it processes a message. Figure 14-8 shows a typical printer abort dialog box, in this case for the next example program PRINT3.

Figure 14-9 shows the relationship between the different elements involved while a printer session is in progress for a program that has an abort procedure. The sole purpose of the dialog box is to allow the user to change the value of the _bPrintContinue variable while printing is in progress. A change in the _bPrintContinue value will be detected the next time a message is processed in the abort function, providing an opportunity for the program to stop the printing activities.

As you can see, setting up a program to allow a print job to be interrupted is not trivial. The reason for the complexity is that the program is basically doing two things at the same time. The printer driver is processing output from the main part of the program, while the abort procedure periodically checks if the user has selected the "Cancel" button on the abort dialog box. As mentioned previously, you will not need to code an abort procedure from scratch every time you want to be able to interrupt a print job. The code in the next example includes a standardized abort procedure that can be incorporated into other programs.

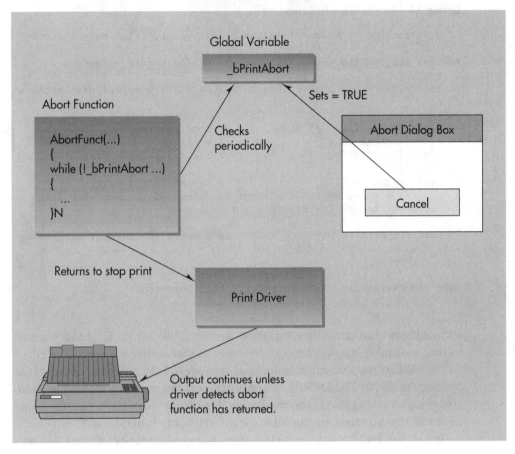

Figure 14-9 Printer Abort Logic Elements

The PRINTCAN Program

The next complete example, PRINT3, is broken up into two portions. The generalized printer abort procedure is stored in the PRINTCAN.CPP and PRINT-CAN.HPP files. The PRINT3.CPP program calls functions within PRINTCAN.CPP to manage the printer abort dialog box and related functions. We will examine PRINTCAN first, and then look at the PRINT3 program.

Listing 14-18 shows the PRINTCAN.HPP file. This file is intended to be included in any program that will need a printer abort dialog box, so the file is a combination of both the resource ID header file and the C++ header file. Note that the **CPrintAbort** class is derived from **CDialog**. This class will be the basis for the modeless dialog box that will be visible during printing operations. The

Listing 14-18 PRINTCAN.HPP Header File

```
// printcan.hpp    header file for printcan.cpp, print cancel dlg box

#define DLI_CANCELBUTTON    1        // dialog box ID number

class CPrintAbort : public CDialog  // derive a modeless dialog class
{
public:
    CPrintAbort (CDC* pPrintDC) ;    // constructor
    ~CPrintAbort () ;                // destructor
    BOOL PrintContinue () ;          // returns printer status
private:
    void OnButton () ;               // cancel button action
        // process WM_CLOSE message to delete dialog box when done
    void OnClose () {delete this ; }

    DECLARE_MESSAGE_MAP()            // prepare for message processing
} ;

        // the printer abort message processing function
BOOL FAR PASCAL EXPORT AbortProc(HDC hDC, int nCode) ;
```

CPrintAbort class definition includes the DECLARE_MESSAGE_MAP() macro so that the dialog box can process messages like any other window.

The **AbortProc()** function is declared separately from any class definition at the bottom of PRINTCAN.HPP. The **AbortProc()** function is a global function, and not part of any class. The reason for this is that we need to pass the exact name of the function in the **CDC::SetAbortProc()** function call. Functions within classes end up having their names changed internally by the C++ compiler during compilation. This "name mangling" is the way the C++ compiler keeps track of which functions belong to which class. Name mangling is normally invisible to the programmer, but becomes an issue if you need to use an exact function name. The **AbortProc()** function in PRINTCAN.HPP is declared as a global function to avoid name mangling. Note that all printer abort procedures must have the exact form declared in Listing 14-18.

Listing 14-19 shows the PRINTCAN.CPP file, which is a combination of the program logic to run a dialog box and the coding of the **AbortProc()** function. The constructor function for the **CPrintAbort** class automatically calls the **CDC::SetAbortProc()** function and passes the name of the **AbortProc()** function as a parameter. If **CDC::SetAbortProc()** returns a negative value, some error occurred, so a message box is displayed. Note the unusual way the **CWnd::Message-Box()** function is called from within the constructor function:

```
AfxGetApp()->m_pMainWnd->MessageBox (...) ;
```

Listing 14-19 PRINTCAN.CPP

```cpp
// printcan.cpp     print cancel dialog box functions

// don't forget to include the printcan.dlg dialog box definition
// in the calling program's resources

#include <afxwin.h>          // class library header file
#include "printcan.hpp"      // header file for this program

                            // declare two global variables:
BOOL _bPrintContinue ;      // TRUE if printing should continue
HWND _hDlg ;                // dialog box window handle

CPrintAbort::CPrintAbort (CDC* pPrintDC)// constructor
{
    _bPrintContinue = TRUE ;             // start with flag set true
    if (pPrintDC->SetAbortProc (AbortProc) < 0)
    {
        AfxGetApp()->m_pMainWnd->MessageBox
            ("Could not set printer abort procedure.",
            "Printing Error",
            MB_OK | MB_ICONEXCLAMATION) ;
    }
    else
    {
        this->Create ("PrintStop") ;  // show the dialog box
        _hDlg = this->m_hWnd ;  // save dialog box window handle
    }
}


CPrintAbort::~CPrintAbort ()      // destructor
{
    this->DestroyWindow () ;      // kill modeless dialog box
}


CPrintAbort::PrintContinue ()     // return current printer status
{
    return _bPrintContinue ;
}

BEGIN_MESSAGE_MAP (CPrintAbort, CDialog)
    ON_COMMAND (DLI_CANCELBUTTON, OnButton)
    ON_WM_CLOSE ()
END_MESSAGE_MAP ()

void CPrintAbort::OnButton ()     // cancel button selected
{
    _bPrintContinue = FALSE ;     // change flag, so printing will stop
    this->DestroyWindow () ;      // kill dialog box
}
```

```
    // Printing abort procedure, process messages during printing
    // Note that this is a global function, not part of a class.

BOOL FAR PASCAL EXPORT AbortProc(HDC hDC, int nCode)
{
    MSG msg;// message structure
            // loop checks bPrintContinue every time a message is sent
    while (_bPrintContinue &&
            ::PeekMessage(&msg, NULL, 0, 0, PM_REMOVE))
    {
        if (_hDlg && !::IsDialogMessage (_hDlg, &msg))
        {
            ::TranslateMessage (&msg);   // send message on to whatever
            ::DispatchMessage (&msg);    // application is active
        }
    }
    return _bPrintContinue ;                 // returns when bPrintContinue
}                                            // == FALSE
```

By using **AfxGetApp()** to retrieve a pointer to the **CWinApp** object, the **CPrintAbort** constructor function can create a message box tied to the main program window without being passed a pointer to the **CWnd** object as a parameter. **AfxGetApp()** fetches this pointer automatically, which helps make the **CPrintAbort** class easy to use in other programs.

If the printer abort procedure was correctly installed, the **CPrintAbort** constructor displays a dialog box named "PrintStop." The PrintStop dialog box definition will be discussed in a moment. One other important detail is that the handle of the dialog box window is saved as the global variable _hDlg_ for use by the **::IsDialogMessage()** function within the body of the abort procedure.

```
this->Create ("PrintStop") ;  // show the dialog box
_hDlg = this->m_hWnd ;  // save dialog box window handle
```

The PRINTCAN.CPP program includes the **CPrintAbort::PrintContinue()** function. This is a public function that can be called by the program using the printer abort dialog box to check whether printing should continue. In a long printing job, the **CPrintAbort::PrintContinue()** function might be called many times.

Don't be alarmed if the description of the abort procedure logic seems unnecessarily complicated. All you will need to do to create a printer abort procedure is include PRINTCAN in another program you are working on. However, it is a good idea to have a general understanding of what PRINTCAN is doing even if you do not need to modify it for other programming projects.

One last file is needed to complete PRINTCAN, the dialog box definition. Listing 14-20 shows the PRINTCAN.DLG dialog box template. This file will be

Listing 14-20 PRINTCAN.DLG Dialog Box Template

```
// printcan.dlg       dialog box definition for printcan.cpp

#include <windows.h>

PrintIcon   ICON    printcan.ico

#define DLI_CANCELBUTTON    1            // dialog box ID number

PrintStop DIALOG 6, 18, 160, 100
STYLE DS_MODALFRAME | WS_POPUP | WS_VISIBLE | WS_CAPTION
CAPTION "Printer Active"
FONT 8, "Helv"
{
    PUSHBUTTON      "CANCEL", DLI_CANCELBUTTON, 45, 69, 64, 14
    LTEXT           "The printer is now running.  Click the CANCEL \
                    button to abort the print job.",
                    -1, 51, 16, 91, 33
    ICON            "PrintIcon", -1, 8, 22, 16, 16
}
```

included in the resource script file of any program that needs to display a print cancel dialog box. Note that the dialog box template includes a static text control and an icon. The only control that the user can activate is a single PUSH-BUTTON control labeled "Cancel."

Counting the icon file used in the dialog box, PRINTCAN consists of four files: PRINTCAN.CPP, PRINTCAN.HPP, PRINTCAN.DLG, and PRINTCAN.ICO (Figure 14-10). You will need to make sure all four files are copied to the same subdirectory as your other program files to make use of PRINTCAN in a project.

THE PRINT3 PROGRAM

The PRINTCAN program is put to work in PRINT3, the last printing example in this chapter. PRINT3 appears as shown in Figure 14-11, displaying two lines of text in the client area. These same two lines are also output on the printer if the

Figure 14-10 PRINTCAN.ICO

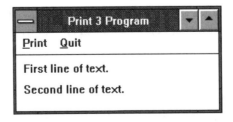

Figure 14-11 The PRINT3 Program

"Print" menu item is selected. Both the client area device context and the printer device context are set to the MM_LOMETRIC mapping mode prior to any output, so the output is aligned properly on both devices.

During the printing process, the abort dialog box (see Figure 14-8) is visible above the PRINT3 program window. With only two lines of text to print, the abort procedure will be visible only for a few seconds if the printer is available. However, if you shut off your printer and use the Windows Control Panel application to turn off the "print manager" option, the PRINT3 program will sit patiently for about 30 seconds with the abort dialog box displayed. During the 30 seconds, you can prove to yourself that the abort procedure really works by selecting the "Cancel" button on the abort dialog box. If you wait the full 30 seconds, the printer driver will display its own error message box, and the printer abort dialog box will vanish.

Listing 14-21 shows the PRINT3.CPP program. PRINT3 is almost identical to the PRINT2 example, except that PRINT3 uses the PRINTCAN printer abort dialog box. To use PRINTCAN requires the following changes:

1. The PRINTCAN.HPP header file is included at the top of PRINT3.CPP.

2. After the printer device context is created, but before output is started, the printer abort procedure is initiated with a single line of code:

```
CPrintAbort PrtDlg (pPrintDC) ;
```

3. The PRINTCAN.CPP file is included in the project file.

4. The PRINTCAN.DLG dialog box template is added to the program's resources.

That is it. The printer abort dialog box will be displayed during the printing operations. The dialog box will automatically be destroyed when the printing function returns because the **CPrintAbort** object is created as an automatic variable. However, destroying the printer abort dialog box does not automatically stop printing. In PRINT3.CPP, the **CPrintAbort::PrintContinue()** function (defined in PRINTCAN.CPP) is checked before printing starts to make sure that the user has not canceled the printing job. If the job was canceled, **CDC::Abort-Doc()** is used to cancel any printing in progress.

The output of PRINT3.CPP is so short that it only checks the status of the printer abort dialog box with the **CPrintAbort::PrintContinue()** function one time. In a program with a lot of output, the **CPrintAbort::PrintContinue()** function would be called many times to make sure that the printing job should continue.

One important detail in the PRINT3.CPP program is that the main program window is disabled by calling the **CWnd::EnableWindow()** function with a value of FALSE while the printer abort dialog box is visible. Disabled windows do not receive messages from Windows, so all messages are processed by the

Listing 14-21 PRINT3.CPP

```cpp
// print3.cpp                    printing with print cancel dialog box

#include <afxwin.h>       // class library header file
#include <string.h>       // for strtok() function
#include "printcan.hpp"   // header file for print cancel dialog box
#include "print3.h"       // header file for resource data
#include "print3.hpp"     // header file for this program


CTheApp theApp ;          // create one CTheApp object - runs program

BOOL CTheApp::InitInstance ()   // override default InitInstance()
{
    m_pMainWnd = new CMainWindow () ;        // create a main window
    m_pMainWnd->ShowWindow (m_nCmdShow) ;    // make it visible
    m_pMainWnd->UpdateWindow () ;            // paint center
    return TRUE ;
}


CMainWindow::CMainWindow () // constructor for main program window
{
    CString title ;          // get program captin from resource data
    title.LoadString (S_PROGRAMCAPTION) ;
    Create (NULL, title, WS_OVERLAPPEDWINDOW, rectDefault,
        NULL, "MyMenu") ;
}


BEGIN_MESSAGE_MAP (CMainWindow, CFrameWnd)
    ON_WM_PAINT ()                       // process WM_PAINT messages
    ON_COMMAND (IDM_PRINT, OnPrint)      // menu items
    ON_COMMAND (IDM_QUIT, OnExit)
END_MESSAGE_MAP ()

void CMainWindow::OnPaint ()          // window painting function
{
    CPaintDC dc(this) ;              // get client device context
    SetDC (&dc) ;                    // initialize dc settings
    OutputStuff (&dc) ;              // send ouput to client area
}

void CMainWindow::OnPrint ()                  // menu item "Print"
{
    char szPrinter [64], *szDriver, *szDevice, *szOutput ;
        // read WIN.INI file section [windows], line "device=..."
    GetProfileString ("windows", "device", "", szPrinter, 64) ;
        // parse string to find device, driver, and output strings
    szDevice = strtok (szPrinter, ",") ;// commas separate fields
    szDriver = strtok (NULL, ",") ;
    szOutput = strtok (NULL, ",") ;
```

```
    pPrintDC = new CDC ;                  // create a printer dc
    if (pPrintDC->CreateDC (szDriver, szDevice, szOutput, NULL))
    {
        SetDC (pPrintDC) ;                // initialize the dc
        this->EnableWindow (FALSE) ;      // disable main window
        CPrintAbort PrtDlg (pPrintDC) ;   // show print abort dlg box
        DOCINFO DocInfo ;
        DocInfo.cbSize = sizeof (DOCINFO) ; // always
        DocInfo.lpszDocName = "Test" ;    // print job name
        DocInfo.lpszOutput = NULL ;       // not output to file
        if (pPrintDC->StartDoc (&DocInfo) != -1)
        {
            pPrintDC->StartPage () ;       // start a new page
            if (PrtDlg.PrintContinue ())// if not cancelled
            {
                OutputStuff (pPrintDC) ;// output to printer dc
                pPrintDC->EndPage () ;  // eject a page
                pPrintDC->EndDoc () ;    // end printing job
            }
            else                        // user cancelled printing
            {
                pPrintDC->AbortDoc () ; // quit output
            }
        }
    }
    this->EnableWindow (TRUE) ;           // enable main window
    delete pPrintDC ;
}

void CMainWindow::OnExit ()               // menu item "Quit"
{
    this->DestroyWindow () ;              // destroy main window,
}                                         // this stops application

void CMainWindow::SetDC (CDC* pdc)         // initialize a device context
{
    pdc->SetMapMode (MM_LOMETRIC) ;        // change mapping mode
    pdc->SetWindowOrg (-20, 50) ;          // move origin
    pdc->SetTextAlign (TA_LEFT | TA_BOTTOM) ;
}

void CMainWindow::OutputStuff (CDC* pdc)// function to output to dc
{                                        // works for screen and printer
    CString string ;
    string.LoadString (S_OUTTEXT1) ;
    pdc->TextOut (0, 0, string, string.GetLength ()) ;
        // determine the height of string output in dc
    CSize TextSize = pdc->GetTextExtent (string,
        string.GetLength ()) ;
    string.LoadString (S_OUTTEXT2) ;
    pdc->TextOut (0, -2 * TextSize.cy, string,
        string.GetLength ()) ;
}
```

logic in the abort function. The main program window is enabled when printing is completed with a second call to **CWnd::EnableWindow()**.

The support files for PRINT3.CPP are shown in Listings 14-22 to 14-25. Note
the inclusion of PRINTCAN.DLG in the PRINT3.RC resource script file (Listing
14-24). The program's icon is shown in Figure 14-12. Don't forget to include
PRINTCAN.CPP in the project file for PRINT3.CPP when you compile. Also note
in Listing 14-25 that the STACKSIZE value has been increased to 10240 bytes.
Microsoft recommends increasing the stack size any time the common dialog
boxes are used.

Listing 14-22 PRINT3.HPP Header File

```
// print3.hpp      header file for print3.cpp

class CMainWindow : public CFrameWnd    // derive a main window class
{
public:
    CMainWindow () ;                     // declare a constructor
private:
    CDC *pPrintDC ;                      // pointer to printer dc
    CPrintAbort* pPrtDlg ;               // pointer to print cancel dlg box
    void OnPaint () ;                    // window painting function
    void OnPrint () ;                    // menu items
    void OnExit () ;
    void SetDC (CDC* pdc) ;              // function to initialize a dc
    void OutputStuff (CDC* pdc) ;        // output function

    DECLARE_MESSAGE_MAP()                // prepare for message processing
} ;

class CTheApp : public CWinApp          // derive an application class
{
public:
    BOOL InitInstance () ;              // declare new InitInstance()
} ;
```

Figure 14-12 PRINT3.ICO Icon Image

Listing 14-23 PRINT3.H Resource ID Header File

```
// print3.h   header file for resource ID numbers

#define IDM_QUIT              1       // menu item ID numbers
#define IDM_PRINT             2

#define S_PROGRAMCAPTION      1       // string table ID numbers
#define S_OUTTEXT1            2
#define S_OUTTEXT2            3
```

Listing 14-24 PRINT3.RC Resource Script File

```
// print3.rc   resource script file

#include <afxres.h>
#include "print3.h"
#include "printcan.dlg"


AFX_IDI_STD_FRAME    ICON     print3.ico     // the program's icon

MyMenu MENU                                   // define the menu
{
    MENUITEM "&Print",          IDM_PRINT
    MENUITEM "&Quit",           IDM_QUIT
}

STRINGTABLE
{
    S_PROGRAMCAPTION    "Print 3 Program"
    S_OUTTEXT1          "First line of text."
    S_OUTTEXT2          "Second line of text."
}
```

Listing 14-25 PRINT3.DEF Module Definition File

```
NAME            print3
DESCRIPTION     'print3 C++ program'
EXETYPE         WINDOWS
STUB            'WINSTUB.EXE'
CODE            PRELOAD MOVEABLE
DATA            PRELOAD MOVEABLE MULTIPLE
HEAPSIZE        4096
STACKSIZE       10240
```

GETTING INFORMATION ABOUT A DEVICE

Although the device context insulates Windows programs from the low-level
details of particular output devices, there are situations where you will want to
find out some of the physical details of the printer or video equipment in use.

For example, you may want to modify the colors a program uses depending on the number of colors the video board is capable of displaying. It is also valuable to be able to determine the size and resolution of the screen or output surface before deciding how big to make detailed pictures.

There are three basic ways to find out details about a physical output device. One is to create a device context for the device, and then read the values stored by Windows for the device. The **CDC::GetDeviceCaps()** function ("get device capabilities") accesses the device context data, returning any single value requested. The second technique is to take advantage of the common dialogs provided by Microsoft for changing and determining printer settings. Common dialogs were introduced with Windows 3.1 to provide dialog boxes that all applications can use for repetitive tasks such as printer setup, obtaining a search string, selecting a color, and so on. Physically, the common dialog boxes are defined in a dynamic link library file COMMDLG.DLL. We will take advantage of a common dialog box later in this chapter in the section *Printer Setup Dialog Boxes*.

The third way to access a device is to call functions in the device driver. For example, Microsoft specifies in its documentation on creating device drivers that the driver must contain the **DeviceCapabilities()** function, which can be called from within a Windows program. We will explore accessing functions in a device driver in the next section, but for now the focus will be on using **CDC::GetDeviceCaps()**.

Using CDC::GetDeviceCaps()

CDC::GetDeviceCaps() is very simple to use. Determining the number of vertical pixels for the video display is a typical use of the function and is shown here. The *this* pointer is assumed to point to a **CWnd** object.

```
CClientDC dc (this) ;  // create dev. context for window
int nVertPix = dc.GetDeviceCaps (VERTRES) ;
```

Note that although the device context was obtained for a window, the device data applies to the entire screen (entire device), not just the portion of the screen occupied by the window. **CDC::GetDeviceCaps()** uses a series of index values, such as VERTRES, to specify the data element requested. These index values are defined in WINDOWS.H. The values that you are most likely to use are summarized in Table 14-3.

Two of the **CDC::GetDeviceCaps()** index values are used to determine the number of colors a device, such as a video display, can show simultaneously. Some video displays, such as 16-color VGA boards, store color data for each primary color in separate blocks of memory called "color planes." The other data format stores all the bits needed to specify a color in adjacent locations in

Value	Meaning
TECHNOLOGY	Determines the type of device. For common devices, the returned value will be equal to DT_PLOTTER, DT_RASDISPLAY (raster display), or DT_RASPRINTER (raster printer).
HORZSIZE	The approximate width of the physical display in millimeters.
VERTSIZE	The approximate height of the physical display in millimeters.
HORZRES	The number of horizontal pixels.
VERTRES	The number of vertical pixels.
LOGPIXELSX	The number of pixels per logical inch horizontally.
LOGPIXELSY	The number of pixels per logical inch vertically.
BITSPIXEL	The number of adjacent color bits per pixel.
PLANES	The number of color planes.

Table 14-3 Common CDC::GetDeviceCaps() Index Values

memory. This is typical for higher resolution systems. Any given display will use only one of these two storage techniques, so either the value returned by **CDC::GetDeviceCaps()** of BITSPIXEL will be 1, or the value returned for PLANES will be 1. The value not equal to one will be the number of bits per pixel used to store colors. You can determine the number of simultaneous colors with this formula:

$$2^{(BITSPIXEL + PLANES - 1)} = \text{Simultaneous Colors}$$

For example, a super VGA board will typically return 8 for BITSPIXEL, and 1 for PLANES, so the number of simultaneous colors is:

$$2^{(8 + 1 - 1)} = 2^8 = 256 \text{ Simultaneous Colors}$$

An Example Using CDC::GetDeviceCaps()

The next example program, called DEVCAP, demonstrates using **CDC::GetDeviceCaps()** for determining physical information about both the video display and the currently selected printer. Figure 14-13 shows DEVCAP in action, displaying information about a system with a super VGA video board and an HP IIP printer. The horizontal and vertical sizes in millimeters for the video system are just Windows' best estimate for the 1,024 by 768 video resolution. The printer horizontal and vertical sizes are more accurate and refer to the printable region on a page. Note that in Figure 14-13 the video board is a 256-color system (2^8), and the printer is a monochrome (black and white) device.

	Video	Printer
Horz. mm	280	203
Vert. mm	210	266
Horz. pixels	1024	2394
Vert. pixels	768	3144
Color bits	8	1
Color planes	1	1

Figure 14-13 The DEVCAP Program

Listing 14-26 shows the DEVCAP.CPP program. DEVCAP uses string table entries for all of the text strings that show up in the DEVCAP window's client area. To simplify displaying the string table entries at different locations, DEVCAP.CPP defines the **CMainWindow::OutStringTable()** function at the end of the listing that displays a given string at an *X,Y* location on the screen.

A similar utility function called **CMainWindow::OutDevCapValue()** is defined to output the numeric value for an entry that the **CDC::GetDeviceCaps()** function obtains from a device context at a given *X,Y* location. **CMainWindow::OutDevCapValue()** is then called a number of times in the **CWnd::OnPaint()** function of DEVCAP.CPP to display each of the device capabilities requested at a different location in the window's client area.

DEVCAP.CPP contains the standard logic for obtaining the installed printer's description from the WIN.INI file. This is done each time a WM_PAINT message is received to create the device context object for the printer. A **CPaintDC** object is also created to hold the device context for the video system, and these two device contexts are used to obtain device capabilities values for the printer and video system, respectively. You would not want to store a printer's characteristics during the program's startup sequence because the user has the freedom to select a new printer at any time.

One shortcut taken for clarity in DEVCAP.CPP is that the physical locations of all the strings and numeric entries are at fixed *X,Y* locations on the screen. A more complete program would use the **CDC::GetTextMetrics()** function to determine the character font height and width, and then calculate the text locations accordingly. This would better assure that the output was spaced properly on the window's client area, regardless of the video resolution of the system.

The support files for DEVCAP.CPP are shown in Listings 14-27 to 14-30. Figure 14-14 shows the program's icon.

Listing 14-26 DEVCAP.CPP

```cpp
// devcap.cpp              example showing device capabilities

#include <afxwin.h>    // class library header file
#include <strstrea.h>  // streams header file
#include <string.h>    // for strtok() function
#include "devcap.h"    // header file for resource data
#include "devcap.hpp"  // header file for this program

CTheApp theApp ;        // create one CTheApp object - runs program

BOOL CTheApp::InitInstance ()    // override default InitInstance()
{
    m_pMainWnd = new CMainWindow () ;          // create a main window
    m_pMainWnd->ShowWindow (m_nCmdShow) ;    // make it visible
    m_pMainWnd->UpdateWindow () ;             // paint center
    return TRUE ;
}


CMainWindow::CMainWindow () // constructor for main program window
{
    CString title ;       // get program caption from resource data
    title.LoadString (S_PROGRAMCAPTION) ;
    Create (NULL, title, WS_OVERLAPPEDWINDOW, rectDefault,
        NULL, "MyMenu") ;
}

BEGIN_MESSAGE_MAP (CMainWindow, CFrameWnd)
    ON_WM_PAINT ()                 // process WM_PAINT messages
    ON_COMMAND (IDM_QUIT, OnExit)   // menu item "Quit"
END_MESSAGE_MAP ()

void CMainWindow::OnPaint ()          // window painting function
{
    CPaintDC PaintDC (this) ;        // get client area device context

    char szPrinter [64], *szDriver, *szDevice, *szOutput ;
        // read WIN.INI file section [windows], line "device=..."
    ::GetProfileString ("windows", "device", "", szPrinter, 64) ;
        // parse string to find device, driver, and output strings
    szDevice = strtok (szPrinter, ",") ;     // commas separate fields
    szDriver = strtok (NULL, ",") ;
    szOutput = strtok (NULL, ",") ;
    CDC PrintDC ;                            // create a printer dc
    PrintDC.CreateDC (szDriver, szDevice, szOutput, NULL) ;

        // show headings; strings from string table entries
    OutStringTable (&PaintDC, S_VIDEOTITLE, 100, 0) ;
```

```
        OutStringTable (&PaintDC, S_PRINTERTITLE, 200, 0) ;
        OutStringTable (&PaintDC, S_HORZSIZE, 0, 20 ) ;
        OutStringTable (&PaintDC, S_VERTSIZE, 0, 40 ) ;
        OutStringTable (&PaintDC, S_HORZRES, 0, 60 ) ;
        OutStringTable (&PaintDC, S_VERTRES, 0, 80 ) ;
        OutStringTable (&PaintDC, S_BITSPIXEL, 0, 100 ) ;
        OutStringTable (&PaintDC, S_PLANES, 0, 120 ) ;
                        // put device capabilities values on screen
        OutDevCapValue (&PaintDC, &PaintDC, HORZSIZE, 100, 20) ;
        OutDevCapValue (&PaintDC, &PrintDC, HORZSIZE, 200, 20) ;
        OutDevCapValue (&PaintDC, &PaintDC, VERTSIZE, 100, 40) ;
        OutDevCapValue (&PaintDC, &PrintDC, VERTSIZE, 200, 40) ;
        OutDevCapValue (&PaintDC, &PaintDC, HORZRES, 100, 60) ;
        OutDevCapValue (&PaintDC, &PrintDC, HORZRES, 200, 60) ;
        OutDevCapValue (&PaintDC, &PaintDC, VERTRES, 100, 80) ;
        OutDevCapValue (&PaintDC, &PrintDC, VERTRES, 200, 80) ;
        OutDevCapValue (&PaintDC, &PaintDC, BITSPIXEL, 100, 100) ;
        OutDevCapValue (&PaintDC, &PrintDC, BITSPIXEL, 200, 100) ;
        OutDevCapValue (&PaintDC, &PaintDC, PLANES, 100, 120) ;
        OutDevCapValue (&PaintDC, &PrintDC, PLANES, 200, 120) ;
}

void CMainWindow::OnExit ()                 // menu item "Quit"
{
    this->DestroyWindow () ;                 // destroy main window,
}                                            // this stops application


    // show string table entry nString at location x,y on OutDC
void CMainWindow::OutStringTable (CPaintDC* OutDC, int nString,
    int x, int y)
{
    CString st ;
    st.LoadString (nString) ;
    OutDC->TextOut (x, y, st, st.GetLength ()) ;
}


    // show device capabilities code value for device DevDC at x,y
    // on device OutDC.  OutDC and DevDC can be the same device,
    // or different devices.
void CMainWindow::OutDevCapValue (CPaintDC* OutDC, CDC* DevDC,
    int code,  int x, int y)
{
    int nRetValue = DevDC->GetDeviceCaps (code) ;
    char cBuf [128] ;
    ostrstream myStream (cBuf, sizeof (cBuf)) ;
    myStream << nRetValue << ends ;
    OutDC->TextOut (x, y, cBuf, lstrlen (cBuf)) ;
}
```

Listing 14-27 DEVCAP.HPP Header File

```
// devcap.hpp    header file for devcap.cpp

class CMainWindow : public CFrameWnd     // derive a main window class
{
public:
    CMainWindow () ;                    // declare a constructor
private:
    void OnPaint () ;                    // window painting function
    void OnExit () ;                     // menu item "Quit"
    // show string table entry nString at location x,y on OutDC
    void OutStringTable (CPaintDC* OutDC, int string, int x, int y) ;
    // show device caps code for device DevDC at location x,y
    void OutDevCapValue (CPaintDC* OutDC, CDC* DevDC, int code,
        int x, int y) ;

    DECLARE_MESSAGE_MAP()                // prepare for message processing
} ;

class CTheApp : public CWinApp      // derive an application class
{
public:
    BOOL InitInstance () ;              // declare new InitInstance()
} ;
```

Listing 14-28 DEVCAP.H Resource ID Header File

```
// devcap.h   header file for resource ID numbers

#define IDM_QUIT            1           // menu item ID numbers
#define IDM_PRINT           2

#define S_PROGRAMCAPTION    1           // string table ID numbers
#define S_PRINTERTITLE      2
#define S_VIDEOTITLE        3
#define S_HORZSIZE          4
#define S_VERTSIZE          5
#define S_HORZRES           6
#define S_VERTRES           7
#define S_BITSPIXEL         8
#define S_PLANES            9
```

Figure 14-14 DEVCAP.ICO Icon Image

Listing 14-29 DEVCAP.RC Resource Script File

```
// devcap.rc  resource script file

#include <afxres.h>
#include "devcap.h"

AFX_IDI_STD_FRAME   ICON    devcap.ico   // the program's icon

MyMenu MENU                              // define the menu
{
    MENUITEM "&Quit",        IDM_QUIT
}


STRINGTABLE
{
    S_PROGRAMCAPTION       "Devcap Program"
    S_PRINTERTITLE         "Printer"
    S_VIDEOTITLE           "Video"
    S_HORZSIZE             "Horz. mm"
    S_VERTSIZE             "Vert. mm"
    S_HORZRES              "Horz. pixels"
    S_VERTRES              "Vert. pixels"
    S_BITSPIXEL            "Color bits"
    S_PLANES               "Color planes"
}
```

Listing 14-30 DEVCAP.DEF Module Definition File

```
NAME           devcap
DESCRIPTION    'devcap C++ program'
EXETYPE        WINDOWS
STUB           'WINSTUB.EXE'
CODE           PRELOAD MOVEABLE
DATA           PRELOAD MOVEABLE MULTIPLE
HEAPSIZE       1024
STACKSIZE      5120
```

PRINTER SETUP DIALOG BOXES

Back in the Windows 2.0 days, most programs required that the Windows Control Panel be used to change printer settings, such as selecting a different paper size. Most Windows 3.x programs provide the handy shortcut of a "Printer Setup" menu item, so you can change printer settings quickly from within the program. Figure 14-15 shows a typical printer setup dialog box.

Displaying a printer setup dialog box is such a common activity that Microsoft introduced a standard approach with Windows 3.1. The printer setup dialog box and several other common dialog boxes (file selection, input of a

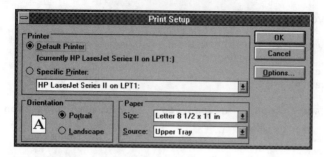

Figure 14-15 A Printer Setup Dialog Box

search string, selecting fonts, color selection, etc.) are part of the Microsoft's "Common Dialogs." The MFC classes make it simple to use these predefined dialog boxes by deriving dialog box classes for each type of dialog box. You will need to include the AFXDLGS.H header file in your program to take advantage of these dialog box classes.

To create a printer setup dialog box like the one shown in Figure 14-15, simply create a **CPrintDialog** object and call the **CDialog::DoModal**() function to display the object.

```
CPrintDialog PrintDlg (TRUE) ;
int nRetValue = PrintDlg.DoModal () ;
```

The **CPrintDialog::DoModal**() function will return either IDOK or IDCANCEL, depending on whether the user terminated the dialog box using the "OK" or "Cancel" button. You can also find out the status of any of the current printer settings using member functions of the **CPrintDialog** class. For example, to find out the number of copies that will be output:

```
int nCopies = PrintDlg.GetCopies () ;
```

Table 14-4 summarizes the member functions of the **CPrintDialog** class that you may find useful in determining what options the user will use for the next printing job. In most cases, these functions provide all of the information that you will need to use a printer for output from a Windows program.

Accessing a Printer Driver's Functions

There are a few situations where you will need to get more information about the specific printer or other output device. For example, you may need to know whether the device supports color output, and the resolution of the device. In order to get at these physical details, you will need to access functions in the printer driver.

Function	Returned Value
CPrintDialog::GetCopies()	Returns the number of copies that will be output.
CPrintDialog::GetDevMode()	Returns a pointer to a character string containing the printer's mode.
CPrintDialog::GetDeviceName()	Returns a pointer to a character string containing the name of the printer device.
CPrintDialog::GetDriverName()	Returns a pointer to a character string containing the name of the printer driver file.
CPrintDialog::GetFromPage()	Returns the starting page number.
CPrintDialog::GetPortName()	Returns a pointer to a character string containing the output port name (like "LPT1").
CPrintDialog::GetToPage()	Returns the ending page number.
CPrintDialog::PrintAll()	Returns TRUE if all pages will be printed.
CPrintDialog::PrintCollate()	Returns TRUE if the output is to be collated.
CPrintDialog::PrintRange()	Returns TRUE if the user entered a range of pages to print.
CPrintDialog::PrintSelection()	Returns TRUE if the user wants to print the current selection in the document.

Table 14-4 CPrintDialog Member Functions

If you think about the concept of calling a function in a printer driver, you may wonder how this is possible. The printer driver is a separate program, and one for which we do not have a source code listing. Under DOS, it would be nearly impossible to call a function in another program. There are two secrets to our ability to call a function in the printer driver under Windows. The first is that Microsoft specifies the names of several functions that all printer drivers should support. This is part of the documentation Microsoft provides with the *Windows Device Driver Development Kit* (DDDK). The other key is that the printer device driver file is a special type of Windows program, called a Dynamic Link Library, or "DLL" for short. DLLs are collections of functions that can be called by other Windows programs to perform tasks.

Although this is the first time we will *explicitly* call a function in a DLL, all of the programs in this book call functions in DLLs. Every time you use a Windows function, such as **CDC::TextOut()**, you are calling a function in a dynamic link library. The common Windows functions reside in DLLs named KERNEL, USER, and GDI. You can find these files in the Windows system directory. Dynamic link libraries are the basic stuff out of which Windows is made. Windows can be added to by simply adding more functions in dynamic link libraries. A printer driver is a typical example of a special feature added to Windows via a DLL.

Driver files are not part of the main portion of Windows and, therefore, do not use the WINDOWS.H file for constants and function declarations. Instead, the Microsoft development tools provide a separate header file called PRINT.H (named DRIVINIT.H under Windows NT). This file contains all of the constants, structure definitions, and function declarations needed to work with driver files from an outside program. For example, there is a *typedef* statement for the **DeviceCapabilities()** function in PRINT.H:

```
typedef DWORD  (CALLBACK* LPFNDEVCAPS)(LPSTR, LPSTR, UINT,
    LPSTR, DEVMODE FAR*);
```

The function type for **DeviceCapabilities()** was given the name LPFNDEVCAPS. These declared types are handy when declaring pointers to functions, as you will see in a moment. If you are working with a device driver's functions, be sure to include the PRINT.H file in your Windows program.

The first step in accessing a function in the printer driver is to load the driver into memory. The **::LoadLibrary()** global Windows function does this, and returns a handle to the file in memory. If the printer driver is already loaded, **::LoadLibrary()** just returns a handle to the driver in memory, without loading another copy. As an example, to load the HPPLC.DRV driver file, you would use the following code:

```
HANDLE hDriver = ::LoadLibrary ("c:\windows\system\hpplc.drv") ;
```

(This **::LoadLibrary()** function call is a bit oversimplified, as you would seldom know in advance that the user will be using the HPPLC.DRV driver. The complete example program PRTDRIV.CPP (shown later in Listing 14-31) demonstrates a more general technique for calling the **::LoadLibrary()** function, after determining the name of the currently installed printer driver.)

If the value returned by **::LoadLibrary()** is greater than 31, the library was successfully loaded. A returned value less than or equal to 31 means that the library was not loaded, probably because the library path/file name was incorrect. Assuming the library was loaded properly, the next step is to obtain the address of a function in the library so that the function can be called. **::GetProcAddress()** returns the address of a function in a DLL, or returns NULL if the function was not found

```
LPFNDEVCAPS lpfnDeviceCaps = (LPFNDEVCAPS) ::GetProcAddress
        (hDriver, "DeviceCapabilities") ;
```

Note that the *lpfnDeviceCaps* returned value from **::GetProcAddress()** is cast to the type LPFNDEVCAPS, defined in the PRINT.H header file. This is important, because the next step is to call the function pointed to by the *lpfnDeviceCaps* address. The C++ compiler will do its normal type checking when this function is called, so correctly casting the pointer to the function keeps the compiler satisfied that there has not been an error in the parameter list passed to the function. Here is an example function call to the **DeviceCapabilities()** function in the HPPLC.DRV printer driver, using the address of the function just obtained with **::GetProcAddress()**:

```
DWORD dwVersion = (* lpfnDeviceCaps) (szPrinter, szOutput,
            DC_DRIVER, NULL, NULL) ;
```

Don't feel bad if this syntax looks a bit odd. You can program in C or C++ for years without running into a need to call a function using a pointer to the function. However, this is valid C++ language syntax, and it is equivalent to calling the **DeviceCapabilities()** function in the printer driver directly:

```
DeviceCapabilites (szPrinter, szOutput, DC_DRIVER, NULL, NULL) ;
```

This direct call to the **DeviceCapabilities()** function would work if you were creating the printer driver, but is not possible from within another Windows program. The C++ compiler has no way of knowing the address of the **DeviceCapabilities()** function in advance and, therefore, cannot compile this function call. The address of the function in the driver must be obtained when the program is running (after the driver is loaded into memory so that the address is known), and a pointer is then used to call the **DeviceCapabilities()** function.

When you are done using the printer driver, you can tell Windows to free the driver from memory with the **::FreeLibrary()** global Windows function. The library will only be physically removed from memory if no other program is currently using the driver. Calling **::FreeLibrary()** is optional because Windows will purge the driver file from memory if it is no longer needed when Windows needs more space in memory.

```
::FreeLibrary (hDriver) ;
```

The DeviceCapabilities() Function

DeviceCapabilities() is an elaborate function, which can return many different pieces of information about an output device. Every company that produces drivers for their printer or output device is expected to support all of the **DeviceCapabilities()** options in their driver file. The full syntax for **DeviceCapabilities()** is shown in Table 14-5. A second table, Table 14-6, lists all the index

DWORD **DeviceCapabilities** (LPSTR *lpDeviceName*, LPSTR *lpPort*, WORD *nIndex*, LPSTR *lpOutput*, LPDEVMODE *lpDevMode*);

Parameter	Meaning
lpDeviceName	LPSTR A pointer to a null-terminated character string containing the printer device name as "PCL/HP LaserJet."
lpPort	LPSTR A pointer to a null-terminated character string containing the name of the port to which the device is connected, such as "LPT1:."
nIndex	WORD Specifies which value to obtain from the device. It can be any of the indices in Table 14-6, all of which are defined in DRIVINIT.H.
lpOutput	LPSTR A pointer to a memory buffer that will hold the device information obtained. The data received in the buffer will depend on the index value, as described in Table 14-6.
lpDevMode	LPDEVMODE Normally set to NULL. In this case, **DeviceCapabilities()** returns the current initialization values for the specified driver. If *lpDevMode* is not NULL, it should contain a pointer to a DEVMODE data structure containing the values to be read by **DeviceCapabilities()**. DEVMODE is defined in DRIVINIT.H.

Table 14-5 DeviceCapabilities() Parameters

values defined in the PRINT.H header file that are used to specify which data value should be returned.

A Printer Driver Access Example

The last example program in this chapter is called PRTDRIV.CPP. This example demonstrates using both the printer setup dialog box and the **DeviceCapabilities()** function with whatever printer driver is currently installed on your system. Figure 14-16 shows a typical example of PRTDRIV running with an HP IIP printer installed. If the "Printer Setup" menu item is selected, the printer setup dialog box defined in the printer driver is displayed, as was shown in Figure 14-15. The exact dialog box displayed will depend on the printer driver, so expect yours to be somewhat different unless you have an HP IIP printer installed.

Listing 14-31 shows the PRTDRIV.CPP program. Each time a WM_PAINT message is processed in **CMainWindow::OnPaint()**, PRTDRIV.CPP creates a character string consisting of the full path name and file name of the currently installed printer driver. This requires several steps. First, the printer driver and output de-

Value	Meaning
DC_BINNAMES	If the printer driver does not support multiple bins, **Device-Capabilities()** returns 0. If multiple bins are supported, **DeviceCapabilities()** returns the number of bins. *lpOutput* should then point to a memory buffer to hold data on the bins. The data consists of an array of integers, each containing the bin ID number (one for each bin). This is followed by the bin names, each 24 characters long. Set *lpOutput* to NULL to simply return the number of bins supported. This is usually done to determine the number of bytes to allocate for the bin numbers and names (26 bytes per bin).
DC_BINS	If *lpOutput* is set to NULL, **DeviceCapabilities()** returns the number of paper bins the printer supports. If *lpOuput* is not NULL, it should contain a pointer to a memory buffer. The buffer will receive an array of WORD values, each containing a bin number.
DC_COPIES (Win 3.1)	**DeviceCapabilities()** returns the maximum number of copies that the printer can produce.
DC_DRIVER	**DeviceCapabilities()** returns the printer driver version number.
DC_DUPLEX	Returns 1 if the printer supports duplex printing, 0 if not.
DC_ENUMRESOLUTIONS	If *lpOutput* is set to NULL, **DeviceCapabilities()** returns the number of output resolutions the printer supports. If *lpOuput* is not NULL, it should contain a pointer to a memory buffer. The buffer will receive an array of groups of two LONG integer values, each containing the horizontal and vertical resolution supported.
DC_EXTRA	Returns the number of bytes of device specific data at the end of the DEVMODE structure for the printer driver.
DC_FIELDS	Returns the bit-field value that specifies which features are supported by the printer driver. This is the same as the *dmFields* element of the DEVMODE structure.
DC_FILEDEPENDENCIES	If *lpOutput* is set to NULL, **DeviceCapabilities()** returns the number of files that need to be loaded to make the printer work. If *lpOuput* is not NULL, it should contain a pointer to a memory buffer. The buffer will receive an array of 64 character long file names, each containing the file name of a file that must be loaded to support the printer.

Table 14-6 DeviceCapabilities() nIndex Values

continued on next page

continued from previous page

Value	Meaning
DC_MAXEXTENT	Returns a POINT structure containing the maximum paper size that the printer can support. These are the largest values that can be placed in the *dmPaperLength* and *dmPaperWidth* elements of the DEVMODE structure.
DC_MINEXTENT	Returns a POINT structure containing the minimum paper size that the printer can support. These are the smallest values that can be placed in the *dmPaperLength* and *dmPaperWidth* elements of the DEVMODE structure.
DC_PAPERS	If *lpOutput* is set to NULL, **DeviceCapabilities()** returns the number of supported paper sizes. This is the normal use of this flag. If *lpOuput* is not NULL, it should contain a pointer to a memory buffer. The buffer will receive an array of WORD values, each containing a supported paper size.
DC_PAPERSIZE	*lpOutput* should contain a pointer to a memory buffer. The buffer will receive an array of POINT values, each containing the horizontal and vertical size in 1/10 mm for supported paper sizes. Use DC_PAPERS first to determine the size of the data buffer needed to contain the POINT data.
DC_SIZE	**DeviceCapabilities()** returns the size of the DEVMODE data structure, not including any driver-specific data following the structure. This is the same as the *dmSize* element of the DEVMODE data structure.
DC_VERSION	**DeviceCapabilities()** returns the Microsoft driver specification number to which the driver conforms.

Table 14-6 DeviceCapabilities() nIndex Values

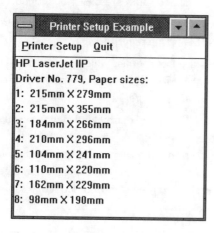

Figure 14-16 The PRTDRIV Program

vice name are extracted from the WIN.INI file, using the same techniques as in the previous examples. Next, the system directory path name is determined using the handy **::GetSystemDirectory()** function. The system directory is where all the driver files are stored for use by Windows. Normally, the system directory has the path name "C:\WINDOWS\SYSTEM," but you cannot safely assume this. The user may be using another drive, and may have renamed the system directory when he or she installed Windows. **::GetSystemDirctory()** copies the current directory name into a character string, correctly including the current drive letter and directory names. There is also a **::GetWindowsDirectory()** function, if you ever need to know the Windows directory ("C:\WINDOWS" by default).

```
char szSysDir [128] ;              // get system directory name
::GetSystemDirectory (szSysDir, 128) ;
```

The full path/file name of the driver file is constructed using the MFC **stream** operators and an **ostrstream** object. One trick here is that the backslash character (\) has a special meaning to the C++ compiler because, normally, it is used to insert tab and newline characters (\t and \n). Use two backslash characters in sequence ("\\") to append a single backslash character to a character string or stream.

```
ostrstream DriveStream (szFullDriver, sizeof (szFullDriver)) ;
DriveStream << szSysDir << "\\" << szDriver << ".DRV" << ends ;
```

Next, the driver file is loaded using the **::LoadLibrary()** function. **::LoadLibrary()** will return a value less than 32 if an error occurred. Otherwise, the returned value is the handle of the driver file in memory.

```
HANDLE hDriver = ::LoadLibrary (szFullDriver) ;
```

Now that you have the handle of the driver file in memory, you can get the address of the **DeviceCapabilities()** function within the driver using the **::GetProcAddress()** function. The returned value is cast to (LPFNDEVCAPS), which is defined in the PRINT.H header file.

```
LPFNDEVCAPS lpfnDeviceCaps = (LPFNDEVCAPS) ::GetProcAddress
          (hDriver, "DeviceCapabilities") ;
```

The pointer to the **DeviceCapabilities()** function in the driver file is then used twice to obtain specific information about the printer. In PRTDRIV.CPP, the driver version number and the supported paper sizes are determined and then output to the parent window's device context. This amounts to a lot of work to get a small amount of data from the printer driver. However, it is much less work than supporting all of the world's printers with your own printer drivers!

You will also want to look at the **CMainWindow::OnSetup()** function, which runs the printer setup dialog box. If the user selects the "OK" button on

Listing 14-31 PRTDRIV.CPP

```
// prtdriv.cpp        using printer setup dialog box and print driver

#include <afxwin.h>          // class library header file
#include <afxdlgs.h>         // common dialogs header file
#include <print.h>           // header file for printer driver info
#include <strstrea.h>        // streams header file
#include <string.h>          // for strtok() function
#include "prtdriv.h"         // header file for resource data
#include "prtdriv.hpp"       // header file for this program

CTheApp theApp ;             // create one CTheApp object - runs program

BOOL CTheApp::InitInstance ()    // override default InitInstance()
{
    m_pMainWnd = new CMainWindow () ;       // create a main window
    m_pMainWnd->ShowWindow (m_nCmdShow) ;   // make it visible
    m_pMainWnd->UpdateWindow () ;           // paint center
    return TRUE ;
}

CMainWindow::CMainWindow () // constructor for main program window
{
    CString title ;      // get program caption from resource data
    title.LoadString (S_PROGRAMCAPTION) ;
    Create (NULL, title, WS_OVERLAPPEDWINDOW, rectDefault,
        NULL, "MyMenu") ;
}

BEGIN_MESSAGE_MAP (CMainWindow, CFrameWnd)
    ON_WM_PAINT ()                       // process WM_PAINT messages
    ON_COMMAND (IDM_SETUP, OnSetup)      // menu item "Setup Printer"
    ON_COMMAND (IDM_QUIT, OnExit)        // menu item "Quit"
END_MESSAGE_MAP ()

void CMainWindow::OnPaint ()             // window painting function
{                                        // gets info from printer driver
    char szPrinter [64], *szDriver, *szDevice, *szOutput ;
    CPaintDC PaintDC (this) ;            // get client area device context
        // read WIN.INI file section [windows], line "device=..."
    ::GetProfileString ("windows", "device", "", szPrinter, 64) ;
        // parse string to find device, driver, and output strings
    szDevice = strtok (szPrinter, ",") ;    // commas separate fields
    szDriver = strtok (NULL, ",") ;
    szOutput = strtok (NULL, ",") ;
                                         // load driver file into memory:
    char szFullDriver [256] ;           // first, make a stream object
    ostrstream DriveStream (szFullDriver, sizeof (szFullDriver)) ;
    char szSysDir [128] ;               // get system directory name
    ::GetSystemDirectory (szSysDir, 128) ;
                                         // build full path/file name
    DriveStream << szSysDir << "\\" << szDriver << ".DRV" << ends ;
                                         // load driver and save handle
    HANDLE hDriver = ::LoadLibrary (szFullDriver) ;
    if ((int)hDriver < 32)                   // if driver not loaded,
```

```
    {                                       // show a message box and return
        CString msg, title ;
        msg.LoadString (S_PRINTDRIVERPROBLEM) ;
        title.LoadString (S_PRINTERROR) ;
        this->MessageBox (msg, title, MB_OK) ;
        return ;
    }                                       // get address of function in driver
    LPFNDEVCAPS lpfnDeviceCaps = (LPFNDEVCAPS) ::GetProcAddress
        (hDriver, "DeviceCapabilities") ;
    POINT PointArray [50] ;         // array to hold paper sizes
    if (lpfnDeviceCaps)                     // if function was found in driver
    {                                       // show device name at top
        PaintDC.TextOut (0, 0, szDevice, lstrlen (szDevice)) ;
                                            // get printer driver version number
        DWORD dwVersion = (* lpfnDeviceCaps) (szPrinter, szOutput,
            DC_DRIVER, NULL, NULL) ;
                                            // load paper sizes into point array
        DWORD dwNumPaperSizes = (* lpfnDeviceCaps) (szPrinter,
            szOutput, DC_PAPERSIZE, (LPSTR) PointArray, NULL) ;
                                            // make a stream for output strings
        char cBuf [128] ;
        ostrstream myStream (cBuf, sizeof (cBuf)) ;
        myStream << "Driver No. " << dwVersion << ",
            Paper sizes:" << ends ;
        PaintDC.TextOut (0, 20, cBuf, lstrlen (cBuf)) ;
        for (int i = 0 ; i < (int) dwNumPaperSizes ; i++)
        {                                   // show each paper size
            myStream.seekp (0) ;// move back to beginning of string
            myStream << i << ": " << PointArray [i].x / 10 << "mm X "
                << PointArray [i].y / 10 << "mm" << ends ;
            PaintDC.TextOut (0, 40 + (i * 20), cBuf, lstrlen (cBuf)) ;
        }
    }
}

void CMainWindow::OnSetup ()       // menu item "Setup Printer"
{
    CPrintDialog PrintDlg (TRUE) ;
    int nRetValue = PrintDlg.DoModal () ;// run printer setup dialog
    if (nRetValue == IDCANCEL)         // user selected "Cancel" button
        MessageBeep (0) ;
    else                                    // user selected "Ok" button
    {                                       // show some setup values in a
        char cBuf [256] ;                   // message box
        ostrstream myStream (cBuf, sizeof (cBuf)) ;
        myStream << "Current printer setup: " <<
            PrintDlg.GetCopies () << "copies, to printer " <<
            PrintDlg.GetDeviceName () << ", on port " <<
            PrintDlg.GetPortName () << ends ;
        this->MessageBox (cBuf, "", MB_OK) ;
    }
}

void CMainWindow::OnExit ()                 // menu item "Quit"
{
    this->DestroyWindow () ;                // destroy main window,
}                                           // this stops application
```

the dialog box, the **CMainWindow::OnSetup()** function displays a message box containing a number of the current printer settings. If the user selects the "Cancel" button, the program simply beeps the computer's speaker.

One shortcut taken in the PRTDRIV.CPP program is that the paper sizes are copied to an array of POINT structures called *PointArray[]*. This is not an ideal practice because no matter how big you make the array, there is always the chance that someone will build a printer with even more supported paper sizes. The preferred practice is to allocate a memory block big enough to hold all of the paper sizes once the number of paper sizes has been determined. This technique is demonstrated in one of the exercises at the end of this chapter.

Listings 14-32 to 14-35 show the support files for PRTDRIV.CPP. The program's icon is shown in Figure 14-17.

Listing 14-32 PRTDRIV.HPP Header File

```
// prtdriv.hpp    header file for prtdriv.cpp

class CMainWindow : public CFrameWnd  // derive a main window class
{
public:
    CMainWindow () ;              // declare a constructor
private:
    void OnPaint () ;            // window painting function
    void OnSetup () ;            // menu item "Setup"
    void OnExit () ;             // menu item "Quit"

    DECLARE_MESSAGE_MAP()        // prepare for message processing
} ;

class CTheApp : public CWinApp  // derive an application class
{
public:
    BOOL InitInstance () ;       // declare new InitInstance()
} ;
```

Listing 14-33 PRTDRIV.H Resource ID Header File

```
// prtdriv.h   header file for resource ID numbers

#define IDM_QUIT                1       // menu item ID numbers
#define IDM_SETUP               2

#define S_PROGRAMCAPTION        1       // string table ID numbers
#define S_PRINTDRIVERPROBLEM    2
#define S_PRINTERROR            3
```

Figure 14-17 PRTDRIV.ICO Icon Image

Listing 14-34 PRTDRIV.RC Resource Script File

```
// prtdriv.rc  resource script file

#include <afxres.h>
#include "prtdriv.h"

AFX_IDI_STD_FRAME   ICON    prtdriv.ico      // the program's icon

MyMenu MENU                                  // define the menu
{
    MENUITEM "&Printer Setup",  IDM_SETUP
    MENUITEM "&Quit",           IDM_QUIT
}


STRINGTABLE
{
    S_PROGRAMCAPTION           "Printer Setup Example"
    S_PRINTDRIVERPROBLEM       "Could not load Printer Driver."
    S_PRINTERROR               "Printer Error"
}
```

Listing 14-35 PRTDRIV.DEF Module Definition File

```
NAME           prtdriv
DESCRIPTION    'prtdriv C++ program'
EXETYPE        WINDOWS
STUB           'WINSTUB.EXE'
CODE           PRELOAD MOVEABLE
DATA           PRELOAD MOVEABLE MULTIPLE
HEAPSIZE       1024
STACKSIZE      10240
```

SUMMARY

Windows supports printers and plotters by using specialized support files called printer drivers. When a printer is installed, the printer driver is added to the Windows system directory, and the driver name is added to the WIN.INI file. When a program outputs text or graphics to the printer, the driver converts the GDI function calls into instructions that the printer understands. During output of text and graphics, the driver is not directly accessed. Simply obtaining a device context handle to the printer with the **CDC::CreateDC()** function allows all of the text and graphics commands to be sent to the printer instead of the screen. Normally, you will want to use a device context mapping mode with fixed scaling, such as MM_LOMETRIC, when working with a printer to avoid having the proportions of the output change depending on the resolution of the printer.

Printers require special commands, such as ejecting a page, that have no equivalent when output is sent to the screen. The **CDC** class provides a number of functions, such as **CDC::StartDoc()** and **CDC::StartPage()**, that send special commands to the printer. The **CDC::SetAbortProc()** function can also be used to notify the printer driver of a function that should process messages while the print job is in progress. This function, called an "abort" function, allows a Windows program to interrupt the print job while it is in progress.

It is sometimes necessary to obtain information about a printer or plotter to determine if it supports color output, what paper sizes are available, and so on. There are three general approaches to obtaining this type of data. The **CDC::GetDeviceCaps()** function allows a program to determine limited information about the printer or plotter, based on the values stored in the device context data. The second method takes advantage of the common dialog classes defined in the AFXDLGS.H header file. The **CPrintDialog** class can be used to display a printer setup dialog box and to obtain information about the current settings. The third method of obtaining information about the printer is to call functions within the printer driver. This is done indirectly by first loading the printer driver into memory with **::LoadLibrary()**, obtaining the address of a function in the driver with **::GetProcAddress()**, and then calling the function. The **DeviceCapabilities()** in the driver file provides a wide range of information about the printer. The PRINT.H header file is provided with the Microsoft programming tools to simplify working with device driver functions.

QUESTIONS

1. The driver file for a printer is stored in the _____ directory. The WIN.INI file is stored in the _____ directory.

2. The line in the WIN.INI file that contains the name of the printer, the printer driver name, and the output device name, starts with the word _____ followed by an equal sign. This will be in the section of WIN.INI that is named _____, surrounded in square brackets.

3. Use the _____ function to create a device context for a printer.

4. The correct way to read a line from the WIN.INI file is to call the _____ function.

5. Specialized graphics output commands, which are part of the **CDC** class and are available to the **CClientDC** or **CPaintDC** classes, must be used to output to a printer. (True/False)

6. Which function is used to begin a printing job?
   a. **CDC::StartDoc()**
   b. **CDC::StartPage()**
   c. **CDC::SetAbortProc()**
   d. **CDC::EndDoc()**

7. Which mapping mode would be the best choice for printing an image that is also displayed in the program's main window client area?
   a. MM_ISOTROPIC
   b. MM_ANISOTROPIC
   c. MM_HIMETRIC
   d. a or b

8. The dialog box that displays the print job "Cancel" button is derived from which of the following classes?
   a. **CDialog**
   b. **CPrintDialog**
   c. **CModalDialog**
   d. b or c

9. The abort procedure is a:
   a. global function
   b. a function that receives and transmits messages
   c. not part of any MFC class
   d. a, b, and c

10. The **CDC::GetDeviceCaps()** function retrieves information about a printer or other output device from:
    a. the printer driver
    b. the WIN.INI file
    c. the device context data
    d. the Windows environment

11. Function prototypes and constant definitions used with printer drivers are declared in the _____ file.

12. The _____ function loads the printer driver into memory. _____ removes it from memory.

13. The _____ function returns the address of a function in a driver or dynamic link library loaded into memory.

EXERCISES

1. The PRTDRIV.CPP program takes a shortcut of using an array of POINT structures to store the paper sizes obtained from the **DeviceCapabilities()** function in the printer driver. This is not an ideal solution because it is always possible that there will be more paper sizes supported than the number of POINT structures in the array, which will cause the program to terminate when Windows detects an attempt to write past the end of the array. Improve PRTDRIV.CPP so that the array of POINT data returned by **DeviceCapabilities()** is stored in a memory block. (Hint: You will need to call **DeviceCapabilities()** twice, once to obtain the number of paper sizes, and a second time to fill the paper size data into the allocated memory block.)

2. Modify the PRINT3.CPP program so that the printer abort procedure beeps the computer's speaker every time a message is processed while the dialog box is visible. When are messages received during printing?

ANSWERS TO QUESTIONS

1. system, windows.
2. device, windows.
3. **CDC::CreateDC()**.
4. **::GetProfileString()**.
5. False. **CClientDC** and **CPaintDC** are both derived from **CDC**, so all of the public functions in **CDC** are available to the derived classes. The same output functions are available in all three classes, such as **CDC::Ellipse()**.
6. a.
7. c.
8. a.

9. d.

10. c.

11. PRINT.H.

12. ::LoadLibrary(), ::FreeLibrary().

13. ::GetProcAddress().

SOLUTIONS TO EXERCISES

1. The complete solution is given under the name C14EXER1 on the source code disks. The changes (which are all in the **CMainWindow::OnPaint()** function) are summarized in Listing 14-36. The key to using an allocated memory block to store the paper size data is that you must determine the number of paper sizes before the block is allocated, so that you know how much space to reserve. This is done by first calling the **DeviceCapabilities()** function in the printer driver with the DC_PAPERS flag. The returned value is the number of paper sizes supported. A memory block of that size is then allocated with the *new* operator. The second call to the **DeviceCapabilities()** function uses the DC_PAPERS flag and copies the paper sizes into the memory block.

   Note the interesting shortcut in the **CDC::TextOut()** function at the bottom of the WM_PAINT logic in Listing 14-36. Array notation is used to reference the specific POINT value in the *pPointArray* memory block, even though *pPointArray* was only declared as a pointer to POINT data

Listing 14-36 Modifications to PRTDRIV.CPP

```
void CMainWindow::OnPaint ()          // window painting function
{                                     // gets info from printer driver
    char szPrinter [64], *szDriver, *szDevice, *szOutput ;
    CPaintDC PaintDC (this) ;         // get client area device context
        // read WIN.INI file section [windows], line "device=..."
    GetProfileString ("windows", "device", "", szPrinter, 64) ;
        // parse string to find device, driver, and output strings
    szDevice = strtok (szPrinter, ",") ;    // commas separate fields
    szDriver = strtok (NULL, ",") ;
    szOutput = strtok (NULL, ",") ;
                                      // load driver file into memory:
    char szFullDriver [256] ;         // first, make a stream object
```

```
ostrstream DriveStream (szFullDriver, sizeof (szFullDriver)) ;
char szSysDir [128] ;          // get system directory name
GetSystemDirectory (szSysDir, 128) ;
                               // build full path/file name
DriveStream << szSysDir << "\\" << szDriver << ".DRV" << ends ;
                               // load driver and save its handle
HANDLE hDriver = LoadLibrary (szFullDriver) ;
if ((int)hDriver < 32)         // if driver not loaded,
{                              // show a message box and return
    CString msg, title ;
    msg.LoadString (S_PRINTDRIVERPROBLEM) ;
    title.LoadString (S_PRINTERROR) ;
    this->MessageBox (msg, title, MB_OK) ;
    return ;
}                              // get address of function in driver
LPFNDEVCAPS lpfnDeviceCaps = (LPFNDEVCAPS)
    GetProcAddress (hDriver, "DeviceCapabilities") ;

if (lpfnDeviceCaps)            // if function was found in driver
{                              // show device name at top
    PaintDC.TextOut (0, 0, szDevice, lstrlen (szDevice)) ;
                               // get printer driver version number
    DWORD dwVersion = (* lpfnDeviceCaps) (szPrinter, szOutput,
        DC_DRIVER, NULL, NULL) ;
                               // find number of paper sizes
    DWORD dwNumPaperSizes = (* lpfnDeviceCaps) (szPrinter,
        szOutput, DC_PAPERS, NULL, NULL) ;
    if (dwNumPaperSizes < 1)// no further action if no paper!
        return ;
                               // allocate space to hold size data
    POINT *pPointArray = new POINT [(int) dwNumPaperSizes] ;
                               // load paper sizes into point array
    (* lpfnDeviceCaps) (szPrinter, szOutput, DC_PAPERSIZE,
        (LPSTR) pPointArray, NULL) ;
                               // make a stream for output strings
    char cBuf [128] ;
    ostrstream myStream (cBuf, sizeof (cBuf)) ;
    myStream << "Driver No. " << dwVersion << ",
        Paper sizes:" << ends ;
    PaintDC.TextOut (0, 20, cBuf, lstrlen (cBuf)) ;
    for (int i = 0 ; i < (int) dwNumPaperSizes ; i++)
    {                          // show each paper size
        myStream.seekp (0) ;   // move back to start of string
        myStream << i << ": " << pPointArray [i].x / 10 << "mm X "
            << pPointArray [i].y / 10 << "mm" << ends ;
        PaintDC.TextOut (0, 40 + (i * 20), cBuf, lstrlen (cBuf)) ;
    }
    delete pPointArray ;
}
}
```

(**POINT *pPointArray**), not as an array of POINT data (**POINT pPointArray[]**). The C++ compiler will allow you to use array notation based on a pointer to a block of data, as long as the data type for the pointer and array notation is the same. Array notation makes it easier to access specific elements of an array, rather than always using and incrementing pointers.

2. Listing 14-37 shows the modified printer abort procedure, which calls **::MessageBeep()** every time a message is processed. If you have the Print Manager turned off and turn your printer off and then run the modified PRINT3 program, you will have enough time to experiment with the program while the print abort dialog box is visible (after about 30 seconds the printer driver will quit trying to print and will display a message box). While the printer abort dialog box is visible, you may note that no messages are processed unless some action is taken, such as moving the mouse or using the keyboard. These actions generate messages, which are then processed by the **AbortProc()** function. The messages interrupt any processing being done by the printer driver, and provide an opportunity to cancel the printer job by selecting the "Cancel" button in the dialog box.

   The complete solution is given under the file names C14EXER2 and PRINTCN2 on the source code disks.

Listing 14-37 Modified Printer Abort Procedure

```
BOOL FAR PASCAL EXPORT AbortProc(HDC hDC, int nCode)
{
    MSG msg;    // message structure
        // loop checks bPrintContinue every time a message is sent
    while (_bPrintContinue &&
        PeekMessage(&msg, NULL, 0, 0, PM_REMOVE))
    {
        ::MessageBeep (0) ;
        if (_hDlg && !IsDialogMessage (_hDlg, &msg))
        {
            TranslateMessage (&msg);    // send message on to whatever
            DispatchMessage (&msg);     // application is active
        }
    }
    return _bPrintContinue ;            // returns when bPrintContinue
}
```

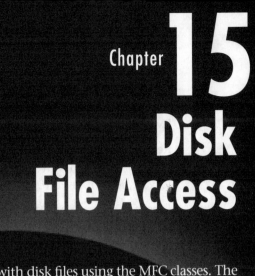

Disk
File Access

There are several ways to work with disk files using the MFC classes. The most direct method is to use the **CFile** class, which provides every function you will need for file access. An alternative is provided by the **fstream** class, which abstracts file operations to allow the use of standard C++ stream syntax (<<, >>, etc.) to send data to and from a disk file.

Besides moving data to and from a disk file, you will also need to allow the user to select which files should be accessed. File selection under Windows involves creating a dialog box that has list boxes for selecting subdirectories and specific files. The MFC classes provide access to a ready-to-use file selection dialog box. This dialog box is tested in this chapter by creating a functioning text editor, although it lacks cut-and-paste operations. These will be added in Chapter 17, *The Clipboard*.

Concepts covered: DOS disk file access, opening a file, reading file data, writing to a file, file position, closing a file, creating a file selection dialog box, SMARTDRV.EXE, attaching a memory block to an edit control.

Key words covered: CFile::modeCreate, CFile::modeRead, CFile::modeWrite, CFile::modeReadWrite, CFile::begin, CFile::current, CFile::end, ios::app, ios::ate, ios::in, ios::out, ios::trunc, ios::binary, ios::beg, ios::cur, ios::end.

Functions covered: CFile::Open(), CFile::Close(), CFile::Read(), CFile::Write(), CFile::GetLength(), CFile::Seek(), fstream::open(), fstream::close(), ostream::seekp(), istream::seekg(), istream::tellg(), CEdit::GetHandle(), CEdit::SetHandle().

Classes covered: CFile, CFileException, fstream, istream, ostream, ios.

HOW WINDOWS PROGRAMS ACCESS FILES

For most operations, Windows contains its own programming logic for accessing the computer's hardware. For example, all of the graphics output in the Windows GDI bypasses MS-DOS and directly accesses the computer's video hardware. However, Windows uses MS-DOS to access disk files. MS-DOS is always loaded in memory when Windows is running, so taking advantage of MS-DOS saves memory space by not duplicating these functions. Using MS-DOS functions also allows Windows to maintain 100% file compatibility with MS-DOS programs, which is a key selling point for the Windows environment. Figure 15-1 shows a comparison between the program logic for graphics output under Windows, and that for disk file access.

Windows NT File Access

Windows NT does not use the MS-DOS operating system for disk file access, so MS-DOS is not loaded before starting Windows NT. Instead, Windows NT is the first (and only) operating system you use to boot your computer. Windows NT includes all of the file access logic to deal with the disk drive hardware. Windows NT has the ability to read and write in MS-DOS-compatible format, which maintains compatibility with MS-DOS systems. This is called the "FAT" file format, which stands for the File Allocation Tables used by MS-DOS to track the location of files on the disk. Initially, most Windows NT users will probably use the FAT file system as they migrate from Windows to Windows NT.

continued on next page

continued from previous page

Windows NT also supports two other file formats. The HPFS (High Performance File System) is designed for the R4000-based computers. The NTFS (New Technology File System) is designed as a replacement for the FAT system on 80x86 CPU-based computers. The NTFS has faster access, better error recovery, and much better security than the older FAT system. The NTFS is ideal for networking applications.

The MFC classes (and Windows NT itself) hide all of the underlying differences between the three file systems. As a programmer, you will be able to create applications that can be compiled without change for either Windows 3.1 or Windows NT.

FILE ACCESS—TWO APPROACHES

Disk files provide an ideal subject for a C++ class object. The file can be thought of as a single object upon which various functions operate. The class libraries supplied with the Microsoft C++ compiler include two different classes for disk file access. The **CFile** class is part of the MFC classes, while the **fstream** class is part of the Microsoft **iostream** class library. Both classes support all of the basic

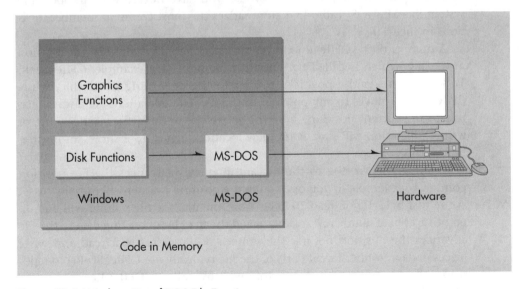

Figure 15-1 Windows Use of DOS File Functions

file operations, such as opening, reading, and writing data to the file. The difference between the two approaches is that the **CFile** class uses a conventional series of functions, such as **Read()**, **Write()**, **Open()**, **Close()**, and so on. The **fstream** class uses similar basic functions, but also uses C++ syntax for sending data to and from a disk file with overloaded operators, such as << and >>.

A logical question at this point is "Which class is best?" The answer boils down to being a matter of personal taste. The **CFile** and **fstream** classes both provide a complete set of functions for file access. One advantage of the **fstream** class is that it provides formatting options. If you need to read or write formatted data (for example, when converting between text and numeric data), the **fstream** class is probably the best choice.

This chapter starts with a simple example that uses the **CFile** class, and then creates a functionally identical application using the **fstream** class. You can compare the two programs and decide for yourself which class you prefer. The author happens to prefer the **fstream** approach because its syntax follows C++ language conventions. The last example in the chapter, which is a simple text editor, uses the **fstream** class.

THE CFILE CLASS

The MFC classes provide the **CFile** class for standard file operations. The functions will probably look familiar to you if you have worked with an operating system like MS-DOS. Table 15-1 summarizes the most common member functions in the **CFile** class.

A number of the **CFile** functions base their operations on a specific location in the file, which is called the "position pointer." For example, **CFile::SeekToBegin()** moves the position pointer to the beginning of the file, while **CFile::Seek()** moves to any position in the file. File operations are always relative to the current position, so if you move the pointer, the next reading or writing operation will start at the new location. Figure 15-2 shows an illustration of this concept.

Reading and writing to the file automatically advances the file position pointer. For example, if you open a file the position pointer will initially be set at the first byte. If you read 20 bytes from the file, the file pointer will end up pointing at byte number 21, ready to read the next byte. Writing data to the file advances the position pointer the same way. Programs that read and write pieces of data from different parts of the file typically use **CFile::Seek()** to reposition the file position pointer, followed by calls to **CFile::Read()** and/or **CFile::Write()**.

Function	Purpose
CFile::Open()	Opens a file for reading or writing data.
CFile::Close()	Closes a file. Access is not possible until the file is again opened.
CFile::Rename()	Changes the name of a file.
CFile::Remove()	Deletes the file.
CFile::Read()	Reads data from the file.
CFile::Write()	Writes data to the file.
CFile::GetLength()	Returns the length of the file.
CFile::Seek()	Moves to a specific location in the file.
CFile::SeekToBegin()	Moves to the beginning of the file.
CFile::SeekToEnd()	Moves to the end of the file.
CFile::GetPosition()	Returns the current position in the file.

Table 15-1 CFile Class Member Functions

One thing to keep in mind with disk files is that they have no intrinsic structure. You can think of a disk file as a long chain of bytes. It is up to the program to maintain the logical organization of a disk file and to interpret the data as it is read.

Opening a Disk File

Before you can take any action on a file, you must alert the operating system that the file will be accessed. This is called "opening" a file. The **CFile** class provides

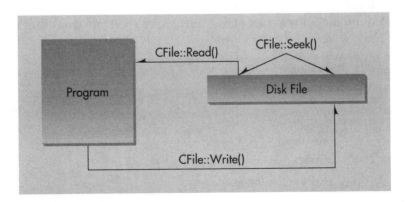

Figure 15-2 The File Position Pointer

two ways of doing this. One is to create a **CFile** object and open the file all at the same time. This takes advantage of the overloaded **CFile** constructor function.

```
CFile MyFile ("FILENAME.TXT", CFile::modeRead) ;
```

The other option is to first create a **CFile** object, and then use the **CFile** object to open a file. This two-step approach is handy because it allows you to declare the **CFile** object as a member of a class in your program without opening a particular file. Later, when you need to access the file, you can call the **CFile::Open()** function.

```
CFile MyFile ;      // create CFile object only
BOOL bStatus = MyFile.Open ("FILENAME.TXT", CFile::modeRead) ;
```

Note that the **CFile::Open()** function returns TRUE if the file was successfully opened, or FALSE if an error occurred. Both methods of opening a file take advantage of predefined flag values to specify what type of operations will be performed on the file. The **CFile::modeRead** flag opens the file for reading only. Any attempt to write to the file will fail if this flag is used. Table 15-2 lists the most common **CFile** flag values. The **CFile** class supports other flag values that are applicable to multiuser (LAN) applications. These advanced uses are not covered in this book.

If **CFile::Open()** returns FALSE, the file was not successfully opened. In most cases the cause is fairly obvious, such as when attempting to open a file that does not exist. In some applications it may be important to find out more specifics about why an attempt to open a file was not successful. The **CFile::Open()** function has an optional third parameter that is a pointer to a **CFileException** object. The **CFileException** class has the sole purpose of handling problems when opening files. Listing 15-1 shows a typical example using the **CFileException** class.

The *m_cause* public member of the **CFileException** class will contain an integer code for the file error if an error occurs. If you look in the AFX.H header file (included automatically as part of AFXWIN.H), you will find that the error codes

Value	Meaning
CFile::modeCreate	Creates a new file. If the file already exists it is opened and truncated to zero bytes.
CFile::modeRead	Opens a file for reading only.
CFile::modeReadWrite	Opens a file for reading and writing.
CFile::modeWrite	Opens a file for writing only.

Table 15-2 CFile Flag Values

15
DISK
FILE ACCESS

Listing 15-1 Using CFileException to Track a File Error

```
CFile MyFile ;
CFileException CFE ;
if (!MyFile.Open ("FILENAME", CFile::modeWrite, &CFE))
{
    int nError = CFE.m_cause ;
    // deal with the specific error here
}
```

Listing 15-2 CFileException Error Codes

```
enum {
    none,               // 0   no error occurred
    generic,            // 1   error, no specific cause
    fileNotFound,       // 2   could not find file
    badPath,            // 3   subdirectory path invalid
    tooManyOpenFiles,   // 4   exceeded DOS limit on open files
    accessDenied,       // 5   file exists, but access denied
    invalidFile,        // 6   the file itself is invalid
    removeCurrentDir,   // 7   requested to remove current dir.
    directoryFull,      // 8   no room in directory list
    badSeek,            // 9   seek operation failed (bad file?)
    hardIO,             // 10  input/output error
    sharingViolation,   // 11  sharing violation
    lockViolation,      // 12  file is locked
    diskFull,           // 13  disk has no additional room
    endOfFile,          // 14  attempt to read past end of file
};
```

are given names using the C++ language *enum* operator. *enum* just numbers a series of names in a sequence. Listing 15-2 shows the file exception codes with the error codes spelled out.

Catching Exceptions

You can also take advantage of the **CFileException** class to trap errors when using the **CFile** constructor function to open a file. This requires you to use the TRY, CATCH, and END_CATCH macros that are defined as part of the MFC classes as part of the "exception handling" logic. Listing 15-3 shows an outline of how to "catch" an "exception" caused by an error in attempting to open a file. The portion of the code that might cause the error follows the TRY macro. The portion of the code that should be executed if an "exception" (error) occurs is surrounded by the CATCH and END_CATCH macros. The **CFileException** and **theException** definitions are included automatically if you include AFXWIN.H in your file, so these values do not need to be declared.

continued on next page

continued from previous page

Listing 15-3 Catching an Exception

```
TRY
{
    CFile File ("testfile.txt", CFile::modeRead) ;
    // do any file operations here
}
CATCH (CFileException, theException)
{
    // do any error messages for file-not-opened here
    return ;
}
END_CATCH
```

The Microsoft documentation includes all sorts of other uses for pre-defined macros that handle exceptions, including errors in memory allocation. The example in Listing 15-3 is the only use of these macros in this book. If you would like to use these macros for error handling, you will want to review Chapter 5 of the *Microsoft C++ Class Libraries Reference* for additional information.

Reading and Writing Data

Once you have the file open, you can read and write data. For example, to create a new file, TESTFILE.TXT, and copy the uppercase alphabet to the file, you would use the code in Listing 15-4. Note that the data is first copied into a memory buffer, and then written as a block to the file using the **CFile::Write()** function. When file access is completed, the **CFile::Close()** function is used to close the file. The data is not safely stored in the file until the file is closed.

Notice in Listing 15-4 that the class name **CFile** is used in front of the flag values, such as **CFile::modeCreate**, rather than using the name of the object *File*. This is because the flags such as **modeCreate** are just constants and are not inherited by objects derived from the class. You will get a compiler error if you attempt to use a flag value like **File::modeCreate** because the **modeCreate** flag is not inherited from the **CFile** class by the *File* object.

When a file is first opened, the file position pointer will point to the beginning of the file. Any call made to **CFile::Read()** or **CFile::Write()** will start on the first byte, and move forward in the file as bytes are read or written. Often, you will want to move to a specific location in the file prior to reading or writing data. This is done with the **CFile::Seek()** function, which moves the file pointer forward or backward in the file. Listing 15-5 shows an example that moves to byte number 10 in the file, and then writes ten bytes of data to the file.

Listing 15-4 Creating a New File

```
CFile File ;
if (!File.Open ("testfile.txt",
    CFile::modeCreate | CFile::modeWrite))
{
    // display an error message
    return ;
}
char* ps = new char [27] ;          // allocate a memory buffer
char* ps2 = ps ;
for (int i = 0 ; i < 26 ; i++)
    *ps2++ = 'A' + i ;              // put in uppercase letters
*ps2 = 0 ;                          // add null byte
File.Write (ps, 27) ;              // write the data to file
File.Close () ;                     // close the file
delete ps ;                         // free the memory block
```

Listing 15-5 Using CFile::Seek()

```
CFile File ;
if (!File.Open ("testfile.txt", CFile::modeReadWrite))
{
    // display an error message
    return ;
}
File.Seek (10, CFile::begin) ;
char TempBuff [] = {"Some text."} ;
File.Write (TempBuff, 10) ;
File.Close () ;
```

The **CFile::Seek()** syntax is summarized in Table 15-3. You can use both positive and negative values for the *lOff* parameter to move the file position pointer forward and backward in the file. A common error is to move past the end of the file, which will invalidate any subsequent reading operations. It is up to your program's logic to keep track of the length of the file to avoid this error. You can use the **CFile::GetLength()** function at any time to determine the current size of the file.

Closing a File

It is easy to forget to close a disk file after it has been opened or created. Until a file is closed, the data is not fully registered on the disk drive. If you forget to close a file, other disk operations may write over some or all of the disk file. The operating system may also run out of file handles if the program continues to open, but not close, files.

```
LONG CFile::Seek (LONG lOff, UINT wFrom) ;
```

Parameter	Meaning
lOff	The number of bytes to move. Positive values move forward in the file, negative values move backward (toward the start of the file).
wFrom	The starting position from which to move the pointer. The **CFile** class defines three flag values that specify the starting point for the **CFile::Seek()** operation. The wFrom parameter should contain one of these values.
CFile::begin	Move the file position pointer lOff bytes relative to the beginning of the file.
CFile::current	Move the file position pointer lOff bytes relative to the current location of the file position pointer.
CFile::end	Move the file position pointer lOff bytes relative to the end of the file. lOff must be either zero or negative.

Table 15-3 CFile::Seek() Syntax

Closing a file is simple—just call the **CFile::Close()** function. Once the file is closed, the **CFile** object no longer holds a valid disk file. If you want to do another operation on the file, you must open it again with **CFile::Open()**.

The SMARTDRV.EXE Program

When you install Windows 3.1, the installation program will add a line to the CONFIG.SYS file on your root directory (usually the C:\ directory) that will cause the SMARTDRV.EXE program to be loaded into memory. SMARTDRV is a disk caching program. This means that SMARTDRV can speed up disk operations by saving recently loaded portions of disk files in memory, rather than always reading and writing from the disk surface. The memory allocated to saving disk file contents is called a "cache." A typical call to load SMARTDRV.EXE is as follows:

```
C:\WINDOWS\SMARTDRV.EXE
```

This line in AUTOEXEC.BAT will run the SMARTDRV.EXE program. The physical size limits of the cache that are optimum for your system will depend on how much memory you have installed.

continued on next page

continued from previous page

SMARTDRV has no way of knowing in advance which files you will be using, and is only effective once a file has been opened. When a disk file is opened, its contents are copied into the SMARTDRV cache. For small files, the entire file will end up copied into the cache. For larger files, the portions of the file that are accessed, and which will fit within the limits of the cache size, will end up copied into the cache. Subsequent disk reading operations that access the portions of the file in the cache will only read the memory contents, and will not physically read from the disk file. You can verify this by noting that the disk drive light does not flash during these file operations.

The result of disk caching is that repeated access to the same files or file portions is very fast. This is a big advantage for Windows applications, which typically store a variety of items as resource data (menus, string tables, etc.) and which may have a number of different elements of the program loaded and unloaded from the disk as the program operates.

A FILE ACCESS EXAMPLE

The first example program in this chapter, imaginatively named FILE1, demonstrates several file operations. Figure 15-3 shows the FILE1 program in operation. When the "Write File" menu item is selected, FILE1 writes the capital letters A-Z to a file named TESTFILE.TXT in the same drive/directory that the FILE1 program resides. Selecting the "Read File" option opens the TESTFILE.TXT file, reads its contents, and displays the contents in the FILE1 window's client area. This is the status shown in Figure 15-3.

The "Append File" menu item also opens the TESTFILE.TXT file, this time to add the digits 0-9 to the end of the file. If the "Read File" menu item is selected after "Append File" is selected once, FILE1 will appear as shown in Figure 15-4. Each time "Append File" is selected, another set of 0-9 digits is appended to the file, lengthening the file.

Figure 15-3 The FILE1 Program After "Write File" and "Read File" Menu Item Selections

Figure 15-4 The FILE1 Program After "Append File" and "Read File" Menu Item Selections

Listing 15-6 shows the FILE1.HPP header file. Note that a **CFile** object named *File* is declared as a private member of the **CMainWindow** class. This will make the *File* object available to all member functions of the **CMain-Window** class. The *File* object will be used for all file operations in the program. Besides the message processing functions for the menu items, FILE1.HPP also declares a function named **StringTableMessageBox()**, which will be used to display message boxes as the program operates.

The FILE1.CPP program is shown in Listing 15-7. The file operations are simplified by always creating a file named "TESTFILE.TXT" in the same directory with the program. This file is created when the user selects the "Write File" menu item, which is mapped to the **CMainWindow::OnWrite()** function.

Listing 15-6 FILE1.HPP Header File

```
// file1.hpp    header file for file1.cpp

class CMainWindow : public CFrameWnd  // derive main window class
{
public:
    CMainWindow () ;               // declare a constructor
private:
    CFile File ;                   // CFile object declared here
    void OnWrite () ;              // write to the disk file
    void OnRead () ;               // read from disk file
    void OnAdd () ;                // append data to disk file
    void OnExit () ;              // menu item "Quit"
    int StringTableMessageBox (int nMessage, int nTitle,
        WORD flags = MB_OK) ;

    DECLARE_MESSAGE_MAP()          // prepare for message processing
} ;

class CTheApp : public CWinApp  // derive an application class
{
public:
    BOOL InitInstance () ;         // declare new InitInstance()
} ;
```

Listing 15-7 FILE1.CPP

```cpp
// file1.cpp                    example using CFile class

#include <afxwin.h>     // class library header file
#include <strstrea.h>   // streams header file
#include "file1.h"      // header file for resource data
#include "file1.hpp"    // header file for this program


CTheApp theApp ;         // create one CTheApp object - runs program

BOOL CTheApp::InitInstance ()    // override default InitInstance()
{
    m_pMainWnd = new CMainWindow () ;        // create a main window
    m_pMainWnd->ShowWindow (m_nCmdShow) ;    // make it visible
    m_pMainWnd->UpdateWindow () ;            // paint center
    return TRUE ;
}


CMainWindow::CMainWindow () // constructor for main program window
{
    CString title ;      // get program caption from resource data
    title.LoadString (S_PROGRAMCAPTION) ;
    Create (NULL, title, WS_OVERLAPPEDWINDOW, rectDefault,
        NULL, "MyMenu") ;
}


BEGIN_MESSAGE_MAP (CMainWindow, CFrameWnd)
    ON_COMMAND (IDM_WRITE, OnWrite)      // menu item "Write File"
    ON_COMMAND (IDM_READ, OnRead)        // menu item "Read File"
    ON_COMMAND (IDM_ADD, OnAdd)          // menu item "Append File"
    ON_COMMAND (IDM_QUIT, OnExit)        // menu item "Quit"
END_MESSAGE_MAP ()

void CMainWindow::OnWrite ()
{
    if (!File.Open ("testfile.txt",
        CFile::modeCreate | CFile::modeWrite))
    {   // show an error message if could not create the file
        StringTableMessageBox (S_NOCREATE, S_FILEERROR,
            MB_OK | MB_ICONHAND) ;
        return ;
    }
    char* ps = new char [27] ;               // allocate a memory buffer
    char* ps2 = ps ;
    for (int i = 0 ; i < 26 ; i++)
        *ps2++ = 'A' + i ;                   // put in uppercase letters
    *ps2 = 0 ;                               // add null byte
    File.Write (ps, 27) ;                    // write the data to file
    File.Close () ;                          // close the file
    delete ps ;                              // free the memory block
    StringTableMessageBox (S_CREATED, S_MESSAGE,
        MB_OK | MB_ICONINFORMATION) ;
}
```

```
void CMainWindow::OnRead ()
{
    if (!File.Open ("testfile.txt", CFile::modeRead))
    {
        StringTableMessageBox (S_NOREAD, S_FILEERROR,
            MB_OK | MB_ICONHAND) ;
        return ;
    }                                        // get file length
    UINT FileLong = (UINT) File.Seek (0, CFile::end) ;
    File.Seek (0, CFile::begin) ;            // go back to beginning
    char* ps = new char [FileLong] ;         // allocate a buffer
    File.Read (ps, FileLong) ;               // copy file to buffer
    File.Close () ;                          // close the file

    CClientDC dc (this) ;                    // get client area dc
    dc.TextOut (0, 0, ps, lstrlen (ps)) ;// show buffer contents
    delete ps ;                              // get rid of buffer
}


void CMainWindow::OnAdd ()
{
    if (!File.Open ("testfile.txt",
        CFile::modeRead | CFile::modeWrite))
    {
        StringTableMessageBox (S_NOREAD, S_FILEERROR,
            MB_OK | MB_ICONHAND) ;
        return ;
    }
            // move to one before end to write over terminal null
    UINT FileLong = (UINT) File.Seek (-1, CFile::end) ;
    char* ps = new char [11] ;          // allocate a buffer
    char* ps2 = ps ;
    for (int i = 0 ; i < 10 ; i++)
        *ps2++ = '0' + i ;              // put in digit characters
    *ps2 = 0 ;                          // add null byte
    File.Write (ps, 11) ;               // write the data to the file
    File.Close () ;                     // close the file
    delete ps ;                         // free the memory block
    StringTableMessageBox (S_NOWTRY, S_MESSAGE,
        MB_OK | MB_ICONINFORMATION) ;
}

void CMainWindow::OnExit ()             // menu item "Quit"
{
    this->DestroyWindow () ;            // destroy main window,
}                                       // this stops application

    // show string table entry nString at location x,y
int CMainWindow::StringTableMessageBox (int nMessage, int nTitle,
    WORD flags)
{
    CString message, title ;
    message.LoadString (nMessage) ;
    title.LoadString (nTitle) ;
    return (this->MessageBox (message, title, flags)) ;
}
```

The contents of the file are read when the user selects "Read File," which is mapped to the **CMainWindow::OnRead()** function. **CMainWindow::On-Read()** exercises the **CFile::Seek()** function to determine the length of the file. The file position pointer returned by **CFile::Seek()** will be equal to the number of bytes in the file if the pointer is positioned at the end. You can also use the **CFile::GetLength()** function to accomplish the same result.

```
UINT FileLong = (UINT) File.Seek (0, CFile::end) ;
File.Seek (0, CFile::begin) ;          // go back to beginning
```

Once the length of the file is known, a buffer to hold the file data can be allocated. The data from the file is then copied into this buffer using the **CFile::Read()** function.

```
char* ps = new char [FileLong] ;       // allocate a buffer
File.Read (ps, FileLong) ;             // copy file to buffer
```

The file is then closed with **CFile::Close()**, and the data displayed on the FILE1 program's main window client area. The file must be reopened to do any further operations, such as the addition of ten digit characters when the user selects the "Append File" menu item. The only trick in appending the ten new characters is to write over the null character at the end of the string. This is done by using **CFile::Seek()** to move one character before the end of the file:

```
UINT FileLong = (UINT) File.Seek (-1, CFile::end) ;
```

Once the file pointer is moved to this position, the subsequent **CFile::Write()** operations add bytes starting at this point. The null character is written over, and a new null character is added to the end of the extended file as the last character written. If the intermediate null character were not written over, functions such as **CDC::TextOut()** would only output the character data up to the first null. Any character data after that point would be hidden.

Throughout FILE1.CPP, you will see the **StringTableMessageBox()** function used to display messages composed of character strings defined in the program's resource script file. The **CMainWindow::StringTableMessageBox()** function is defined at the end of FILE1.CPP. This is a simple and very useful function that you will see in a number of example programs in this book. Both the message box title and internal text strings are passed to the function using the string table ID numbers. By default, the function displays a single "OK" button, although you can pass standard **CWnd::MessageBox()** flag values (such as MB_OKCANCEL) as the optional third parameter.

The remaining support files for FILE1.CPP are shown in Listings 15-8 to 15-10. Figure 15-5 shows the program's icon.

Listing 15-8 FILE1.H Resource ID Header File

```
// file1.h  header file for resource ID numbers

#define IDM_WRITE          1        // menu item ID numbers
#define IDM_READ           2
#define IDM_ADD            3
#define IDM_QUIT          10

#define S_PROGRAMCAPTION   1        // string table ID numbers
#define S_NOCREATE         2
#define S_FILEERROR        3
#define S_CREATED          4
#define S_MESSAGE          5
#define S_NOREAD           6
#define S_NOOPEN           7
#define S_NOWTRY           8
```

Listing 15-9 FILE1.RC Resource Script File

```
// file1.rc  resource script file

#include <afxres.h>
#include "file1.h"

AFX_IDI_STD_FRAME   ICON    file1.ico       // the program's icon

MyMenu MENU                                 // define the menu
{
    MENUITEM "&Write File",     IDM_WRITE
    MENUITEM "&Read File",      IDM_READ
    MENUITEM "&Append File",    IDM_ADD
    MENUITEM "&Quit",           IDM_QUIT
}

STRINGTABLE
{
    S_PROGRAMCAPTION    "File 1 Program"
    S_NOCREATE          "Could not create file TESTFILE.TXT"
    S_FILEERROR         "File Error"
    S_CREATED           "Created file TESTFILE.TXT"
    S_MESSAGE           "Message"
    S_NOREAD            "Could not read file TESTFILE.TXT"
    S_NOOPEN            "Could not open file TESTFILE.TXT"
    S_NOWTRY            "Now try reading file"
}
```

Figure 15-5 FILE1.ICO Icon Image

Listing 15-10 FILE1.DEF Module Definition File

```
NAME          file1
DESCRIPTION   'file1 C++ program'
EXETYPE       WINDOWS
STUB          'WINSTUB.EXE'
CODE          PRELOAD MOVEABLE
DATA          PRELOAD MOVEABLE MULTIPLE
HEAPSIZE      1024
STACKSIZE     5120
```

THE FSTREAM CLASS

The **CFile** class provides a familiar set of functions for programmers who have been using the MS-DOS file system. However, the Microsoft **iostream** classes provide an alternative family of classes that abstracts disk files to represent an output stream object. The **fstream** class (one of the **iostream** classes) allows you to send and receive data from a disk file using standard C++ stream operators, such as >> and <<. The **fstream** class is defined in the FSTREAM.H header file, not in the standard AFXWIN.H header. Table 15-4 shows a comparison of the primary functions in the **CFile** and **fstream** classes.

The **fstream** class is interesting in that it inherits from both an input and output stream class. This complex inheritance path is shown in Figure 15-6. The inheritance path is important because you may need to use functions in not only the **fstream** class, but also in **iostream**, **ostream**, **istream**, and the **ios** base class. Public member functions in all of these classes are available to any **fstream** object. For example, we will use the **ostream::seekp()** function to move

CFile Class	fstream Class	Purpose
CFile::Open	fstream::open()	Open a file.
CFile::Close()	fstream::close()	Close a file.
CFile::Read()	istream::operator >>	Read data from a file.
CFile::Write()	ostream::operator <<	Write data to a file.
CFile::Seek()	istream::seekg() ostream::seekp()	Move to a new position in the file.
CFile::GetPosition()	istream::tellg() ostream::tellp()	Return current position in the file.

Table 15-4 Common CFile Versus fstream Class Member Functions

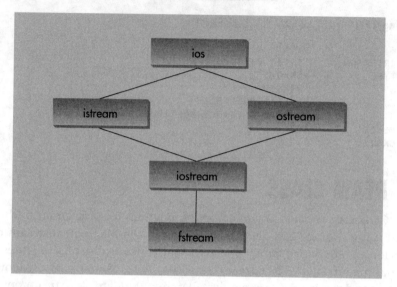

Figure 15-6 The fstream Class Inheritance

to a new location in a file created using a **fstream** object. You could also use the **istream::seekg()** function for the same task because the **fstream** class inherits from both **ostream** and **istream**. You will need to keep the inheritance path in mind when looking up functions in the MFC documentation, because the function you need may reside in any of the classes shown in Figure 15-6.

Opening a disk file using the **fstream** class is similar to using the **CFile** class. There are two basic methods. One method is to create an **fstream** object and open a file all in one call to the **fstream** constructor function:

```
fstream FileStream ("filename", ios::out, filebuf::sh_none) ;
```

This line creates an **fstream** object named *FileStream*, and opens the disk file FILENAME for output. The meaning of the parameters will be explained in a moment. The second method of opening a file is to first create an **fstream** object, and later call the **fstream::open()** function to open the disk file:

```
fstream FileStream ;    // create the fstream object first
FileStream.open ("filename", ios::out, filebuf::sh_none) ;
```

The advantage of using the two-step method of opening a file is that the **fstream** object can be declared as a member object of a class, and then later used to open a file. This will be demonstrated with the next example program. Both methods use the same three parameters when opening the file. The first parameter is the name of the file. This can be a full path/file name, such as "C:\TEXT\MYFILE.TXT." The second parameter specifies one or more flag values,

File Mode	Meaning
ios::app	(Append) New bytes are always written to the end of the file, regardless of the last call to **ostream::seekp()**.
ios::ate	(At End) Moves to the end of the file when opened, but **ostream::seekp()** can be used to change the file position pointer for subsequent write operations.
ios::in	(Input) The file is opened for input.
ios::out	(Output) The file is opened for output.
ios::trunc	(Truncate) If the file already exists, its contents are discarded. If the file does not already exist, a new file is created.
ios::nocreate	If the file does not already exist, a new file is not created.
ios::noreplace	If the file already exists, the function fails (no harm to an existing file).
ios::binary	Opens a file in binary mode. The default mode is text.

Table 15-5 fstream::open() Mode Flags

such as **ios::out**, that specify the file mode when opened. These flag values are defined in FSTREAM.H and summarized in Table 15-5. Note that two or more of these flags can be combined using the C++ language binary OR operator (|).

The third parameter passed to **fstream::open()** is the file protection flag. This should be one of the values shown in Table 15-6. The *filebuff::sh_read* and *filebuff:sh_write* modes can be combined with the binary OR operator (|). File sharing is important in applications where more than one user may access the same database at one time. Some database programs allow many users to read data at one time, but only one is allowed to write, so as to avoid conflicts where two programs are attempting to change the same entry at one time.

Once you have created an **fstream** object, you can use the overloaded << and >> operators to send and receive data to or from the file. The >> operator is

Flag	Meaning
filebuff::sh_compat	Compatibility (share) mode. Multiple access allowed.
filebuff::sh_none	Exclusive mode—no sharing allowed.
filebuff::sh_read	Read sharing is allowed.
filebuff::sh_write	Write sharing is allowed.

Table 15-6 fstream::open() Protection Flags

inherited from the **istream** (input stream) class, while << is inherited from **ostream** (output stream). Both operators are heavily overloaded, so you can send character data, integers, longs, floats, and even other stream objects as data. Listing 15-11 shows a typical sequence of function calls that writes a short character string to a file named "TESTFILE.TXT."

The **fstream::is_open()** function returns a nonzero value if the file is opened, or zero if an error occurred. As you can see, sending data to a file is pretty simple using the **fstream** class. Reading data from a file is a bit more complex because you will usually need to determine how long the file is before allocating memory to hold the file's data. Listing 15-12 shows a comparable example that copies the contents of the "TESTFILE.TXT" disk file into a memory buffer. The length of the file is determined by first calling the **istream::seekg()** function to move to the end of the file, and then using **istream::tellg()** to return the value of the file position pointer. The value of the pointer at the end of the file is the number of bytes in the file, returned as a *streampos* (integer) value. Note that **istream::seekg()** and **istream::tellg()** are from the input stream class **istream** because we are reading (getting input) from the file.

The **istream::seekg()** function works just like the **CFile::Seek()** function we used in the first example program. The first parameter specifies the number of bytes

Listing 15-11 Writing to a File

```
fstream FStream ;
FStream.open ("testfile.txt", ios::out, filebuf::sh_none) ;
if (FStream.is_open)          // check if file opened OK
{
    FStream << "This data sent to the file." ;
    FStream.close () ;
}
```

Listing 15-12 Reading from a File

```
fstream FStream ;
FStream.open ("testfile.txt", ios::in, filebuf::sh_none) ;
if (FStream.is_open)
{
    FStream.seekg (0, ios::end) ;            // move to end of stream
    streampos pos = FStream.tellg () ;       // returns file length
    FStream.seekg (0, ios::beg) ;            // go back to beginning
    char* cBuf = new char [(int) pos] ;      // allocate a buffer

    FStream >> cBuf ;                        // copy file to buffer
    FStream.close () ;                       // close the file
    // do something with the data
    delete cBuf ;
}
```

Flag	Meaning
ios::beg	Movement in the file is relative to the beginning of the file.
ios::cur	Movement in the file is relative to the current position.
ios::end	Movement in the file is relative to the end of the file.

Table 15-7 istream::seekg() and ostream::seekp() Flags

to move in the file. Positive values move toward the end of the file, while negative values move toward the beginning. The second parameter specifies the starting point for the movement. Table 15-7 summarizes the flag values that can be used with **istream::seekg()**. The **ostream::seekp()** function is used for moving in a file opened for output, and uses the same parameters and flags as **istream::seekg()**.

An Example Program Using the fstream Class

The next example program, FILESTRM, uses the **fstream** class to accomplish the same activities as the previous example, FILE1. In both cases, a file named TESTFILE.TXT is created, written to, and read from, based on menu item selections. Figure 15-7 shows the FILESTRM program after the user has selected the "Write File," "Append File," and "Read File" menu items. "Write File" writes the uppercase alphabet to TESTFILE.TXT. "Append File" adds the digit characters "0" to "9" to the end of the file. "Read File" reads TESTFILE.TXT and displays the string in the program window's client area. You can select "Append File" as many times as you like. The file gets ten characters longer each time "Append File" is selected. Selecting "Write File" again reduces the file to its initial state of containing only 26 characters plus a terminal null character.

Listing 15-13 shows the FILESTRM.HPP header file. Note that an **fstream** object is declared as a private member of the **CMainWindow** class. Otherwise, the file is identical to FILE1.HPP.

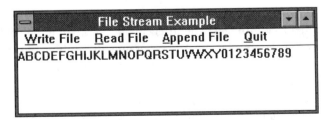

Figure 15-7 The FILESTRM Program

635

Listing 15-13 FILESTRM.HPP Header File

```
// filestrm.hpp    header file for filestrm.cpp

class CMainWindow : public CFrameWnd// derive a main window class
{
public:
    CMainWindow () ;                     // declare a constructor
private:
    fstream FStream ;                    // file stream object
    void OnWrite () ;                    // write to the disk file
    void OnRead () ;                     // read from disk file
    void OnAdd () ;                      // append data to disk file
    void OnExit () ;                     // menu item "Quit"
    // show string table entry nString at location x,y
    int StringTableMessageBox (int nMessage, int nTitle,
        WORD flags = MB_OK) ;

    DECLARE_MESSAGE_MAP()                // prepare for message processing
} ;

class CTheApp : public CWinApp          // derive an application class
{
public:
    BOOL InitInstance () ;              // declare new InitInstance()
} ;
```

Listing 15-14 shows the FILESTRM.CPP program. Rather than construct a memory buffer containing all the data to be written to the file, FILESTRM.CPP copies the letters and digits individually to the file using the << operator. The << operator is overloaded to copy character data (as well as many other types of data) to a file, so the only trick is to make sure that the data is cast to (char) before sending it. For example, the digit characters are added to the end of TESTFILE.TXT with the following sequence:

```
FStream.seekp (-1, ios::end) ; // back up 1, over null byte
for (int i = 0 ; i < 10 ; i++)
 FStream << (char) ('0' + i) ; // write 10 digits
FStream << (char) 0 ; // add terminal null
```

Without the (char) cast, the data in the quantity ('0' + i) would be interpreted by the compiler as an integer. The integer (number) would be copied to the file, not its character representation. The program will run fine, but the data in the file will be a sequence of integers and will not be displayed properly by **CDC::TextOut()** unless you do some formatting.

The remaining support files for FILESTRM.CPP are shown in Listings 15-15 to 15-17. These are essentially identical to their FILE1 counterparts. Figure 15-8 shows the FILESTRM.ICO icon image.

Listing 15-14 FILESTRM.CPP

```cpp
// filestrm.cpp              example using fstream class

#include <afxwin.h>          // class library header file
#include <strstrea.h>        // streams header file
#include <fstream.h>         // file streams header file
#include "filestrm.h"        // header file for resource data
#include "filestrm.hpp"      // header file for this program

CTheApp theApp ;         // create one CTheApp object - runs program

BOOL CTheApp::InitInstance ()    // override default InitInstance()
{
    m_pMainWnd = new CMainWindow () ;         // create a main window
    m_pMainWnd->ShowWindow (m_nCmdShow) ;     // make it visible
    m_pMainWnd->UpdateWindow () ;             // paint center
    return TRUE ;
}


CMainWindow::CMainWindow () // constructor for main program window
{
    CString title ;      // get program caption from resource data
    title.LoadString (S_PROGRAMCAPTION) ;
    Create (NULL, title, WS_OVERLAPPEDWINDOW, rectDefault,
        NULL, "MyMenu") ;
}

BEGIN_MESSAGE_MAP (CMainWindow, CFrameWnd)
    ON_COMMAND (IDM_WRITE, OnWrite)      // menu item "Write File"
    ON_COMMAND (IDM_READ, OnRead)        // menu item "Read File"
    ON_COMMAND (IDM_ADD, OnAdd)          // menu item "Append File"
    ON_COMMAND (IDM_QUIT, OnExit)        // menu item "Quit"
END_MESSAGE_MAP ()

void CMainWindow::OnWrite ()     // create TESTFILE.TXT file
{
    FStream.open ("testfile.txt", ios::out, filebuf::sh_none) ;
    if (!FStream.is_open)        // if error show message and return
    {
        StringTableMessageBox (S_NOCREATE, S_FILEERROR,
            MB_OK | MB_ICONHAND) ;
        return ;
    }
    for (int i = 0 ; i < 26 ; i++)
        FStream << (char) ('A' + i) ;  // write alphabet

    FStream << (char) 0 ;                    // write null char
    FStream.close () ;                       // close the file
    StringTableMessageBox (S_CREATED, S_MESSAGE,
        MB_OK | MB_ICONINFORMATION) ;
}
```

```
void CMainWindow::OnRead ()        // read file and show contents
{
    FStream.open ("testfile.txt", ios::in, filebuf::sh_none) ;
    if (!FStream.is_open)          // if error show message and return
    {
        StringTableMessageBox (S_NOREAD, S_FILEERROR,
            MB_OK | MB_ICONHAND) ;
        return ;
    }
    FStream.seekg (0, ios::end) ;        // move to end of stream
    streampos pos = FStream.tellg () ;   // returns file length
    FStream.seekg (0, ios::beg) ;        // go back to beginning
    char* cBuf = new char [(int) pos] ;  // allocate a buffer

    FStream >> cBuf ;                    // copy file to buffer
    FStream.close () ;                   // close the file
    CClientDC dc (this) ;                // get client area dc
    dc.TextOut (0, 0, cBuf, lstrlen (cBuf) ) ;  // show string
    delete cBuf ;                        // delete the buffer
}

void CMainWindow::OnAdd ()
{
    FStream.open ("testfile.txt", ios::in | ios::out,
        filebuf::sh_none) ;
    if (!FStream.is_open)    // if error show message and return
    {
        StringTableMessageBox (S_NOOPEN, S_FILEERROR,
            MB_OK | MB_ICONHAND) ;
        return ;
    }
    FStream.seekp (-1, ios::end) ;  // back up 1, over null byte

    for (int i = 0 ; i < 10 ; i++)
        FStream << (char) ('0' + i) ;  // write 10 digits

    FStream << (char) 0 ;               // add terminal null
    FStream.close () ;                  // close the file
    StringTableMessageBox (S_NOWTRY, S_MESSAGE,
        MB_OK | MB_ICONINFORMATION) ;
}

void CMainWindow::OnExit ()          // menu item "Quit"
{
    this->DestroyWindow () ;         // destroy main window,
}                                    // this stops application

    // show string table entry nString at location x,y
int CMainWindow::StringTableMessageBox (int nMessage,
    int nTitle, WORD flags)
{
    CString message, title ;
    message.LoadString (nMessage) ;
    title.LoadString (nTitle) ;
    return (this->MessageBox (message, title, flags)) ;
}
```

Listing 15-15 FILESTRM.RC Resource Script File

```
// filestrm.rc   resource script file

#include <afxres.h>
#include "filestrm.h"

AFX_IDI_STD_FRAME   ICON   filestrm.ico       // the program's icon

MyMenu MENU                                    // define the menu
{
    MENUITEM "&Write File",      IDM_WRITE
    MENUITEM "&Read File",       IDM_READ
    MENUITEM "&Append File",     IDM_ADD
    MENUITEM "&Quit",            IDM_QUIT
}

STRINGTABLE
{
    S_PROGRAMCAPTION    "File Stream Example"
    S_NOCREATE          "Could not create file TESTFILE.TXT"
    S_FILEERROR         "File Error"
    S_CREATED           "Created file TESTFILE.TXT"
    S_MESSAGE           "Message"
    S_NOREAD            "Could not read file TESTFILE.TXT"
    S_NOOPEN            "Could not open file TESTFILE.TXT"
    S_NOWTRY            "Now try reading file"
}
```

Listing 15-16 FILESTRM.H Resource ID Header File

```
// filestrm.h   header file for resource ID numbers

#define IDM_WRITE            1       // menu item ID numbers
#define IDM_READ             2
#define IDM_ADD              3
#define IDM_QUIT            10

#define S_PROGRAMCAPTION     1       // string table ID numbers
#define S_NOCREATE           2
#define S_FILEERROR          3
#define S_CREATED            4
#define S_MESSAGE            5
#define S_NOREAD             6
#define S_NOOPEN             7
#define S_NOWTRY             8
```

Figure 15-8 FILESTRM.ICO Icon Image

Listing 15-17 FILESTRM.DEF Module Definition File

```
NAME            filestrm
DESCRIPTION     'filestrm C++ program'
EXETYPE         WINDOWS
STUB            'WINSTUB.EXE'
CODE            PRELOAD MOVEABLE
DATA            PRELOAD MOVEABLE MULTIPLE
HEAPSIZE        1024
STACKSIZE       5120
```

USING A FILE SELECTION DIALOG BOX

One of the hallmarks of a good Windows application is the simple way you can select a file, or change disk subdirectories. Gone are the days of early MS-DOS programs that required you to remember subdirectory and file names. Most Windows programs allow file and subdirectory selection with a simple dialog box, such as the one shown in Figure 15-9. Subdirectories are selected with the right list box, and files with the left one. File names can also be entered by typing in the edit control at the upper left corner. The two combo boxes at the bottom of the dialog box allow the file display to be limited to a range of file names (such as *.TXT) and also allow the user to select a different disk drive.

File selection is such a common activity that Microsoft included the file selection dialog box in the Windows "common dialogs" collection. In the last chapter, we used a common dialog box to set up the printer. The file selection dialog box is just as easy to create, and will save you hundreds of lines of programming code compared with creating a similar dialog box from scratch.

The AFXDLGS.H header file declares the **CFileDialog** class, which is derived from the **CModalDialog** class for modal dialog boxes. You will need to include the AFXDLGS.H header file in your program to use the dialog box. The

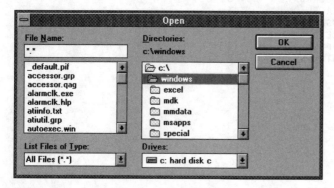

Figure 15-9 A File Selection Dialog Box

constructor function for the **CFileDialog** class takes a number of parameters. A typical sequence that creates the file dialog box shown in Figure 15-9 is shown in Listing 15-18. First, the **CFileDialog** object named *FDialog* is created using a constructor function. Then, the **CDialog::DoModal()** function is executed to display the dialog box. **CDialog::DoModal()** will return IDOK if the user made a selection. If a selection was made, the full path/file name is extracted from the **CFileDialog** object using **CFileDialog::GetPathName()**. In Listing 15-18, the path/file name is copied into the **CString** object named *FileName*.

Listing 15-19 and Table 15-8 summarize the meaning of all the parameters passed to the constructor. The only tricky part is the definition of the file name filters. A filter string like "C Files |*.c" will display the text "C Files" in the lower

Listing 15-18 Creating and Displaying a File Selection Dialog Box

```
CFileDialog FDialog (TRUE, "TXT", "*.*",      // run file dialog
    OFN_HIDEREADONLY | OFN_OVERWRITEPROMPT,
    "All Files (*.*)|*.*|Text Files (*.TXT)|*.TXT||") ;
if (FDialog.DoModal () != IDOK)      // run file dialog box
    return ;                         // user selected cancel
CString FileName = FDialog.GetPathName () ; // get path/file name
```

Parameter	Meaning
bOpenFileDialog	Set to TRUE for a file open dialog box, or FALSE for a file save dialog box.
lpszDefExt	A pointer to a character string containing the default file extension. This extension will be added automatically if the user does not specify an extension. The default NULL value does not append a file extension.
lpszFileName	A pointer to a character string containing the initial file name. (default == NULL).
dwFlags	One or more flag values that allow you to alter the appearance and behavior of the file selection dialog box. These flag values are declared in the COMMDLG.H header file that is included by AFXDLGS.H. The flags and their meanings are shown in Table 15-9. The default is OFN_HIDEREADONLY	OFN_OVERWRITEPROMPT.
lpszFilter	A pointer to a character string containing the file filter strings. Be sure to terminate the string with a "||". See the example and discussion above for how to format the filter string.
pParentWnd	A pointer to the parent window object.

Table 15-8 CFileDialog Constructor Parameters

Listing 15-19 CFileDialog Constructor Declaration (AFXDLGS.H)

```
CFileDialog(BOOL bOpenFileDialog,
    LPCSTR lpszDefExt = NULL,
    LPCSTR lpszFileName = NULL,
    DWORD dwFlags = OFN_HIDEREADONLY | OFN_OVERWRITEPROMPT,
    LPCSTR lpszFilter = NULL,
    CWnd* pParentWnd = NULL);
```

Flag	Meaning
OFN_ALLOWMULTISELECT	Specifies that the "File Name" list box allows multiple selections.
OFN_CREATEPROMPT	Specifies that the dialog function should query the user as to whether or not they want to create a file that does not currently exist. (This flag automatically sets the OFN_PATHMUSTEXIST and OFN_FILEMUSTEXIST flags.)
OFN_FILEMUSTEXIST	Specifies that the user can only enter names of existing files in the "File Name" entry field. If this flag is set and the user enters an invalid file name in the File Name entry field, the dialog function will display a warning in a message box. (This flag causes the OFN_PATHMUSTEXIST flag to also be set.)
OFN_HIDEREADONLY	Hides the read-only check box.
OFN_NOCHANGEDIR	Forces the dialog box to set the current directory back to what it was when the dialog was invoked.
OFN_OVERWRITEPROMPT	Causes the "Save As" dialog box to generate a message box if the selected file already exists. The user must confirm whether to overwrite the file.
OFN_PATHMUSTEXIST	Specifies that the user can only enter valid path names. If this flag is set and the user enters an invalid path name in the "File Name" entry field, the dialog function will display a warning in a message box.
OFN_READONLY	Causes the "Read only" check box to be initially checked when the dialog box is created.
OFN_SHOWHELP	Causes the dialog box to show the Help push button. This makes a simple help screen available if the Help button is selected. The parent window must not be NULL if this option is specified.

Table 15-9 CFileDialog Flag Values (Defined in COMMDLG.H)

left combo box (Figure 15-9), and will display only files that match the search filter "*.c". You can put as many of the filter definitions as you like in the parameter list, separating each with the vertical bar character (|). The end of the file filters must be marked with two vertical bars (||).

CREATING A TEXT EDITOR

The last example program in this chapter is called FILE2. FILE2 is a simple text editor that puts the file selection dialog box and the **fstream** classes to work. Figure 15-10 shows the FILE2 program editing the CONFIG.SYS file. FILE2 contains a big edit control that occupies the entire main program window client area. The edit control does all the work of displaying any text file that is loaded into memory, and allowing the text to be edited. From a programming point of view, essentially all of the FILE2.CPP program consists of the logic to read and write disk file data. The built-in logic of the edit control handles just about everything else. FILE2.CPP is a striking example of the amount of built-in power available in the Windows programming environment.

The edit control that fills the FILE2 program's client area has both a vertical and a horizontal scroll bar. They are part of the edit control window, not the FILE2 main program window. Edit controls automatically scroll their contents if scroll bars are attached. Note in Figure 15-10 that the left side of the scroll bar is slightly offset from the edge of the window border. This gap is caused by positioning the edit control five pixels from the left border of the main program window. The five pixel gap keeps the text from being flush against the border, which would make it difficult to read the first character of every line.

How Edit Controls Store Text

In order to exchange data between an edit control and a file, you will need to know how an edit control stores text data. All of the text in an edit control is

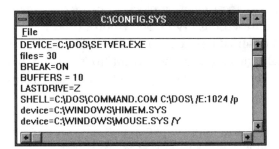

Figure 15-10 The FILE2 Program

stored in a local memory block that is maintained by the Windows environment. The size of the block is automatically adjusted to match the amount of text. Because local blocks are stored in the program's local data segment, the amount of text data is limited to 64K, less the size of the stack and local heap. This means that you cannot edit huge text files using an edit control. The Windows Notepad application is just an elaborate edit control, which limits the amount of data that can be handled by this application.

You can retrieve the handle of an edit control's local memory block using the **CEdit::GetHandle()** function. You can also pass a handle of a new local memory block to the edit control using the **CEdit::SetHandle()** function. If you use these functions, you must be careful not to destroy the memory block used by the edit control without replacing the block with a new one. The **CLocalBlock** class developed in Chapter 12, *Managing Memory*, has a *Permanence* flag that stops the physical memory block attached to a **CLocalBlock** object from being freed when the **CLocalBlock** object is destroyed. The *Permanence* flag was included in the **CLocalBlock** class specifically to allow using the **CLocalBlock** class with edit controls.

The text data is stored as one long character string within the local memory block used by the edit control. The only null character is the last character in the file. Ends of lines are marked with the character sequence CR, CR, LF. If the edit control is too narrow to show an entire line, the line will be wrapped and the sequence CR, LF will be inserted to mark the end of the line. The double CR, CR marking "hard" end-of-line positions causes a bit of complication when reading the data in an edit control, as we will see in a moment.

Copying data from a disk file to an edit control is simple. Edit controls are windows and the text within the edit control is the edit window's caption. You can use the **CWnd::SetWindowText()** function to pass a long character string to the edit control. The text string will be displayed within the edit control's client area. Listing 15-20 shows a typical sequence of function calls that open a file and copy the contents of the file into an edit control named *EditCntl*. In this case, the file data is initially read into a local memory block named *ReadMemBlock*, and then copied into the edit control using **CWnd::SetWindowText()**.

Copying the contents of an edit control to a file is a bit tricky. The most obvious method is to obtain the handle of the edit control's memory block and copy every byte to a file. For example, Listing 15-21 shows an example that copies the contents of an edit control named *EditCntl* to an **fstream** object named *FStream*.

The problem with the direct technique shown in Listing 15-21 is that the data within the edit control's memory block is transferred exactly as is. The unusual byte sequence CR, CR, LF marking end-of-line positions in the file ends up copied

Listing 15-20 Copying a File into an Edit Control

```
FStream.open (FileName, ios::in, filebuf::sh_read) ;
if (!FStream.is_open)          // if error show message and return
{
    // show an error message
    return ;
}
FStream.seekg (0, ios::end) ;          // move to end of stream
int nBytes = (int) FStream.tellg () ;   // returns file length
FStream.seekg (0, ios::beg) ;    // go back to beginning
                // allocate local memory block for edit control
CLocalBlock ReadMemBlock ;        // memory block for reading file
                                  // make big enough to hold file
if (!ReadMemBlock.resize (nBytes + 1))  // if could not allocate
{
    // show an error message
    return ;
}
char* pStr = ReadMemBlock.lock () ; // lock block in memory
FStream.setmode (filebuf::binary) ; // treat file as binary data
FStream.read (pStr, nBytes) ;        // read file into block
FStream.close () ;                   // close the file
*(pStr + nBytes) = 0 ;               // put null char at end
EditCntl.SetWindowText (pStr) ; // pass text to edit control
```

Listing 15-21 Direct Transfer of Edit Control Data

```
HANDLE hEditText = EditCntl.GetHandle () ;
CLocalBlock EditTextBlock ;                  // create local block
EditTextBlock.sethandle (hEditText, TRUE) ; // attach edit block
// note permanence flag set to TRUE, so edit cntl block not freed
PSTR pEditText = EditTextBlock.lock () ;    // lock block
FStream << pEditText ;                       // copy data to file
EditTextBlock.unlock () ;                    // unlock block
FStream.close () ;                           // close the file
```

to the disk file. If you then read the file with a normal text editor, the extra CR characters will show up as unprintable characters, and may confuse the editor.

A better technique for copying the text from an edit control to a disk file is to read each line in the edit control separately. This gives you an opportunity to append the normal CR, LF byte sequence at the end of each line, rather than the CR, CR, LF sequence used internally to the edit control. Listing 15-22 shows an example of program logic that reads each line in the *EditCntl* edit control and copies the lines to the **fstream** object *FStream*.

The **CEdit::GetLineCount()** function returns the number of lines in the edit control's memory block. The **CEdit::GetLine()** function copies a specific line of text from the edit control to a memory buffer. You can find the position of the first byte in a given line of text using the **CEdit::LineIndex()** function. The index

Listing 15-22 Line-at-a-Time Transfer of Edit Control Data

```
int nLines = EditCntl.GetLineCount () ; // get number of lines
int nLong, nIndex ;
char cBuf [256] ;
for (int i = 0 ; i < nLines ; i++)
{
    EditCntl.GetLine (i, cBuf, 256) ; // read each line
    nIndex = EditCntl.LineIndex (i) ; // get pos of start of line
    nLong = EditCntl.LineLength (nIndex) ;  // find linelength
    cBuf [nLong] = 0 ;                 // null terminate the string
    FStream << cBuf << endl ;          // send it to the file
}                              // endl == addition of newline CR/LF
FStream.close () ;                     // close the file
```

is the number of bytes from the start of the memory block to the first character of a given line. The first line is numbered zero. The length of a line, not counting CR and LF characters at the end, can be determined with **CEdit::LineLength()**. Refer to Chapter 5, *Window Controls*, if the **CEdit** class functions do not look familiar.

Note in Listing 15-22 that a normal CR, LF character pair is added to the end of each line as it is sent to the **fstream** object *FStream* using the *endl* constant. *endl* stands for "end of line," and appends a CR, LF pair to the data being sent to the **fstream** object. This creates a "normal" text file without the extra CR characters.

The FILE2 Simple Editor

Now that you have the background of how file selection dialog boxes and edit controls are used, let's look at the C++ program for the minimal editor. Listing 15-23 shows the FILE2.HPP header file. The **CMainWindow** class includes a **CEdit** object *EditCntl* that will contain the edit control that covers the main program window client area, a **CString** object *FileName* that will hold the name of the file being edited, and an **fstream** object *FStream* that will be the file object. Note that a **CWnd::OnSize()** function is declared, so the program will process WM_SIZE messages.

Listing 15-24 shows the FILE2.CPP program. This example closely follows the previous discussions of how to display file selection dialog boxes, and how to copy data to and from a disk file and edit control. Note that the edit control is resized to fit the main program window's client area every time a WM_SIZE message is processed. FILE2.CPP also uses the **CMainWindow::StringTable-MessageBox()** function from the previous examples in this chapter to display message boxes.

Listing 15-23 FILE2.HPP Header File

```cpp
// file2.hpp     header file for file2.cpp

class CMainWindow : public CFrameWnd  // derive a main window class
{
public:
    CMainWindow () ;                   // declare a constructor
private:
    CEdit EditCntl ;                   // create an edit object
    CString FileName ;                 // string to hold file name
    fstream FStream ;                  // file stream object
    void OnNew () ;                    // clear edit area
    void OnOpen () ;                   // open a file
    void OnSave () ;                   // write to a file
    void OnAbout () ;                  // show about box
    void OnExit () ;                   // menu item "Quit"
                                       // process selected messages
    void OnSize (UINT nType, int cx, int cy) ;

    // show string table entry nString at location x,y
    int StringTableMessageBox (int nMessage, int nTitle,
        WORD flags = MB_OK) ;

    DECLARE_MESSAGE_MAP()              // prepare for message processing
} ;

class CTheApp : public CWinApp        // derive an application class
{
public:
    BOOL InitInstance () ;            // declare new InitInstance()
} ;
```

Listing 15-24 FILE2.CPP

```cpp
// file2.cpp         simple text editor using file selection dialogs

#include <afxwin.h>        // class library header file
#include <strstrea.h>      // streams header file
#include <afxdlgs.h>       // common dialogs header file
#include <fstream.h>       // file streams header file
#include "winmem.hpp"      // windows memory block header file
#include "file2.h"         // header file for resource data
#include "file2.hpp"       // header file for this program

CTheApp theApp ;           // create one CTheApp object - runs program

BOOL CTheApp::InitInstance ()    // override default InitInstance()
{
    m_pMainWnd = new CMainWindow () ;       // create a main window
    m_pMainWnd->ShowWindow (m_nCmdShow) ;   // make it visible
    m_pMainWnd->UpdateWindow () ;           // paint center
    return TRUE ;
}
```

```
CMainWindow::CMainWindow () // constructor for main program window
{
    CString title ;        // get program caption from resource data
    title.LoadString (S_PROGRAMCAPTION) ;
    Create (NULL, title, WS_OVERLAPPEDWINDOW, rectDefault,
        NULL, "MyMenu") ;
    CRect ControlRect (0, 0, 1, 1) ;// rect to hold edit size
                                    // create multiline edit control
    EditCntl.Create (WS_CHILD | WS_VISIBLE | ES_MULTILINE |
        WS_VSCROLL | WS_HSCROLL | ES_AUTOHSCROLL | ES_AUTOVSCROLL,
        ControlRect, this, NULL) ;
    FileName = "*.*" ;            // initialize with default file name
}

BEGIN_MESSAGE_MAP (CMainWindow, CFrameWnd)
    ON_COMMAND (IDM_NEW, OnNew)          // menu item "New File"
    ON_COMMAND (IDM_OPEN, OnOpen)        // menu item "Open File"
    ON_COMMAND (IDM_SAVE, OnSave)        // menu item "Save File"
    ON_COMMAND (IDM_ABOUT, OnAbout)      // menu item "About File2"
    ON_COMMAND (IDM_QUIT, OnExit)        // menu item "Quit"
    ON_WM_SIZE ()                        // process WM_SIZE messages
END_MESSAGE_MAP ()

void CMainWindow::OnNew ()               // menu item "New File"
{
    EditCntl.SetWindowText ("") ;        // clear the edit area
    CString title ;                      // get default program caption
    title.LoadString (S_PROGRAMCAPTION) ;
    this->SetWindowText (title) ;        // change main window title
    FileName = "*.*" ;
}


void CMainWindow::OnOpen ()              // open a file and read data
{
    CFileDialog FDialog (TRUE, "TXT", "*.*",
        OFN_HIDEREADONLY | OFN_OVERWRITEPROMPT,
        "All Files (*.*)|*.*|Text Files (*.TXT)|*.TXT||") ;
    if (FDialog.DoModal () != IDOK)      // run file dialog box
        return ;                         // user selected cancel
    FileName = FDialog.GetPathName () ; // get path/file name string
    this->SetWindowText (FileName) ;     // file name is caption
                                         // open the file for reading
    FStream.open (FileName, ios::in, filebuf::sh_read) ;
    if (!FStream.is_open)                // if error show message and return
    {
        StringTableMessageBox (S_FILENOTOPEN, S_FILEERROR,
            MB_OK | MB_ICONHAND) ;
        return ;
    }
```

```
    FStream.seekg (0, ios::end) ;         // move to end of stream
    int nBytes = (int) FStream.tellg () ;   // returns file length
    FStream.seekg (0, ios::beg) ;         // go back to beginning
                    // allocate local memory block for edit control
    CLocalBlock ReadMemBlock ;         // memory block for reading file
                                       // make big enough to hold file
    if (!ReadMemBlock.resize (nBytes + 2))  // if could not allocate
    {                                       // show error and return
        StringTableMessageBox (S_NOTALLOC, S_MEMERROR,
            MB_OK | MB_ICONHAND) ;
        return ;
    }
    char* pStr = ReadMemBlock.lock () ; // lock block in memory
    FStream.setmode (filebuf::binary) ; // treat file as binary data
    FStream.read (pStr, nBytes) ;         // read file into block
    FStream.close () ;                    // close the file
    *(pStr + nBytes) = 0 ;                // put null char at end
    EditCntl.SetWindowText (pStr) ; // pass text to edit control
}                                      // mem block freed automatically

void CMainWindow::OnSave ()            // copy edit cntl contents to file
{
    CFileDialog FDialog (FALSE, "TXT", FileName,    // run file dlg
        OFN_HIDEREADONLY | OFN_OVERWRITEPROMPT,
        "All Files (*.*)|*.*|Text Files (*.TXT)|*.TXT||") ;
    if (FDialog.DoModal () != IDOK)        // run file dialog box
        return ;                           // user selected cancel
    FileName = FDialog.GetPathName () ; // get full path/file name
    this->SetWindowText (FileName) ;    // file name is the caption
    FStream.open (FileName, ios::out, filebuf::sh_write) ;
    if (!FStream.is_open)          // if error show message and return
    {
        StringTableMessageBox (S_FILENOTOPEN, S_FILEERROR,
            MB_OK | MB_ICONHAND) ;
        return ;
    }
    int nLines = EditCntl.GetLineCount () ; // get number of lines
    int nLong, nIndex ;
    char cBuf [256] ;
    for (int i = 0 ; i < nLines ; i++)
    {
        EditCntl.GetLine (i, cBuf, 256) ; // read line in edit cntl
        nIndex = EditCntl.LineIndex (i) ; // get pos of start of line
        nLong = EditCntl.LineLength (nIndex) ;    // find line length
        cBuf [nLong] = 0 ;                 // null terminate the string
        FStream << cBuf << endl ;      // send it to the file
    }                                  // endl == addition of newline
    FStream.close () ;                 // close the file
}
```

```
void CMainWindow::OnAbout ()
{
    StringTableMessageBox (S_ABOUTTEXT, S_ABOUTCAPTION) ;
}

void CMainWindow::OnExit ()                // menu item "Quit"
{
    this->DestroyWindow () ;               // destroy main window,
}                                          // this stops application

void CMainWindow::OnSize (UINT nType, int cx, int cy)
{       // resize edit control to always fit inside parent window.
    EditCntl.MoveWindow (5, 0, cx - 5, cy) ;
}       // Use offset of 5 for left border

    // show string table entry nString at location x,y
int CMainWindow::StringTableMessageBox (int nMessage, int nTitle,
    WORD flags)
{
    CString message, title ;
    message.LoadString (nMessage) ;
    title.LoadString (nTitle) ;
    return (this->MessageBox (message, title, flags)) ;
}
```

The remaining support files for FILE2.CPP are shown in Listings 15-25 to 15-27. Note that the stack size is set equal to 10K in the module definition file. The common dialog boxes make heavy use of the stack, so you should use a 10K minimum stack size if you use any of the common dialog box functions. The program's icon is shown in Figure 15-11. Don't forget to include the WINMEM.CPP program in the project file when you compile FILE2.

Listing 15-25 FILE2.H Resource ID Header File

```
// file2.h  header file for resource ID numbers

#define IDM_NEW              1        // menu item ID numbers
#define IDM_OPEN             2
#define IDM_SAVE             3
#define IDM_ABOUT            4
#define IDM_QUIT            10

#define S_PROGRAMCAPTION     1        // string table ID numbers
#define S_FILENOTOPEN        2
#define S_NOTALLOC           3
#define S_MEMERROR           4
#define S_ABOUTTEXT          5
#define S_ABOUTCAPTION       6
#define S_FILEERROR          7
```

Listing 15-26 FILE2.RC Resource Script File

```
// file2.rc   resource script file

#include <afxres.h>
#include "file2.h"

AFX_IDI_STD_FRAME   ICON    file2.ico      // the program's icon

MyMenu MENU                                // define the menu
{
    POPUP    "&File"
    {
        MENUITEM "&New File",   IDM_NEW
        MENUITEM "&Open File",  IDM_OPEN
        MENUITEM "&Save File",  IDM_SAVE
        MENUITEM SEPARATOR
        MENUITEM "&About",      IDM_ABOUT
        MENUITEM "&Quit",       IDM_QUIT
    }
}


STRINGTABLE
{
    S_PROGRAMCAPTION    "File 2 - Simple Editor"
    S_FILENOTOPEN       "Could Not Open File"
    S_NOTALLOC          "Could not allocate memory."
    S_MEMERROR          "Memory Error"
    S_ABOUTTEXT         "Simple Editor Application"
    S_ABOUTCAPTION      "File 2 Program"
    S_FILEERROR         "File Error"
}
```

Listing 15-27 FILE2.DEF Module Definition File

```
NAME            file2
DESCRIPTION     'file2 C++ program'
EXETYPE         WINDOWS
STUB            'WINSTUB.EXE'
CODE            PRELOAD MOVEABLE
DATA            PRELOAD MOVEABLE MULTIPLE
HEAPSIZE        1024
STACKSIZE       10240
```

Figure 15-11 FILE2.ICO Icon Image

SUMMARY

Windows programs use DOS for disk file operations. This reduces the amount of memory consumed by Windows because DOS is always loaded before Windows is started. Using DOS file operations also has the advantage of ensuring that files created with Windows applications are compatible at the operating system level with files created with DOS programs. The actual organization of the data within the file may be different between DOS and Windows programs, just as different DOS programs have different structures within their file data.

Windows NT does not use MS-DOS for file access. Instead, Windows NT has its own built-in file logic. This underlying difference is hidden by Windows NT and the MFC classes. You can use the MFC classes to create programs that will compile and run under both systems without modification.

The MFC classes provide several methods of working with disk files. This chapter explored both the **CFile** class and the **fstream** class. The **CFile** class provides conventional file operations for opening, reading, writing, and closing a disk file. The **fstream** class provides the same functionality, but also has the convenience of overloaded operators (such as << and >>) to simplify input and output from the file. In both cases, a file must be opened before any file activity can take place. As soon as the file operations are completed, you should close the file to make sure that the data is recorded on disk.

Windows programs generally make it easy for the user to select a file and/or file subdirectory using a file selection dialog box. The **CFileDialog** class provides ready-to-use file selection dialog boxes. The **CFileDialog** class takes advantage of the common dialogs provided with Windows 3.1 and above. The **CFile-Dialog** class was used in the FILE2 example program, which is a minimal text editor. FILE2 will be improved by adding cut-and-paste operations in Chapter 17, *The Clipboard*.

QUESTIONS

1. To open a file using the **CFile** class, use the _____ function. To open a file using the **fstream** class, use the _____ function.
2. The low-level operations that work with disk files are part of Windows 3.1. (True/False)
3. When file operations using a **CFile** object are complete, the _____ function from the **CFile** class must be called to ensure that the file is closed and that all data is physically recorded on the disk media.

4. To move to a location in an open file 25 bytes before the end of the file, use the following call to the **CFile::Seek** function for the **CFile** object **fileobj**:
   a. **fileobj.Seek (25, CFile::end)**
   b. **fileobj.Seek (-25, CFile::end)**
   c. **fileobj.Seek (-25, CFile::begin)**
   d. none of the above

5. Use the _____ function to link a local memory buffer containing text to an edit control.

6. **CFile::Open()** will return a value of _____ if the file could not be opened.

7. To add new data to the end of an existing file, the entire contents of the file must be created in a memory block, and then copied to the disk file. (True/False)

8. The **CFileDialog** class creates a:
   a. system modal dialog box
   b. modal dialog box
   c. modeless dialog box
   d. child window

9. You can put a character string into the edit area of an edit control with the _____ function.

10. The text in an edit control is actually stored in a global memory block. (True/False)

EXERCISES

1. Modify the FILE1.CPP program so that the initial character string copied to the TESTFILE.TXT file is a string table entry in the program's resource script file, rather than the alphabet.

2. Modify the FILE1.CPP program so that the "Append File" menu item causes every other character to be changed to lowercase in the disk file, as shown in Figure 15-12. Make the changes to the disk file without reading the file into memory. In other words, write the new lowercase characters to the disk file individually.

Chapter 15, Exercise 2	▼	▲

Write File   Read File   Append File   Quit
aBcDeFgHiJkLmNoPqRsTuVwXyZ

Figure 15-12 The C15EXER2 Program

ANSWERS TO QUESTIONS

1. CFile::Open(), fstream::open().
2. False. Windows uses the MS-DOS file functions. However, Windows NT has its own file access functions, and does not use MS-DOS.
3. CFile::Close().
4. b.
5. CEdit::SetHandle().
6. FALSE or zero.
7. False. You can append data to an existing file without changing the current file contents.
8. b.
9. CWnd::SetWindowText().
10. False. The text in an edit control is stored in a local memory block.

SOLUTIONS TO EXERCISES

1. First, add a new entry in the program's resource ID header file for the ID number of the new string table entry:

```
#define S_FILETEXT          9
```

Second, add the new string table entry to the program's resource script file:

```
S_FILETEXT          "This is a stringtable text entry."
```

Finally, modify the program so that the string table entry is copied to a buffer, and the buffer then copied to the disk file. You can either allocate a local memory buffer, or just use a **CString** object, as shown in Listing 15-28.

The complete solution is given under the file name C15EXER1 on the source code disks.

2. The key to changing every other character in the disk file is to repeatedly call the **CFile::Seek()** function to move forward in the file. Listing 15-29 shows the modifications to the FILE1.CPP program for the portion that handles the selection of the "Append File" menu item. **CFile::Write()** is called to write only one character at a time. Writing a character advances the file position pointer one byte in the file. To write on every second location, **CFile::Seek()** is then called to advance one more byte.

Listing 15-28 Modifications to FILE1.CPP

```
if (!File.Open ("testfile.txt",
    CFile::modeCreate | CFile::modeWrite))
{
    StringTableMessageBox (S_NOCREATE, S_FILEERROR,
        MB_OK | MB_ICONHAND) ;
    return ;
}
CString string ;                        // create a string object
string.LoadString (S_FILETEXT) ;    // fill string from resources
File.Write (string, string.GetLength ()) ; // write to the file
File.Close () ;                         // close the file
```

Listing 15-29 Solution to Chapter 15 Exercise 2

```
if (!File.Open ("testfile.txt",
    CFile::modeRead | CFile::modeWrite))
{
    StringTableMessageBox (S_NOREAD, S_FILEERROR,
        MB_OK | MB_ICONHAND) ;
    return ;
}
char cBuf [2] = " " ;
for (int i = 0 ; i < 26 ; i += 2)
{
    cBuf [0] = 'a' + i ;   // lowercase letters to cBuf
    File.Write (cBuf, 1) ; // write one char, advancing one byte
    File.Seek (1, CFile::current) ; // advance one more byte
}
File.Close () ;                 // close the file
```

## Chapter 16

Bitmaps

So far, the example programs using graphics in this book have called GDI functions, such as **CDC::Ellipse()** and **CDC::Rectangle()**, to do the drawing. GDI functions are ideal for geometric shapes, but are not convenient for realistic images like a person's face. More realistic images can be created with painting programs, such as the Windows Paint application, which allow the color of each pixel to be edited. These images are known as bitmaps, as each color "bit" of the picture is stored individually. We have been using a limited form of bitmap for the program icon images that were created with the Microsoft Image Editor. Icons are small bitmaps, but they are limited to certain sizes that Windows can conveniently display when an application is minimized. The image editor also allows you to create and save images of any size using the Windows bitmap format, limited only by the resolution of your system's video equipment.

Bitmaps are records of each pixel's color in a picture drawn on a computer's screen. Bitmaps have the advantage of being able to save any picture, no matter how complex. The disadvantage of bitmaps is that they take up a lot of space because every pixel's color must be recorded individually. The MFC classes support the **CDC** and **CBitmap** classes, which provide a number of useful functions for manipulating bitmap images. You can use a bitmap as a brush pattern, stretch and shrink bitmap images, and paste them on the screen with different effects depending on the screen image "under" the bitmap.

Bitmaps also find their way into animated graphics. Windows allows you to "draw" on a memory bitmap. Memory bitmaps imitate the screen's organization for saving each pixel's color. When all of the drawing is completed, the memory bitmap can be "pasted" onto the screen, making the complete image visible at once. The advantage is that the drawing operations take place in the background, so the user sees the complete new image appear in one quick action.

Concepts covered: Loading a bitmap resource, creating a memory device context, displaying a bitmap, stretching or shrinking a bitmap, raster operation codes, filling an area with a bitmap brush, device dependent versus device independent bitmaps.

Key words covered: BLACKNESS, DSTINVERT, MERGECOPY, MERGEPAINT, NOTSRCCOPY, NOTSRCERASE, PATCOPY, PATINVERT, PATPAINT, SRCAND, SRCCOPY, SRCERASE, SRCINVERT, SRCPAINT, WHITENESS, BITMAP, DIB.

Functions covered: CBitmap::LoadBitmap(), CDC::CreateCompatibleDC(), CDC::BitBlt(), CDC::StretchBlt(), CBrush::CreatePatternBrush(), CDC::PatBlt().

Classes covered: CBitmap.

HOW BITMAPS STORE IMAGES

Imagine that you have been using the Windows Paintbrush application to draw a picture. Although Paintbrush allows you to draw rectangles, lines, and other objects, the actual data for the picture is recorded one pixel at a time. Each pixel can have a different color, so if you save the color of each pixel, you have captured the entire image. This is exactly what Paintbrush does when it saves a picture as a bitmap file. Figure 16-1 illustrates the relationship between a picture and the bitmap data that stores the image.

The amount of data it takes to store a bitmap depends on the size of the picture, and on the number of colors the bitmap uses. For black and white systems, only one bit is needed for each pixel. The bit can be set to one for white

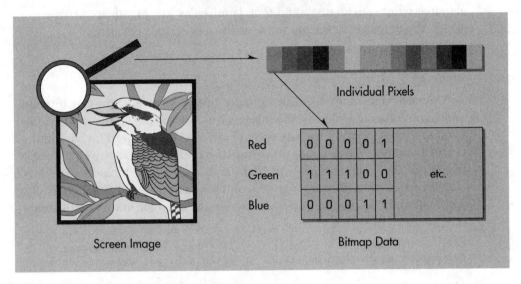

Figure 16-1 How a Bitmap Stores Image Data

and to zero for black. For color images, more bits are required. A 16-color VGA display requires four bits per pixel, while a "true color" display needs three bytes (24 bits) per pixel to specify each color.

Bitmaps are not efficient ways to store large images. For example, saving a VGA screen requires 640 x 480 x 4 = 806,400 bits, or about 100K of storage. Normally, you will use bitmaps for smaller images, particularly images that are difficult to re-create using GDI functions, such as **CDC::Rectangle()** and **CDC::Ellipse()**. Bitmaps are easy to create. You can use the Windows Paintbrush application or the Microsoft Image Editor. Both Paintbrush and Image Editor can save images as bitmap files with the extension ".BMP."

Loading a Bitmap File

The most common use of bitmaps is to display small images as part of a program's operations. Bitmaps do not change as the program operates (bitmaps are static data), so the ideal place to store bitmap information is with the program's resources. First, create the bitmap image using your favorite editor and save it in the same subdirectory that you will use for your program files. Second, add a BITMAP line to your program's resource script file as follows:

```
ImageBmp    BITMAP  image.bmp
```

This adds the data in the IMAGE.BMP bitmap file to the program's resources, and gives the bitmap data the name "ImageBmp." The format of this line in the resource script statement should look familiar, as it is identical to the way in which cursor images and icons are added to a program's resources.

```
ImageBmp    BITMAP   image.bmp
HandCurs    CURSOR   hand.cur
ProgIcon    ICON     test.ico
```

Cursor images and icons are actually just specialized forms of bitmaps, which must use certain sizes and limited colors. Bitmap data is the most flexible, because the bitmap can have any size and can take advantage of high resolution color equipment. When you want to display a bitmap, the bitmap data must be read from the program's resource data and loaded into memory. The MFC classes provide the **CBitmap** class for common manipulations, such as loading a bitmap from the program's resource script file. The **CBitmap::LoadBitmap()** function does this.

```
CBitmap MyBitmap ;                  // create a CBitmap object
CBitmap.LoadBitmap ("ImageBmp") ;   // load bitmap resource data
```

Displaying a Bitmap

With the bitmap data loaded into memory, you are ready to display the bitmap image on the screen. This is a little more involved than you might expect. Windows uses the concept of a *memory device context* to convert from the format of the bitmap data file to the physical format used by the screen display or printer. A memory device context is just like the device context for the screen or printer, except that it is not tied to a specific device. You must select a bitmap into the memory device context before it can be displayed on a physical device. Selecting the bitmap into a memory device context gives Windows a chance to figure out if the color data needs to be organized in color planes (like a VGA card uses) or organized by using adjacent color bits (for higher color resolution video cards). The steps needed to display a bitmap are

1. Load the bitmap data into memory with **CBitmap::LoadBitmap()**.
2. Create a memory device context with **CDC::CreateCompatibleDC()**.
3. Select the bitmap into the memory device context with **CDC::SelectObject()**.
4. Copy the bitmap from the memory device context to the output device context with **CDC::BitBlt()**.

Figure 16-2 illustrates how these functions interact to produce the final bitmap image. The **CDC::CreateCompatibleDC()** function creates a memory device context with the same physical attributes as the device context of your video system or printer. When you call **CDC::SelectObject()** and select the

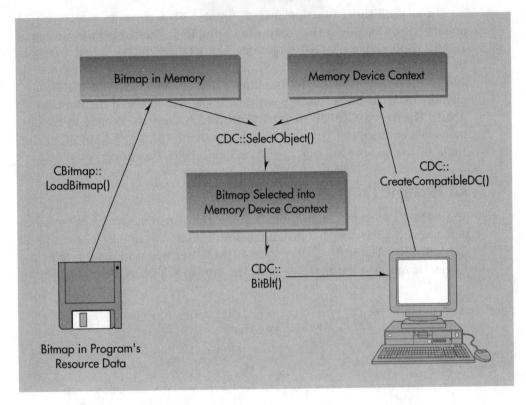

Figure 16-2 Steps to Display a Bitmap Image

bitmap into the memory device context, Windows sets up the bitmap data with the exact sequence of bits needed to display the data on the physical device. This makes the last step, calling **CDC::BitBlt()**, very fast. **CDC::BitBlt()** stuffs the bitmap bits from the memory device context right into the output device. Listing 16-1 demonstrates a typical sequence of function calls to display a bitmap. The *this* pointer is assumed to point to a **CWnd** or **CFrameWnd** object.

Listing 16-1 Displaying a Bitmap

```
CBitmap MyBitmap ;
MyBitmap.LoadBitmap ("ImageBmp") ;   // load bitmap from resources
CClientDC cDC (this) ;               // get client area dc
CDC MemDC ;                          // create second CDC object
MemDC.CreateCompatibleDC (&cDC) ;    // create memory dc
MemDC.SelectObject (&MyBitmap) ;     // select bmp into mem. dc
                         // show upper right corner at 10,20
cDC.BitBlt (10, 20, 32, 32, &MemDC, 0, 0, SRCCOPY) ;
```

The **CDC::BitBlt()** function takes a number of parameters, which can be understood by looking at the last line in Listing 16-1. The bitmap was created as a 32 by 32 pixel image, stored as resource data. **CDC::BitBlt()** is called to display the image at location 10,20 on the window's client area, with an output height and width of 32 pixels each. The bitmap data is obtained from the *MemDC* memory device context, starting with the upper left corner of the bitmap (0,0 point). The flag "SRCCOPY" tells **CDC::BitBlt()** to copy the bitmap to the output device context, covering up any pixels under the bitmap's 32 by 32 square. Table 16-1 shows the full syntax of the **CDC::BitBlt()** function.

An Example Program Using BitBlt()

The BITMAP1 program demonstrates loading a bitmap from a program's resource data, and displaying the bitmap using a memory device context and **CDC::BitBlt()**. Figure 16-3 shows the BITMAP1 program in action, after the "Show" menu item has been selected. The bitmap is a 64 by 64 pixel, 16-color

```
BOOL  CDC::BitBlt(int X, int Y, int nWidth, int nHeight, CDC* pSrcDC,
      int XSrc, int YSrc, DWORD dwRop) ;
```

Parameter	Meaning
X	The logical X-coordinate of the upper left corner of the destination rectangle.
Y	The logical Y-coordinate of the upper left corner of the destination rectangle.
nWidth	The width in logical units of the destination rectangle.
nHeight	The height in logical units of the destination rectangle.
pSrcDC	A pointer to the device context from which the bitmap will be copied. This is normally a memory device context created with **CDC::CreateCompatibleDC()**. A bitmap is loaded into the memory device context using **CDC::SelectObject()**.
XSrc	The logical X-coordinate of the upper left corner in the source bitmap. Normally, zero for the whole bitmap.
YSrc	The logical Y-coordinate of the upper left corner in the source bitmap. Normally, zero for the whole bitmap.
dwRop	One of the raster operation codes. Fifteen of the 256 possibilities have names defined in WINDOWS.H. You will most often use the SRCCOPY code for this parameter. The remainder are explained later in this chapter, under the heading *Raster Operation Codes*.

Table 16-1 CDC::BitBlt() Syntax

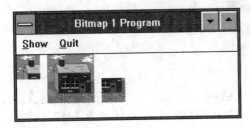

Figure 16-3 The BITMAP1 Program

bitmap created with the Microsoft Image Editor. The center image in Figure 16-3 is the complete bitmap. The left and right images demonstrate the **CDC::BitBlt()** function's ability to display portions of a bitmap image. The left image is the upper left quarter of the bitmap, while the right image shows the lower right quarter.

The first step in creating the BITMAP1 program is to create a 64 by 64 pixel bitmap to display. The source code disks include a bitmap named HOUSE.BMP. Figure 16-4 shows a blowup of the HOUSE bitmap in the work area of the Microsoft Image Editor application.

With the bitmap saved as the HOUSE.BMP file, you are ready to add the bitmap data to the program's resources. Listing 16-2 shows the BITMAP1.RC file, which includes both the program's icon file and the HOUSE.BMP file as resource data, along with a simple menu definition and a short string table.

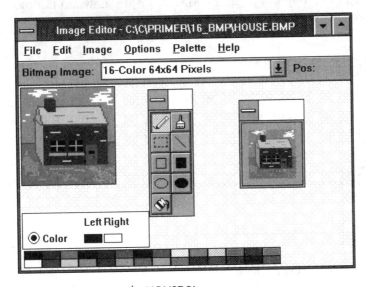

Figure 16-4 Creating the HOUSE Bitmap

Listing 16-2 BITMAP1.RC Resource Script File

```
// bitmap1.rc  resource script file

#include <afxres.h>
#include "bitmap1.h"

AFX_IDI_STD_FRAME   ICON    bitmap1.ico      // the program's icon
HouseBmp            BITMAP  house.bmp        // a bitmap file

MyMenu MENU                                  // define the menu
{
    MENUITEM "&Show",       IDM_SHOW
    MENUITEM "&Quit",       IDM_QUIT
}


STRINGTABLE
{
    S_PROGRAMCAPTION      "Bitmap 1 Program"
}
```

The BITMAP1.CPP program (Listing 16-3) follows the previous discussion of loading and displaying bitmaps. The only change is that three calls to the **CDC::BitBlt()** function are made to display different portions of the HOUSE bitmap. Note that the **CBitmap** object and memory device context are created as automatic variables, and are deleted automatically when the **CMainWindow::OnShow()** function returns.

The remaining support files for BITMAP1.CPP are shown in Listings 16-4 to 16-6. Figure 16-5 shows the program's icon.

STRETCHING A BITMAP

The **CDC::BitBlt()** function is delightfully fast, once the bitmap data has been selected into a memory device context. You can happily "blit" the same image all over the output device context. Although **CDC::BitBlt()** can output pieces

Figure 16-5 BITMAP1.ICO Icon Image

Listing 16-3 BITMAP1.CPP

```cpp
// bitmap1.cpp              example displaying a bitmap file

#include <afxwin.h>      // class library header file
#include "bitmap1.h"     // header file for resource data
#include "bitmap1.hpp"   // header file for this program

CTheApp theApp ;          // create one CTheApp object - runs program

BOOL CTheApp::InitInstance ()   // override default InitInstance()
{
    m_pMainWnd = new CMainWindow () ;        // create a main window
    m_pMainWnd->ShowWindow (m_nCmdShow) ;    // make it visible
    m_pMainWnd->UpdateWindow () ;            // paint center
    return TRUE ;
}


CMainWindow::CMainWindow ()      // constructor for window
{
    CString title ;       // get program caption from resource data
    title.LoadString (S_PROGRAMCAPTION) ;
    Create (NULL, title, WS_OVERLAPPEDWINDOW, rectDefault,
        NULL, "MyMenu") ;
}


BEGIN_MESSAGE_MAP (CMainWindow, CFrameWnd)
    ON_COMMAND (IDM_SHOW, OnShow)        // respond to menu items
    ON_COMMAND (IDM_QUIT, OnExit)
END_MESSAGE_MAP ()

void CMainWindow::OnShow ()       // respond to menu item "Show"
{
    CBitmap ABitmap ;
    ABitmap.LoadBitmap ("HouseBmp") ;   // load bitmap from resources
    CClientDC cDC (this) ;              // get client area dc
    CDC MemDC ;
    MemDC.CreateCompatibleDC (&cDC) ;   // create memory dc
    MemDC.SelectObject (&ABitmap) ;
                                // show upper right corner at 0,0
    cDC.BitBlt (0, 0, 32, 32, &MemDC, 0, 0, SRCCOPY) ;
                                // show entire bitmap at 42,0
    cDC.BitBlt (42, 0, 64, 64, &MemDC, 0, 0, SRCCOPY) ;
                                // show lower right corner at 116,32
    cDC.BitBlt (116, 32, 32, 32, &MemDC, 32, 32, SRCCOPY) ;
}

void CMainWindow::OnExit ()       // respond to menu item "Quit"
{
    this->DestroyWindow () ;      // destroy main window,
}                                 // this stops application
```

Listing 16-4 BITMAP1.HPP Header File

```
// bitmap1.hpp    header file for bitmap1.cpp

class CMainWindow : public CFrameWnd    // derive a main window class
{
public:
    CMainWindow () ;                     // declare a constructor
private:
    void OnShow () ;                     // display bitmap
    void OnExit () ;                     // stop application

    DECLARE_MESSAGE_MAP()
} ;

class CTheApp : public CWinApp          // derive an application class
{
public:
    BOOL InitInstance () ;               // declare new InitInstance()
} ;
```

Listing 16-5 BITMAP1.H Resource ID Header File

```
// bitmap1.h  header file for resource ID numbers

#define IDM_SHOW           1    // menu item ID numbers
#define IDM_QUIT           2

#define S_PROGRAMCAPTION   1    // string table ID number
```

Listing 16-6 BITMAP1.DEF Module Definition File

```
NAME           bitmap1
DESCRIPTION    'bitmap1 C++ program'
EXETYPE        WINDOWS
STUB           'WINSTUB.EXE'
CODE           PRELOAD MOVEABLE
DATA           PRELOAD MOVEABLE MULTIPLE
HEAPSIZE       1024
STACKSIZE      5120
```

of a bitmap, it cannot increase or reduce the size of a bitmap. The **CDC** class includes the **CDC::StretchBlt()** function as an alternative to **CDC::BitBlt()** when the bitmap needs to be changed in size. **CDC::StretchBlt()** takes the same parameters as **CDC::BitBlt()**, plus two more. You specify not only the location of the top left corner of the output bitmap, but also its width and length. The source bitmap will be stretched or compressed to fill out the specified size. Table 16-2 lists the syntax of the **CDC::StretchBlt()** function.

```
BOOL    CDC::StretchBlt(int X, int Y, int nWidth, int nHeight, CDC*
        pSrcDC, int XSrc, int YSrc, int nSrcWidth, int nSrcHeight,
        DWORD dwRop) ;
```

Parameter	Meaning
X	The logical X-coordinate of the upper left corner of the bitmap on the output device context.
Y	The logical Y-coordinate of the upper left corner of the bitmap on the output.
nWidth	The width in logical units of the output bitmap.
nHeight	The height in logical units of the output bitmap.
pSrcDC	A pointer to the device context object from which the bitmap will be copied. This is normally a memory device context created with **CDC::CreateCompatibleDC()**. A bitmap is loaded into the memory device context using **CDC::SelectObject()**.
XSrc	The logical X-coordinate of the upper left corner of the source bitmap. Normally zero.
YSrc	The logical Y-coordinate of the upper left corner of the source bitmap. Normally zero.
nSrcWidth	The width of the source bitmap in logical units. If the default coordinate system is being used for *pSrcDC*, this is the width in pixels.
nSrcHeight	The height of the source bitmap in logical units. If the default coordinate system is being used for *pSrcDC*, this is the height in pixels.
dwRop	One of the raster operation codes. Fifteen of the 256 possibilities have names defined in WINDOWS.H. You will most often use the code SRCCOPY for this parameter. The remaining codes are explained later in this chapter, under the heading *Raster Operation Codes*.

Table 16-2 CDC::StretchBlt() Syntax

Using CDC::StretchBlt()

The BITMAP2 example program demonstrates the **CDC::StretchBlt()** function by both shrinking and expanding the HOUSE.BMP bitmap image used in the last example. Figure 16-6 shows the BITMAP2 program in operation. From left to right, the images are 1) half size; 2) full size; 3) doubled size; and 4) four times original size, but only displaying the upper left corner of the image. All of these images are created with calls to the **CDC::StretchBlt()** function, shrinking and expanding the same bitmap image after it has been selected into a memory device context.

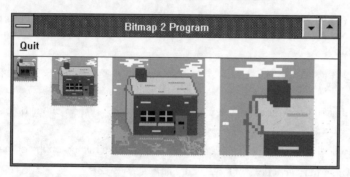

Figure 16-6 The BITMAP2 Program

If you examine the diagonal lines in Figure 16-6, you will notice that the lines become increasingly jagged as the image is enlarged. This is inevitable because the **CDC::StretchBlt()** function simply adds pixels with the same colors as the original pixels to fill in the image as it is expanded. Although it is not obvious in looking at the smallest image in Figure 16-6, **CDC::StretchBlt()** eliminates pixels when the image is reduced in size. You can change the logic used to eliminate pixels using the **CDC::SetStretchBltMode()** function; however, no matter what you do, pixels must disappear for an image to become smaller. As a general rule, bitmaps become unacceptably altered when they are increased or decreased in size by more than a factor of two. If you need broader scaling than this, consider storing multiple bitmaps of the same image, each with different sizes.

Listing 16-7 shows the BITMAP2.CPP program. BITMAP2.CPP is almost identical to the previous BITMAP1.CPP example, except that the **CDC::StretchBlt()** function has been substituted for the **CDC::BitBlt()** function. **CDC::StretchBlt()** is not as fast as **CDC::BitBlt()**, so you will only want to use **CDC::StretchBlt()** if the bitmap must be changed in scale. The other change to BITMAP2.CPP is that the painting logic has been placed in the WM_PAINT message processing section, so the images are automatically repainted.

The support files for BITMAP2.CPP are shown in Listings 16-8 to 16-11. Figure 16-7 shows the program's icon.

Figure 16-7 BITMAP2.ICO Icon Image

Listing 16-7 BITMAP2.CPP

```cpp
// bitmap2.cpp                example using StretchBlt

#include <afxwin.h>        // class library header file
#include "bitmap2.h"       // header file for resource data
#include "bitmap2.hpp"     // header file for this program

CTheApp theApp ;           // create one CTheApp object - runs program

BOOL CTheApp::InitInstance ()    // override default InitInstance()
{
    m_pMainWnd = new CMainWindow () ;        // create a main window
    m_pMainWnd->ShowWindow (m_nCmdShow) ;    // make it visible
    m_pMainWnd->UpdateWindow () ;            // paint center
    return TRUE ;
}


CMainWindow::CMainWindow ()       // constructor for window
{
    CString title ;       // get program caption from resource data
    title.LoadString (S_PROGRAMCAPTION) ;
    Create (NULL, title, WS_OVERLAPPEDWINDOW, rectDefault,
        NULL, "MyMenu") ;
}

BEGIN_MESSAGE_MAP (CMainWindow, CFrameWnd)
    ON_WM_PAINT ()                      // process WM_PAINT msg
    ON_COMMAND (IDM_QUIT, OnExit)       // respond to menu items
END_MESSAGE_MAP ()

void CMainWindow::OnPaint ()            // process WM_PAINT msg
{
    CBitmap ABitmap ;
    ABitmap.LoadBitmap ("HouseBmp") ;   // load bitmap from resources
    CPaintDC cDC (this) ;               // get client area dc
    CDC MemDC ;
    MemDC.CreateCompatibleDC (&cDC) ;   // create memory dc
    MemDC.SelectObject (&ABitmap) ;
    cDC.StretchBlt (0, 0, 32, 32, &MemDC, 0, 0, 64, 64, SRCCOPY) ;
    cDC.StretchBlt (52, 0, 64, 64, &MemDC, 0, 0, 64, 64, SRCCOPY) ;
    cDC.StretchBlt (136, 0, 128, 128, &MemDC, 0, 0, 64, 64,
        SRCCOPY);
    cDC.StretchBlt (284, 0, 128, 128, &MemDC, 0, 0, 32, 32,
        SRCCOPY);
}


void CMainWindow::OnExit ()     // respond to menu item "Quit"
{
    this->DestroyWindow () ;    // destroy main window,
}                               // this stops application
```

Listing 16-8 BITMAP2.HPP Header File

```
// bitmap2.hpp    header file for bitmap2.cpp

class CMainWindow : public CFrameWnd    // derive a main window class
{
public:
    CMainWindow () ;                     // declare a constructor
private:
    void OnPaint () ;                    // process WM_PAINT
    void OnExit () ;                     // stop application

    DECLARE_MESSAGE_MAP()
} ;

class CTheApp : public CWinApp          // derive an application class
{
public:
    BOOL InitInstance () ;               // declare new InitInstance()
} ;
```

Listing 16-9 BITMAP2.H Resource ID Header File

```
// bitmap2.h   header file for resource ID numbers

#define IDM_QUIT           1   // menu item ID numbers

#define S_PROGRAMCAPTION   1   // string table ID number
```

Listing 16-10 BITMAP2.RC Resource Script File

```
// bitmap2.rc   resource script file

#include <afxres.h>
#include "bitmap2.h"

AFX_IDI_STD_FRAME    ICON     bitmap2.ico   // the program's icon
HouseBmp             BITMAP   house.bmp     // a bitmap file

MyMenu MENU                                 // define the menu
{
    MENUITEM "&Quit",        IDM_QUIT
}

STRINGTABLE
{
    S_PROGRAMCAPTION     "Bitmap 2 Program"
}
```

Listing 16-11 BITMAP2.DEF Module Definition File

```
NAME            bitmap2
DESCRIPTION     'bitmap2 C++ program'
EXETYPE         WINDOWS
STUB            'WINSTUB.EXE'
CODE            PRELOAD MOVEABLE
DATA            PRELOAD MOVEABLE MULTIPLE
HEAPSIZE        1024
STACKSIZE       5120
```

RASTER OPERATION CODES

In the previous examples, the **CDC::BitBlt()** and **CDC::StretchBlt()** functions were called using the SRCCOPY constant. For example, in the BITMAP2 program, the first picture is drawn with the function call:

```
cDC.StretchBlt (0, 0, 32, 32, &MemDC, 0, 0, 64, 64, SRCCOPY) ;
```

SRCCOPY, a constant defined in WINDOWS.H, is referred to as a "raster operation code." Raster operations take place on a raster device, which is a device that draws using individual dots, such as a typical video monitor or laser printer. The opposite of a raster device is a vector device that draws using lines. The most common vector device is a plotter that moves pens in lines to draw images. Bitmaps are clearly associated with raster devices, as a bitmap is just a method of storing the color of each pixel on the screen.

When using functions like **CDC::BitBlt()** and **CDC::StretchBlt()**, it is possible to do more than just copy the bitmap onto the output device. These functions can look at the pixels currently on the screen and combine those pixel colors with the bitmap's pixel colors to produce the final image. The combining of the screen pixels and the bitmap pixels is done with binary logic (binary AND, OR, NOT, etc.), sometimes called "raster" logic. Figure 16-8 shows two examples, using a simple monochrome bitmap for both the source bitmap and the destination screen. The same type of logic can be applied to color bitmaps by taking the red, green, and blue elements of each pixel's color individually.

To make life even more interesting, Windows can also include the currently selected brush pattern in the binary logic. With three bitmaps (source bitmap, destination bitmap, and the brush pattern), there are a total of 256 possible combinations that can be created. Fortunately, you are unlikely to need more than two or three of these combinations. The WINDOWS.H header file gives names to the 15 most common raster operations, which are listed in

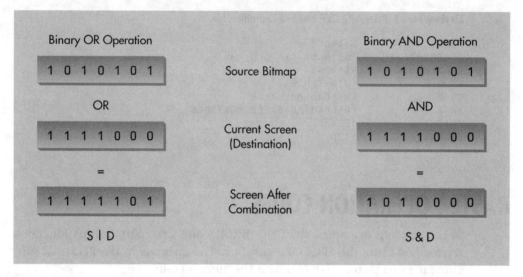

Figure 16-8 Raster Logic for a Monochrome Bitmap

Table 16-3. For the Boolean codes, "S" is the source bitmap, "D" is the destination bitmap (usually the screen), and "P" is the currently selected brush (called a "pattern") of the output device context. The Boolean operators follow these conventions: AND = &, NOT = ~, OR = |, XOR = ^.

Several of the raster operation codes in Table 16-3 deserve special mention. The SRCCOPY operator just copies the bitmap onto the destination, which is the most common requirement. The BLACKNESS and WHITENESS operators make the bitmap area all black or all white, respectively. These operators have the advantage of being able to set the bitmap handle to NULL, because the bitmap is not used to create the final image. DSTINVERT, PATINVERT, and SCRINVERT have the interesting property that painting the same bitmap at the same location twice causes the bitmap to disappear. This can be useful in animation because it is simple to make the "old" image disappear by painting the image a second time at the same location.

An Example Using Raster Operation Codes

The next example program, BITMAP3, demonstrates all fifteen of the raster operation codes listed in Table 16-3. Figure 16-9 shows the BITMAP3 program in operation. The black and white illustration does not do the program justice, so be sure to create and run this example to get the full visual effect. The same bitmap is displayed all 15 times, but it looks different in each case because a different raster operation code is applied. The unadulterated source bitmap can

Value	Meaning
BLACKNESS	Turns all output black. (0)
DSTINVERT	Inverts the destination bitmap. (~D)
MERGECOPY	The source and pattern bitmaps are combined with the Boolean AND operator. (P & S)
MERGEPAINT	The inverted source and destination bitmaps are combined with the Boolean OR operator. (~S | D)
NOTSRCCOPY	Inverts the source bitmap, then copies it to the destination. (~S)
NOTSRCERASE	Inverts the result of combining the source and destination bitmaps using the Boolean OR operator. (~(S | D))
PATCOPY	Copies the pattern to the destination. (P)
PATINVERT	Combines the destination bitmap with the pattern using the Boolean OR operator. (P ^ D)
PATPAINT	P | ~(S | D)
SRCAND	Combines the source and destination bitmaps with the Boolean AND operator. (S & D)
SRCCOPY	Copies the source to the destination. (S)
SRCERASE	S & ~ D
SRCINVERT	Combines the source and destination bitmaps using the Boolean XOR operator. (S ^ D)
SRCPAINT	Combines the source and destination bitmaps using the Boolean OR operator. (S | D)
WHITENESS	Turns all output white. This is a quick way to blank a device context. (1)

For the Boolean codes, "S" is the source bitmap, "D" is the destination bitmap (usually the screen), and "P" is the currently selected brush (called a "pattern") of the output device context. The Boolean operators follow these conventions: AND = &, NOT = ~, OR = |, XOR = ^.

Table 16-3 Raster Operation Codes for CDC::BitBlt() and CDC::StretchBlt()

be seen in the lower left corner, above the SRCCOPY raster operation code. The background is a black and white bitmap pattern, with tiles that appear roughly like bricks. The inverted image above the DSTINVERT raster code shows the brick pattern more clearly, as the colors are reversed. The selected brush has a blue, diagonal cross pattern, visible above the PATCOPY raster code.

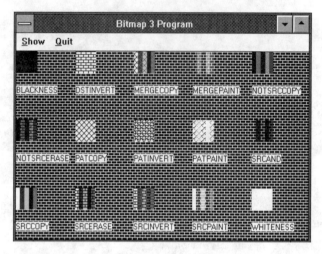

Figure 16-9 The BITMAP3 Program After Selecting the "Show" Menu Item

An interesting experiment you can do with BITMAP3 is to select the "Show" menu item more than once. Figure 16-10 shows the result after a second click. The bitmap images drawn with the DSTINVERT, PATINVERT, and SRCINVERT raster codes all disappear, and several others change colors. The reason for these changes is that in painting the second time, the raster codes that involve comparisons with the screen now have a different starting point. Selecting "Show" a third time restores all of the bitmaps to their previous states.

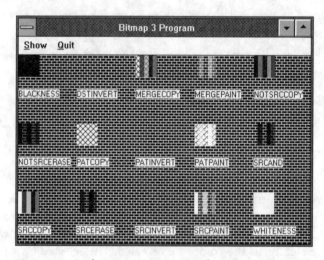

Figure 16-10 The BITMAP3 Program After Selecting the "Show" Menu Item a Second Time

The BITMAP3 Program

The BITMAP3 program uses a new programming technique to paint the client area with a brick pattern. The brick bitmap was created with the Image Editor and stored as a bitmap file. BITMAP3 includes this bitmap in its resource data, and names the bitmap data "BrickBrush." The two keys to painting with a bitmap brush are to use the **CBrush::CreatePatternBrush()** function to create a brush from a bitmap, and to use the **CDC::PatBlt()** function to fill an area using the currently selected brush. Listing 16-12 shows the **CWnd::OnPaint()** function from BITMAP3.CPP, which paints the client area with a pattern named "BrickBrush." The *nXclient* and *nYclient* variables are private integers of the **CMainWindow** class, which are used to store the current size of the client area.

The **CDC::PatBlt()** function has a limited set of raster operation codes, which are listed in Table 16-4. **PatBlt()** only works with the destination bitmap and the current brush pattern, and does not use a second bitmap like **CDC::Bit-Blt()** and **CDC::StretchBlt()**. **CDC::PatBlt()**, therefore, has fewer possible raster operation codes.

Listing 16-12 Painting with a Pattern Brush

```
void CMainWindow::OnPaint ()          // process WM_PAINT messages
{                                     // paint with brick pattern brush
    CPaintDC dc (this) ;                     // get client area dc
    CBitmap BrickBmp ;
    BrickBmp.LoadBitmap ("BrickBrush") ;   // load the pattern bmp
    CBrush brush ;
    brush.CreatePatternBrush (&BrickBmp) ;  // convert bmp into brush
    dc.SelectObject (&brush) ;              // select brush into dc
                                           // use brush to paint area
    dc.PatBlt (0, 0, nXclient, nYclient, PATCOPY) ;
}
```

Value	Meaning
BLACKNESS	Turns all output black. (0)
DSTINVERT	Inverts the destination bitmap. (~D)
PATCOPY	Copies the pattern to the destination. (P)
PATINVERT	Combines the destination bitmap with the pattern using the Boolean OR operator. (P | D)
WHITENESS	Turns all output white. This is a quick way to blank a device context. (1)

Table 16-4 Raster Operation Codes for PatBlt()

Listing 16-13 shows the complete BITMAP3.CPP program. The bitmap images are not displayed until the user selects the "Show" menu item. The bitmap is selected into the memory device context, while the crosshatched brush is selected into the output device context, prior to painting the 15 copies of the bitmap image. All 15 of the predefined raster operation codes in WINDOWS.H are loaded into a static DWORD array *dwRasterOp[]*. This makes it easy for **CDC::BitBlt()** to be called 15 times, each time with a different raster operation code. In addition, the name of the raster operation code is displayed under each bitmap. The raster operation code names are defined as consecutive entries in the program's string table in the resource script file. The **CMainWindow::StringAtPoint()** function defined towards the end of BITMAP3.CPP writes each string under the bitmap.

The bitmaps for both the brick brush and the colored square were created using the Image Editor. Figures 16-11 and 16-12 show the two images. The color bands in the 64 by 64 pixel COLORS.BMP bitmap are (from left to right) white, red, yellow, blue, and green. The BRIKBRSH bitmap is black and white, and only 8 by 8 pixels in size. If you attempt to use a larger bitmap with the **CBrush::CreatePatternBrush()** function, only the upper left 8 by 8 pixel square will be used because Windows brushes are limited to 8 by 8 pixels.

One other item of interest in BITMAP3.CPP is the **CMainWindow::StringAtPoint()** function. This function is used to write the names of the raster operation codes under the graphic images on the main program window. The names of the raster operations codes are stored in a string table in the program's resource script file BITMAP3.RC (Listing 16-16). **CMainWindow::StringAtPoint()** writes a specific string table entry at an *X,Y* position on the main program window's client area. You may find this function useful in other programs that use string table data for output to the display.

Listings 16-14 to 16-17 show the remaining support files for BITMAP3.CPP. The program's icon is shown in Figure 16-13.

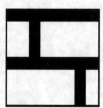

Figure 16-11 BRIKBRSH.BMP

Figure 16-12 COLORS.BMP

Listing 16-13 BITMAP3.CPP

```cpp
// bitmap3.cpp              example showing raster operation codes

#include <afxwin.h>     // class library header file
#include "bitmap3.h"    // header file for resource data
#include "bitmap3.hpp"  // header file for this program


CTheApp theApp ;        // create one CTheApp object - runs program

BOOL CTheApp::InitInstance ()   // override default InitInstance()
{
    m_pMainWnd = new CMainWindow () ;       // create a main window
    m_pMainWnd->ShowWindow (m_nCmdShow) ;   // make it visible
    m_pMainWnd->UpdateWindow () ;           // paint center
    return TRUE ;
}


CMainWindow::CMainWindow ()      // constructor for window
{
    CString title ;      // get program caption from resource data
    title.LoadString (S_PROGRAMCAPTION) ;
    Create (NULL, title, WS_OVERLAPPEDWINDOW, rectDefault,
        NULL, "MyMenu") ;
}

BEGIN_MESSAGE_MAP (CMainWindow, CFrameWnd)
    ON_COMMAND (IDM_SHOW, OnShow)           // respond to menu items
    ON_COMMAND (IDM_QUIT, OnExit)
    ON_WM_PAINT ()                          // respond to WM_PAINT
    ON_WM_SIZE ()                           // and WM_SIZE messages
END_MESSAGE_MAP ()

void CMainWindow::OnShow ()      // respond to menu item "Show"
{
    DWORD dwRasterOp [15] = {BLACKNESS, DSTINVERT, MERGECOPY,
        MERGEPAINT, NOTSRCCOPY, NOTSRCERASE, PATCOPY, PATINVERT,
        PATPAINT, SRCAND, SRCCOPY, SRCERASE, SRCINVERT, SRCPAINT,
        WHITENESS} ;

    CBitmap ABitmap ;
    ABitmap.LoadBitmap ("ColorsBmp") ;  // load bitmap from resources
    CClientDC cDC (this) ;              // get client area dc
    cDC.SelectStockObject (ANSI_VAR_FONT) ; // pick a small font
    CDC MemDC ;
    MemDC.CreateCompatibleDC (&cDC) ;   // create memory dc
    MemDC.SelectObject (&ABitmap) ;
    CBrush brush ;                      // create a pattern brush
    brush.CreateHatchBrush (HS_DIAGCROSS, RGB (0, 0, 255)) ;
```

```
        cDC.SelectObject (&brush) ;
        for (int i = 0 ; i < 5 ; i++)          // draw same bitmap with
        {                                      // 15 different ROP codes
            for (int j = 0 ; j < 3 ; j++)
            {
                cDC.BitBlt (90 * i, 100 * j, 32, 32,
                    &MemDC, 0, 0, dwRasterOp [i + (5 * j)]) ;
                StringAtPoint (&cDC, 90 * i, 50 + (100 * j),
                    S_BLACKNESS + i + (5 * j)) ;
            }
        }
}                      // all objects are automatic, so no cleanup required

void CMainWindow::OnExit ()        // respond to menu item "Quit"
{
    this->DestroyWindow () ;       // destroy main window,
}                                  // this stops application

void CMainWindow::StringAtPoint (CDC* pDC, int X, int Y, int nString)
{
    CString string ;
    string.LoadString (nString) ;
    pDC->TextOut (X, Y, string, string.GetLength ()) ;
}

void CMainWindow::OnPaint ()            // process WM_PAINT messages
{                                       // paint with brick pattern brush
    CPaintDC dc (this) ;                    // get client area dc
    CBitmap BrickBmp ;
    BrickBmp.LoadBitmap ("BrickBrush") ;    // load the pattern bmp
    CBrush brush ;
    brush.CreatePatternBrush (&BrickBmp) ;  // convert bmp into brush
    dc.SelectObject (&brush) ;              // select brush into dc
                                            // use brush to paint area
    dc.PatBlt (0, 0, nXclient, nYclient, PATCOPY) ;
}

void CMainWindow::OnSize (UINT nType, int cx, int cy)
{
    nXclient = cx ;                    // save client area size
    nYclient = cy ;
}
```

Figure 16-13 BITMAP3.ICO Icon Image

Listing 16-14 BITMAP3.HPP Header File

```cpp
// bitmap3.hpp     header file for bitmap3.cpp

class CMainWindow : public CFrameWnd     // derive a main window class
{
public:
    CMainWindow () ;                      // declare a constructor
private:
    int nXclient, nYclient ;              // save client area size
    void OnShow () ;                      // display bitmap
    void OnExit () ;                      // stop application

    void OnPaint () ;
    void OnSize (UINT nType, int cx, int cy) ;

    void StringAtPoint (CDC* pDC, int X, int Y, int nString) ;

    DECLARE_MESSAGE_MAP()                 // prepare for message processing
} ;

class CTheApp : public CWinApp          // derive an application class
{
public:
    BOOL InitInstance () ;                // declare new InitInstance()
} ;
```

Listing 16-15 BITMAP3.H Resource ID Header File

```cpp
// bitmap3.h  header file for resource ID numbers

#define IDM_SHOW            1   // menu item ID numbers
#define IDM_QUIT            2

#define S_PROGRAMCAPTION    1   // string table ID numbers
#define S_BLACKNESS         2
#define S_DSTINVERT         3
#define S_MERGECOPY         4
#define S_MERGEPAINT        5
#define S_NOTSRCCOPY        6
#define S_NOTSRCERASE       7
#define S_PATCOPY           8
#define S_PATINVERT         9
#define S_PATPAINT          10
#define S_SRCAND            11
#define S_SRCCOPY           12
#define S_SRCERASE          13
#define S_SRCINVERT         14
#define S_SRCPAINT          15
#define S_WHITENESS         16
```

Listing 16-16 BITMAP3.RC Resource Script File

```
// bitmap3.rc  resource script file

#include <afxres.h>
#include "bitmap3.h"

AFX_IDI_STD_FRAME    ICON      bitmap3.ico      // the program's icon
BrickBrush           BITMAP    brikbrsh.bmp     // bitmap files
ColorsBmp            BITMAP    colors.bmp

MyMenu MENU                                      // define the menu
{
    MENUITEM "&Show",        IDM_SHOW
    MENUITEM "&Quit",        IDM_QUIT
}

STRINGTABLE
{
    S_PROGRAMCAPTION    "Bitmap 3 Program"
    S_BLACKNESS         "BLACKNESS"
    S_DSTINVERT         "DSTINVERT"
    S_MERGECOPY         "MERGECOPY"
    S_MERGEPAINT        "MERGEPAINT"
    S_NOTSRCCOPY        "NOTSRCCOPY"
    S_NOTSRCERASE       "NOTSRCERASE"
    S_PATCOPY           "PATCOPY"
    S_PATINVERT         "PATINVERT"
    S_PATPAINT          "PATPAINT"
    S_SRCAND            "SRCAND"
    S_SRCCOPY           "SRCCOPY"
    S_SRCERASE          "SRCERASE"
    S_SRCINVERT         "SRCINVERT"
    S_SRCPAINT          "SRCPAINT"
    S_WHITENESS         "WHITENESS"
}
```

Listing 16-17 BITMAP3.DEF Module Definition File

```
NAME            bitmap3
DESCRIPTION     'bitmap3 C++ program'
EXETYPE         WINDOWS
STUB            'WINSTUB.EXE'
CODE            PRELOAD MOVEABLE
DATA            PRELOAD MOVEABLE MULTIPLE
HEAPSIZE        1024
STACKSIZE       5120
```

DRAWING ON A MEMORY BITMAP

So far in this book, we have used the GDI functions like **CDC::LineTo()** and **CDC::Rectangle()** to output GDI commands to "real" devices for the screen and the printer. It turns out that you can also use the GDI functions to "draw" on a memory device context. You can do all sorts of output on the memory device context, and then copy the finished image all at once to a "real" device context using **CDC::BitBlt()**. Although you can use the GDI functions to draw on a bitmap file/resource loaded into memory, normally you will want to create a blank bitmap in memory before using the GDI functions.

In this book, we will refer to a bitmap selected into a memory device context as a "memory bitmap." (The Microsoft documentation simply refers to the memory device context, without naming the bitmap selected into the memory device context.) The **CDC::CreateCompatibleBitmap()** function creates a blank memory bitmap. Listing 16-18 shows a typical program fragment, which creates a 100 pixel wide by 100 pixel high memory bitmap, draws a rectangle on the memory bitmap, and then copies the entire memory device context to the screen device context.

Drawing on a memory bitmap probably sounds like a roundabout way to produce an image. Normally, it is easier to just draw on the output device context, and skip the intermediate steps required to create a memory bitmap. However, there are situations where doing all of the drawing on a memory bitmap and copying the final picture to the output device with a single call to **CDC::BitBlt()** produces a much better effect. The advantage of drawing to the memory bitmap is that all of the GDI operations are invisible to the user. The drawing is made visible only when the final bitmap is copied to the output device context with **CDC::BitBlt()** or **CDC::StretchBlt()**. **CDC::BitBlt()** is a fast function, much faster than the GDI functions, such as **CDC::Rectangle()** and **CDC::Ellipse()**. By drawing on a memory bitmap, and then "blitting" the finished image to the output device, the image appears in an instant, rather than gradually taking shape as each GDI function does its work.

Listing 16-18 Painting on a Memory Device Context

```
CClientDC dc (this) ;          // get client area device context
CDC memDC ;                    // create a second CDC object
memDC.CreateCompatibleDC (&dc) ;    // make it a memory device context
CBitmap memBitmap ;                 // create 100 X 100 memory bitmap
memBitmap.CreateCompatibleBitmap (&dc, 100, 100) ;
CBitmap* pBmp = memDC.SelectObject (&memBitmap) ;
memDC.Rectangle (10, 10, 90, 90) ;  // paint rectangle on memory bmp
    // now copy the whole image to the client area dc using BitBlit
dc.BitBlt (0, 0, 100, 100, &memDC, 0, 0, SRCCOPY) ;
```

Memory Bitmaps and Animation

The most common situation that demands the use of memory bitmaps is animation. Even simple animated sequences are jittery if you attempt to move objects by painting and repainting each object using GDI functions directly on the output device. A better way to animate is to do all of the changes on a memory bitmap, and then "blit" the finished picture onto the screen. This technique can be applied to the entire screen at once, or to individual portions that are changing. In general, it is best to limit the size of the memory bitmap to a relatively small portion of the screen that is changing to minimize the time delays in repainting.

The last example program in this chapter, BITMAP4, demonstrates using memory bitmaps for animation by animating a moving ball image. BITMAP4 uses both direct GDI function calls to the screen, and a memory bitmap to paint the background, so you can compare the two techniques. Figure 16-14 shows the running BITMAP4 program, which is similar to the GRAPHIC2 example program in Chapter 4, *Text and Graphics Output*. Selecting the "On" menu item causes a red ball to bounce around in the window's client area.

If the "Blit Drawing" menu item has been selected, the ball appears to move steadily. The speed of the ball will depend on the size of the BITMAP4 window. The larger the window, the slower the drawing, because the program will repaint the entire client area for each movement of the ball. If the "Direct GDI" menu item is selected, the ball moves faster, and the image becomes fuzzy, because it changes constantly. With the GDI technique, the speed of the ball is not affected by the size of the program window because only the ball itself is drawn, not the entire client area.

The "Blit Drawing" option shows a clear image of the ball moving because all of the drawing operations are done on a memory bitmap. When the image is complete, the finished picture of the entire client area, including the ball, is

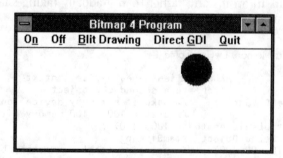

Figure 16-14 The BITMAP4 Program

"blit" onto the screen. With the "Direct GDI" option, the ball is drawn on the screen's device context. Each GDI action, erasing the ball at the old location and drawing it again at the new location, is visible to the user and causes the ball to appeart to flicker on the screen as it moves.

The BITMAP4 program consists of two groups of source code files. The BALL2.CPP and BALL2.HPP files define the routines used to draw a moving ball on the screen. BITMAP4.CPP and its support files define the program window and menu, and use the BALL2.CPP functions to animate the moving ball image.

Listing 16-19 shows the BALL2.HPP header file. This is similar to the BALL.HPP file from Chapter 4, *Text and Graphics Output*. The main difference is that there are now two ball drawing functions: **MovingBall::DrawBall()** and **MovingBall::DrawBallBlt()**. The latter uses a memory device context to draw the moving ball.

Listing 16-20 shows the BALL2.CPP program file. The **MovingBall::Draw-BallBlt()** function draws the moving ball by first creating a memory device context, drawing the ball at a new location on the memory DC, and then "blitting" the entire memory DC onto the BITMAP4 window's client area.

Listing 16-19 BALL2.HPP Header File

```
// ball2.hpp   header file for moving ball routines in ball2.cpp

#define BALLRAD     20          // ball radius
#define VELOCITY    5           // pixels per move velocity
#define MINRAD      15          // how close ball can get to edge

class MovingBall                // moving ball class
{
public:
    MovingBall (CWnd* pWnd) ;            // constructor
    void BallOn () {bBallOn = TRUE ;}    // turns ball on
    void BallOff () {bBallOn = FALSE ;}  // turns ball off
    int IsBallOn () {return bBallOn ;}   // query status of ball
    void MoveBall () ;                   // move ball to next location
    void DrawBall () ;                   // draw ball at location
    void DrawBallBlt () ;                // draw ball using mem dc
private:
    BOOL bBallOn ;                       // true if ball is visible
    int nX, nY ;                         // current ball position
    int nVelX, nVelY ;                   // current ball velocity
    CWnd* pWindow ;                      // save window handle
} ;
```

Listing 16-20 BALL2.CPP

```cpp
// ball2.cpp    moving ball routines

#include <afxwin.h>            // class library header file
#include "ball2.hpp"           // header for this program file

MovingBall::MovingBall (CWnd* pWnd)      // constructor for moving ball
{
    pWindow = pWnd ;                     // initialize private variables
    bBallOn = FALSE ;
    nX = nY = BALLRAD ;
    nVelX = nVelY = VELOCITY ;
}

void MovingBall::DrawBall ()    // draw red ball using direct GDI
{
    if (!bBallOn)                       // do nothing if ball is not to move
        return ;

    CRect ClientRect ;
    pWindow->GetClientRect (&ClientRect) ;  // get client area size
    int Cwide = ClientRect.Width () ;
    int Ctall = ClientRect.Height () ;

    CClientDC dc(pWindow) ;                 // get client area dct
    CBrush Wbrush (RGB (255, 255, 255)) ;   // use white brush to fill
    dc.SelectObject (&Wbrush) ;             // the memory dc.
    dc.SelectStockObject (NULL_PEN) ;       // null pen, so no border
    dc.Rectangle (0, 0, Cwide, Ctall) ;     // fill dc

    CBrush Rbrush (RGB (255, 0, 0)) ;       // red brush for ball
    dc.SelectObject (&Rbrush) ;             // into dc for window
                                   // to draw ball using Ellipse()
    dc.Ellipse (nX - BALLRAD, nY - BALLRAD, nX + BALLRAD,
        nY + BALLRAD) ;
    dc.SelectStockObject (BLACK_PEN) ;   // select stock objects to
    dc.SelectStockObject (WHITE_BRUSH) ;// free pen and brush from dc
}

void MovingBall::DrawBallBlt ()  // draw red ball using memory dc
{
    if (!bBallOn)                       // do nothing if ball is not to move
        return ;

    CRect ClientRect ;
    pWindow->GetClientRect (&ClientRect) ;  // get client area size
    int Cwide = ClientRect.Width () ;
    int Ctall = ClientRect.Height () ;
```

```
    CClientDC dc(pWindow) ;                    // get client area dc
    CDC memDC ;
    memDC.CreateCompatibleDC (&dc) ;           // create memory dc
    CBitmap memBitmap ;                        // create memory bitmap
    memBitmap.CreateCompatibleBitmap (&dc, Cwide, Ctall) ;
    CBitmap* pBmp = memDC.SelectObject (&memBitmap) ;

    CBrush Wbrush (RGB (255, 255, 255)) ;   // use white brush and pen
    memDC.SelectObject (&Wbrush) ;             // to fill the memory dc ;
    memDC.SelectStockObject (WHITE_PEN) ;
    memDC.Rectangle (0, 0, Cwide, Ctall) ;

    CBrush Rbrush (RGB (255, 0, 0)) ; // red brush for ball interior
    memDC.SelectObject (&Rbrush) ;     // to draw ball using ellipse()
    memDC.Ellipse (nX - BALLRAD, nY - BALLRAD, nX + BALLRAD,
        nY + BALLRAD) ;

    // now copy the ball image to the client area dc using BitBlit
    dc.BitBlt (0, 0, Cwide, Ctall, &memDC, 0, 0, SRCCOPY) ;
    memDC.SelectStockObject (BLACK_PEN) ;   // select stock objects to
    memDC.SelectStockObject (WHITE_BRUSH) ; // free pen and brush
    memDC.SelectObject (pBmp) ;
}

void MovingBall::MoveBall ()     // move ball to new location
{
    CRect   ClientRect ;
    int     nXSize, nYSize ;

    if (!bBallOn)                   // do nothing if ball is not to move
        return ;

    pWindow->GetClientRect (&ClientRect) ;  // get client area bounds
    nXSize = ClientRect.Width () ;
    nYSize = ClientRect.Height () ;

    nX += nVelX ;                   // move ball's location by velocity
    nY += nVelY ;                   // units in both directions
            // check if user moved walls, covering up the ball
    if (nY > nYSize)
        nY = 2 * BALLRAD ;          // if so, put in a safe place
    if (nX > nXSize)
        nX = 2 * BALLRAD ;
            // reverse direction if within MINRAD of a wall
    if (nY < MINRAD || nYSize - nY < MINRAD)
        nVelY *= -1 ;               // mult by -1 reverses direction
    if (nX < MINRAD || nXSize - nX < MINRAD)
        nVelX *= -1 ;
}
```

The **CWnd::GetClientRect()** function is used to determine the size of the BITMAP4 window's client area before creating the memory device context. Once the memory device context is created, standard GDI painting functions are used to paint the ball. When the complete image of the window's client area is ready in the memory DC, the entire image is copied onto the "real" device context for the BITMAP4 program window.

Note at the bottom of the **MovingBall::DrawBallBlt()** function that care is taken to displace any new pens or brushes from the memory device context before the pens and brushes are deleted (they are deleted automatically when the function returns). This is the same procedure used with any "real" device context to avoid having a device context contain a pointer to a nonexistent GDI object. The memory bitmap itself is also a GDI object. **MovingBall::DrawBallBlt()** saves a pointer (*pBmp*) to the memory device context's original bitmap when the memory bitmap is selected into the device context.

```
CBitmap memBitmap ;                        // create memory bitmap
memBitmap.CreateCompatibleBitmap (&dc, Cwide, Ctall) ;
CBitmap* pBmp = memDC.SelectObject (&memBitmap) ;
```

The *pBmp* pointer is then used to displace the new memory bitmap from the memory device context in the last line of the **MovingBall::DrawBallBlt()** function.

```
memDC.SelectObject (pBmp) ;
```

Think of a memory bitmap as being another GDI object, just like a pen or brush. It is selected into the memory device context to provide a surface for GDI painting operations, and should be selected out of the device context before the memory bitmap is deleted.

Listings 16-21 to 16-25 show the BITMAP4 files. These files are almost identical to the GRAPHIC2 program introduced in Chapter 4, *Text and Graphics Output*. The main change is to provide a choice between the two methods of drawing the moving ball: direct GDI operations or using a memory device context. All of the drawing operations are in the BALL2.CPP file. All BITMAP4.CPP does is process menu selections and call the appropriate drawing functions during periods when the system is not busy. The **CWinApp::OnIdle()** virtual function is called automatically whenever the system has free time, which provides an ideal point to call the drawing functions. The global variable *_BlitOn* is used to keep track of whether the user has selected the GDI or memory device context drawing method. Figure 16-15 shows the program's icon.

Listing 16-21 BITMAP4.CPP

```cpp
// bitmap4.cpp              example using memory dc for animation

#include <afxwin.h>      // class library header file
#include "ball2.hpp"     // header file for moving ball object
#include "bitmap4.h"     // header file for resource data
#include "bitmap4.hpp"   // header file for this program

CTheApp theApp ;         // create one CTheApp object - runs program
MovingBall* Ball ;       // pointer to MovingBall object
BOOL _BlitOn = FALSE ;   // track of method used for drawing ball

BOOL CTheApp::InitInstance ()   // override default InitInstance()
{
    m_pMainWnd = new CMainWindow () ;         // create a main window
    m_pMainWnd->ShowWindow (m_nCmdShow) ;     // make it visible
    m_pMainWnd->UpdateWindow () ;             // paint center
    return TRUE ;
}

BOOL CTheApp::OnIdle (LONG lCount)  // draw ball in idle periods
{
    if (lCount > 100)    // if no activity for more than .1 second
    {
        Ball->MoveBall () ;      // move ball during idle time
        if (_BlitOn)
            Ball->DrawBallBlt () ;  // draw ball using mem dc
        else
            Ball->DrawBall () ;      // draw ball using direct gdi
    }
    return TRUE ;
}

CMainWindow::CMainWindow ()            // constructor for window
{
    CString title ;                    // get program caption
    title.LoadString (S_PROGRAMCAPTION) ;
    Create (NULL, title, WS_OVERLAPPEDWINDOW, rectDefault,
        NULL, "MyMenu") ;
    Ball = new MovingBall (this) ;  // create one moving ball
}

BEGIN_MESSAGE_MAP (CMainWindow, CFrameWnd)
    ON_COMMAND (IDM_ON, OnOn)     // menu items
    ON_COMMAND (IDM_OFF, OnOff)
    ON_COMMAND (IDM_BLIT, OnBlit)
    ON_COMMAND (IDM_GDI, OnGdi)
    ON_COMMAND (IDM_QUIT, OnExit)
    ON_WM_CLOSE ()
END_MESSAGE_MAP ()

void CMainWindow::OnOn ()          // menu item "On"
{
    Ball->BallOn () ;
}
```

```
void CMainWindow::OnOff ()          // menu item "Off"
{
    Ball->BallOff () ;
}


void CMainWindow::OnBlit ()         // menu item "Blit Drawing"
{
    _BlitOn = TRUE ;
}


void CMainWindow::OnGdi ()          // menu item "Direct GDI"
{
    _BlitOn = FALSE ;
}


void CMainWindow::OnExit ()         // respond to menu item "Quit"
{
    Ball->BallOff () ;
    this->DestroyWindow () ;        // destroy main window,
}                                   // this stops application

void CMainWindow::OnClose ()        // process WM_CLOSE message - sent
{                                   // when program is about to terminate
    delete Ball ;                   // free ball object from memory
}
```

Listing 16-22 BITMAP4.HPP Header File

```
// bitmap4.hpp     header file for bitmap4.cpp

class CMainWindow : public CFrameWnd     // derive a main window class
{
public:
    CMainWindow () ;                // declare a constructor
private:
    BOOL bDrawOn ;
    CDC cDC, MemDC ;
    void OnOn () ;                  // menu items
    void OnOff () ;
    void OnBlit () ;
    void OnGdi () ;
    void OnExit () ;

    void OnClose () ;              // process WM_CLOSE
    DECLARE_MESSAGE_MAP()          // prepare for message processing
} ;

class CTheApp : public CWinApp   // derive an application class
{
public:
    BOOL InitInstance () ;               // declare new InitInstance()
    BOOL OnIdle (LONG lCount) ;          // idle time processing
} ;
```

Listing 16-23 BITMAP4.H Resource ID Header File

```
// bitmap4.h  header file for resource ID numbers

#define IDM_ON        1          // menu item ID numbers
#define IDM_OFF       2
#define IDM_BLIT      3
#define IDM_GDI       4
#define IDM_QUIT      10

#define S_PROGRAMCAPTION   1     // string table ID number
```

Listing 16-24 BITMAP4.RC Resource Script File

```
// bitmap4.rc  resource script file

#include <afxres.h>
#include "bitmap4.h"

AFX_IDI_STD_FRAME   ICON   bitmap4.ico     // the program's icon

MyMenu MENU                                 // define the menu
{
    MENUITEM "O&n",              IDM_ON
    MENUITEM "O&ff",             IDM_OFF
    MENUITEM "&Blit Drawing",    IDM_BLIT
    MENUITEM "Direct &GDI",      IDM_GDI
    MENUITEM "&Quit",            IDM_QUIT
}

STRINGTABLE
{
    S_PROGRAMCAPTION    "Bitmap 4 Program"
}
```

Listing 16-25 BITMAP4.DEF Module Definition File

```
NAME            bitmap4
DESCRIPTION     'bitmap4 C++ program'
EXETYPE         WINDOWS
STUB            'WINSTUB.EXE'
CODE            PRELOAD MOVEABLE
DATA            PRELOAD MOVEABLE MULTIPLE
HEAPSIZE        1024
STACKSIZE       10240
```

Figure 16-15 BITMAP4.ICO Icon Image

You should experiment with BITMAP4 and different parent window sizes. The speed of the ball is not affected by the size of the window when the direct GDI functions are used because only the ball itself is being repainted. However, the speed of the ball falls off rapidly as the size of the window increases if the memory device context method is used. This is because the entire client area is being repainted in memory before each "movement" of the ball. The number of pixels goes up as the square of the size of the window. The number of computations the program must do to repaint the entire client area is proportional to the number of pixels, so a big client area results in a lot of calculations and a slow program. You can get a rough feel for the maximum practical size of an area that can be painted in a memory device context by experimenting with BITMAP4. Remember that in a real program a moving image typically only moves a few pixels, so it is not necessary to repaint the entire client area to simulate movement of a small object.

BITMAP DATA INTERNAL FORMAT

Up to this point, we have managed to manipulate bitmaps using the **CBitmap** class without being concerned with the internal format of the data. One of the advantages of using the MFC classes is that normally you will not need to concern yourself with the internal representation of the data in a bitmap, or any other GDI object. However, the **CBitmap** class only covers the simplest form of bitmap objects. You may need to support more than the basic types of bitmap if your application is expected to work on systems with different levels of color support.

If you dig into the internal details of the data that the **CBitmap** class manipulates, you will discover that there are two different data formats used by Windows to store bitmap data. For the most part, Windows converts automatically between these two formats, so you will not deal with the data in the bitmap structure directly in most cases. However, you may run into the terminology used to describe the different types of bitmaps, and you may need to occasionally deal with the bitmap data.

The **CBitmap** class works primarily with the simplest type of bitmap, which is the BITMAP format, sometimes called the "device-dependent bitmap" (DDB) or "old" bitmap format. The BITMAP format is device-dependent because the data stored with the bitmap has the numeric values for the color of each pixel, but does not have data to specify the color value of each possible pixel (how "red" red is, etc.). In other words, the BITMAP format assumes that you will display the bitmap on the same type of display that was used to create the BITMAP. If the bitmap is displayed on another type of display with a different color resolution, the colors of the bitmap image may end up completely wrong.

Because of this problem, the BITMAP format is used primarily for manipulating images in memory, but not for storing bitmap data on disk files. The BITMAP data structure is defined in WINDOWS.H as shown in Listing 16-26.

The BITMAP structure has two different ways to specify the number of color bits used in the pixel data. *bmPlanes* is the number of color planes a device, such as a VGA display, may use. If this value is used, then *bmBitsPixel* will be set to one. *bmBitsPixel* is the number of color bits per pixel for a device that does not use color planes, such as a high-end "true color" display. If this value is used, *bmPlanes* will be set to one. The **CBitmap::CreateCompatibleBitmap()** function sets these color values to match a physical device, so you do not have to know in advance how the colors are stored by the video system. The actual pixel data is stored in a memory buffer pointed to by *bmBits*. This buffer is usually immediately after the header data in memory, as shown in Figure 16-16.

The DIB Format

The device-independent bitmap (DIB) was introduced with Windows 3.0 as a solution to the shortcomings of the old BITMAP (DDB) format. The difference between DIBs and DDBs is that DIBs include a table of the colors the bitmap will

Listing 16-26 BITMAP Structure

```
typedef struct tagBITMAP
  {
    int      bmType;          // always zero
    int      bmWidth;         // width in pixels
    int      bmHeight;        // height in pixels
    int      bmWidthBytes;    // bytes per line of data
                              // must be a multiple of 2
    BYTE     bmPlanes;        // the number of color planes
    BYTE     bmBitsPixel;     // the number of bits per pixel
    LPSTR    bmBits;          // far pointer to the bitmap data
  } BITMAP;
typedef BITMAP              *PBITMAP;
typedef BITMAP NEAR         *NPBITMAP;
typedef BITMAP FAR          *LPBITMAP;
```

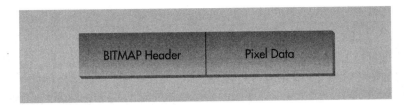

Figure 16-16 The DDB Bitmap Format in Memory

use. This allows a program to read the color data, adjust the color palette being used on the screen, and then display the bitmap image. Adjusting the color palette is an advanced subject, and not covered in this book (see Chapter 12 of *The Waite Group's Windows API Bible* for a discussion color palette control). However, we used the DIB format indirectly in the examples in this chapter, as Windows uses this format for bitmap disk files. The Paintbrush application and the Microsoft Image Editor save their output as DIB data. The DIB bitmap data is automatically converted to the BITMAP (DDB) format when the data is loaded into memory with the **CBitmap::LoadBitmap()** function.

An important difference between the BITMAP and DIB formats is that only the BITMAP format can be selected into a device context. The DIB format is best thought of as a disk file format, used to preserve the color information. The BITMAP format is the low-level data about an image that can be directly "blit" to a location on the screen. The header format for a DIB is more complex than for the simple BITMAP. The DIB format consists of three sections, shown in Figure 16-17. This is the format you would use if you were to load raw DIB data into memory with **::LoadResource()**, instead of automatically converting the DIB data to BITMAP format using **CBitmap::LoadBitmap()**.

WINDOWS.H includes the definitions for both the BITMAPINFOHEADER and RGBQUAD structures, which are shown in Listing 16-27.

Although similar to the BITMAP header structure, BITMAPINFOHEADER contains some added fields. The *biBitCount* element contains the number of color bits per pixel. This will be 1, 4, 8 or 24 bits. Table 16-5 describes the meaning of these values.

The *biCompression* element contains a value to define how the bitmap data is compressed to save space. If it is set to BI_RGB, no compression is used. BI_RLE4 is a 4 bits-per-pixel run length encoding compression. BI_RLE8 is an 8 bits-per-pixel compression.

biSizeImage is the bitmap size in bytes. Each row of pixel data must terminate on a 32-bit (DWORD) boundary. If a row of pixels, with the specified number of color bits per pixel, does not end at an even 32-bit number, the remainder is padded with zero bits.

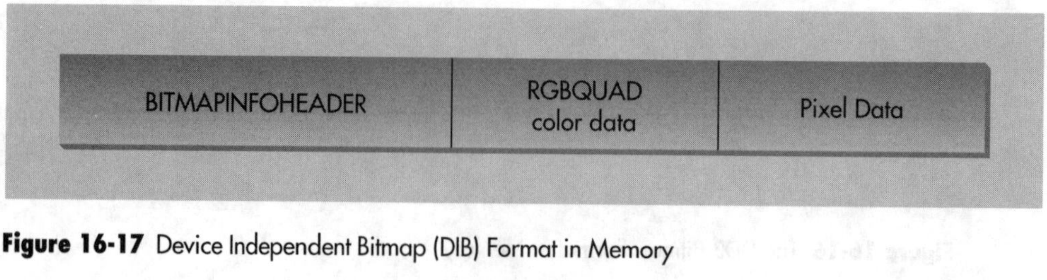

| BITMAPINFOHEADER | RGBQUAD color data | Pixel Data |

Figure 16-17 Device Independent Bitmap (DIB) Format in Memory

Listing 16-27 BITMAPINFOHEADER and RGBQUAD Structures

```
typedef struct tagBITMAPINFOHEADER{
    DWORD    biSize;            // size of BITMAPINFOHEADER
    DWORD    biWidth;           // width in pixels
    DWORD    biHeight;          // height in pixels
    WORD     biPlanes;          // always 1
    WORD     biBitCount;        // color bits per pixel
                                // must be 1, 4, 8 or 24
    DWORD    biCompression;     // BI_RGB, BI_RLE8
                                // or BI_RLE4
    DWORD    biSizeImage;       // total bytes in image
    DWORD    biXPelsPerMeter;   // 0, or opt. h res.
    DWORD    biYPelsPerMeter;   // 0, or opt. v res.
    DWORD    biClrUsed;         // normally 0, can set a
                                // lower no. colors than biBitCount
    DWORD    biClrImportant;    // normally 0
} BITMAPINFOHEADER;

typedef struct tagRGBQUAD
{
    BYTE     rgbBlue;           // blue element of the color
    BYTE     rgbGreen;          // green element of the color
    BYTE     rgbRed;            // red element of the color
    BYTE     rgbReserved;
} RGBQUAD;
```

The *biXPelsPerMeter* and *biYPelsPerMeter* values can be used to encode the bitmap resolution in pixels per meter, although these values are not required (can be set to zero). *biClrUsed* specifies the number of color values in the color table (described below) that are actually used. Normally set to zero, meaning that all colors are used. This value must be set to zero if the bitmap is compressed. *biClrImportant* specifies the number of critical colors. Normally set to zero, meaning that all of the colors are important.

Color Bits	Number of Colors
1	A monochrome bitmap. Each bit in the bitmap data will represent one pixel.
4	A bitmap with 16 colors. Each pixel requires 4 bits of information in the bitmap data. The 4 bits represent an index in the color table.
8	A bitmap with 256 colors. Each pixel requires a byte of information in the bitmap data. The byte value represents an index into the color table.
24	A bitmap with 2^{24} colors. Each pixel requires 3 bytes of information, representing the RGB (Red, Green, Blue) color bytes.

Table 16-5 Color Resolutions

After the BITMAPINFOHEADER structure, a DIB will contain the color table. This is a set of RGBQUAD data structures, holding the RGB color for each of the colors used in the bitmap. There will be as many RGBQUAD entries as there are color choices in the bitmap. For example, if *biBitCount* is 4, there will be 16 color possibilities, requiring 16 RGBQUAD elements to define, taking up 16 * 4 = 64 bytes of space. This assumes *biClrUsed* is set to zero. If *biClrUsed* is set to a value above zero, that value will be the number of RGBQUAD elements.

WINDOWS.H includes two other structure definitions that are useful in manipulating DIBs. The BITMAPINFO structure simply combines the first two parts of a DIB into one structure, as shown in Listing 16-28.

The last structure is used only when DIBs are stored to disk. The BITMAPFILEHEADER structure (Listing 16-29) is the first part of a bitmap stored as a disk file. This is how the Windows PaintBrush and SDKPaint applications store their outputs. Figure 16-18 shows how the DIB data is arranged in a disk file.

Listing 16-28 BITMAPINFO Structure

```
typedef struct tagBITMAPINFO {
    BITMAPINFOHEADER    bmiHeader;
    RGBQUAD             bmiColors[1];
} BITMAPINFO;
```

Listing 16-29 BITMAPFILEHEADER Structure

```
typedef struct tagBITMAPFILEHEADER {
    WORD    bfType;         // always equal to 'BM'
    DWORD   bfSize;         // size of file in DWORDs
    WORD    bfReserved1;    // set to zero
    WORD    bfReserved2;    // set to zero
    DWORD   bfOffBits;      // byte offset from BITMAPFILEHEADER to
                            // bitmap pixel data in the file
} BITMAPFILEHEADER;
typedef BITMAPFILEHEADER FAR    *LPBITMAPFILEHEADER;
typedef BITMAPFILEHEADER        *PBITMAPFILEHEADER;
```

Figure 16-18 Device Independent Bitmap Format as a Disk File

The MFC classes do not provide direct support for DIB bitmaps. However, the Windows API includes a full selection of global functions for working with DIBs. Typically, a program that takes advantage of DIB bitmaps will also use advanced techniques for manipulating color palettes (also not supported in the MFC classes). Both of these techniques are beyond the scope of this book. Refer to Chapters 12 and 15 of *The Waite Group's Windows API Bible* for details and C language example programs.

SUMMARY

Bitmaps record every pixel of an image drawn with a raster device, such as a video screen. Bitmaps have the advantage of being able to store any image, but they take up a lot of space. The amount of memory and/or disk space consumed by a bitmap depends on the size of the image stored, and on the number of colors possible per pixel. Bitmaps are commonly used to store smaller images, but they take too much disk space and memory to store large amounts of graphic data, such as long sequences of complete screen images.

The most common way Windows programs use bitmaps is to include bitmap files in the program's resource data. Bitmaps can be created with the image editors that come with the Windows programming tools, or with the Windows PaintBrush application. Bitmap files are included in a program's resource data by using the BITMAP statement. The **CBitmap::LoadBitmap()** function loads the bitmap into memory from the resource data. To display the bitmap, the bitmap must be selected into a memory device context created with **CDC::CreateCompatibleDC()**, and then copied to the device context of screen or printer using **CDC::BitBlt()** or **CDC::StretchBlt()**. **CDC::BitBlt()** merely copies the bitmap to a device, while **CDC::StretchBlt()** can stretch or compress the image as it is copied.

When a bitmap image is copied to a device context, the bitmap pixels can be altered depending on the colors of the pixels that will be covered up by the bitmap, and by the colors of the brush currently selected into the output device context. The different possible combinations of these three colors are controlled using raster operation codes. The most common raster operation code is SRCCOPY, which simply copies the bitmap to the output device without considering the color of the current pixels on the device or the current brush. Other raster codes are given names in WINDOWS.H, and perform more complex operations when **CDC::BitBlt()** or **CDC::StretchBlt()** is called.

One other use of bitmaps is to allow drawing on a memory bitmap. This is ideal for animation and complex drawing operations. Drawing on a memory bitmap allows all of the drawing to be done in the background, and then the final image to be "blit" to the screen using **CDC::BitBlt()** or **CDC::StretchBlt()**. **CDC::CreateCompatibleBitmap()** creates a memory bitmap, which can be selected into a memory device context created with **CDC::CreateCompatibleDC()**. Normal GDI functions like **CDC::LineTo()** and **CDC::Rectangle()** can be used to draw on a bitmap in memory, just like any other device context.

QUESTIONS

1. When a bitmap file is included in a program's resource script file, the bitmap is given a name. This name does not have to be the same as the bitmap file name, and it is used to locate the bitmap data in the finished program's resources. (True/False)

2. The _____ function loads a bitmap into memory.

3. Before a bitmap can be displayed, it must be selected into a _____ device context created with the _____ function.

4. The **CDC::BitBlt()** function copies a bitmap from the _____ to a physical output device.
   a. bitmap in the resource data
   b. bitmap in memory
   c. bitmap selected into a memory device context
   d. bitmap file

5. The **CDC::BitBlt()** function also has the ability to stretch or compress a bitmap image. (True/False)

6. The raster operation code to copy the source bitmap to the destination device without changing the source bitmap is _____.

7. Which of the following raster operation codes would make the source bitmap alternately appear and disappear is it was repeatedly "blit" onto the output device context?
   a. SRCERASE
   b. SRCINVERT
   c. SRCCOPY
   d. SRCAND

8. The _____ function fills a rectangular area with the currently selected pattern brush.

9. Which function is used to load an 8 by 8 pixel bitmap from resources and convert it into a brush that can be used in GDI painting operations?
   a. **CBitmap::LoadBitmap()**
   b. **CBrush::CreatePatternBrush()**
   c. **CDC::SelectObject()**
   d. a, b, and c

10. To execute a function during periods when no other activities are taking place, put the function call within the _____ function of the **CWinApp** MFC class.

11. Use the _____ function to create a blank memory bitmap that can be selected into a memory device context for drawing.

EXERCISES

1. Modify the BITMAP2 program so that the HOUSE.BMP file is displayed only once, but is stretched to fill the client area.

2. Modify the BITMAP4 program so that a small bitmap, such as a picture of an airplane, is moved around the main program window's client area instead of the red ball.

ANSWERS TO QUESTIONS

1. True.
2. **CBitmap::LoadBitmap()**.
3. memory, **CDC::CreateCompatibleDC()**.
4. c.
5. False. The **CDC::StretchBlt()** function stretches and compresses bitmap images.
6. SRCCOPY.
7. b.
8. **CDC::PatBlt()**.
9. d.
10. **CWinApp::OnIdle()**.
11. **CDC::CreateCompatibleBitmap()**.

SOLUTIONS TO EXERCISES

1. The only changes needed are to process WM_SIZE messages to determine the window's client area dimensions, and to use these values when calling **CDC::StretchBlt()**. Listing 16-30 shows the modifications to BITMAP2.CPP. You will also need to declare the **CMainWindow::OnSize()** function in the program's header file.

   The complete solution is under the file name C16EXER1 on the source code disks.

2. First you will need to create a small bitmap image and include it in the program's resources.

   ```
   Airplane              BITMAP  airplane.bmp    // bitmap data
   ```

   All of the drawing functions are within the BALL2.CPP program. The modifications to BALL2.CPP are shown in Listing 16-31. The direct GDI

Listing 16-30 Modifications to BITMAP2.CPP

```
BEGIN_MESSAGE_MAP (CMainWindow, CFrameWnd)
    ON_WM_PAINT ()                          // process WM_PAINT msg
    ON_WM_SIZE ()                           // and WM_SIZE
    ON_COMMAND (IDM_QUIT, OnExit)           // respond to menu items
END_MESSAGE_MAP ()

void CMainWindow::OnPaint ()                // process WM_PAINT msg
{
    CBitmap ABitmap ;
    ABitmap.LoadBitmap ("HouseBmp") ;       // load bitmap from resources
    CPaintDC cDC (this) ;                   // get client area dc
    CDC MemDC ;
    MemDC.CreateCompatibleDC (&cDC) ;       // create memory dc
    MemDC.SelectObject (&ABitmap) ;
    cDC.StretchBlt (0, 0, nClientX, nClientY, &MemDC,
        0, 0, 64, 64, SRCCOPY) ;
}

void CMainWindow::OnSize (UINT nType, int cx, int cy)
{
    nClientX = cx ;                         // save client area size
    nClientY = cy ;
}
```

drawing is fairly simple. The interesting case is in the **MovingBall::Draw-BallBlt()** function. The bitmap is selected into the memory device context *MemDC*. The *MemDC* image is "blit" onto the larger *memDC* memory device context that contains a memory image of the entire client area. Finally, the entire *memDC* image is "blit" onto the window's client area to make the image visible.

The complete solution is given under the file names C16EXER2 and BALL3 on the source code disks.

Listing 16-31 Modifications to BALL2.CPP

```
void MovingBall::DrawBall ()      // draw red ball using direct GDI
{
    if (!bBallOn)                 // do nothing if ball is not to move
        return ;

    CClientDC dc(pWindow) ;                    // get client area dc
    CBitmap ABitmap ;
    ABitmap.LoadBitmap ("Airplane") ;   // load bitmap from resources
    CDC MemDC ;
    MemDC.CreateCompatibleDC (&dc) ;    // create memory dc
    MemDC.SelectObject (&ABitmap) ;

    dc.BitBlt (nX, nY, 32, 32, &MemDC, 0, 0, SRCCOPY) ;
}

void MovingBall::DrawBallBlt ()  // draw red ball using memory dc
{
    if (!bBallOn)                        // do nothing if ball is not to move
        return ;

    CRect ClientRect ;
    pWindow->GetClientRect (&ClientRect) ;  // get client area size
    int Cwide = ClientRect.Width () ;
    int Ctall =  ClientRect.Height () ;

    CClientDC dc(pWindow) ;              // get client area device context
    CDC memDC ;
    memDC.CreateCompatibleDC (&dc) ;// create memory device context
    CBitmap memBitmap ;                  // create memory bitmap
    memBitmap.CreateCompatibleBitmap (&dc, Cwide, Ctall) ;
    CBitmap* pBmp = memDC.SelectObject (&memBitmap) ;

    CBrush Wbrush (RGB (0, 255, 255)) ; // use blue brush and pen to
    memDC.SelectObject (&Wbrush) ;       // fill the memory dc ;
    memDC.SelectStockObject (WHITE_PEN) ;
    memDC.Rectangle (0, 0, Cwide, Ctall) ;
```

```
CBitmap ABitmap ;
ABitmap.LoadBitmap ("Airplane") ;    // load bitmap from resources
CDC MemDC ;
MemDC.CreateCompatibleDC (&dc) ;    // create memory dc
MemDC.SelectObject (&ABitmap) ;
memDC.BitBlt (nX, nY, 32, 32, &MemDC, 0, 0, SRCCOPY) ;

        // now copy the image to the client area dc using BitBlit
dc.BitBlt (0, 0, Cwide, Ctall, &memDC, 0, 0, SRCCOPY) ;
memDC.SelectObject (pBmp) ;
}
```

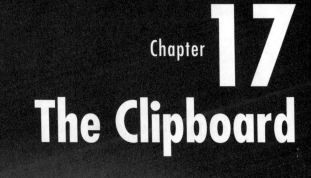

Chapter 17

The Clipboard

One of the pleasures of using the Windows environment is the ability to cut text and graphics from one application and paste it into another application. This ability is shared by almost all Windows applications because the Windows environment provides the Clipboard as a common mechanism for exchanging data. The Clipboard is just a memory block that Windows maintains. Applications can pass data to the Clipboard or read the contents of the Clipboard. Because the Clipboard is maintained by the Windows environment, its contents are available to any running application.

The most common types of data exchanged via the Clipboard are text and bitmaps. There are a number of formats available for Clipboard data, and you can invent your own formats for specialized data, such as spreadsheet cells. Although the Clipboard is most often used to exchange data between separate programs, you may find the Clipboard convenient for cut and paste operations within a single program.

This chapter demonstrates several uses of the Clipboard, including copying and retrieving both text and graphics. The simple text editor introduced in Chapter 15, *Disk File Access*, is also improved at the end of the chapter by adding cut, paste, copy, and delete functions that take advantage of the Clipboard. The final result, called SIMPEDIT, is a basic text editor that you can include in other programming projects.

Concepts covered: Clipboard viewers, passing a memory block to the Clipboard, Clipboard formats, reading Clipboard data, delayed rendering of Clipboard data, passing text from an edit control to and from the Clipboard.

Key words covered: CF_TEXT, CF_BITMAP, CF_OEMTEXT.

Functions covered: CWnd::OpenClipboard(), ::CloseClipboard(), ::EmptyClipboard(), ::SetClipboardData(), ::GetClipboardData(), AfxGetResourceHandle(), ::IsClipboardFormatAvailable(), CBitmap::FromHandle(), ::RegisterClipboardFormat(), CGdiObject::GetObject(), CEdit::Copy(), CEdit::Paste(), CEdit::Cut().

Messages covered: WM_COPY, WM_CUT, WM_PASTE, WM_RENDERALLFORMATS, WM_RENDERFORMAT, WM_DESTROYCLIPBOARD.

HOW THE CLIPBOARD WORKS

One thing to clear up right away is that the Windows application called CLIPBRD.EXE that comes with Windows is *not* the Clipboard. CLIPBRD.EXE (shown in Figure 17-1) is a clipboard viewer, not the Clipboard itself. Clipboard viewer applications show you what type of data is currently in the Clipboard. For example, Figure 17-1b shows the clipboard viewer displaying some bitmap data.

When you use the "Copy" or "Cut" menu items in Paintbrush, Notepad, or Windows Write, you are copying data to the Clipboard. If you are running the clipboard viewer, the data will show up in CLIPBRD's client area. If the data selected was text, text will appear in CLIPBRD's client area. If the data selected was a bitmap image, the bitmap will be displayed by CLIPBRD. When you select the "Paste" menu item from these applications, you are copying data from the Clipboard to the application. Windows keeps track of the type of data being stored in the Clipboard as the "clipboard format." Typical formats are named CF_TEXT for text data, and CF_BITMAP for bitmaps.

For all types of data, the data being transferred is stored in a global memory block. If the application needs to send some data to the Clipboard, the data is first copied into the global memory block. The data block is then transferred to

a) CLIPBRD Icon   b) CLIPBRD in Operation

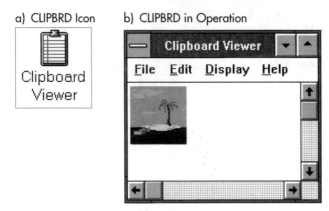

Figure 17-1 The CLIPBRD.EXE Clipboard Viewer

the Windows Clipboard, which takes ownership of the block. When Windows owns the block, the data in the block is said to be "in the Clipboard." Figure 17-2 illustrates the process of transferring a data block to Windows. Keep in mind that Windows, the application program(s), and the memory block are all in memory before and after the block is transferred to the Clipboard. It is the ownership of the block that is transferred to Windows.

Once the memory block has been transferred to the Windows Clipboard, it is no longer related to the program that created the block. The Windows environment has complete ownership of the Clipboard data. Any application can

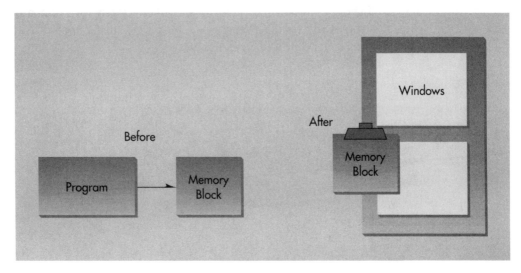

Figure 17-2 Transferring a Memory Block to the Clipboard

request access to the data in the Clipboard, although the data can only be read, not modified. The block will continue to be attached to the Windows Clipboard until a program empties the Clipboard, or passes another block with the same type of data to Windows. Windows can only keep one memory block at a time for any given clipboard format, so any new data displaces the old data block. Windows automatically frees the old global memory block when it is displaced from the Clipboard.

BASIC CLIPBOARD FUNCTIONS

From a programming standpoint, the Clipboard is easy to use, and boils down to understanding five functions that are summarized in Table 17-1. Notice that only the **CWnd::OpenClipboard()** function is a member of an MFC class. The others are global functions.

As an example, let's copy some text into the Clipboard. The first step is to allocate a global memory block, and copy data into the block. The **CGlobalBlock** class we created back in Chapter 12, *Managing Memory*, is ideal for allocating blocks for use by the Clipboard. This requires that you include the WINMEM.CPP program in any project that uses the **CGlobalBlock** class, and include the WINMEM.HPP header file in your .CPP source file. The **CGlobalBlock** class constructor function includes the *Permanence* flag, which allows memory blocks to be allocated that are not automatically freed from memory when the **CGlobalBlock** object is destroyed. The *Permanence* flag was included specifically to allow the **CGlobalBlock** class to be used effectively for Clipboard data. Listing 17-1 shows an example that copies some text to the Clipboard. The *this* pointer is assumed to point to a **CWnd** object.

Function	Meaning
CWnd::OpenClipboard()	Opens the Clipboard for access by the program.
::EmptyClipboard()	Frees all data now in the Clipboard.
::GetClipboardData()	Retrieves a handle to read-only data in the Clipboard.
::SetClipboardData()	Passes a memory block to the Clipboard.
::CloseClipboard()	Closes the Clipboard.

Table 17-1 Basic Clipboard Functions

Listing 17-1 Copying Text to the Clipboard

```
// create a global memory block object with permanence TRUE
CGlobalBlock GClipMem (10, GMEM_MOVEABLE, TRUE) ;
GClipMem = (LPSTR) "Some text data" ; // copy text to block
if (this->OpenClipboard ())                // open the clipboard
{
    ::EmptyClipboard () ;        // get rid of all clipboard data
    ::SetClipboardData (CF_TEXT, GClipMem.gethandle ()) ;
    ::CloseClipboard () ;        // add block as CF_TEXT and close
}
```

The example in Listing 17-1 takes advantage of the **CGlobalBlock** overloaded assignment operator (=) to copy a short text string into the *GClipMem* memory block. Once a memory block is ready, the Clipboard is opened with **CWnd::OpenClipboard()**. Only one application can open the Clipboard at any one time, so **CWnd::OpenClipboard()** both opens the Clipboard and keeps any other application from accessing the Clipboard. Internally, Windows tracks which window object loaded data into the Clipboard, which is why the **CWnd::OpenClipboard()** function is a member of the **CWnd** class. Any time you open the Clipboard with **CWnd::OpenClipboard()**, you are telling the Windows environment which program window will be using the Clipboard.

If the Clipboard was available (not currently opened by another application), **CWnd::OpenClipboard()** will return TRUE. The Clipboard is emptied of all data with **::EmptyClipboard()**, and then given the new data block with **::SetClipboardData()**. We will examine the parameters passed to **::SetClipboardData()** in a moment. Finally, the Clipboard is closed using **::CloseClipboard()**, so that other programs can again access the Clipboard. Closing the Clipboard does *not* delete the data in the Clipboard. Think of closing the Clipboard as being similar to closing a disk file. Closing the Clipboard makes sure that the data is properly registered in the Clipboard so any application can later retrieve it.

Note that the **::SetClipboardData()** function's second parameter is the handle of the memory block being passed to Windows, not the address of the memory block. The **CGlobalBlock::GetHandle()** function returns the memory handle for a block allocated with the **CGlobalBlock** class. Windows uses the handle of the memory block instead of the block's address so the block can be moveable in memory. You cannot use the C++ *new* operator to allocate a block for the Clipboard because the block's handle is used by Windows. There is no way to obtain a unique handle for a memory block allocated by the *new* operator.

The same application will probably need to be able to read the Clipboard data. The only trick to remember is that the data in the Clipboard belongs to

Windows, so the block is read-only data once it is in the Clipboard. You will need to copy the Clipboard data to a memory buffer within your program before the data is used if you are going to modify the Clipboard data in any way. Listing 17-2 shows a typical example, which copies the Clipboard text data into the **CString** object **string**.

CLIPBOARD FORMATS

You probably noticed in the previous section that the **::SetClipboardData()** and **::GetClipboardData()** functions used the CF_TEXT constant. CF_TEXT is defined in WINDOWS.H, and is a clipboard format for simple text data. Table 17-2 shows the most common predefined clipboard formats.

In addition to the predefined clipboard formats, an application can create a special clipboard format. Spreadsheet programs typically create their own clipboard format for cutting and pasting the contents of spreadsheet cells. The **::RegisterClipboardFormat()** function creates a clipboard format, based on a text name string. Once the new clipboard format is registered, the returned value from **::RegisterClipboardFormat()** can be used in place of a predefined format, such as CF_TEXT, when calling **::SetClipboardData()** and **::GetClipboardData()**. A custom clipboard format will be demonstrated in the second example program in this chapter.

Listing 17-2 Reading Clipboard Data

```
if (this->OpenClipboard ()) // if clipboard is not already open
{                           // get the handle to clipboard data
    HANDLE hClipMem = ::GetClipboardData (CF_TEXT) ;
    CString string ;        // create a CString object
    if (hClipMem)           // if there is some CF_TEXT data
    {
        CGlobalBlock GClipMem ;    // create a global mem object
            // attach the clipboard handle to global block
        GClipMem.sethandle (hClipMem, TRUE) ;   // permanence TRUE
        LPSTR lpClip = GClipMem.lock () ;        // lock the block
        if (lpClip)
            string = lpClip ;   // copy contents to CString object
        else
            string = " " ;      // error - just put in blank
        GClipMem.unlock () ;
    }                   // GClipMem automatically destroyed
    ::CloseClipboard () ;
    // use the CString object here
}
```

Value	Meaning
CF_BITMAP	A bitmap.
CF_DIB	A memory block containing a device-independent bitmap (DIB). The block will contain a BITMAPINFO data structure followed by the bitmap bits (see Chapter 16, *Bitmaps*).
CF_DIF	Software Arts' Data Interchange Format.
CF_METAFILEPICT	A metafile picture. See Chapter 23 of *The Waite Group's Windows API Bible* for a description of metafiles.
CF_OEMTEXT	A memory block containing only OEM text characters. Each line is ended with a CR-LF pair. A NULL byte marks the end of the text. This is the format Windows uses to transfer data between non-Windows and Windows applications.
CF_OWNERDISPLAY	The Clipboard owner is responsible for painting the Clipboard.
CF_PALETTE	A handle to a color palette.
CF_TEXT	A memory block containing text characters. Each line is ended with a CR-LF pair. A NULL byte marks the end of the text. This is the standard format for exchanging text between Windows applications.
CF_TIFF	Tag Image File Format. This is data format used by a number of graphics programs for exchanging bitmap data.

Table 17-2 Predefined Clipboard Formats

The most obvious reason for clipboard formats is to make sure that the data in the Clipboard is in the format that the program expects. It would be a disaster for a program to expect to read text data when the memory block contains a bitmap. A more subtle reason for using clipboard formats is that a program can save data to the Clipboard in more than one format at the same time. Although the Clipboard can only hold one memory block at a time with the CF_TEXT format, the Clipboard can contain several memory blocks at once, as long as each has a different format. Figure 17-3 shows this situation, with three clipboard memory formats in place at one time.

A program that wants to read the Clipboard data can look to see which formats are available. The **::IsClipboardFormatAvailable**() function comes in handy to see what data is in the Clipboard to be read. The program can start out with the most desirable format, and load it if it is available. For example, the spreadsheet would read the specialized format for storing a spreadsheet cell in

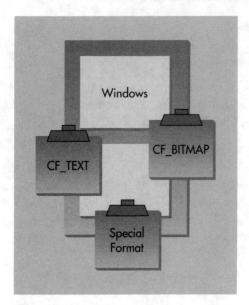

Figure 17-3 Multiple Clipboard Formats

preference to the simple CF_TEXT format, as the CF_TEXT format would just pass the cell's contents, and not any special formatting information. If the most desirable format is not available, the program can use a less sophisticated format, as shown in Listing 17-3.

Many Windows applications take advantage of multiple clipboard formats. For example, Word for Windows loads five different formats into the Clipboard when a selection of text is copied or cut. The most desirable format is the special "Rich text format" that Word for Windows uses to cut and paste text, including all text formatting information. Word for Windows also copies the selected text in the CF_TEXT and CF_OEMTEXT formats, so that other programs, which do not support the "Rich Text" format, can at least copy the text characters from data placed on the Clipboard. Word for Windows will also read and write several forms of graphical data including DDB and DIB bitmaps, allowing the user to paste pictures directly into a document via the Clipboard.

Listing 17-3 Checking for a Clipboard Format

```
if (::IsClipboardFormatAvailable (CF_TEXT))
    // read that data
else if (::IsClipboardFormatAvailable (CF_OEMTEXT))
    // second choice, read OEM text
```

CLIPBOARD LIMITATIONS

There is a basic limitation to the Clipboard that you should keep in mind when designing Windows applications. The Clipboard is designed to hold data from only one program at any one time. If the application supports multiple clipboard formats, the contents in each of the formats is expected to reflect the same basic data. For example, if you copy text into the Clipboard using Word for Windows, the same text string will be saved in several clipboard formats. The CF_TEXT format block will contain just the text characters, while special clipboard formats, such as "Rich Text," will contain the text *and* formatting data (font, boldface, underline, etc.). Word for Windows could also have a bitmap image of the text string copied to the Clipboard along with several text formats. The bitmap version would be suitable for pasting the character data into a paint program. Most paint programs recognize the CF_TEXT format, so saving the text data as a bitmap is not necessary, but it *is* possible to save both text and bitmap data to the Clipboard at the same time.

If you have several applications running at the same time, copying data to the Clipboard from one application will result in any data currently in the Clipboard being lost. This is because applications call **::EmptyClipboard()** before copying their own data to the Clipboard. Every running application can then read the new data, if the application supports one of the formats in the Clipboard.

A simple way of describing this limitation from the user's point of view is: "The clipboard only holds one object at a time." As a programmer, you will realize that the "one object" may be stored using several clipboard formats. There is no reason to burden the user with this knowledge. He or she can happily cut and paste data between applications without any thought of the subtle differences in data formats used by different programs.

A SIMPLE CLIPBOARD EXAMPLE

The first example program in this chapter, CLIPBRD1, demonstrates the basic clipboard functions. Figure 17-4 shows CLIPBRD1 running, after both the "Copy

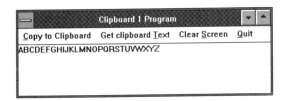

Figure 17-4 The CLIPBRD1 Program

to Clipboard" and "Get clipboard Text" menu items were selected. CLIPBRD1 copies the uppercase alphabet to a memory block, and sends the block to the Clipboard when "Copy to Clipboard" is selected.

Because CLIPBRD1 uses the Clipboard to copy and retrieve data, the text is available to other applications. Here are some experiments that you can try using CLIPBRD1.

1. After selecting the "Copy to Clipboard" menu item in CLIPBRD1, start the Notepad or Windows Write application, and select "Paste." The uppercase alphabet will be copied from the Clipboard into your document.

2. Start the Windows clipboard viewer application while CLIPBRD1 is running. The contents inside the clipboard viewer will change to the alphabet when "Copy to Clipboard" is selected in CLIPBRD1.

3. Highlight a block of text from within the Notepad application, and then select Notepad's "Copy" menu item. The next time the "Get clipboard Text" menu item is selected in CLIPBRD1, the text copied in Notepad will be displayed in CLIPBRD1's client area. The text will end up all on one line, as CLIPBRD1 makes no attempt to format text data.

As you can see from these examples, CLIPBRD1 succeeds in exchanging text data with a wide range of other applications. Windows makes it so easy to use the Clipboard that it is almost criminal not to support the Clipboard in a Windows application.

The complete CLIPBRD1.CPP program is shown in Listing 17-4. This is about as simple as a program that supports the Clipboard can be, as only the CF_TEXT format is supported. When the user selects the "Copy to Clipboard" menu item, the **CMainWindow::OnSend()** message processing function is executed. The uppercase alphabet is copied into a global memory block, and the block is then passed to the Clipboard using **::SetClipboardData()** and the CF_TEXT clipboard format. Note that the WINMEM.HPP file is included at the top of CLIPBRD1.CPP so the **CGlobalBlock** class from Chapter 12, *Managing Memory*, can be used to manage memory blocks exchanged with the Clipboard. The third parameter passed to the **CGlobalBlock** constructor function sets the *Permanence* flag to TRUE, so the block is not freed from memory when the **CGlobalBlock** object is destroyed.

```
CGlobalBlock GClipMem (27, GMEM_MOVEABLE, TRUE) ;
```

When the user selects the "Get clipboard Text" menu item, the **CMainWindow::OnGet()** message processing function is executed. When **::GetClipboardData()** is called with the CF_TEXT clipboard format, the returned value will be NULL if data with the CF_TEXT format is not currently

available in the Clipboard. This keeps CLIPBRD1 from attempting to display bitmap, or other nontext data if CF_TEXT data is not available.

Assuming the CF_TEXT data is loaded into the Clipboard, the **CMainWindow::OnGet()** function displays the text on the CLIPBRD1 window's client area. The **::GetClipboardData()** function returns a handle to the Clipboard data, not the address of the data. To obtain the address, the Clipboard handle is first attached to the **CGlobalBlock** object *GClipMem* using the **CGlobalBlock::SetHandle()** function. The **CGlobalBlock::lock()** function can then be used to lock the memory block so the address is fixed in memory.

```
CGlobalBlock GClipMem  ;  // create a global mem object
GClipMem.sethandle (hClipMem, TRUE) ;   // permanence TRUE
LPSTR lpClip = (LPSTR) GClipMem.lock () ;       // lock the block
```

Clipboard data is always read-only, meaning that you cannot modify the data even if the block is locked in memory. The Clipboard data belongs to Windows, not to your application. In the CLIPBRD1.CPP program, the text read from the Clipboard is simply displayed on the screen without modification. Because displaying the text is a read-only activity, the Clipboard data can be displayed without first copying it to a memory object controlled by the program. The **CDC::TextOut()** function is used to display the character data.

```
if (lpClip)         // only reading data, so no need
{                   // to copy to another block
    CClientDC dc (this) ;
    dc.TextOut (0, 0, lpClip, ::lstrlen (lpClip)) ;
}
```

After the Clipboard data is used, the data block should be unlocked. The application using the Clipboard should also call the **::CloseClipboard()** function to release the Clipboard for use by other applications.

```
GClipMem.unlock () ;
::CloseClipboard () ;
```

As you can see from the simplicity of CLIPBRD1.CPP, supporting Clipboard operations is not difficult under Windows.

Listings 17-5 to 17-8 show the support files for CLIPBRD1.CPP. The program's icon is shown in Figure 17-5.

Figure 17-5 CLIPBRD1.ICO Icon Image

Listing 17-4 CLIPBRD1.CPP

```cpp
// clipbrd1.cpp              simple demonstration using clipboard

#include <afxwin.h>          // class library header file
#include "winmem.hpp"        // memory functions from chapter 12
#include "clipbrd1.h"        // header file for resource data
#include "clipbrd1.hpp"      // header file for this program

CTheApp theApp ;             // create one CTheApp object - runs program

BOOL CTheApp::InitInstance ()    // override default InitInstance()
{
    m_pMainWnd = new CMainWindow () ;        // create a main window
    m_pMainWnd->ShowWindow (m_nCmdShow) ;    // make it visible
    m_pMainWnd->UpdateWindow () ;            // paint center
    return TRUE ;
}

CMainWindow::CMainWindow ()      // constructor for window
{
    CString title ;      // get program caption from resource data
    title.LoadString (S_PROGRAMCAPTION) ;
    Create (NULL, title, WS_OVERLAPPEDWINDOW, rectDefault,
        NULL, "MyMenu") ;
}

BEGIN_MESSAGE_MAP (CMainWindow, CFrameWnd)
    ON_COMMAND (IDM_SENDCLIP, OnSend)
    ON_COMMAND (IDM_GETCLIP, OnGet)
    ON_COMMAND (IDM_CLEAR, OnClear)
    ON_COMMAND (IDM_QUIT, OnExit)
END_MESSAGE_MAP ()

void CMainWindow::OnSend ()      // "Copy to Clipboard" menu item
{       // create a global memory block object with permanence TRUE
    CGlobalBlock GClipMem (27, GMEM_MOVEABLE, TRUE) ;
    char cBuf [27] ;                 // create a character buffer
    for (int i = 0 ; i < 26 ; i++)
        cBuf [i] = 'A' + i ;         // put in 26 characters
    cBuf [i] = 0 ;                   // and ending null
    GClipMem = (LPSTR) cBuf ;    // copy buffer to block
    if (this->OpenClipboard ())      // open the clipboard
    {
        ::EmptyClipboard () ;        // get rid of all clipboard data
        ::SetClipboardData (CF_TEXT, GClipMem.gethandle ()) ;
        ::CloseClipboard () ;        // add block as CF_TEXT and close
    }
}       // CClipBlock object destroyed here, but handle is "permanent"
```

```
void CMainWindow::OnGet ()          // "Get clipboard text" menu item
{
    if (this->OpenClipboard ()) // if clipboard is not already open
    {                           // get the handle to clipboard data
        HANDLE hClipMem = ::GetClipboardData (CF_TEXT) ;
        if (hClipMem)           // if there is some CF_TEXT data
        {
            CGlobalBlock GClipMem  ; // create a global mem object
                // attach the clipboard handle to global block
            GClipMem.sethandle (hClipMem, TRUE) ;   // permanence TRUE
            LPSTR lpClip = (LPSTR) GClipMem.lock () ;       // lock the block
            if (lpClip)         // only reading data, so no need
            {                   // to copy to another block
                CClientDC dc (this) ;
                dc.TextOut (0, 0, lpClip, ::lstrlen (lpClip)) ;
            }
            GClipMem.unlock () ;
        }                           // GClipMem automatically destroyed
        ::CloseClipboard () ;
    }
}

void CMainWindow::OnClear ()     // "Clear screen" menu item
{
    this->Invalidate () ;
}

void CMainWindow::OnExit ()      // "Quit" menu item
{
    this->DestroyWindow () ;     // destroy main window,
}                                // this stops application
```

Listing 17-5 CLIPBRD1.HPP Header File

```
// clipbrd1.hpp    header file for clipbrd1.cpp

class CMainWindow : public CFrameWnd     // derive a main window class
{
public:
    CMainWindow () ;                     // declare a constructor
private:
    void OnSend () ;                     // process menu items
    void OnGet () ;
    void OnClear () ;
    void OnExit () ;

    DECLARE_MESSAGE_MAP()                // prepare for message processing
} ;

class CTheApp : public CWinApp     // derive an application class
{
public:
    BOOL InitInstance () ;               // declare new InitInstance()
} ;
```

Listing 17-6 CLIPBRD1.H Resource ID Header File

```
// clipbrd1.h  header file for resource ID numbers

#define IDM_SENDCLIP        1        // menu item ID numbers
#define IDM_GETCLIP         2
#define IDM_CLEAR           3
#define IDM_QUIT            4


#define S_PROGRAMCAPTION    1        // string table ID number
```

Listing 17-7 CLIPBRD1.RC Resource Script File

```
// clipbrd1.rc  resource script file

#include <afxres.h>
#include "clipbrd1.h"

AFX_IDI_STD_FRAME   ICON   clipbrd1.ico   // the program's icon

MyMenu MENU                                // define the menu
{
    MENUITEM "&Copy to Clipboard",  IDM_SENDCLIP
    MENUITEM "Get clipboard &Text", IDM_GETCLIP
    MENUITEM "Clear &Screen",       IDM_CLEAR
    MENUITEM "&Quit",               IDM_QUIT
}


STRINGTABLE
{
    S_PROGRAMCAPTION    "Clipboard 1 Program"
}
```

Listing 17-8 CLIPBRD1.DEF Module Definition File

```
NAME          clipbrd1
DESCRIPTION   'clipbrd1 C++ program'
EXETYPE       WINDOWS
STUB          'WINSTUB.EXE'
CODE          PRELOAD MOVEABLE
DATA          PRELOAD MOVEABLE MULTIPLE
HEAPSIZE      1024
STACKSIZE     5120
```

MULTIPLE CLIPBOARD FORMATS

The next example program, CLIPBRD2, demonstrates saving multiple clipboard formats at the same time, and also creates a special clipboard format for saving numeric data. Figure 17-6 shows CLIPBRD2 running, displaying bitmap data

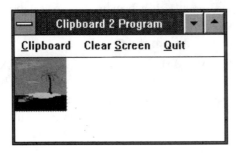

Figure 17-6 CLIPBRD2 Program Displaying a Bitmap

obtained from the Clipboard. Figure 17-7 shows CLIPBRD2 after obtaining both CF_TEXT and a special numeric format from the Clipboard. CLIPBRD2 is an extreme example of Windows' ability to handle multiple clipboard formats at the same time. Normally, data passed to the Clipboard with different formats would represent different ways of saving the same basic data, such as different text formats. CLIPBRD2 manages to save three entirely different types of data in the Clipboard at the same time, so you can verify that each of the data types is independently stored.

You can do a few experiments when CLIPBRD2 is running to demonstrate the impact of saving multiple clipboard formats at the same time.

1. After CLIPBRD2 is running and has been used to copy data to the Clipboard, start the Paintbrush application. If you select the "Paste" menu item in Paintbrush, the same bitmap shown in Figure 17-7 will appear in the Paintbrush client area. This is because Paintbrush reads and writes the CF_BITMAP clipboard format, which CLIPBRD2 uses to copy the bitmap to the Clipboard.

2. If you select "Paste" from within the Notepad application after CLIPBRD2 has copied data to the Clipboard, the text string (all the uppercase letters)

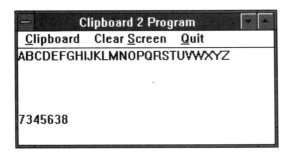

Figure 17-7 CLIPBRD2 Program Displaying CF_TEXT and a Special Format

will appear in the Notepad client area. This is because Notepad supports the CF_TEXT clipboard format. Notepad does not support the CF_BITMAP format, so the bitmap data is not copied from the Clipboard.

3. Some applications, such as Windows Write, support both the CF_TEXT and CF_BITMAP formats. If you select the "Paste" menu item, only the text string will be copied to the Windows Write client area. This is because Windows Write considers CF_TEXT to be a preferable format, compared to CF_BITMAP, if both formats are available. However, if you choose the "Paste Special" menu item, Windows Write will allow you to select either the bitmap or the text data in the Clipboard. Figure 17-8 shows Windows Write after both formats have been "pasted" from the Clipboard.

The complete CLIPBRD2.CPP program is shown in the next section. This is a more complex example, so let's break it down. CLIPBRD2 puts three different types of data in the Clipboard when the "Copy to Clipboard" menu item is selected. This requires allocation of three separate global memory blocks. Each block is filled with the right type of data, and then passed to the Clipboard with **::SetClipboardData()**. The text data in CLIPBRD2 is again just the uppercase letters A-Z, copied into a global memory block as shown in Listing 17-9.

The bitmap image is stored in the program's resources with the name "IslandBMP." The island image was created with the Image Editor, and saved as a bitmap file (ISLAND.BMP on the source code disks). All previous examples have used the **CBitmap::LoadBitmap()** function to load a bitmap into memory. **CBitmap::LoadBitmap()** works fine, except that it has the built-in property of freeing the bitmap data from memory when the **CBitmap** object is

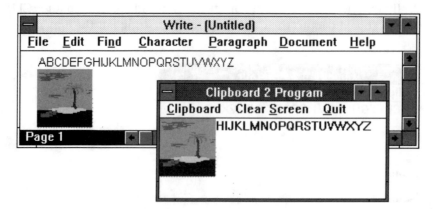

Figure 17-8 Windows Write Obtaining Data from CLIPBRD2 via the Clipboard

deleted. You can use the **CBitmap::LoadBitmap()** function with the Clipboard if you are careful to avoid deleting the **CBitmap** object while the bitmap is stored in the Clipboard (the **CGdiObject::GetSafeHandle()** function returns the memory handle of a loaded GDI object such as a bitmap). However, it is simpler to load the bitmap directly into memory using the low-level functions for manipulating bitmap data. Listing 17-10 shows how this is done.

The global function **::AfxGetResourceHandle()** returns the memory handle for the program's resources. The **::LoadBitmap()** function finds the BITMAP resource data named "IslandBMP" and returns the memory handle. This memory handle is exactly what is needed to pass the bitmap data to the Clipboard. The **::LoadBitmap()** function is not attached to any class and has no destructor function. You can, therefore, be confident that the bitmap data will not be inadvertently freed from memory.

This leaves one more clipboard format. CLIPBRD2 registers a new clipboard format called "DIGITS" with Windows. The WORD value returned from the **::RegisterClipboardFormat()** function is the ID number for this special format. Listing 17-11 shows the registration of the special clipboard format and the creation of another **CGlobalBlock** object to hold the data. In this case, a series of seven digit characters are copied to the global block. There is actually nothing "special" about this data, so the CF_TEXT format could have been used.

At this point CLIPBRD2 has three memory blocks loaded with data and has registered the new clipboard format "DIGITS." The only step left is to pass these

Listing 17-9 Loading Text Data into a Global Memory Block

```
CGlobalBlock GTextBlock (27, GMEM_MOVEABLE, TRUE) ;
LPSTR pStr = (LPSTR) GTextBlock.lock () ;
for (int i = 0 ; i < 26 ; i++)
    *pStr++ = 'A' + i ;        // put in 26 characters
*pStr = 0 ;                    // and ending null
GTextBlock.unlock () ;         // leave the block unlocked
```

Listing 17-10 Loading the Bitmap Data into Memory

```
HBITMAP hBitmap = ::LoadBitmap (AfxGetResourceHandle (),
    "IslandBMP") ;
```

Listing 17-11 Registering a Special Clipboard Format

```
wClipFormat = ::RegisterClipboardFormat ("DIGITS") ;
    // create another global object with "permanence" set TRUE
CGlobalBlock GSpecBlock (32, GMEM_MOVEABLE, TRUE) ;
GSpecBlock = "7345638" ;    // copy digits to block
```

three memory blocks to the Clipboard using the **::SetClipboardData()** function, as shown in Listing 17-12.

Note how the *wClipFormat* WORD value returned by **::RegisterClipboardFormat()** is used just like the predefined CF_TEXT and CF_BITMAP formats to pass a format to the Windows Clipboard. The Clipboard now holds all three memory blocks. The remainder of the CLIPBRD2.CPP listing deals with retrieving the Clipboard data so it can be displayed. Getting the CF_TEXT data is done identically to the previous CLIPBRD1.CPP program, and is not repeated here. Displaying the bitmap is a little more involved. Listing 17-13 shows the portion that displays the bitmap image retrieved from the Clipboard.

The handle of the memory block containing the bitmap in the Clipboard is retrieved with **::GetClipboardData()**, and selected into a memory device context created with **CDC::CreateCompatibleDC()**. The **CBitmap::FromHandle()** function passes the bitmap data handle to a **CBitmap** object so that we can use the normal **CBitmap** class functions. The only problem is figuring out how big the bitmap should be. CLIPBRD2.CPP uses the handy **CGdiObject::GetObject()** function to read the beginning of the memory block and copy the data into a BITMAP structure. (Review Chapter 16, *Bitmaps*, if you do not remember the details of the BITMAP structure.) The *bmWidth* and *bmHeight* elements of the BITMAP structure are then used to specify the correct width and height of the bitmap to display. **CDC::BitBlt()** does the work of copying the bitmap data to the window's client area.

Retrieving the special "DIGITS" clipboard format data is similar to retrieving CF_TEXT data. The **::GetClipboardData()** function is called using the *wClipFormat* WORD value that was returned by **::RegisterClipboardFormat()** when the new format was registered, as shown in Listing 17-14.

Note in these examples that the **::IsClipboardFormatAvailable()** function is not used to determine if one of the three formats is available before attempting to read the data. The **::GetClipboardData()** function will return NULL if the

Listing 17-12 Sending Three Clipboard Formats

```
if (this->OpenClipboard ()) // open the clipboard
{
    ::EmptyClipboard () ;    // get rid of all clipboard data
                             // put text data in clipboard
    ::SetClipboardData (CF_TEXT, GTextBlock.gethandle ()) ;
                             // and bitmap data
    ::SetClipboardData (CF_BITMAP, hBitmap) ;
                             // and special clipboard format
    ::SetClipboardData (wClipFormat, GSpecBlock.gethandle ()) ;
    ::CloseClipboard () ;    // close clipboard
}
```

Listing 17-13 Reading and Displaying Bitmap Data from the Clipboard

```
void CMainWindow::OnGetBmp ()    // "Get clipboard BMP" menu item
{
    if (this->OpenClipboard ()) // if clipboard is not already open
    {                           // get the handle to clipboard data
        HANDLE hClipMem = ::GetClipboardData (CF_BITMAP) ;
        if (hClipMem)           // if there is some CF_BITMAP data
        {
            CBitmap bmp, *pBmp ;    // create a CBitmap object, link
            pBmp = bmp.FromHandle (hClipMem) ;// to clipboard handle
            BITMAP bmpInfo ;        // create BITMAP structure
            // copy data into BITMAP structure to get bitmap size
            pBmp->GetObject (sizeof (BITMAP), &bmpInfo) ;

            CClientDC dc (this) ;   // get client area DC
            CDC MemDC ;             // create memory dc compatible
            MemDC.CreateCompatibleDC (&dc) ;// with client area dc
            MemDC.SelectObject (pBmp) ; // select bitmap int mem dc
                                    // display complete bitmap
            dc.BitBlt (0, 0, bmpInfo.bmWidth, bmpInfo.bmHeight,
                &MemDC, 0, 0, SRCCOPY) ;
        }
        ::CloseClipboard () ;
    }
}
```

Listing 17-14 Reading the Special Clipboard Format

```
void CMainWindow::OnGetSpecial ()    // "Get Special data" menu item
{
    if (this->OpenClipboard ()) // if clipboard is not already open
    {                           // get the handle to clipboard data
        HANDLE hClipMem = ::GetClipboardData (wClipFormat) ;
        if (hClipMem)               // if there is special format data
        {
            CGlobalBlock GSpecBlock ;   // make a GClipBlock object
            GSpecBlock.sethandle (hClipMem, TRUE) ;
            LPSTR lpClip = (LPSTR) GSpecBlock.lock () ;   // lock the block
            if (lpClip)             // only reading data, so no need
            {                       // to copy to another block
                CClientDC dc (this) ;
                dc.TextOut (0, 70, lpClip, lstrlen (lpClip)) ;
            }
            GSpecBlock.unlock () ;
        }
        ::CloseClipboard () ;
    }
}
```

specified format is not available, even if a memory block with some other format is currently selected into the Clipboard. This stops applications from reading the wrong type of data by accident.

CLIPBRD2 Listings

Listing 17-15 shows the complete CLIPBRD2.CPP program. The support files are shown in Listings 17-16 to 17-19. Figure 17-9 shows the bitmap displayed by the program. Figure 17-10 shows the program's icon.

Listing 17-15 CLIPBRD2.CPP

```
// clipbrd2.cpp                  clipboard use with multiple formats

#include <afxwin.h>       // class library header file
#include "winmem.hpp"     // memory functions from chapter 12
#include "clipbrd2.h"     // header file for resource data
#include "clipbrd2.hpp"   // header file for this program

CTheApp theApp ;          // create one CTheApp object - runs program

BOOL CTheApp::InitInstance ()   // override default InitInstance()
{
    m_pMainWnd = new CMainWindow () ;        // create a main window
    m_pMainWnd->ShowWindow (m_nCmdShow) ;    // make it visible
    m_pMainWnd->UpdateWindow () ;            // paint center
    return TRUE ;
}

CMainWindow::CMainWindow ()       // constructor for window
{
    CString title ;      // get program caption from resource data
    title.LoadString (S_PROGRAMCAPTION) ;
    Create (NULL, title, WS_OVERLAPPEDWINDOW, rectDefault,
        NULL, "MyMenu") ;
}

BEGIN_MESSAGE_MAP (CMainWindow, CFrameWnd)
    ON_COMMAND (IDM_SENDCLIP, OnSend)
    ON_COMMAND (IDM_GETTEXT, OnGetText)
    ON_COMMAND (IDM_GETBMP, OnGetBmp)
    ON_COMMAND (IDM_GETSPECIAL, OnGetSpecial)
    ON_COMMAND (IDM_CLEAR, OnClear)
    ON_COMMAND (IDM_QUIT, OnExit)
END_MESSAGE_MAP ()

void CMainWindow::OnSend ()       // "Copy to Clipboard"
{       // create a memory block object with "permanence" set TRUE
    CGlobalBlock GTextBlock (27, GMEM_MOVEABLE, TRUE) ;
    LPSTR pStr = (LPSTR) GTextBlock.lock () ;
    for (int i = 0 ; i < 26 ; i++)
        *pStr++ = 'A' + i ;        // put in 26 characters
    *pStr = 0 ;                    // and ending null
```

```
        GTextBlock.unlock () ;        // leave the block unlocked
            // load bitmap from resource data - load directly rather
            // than using a CBitmap object to avoid CBitmap destructor
        HBITMAP hBitmap = ::LoadBitmap (AfxGetResourceHandle (),
            "IslandBMP") ;
                                    // register a new clipboard format
        wClipFormat = ::RegisterClipboardFormat ("DIGITS") ;
            // create another global object with "permanence" set TRUE
        CGlobalBlock GSpecBlock (32, GMEM_MOVEABLE, TRUE) ;
        GSpecBlock = "7345638" ;     // copy digits to block

        if (this->OpenClipboard ()) // open the clipboard
        {
            ::EmptyClipboard () ;    // get rid of all clipboard data
                                    // put text data in clipboard
            ::SetClipboardData (CF_TEXT, GTextBlock.gethandle ()) ;
                                    // and bitmap data
            ::SetClipboardData (CF_BITMAP, hBitmap) ;
                                    // and special clipboard format
            ::SetClipboardData (wClipFormat, GSpecBlock.gethandle ()) ;
            ::CloseClipboard () ;    // close clipboard
        }
}

void CMainWindow::OnGetText ()  // "Get clipboard Text" menu item
{
    if (this->OpenClipboard ()) // if clipboard is not already open
    {                           // get the handle to clipboard data
        HANDLE hClipMem = ::GetClipboardData (CF_TEXT) ;
        if (hClipMem)           // if there is some CF_TEXT data
        {
            CGlobalBlock GTextBlock ;  // make a GClipBlock object
        // attach handle to mem object with "permanence" set TRUE
            GTextBlock.sethandle (hClipMem, TRUE) ;
            LPSTR lpClip = (LPSTR) GTextBlock.lock () ;  // lock block
            if (lpClip)
            {
                CClientDC dc (this) ;
                dc.TextOut (0, 0, lpClip, lstrlen (lpClip)) ;
            }
            GTextBlock.unlock () ;
        }                       // mem object destroyed here, but
        ::CloseClipboard () ;   // handle remains valid because
    }                           // "permanence" was set TRUE
}

void CMainWindow::OnGetBmp ()   // "Get clipboard BMP" menu item
{
    if (this->OpenClipboard ()) // if clipboard is not already open
    {                           // get the handle to clipboard data
        HANDLE hClipMem = ::GetClipboardData (CF_BITMAP) ;
```

```
        if (hClipMem)              // if there is some CF_BITMAP data
        {
            CBitmap bmp, *pBmp ;    // create a CBitmap object, link
            pBmp = bmp.FromHandle (hClipMem) ;// to clipboard handle
            BITMAP bmpInfo ;         // create BITMAP structure
            // copy data into BITMAP structure to get bitmap size
            pBmp->GetObject (sizeof (BITMAP), &bmpInfo) ;

            CClientDC dc (this) ;    // get client area DC
            CDC MemDC ;              // create memory dc compatible
            MemDC.CreateCompatibleDC (&dc) ;// with client area dc
            MemDC.SelectObject (pBmp) ; // select bitmap int mem dc
                                     // display complete bitmap
            dc.BitBlt (0, 0, bmpInfo.bmWidth, bmpInfo.bmHeight,
                &MemDC, 0, 0, SRCCOPY) ;

        }
        ::CloseClipboard () ;
    }
}


void CMainWindow::OnGetSpecial ()    // "Get Special data" menu item
{
    if (this->OpenClipboard ()) // if clipboard is not already open
    {                           // get the handle to clipboard data
        HANDLE hClipMem = ::GetClipboardData (wClipFormat) ;
        if (hClipMem)           // if there is special format data
        {
            CGlobalBlock GSpecBlock ;   // make a GClipBlock object
            GSpecBlock.sethandle (hClipMem, TRUE) ;
            LPSTR lpClip = (LPSTR) GSpecBlock.lock () ;    // lock the block
            if (lpClip)          // only reading data, so no need
            {                    // to copy to another block
                CClientDC dc (this) ;
                dc.TextOut (0, 70, lpClip, lstrlen (lpClip)) ;
            }
            GSpecBlock.unlock () ;
        }
        ::CloseClipboard () ;
    }
}


void CMainWindow::OnClear ()     // "Clear screen" menu item
{
    this->Invalidate () ;
}

void CMainWindow::OnExit ()      // "Quit" menu item
{
    this->DestroyWindow () ;     // destroy main window,
}                                // this stops application
```

Listing 17-16 CLIPBRD2.HPP Header File

```
// clipbrd2.hpp    header file for clipbrd2.cpp

class CMainWindow : public CFrameWnd    // derive a main window class
{
public:
    CMainWindow () ;            // declare a constructor
private:
    WORD wClipFormat ;         // special clipboard format
    void OnSend () ;           // process menu items
    void OnGetText () ;
    void OnGetBmp () ;
    void OnGetSpecial () ;
    void OnClear () ;
    void OnExit () ;

    DECLARE_MESSAGE_MAP()      // prepare for message processing
} ;

class CTheApp : public CWinApp  // derive an application class
{
public:
    BOOL InitInstance () ;     // declare new InitInstance()
} ;
```

Listing 17-17 CLIPBRD2.H Resource ID Header File

```
// clipbrd2.h  header file for resource ID numbers

#define IDM_SENDCLIP      1       // menu item ID numbers
#define IDM_GETTEXT       2
#define IDM_GETBMP        3
#define IDM_GETSPECIAL    4
#define IDM_CLEAR         5
#define IDM_QUIT          6

#define S_PROGRAMCAPTION  1       // string table ID number
```

Figure 17-9 ISLAND.BMP Bitmap

Figure 17-10 CLIPBRD2.ICO Icon Image

Listing 17-18 CLIPBRD2.RC Resource Script File

```
// clipbrd2.rc   resource script file

#include <afxres.h>
#include "clipbrd2.h"

AFX_IDI_STD_FRAME    ICON    clipbrd2.ico    // the program's icon
IslandBMP            BITMAP  island.bmp      // a bitmap to show

MyMenu MENU                                  // define the menu
{
    POPUP   "&Clipboard"
    {
        MENUITEM "&Copy to Clipboard",  IDM_SENDCLIP
        MENUITEM "Get clipboard &Text", IDM_GETTEXT
        MENUITEM "Get clipboard &BMP",  IDM_GETBMP
        MENUITEM "Get &Special data",   IDM_GETSPECIAL
    }
    MENUITEM "Clear &Screen",        IDM_CLEAR
    MENUITEM "&Quit",                IDM_QUIT
}


STRINGTABLE
{
    S_PROGRAMCAPTION    "Clipboard 2 Program"
}
```


Listing 17-19 CLIPBRD2.DEF Module Definition File

```
NAME            clipbrd2
DESCRIPTION     'clipbrd2 C++ program'
EXETYPE         WINDOWS
STUB            'WINSTUB.EXE'
CODE            PRELOAD MOVEABLE
DATA            PRELOAD MOVEABLE MULTIPLE
HEAPSIZE        1024
STACKSIZE       5120
```

DELAYED RENDERING OF CLIPBOARD DATA

Programs like Word for Windows that supply four or five clipboard formats at once could waste a lot of time and memory space if all five formats were copied to the Clipboard each time the "Copy" or "Cut" menu items were selected. It is unlikely that more than one of the clipboard formats will be read at any one time. This leaves the other format's memory blocks unused.

Fortunately, Windows provides an intelligent alternative to simply copying all of the data to the Clipboard. An application sending data to the Clipboard can register the clipboard format without passing any data. This is done by passing null (zero) as the handle to the data block when **::SetClipboardData()** is called. Listing 17-20 shows an example, which passes a null data handle for the CF_TEXT clipboard format.

The effect of passing a null handle with **::SetClipboardData()** is illustrated in Figure 17-11. The Clipboard does not receive any data, but records that the window will supply CF_TEXT data on demand. Windows knows which window

Listing 17-20 Delayed Rendering of CF_TEXT Format

```
if (this->OpenClipboard ()) // open the clipboard
{
    ::EmptyClipboard () ;    // get rid of all clipboard data
    ::SetClipboardData (CF_TEXT, NULL) ; // NULL data handle
    ::CloseClipboard () ;    // close clipboard
}
```

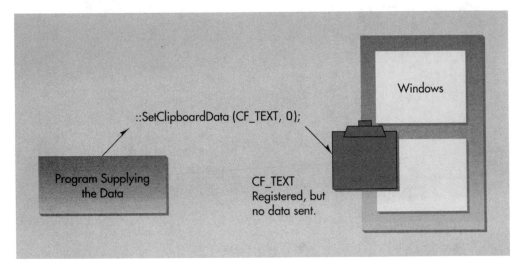

Figure 17-11 Preparing the Clipboard for Delayed Rendering

will supply the data because Windows records the window object that called the **CWnd::OpenClipboard()** function.

When an application attempts to read CF_TEXT data from the Clipboard, several actions take place to supply the data. Figure 17-12 shows the sequence of events. The program requesting CF_TEXT data from the Clipboard calls the **::GetClipboardData()** function. Windows recognizes that the CF_TEXT data needs to be loaded, and sends a WM_RENDERFORMAT message to the window that called **::SetClipboardData()** with the null handle. That program calls **::SetClipboardData()** again, but this time passes a handle to a memory block containing the data. Finally, Windows passes the handle to the data block to the program that requested the data.

One of the interesting aspects of delayed rendering is that the program requesting the data cannot tell the difference between data already in the Clipboard and data supplied later via delayed rendering. In either case, the requester program receives a handle to the memory block containing the data when the **::GetClipboardData()** function returns. In the delayed rendering case, the requester program stops executing while it waits for the data block to be supplied by the supplier program. Windows passes execution to the supplier program by

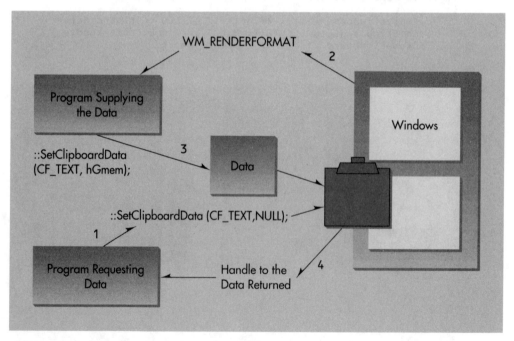

Figure 17-12 Retrieving Clipboard Data—Delayed Rendering Case

sending the WM_RENDERFORMAT message, and does not give control back to the requester program until the handle to the Clipboard data block is returned. All of these actions occur transparently. The user just sees the data being pasted as expected.

WM_RENDERALLFORMATS and WM_DESTROYCLIPBOARD

There are a couple of other situations that pop up when an application uses delayed rendering. One is when the program supplying data is terminated before the Clipboard data is requested. A program that is not running cannot supply data, so some trickery is required. Windows gets around this problem by sending the supplying program a WM_RENDERALLFORMATS message before the program terminates. Programs that supply Clipboard data are expected to send memory blocks containing data with all the clipboard formats they support when a WM_RENDERALLFORMATS message is received. The result is that the data is put in the Clipboard before the program terminates, so it can still be obtained later by another program.

WM_RENDERALLFORMATS will only be sent to a program that has called **::SetClipboardData()** with a null memory block handle, but has not yet supplied the data. The message is sent as the program terminates, after the program's window has been destroyed. Putting the appropriate data blocks back into the Clipboard is a "last gasp" effort the program makes before it dies.

Another message that programs supplying Clipboard data will receive is WM_DESTROYCLIPBOARD. This message sounds serious, but all it means is that an application (usually another program) has called the **::EmptyClipboard()** function. The idea is that the supplier program may be holding onto one or more memory blocks for delayed rendering. If another application calls **::EmptyClipboard()**, the old Clipboard data is no longer needed, so the supplier program can free any memory blocks that contain data. WM_DESTROYCLIPBOARD will only be received if the supplier program has called the **::SetClipboardData()** using a null data handle for delayed rendering, but has not supplied the data.

A Delayed Rendering Example

The DELREND program was designed to demonstrate delayed clipboard rendering. When the "Copy to Clipboard" menu item is selected, DELREND passes the Clipboard the CF_TEXT clipboard format and a null data handle. This tells Windows that DELREND will supply text data on demand. For example, if you then open the Notepad application and select "Edit/Paste," Notepad will attempt to read the Clipboard data. Initially, there is no data in the Clipboard, so Windows sends DELREND a WM_RENDERFORMAT message for the CF_TEXT format. DELREND processes this message, and passes a memory block containing the text data to the Clipboard. Windows then returns control to Notepad, which reads the text data in the Clipboard and copies it to the Notepad client area. Figure 17-13 shows the DELREND program on top of the Notepad application after the "Edit/ Paste" menu item has been selected in Notepad.

When the "Copy to Clipboard" menu item is selected, DELREND calls the **::SetClipboardData()** function, passing a null handle for delayed rendering of the CF_TEXT format. Nothing else happens unless an application tries to read the CF_TEXT data in the Clipboard. Windows then sends the WM_RENDERFORMAT message to DELREND, and expects the program to supply a data block containing the text. The text is actually a custom resource, included in the program's resource script file that uses the custom resource name "TEXT." The text data for the program is in a separate file PARAGRPH.TXT, which is included in the resource data with the following line in the resource script file DELREND.RC:

```
Paragraph   TEXT    paragrph.txt    // custom resource file
```

Resource data is read-only, so to give the text data to the Clipboard, the resource data must be copied into a global memory block. DELREND.CPP takes advantage of the **StringResource** classes developed back in Chapter 11, *Other Resources*. The **StringResource** class is declared in the STRRES.HPP header file and uses the STRRES.CPP program.

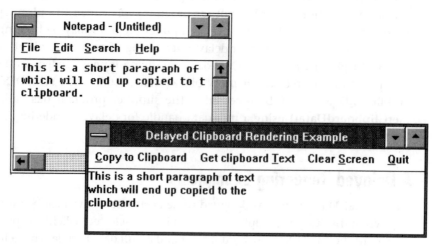

Figure 17-13 The Notepad and DELREND Programs

When a WM_RENDERFORMAT message is sent to the program window, the message map passes execution to the **CWnd::OnRenderFormat()** message processing function. The *nParameter* value sent with the message is set equal to the clipboard format code. The program receiving WM_RENDERFORMAT must check to make sure that the requested format is one that the program supports. DELREND only supports the CF_TEXT format, so this is the only case considered. Listing 17-21 shows the **CWnd::OnRenderFormat()** function from DELREND.CPP

One important point in processing the WM_RENDERFORMAT message is that there is no call to **::OpenClipboard()** or **::CloseClipboard()**. This is because whatever application is requesting the data (it may be DELREND itself) has already opened the Clipboard. All DELREND must do is call the **::SetClipboardData()** function to pass the data block to the Clipboard.

Because DELREND only supports the CF_TEXT clipboard format, responding to the WM_RENDERALLFORMATS message is not very different from responding to a WM_RENDERFORMAT message for the CF_TEXT format. One important difference is that the Clipboard must be opened and closed when responding to WM_RENDERALLFORMATS. WM_RENDERALLFORMATS is sent when the program is terminating, not when another program has requested Clipboard data. The Clipboard will not be open when the WM_RENDERALLFORMATS message is received.

Delayed rendering is a bit more complex than directly copying data to the Clipboard. However, delayed rendering is the best technique to use if large amounts of data are to be sent to the Clipboard, or if more than one clipboard format is supported.

Listing 17-21 Processing the WM_RENDERFORMAT Message

```
void CMainWindow::OnRenderFormat (UINT nFormat)
{
    if (nFormat != CF_TEXT) // this app only renders CF_TEXT format
        return ;
        // use the StringResource object to load in resource data
    StringResource StrRes ("paragraph", "TEXT") ;
        // allocate "permanent" block to pass to clipboard
    CGlobalBlock ClipBlock (StrRes.GetLength (),
        GMEM_MOVEABLE, TRUE) ;
        // copy the resource string into the global memory block
    ClipBlock = (LPSTR) StrRes.GetString () ;
    ::SetClipboardData (CF_TEXT, ClipBlock.gethandle ()) ;
    ::CloseClipboard () ;        // close clipboard
}
```

DELREND Listings

Listing 17-22 shows the DELREND.CPP program. The support files are shown in
Listings 17-23 to 17-27. Figure 17-14 shows the program's icon.

Listing 17-22 DELEREND.CPP

```
// delrend.cpp                  clipboard use with multiple formats

#include <afxwin.h>        // class library header file
#include "winmem.hpp"      // memory functions from chapter 12
#include "strres.hpp"      // resource functions from chapter 11
#include "delrend.h"       // header file for resource data
#include "delrend.hpp"     // header file for this program

CTheApp theApp ;           // create one CTheApp object - runs program

BOOL CTheApp::InitInstance ()     // override default InitInstance()
{
    m_pMainWnd = new CMainWindow () ;       // create a main window
    m_pMainWnd->ShowWindow (m_nCmdShow) ;   // make it visible
    m_pMainWnd->UpdateWindow () ;           // paint center
    return TRUE ;
}


CMainWindow::CMainWindow ()        // constructor for window
{
    CString title ;     // get program caption from resource data
    title.LoadString (S_PROGRAMCAPTION) ;
    Create (NULL, title, WS_OVERLAPPEDWINDOW, rectDefault,
        NULL, "MyMenu") ;
}

BEGIN_MESSAGE_MAP (CMainWindow, CFrameWnd)
    ON_COMMAND (IDM_SENDCLIP, OnSend)
    ON_COMMAND (IDM_GETTEXT, OnGetText)
    ON_COMMAND (IDM_CLEAR, OnClear)
    ON_COMMAND (IDM_QUIT, OnExit)
    ON_WM_RENDERFORMAT ()
    ON_WM_RENDERALLFORMATS ()
END_MESSAGE_MAP ()

void CMainWindow::OnSend ()        // "Copy to Clipboard" menu item
{                                  // set clipboard->delayed rendering
    if (this->OpenClipboard ()) // open the clipboard
    {
        ::EmptyClipboard () ;    // get rid of all clipboard data
        ::SetClipboardData (CF_TEXT, NULL) ; // NULL data handle
        ::CloseClipboard () ;    // close clipboard
    }
}
```

```
void CMainWindow::OnGetText ()   // "Get clipboard Text" menu item
{
    if (this->OpenClipboard ()) // if clipboard is not already open
    {                           // get the handle to clipboard data
        HANDLE hClipMem = ::GetClipboardData (CF_TEXT) ;
        if (hClipMem)           // if there is some CF_TEXT data
        {
            CGlobalBlock GTextBlock ;    // make a GClipBlock
        // attach handle to mem object with "permanence" set TRUE
            GTextBlock.sethandle (hClipMem, TRUE) ;
            LPSTR lpClip = GTextBlock.lock () ;    // lock block
            if (lpClip)
            {
                CClientDC dc (this) ;
                CRect rClient ;      // get client area rectangle
                this->GetClientRect (&rClient) ;
                dc.DrawText (lpClip, lstrlen (lpClip), rClient,
                    DT_LEFT | DT_WORDBREAK) ;
            }
            GTextBlock.unlock () ;
        }                              // mem object destroyed here,
        ::CloseClipboard () ;         // handle remains valid because
    }                                 // "permanence" was set TRUE
}

void CMainWindow::OnClear ()      // "Clear screen" menu item
{
    this->Invalidate () ;
}

void CMainWindow::OnExit ()       // "Quit" menu item
{
    this->DestroyWindow () ;      // destroy main window,
}                                 // this stops application

    // Clipboard got a request for a format - fill if CF_TEXT
void CMainWindow::OnRenderFormat (UINT nFormat)
{
    if (nFormat != CF_TEXT) // this app only renders CF_TEXT format
        return ;
        // use the StringResource object to load in resource data
    StringResource StrRes ("paragraph", "TEXT") ;
        // allocate "permanent" block to pass to clipboard
    CGlobalBlock ClipBlock (StrRes.GetLength (),
        GMEM_MOVEABLE, TRUE) ;
        // copy the resource string into the global memory block
    ClipBlock = (LPSTR) StrRes.GetString () ;
    ::SetClipboardData (CF_TEXT, ClipBlock.gethandle ()) ;
    ::CloseClipboard () ;         // close clipboard
}
```

```
    // app is terminating, just render the CF_TEXT format
void CMainWindow::OnRenderAllFormats ()
{
    StringResource StrRes ("paragraph", "TEXT") ;
    CGlobalBlock ClipBlock (StrRes.GetLength (),
        GMEM_MOVEABLE, TRUE) ;
    ClipBlock = (LPSTR) StrRes.GetString () ;
    if (this->OpenClipboard ())      // if clipboard is not open
    {
        ::SetClipboardData (CF_TEXT, ClipBlock.gethandle ()) ;
        ::CloseClipboard () ;         // close clipboard
    }
}
```

Listing 17-23 DELREND.HPP Header File

```
class CMainWindow : public CFrameWnd     // derive a main window class
{
public:
    CMainWindow () ;                    // declare a constructor
private:
    WORD wClipFormat ;                  // special clipboard format
    void OnSend () ;                    // process menu items
    void OnGetText () ;
    void OnClear () ;
    void OnExit () ;

                                        // process selected messages
    void OnRenderFormat (UINT nFormat) ;
    void OnRenderAllFormats () ;


    DECLARE_MESSAGE_MAP()               // prepare for message processing
} ;

class CTheApp : public CWinApp      // derive an application class
{
public:
    BOOL InitInstance () ;              // declare new InitInstance()
} ;
```

Listing 17-24 DELREND.H Resource ID Header File

```
// delrend.h  header file for resource ID numbers

#define IDM_SENDCLIP        1      // menu item ID numbers
#define IDM_GETTEXT         2
#define IDM_CLEAR           3
#define IDM_QUIT            4

#define S_PROGRAMCAPTION    1          // string table ID number
```

Listing 17-25 DELREND.RC Resource Script File

```
// delrend.rc   resource script file

#include <afxres.h>
#include "delrend.h"

AFX_IDI_STD_FRAME    ICON      delrend.ico     // the program's icon
Paragraph            TEXT      paragrph.txt    // custom resource file

MyMenu MENU                                    // define the menu
{
    MENUITEM "&Copy to Clipboard",   IDM_SENDCLIP
    MENUITEM "Get clipboard &Text",  IDM_GETTEXT
    MENUITEM "Clear &Screen",        IDM_CLEAR
    MENUITEM "&Quit",                IDM_QUIT
}


STRINGTABLE
{
    S_PROGRAMCAPTION     "Delayed Clipboard Rendering Example"
}
```

Listing 17-26 DELREND.DEF Module Definition File

```
NAME            delrend
DESCRIPTION     'delrend C++ program'
EXETYPE         WINDOWS
STUB            'WINSTUB.EXE'
CODE            PRELOAD MOVEABLE
DATA            PRELOAD MOVEABLE MULTIPLE
HEAPSIZE        1024
STACKSIZE       5120
```

Listing 17-27 PARAGRPH.TXT

```
This is a short paragraph of text
that will end up copied to the
Clipboard.
```

Figure 17-14 DELREND.ICO Icon Image

USING THE CLIPBOARD WITH AN EDIT CONTROL

A number of the previous examples in this book have taken advantage of edit controls as a simple means of getting text input from the user. It turns out that Windows has built-in support of cut-and-paste operations for text selected within an edit control. Text is selected in an edit control by holding down the left mouse button and dragging the mouse cursor over a block of text. The selected text ends up highlighted in reverse video, as shown in Figure 17-15. You can also hold down the (SHIFT) key and select an area of text using the arrow keys.

Once a block of text has been highlighted, it can be copied to the Clipboard by sending the edit control a WM_COPY message. This is typically done in response to the user selecting the "Copy" menu item, from the "Edit" menu. Essentially all Windows editors support this menu convention. Here is a typical call to **CWnd::SendMessage()**, sending the WM_COPY message to the **CEdit** object named **EditCntl**:

```
EditCntl.SendMessage (WM_COPY, 0, 0L) ;
```

The WM_COPY message does not use the *wParam* and *lParam* parameters, so they are just set to zero. When the edit control receives the WM_COPY message, the selected text is automatically copied to the Clipboard using the CF_TEXT clipboard format. The **CEdit** class provides an even simpler alternative to explicitly sending the WM_COPY message. Calling the **CEdit::Copy()** function results in the WM_COPY message being sent to the edit control, and the selected text is copied to the Clipboard.

```
EditCntl.Copy () ;
```

You can then paste the text elsewhere in the same edit control, or in a completely different application. Pasting text from the Clipboard into the edit control is just as simple. The **CEdit::Paste()** function does all the work, assuming that

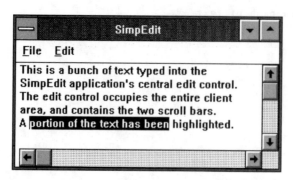

Figure 17-15 Text Highlighted in an Edit Control

there is CF_TEXT data in the Clipboard before the message is sent. **CEdit::Paste()** is equivalent to sending a WM_PASTE message to the edit control.

```
EditCntl.Paste () ;
```

The pasted text ends up at the current insertion point in the edit control. The insertion point is where the blinking caret appears when the edit control has the input focus. You can also cut the selected text out of the edit control, so that the selected text ends up in the Clipboard, but vanishes from the edit control. The **CEdit::Cut()** function does this magic by sending a WM_CUT message to the edit control.

```
EditCntl.Cut () ;
```

One last operation that you may want to implement is to allow deletion of the selected text in the edit control, without copying the data to the Clipboard. There is no specific message to do this, but it is easily done. Just cut the selected text to the Clipboard, and then empty the Clipboard.

```
EditCntl.Cut () ;
if (this->OpenClipboard ())
{
    ::EmptyClipboard () ;
    ::CloseClipboard () ;
}
```

Adding Clipboard Functionality to a Simple Editor

In Chapter 15, *Disk File Access*, the FILE2 program was created to demonstrate using the file selection dialog box. The last example in this chapter, SIMPEDIT, builds on FILE2 to create a fairly complete text editor. SIMPEDIT is shown in Figure 17-16, editing its own source code. (There is something wonderfully recursive about editing a program with itself.)

```
┌─────────────────────────────────────────────────────┐
│  ═        D:\C\17_CLIP\SIMPEDIT.CPP          ▼  ▲    │
│  File   Edit                                          │
├─────────────────────────────────────────────────────┤
│ // simpedit.cpp   simple text editor using file selection dialogs │
│                                                       │
│ #include <afxwin.h>      // class library header file │
│ #include <strstrea.h>    // streams header file       │
│ #include <afxdlgs.h>     // common dialogs header file │
│ #include <fstream.h>     // file streams header file   │
│ #include "winmem.hpp"     // windows memory block header file │
│ #include "simpedit.h"    // header file for resource data │
│ #include "simpedit.hpp"   // header file for this program │
│                                                       │
│ CTheApp theApp ;       // create one CTheApp object - runs program │
└─────────────────────────────────────────────────────┘
```

Figure 17-16 The SIMPEDIT Program

The SIMPEDIT.CPP in Listing 17-28 is just like FILE2.CPP from Chapter 15, *Disk File Access*, except that the cut, paste, copy, and delete operations have been added exactly as shown in the previous section. SIMPEDIT also uses the common dialog procedures for displaying a file selection dialog box.

The remaining support files for SIMPEDIT.CPP are shown in Listings 17-29 to 17-32. Figure 17-17 shows the program's icon. Note that keyboard accelerators have been added for the main menu selections in the resource script file, following the conventions used by Notepad, Windows Write, and many other Windows applications. (Microsoft quietly changed these conventions with the Windows 3.1 release from the earlier conventions that were even more arbitrary.) Don't forget to include WINMEM.CPP in your project file when compiling SIMPEDIT.CPP.

Listing 17-28 SIMPEDIT.CPP

```
// simpedit.cpp    simple text editor using file selection dialogs

#include <afxwin.h>        // class library header file
#include <strstrea.h>      // streams header file
#include <afxdlgs.h>       // common dialogs header file
#include <fstream.h>       // file streams header file
#include "winmem.hpp"      // windows memory block header file
#include "simpedit.h"      // header file for resource data
#include "simpedit.hpp"    // header file for this program

CTheApp theApp ;         // create one CTheApp object - runs program

BOOL CTheApp::InitInstance ()   // override default InitInstance()
{
    m_pMainWnd = new CMainWindow () ;       // create a main window
    m_pMainWnd->ShowWindow (m_nCmdShow) ;   // make it visible
    m_pMainWnd->UpdateWindow () ;           // paint center
    return TRUE ;
}


CMainWindow::CMainWindow ()      // constructor for main program window
{
    CString title ;         // get program caption from resource data
    title.LoadString (S_PROGRAMCAPTION) ;
    Create (NULL, title, WS_OVERLAPPEDWINDOW, rectDefault,
        NULL, "MyMenu") ;
    CRect ControlRect (0, 0, 1, 1) ;// rect to hold init edit size
                                    // create multiline edit control
```

```
    EditCntl.Create (WS_CHILD | WS_VISIBLE | ES_MULTILINE |
        WS_VSCROLL | WS_HSCROLL | ES_AUTOHSCROLL | ES_AUTOVSCROLL,
        ControlRect, this, NULL) ;
    FileName = "*.*" ;            // initialize with default file name
}

BEGIN_MESSAGE_MAP (CMainWindow, CFrameWnd)
    ON_COMMAND (IDM_NEW, OnNew)         // menu item "New File"
    ON_COMMAND (IDM_OPEN, OnOpen)       // menu item "Open File"
    ON_COMMAND (IDM_SAVE, OnSave)       // menu item "Save File"
    ON_COMMAND (IDM_ABOUT, OnAbout)     // menu item "About File2"
    ON_COMMAND (IDM_QUIT, OnExit)       // menu item "Quit"
    ON_COMMAND (IDM_COPY, OnCopy)       // menu item "Copy"
    ON_COMMAND (IDM_CUT, OnCut)         // menu item "Cut"
    ON_COMMAND (IDM_DELETE, OnDelete)   // menu item "Delete"
    ON_COMMAND (IDM_PASTE, OnPaste)     // menu item "Paste"
    ON_WM_SIZE ()                       // process WM_SIZE messages
END_MESSAGE_MAP ()

void CMainWindow::OnNew ()          // menu item "New File"
{
    EditCntl.SetWindowText ("") ;   // clear the edit area
    CString title ;                 // get default program caption
    title.LoadString (S_PROGRAMCAPTION) ;
    this->SetWindowText (title) ;   // change main window title
    FileName = "*.*" ;              // reset with default file name
}

void CMainWindow::OnOpen ()         // open a file and read data
{
    CFileDialog FDialog (TRUE, "TXT", "*.*",    // run file dlg
        OFN_HIDEREADONLY | OFN_OVERWRITEPROMPT,
        "All Files (*.*)|*.*|Text Files (*.TXT)|*.TXT||") ;
    if (FDialog.DoModal () != IDOK) // run file selection dialog box
        return ;                    // user selected cancel or close
    FileName = FDialog.GetPathName () ; // get full path/file name
    this->SetWindowText (FileName) ;// file name is the window caption
                                    // open the file for reading
    FStream.open (FileName, ios::in, filebuf::sh_read) ;
    if (!FStream.is_open)           // if error show message, return
    {
        StringTableMessageBox (S_FILENOTOPEN, S_FILEERROR,
            MB_OK | MB_ICONHAND) ;
        return ;
    }
    FStream.seekg (0, ios::end) ;   // move to end of stream
    int nBytes = (int) FStream.tellg () ;   // returns file length
    FStream.seekg (0, ios::beg) ;   // go back to beginning
                    // allocate local memory block for edit control
    CLocalBlock ReadMemBlock ;      // memory block for reading file
                                    // make big enough to hold file
```

```
    if (!ReadMemBlock.resize (nBytes + 2))  // if could not allocate
    {                                 // show error and return
        StringTableMessageBox (S_NOTALLOC, S_MEMERROR,
            MB_OK | MB_ICONHAND) ;
        return ;
    }
    char* pStr = (char *) ReadMemBlock.lock () ; // lock block
    FStream.setmode (filebuf::binary) ; // treat file as binary
    FStream.read (pStr, nBytes) ;       // read file into block
    FStream.close () ;                  // close the file
    *(pStr + nBytes) = 0 ;           // put two null chars at end
    *(pStr + nBytes + 1) = 0 ;
    EditCntl.SetWindowText (pStr) ; // pass text to edit control
}                                    // mem block freed automatically

void CMainWindow::OnSave ()      // copy edit cntl contents to file
{
    CFileDialog FDialog (FALSE, "TXT", "*.*",   // run file dlg
        OFN_HIDEREADONLY | OFN_OVERWRITEPROMPT,
        "All Files (*.*)|*.*|Text Files (*.TXT)|*.TXT||") ;
    if (FDialog.DoModal () != IDOK) // run file selection dialog box
        return ;                    // user selected cancel or close
    FileName = FDialog.GetPathName () ; // get full path/file name
    this->SetWindowText (FileName) ;// file name is the caption
    FStream.open (FileName, ios::out, filebuf::sh_write) ;
    if (!FStream.is_open)           // if error show message and return
    {
        StringTableMessageBox (S_FILENOTOPEN, S_FILEERROR,
            MB_OK | MB_ICONHAND) ;
        return ;
    }
    int nLines = EditCntl.GetLineCount () ; // get # of lines of text
    int nLong, nIndex ;
    char cBuf [256] ;
    for (int i = 0 ; i < nLines ; i++)
    {
        EditCntl.GetLine (i, cBuf, 256) ;   // read each line
        nIndex = EditCntl.LineIndex (i) ;   // get pos of start
        nLong = EditCntl.LineLength (nIndex) ;   // find length
        cBuf [nLong] = 0 ;                       // null terminate
        FStream << cBuf << endl ;       // send it to the file
    }                                    // endl == addition of newline
    FStream.close () ;                   // close the file
}

void CMainWindow::OnAbout ()
{
    StringTableMessageBox (S_ABOUTTEXT, S_ABOUTCAPTION,
        MB_OK | MB_ICONINFORMATION) ;
}
```

```
void CMainWindow::OnCopy ()
{
    EditCntl.Copy () ;
}

void CMainWindow::OnCut ()
{
    EditCntl.Cut () ;
}

void CMainWindow::OnDelete ()
{
    EditCntl.Cut () ;
    if (this->OpenClipboard ())
    {
        ::EmptyClipboard () ;
        ::CloseClipboard () ;
    }
}

void CMainWindow::OnPaste ()
{
    EditCntl.Paste () ;
}

void CMainWindow::OnExit ()            // menu item "Quit"
{
    this->DestroyWindow () ;           // destroy main window,
}                                      // this stops application

void CMainWindow::OnSize (UINT nType, int cx, int cy)
{       // resize edit control to always fit inside parent window.
    EditCntl.MoveWindow (5, 0, cx - 5, cy) ;
}       // Use offset of 5 for left border

    // show string table entry nString at location x,y
int CMainWindow::StringTableMessageBox (int nMessage,
    int nTitle, WORD flags)
{
    CString message, title ;
    message.LoadString (nMessage) ;
    title.LoadString (nTitle) ;
    return (this->MessageBox (message, title, flags)) ;
}
```

Figure 17-17 SIMPEDIT.ICO Icon Image

Listing 17-29 SIMPEDIT.HPP Header File

```
// simpedit.hpp    header file for simpedit.cpp

class CMainWindow : public CFrameWnd  // derive a main window class
{
public:
    CMainWindow () ;               // declare a constructor
private:
    CEdit EditCntl ;               // create an edit object
    CString FileName ;             // string to hold file name
    fstream FStream ;              // file stream object
    void OnNew () ;                // clear edit area
    void OnOpen () ;               // open a file
    void OnSave () ;               // write to a file
    void OnAbout () ;              // show about box
    void OnExit () ;               // menu item "Quit"

    void OnCopy () ;               // cut and paste menu items
    void OnCut () ;
    void OnDelete () ;
    void OnPaste () ;
                                   // process selected messages
    void OnSize (UINT nType, int cx, int cy) ;

    // show string table entry nString at location x,y
    int StringTableMessageBox (int nMessage, int nTitle,
        WORD flags = MB_OK) ;

    DECLARE_MESSAGE_MAP()          // prepare for message processing
} ;

class CTheApp : public CWinApp  // derive an application class
{
public:
    BOOL InitInstance () ;                 // declare new InitInstance()
} ;
```

Listing 17-30 SIMPEDIT.H Resource ID Header File

```
// simpedit.h  header file for resource ID numbers

#define IDM_NEW           1      // menu item ID numbers
#define IDM_OPEN          2
#define IDM_SAVE          3
#define IDM_ABOUT         4
#define IDM_COPY          5
#define IDM_CUT           6
#define IDM_PASTE         7
#define IDM_DELETE        8
#define IDM_QUIT          9
```

```
#define S_PROGRAMCAPTION    1         // string table ID numbers
#define S_FILENOTOPEN       2
#define S_NOTALLOC          3
#define S_MEMERROR          4
#define S_ABOUTTEXT         5
#define S_ABOUTCAPTION      6
#define S_FILENOTCREATE     7
#define S_FILEOPEN          8
#define S_FILEWRITE         9
#define S_FILEERROR        10
```

Listing 17-31 SIMPEDIT.RC Resource Script File

```
// simpedit.rc   resource script file

#include <windows.h>
#include <afxres.h>
#include "simpedit.h"


AFX_IDI_STD_FRAME   ICON    simpedit.ico        // the program's icon

MyMenu MENU                                     // define the menu
{
    POPUP    "&File"
    {
        MENUITEM "&New File",    IDM_NEW
        MENUITEM "&Open File",   IDM_OPEN
        MENUITEM "&Save File",   IDM_SAVE
        MENUITEM SEPARATOR
        MENUITEM "&About",       IDM_ABOUT
        MENUITEM "&Quit",        IDM_QUIT
    }
    POPUP    "&Edit"
    {
        MENUITEM "Cu&t      Cntl+X"     IDM_CUT
        MENUITEM "&Copy     Cntl+C"     IDM_COPY
        MENUITEM "&Paste    Cntl+V"     IDM_PASTE
        MENUITEM "&Delete   Del"        IDM_DELETE
    }
}


MyAccel     ACCELERATORS
{
    VK_DELETE,    IDM_DELETE,      VIRTKEY
    "X",          IDM_CUT,         VIRTKEY, CONTROL
    "C",          IDM_COPY,        VIRTKEY, CONTROL
    "V",          IDM_PASTE,       VIRTKEY, CONTROL
    VK_F2,        IDM_SAVE,        VIRTKEY
    VK_F3,        IDM_OPEN,        VIRTKEY
}
```

```
STRINGTABLE
{
    S_PROGRAMCAPTION      "SimpEdit"
    S_FILENOTOPEN         "Could Not Open File"
    S_NOTALLOC            "Could not allocate memory."
    S_MEMERROR            "Memory Error"
    S_ABOUTTEXT           "Simple Editor Application"
    S_ABOUTCAPTION        "Simple Editor Program"
    S_FILENOTCREATE       "Could not open or create file."
    S_FILEOPEN            "Open a file."
    S_FILEWRITE           "Write data to a file."
    S_FILEERROR           "File Error"
}
```

Listing 17-32 SIMPEDIT.DEF Module Definition File

```
NAME             simpedit
DESCRIPTION      'simpedit C++ program'
EXETYPE          WINDOWS
STUB             'WINSTUB.EXE'
CODE             PRELOAD MOVEABLE
DATA             PRELOAD MOVEABLE MULTIPLE
HEAPSIZE         1024
STACKSIZE        10240
```

SUMMARY

Windows applications use the Clipboard to exchange information. Usually the information is a block of text or a figure that has been selected and "Cut" or "Copied" to the Clipboard. Once data has been sent to the Clipboard, any application can read the information. Clipboard data is owned by Windows, not by the program that created the data, so data in the Clipboard cannot be modified (read-only data).

Physically, Clipboard data resides in one or more global memory blocks that have been sent to Windows. The application program sending information to the Clipboard must first allocate a global memory block, and copy data into the block. The Clipboard is then opened by calling the **CWnd::OpenClipboard()** function. Only one program can have the Clipboard open at any one time. Usually, the **::EmptyClipboard()** function is then called to free any memory blocks currently attached to the Clipboard. The **::SetClipboardData()** function transfers the memory block from the program to Windows, making the block the property of Windows. Finally, **::CloseClipboard()** closes the Clipboard, so another application can open it and read the data.

To read data from the Clipboard, the Clipboard is first opened using **CWnd::OpenClipboard()**. The handle of the global memory block in the Clipboard is obtained with **::GetClipboardData()**. **::CloseClipboard()** must again be used to close the Clipboard, allowing other programs to access the same data. The Clipboard can contain data in more than one format at one time. The common formats are given names like CF_TEXT and CF_BITMAP in WINDOWS.H. An application can also create a custom clipboard format using the **::RegisterClipboardFormat()** function.

Windows also supports a more advanced technique for sending data to the Clipboard for cases where a program transmits large amounts of data to the Clipboard, or supports several clipboard formats at the same time. "Delayed rendering" of the Clipboard allows a program to register that one or more clipboard formats are available, but not send the data to the Clipboard unless an application requests it. To establish a clipboard format with delayed rendering, the **::SetClipboardData()** function is called with NULL (zero) in place of the handle to the global memory block. If the Clipboard data is requested, Windows will send the supplying program a WM_RENDERFORMAT message. The supplying program then transmits the data to the Clipboard using **::SetClipboardData()**, passing a handle to a global memory block. Programs supporting delayed rendering should also process the WM_RENDERALLFORMATS message, which tells the program to copy any pending clipboard information to the Clipboard right before the application terminates. The WM_DESTROYCLIPBOARD message can also be processed, which alerts the program supplying clipboard data that **::EmptyClipboard()** has been called, so any pending information for the Clipboard can be discarded.

Edit controls have built-in support of cut-and-paste operations using the Clipboard. Any text highlighted in the edit control can be copied to the Clipboard using **CEdit::Copy()**. The **CEdit::Cut()** function deletes the selected text from the edit control and copies it to the Clipboard. Both messages use the CF_TEXT clipboard format. CF_TEXT data in the Clipboard can be pasted into an edit control using **CEdit::Paste()**.

In the course of the several example programs in this chapter, we used the **StringResource** class developed in Chapter 11, *Other Resources*, and the **CGlobalBlock** class developed in Chapter 12, *Managing Memory*. This approach is typical of the normal process of writing programs using C++. Well-designed objects can be used without modification in a variety of programs. The more objects you create, the fewer objects you will need to invent from scratch for successive projects. The ideal C++ program consists of a few abstract operations based on a solid collection of existing classes.

QUESTIONS

1. Memory blocks sent to the Clipboard become the property of Windows, but another application can get read and/or write access to the memory block using the **::GetClipboardData()** function. (True/False)

2. When the clipboard viewer program is operating, the clipboard viewer reads the Clipboard data, which stops other applications from doing "Paste" operations. (True/False)

3. When one application has the Clipboard open, the only other applications that can open the Clipboard are
   a. other applications reading data
   b. other applications writing data
   c. no other application
   d. a and b

4. The type of memory block passed to the Clipboard is a:
   a. global memory block
   b. local memory block
   c. global memory block allocated with a clipboard format flag such as CF_TEXT
   d. none of the above

5. The Clipboard can hold only one memory block at one time. (True/False)

6. To establish delayed rendering of a clipboard format, the handle to the memory block passed with **::SetClipboardData()** should be _____.

7. The **CEdit::Copy** Function copies text to the Clipboard from an edit control. The text copied is
   a. the entire edit control's contents
   b. text currently selected in the edit control
   c. text from the current insertion point to the end of the edit control
   d. none of the above

8. The difference between using **CEdit::Copy()** and **CEdit::Cut()** is
   a. only **CEdit::Copy()** sends data to the Clipboard
   b. **CEdit::Cut()** also deletes the currently selected text
   c. the two functions use different clipboard formats
   d. none of the above

9. To create a custom clipboard format, call the _____ function.

EXERCISES

1. Modify the CLIPBRD1.CPP program so that both the CF_TEXT and CF_OEMTEXT clipboard formats can be displayed when the "Get clipboard Text" menu item is selected. Display the CF_TEXT format in preference to CF_OEMTEXT. Test your program by copying some data from an MS-DOS window to the Clipboard and displaying it in the window's client area.

2. Modify the DELREND.CPP program so that both CF_TEXT and CF_OEMTEXT clipboard formats are supported. You can use the same resource text data for both clipboard formats, as the characters in the PARAGRPH.TXT file are all common to both the ANSI and OEM character sets. Test your program by opening an MS-DOS window and pasting the OEM text into the DOS window.

ANSWERS TO QUESTIONS

1. False. Clipboard data is always read-only.
2. False. The clipboard viewer does not stop applications from reading Clipboard data.
3. c.
4. a.
5. False. Multiple clipboard formats can be sent to the Clipboard at one time, but no more than one memory block with any single clipboard format can be saved to the Clipboard at any one time.
6. NULL or zero.
7. b.
8. b.
9. ::RegisterClipboardFormat().

SOLUTIONS TO EXERCISES

1. The only changes necessary are to look for both the CF_TEXT and CF_OEMTEXT clipboard formats in the **CMainWindow::OnGet()** function. Listing 17-33 shows the modified **CMainWindow::OnGet()** function.

Listing 17-33 Modifications to CLIPBRD1.CPP

```
void CMainWindow::OnGet ()        // "Get clipboard text" menu item
{
    if (this->OpenClipboard ()) // if clipboard is not already open
    {                           // get the handle to clipboard data
        HANDLE hClipMem = ::GetClipboardData (CF_TEXT) ;
        if (!hClipMem)          // if no TEXT data, try OEMTEXT
            hClipMem = ::GetClipboardData (CF_OEMTEXT) ;
        if (hClipMem)           // if there is some data to read
        {
            CGlobalBlock GClipMem ;    // create a global mem object
                // attach the clipboard handle to global block
            GClipMem.sethandle (hClipMem, TRUE) ;   // permanence TRUE
            LPSTR lpClip = GClipMem.lock () ;       // lock the block
            if (lpClip)          // only reading data, so no need
            {                    // to copy to another block
                CClientDC dc (this) ;
                dc.TextOut (0, 0, lpClip, lstrlen (lpClip)) ;
            }
            GClipMem.unlock () ;
        }                        // GClipMem automatically destroyed
        ::CloseClipboard () ;
    }
}
```

Note how the CF_TEXT format is selected if available. The CF_OEM-
TEXT format is checked only if the **::GetClipboardData()** function does
not find CF_TEXT data in the Clipboard. The complete solution to this
exercise is under the file name C17EXER1 on the source code disks.

2. Both the WM_RENDERALLFORMATS and WM_RENDERFORMAT logic of
the DELREND.CPP program must be modified to provide both CF_TEXT
and CF_OEMTEXT clipboard data on demand. Listing 17-34 shows the
changes to DELREND.CPP. The complete solution is under the file name
C17EXER2 on the source code disks.

Listing 17-34 Changes to DELREND.CPP

```
void CMainWindow::OnSend ()        // "Copy to Clipboard" menu item
{                                  // set clipboard->delayed rendering
    if (this->OpenClipboard ()) // open the clipboard
    {
        ::EmptyClipboard () ;       // get rid of all clipboard data
        ::SetClipboardData (CF_TEXT, NULL) ;    // NULL data handle
        ::SetClipboardData (CF_OEMTEXT, NULL) ; // two formats
        ::CloseClipboard () ;       // close clipboard
    }
}
```

```
void CMainWindow::OnGetText ()  // "Get clipboard Text" menu item
{
    if (this->OpenClipboard ()) // if clipboard is not already open
        {                              // get the handle to clipboard data
        HANDLE hClipMem = ::GetClipboardData (CF_TEXT) ;
        if (!hClipMem)                 // if no TEXT data, try OEMTEXT
            hClipMem = ::GetClipboardData (CF_OEMTEXT) ;
        if (hClipMem)                  // if there is some CF_TEXT data
            {
            CGlobalBlock GTextBlock ;   // make a GClipBlock object
            // attach handle to mem object with "permanence" set TRUE
            GTextBlock.sethandle (hClipMem, TRUE) ;
            LPSTR lpClip = GTextBlock.lock () ;   // lock the block
            if (lpClip)
                {
                CClientDC dc (this) ;
                CRect rClient ;          // get client area rectangle
                this->GetClientRect (&rClient) ;
                dc.DrawText (lpClip, lstrlen (lpClip), rClient,
                    DT_LEFT | DT_WORDBREAK) ;
                }
            GTextBlock.unlock () ;
            }                              // mem object destroyed here, but
        ::CloseClipboard () ;          // handle remains valid because
        }                              // "permanence" was set TRUE
}


// Clipboard got a request for data - fill if CF_TEXT or CF_OEMTEXT
void CMainWindow::OnRenderFormat (UINT nFormat)
{
    if (nFormat == CF_TEXT || nFormat == CF_OEMTEXT)
        {
        // use the StringResource object to load in resource data
        StringResource StrRes ("paragraph", "TEXT") ;
        // allocate "permanent" block to pass to clipboard
        CGlobalBlock ClipBlock (StrRes.GetLength (),
            GMEM_MOVEABLE, TRUE) ;
        // copy the resource string into the global memory block
        ClipBlock = (LPSTR) StrRes.GetString () ;
        if (nFormat == CF_OEMTEXT)
            ::SetClipboardData (CF_OEMTEXT, ClipBlock.gethandle ()) ;
        else
            ::SetClipboardData (CF_TEXT, ClipBlock.gethandle ()) ;
        }
}
    // app is terminating, just render the CF_TEXT format
void CMainWindow::OnRenderAllFormats ()
{
    StringResource StrRes ("paragraph", "TEXT") ;
```

```
CGlobalBlock ClipBlock (StrRes.GetLength (),
    GMEM_MOVEABLE, TRUE) ;
ClipBlock = (LPSTR) StrRes.GetString () ;
if (this->OpenClipboard ()) // if clipboard is not already open
{
    ::SetClipboardData (CF_TEXT, ClipBlock.gethandle ()) ;
    ::SetClipboardData (CF_OEMTEXT, ClipBlock.gethandle ()) ;
    ::CloseClipboard () ;   // close clipboard
}
}
```

## Chapter 18

Dynamic Link Libraries

Dynamic Link Libraries, or "DLLs" for short, provide groups of functions for other Windows applications to use. One DLL can be accessed by any number of applications at the same time. DLLs are an efficient use of memory if the same functions are needed by several applications, since only one copy of the DLL is required. For the programmer, DLLs provide the ultimate in reusable code. Once a DLL is compiled and debugged, it never needs to be compiled or linked into another program again. DLLs become an extension of the Windows environment, adding new functions to those already provided in Windows. Windows itself can be thought of as a collection of DLLs because the low-level code for functions like **CWnd::Create()** and **CDC::BitBlit()** reside in DLLs like KERNEL and GDI. The MFC classes simply organize the functions that are supported in Windows' DLLs.

Dynamic link libraries are simpler to create than complete Windows programs because they do not have a visible window. However, there are a few unique aspects to programming DLLs that must be kept in mind to avoid problems. These unique properties stem from the fact that functions in one DLL can be called by any number of Windows application programs during the same Windows session. Compiling DLLs also requires slight changes to the compiler and linker settings to produce the right code in the finished program.

This chapter first creates a simple DLL, containing one string manipulation function. The three different methods for calling a function from another Windows program are explained. The chapter concludes by converting the selection dialog box (created in Chapter 10, *Dialog Boxes*) to a DLL. This demonstrates a more complex DLL that uses several MFC classes and contains its own resource data.

Concepts covered: Runtime libraries versus DLLs, separation of the stack and data segments, ordinal numbers, compiler/linker settings to create a DLL, exporting a function, importing a function, import libraries, resource data in a DLL.

Key words covered: LIBRARY, EXPORTS, IMPORTS, SINGLE.

Functions covered: CWinApp::InitInstance().

COMPILER RUNTIME LIBRARIES

The core C++ language is reasonably small, and lacks many basic features. Instead of adding functions like **::strlen()** to the core language, C++ takes advantage of runtime libraries. During the development of a program, if you need a function like **::strlen()**, the linker extracts this code from one of the libraries, and adds it to your finished program. Figure 18-1 illustrates linking a program that requires two functions from a runtime library. Only the functions used by the program are extracted from the library. The code from the library file is physically added to your finished program, and acts just as if you had written the function in your own program's code. Runtime libraries are a huge time saver for C++ programmers, as they save you from constantly retyping code for basic functions like ::strlen().

Runtime library files have the extension ".LIB" and are always associated with a header file that contains the function declarations for the functions in the library. Several of the example programs in this book have used runtime library files for the functions not supported by Windows, such as **::strtok()**

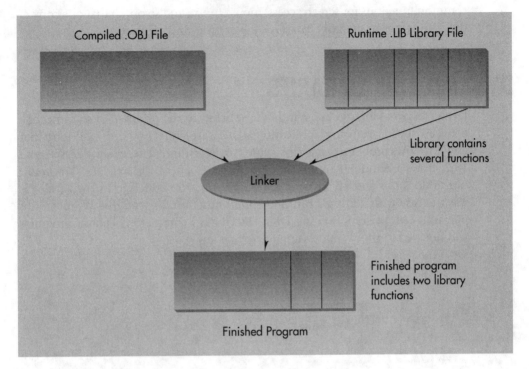

Figure 18-1 Adding Runtime Library Functions to a Program

(string token). To use the **::strtok()** function, the header file STRING.H is included at the top of the C++ program:

```
#include <string.h>
```

The angle brackets around the header file name tell the compiler to look in the compiler subdirectories for the file, rather than in the working directory. The header file includes the declaration of the **::strtok()** function, so that the compiler knows what type of arguments the function should be passed. The compiler and linker take care of extracting the **::strtok()** function's code from a runtime library, and add the code to the finished program.

Runtime libraries are ideal for an environment like MS-DOS, where each program runs by itself. However, Windows allows many programs to run at the same time. All Windows programs need to access the screen, check the mouse and keyboard, allocate memory, and perform numerous other functions. Windows programs would be enormous if all of this logic had to be added to each program via runtime libraries. To be efficient, Windows programs need to be able to share common functions for screen access, mouse input, and so on, so that one copy of these functions in memory can service every running application.

DYNAMIC LINK LIBRARIES

Dynamic Link Libraries are Windows' solution to the problem of sharing code between several running applications. DLLs are collections of functions that any Windows program can access, which are maintained in separate files. Figure 18-2 shows a Windows application that accesses a function in a DLL. The application does not end up with a copy of the function added to its own code, as was the case with adding a runtime library function. Instead, the Windows application calls the function in a DLL. The DLL is a completely separate program, and not tied to the Windows application in any way.

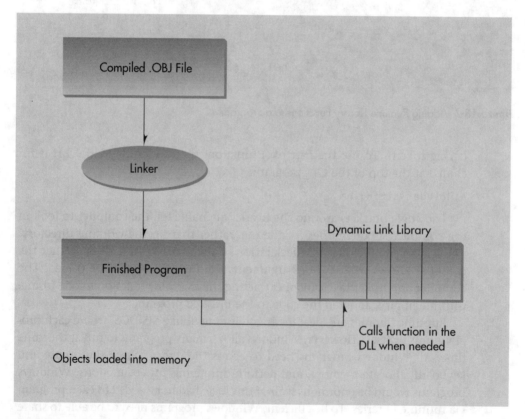

Figure 18-2 Windows Application Using a Function in a DLL

Although Figure 18-2 shows only one Windows application calling a function in the DLL, there is no limit to how many applications can make use of the same DLL. As you may have already guessed, all of the Windows functions that we have been calling, such as **::GlobalAlloc()** and **CDC::Rectangle()**, reside in DLLs supplied by Windows. This is how Windows programs get their basic functionality. The DLLs for Windows are stored in the Windows system directory (C:\WINDOWS\SYSTEM by default) and have names like USER.EXE and GDI.EXE. One confusing aspect of DLLs is that they can have the file extension ".EXE," ".DLL," or ".DRV." If you look in your computer's system directory, you will find all three types of files, all of which are DLLs.

MFC Class Libraries

The MFC classes themselves are interesting hybrids between runtime libraries and DLLs. The statement that the "**CDC::Rectangle()** function resides in one of Windows' DLLs" is not completely accurate. If you look into the definitions of the MFC functions, you will find the **CDC::Rectangle()** function defined as follows:

```
inline BOOL CDC::Rectangle(int x1, int y1, int x2, int y2)
    { return ::Rectangle(m_hDC, x1, y1, x2, y2); }
```

This inline function definition is in the file AFXWIN.INL, which is included with the AFXWIN.H header file. When you use the **CDC::Rectangle()** function, all that really happens is that a global Windows function named **::Rectangle()** is called. The advantage of using the **CDC** class is that it keeps track of the memory handle of the device context (named *m_hDC*), and releases the device context automatically when the **CDC** object is destroyed. Outside of these cleanup activities, the member functions in the **CDC** class are just indirect ways to call global functions like **::Rectangle()** that reside in the DLLs that make up the Windows environment.

Even the simple inline **CDC::Rectangle()** function takes a few bytes to pass the parameters to the global **::Rectangle()** function. That bit of code is stored in the MFC runtime libraries that are included when you compile a program using the MFC classes. The global **::Rectangle()** function that physically draws a rectangle with the currently selected pen and brush takes a lot more code. That part of the code resides in Windows' DLLs.

Although most of the MFC functions are as simple as **CDC::Rectangle()**, there are exceptions. The **CWinApp** class in particular contains a lot of code, including many calls to global Windows functions. The general design of the MFC classes is to provide as "thin a wrapping" of C++ classes as possible around the global Windows functions, while still taking advantage of the power of C++ classes for inheritance, constructors, destructors, virtual functions, and so on.

The result is that programming with the MFC classes retains the same "feel" as working directly with the global Windows functions, but it takes fewer lines of program code and avoids many common programming traps.

How DLLs Work

When you run a normal Windows program, its presence is made obvious by the appearance of the program's window on the screen. The physical program exists as a block of memory occupied by the program's code and data segments. DLLs generally consist of a series of functions that other programs use, and they do not display a visible window. DLLs also have a slightly different structure in memory than regular Windows application programs, which is illustrated in Figure 18-3.

DLLs do not have their own stack, but instead use the stack of any program calling a function in the DLL. As you may recall from Chapter 1, *How Windows Works*, the stack is used for automatic variables (variables declared within a function, and without the "static" prefix). Having DLLs use the stack of the program calling a function in the DLL makes sense if you consider that one DLL could be accessed by hundreds of different Windows applications. Automatic variables

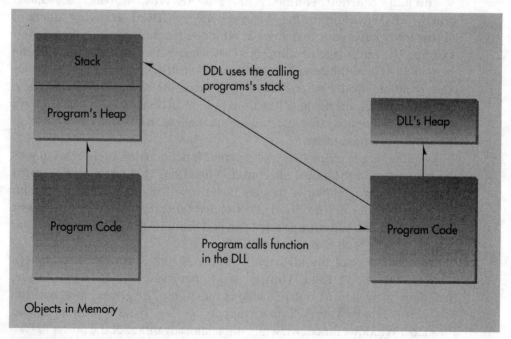

Figure 18-3 A DLL Loaded into Memory

declared within the DLL's functions end up spread around through all of the stacks of the calling programs, rather than piling up in a single stack of a DLL.

Problems with Static Variables in DLLs

As shown in Figure 18-3, DLLs have their own local heap for storing static variables. If you declare a character string in the DLL's code such as:

```
char    cBuf [] = "This is static text." ;
```

the text will be stored in the DLL's local heap. Global variables declared in the DLL's code will also be stored in the DLL's heap. This leads to some interesting situations when more than one Windows application is calling the same functions in a DLL. Imagine that the DLL stores an integer counter as a static variable, as shown in Figure 18-4. Any program that calls the DLL function results in the same static integer being incremented. This can foul things up in a hurry if each of the calling applications is not aware that other applications can change the value of the static variable.

Because there is only a single data heap for a DLL, static variables in DLLs are generally limited to things like text strings and variables that keep track of how many different programs are accessing the DLL. For a DLL to manage data for

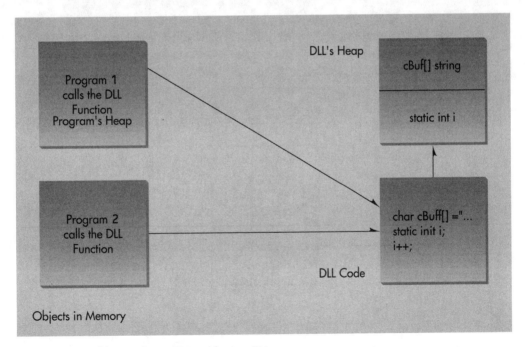

Figure 18-4 Problems with Static Variables in a DLL

calling programs, the DLL will generally need to allocate separate memory blocks for each calling program's data. A common practice is to use the calling program's instance handle (obtained with **AfxGetInstanceHandle()**) as a unique ID value to keep track of which data block belongs to which program. Figure 18-5 shows a typical DLL in memory, having allocated memory blocks for each of the programs currently accessing the DLL's functions.

Another interesting aspect of DLLs is that global memory blocks allocated within the DLL are "owned" by the application calling the DLL, not by the DLL itself. This means that blocks allocated by Program 1 (see Figure 18-5) will be freed if Program 1 is terminated, even if the DLL is still in memory to serve Program 2. Normally, this is desirable behavior, but it can cause problems if you try to allocate all the DLL's memory needs when the DLL is first started. Remember that a DLL will be started by another application calling the DLL, so the memory blocks allocated by the DLL when it starts will be owned by the application that first called the DLL. Those memory blocks will be freed when the first application terminates, even if other applications are using the DLL. This is a fairly subtle error, and may not show up in casual testing, so be sure to test your DLLs with multiple applications (or application instances) using the same DLL.

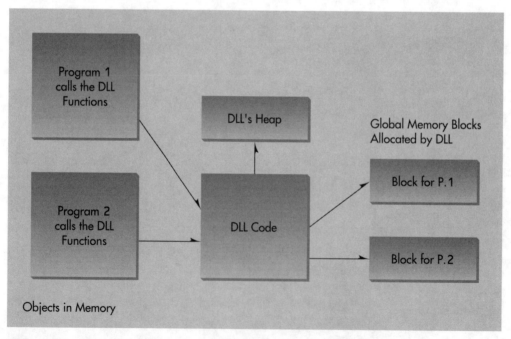

Figure 18-5 DLL Managing Separate Memory Blocks for Each Calling Program

WRITING A DLL USING MFC CLASSES

The **CWinApp** class that has been used in every example program in this book can also be used to create DLLs. The only special requirement is that you must compile the program using the large memory model. This makes all the addresses of both functions and data in the DLL far addresses. This is appropriate for DLLs because they will always be in different segments from the program that calls the DLL.

Creating New MFC Library Files

As supplied by Microsoft, the Microsoft C++ 7.0 disks do not include large model versions of the library files. You are required to compile the MFC source code to create your own library files. Fortunately, an automated method for producing new libraries is supplied with the library files. You will need about a megabyte of hard disk space for each library you create. To create a large model library:

1. Open an MS-DOS window.

2. Change directories to the MFC source code directory. By default, this is C:\C700\MFC\SRC.

3. Type the command line:

   ```
   NMAKE MODEL=L TARGET=W DLL=1 DEBUG=0 CODEVIEW=0
   ```

   This command line will initiate a compilation of all of the MFC source code files and build the large model libraries.

4. If you plan to use the debugger, you will want to do a second compile to create debug versions of the library files:

   ```
   NMAKE MODEL=L TARGET=W DLL=1 DEBUG=1 CODEVIEW=1
   ```

5. To delete all of the object files created during compilation (saving disk space), type the following command line:

   ```
   NMAKE CLEAN
   ```

6. Type EXIT to quit the MS-DOS window. You now have the library files you need to create DLLs using the MFC classes. Use the File Manager to verify that the LAFXDW.LIB (non-debug) and/or LAFXDWD.LIB (debug) runtime library was created and stored in your MFC\LIB subdirectory.

   The fact that the MFC classes require DLLs to be created using the large memory model does not affect applications that call functions residing in the

DLL. You can use functions in a DLL from within an application compiled with the small, medium, or large memory models. In all cases, you will need to use *far* pointers to pass data to and from a DLL, but *far* pointers are available in all memory models. The first example program demonstrates exchanging data between a small memory model application and a large model DLL.

Outline of a DLL

Listing 18-1 shows the outline of a DLL created using the MFC classes. As with normal Windows application programs, DLLs are created by deriving a class from the **CWinApp** class. In Listing 18-1, the name of the derived class is **CDemoDLL**. Within the **CDemoDLL** class definition are two public functions. The first is the mandatory **CWinApp::InitInstance()** virtual function. You must always declare an **InitInstance()** function for your derived class. The **InitInstance()** function will be called when the DLL is first loaded into memory and provides a place to do initialization. In Listing 18-1, the **CDemoDLL::InitInstance()** function just returns TRUE, meaning that initialization was successful. Returning FALSE terminates the DLL.

Listing 18-1 Outline of a DLL

```
// outline.dll

#include <afxwin.h>              // class library header file

class CDemoDLL : public CWinApp       // derive class from CWinApp
{
public:
    virtual BOOL InitInstance () ;  // InitInstance() is required
                                    // use default constructor
    CDemoDLL (const char* pszName) : CWinApp (pszName) { }
} ;

BOOL CDemoDLL::InitInstance ()        // runs when DLL is loaded
{
    // initialization routines go here
    return TRUE ;
}

CDemoDLL demoDLL ("Demo DLL") ;       // create CDemoDLL object
                                      // loads and runs DLL

extern "C"                            // for C language compatibility
void FAR PASCAL _export DllFunction (/* parameter list */)
{   // function does not need to be void, can return a value
    // code for function here
}
```

The other public function in the **CDemoDLL** class is the constructor function. The example just calls the default **CWinApp** class constructor function, passing a character string as the single parameter. The **CWinApp** constructor does all the work of setting up the DLL in memory.

```
CDemoDLL demoDLL ("Demo DLL") ;
```

Creating the object **demoDLL** results in the **CDemoDLL** constructor function being called. The character string "Demo DLL" is passed via the constructor function and becomes the name of the program module. You can just pass NULL in place of a character string. In this case, the DLL's file name becomes the name of the module.

DLL Function Declarations

At the bottom of Listing 18-1 is a prototype for a function in a DLL that could be called from outside of the DLL. The function type is

```
extern "C" void FAR PASCAL _export
```

This remarkably long function type specifies several important properties of the function that are summarized in Table 18-1. The Microsoft documentation suggests casting all functions in DLLs as extern "C" so that the function can be called by

Type	Meaning
extern "C"	The function is a C language function, not a C++ function.
void	The function has a return type of void (no returned value). DLL functions can return any value including int, long, far pointers, etc.
FAR	The function has a far address, meaning that the function address will be in a different segment than that of the program calling the DLL's function.
PASCAL	The PASCAL (not C) convention is used to store the function's parameters on the stack. Essentially, all Windows functions use the PASCAL convention for efficiency.
_export	The function will be exported, allowing other Windows applications to call the function using Windows' dynamic linking mechanism. Only exported functions can be called from outside of a program. Using the _export compiler key word avoids needing to list exported functions in the EXPORTS section of a program's module definition file (the original Windows programming practice).

Table 18-1 DLL Function Type Explanation

both C and C++ programs. We will see later in this chapter that a normal C++ function can also be put into a DLL, but this limits access to only C++ programs.

An Example DLL

The first example DLL in this chapter is named REVSTR.DLL. It provides a function named **StrRev()** that reverses the order of the characters in a global memory block. **StrRev()** will be used in another Windows program to print a text string backwards. Any number of Windows programs can access the **StrRev()** function in the same Windows session. Spelling things backwards is probably not something you do every day, but the REVSTR example has the advantage of demonstrating a number of features in a DLL, without a complex internal operation to confuse matters. This section examines the coding of the DLL's source code file. The next section will explain compiling the file to make a finished DLL, followed by an example Windows application that uses **StrRev()**.

Listing 18-2 shows the source code for the DLL. The **StrRev()** function reverses the order of the bytes in a global memory buffer. **StrRev()** works by copying the contents of the input memory block into a temporary global memory block in reverse order, and then it copies the contents of the temporary block back into the input block.

The top portion of REVSTR.CPP follows the minimal outline for creating a DLL using the MFC classes. The coding of the **StrRev()** function is a bit more interesting. Note that the low-level memory allocation functions, such as **::GlobalAlloc()** and **::GlobalLock()**, are used rather than the **CGlobalBlock** class developed in Chapter 12, *Managing Memory*. **StrRev()** is coded to be as small and efficient as possible. This is typical of the approach you might take to create a DLL containing a number of utility functions that will be called frequently.

Note that *far* pointers are used throughout the **StrRev()** function. The DLL will reside in a different data segment than the application that calls the function, so *far* pointers are used in all cases (remember that "LPSTR" is equivalent to "char far *" in WINDOWS.H).

Module Definition File for a DLL

The module definition file for a DLL is a bit different from that for a Windows application. Listing 18-3 shows the REVSTR.DEF file, with the key changes highlighted. In place of the NAME statement, DLLs use the LIBRARY statement to name the file. Note that the DATA statement includes the key word SINGLE, in place of the usual MULTIPLE. This is because the DLL will have a single data

Listing 18-2 REVSTR.CPP Source Code for a DLL

```cpp
// revstr.cpp    source code for a simple DLL - reverses string

#include <afxwin.h>          // class library header file
#include "revstr.h"          // interface header file

class CMyDLL : public CWinApp       // derive class from CWinApp
{
public:
    virtual BOOL InitInstance () ;  // InitInstance() is required
                                    // use default constructor
    CMyDLL (const char* pszName) : CWinApp (pszName) { }
} ;

BOOL CMyDLL::InitInstance ()        // runs when DLL is loaded
{
    // no initialization to do in this simple example
    return TRUE ;
}

CMyDLL ExampleDLL ("Demo DLL") ;    // create CMyDLL object
                                    // loads and runs DLL

// The StrRev() function reverses the order of the bytes in a
// global memory block.  The bytes are copied temporarily into
// the _hgMem block, and then copied back into the input block.
// Returns TRUE if all OK, FALSE on error.

extern "C"
BOOL FAR PASCAL _export StrRev (LPSTR lpSource, int nLong)
{
    int     i ;
    HANDLE  hgMem ;
    LPSTR   lpDest, lps, lpd ;

        // allocate temporary buffer, length + 1 for terminal null
    hgMem = ::GlobalAlloc (GMEM_MOVEABLE | GMEM_DISCARDABLE,
        (LONG) (nLong + 1)) ;
    if (hgMem)
    {
        lpDest = ::GlobalLock (hgMem) ; // lock both blocks
        lpd = lpDest ;                  // points to start of dest
        lps = lpSource + nLong - 1 ;    // points to end of source

        for (i = 0 ; i < nLong ; i++)   // reverse copy to dest
            *lpd++ = *lps-- ;

        for (i = 0 ; i < nLong ; i++)   // copy back to source
            *lpSource++ = *lpDest++ ;

        ::GlobalFree (hgMem) ;          // free temp buffer
        return (TRUE) ;
    }
    return (FALSE) ;
}
```

Listing 18-3 REVSTR.DEF Module Definition File

```
LIBRARY         revstr
DESCRIPTION     'revstr C++ DLL'
EXETYPE         WINDOWS
STUB            'WINSTUB.EXE'
CODE            PRELOAD MOVEABLE DISCARDABLE
DATA            PRELOAD MOVEABLE SINGLE
HEAPSIZE        1024
```

segment, and there will never be more than one instance of the DLL in memory at any one time. REVSTR.DEF uses the PRELOAD option, meaning that the DLL will be loaded when the calling program starts up. You can also use LOAD-ONCALL, which will delay loading the DLL until a function in the DLL is called. LOADONCALL would be more appropriate if the functions within the DLL are not likely to be called immediately.

A change that you might miss in Listing 18-3 is that there is no STACK statement. This is because the DLL will use the stack of any program calling the DLL's functions. The DLL does have a local data segment that is sized with the HEAPSIZE statement.

The information in the module definition file is used by the linker to correctly build the finished DLL. An older programming practice that is falling out of use is to include the names of any functions that will be called from outside the DLL in the exports section of the module definition file. For example, REVSTR.DEF could have the line:

```
EXPORTS     StrRev  @1
```

The EXPORTS statement explicitly tells the linker that the **StrRev()** function will be called from outside the REVSTR program. The @1 notation assigns the **StrRev()** function the "ordinal number" of one. We will see how ordinal numbers are used later in the chapter.

The EXPORTS statement is not required in REVSTR.DEF because the _export key word was included in the function declaration for the **StrRev()** function in REVSTR.CPP (Listing 18-2). The export status of the function is passed to the linker by the compiler, so it is not necessary to explicitly tell the linker which functions are to be exported. The _export key word is a fairly new addition to C++ compiler syntax and was not available when Windows was originally developed. Many programmers still use the module definition file to declare exported functions.

The REVSTR DLL is so simple that it does not need resource data. DLLs can use resource data, as will be demonstrated later in this chapter. Because DLLs do not have a visible window, there is no need for a program icon.

Header File for a DLL

One last file that is needed in creating the DLL is a header file. The REVSTR.H file (Listing 18-4) includes the function prototype for the exported function **StrRev()**. This is used in the REVSTR.CPP program, and will be used later in the Windows program that calls the **StrRev()** function.

Creating a DLL with PWB

Creating a DLL from within Programmer's Workbench (PWB) is identical to creating a Windows application, except that you select different compiler options. Here are the steps to create REVSTR.DLL:

1. Open (create) the project file REVSTR.MAK. Add the files REVSTR.CPP and REVSTR.DEF to the project. REVSTR does not have any resource data, so there will be no resource script file in the project.

2. Select the "Options/Language Options/C++ Compiler Options." menu item (a dialog box will appear). Select "Large memory model," "80286 Processor," "Warning Level 3," and "Release Options."

3. From the same "C++ Compiler Options" dialog box opened in the previous step, select "Additional Global Options," which will cause another dialog box to appear. Select "Protected-Mode DLL," "Use MFC Libraries," and "Use Pre-compiled Headers." Enter the include file name of AFXWIN.H. Select the "OK" button on both dialog boxes to save your selections.

4. Select the "Project/Build" menu item to compile the project. PWB will create the files REVSTR.OBJ, REVSTR.DLL, and REVSTR.LIB. The LIB file will be explained in a moment.

Using the DLL

To put the REVSTR.DLL dynamic link library to work, you will need to write a Windows application that uses the only function REVSTR.DLL exports: **StrRev()**. The next example program, DLLCALL, will use the **StrRev()** function to reverse the order of the characters in a character string. Figure 18-6 shows the DLLCALL program window, after the "Show Strings" menu item was selected.

Listing 18-4 REVSTR.H Header File

```
// revstr.h    interface file for revstr.dll

extern "C"
BOOL FAR PASCAL _export StrRev (LPSTR lpSource, int nLong) ;
```

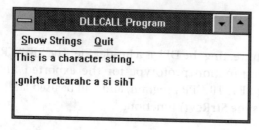

Figure 18-6 The DLLCALL Program

The first step in using a function in a DLL is to let your application program know where to find the function. This can be done in several ways. The most direct method is to add an IMPORTS section to the Windows application's module definition file. Listing 18-5 shows the DLLCALL.DEF file, with the IMPORTS section shown at the end. The IMPORTS statement tells the linker that the function named **StrRev()** will be found in the DLL named REVSTR. A period is used to separate the DLL file name from the function name.

Windows programs can import any number of functions from various DLLs. For example, the following IMPORT statement would allow the program to import three functions from two different DLLs.

```
IMPORTS         DLLONE.OneFunc
                DLLONE.TwoFunc
                DLLTWO.ThreeFunc
```

Once you have added the DLL function names to the application's module definition file, you can use the functions in the DLL just as if they were part of the application itself. Listing 18-6 shows the complete DLLCALL.CPP program, which uses the **StrRev()** function to reverse the order of the characters in a character string. The character string is loaded into a global memory block from the program's resource data using the **CString::LoadString()** function. After the string is displayed once with the characters in the correct order, **StrRev()** is

Listing 18-5 DLLCALL.DEF Module Definition File

```
NAME            dllcall
DESCRIPTION     'dllcall application'
EXETYPE         WINDOWS
STUB            'WINSTUB.EXE'
CODE            PRELOAD MOVEABLE
DATA            PRELOAD MOVEABLE MULTIPLE
HEAPSIZE        1024
STACKSIZE       5120
IMPORTS         REVSTR.StrRev
```

Listing 18-6 DLLCALL.CPP

```cpp
// dllcall.cpp                      example using strrev.dll

#include <afxwin.h>         // class library header file
#include "winmem.hpp"       // memory functions from chapter 12
#include "revstr.h"         // header file for dll
#include "dllcall.h"        // header file for resource data
#include "dllcall.hpp"      // header file for this program


CTheApp theApp ;            // create one CTheApp object - runs program

BOOL CTheApp::InitInstance ()   // override default InitInstance()
{
    m_pMainWnd = new CMainWindow () ;        // create a main window
    m_pMainWnd->ShowWindow (m_nCmdShow) ;    // make it visible
    m_pMainWnd->UpdateWindow () ;            // paint center
    return TRUE ;
}


CMainWindow::CMainWindow ()        // constructor for window
{
    CString title ;        // get program caption from resource data
    title.LoadString (S_PROGRAMCAPTION) ;
    Create (NULL, title, WS_OVERLAPPEDWINDOW, rectDefault,
        NULL, "MyMenu") ;
}


BEGIN_MESSAGE_MAP (CMainWindow, CFrameWnd)
    ON_COMMAND (IDM_SHOW, OnShow)
    ON_COMMAND (IDM_QUIT, OnExit)
END_MESSAGE_MAP ()

void CMainWindow::OnShow ()        // respond to menu item "Show"
{
    CClientDC dc (this) ;
    CString string ;
    string.LoadString (S_EXAMPLESTRING) ;
    dc.TextOut (0, 0, string, string.GetLength ()) ;

    CGlobalBlock Glob (128) ;
    Glob = (LPSTR) (const char*) string ;
    LPSTR lpStr = Glob.lock () ;
    StrRev (lpStr, string.GetLength ()) ;
    dc.TextOut (0, 30, lpStr, lstrlen (lpStr)) ;
}


void CMainWindow::OnExit ()        // respond to menu item "Quit"
{
    this->DestroyWindow () ;    // destroy main window,
}                               // this stops application
```

called to reverse the characters. The string is then output again. One other important detail in the DLLCALL.CPP program file is that the DLL header file REVSTR.H is included at the top of the listing. This header file (shown in Listing 18-4) includes the function declaration for the **StrRev()** function. This lets the compiler know what parameter types will be passed to the **StrRev()** function, even though the function resides in a DLL.

The remaining support files for DLLCALL.CPP are shown in Listings 18-7 to 18-9. Figure 18-7 shows the program's icon.

Listing 18-7 DLLCALL.HPP Header File

```
// dllcall.hpp    header file for dllcall.cpp

class CMainWindow : public CFrameWnd    // derive a main window class
{
public:
    CMainWindow () ;                    // declare a constructor
private:
    void OnShow () ;                    // respond to menu items
    void OnExit () ;

    DECLARE_MESSAGE_MAP()               // prepare for message processing
} ;

class CTheApp : public CWinApp          // derive an application class
{
public:
    BOOL InitInstance () ;              // declare new InitInstance()
} ;
```

Listing 18-8 DLLCALL.H Resource ID Header File

```
// dllcall.h  header file for resource ID numbers

#define IDM_SHOW             1    // menu item ID numbers
#define IDM_QUIT             2

#define S_PROGRAMCAPTION     1    // string table ID numbers
#define S_EXAMPLESTRING      2
```

Figure 18-7 DLLCALL.ICO Icon Image

Listing 18-9 DLLCALL.RC Resource Script File

```
// dllcall.rc  resource script file

#include <afxres.h>
#include "dllcall.h"

AFX_IDI_STD_FRAME   ICON   dllcall.ico    // the program's icon

MyMenu MENU                                // define the menu
{
    MENUITEM "&Show Strings",   IDM_SHOW
    MENUITEM "&Quit",           IDM_QUIT
}

STRINGTABLE
{
    S_PROGRAMCAPTION    "DLLCALL Program"
    S_EXAMPLESTRING     "This is a character string."
}
```

You can compile the DLLCALL program using any compiler memory model you choose. The small memory model is probably the most appropriate. There is no problem using the **StrRev()** function in the DLL from within a small model program because the pointer passed to **StrRev()** is a *far* pointer. *Far* pointers always contain the segment and offset values required to reference a function or data in another segment regardless of the memory model in use. The memory model *does* affect the default pointer type, so a pointer declared **char *** would be a *near* pointer in a small memory model program, but a *far* pointer with the medium or large memory models. **char far *** is always a *far* pointer, as is LPSTR.

Alternate Ways to Reference DLL Functions

In the DLLCALL program, the linker was told the name of the DLL file containing the **StrRev()** function by putting an IMPORTS statement in the DLLCALL.DEF module definition file. There is another shortcut method you can use. Remember back in the discussion of the module definition file for the DLL, the EXPORTS part of the REVSTR.DEF file could include the "ordinal number" for the **StrRev()** function as "@1." This is shown again in Listing 18-10.

Ordinal numbers for exported functions in DLLs are optional, but they allow you to refer to the exported function by its number, rather than the function's name. For example, the Windows application that uses the **StrRev()** function could have a module definition file like the one shown in Listing 18-11. The name of the **StrRev()** function has been replaced by the function's ordinal number.

Listing 18-10 REVSTR.DEF Module Definition File

```
LIBRARY         revstr
DESCRIPTION     'revstr application'
EXETYPE         WINDOWS
STUB            'WINSTUB.EXE'
CODE            PRELOAD MOVEABLE DISCARDABLE
DATA            PRELOAD MOVEABLE SINGLE
HEAPSIZE        1024
EXPORTS         StrRev    @1
```

Listing 18-11 DLLCALL.DEF Using the Ordinal Number for StrRev()

```
NAME            dllcall3
DESCRIPTION     'dllcall3 application'
EXETYPE         WINDOWS
STUB            'WINSTUB.EXE'
CODE            PRELOAD MOVEABLE
DATA            PRELOAD MOVEABLE MULTIPLE
HEAPSIZE        1024
STACKSIZE       5120
EXPORTS         WndProc
IMPORTS         StrRev = REVSTR.1
```

The advantage of using the ordinal number for a function is that it produces slightly smaller and faster code. The disadvantage is that it is easy to get the function numbers mixed up if the DLL contains a large number of exported functions. In general, ordinal numbers should be used only if the program's performance is critically important.

One little trick that you might find useful with the IMPORTS section of a module definition file is to rename the function as it is imported. For example, the line:

```
IMPORTS         StringReverse = REVSTR.1
```

would give the **StrRev()** function (ordinal number one) the alias **StringReverse()** within the program importing the function. The meaning of the parameters passed to the function and the function's returned value are not affected. Do not use the alias technique unless you have a compelling reason to rename a function, because it makes programs very difficult to document (the same function ends up having more than one name).

IMPORT LIBRARIES

If there are a number of exported functions, the best technique is to summarize all of the functions in an import library. Import libraries allow you to forget about adding function names or ordinal numbers to the IMPORTS section of the Windows application's .DEF file. Instead, you collect all the names of the functions in the DLL in a single library file that can be included in the linking process. Figure 18-8 shows the effect of including an import library when creating a Windows application.

The import library tells the linker which DLLs contain the functions that the application needs. Unlike runtime libraries, import libraries do not add the functions from the DLL to the Windows application. Import libraries only contain the references to the locations of functions in DLLs. When the Windows application calls a function in a DLL, the DLL is loaded into memory (if it is not already loaded) and the function is executed within the DLL's code.

Creating an Import Library

The PWB will automatically create an import library for any project file that is compiled to make a DLL. PWB does this by calling the IMPLIB.EXE program at the end of the compile/link process. You can also run the IMPLIB.EXE program separately from within an MS-DOS window. For example, to create the REVSTR.LIB library, open a DOS window, move to the subdirectory containing your DLL and its .DEF file, and type in the following line:

```
implib revstr.lib revstr.dll
```

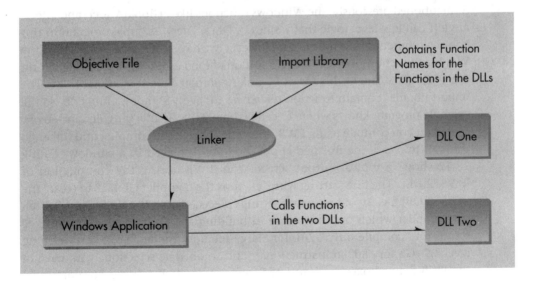

Figure 18-8 Using an Import Library

This will work if the library containing IMPLIB.EXE is in your current DOS PATH. Otherwise, spell out the full path name for IMPLIB, such as:

```
c:\c700\bin\implib revstr.lib revstr.dll
```

Using an Import Library

As mentioned previously, once you have created an import library, you do not need to list the imported function names in the IMPORTS section of the Windows application's module definition file. All you need to do is to add the import library file to the list of files that the linker uses to build the finished program. For example, to compile DLLCALL using the REVSTR.LIB import library, include the following file names in the project file:

```
dllcall.cpp
dllcall.def
dllcall.rc
revstr.lib
```

The reference to the **StrRev()** function being in the REVSTR.DLL file will be extracted from the REVSTR.LIB import library during the linking step. Using import libraries is a lot easier than needing to always remember to update the program's module definition file each time a function is called in a DLL.

The Big Picture on Import Libraries

As mentioned previously, the Windows functions like **::GlobalAlloc()** and **::Rectangle()** call low-level logic that resides in DLLs. Every example program in this book calls functions in these DLLs. However, we have not needed to list all of the Windows functions in the IMPORTS section of each example's module definition file. PWB takes care of this for us by linking import libraries automatically. The import libraries contain function references for every Windows function, so the example program knows where to call **::GlobalAlloc()**, **::Rectangle()**, and so on.

When you compile using PWB, the various steps the compiler and linker go through to create the finished application are displayed in a window. Listing 18-12 shows a typical output screen from PWB during the compilation of REVSTR.DLL. The line starting with "cl" runs the compiler CL.EXE to create the REVSTR.OBJ file. All of the switch settings preceded with the slash character tell the compiler which options to use in building the program. For example, /c stands for "compile only," /AL for "large memory model," /W3 for "warning level 3," /G2 for "80286 instructions," and so on. The selections you make in the PWB dialog boxes are translated into these switch settings automatically, saving you the trouble of having to remember this long list of switches.

Listing 18-12 PWB Build Results Display

```
        NMAKE  /a /f D:\C\18_DLL\REVSTR.MAK all

Microsoft (R) Program Maintenance Utility   Version 1.20
Copyright (c) Microsoft Corp 1988-93. All rights reserved.

Microsoft (R) C/C++ Optimizing Compiler Version 7.00
Copyright (c) Microsoft Corp 1984-1993. All rights reserved.

cl /Ycafxwin.h /c /AL /W3 /G2 /GD /Yuafxwin.h /Zp /BATCH
   /f /Ob1 /Od /Og /Oe /Gs /FoREVSTR.obj REVSTR.CPP
revstr.cpp

        echo > NUL @REVSTR.lrf
        link @REVSTR.lrf

Microsoft (R) Segmented Executable Linker  Version 5.30
Copyright (C) Microsoft Corp 1984-1993.  All rights reserved.

Object Modules [.obj]: REVSTR.obj
Run File [REVSTR.exe]: REVSTR.dll
List File [nul.map]: NUL
Libraries [.lib]:  +
Libraries [.lib]: LIBW.LIB +
Libraries [.lib]: LAFXCW +
Libraries [.lib]: /NOD:LLIBCE +
Libraries [.lib]: LDLLCEW
Definitions File [nul.def]: REVSTR.DEF /BATCH /ONERROR:NOEXE /NOF /NOPACKC;
        implib REVSTR.lib REVSTR.dll

Microsoft (R) Import Library Manager  Version 1.30
Copyright (C) Microsoft Corp 1984-1993.  All rights reserved.
```

Toward the bottom of Listing 18-12, you can see that the linker (Microsoft (R) Segmented Executable Linker) is executed. The input file is REVSTR.OBJ and the output (run file) is REVSTR.DLL. The linker also reads several library files. The LIBW.LIB file is a runtime library containing startup code and other functions that are added to your Windows application to do low-level tasks, such as setting up the application's local heap when it is first loaded. You can think of this runtime library as containing the "secret functions" that your Windows application needs to get started. Microsoft provides documentation of these secret functions to developers of Windows programming tools, but most Windows programmers can take their existence for granted. There are plenty of Windows functions to work with without worrying about the secret ones.

LAFXCW.LIB is the large model library for the MFC classes that you created earlier. Portions of this library are added to your program when you use MFC classes. LLIBCE.LIB and LDLLCEW.LIB are the import libraries that contain the locations of all the built-in Windows functions like ::**GlobalAlloc**(). This is how your program finds where to call all these Windows functions. There are different libraries for each compiler memory model. The first letter of the library name matches the model, S = small, M = medium, L = large, and so on.

At the bottom of Listing 18-12, you will see that PWB executed the IMPLIB.EXE program to create the REVSTR.LIB import library for REVSTR.DLL. If you have a more complex program with a number of .CPP files, all of the exported functions in the project will be referenced in the library file.

Programming Considerations for DLLs

When you write a DLL, there are a few things you need to keep in mind that do not apply to Windows applications:

1. The DLL will be in a different segment from the application calling functions in the DLL. Declare all exported functions FAR (usually FAR PASCAL), and use *far* pointers for addresses.

2. The DLL will have its own static data, which will be common to all of the applications calling functions in the DLL. Don't store data for the calling applications in static variables, which might cause an error if two or more applications are using the DLL at the same time. For example, do not store the current record number in a database as a single static number, if two or more application programs can change the record number.

3. The DLL will use the stack of the calling program(s), which will be in a separate segment from the DLL's static data on the local heap. This can cause problems, particularly if you use runtime library functions that assume the stack and static data are in the same segment. Any function that uses *near* pointers to data will fail.

4. When you allocate global memory blocks from within a DLL, the memory blocks belong to the application calling the DLL, not to the DLL itself. This is how Windows gets around "sharing violations," where two different applications attempt to access the same block of memory. Memory blocks allocated by the DLL will be freed if the application that called the DLL is terminated.

A MORE COMPLETE DLL EXAMPLE

Back in Chapter 10, *Dialog Boxes*, we created a generic dialog box, LISTDLG, that allowed the user to select an item from a list of character strings (the DIALG3 example program in Chapter 10 uses the LISTDLG dialog box). A generic dialog

box that allows the user to make a selection from a list of items is an ideal subject for a DLL. By using a DLL, the same code can be reused in many projects without recompiling, and can be called by any number of application programs in the same Windows session.

The next example program creates the LISTDLG.DLL program, and then uses it to show a list of cars. The program that uses LISTDLG.DLL is called CALLIST. Figure 18-9 shows the CALLIST program after the "List Box" menu item was selected. The user can select any of the items in the list box. The current selection is then displayed in the CALLIST client area.

The LISTDLG.DLL will include resource data because the dialog box is defined in LISTDLG.RC. In addition, LISTDLG.DLL will demonstrate that DLLs can contain C++ functions, not just the C language functions demonstrated in the last example. Using C++ functions within the DLL has the side effect of requiring that both the DLL and the calling program (CALLIST) be compiled with the same (large) memory model. Using C++ functions also means that you would not be able to use the list dialog box from a C language program. (By this point the author assumes that you are completely converted to C++ and would never consider using the C language again! Of course, you might get stuck with supporting a large existing C program....)

Creating LISTDLG.DLL

Listing 18-13 shows the LISTDLG.HPP header file. LISTDLG is complex enough that it is better to put the class definitions in a separate file. The **CListDlgDLL** class is derived from the **CWinApp** MFC class to form the basis for the application. The

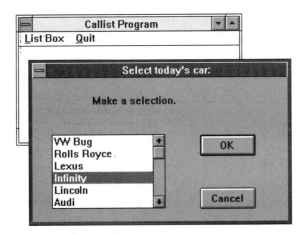

Figure 18-9 The CALLIST Program Displaying the LISTDLG Dialog Box

required virtual function **InitInstance()** is declared, along with a simple constructor function that just calls the **CWinApp** default constructor. This portion of LISTDLG.HPP is identical to the class definition in the previous example.

The LISTDLG.HPP header file also derives the **CListDialog** class from **CModalDialog**. This will be the modal dialog box class. The coding of the **CListDialog** class is almost identical to the LISTDLG example in Chapter 10, *Dialog Boxes.* You do not need to do anything special to create a dialog box from within a DLL.

Listing 18-14 shows the LISTDLG.CPP program. A **CListDlgDLL** object named *demoDLL* is created at the top of the listing. Creating this object causes the constructor function to be executed, which loads and initializes the DLL in memory. The **CListDlgDLL::InitInstance()** function is called during the

Listing 18-13 LISTDLG.HPP Header File

```
// listdlg.hpp           header file for listdlg.cpp

class CListDlgDLL : public CWinApp  // derive class from CWinApp
{
public:
    virtual BOOL InitInstance () ;  // InitInstance() is required
                                    // use default constructor
    CListDlgDLL (const char* pszName) : CWinApp (pszName) { }
} ;


                                // derive class from CModalDialog
class CListDialog : public CModalDialog
{
public:                         // constructor
    CListDialog (CWnd* pParent, CStringList* inList,
        CString* title) : CModalDialog ("ListDialog", pParent)
    {
        pList = inList ;
        pTitle = title ;
    }
private:
    int nChoice ;                       // current selection no.
    CStringList* pList ;                // pointer to string list
    CListBox* pListBox ;                // pointer to list box
    CString* pTitle ;                   // pointer to title
    BOOL OnInitDialog () ;              // override default
    void OnListBoxSel () ;
    void OnOkBtn () {EndDialog (nChoice) ; }
    void OnCancelBtn () {EndDialog (-1) ; }

    DECLARE_MESSAGE_MAP ()              // message map for dialog
} ;
```

Listing 18-14 LISTDLG.CPP

```cpp
// listdlg.cpp            dialog box for displaying list for
selection

#include <afxwin.h>       // class library header file
#include <afxcoll.h>      // for list objects
#include "listdlg.h"      // interface header file
#include "listdlg.hpp"    // class definitions

CListDlgDLL demoDLL ("ListDlg") ;     // create CListDlgDLL object
                                      // loads and runs DLL

BOOL CListDlgDLL::InitInstance ()     // runs when DLL is loaded
{
    // no initialization to do in this example
    return TRUE ;
}

    // C++ language interface function to run dll - called by
    // program that uses the DLL to start the dialog box
int FAR PASCAL _export DoListDlg (CWnd FAR * Parent,
    CStringList FAR * List, CString FAR * Title)
{
    CListDialog* pListDialog =
        new CListDialog (Parent, List, Title) ;
    int nRet = pListDialog->DoModal () ;  // run dialog box
    delete pListDialog ;
    return nRet ;
}

    // function called just before dialog box becomes visible
BOOL CListDialog::OnInitDialog ()
{
    nChoice = -1 ;                    // -1 means no choice made
    this->SetWindowText (*pTitle) ; // ** change window title **
    int nItems = pList->GetCount(); // get number of list items
    if (nItems > 0)
    {                                 // get the list box control
        pListBox = (CListBox*) GetDlgItem(DLI_LISTBOX);
        pListBox->ResetContent();     // empty list box contents
                                      // move to top of string list
        POSITION pos = pList->GetHeadPosition();
        for (int i = 0; i < nItems; i++)
        {                             // copy list item to list box
            CString Str = pList->GetNext(pos);
            pListBox->AddString(Str);
        }
    }
    return TRUE ;
}
```

```
BEGIN_MESSAGE_MAP (CListDialog, CModalDialog)
    ON_COMMAND (DLI_CANCEL, OnCancelBtn)      // defined in .hpp
    ON_COMMAND (DLI_OK, OnOkBtn)              // defined in .hpp
    ON_LBN_SELCHANGE (DLI_LISTBOX, OnListBoxSel)// defined below
END_MESSAGE_MAP ()

void CListDialog::OnListBoxSel ()     // user made selection
{
    nChoice = pListBox->GetCurSel () ; // save selection no.
}
```

startup sequence, but does not do anything other than return TRUE. No special initializations need to be done in LISTDLG when the DLL is first loaded.

The pivotal function in LISTDLG.CPP is **DoListDlg()**. This is a global function (not tied to any class) and is declared int FAR PASCAL _export. The lack of an extern "C" declaration means that the function will use the default C++ calling conventions for the compiler. In other words, **DoListDlg()** is a C++ function. **DoListDlg()** is the function that other application programs will call to display a list box and determine which item in the list was selected.

DoListDlg() receives three parameters. The *Parent* value is a pointer to the parent window **CWnd** object. This is critical in a DLL because the DLL does not have a window of its own, and must "borrow" a window from the calling program in order to display the dialog box. The second parameter *List* is a pointer to a **CStringList** object containing the list of character strings to display. This is how the calling program passes the list to the dialog box. Finally, the *Title* parameter just passes a pointer to a **CString** object containing the string to display in the dialog box caption bar.

All **DoListDlg()** does is create a **CListDialog** object (passing the three parameters to this object) and execute **CDialog::DoModal()** to make the dialog box visible. The dialog box remains visible until the user selects the "OK" or "Cancel" button. **DoListDlg()** returns an integer value corresponding to the item selected by the user. If the user selects the "Cancel" button on the dialog box, **DoListDlg()** returns –1. This returned value is how the calling program knows which item was selected.

The remainder of the LISTDLG.CPP program is copied from the LISTDLG example in Chapter 10, *Dialog Boxes*. In order to call the **DoListDlg()** function from another program, it is necessary to include a function declaration so the compiler knows the function and parameter types. The declaration for **DoListDlg()** is in the LISTDLG.H header file, shown in Listing 18-15. This type of header file is sometimes called an "interface file" because it defines the interface between the calling program and the DLL. Only the **DoListDlg()** function is visible to the calling program. The internal workings of the dialog box are all hidden away inside the DLL.

Listing 18-16 shows the LISTDLG.RC resource script file, which defines the dialog box. There are no special requirements for resources used in DLLs, so the dialog box definition from Chapter 10, *Dialog Boxes*, can be used here without modification.

Listing 18-17 shows the LISTDLG.DEF module definition file. The .DEF file does not include an EXPORTS section because the **DoListDlg()** function was

Listing 18-15 LISTDLG.H Interface File

```
// listdlg.h                interface file for listdlg.dll

#define DLI_LISTBOX     102      // dialog box control IDs
#define DLI_CANCEL      101
#define DLI_OK          100

int FAR PASCAL _export DoListDlg (CWnd FAR * Parent,
    CStringList FAR * List, CString FAR * Title) ;
```

Listing 18-16 LISTDLG.RC Resource Script File

```
// listdlg.rc      dialog box definition

#include "windows.h"
#include "listdlg.h"

ListDialog DIALOG 9, 21, 174, 95
STYLE DS_MODALFRAME | WS_POPUP | WS_CAPTION | WS_SYSMENU
{
    CONTROL "", DLI_LISTBOX, "LISTBOX", LBS_NOTIFY | LBS_HASSTRINGS |
        WS_CHILD | WS_VISIBLE | WS_BORDER | WS_VSCROLL, 14, 38, 76, 53
    DEFPUSHBUTTON "OK", DLI_OK, 114, 38, 38, 14,
        WS_CHILD | WS_VISIBLE | WS_TABSTOP
    PUSHBUTTON "Cancel", DLI_CANCEL, 114, 73, 38, 14, WS_CHILD |
        WS_VISIBLE | WS_TABSTOP
    CONTROL "Make a selection.", -1, "STATIC", SS_LEFT | WS_CHILD |
        WS_VISIBLE, 41, 11, 78, 20
}
```

Listing 18-17 LISTDLG.DEF Module Definition File

```
LIBRARY         listdlg
DESCRIPTION     'listdlg C++ DLL'
EXETYPE         WINDOWS
STUB            'WINSTUB.EXE'
CODE            PRELOAD MOVEABLE DISCARDABLE
DATA            PRELOAD MOVEABLE SINGLE
HEAPSIZE        10240
```

declared with the _export key word, and there are no plans to use the ordinal number technique for calling **DoListDlg()**. Notice again the LIBRARY key word is used in the .DEF file for a DLL in place of NAME for an application program.

In summary, converting the LISTDLG code to a DLL is fairly simple. The main change is to add the derivation of a new class from **CWinApp** to run the DLL, with the associated constructor and **InitInstance()** functions. The other change is to design an interface function named **DoListDlg()** that is exported, so it can be called from another program. The majority of the code and the program's resources are not affected by being placed in a DLL.

Using the DLL

The last example program in this chapter is CALLIST, which uses LISTDLG.DLL to display a list of cars. Figure 18-9 in the previous section shows the appearance of CALLIST when the dialog box is displayed. Figure 18-10 shows the CALLIST program after the user selected a car. If the user selects a car, the name of the car is displayed in the program's client area. If the user selects the "Cancel" button on the dialog box, the string "Nothing Selected" is displayed.

Listing 18-18 shows the CALLIST.CPP program. The program is remarkably short because all the dialog box logic is in the DLL. CALLIST.CPP builds a list of car names in a **CStringList** object named *MenuList* and puts the title string "Select today's car::" in a **CString** object named *Title*. Once these data items are ready, the process of displaying the list box boils down to one line of code:

```
int nRetVal = DoListDlg (this, &MenuList, &Title) ;
```

LISTDLG.DLL takes care of all the dialog box activities and does not return control to CALLIST until the user has selected "OK" or "Cancel." CALLIST then displays the name of the selected car by fetching the string from **CStringList**. If the user selects the "Cancel" button, **DoListDlg()** returns –1, so the "Nothing Selected" string is displayed.

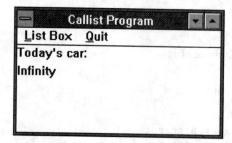

Figure 18-10 CALLIST Program After a Selection

Listing 18-18 CALLIST.CPP

```cpp
// callist.cpp              using listdlg.dll dialog box
// note: this program must be compiled with the large memory model
// to work properly with the (large model) dll

#include <afxwin.h>      // class library header file
#include <afxcoll.h>     // for list objects
#include "callist.h"      // header file for resource data
#include "callist.hpp"    // header file for this program
#include "listdlg.h"      // interface file for listdlg.dll


CTheApp theApp ;          // create one CTheApp object - runs program

BOOL CTheApp::InitInstance ()    // override default InitInstance()
{
    m_pMainWnd = new CMainWindow () ;      // create a main window
    m_pMainWnd->ShowWindow (m_nCmdShow) ;  // make it visible
    m_pMainWnd->UpdateWindow () ;          // paint center
    return TRUE ;
}


CMainWindow::CMainWindow ()        // constructor for window
{
    CString title ;      // get program caption from resource data
    title.LoadString (S_PROGRAMCAPTION) ;
    Create (NULL, title, WS_OVERLAPPEDWINDOW, rectDefault,
        NULL, "MyMenu") ;
}


BEGIN_MESSAGE_MAP (CMainWindow, CFrameWnd)
    ON_COMMAND (IDM_DIALOG, OnDialog)
    ON_COMMAND (IDM_QUIT, OnQuit)
END_MESSAGE_MAP ()

void CMainWindow::OnDialog ()    // respond to menu item "Pick"
{
    this->Invalidate () ;        // clear the client area

    CStringList MenuList ;       // make a list of strings
    MenuList.AddHead ("BMW") ;
    MenuList.AddHead ("Mercedes") ;
    MenuList.AddHead ("Audi") ;
    MenuList.AddHead ("Lincoln") ;
    MenuList.AddHead ("Infinity") ;
    MenuList.AddHead ("Lexus") ;
```

```
          MenuList.AddHead ("Rolls Royce") ;
          MenuList.AddHead ("VW Bug") ;
                                   // make a CString for title
          CString Title ("Select today's car:") ;
                          // call list dialog box function in dll
          int nRetVal = DoListDlg (this, &MenuList, &Title) ;
                          // display the choice in client area
          CClientDC dc (this) ;
          CString string ("Today's car:") ;
          dc.TextOut (0, 0, string, string.GetLength ()) ;
          if (nRetVal != -1)
          {              // extract selected string from list
              POSITION Pos = MenuList.FindIndex (nRetVal) ;
              string = MenuList.GetAt (Pos) ;
          }
          else
              string = "( Nothing Selected )" ;
          dc.TextOut (0, 20, string, string.GetLength ()) ;
      }


      void CMainWindow::OnQuit ()      // respond to menu item "Quit"
      {
          this->DestroyWindow () ;     // destroy main window,
      }                                // this stops application
```

Listings 18-19 to 18-22 show the remaining support files for CALLIST.CPP. Figure 18-11 shows the program's icon. Don't forget to use the large memory model when compiling CALLIST.CPP, and to include the LISTDLG.LIB import library in the project list so that the linker can find the function(s) in the DLL. If you have not already done so, you will need to create a large model runtime library for a Windows application (not DLL) using the MFC classes. See the section entitled *Creating New MFC Library Files* earlier in this chapter for instructions on how to do this. A typical command line to create a large model library for an application is

```
NMAKE MODEL=L TARGET=W DLL=0 DEBUG=0 CODEVIEW=0
```

This MS-DOS command line would create the LAFXCW.LIB library without debugging information. For debugging information use

```
NMAKE MODEL=L TARGET=W DLL=0 DEBUG=1 CODEVIEW=1
```

This will create the LAFXCWD.LIB library. PWB will pick the correct library file depending on which compiler memory model and debugging options you select.

Listing 18-19 CALLIST.HPP Header File

```
// callist.hpp    header file for callist.cpp

class CMainWindow : public CFrameWnd    // derive a main window class
{
public:
    CMainWindow () ;            // declare a constructor
private:
    void OnDialog () ;         // runs dialog box
    void OnQuit () ;           // stop application

    DECLARE_MESSAGE_MAP()      // prepare for message processing
} ;

class CTheApp : public CWinApp // derive an application class
{
public:
    BOOL InitInstance () ;     // declare new InitInstance()
} ;
```

Listing 18-20 CALLIST.H Resource ID Header File

```
// callist.h  header file for resource ID numbers

#define IDM_DIALOG          1        // menu item ID numbers
#define IDM_QUIT            2

#define S_PROGRAMCAPTION    1        // string table ID number
```

Listing 18-21 CALLIST.RC Resource Script File

```
// callist.rc  resource script file

#include <windows.h>
#include <afxres.h>
#include "callist.h"

AFX_IDI_STD_FRAME   ICON    callist.ico // the program's icon

MyMenu MENU                         // define the menu
{
    MENUITEM "&List Box",       IDM_DIALOG
    MENUITEM "&Quit",           IDM_QUIT
}

STRINGTABLE
{
    S_PROGRAMCAPTION    "Callist Program"
}
```

Figure 18-11 CALLIST.ICO Icon Image

Listing 18-22 CALLIST.DEF Module Definition File

```
NAME            callist
DESCRIPTION     'callist C++ program'
EXETYPE         WINDOWS
STUB            'WINSTUB.EXE'
CODE            PRELOAD MOVEABLE
DATA            PRELOAD MOVEABLE MULTIPLE
HEAPSIZE        1024
STACKSIZE       5120
```

SUMMARY

Dynamic link libraries are the basic building blocks of Windows. DLLs provide reusable code that can be shared by any number of applications at the same time. You can add to Windows by writing your own DLLs, which is an efficient way to keep utility functions for your own use in future projects. The MFC **CWinApp** class can be used as the basis for a DLL by deriving a new class from **CWinApp**. You will need to write an **InitInstance()** function for your derived class, which should return TRUE if no problems were encountered during initialization.

When a DLL is loaded into memory, it has its own data segment, but it uses the stack of any application that calls a function in the DLL. This separation of the segment containing the stack and data segment has several side effects. One is that DLLs will not behave properly if you attempt to use functions that assume the stack and data segments are the same. This is a common fault of compiler runtime library functions. Always use *far* pointers when writing DLLs so that the complete segment and offset values are passed for addresses. Another effect is that the static data stored in the data segment is common to every application that calls functions in the DLL. Avoid situations where one application calling the DLL changes a value in a static variable, which then affects the next application calling the DLL.

Memory blocks allocated within the DLL are owned by the application calling the DLL, not by the DLL itself. This causes memory blocks allocated by the DLL to be freed when the application that loaded the DLL is terminated. This is normally desirable behavior, but can cause problems if you allocate memory blocks in the **CWinApp::InitInstance()** function, and then expect the blocks to continue to exist after the application that loaded the DLL has terminated.

There are several ways for a Windows application to reference functions in a DLL. One way is to list the function names in the IMPORTS section of the application's module definition statement. You can either reference the function by name, or use the function's ordinal number. For larger collections of functions, it is best to create an import library. Import libraries are included in the linking process for creating a Windows application, and provide the linker with the DLL file name and function addresses for imported functions used by the application.

QUESTIONS

1. When you include a runtime library file in a C++ program, the entire contents of the runtime library are added to your program, even if you do not use all the functions in the runtime library. (True/False)

2. Each DLL has its own stack to store automatic variables. (True/False)

3. Static data in the DLL's data segment can be accessed by any application calling the DLL. (True/False)

4. The _____ virtual function in the **CWinApp** class is executed when the DLL is loaded into memory.

5. Resource data cannot be included with a DLL because DLLs do not have their own stack. (True/False)

6. The **CWinApp::InitInstance()** function:
   a. is declared as a virtual function in the **CWinApp** class
   b. must be defined for the class you derive from **CWinApp** for the DLL
   c. should return TRUE if no problems occurred during the execution of CWinApp::InitInstance()
   d. a, b, and c

7. The module definition file for a DLL uses the key word _____ in place of NAME.

8. The STACK statement in the module definition file for a DLL should be set to:
   a. 1024
   b. 5120
   c. the size should depend on the amount of data stored
   d. there is no STACK statement in the .DEF file for a DLL

9. The DATA statement for the module definition file of a DLL should contain the key word SINGLE in place of MULTIPLE. (True/False)

10. If a function in a DLL is declared FAR PASCAL, it does not need to use the _export key word or be listed in the EXPORTS section of the module definition file to be called by another application. (True/False)

EXERCISES

1. Modify the DLLCALL program so that the **StrRev()** function is imported from REVSTR.DLL using the ordinal number of the function.

2. Modify the DLLCALL program again, so the **StrRev()** function is imported from REVSTR.DLL using an import library.

ANSWERS TO QUESTIONS

1. False. Only the functions used by the program are loaded from the runtime library.

2. False. DLLs use the calling application(s) stack.

3. True.

4. **InitInstance()**.

5. False. Resource data can be included with a DLL. Resource data is not related to the stack in any way.

6. d.

7. LIBRARY.

8. d.

9. True.

10. False. Exported functions must either have _export defined right before the function name in the function declaration or be listed in the exports section of the DLL's module definition file. You can do both without causing an error.

SOLUTIONS TO EXERCISES

1. You must add an EXPORTS declaration to the REVSTR.DEF module definition file giving the **StrRev()** function an ordinal number. Listing 18-23 shows the modified REVSTR.DEF file, which equates **StrRev()** with ordinal number one.

The only change needed to DLLCALL is to modify the module definition file, replacing the **StrRev()** function name with its ordinal number (one). Listing 18-24 shows the modified module definition file, which uses the ordinal number.

The complete solution is given under the file names C18EXER1 and REVSTR1 on the source code disks.

Listing 18-23 Changes to REVSTR1.DEF Module Definition File

```
LIBRARY          revstr1
DESCRIPTION      'revstr1 C++ DLL'
EXETYPE          WINDOWS
STUB             'WINSTUB.EXE'
CODE             PRELOAD MOVEABLE DISCARDABLE
DATA             PRELOAD MOVEABLE SINGLE
HEAPSIZE         1024
EXPORTS          StrRev @1
```

Listing 18-24 Changes to DLLCALL.DEF Module Definition File

```
NAME             c18exer1
DESCRIPTION      'c18exer1 application'
EXETYPE          WINDOWS
STUB             'WINSTUB.EXE'
CODE             PRELOAD MOVEABLE
DATA             PRELOAD MOVEABLE MULTIPLE
HEAPSIZE         1024
STACKSIZE        5120
IMPORTS          StrRev = REVSTR1.1
```

2. If an import library is used, the application's module definition file does not need to include the IMPORTS statement, as shown in Listing 18-25.

You will need to create an import library from the REVSTR.DLL library using either the IMPLIB.EXE program, or by taking advantage of the PWB automatically calling IMPLIB.EXE when it creates a DLL. The import library will be named REVSTR.LIB, and will need to be included in the project file for the DLLCALL program. The complete program is included under the file name C18EXER2 on the source code disks.

Listing 18-25 Module Definition File

```
NAME            dllcall2
DESCRIPTION     'dllcall2 application'
EXETYPE         WINDOWS
STUB            'WINSTUB.EXE'
CODE            PRELOAD MOVEABLE
DATA            PRELOAD MOVEABLE MULTIPLE
HEAPSIZE        1024
STACKSIZE       5120
```

Windows NT

Microsoft's new version of Windows, called Windows NT, is a completely re-written operating system. Microsoft made every effort to make NT look as similar to Windows 3.1 as possible. The familiar Program Manager, Notepad, File Manager, and other applications look and function just like Windows 3.1. However, NT includes extensive built-in support for Local Area Networks (LANs) and other group-related activities, such as security checks, administrative control over system configuration, and many other features. NT is also more able to handle errant programs than Windows 3.1 due to the use of special features of the 80386 and 80486 chips.

From a programmer's point of view, Windows NT preserves essentially all of the Windows 3.1 API functions, but adds many new ones. C programmers converting Windows 3.1 programs to NT are required to make a few minor changes to the code to deal with low-level differences in the way NT stores message data and pointers. C++ programmers using the MFC classes have even less work to do. The MFC classes hide all of the differences between Windows 3.1 and Windows NT, allowing the same program to be compiled for either system. You still need to be aware of the differences between Windows NT and Windows 3.1 if you plan to write MFC-based programs that will be compiled for both operating systems. This chapter summarizes the underlying differences between the two operating systems.

WINDOWS NT—USER'S PERSPECTIVE

Although Windows NT looks just like Windows 3.1, users will notice differences. NT is designed with Local Area Networks (LANs) in mind. Besides built-in LAN support, NT includes security features that make it much easier for a LAN system administrator to support a group of linked computers. For example, each user has a password and security level. Most users will not be able to directly change their own configuration information—a welcome relief for administrators who had to keep up with all the ways the WIN.INI and SYSTEM.INI files can be corrupted in the Windows 3.1 environment.

NT does away with WIN.INI and SYSTEM.INI as text files, and replaces them with a system database on each computer. Typically, the system administrator will maintain the database for each user. NT tracks version information for applications, so the administrator can update all copies of an application via the LAN, and only update systems with older versions of the software. Low-level electronic mail support is also built into NT, which should provide for direct integration of mail into many NT applications.

Windows NT is considerably better protected against system crashes than previous versions of Windows. Earlier versions of Windows have been constrained by the limitations of the older 80286 CPU chips that Windows 3.1 continues to support. Windows NT was designed from scratch to take advantage of the memory protection features of the 80386 and higher CPUs. The result is that applications that attempt to write on another application's memory area are terminated gracefully without crashing the system. It is still possible to crash NT, but it is a lot more difficult. "Run away" applications can also be terminated, because NT interrupts applications to switch processing time between programs. Although Windows 3.1 did improve "crash resistance" compared with earlier versions, Windows 3.1 still relies on each program to share system resources with all others, and provides no protection if one application falls into an infinite loop and takes over the system.

Windows NT was designed to be ported to different types of computers. Besides the Intel 80386/80486 family, Windows NT runs on MIPS R4000 computers, which use a reduced instruction set (RISC) CPU. Additional CPUs are expected to be supported in the future. This opens the possibility of having a consistent platform for both users and developers across a wide range of computers.

Unlike Windows 3.1 which runs on top of MS-DOS, Windows NT is a self-contained operating system. All of the file access operations are built into NT, rather than relying on MS-DOS. An interesting offshoot of this change is that NT will support several different file systems. NT supports the MS-DOS disk format to provide compatibility with earlier versions of Windows. The MS-DOS format is known as "FAT" under NT, referring to the file allocation tables used in that system. NT will also support the NTFS (New Technology File System) on the 80x86 family of computers, which provides faster access speeds, file security features, and supports file names longer than the 8 + 3 character format used by MS-DOS. NTFS is designed for data-intensive applications, such as database programs and LAN database servers.

WINDOWS NT—PROGRAMMER'S VIEW

The biggest change from a programmer's point of view is that Windows NT is a 32-bit operating system. This means that every address is a 32-bit value, in place of the old segment/offset model used in Windows 3.1 and MS-DOS. You no longer need to think about NEAR and FAR addresses. Every address is 32 bits wide and can specify a location in a 2 gigabyte logical memory area. Artificial limitations, such as the 64K limit on a segment under Windows 3.1, also disappear with Windows NT. For all practical purposes, Windows NT allows you to allocate memory areas of any useful size.

The fact that NEAR and FAR addresses have no significance under Windows NT does not mean that you must go back into your code and purge every reference to *near* and *far* pointers. These declarations are simply ignored by the 32-bit compiler, which makes all pointers 32 bits wide. There is a slight performance penalty for this approach compared with carefully crafted code that optimizes the use of *near* and *far* pointers. However, for the vast majority of applications this performance penalty will not be noticed, and the simplicity of eliminating the distinction between different types of pointers will remove a longstanding source of programming errors.

Microsoft also preserved the distinction between an application's local data segment and the global heap. You can still call functions like **::LocalAlloc()** to allocate in the application's local heap, and **::GlobalAlloc()** to allocate in the global heap. The local heap is not limited to 64K and uses 32-bit pointers just like the global heap.

The 32-bit nature of Windows NT has more subtle effects. Integers and handles are 32-bit values under NT, but only 16-bit values under Windows 3.1. This does not cause any portability problems because int, UINT, and HANDLE are compiled to 32-bit quantities under Windows NT, and to 16-bit quantities under Windows 3.1. As long as your code does not make any assumptions about the size of a data type or object, the program will compile without error under either system. However, if you have gotten into some "bad" habits, such as declaring handles as WORD values instead of using HANDLE, your program will not compile properly under Windows NT. These errors are usually easy to find because the compiler will catch them as type mismatches. The more difficult errors to find typically involve improper uses of casts to convert one type to another.

Windows NT is a message-based operating system, just like Windows 3.1. The messages have the same ID values (for example, WM_CLOSE and WM_SIZE). C programmers must make slight adjustments to their code when porting a program to Windows NT because Windows NT organizes the memory block that holds the message data differently. NT does this to efficiently process 32-bit data, while Windows 3.1 is optimized around 16-bit data. The MFC classes hide these differences completely. If you use C++ and the MFC classes, the message processing functions are identical under both NT and Windows 3.1.

Windows NT includes the full set of GDI functions for text and graphics output. They work exactly like the Windows 3.1 equivalents. All of the file functions work the same way, regardless of which file system is in use. Microsoft included the multimedia extensions in Windows NT, as well as the common dialog boxes that are used in several examples in this book. In short, if you could do it under Window 3.1, you can do it with Windows NT.

UNIQUE FEATURES OF WINDOWS NT

If you are willing to give up compatibility with Windows 3.1, you can take advantage of unique features built into Windows NT that have no equivalent in earlier forms of Windows. These features are not supported by the MFC classes (for reasons of compatibility), so you will need to create your own classes to effectively use these new features with the C++ language.

Perhaps the most significant unique feature is the ability of one running application to have more than one "thread" of execution. This is a concept shared with the OS/2 operating system, and is potentially very useful for certain types of programs. To understand threads, it is helpful to first think about a Windows 3.1 session with several applications running. Windows has the ability to switch between the different programs in the same session. For example, if you have three copies of the Clock application running, all three will continue to advance. Windows diverts messages to each of the clocks as required to initiate actions (WM_TIMER messages to advance the clock). Each of the clock applications has equal access to the system.

Now consider an application that is very complex, and that needs to do some background calculations or database searches while the user continues to interact with the program window. You can do this type of activity under Windows 3.1 to a limited extent by taking advantage of the **CWinApp::OnIdle()** function that gets access to the system when nothing else is going on. However, if the system continues to be busy, **CWinApp::OnIdle()** will never get called, and background calculations will not take place.

Windows NT offers several improvements. The foundation behind these improvements is that NT does not rely solely upon applications giving up control to switch execution between running programs. NT actively interrupts programs and switches to other applications on a timed basis, even if one

application is in the middle of a calculation. The registers and memory values of the interrupted application are all preserved, so the switching does not affect the final outcome of the calculation. However, other applications will get "slices of time" during the execution of a long calculation. This is sometimes called "preemptive multitasking."

Windows NT also allows one application to have more than one "thread" of execution. A thread is like a program within a program. Each thread will receive its own "slice of time" as Windows NT switches between running programs. An application with several threads will receive more access to the CPU than an application with only a single thread. One thread can be used for processing input from the user, while a second thread looks up values in a database to fill in the screen. Windows NT also allows threads to have different priority values, with higher priority threads receiving more access to the CPU.

Another advanced feature supported by Windows NT is the ability for two or more applications to share a memory area. This is similar to having more than one program read and write from the same disk file, except that the data exists in memory. The word "pipes" is used to describe linking programs together using this mechanism. Pipes provide an alternative to the dynamic data exchange (DDE) mechanism supported in both Windows 3.1 and Windows NT. Pipes offer features not available via DDE, such as security levels, but at the cost of losing compatibility with Windows 3.1.

All of the memory features of Windows NT are supported by a virtual memory manager. Windows NT will write blocks of memory off to disk to make room in RAM. During installation, Windows NT will create a file called PAGEFILE.SYS on the root directory of the hard disk containing NT. This file is used as the temporary home for data copied from memory. A typical system running NT will have 16M of RAM memory, and a 20M PAGEFILE.SYS file, resulting in a "virtual" memory size of 36M. That is enough memory for even the most slug-like application.

COMPILING NT PROGRAMS

The final development tools were not available with the Windows NT Beta release. Microsoft had ported the Image Editor and Dialog Box Editor to NT. These applications are identical under NT and Windows 3.1. However, the conversion of the integrated development environment to Windows NT was not completed, so developers had to compile using the conventional tools of NMAKE files calling the compiler and linker directly. Listing A-1 shows a typical NMAKE file for compiling the MINIMAL3 program from Chapter 3, *First Programming Experiments*. Explaining all the nuances of NMAKE files is beyond the scope of this book, although there is a brief description in Appendix D, *Command Line Compilation*.

MINIMAL3.NT uses macro substitution to make the file a bit more readable. For example, the string "minimal3" is substituted anywhere in the listing that the macro $(target) is located because of the macro definition:

```
target = minimal3
```

The 32-bit C++ compiler, CL386, replaces the CL compiler used to compile Windows 3.1 programs. There is also a new linker named COFF and a new library manager named LIB. LIB manages both runtime and dynamic link libraries. In the Beta release, the RC resource compiler had not been finalized, and was not producing 32-bit aligned .RES data. This required that the CVTRES utility be used to convert the 16-bit .RES data into 32-bit aligned data appropriate for a Windows NT application. This portion of the compile/link cycle will be streamlined by the time of the commercial release. The Beta release also

Listing A-1 MINMAL3.NT Windows NT NMAKE File

```
# Windows NT NMAKE file for MINIMAL3
# assumes that the LIB environment variable is set to
# the subdirectory containing the compiler library files

target = minimal3
cflags = -c -G3d -W3 -Di386=1 -D_NTWIN -D_WINDOWS
cvars = -DWIN32 -DWINVER=0x030a -YuAFXWIN.H
guiflags = -subsystem:windows -entry:WinMainCRTStartup
mfclibs = \mstools\mfc\lib\nafxcw.lib \mstools\mfc\lib\libcxx.lib
guilibs = $(LIB)\libc.lib $(LIB)\ntdll.lib \
$(LIB)\kernel32.lib $(LIB)\user32.lib $(LIB)\gdi32.lib \
$(LIB)\comdlg32.lib $(LIB)\userrtl.lib

all: $(target).exe

$(target).obj: $(target).cpp $(target).hpp
    cl386 $(cflags) $(cvars) $(target).cpp

$(target).res: $(target).rc
    rc -r -fo $(target).tmp $(target).rc
    cvtres -$(CPU) $(target).tmp -o $(target).res
    del $(target).tmp

$(target).exe: $(target).obj $(target).def $(target).res
    coff -link $(guiflags) -out:$(target).exe $(target).obj \
    $(target).res $(mfclibs) $(guilibs)
```

required that a long list of library file names be passed to the linker. This list will probably be shortened by combining many of the libraries.

Module definition files continue to be used in the Windows NT compile/link cycle. The STUB and EXETYPE statements are not needed under NT, and are just ignored if present (for compatibility with Windows 3.1 files where they are required). Including a VERSION statement in the .DEF file is highly recommended so each program has an embedded version number as a basis for future updates. If you leave out a VERSION statement in the program's .DEF file, the version number 0.0 will be embedded in the file by default.

Prior to running the compiler, several environment variables are set using a batch file named SETENV.BAT (Listing A-2). The LIB and CPU environment variables are inserted by the NMAKE utility as it reads the NMAKE file.

The MINMAL3 program is created by simply executing the NMAKE command:

```
NMAKE /F MINIMAL3.NT
```

COMPATIBILITY

The only compatibility problems that showed up in testing the examples in this book under Windows NT involved the **AfxRegisterWindowClass()** function. Under Windows 3.1, you can use a shortcut notation to pass the ID value for a stock brush to this function. For example, a typical call to **AfxRegisterWindowClass()** under Windows 3.1 is shown here:

```
ClassName = AfxRegisterWndClass (CS_HREDRAW | CS_VREDRAW,
    AfxGetApp()->LoadStandardCursor (IDC_ARROW),
    LTGRAY_BRUSH + 1 ,
    AfxGetApp()->LoadStandardIcon (IDI_APPLICATION) ) ;
```

The shortcut LTGRAY_BRUSH + 1 results in the window class using the stock light gray brush for painting the client area. This usage generates an error under Windows NT because the compiler expects a handle to a brush as the third

Listing A1-2 SETENV.BAT

```
set path=d:\mstools\bin;%path%
set lib=d:\mstools\lib
set
include=d:\mstools\mfc\include;d:\mstools\h\strict;d:\mstools\h;
set cpu=i386
```

parameter. However, it is a simple matter to use the global function **::GetStockObject()** to fetch a handle to any stock object, as shown here:

```
ClassName = AfxRegisterWndClass (CS_HREDRAW | CS_VREDRAW,
    AfxGetApp()->LoadStandardCursor (IDC_ARROW),
    ::GetStockObject (LTGRAY_BRUSH) ,
    AfxGetApp()->LoadStandardIcon (IDI_APPLICATION) ) ;
```

The Beta release of Windows NT did not support creation of dynamic link libraries (DLLs) using the MFC classes, so the examples in Chapter 18, *Dynamic Link Libraries,* could not be tested under Windows NT. DLL support is expected in the release version.

FINAL COMMENTS

Microsoft has met its objective of making the MFC classes work for both Windows 3.1 and Windows NT applications. Moving an application written with the MFC classes from one environment to the other requires only setting up the compiler and linker. The source code itself is not affected.

Virtual
Key Codes

These values are passed with the WM_KEYDOWN and WM_KEYUP messages to the **CWnd::OnKeyDown()** and **CWnd::OnKeyUp()** message response functions.

Virtual Key Code	Value (HEX)	Meaning
A–Z	0x41–0x5A	The virtual key code for the letters is the same as the ANSI code. Use the uppercase letter in single quotes for the virtual key code ('A').
0–9 (at keyboard top)	0x30–0x39	The virtual key code for the digit keys at the top of the keyboard is the same as the ANSI code. Use the digit in single quotes for the virtual key code ('1').
VK_ACCEPT	0x1E	Kanji only (Japanese characters)
VK_ADD	0x6B	Plus key
VK_BACK	0x08	[BACKSPACE]
VK_CANCEL	0x03	[CONTROL]-[BREAK]
VK_CAPITAL	0x14	[SHIFT LOCK]
VK_CLEAR	0x0C	Clear key (Numeric keypad 5)
VK_CONTROL	0x11	[CONTROL]
VK_CONVERT	0x1C	Kanji only (Japanese characters)
VK_DECIMAL	0x6E	Decimal point
VK_DELETE	0x2E	[DELETE]
VK_DIVIDE	0x6F	Divide (/) key
VK_DOWN	0x28	[↓] (down arrow)
VK_END	0x23	[END]

continued on next page

continued from previous page

Virtual Key Code	Value (HEX)	Meaning
VK_ESCAPE	0x1B	(ESC) (Escape)
VK_EXECUTE	0x2B	Execute key (if any)
VK_F1	0x70	Function keys
VK_F2	0x71	
VK_F3	0x72	
VK_F4	0x73	
VK_F5	0x74	
VK_F6	0x75	
VK_F7	0x76	
VK_F8	0x77	
VK_F9	0x78	
VK_F10	0x79	
VK_F11	0x7A	Enhanced keyboard only
VK_F12	0x7B	Enhanced keyboard only
VK_F13	0x7C	Specialized keyboards only
VK_F14	0x7D	Specialized keyboards only
VK_F15	0x7E	Specialized keyboards only
VK_F16	0x7F	Specialized keyboards only
VK_HIRAGANA	0x18	Kanji only (Japanese characters)
VK_HOME	0x24	(HOME)
VK_INSERT	0x2D	(INS) (Insert)
VK_KANA	0x15	Kanji only (Japanese characters)
VK_KANJI	0x19	Kanji only (Japanese characters)
VK_LBUTTON	0x01	Left mouse button
VK_LEFT	0x25	(←) (left arrow)
VK_MBUTTON	0x04	Middle mouse button
VK_MENU	0x12	Menu key (if any)
VK_MODECHANGE	0x1F	Kanji only (Japanese characters)
VK_MULTIPLY	0x6A	Multiply key

continued on next page

B

VIRTUAL
KEY CODES

continued from previous page

Virtual Key Code	Value (HEX)	Meaning
VK_NEXT	0x22	Next
VK_NONCONVERT	0x1D	Kanji only (Japanese characters)
VK_NUMLOCK	0x90	(NUM LOCK)
VK_NUMPAD0	0x60	The numeric keypad keys
VK_NUMPAD1	0x61	
VK_NUMPAD2	0x62	
VK_NUMPAD3	0x63	
VK_NUMPAD4	0x64	
VK_NUMPAD5	0x65	
VK_NUMPAD6	0x66	
VK_NUMPAD7	0x67	
VK_NUMPAD8	0x68	
VK_NUMPAD9	0x69	
VK_PAUSE	0x13	(PAUSE)
VK_PRINT	0x2A	(PRINT SCREEN) (Windows versions below 3.0)
VK_PRIOR	0x21	(PGUP) (page up)
VK_RBUTTON	0x02	Right mouse button
VK_RETURN	0x0D	(RETURN)
VK_RIGHT	0x27	(→) (right arrow)
VK_ROMAJI	0x16	Kanji only (Japanese characters)
VK_SELECT	0x29	Select key (if any)
VK_SEPARATOR	0x6C	Separator key (if any)
VK_SHIFT	0x10	(SHIFT)
VK_SNAPSHOT	0x2C	(PRINT SCREEN) (Windows 3.0 and later)
VK_SPACE	0x20	Space bar
VK_SUBTRACT	0x6D	Subtract key
VK_TAB	0x09	(TAB)
VK_UP	0x26	(↑) (up arrow)
VK_ZENKAKU	0x17	Kanji only (Japanese characters)

Mouse Hit Test Codes

The mouse hit test codes are transmitted with Windows messages that are sent to a program when the mouse cursor is over a nonclient portion of a window, such as the border or caption area. Normally, processing nonclient area messages is left to the built-in Windows logic, which performs the familiar activities of moving and resizing windows, highlighting menu selections, and so on. However, Windows provides the flexibility for a program to process these messages for itself, overriding the default behaviors.

Mouse hit test codes are used to encode which portion of the nonclient area of a window is beneath the mouse. In an MFC class-based program, these codes are processed by the message processing functions shown in Table C-1.

Message	Message Processing Function
WM_MOUSEACTIVATE	OnMouseActivate(),
WM_NCHITTEST	OnNcHitTest(),
WM_NCLBUTTONDBLCLK	OnNcLButtonDblClk(),
WM_NCLBUTTONDOWN	OnNcLButtonDown(),
WM_NCLBUTTONUP	OnNcLButtonUp(),
WM_NCMBUTTONDBLCLK	OnNcMButtonDblClk(),
WM_NCMBUTTONDOWN	OnNcMButtonDown(),
WM_NCMBUTTONUP	OnNcMButtonUp(),
WM_NCMOUSEMOVE	OnNcMouseMove(),
WM_NCPAINT	OnNcPaint(),
WM_NCRBUTTONDBLCLK	OnNcRButtonDblClk(),

Table C-1 Message Processing Functions Using Mouse Hit Test Codes

continued on next page

continued from previous page

Message	Message Processing Function
WM_NCRBUTTONDOWN	OnNcRButtonDown(),
WM_NCRBUTTONUP	OnNcRButtonUp(),
WM_SETCURSOR	OnSetCursor()

Table C-1 Message Processing Functions Using Mouse Hit Test Codes

Table C-2 lists all of the mouse hit test codes. A hit test value is passed as the *nHitTest* parameter in all of the message processing functions.

Code	Numeric Value	Code	Numeric Value
HTERROR	(-2)	HTLEFT	10
HTTRANSPARENT	(-1)	HTRIGHT	11
HTNOWHERE	0	HTTOP	12
HTCLIENT	1	HTTOPLEFT	13
HTCAPTION	2	HTTOPRIGHT	14
HTSYSMENU	3	HTBOTTOM	15
HTGROWBOX	4	HTBOTTOMLEFT	16
HTSIZE	HTGROWBOX	HTBOTTOMRIGHT	17
HTMENU	5	HTSIZEFIRST	HTLEFT
HTHSCROLL	6	HTSIZELAST	HTBOTTOMRIGHT
HTVSCROLL	7		
HTREDUCE	8		
HTZOOM	9		

Table C-2 Mouse Hit Test Codes

Command Line Compilation

Throughout this book, the assumption has been that you are using the Microsoft Programmer's Workbench for all compilations. PWB is a convenient tool because it automates many of the mundane details of creating a Windows program. However, you may prefer to use another editor to write and edit program files. In this case, you will probably find it more convenient to compile from the MS-DOS command line, rather than using PWB strictly for compilation.

Microsoft supplies the NMAKE utility to help automate the compile/link cycle from the MS-DOS command line. The idea is that you build a short file that describes which files need to be compiled and linked. The NMAKE utility reads this file and then looks at the date and time of each of the files. Any files that have been edited will have a more recent date and time than the output of the compiler. The NMAKE utility then executes the appropriate commands to update the files using the compiler and linker.

Listing D-1 shows a simple file that the NMAKE utility reads in order to update the MINIMAL3 program in Chapter 3, *First Programming Experiments*. All you would need do to compile/link the MINIMAL3 program would be to type:

```
NMAKE /F MINIMAL3.NMK
```

from the MS-DOS command line. The NMAKE utility will read the MINIMAL3.NMK file, decide which files need updating, and do all the appropriate steps to create an updated MINIMAL3.EXE program file.

The first line in Listing D-1 starting with a # character is just a comment. Any text following a # character on a line is a comment. The first line that does anything is

```
minimal3.exe : minimal3.obj minimal3.def minimal3.res
```

This line tells NMAKE to compare the file date/times of MINIMAL3.EXE with those of the three files listed to the right of the colon. If any of the files to the right of the colon is newer than MINIMAL3.EXE then MINIMAL3.EXE needs to

Listing D-1 MINIMAL3.NMK NMAKE File

```
# minimal3.nmk  Microsoft C++ NMAKE file for minimal3

minimal3.exe : minimal3.obj minimal3.def minimal3.res
    link /NOD minimal3, ,NUL,libw slibcew safxcw, minimal3.def;
    rc minimal3.res minimal3.exe

minimal3.res : minimal3.rc minimal3.h
    rc -r minimal3.rc

minimal3.obj : minimal3.cpp minimal3.hpp
    cl /f /c /Zi /Od /W3 /G2 /AS minimal3.cpp
```

be updated. The file to the left of the colon is called the "target file" and the file or files to the right of the colon are called the "dependent files."

If NMAKE finds that MINIMAL3.EXE needs to be updated, NMAKE executes any indented lines following the comparison line. In this case, the linker (LINK.EXE) and the resource compiler (RC.EXE) are both run to update MINIMAL3.EXE. The link command line is rather long because you need to spell out the names of all of the library files that are used to create the finished .EXE program. Refer to Chapter 18, *Dynamic Link Libraries*, for a description of the contents of these library files.

Similar comparisons are done in Listing D-1 to determine if the program's resources need to be compiled. If MINIMAL3.RES is older than MINIMAL3.RC or MINIMAL3.H, MINIMAL3.RC should be recompiled using the resource compiler. The -r switch tells RC.EXE to just compile the resources, and not to add them to the finished .EXE program yet. The previous call to RC.EXE under the linking step adds the MINIMAL3.RES resource data to the finished .EXE program.

If MINIMAL3.OBJ needs updating, the C++ compiler (CL.EXE) is run to recompile MINIMAL3.CPP. The compiler takes a number of command line switch settings that are summarized in Table D-1.

The linker also uses command line switches. Normally, only the /NOD switch, which specifies that the linker should not search the default libraries for functions, is used. This is important for Windows applications, otherwise the linker will run into multiple copies of a number of low-level functions. If you are planning to debug the application with CodeView for Windows, you will also need to use the /COD switch, which tells the linker to add debugging information to the program.

One of the interesting things about the NMAKE utility is that it can figure out the chain of dependent files in an NMAKE file. It does not matter if you put the linking step ahead of the compilation step. NMAKE will detect that

Switch	Meaning
/f	Fast compile.
/c	Compile only—do not invoke linker yet.
/Od	Do not optimize (saves compile time during development).
/Zi	Adds line numbers to the object file—ready for debugging.
/W3	Warning level 3 (lots of messages).
/G2	Use 80286 instructions.
/AS	Use small memory model.
/YcAFXWIN.H	Create the AFXWIN.PCH pre-compiled header file.
/YuAFXWIN.H	Use the AFXWIN.PCH pre-compiled header file created previously using the /YcAFXWIN.H command line option.

Table D-1 C++ Compiler Switches

MINIMAL3.OBJ must be created before MINIMAL3.EXE can be updated and proceed accordingly.

Advanced NMAKE Files

To compile efficiently using the MFC classes requires you to take advantage of pre-compiled header files. This keeps the compiler from needing to go through the entire AFXWIN.H header file each time you compile. You can take advantage of another feature of the NMAKE utility to allow the same NMAKE file to cover both the creation of the pre-compiled header file and later use of that file. Listing D-2 shows a more advanced NMAKE file for MINIMAL3 that uses the *if*, *else*, and *endif* conditional switches to turn different parts of the NMAKE file on and off.

The MINIMAL3.NMK file detects whether the flags DEBUG and/or MAKEPCH are set equal to one. For example, for the first compilation you will need to create the AFXWIN.PCH pre-compiled header file:

```
NMAKE /F MINMAL3.NMK MAKEPCH=1
```

This NMAKE command line sets the MAKEPCH flag equal to one, so the portion of the MINIMAL3.NMK file including the compiler switch /YcAFXWIN.H is executed. This tells the compiler to create the pre-compiled header file. Later you could compile quickly using the pre-compiled header:

```
NMAKE /F MINIMAL3.NMK
```

Listing D-2 MINIMAL3.NMK Complete NMAKE File

```
# minimal3.nmk  Microsoft C++ NMAKE file for minimal3
# execute with: nmake \f minimal3.nmk MAKEPCH=1 first to make
#   pre-compiled header file AFXWIN.PCH, then drop flag or use
#   MAKEPCH=0 for fast  compilation.  Default is fast compile using
#   a PCH header file.  execute with: nmake \f minimal3.nmk DEBUG=1
#   to prepare for codeview for Windows debugging

!if "$(DEBUG)"=="1"         # add symolic data to exe for cvw
minimal3.exe : minimal3.obj minimal3.def minimal3.res
    link /NOD /COD minimal3, , ,libw slibcew safxcw, minimal3.def;
    rc minimal3.res minimal3.exe
!else                       # faster compile if no codeview data
minimal3.exe : minimal3.obj minimal3.def minimal3.res
    link /NOD minimal3, ,NUL,libw slibcew safxcw, minimal3.def;
    rc minimal3.res minimal3.exe
!endif

minimal3.res : minimal3.rc minimal3.h
    rc -r minimal3.rc

!if "$(MAKEPCH)"=="1"       # make pre-compiled header for afxwin.h
minimal3.obj : minimal3.cpp minimal3.hpp
    cl /f /c /Zi /Od /W3 /G2 /AS /YcAFXWIN.H minimal3.cpp
!else                       # use pre-compiled header
minimal3.obj : minimal3.cpp minimal3.hpp
    cl /f /c /Zi /Od /W3 /G2 /AS /YuAFXWIN.H minimal3.cpp
!endif
```

You can also take advantage of the DEBUG switch to prepare the MINIMAL3.EXE program for debugging:

```
NMAKE /F MINIMAL3.NMK DEBUG=1
```

You can get much more advanced than these NMAKE files using the NMAKE macro language features. However, for the simple programs in this book the conditional features are all you will need.

Compiling a DLL

One last file to examine is the NMAKE file that compiles LISTDLG.DLL from Chapter 18, *Dynamic Link Libraries*. The library names and compiler options used when compiling a DLL are slightly different than those for a Windows application. Listing D-3 shows the LISTDLG.NMK NMAKE file.

The source code disks include NMAKE files for every program in the book. The NMAKE files use the extension .NMK to differentiate them from the .MAK files created by PWB. Actually, PWB uses the NMAKE utility to do all compilations. If

Listing D-3 LISTDLG.NMK NMAKE File

```
# nmake file for listdlg.dll
# execute with: nmake \f callist.nmk MAKEPCH=1 first to make
#   pre-compiled header file STRSTREA.PCH, then drop flag or use
#   MAKEPCH=0 for fast  compilation.  Default is fast compile using
#   a PCH header file.  execute with: nmake \f callist.nmk DEBUG=1
#   to prepare for codeview for Windows debugging.

!if "$(DEBUG)"=="1"         # add symolic data to exe for cvw
listdlg.dll : listdlg.obj listdlg.def listdlg.res listdlg.def
    link /NOD /COD /MAP listdlg, listdlg.dll, nul, \
        lafxdw libw ldllcew, listdlg.def
    rc listdlg.res listdlg.dll
    implib listdlg.lib listdlg.dll
!else                       # faster compile if no codeview data
listdlg.dll : listdlg.obj listdlg.def listdlg.res listdlg.def
    link /NOD listdlg, listdlg.dll, nul, \
        lafxdw libw ldllcew, listdlg.def
    rc listdlg.res listdlg.dll
    implib listdlg.lib listdlg.dll
!endif

listdlg.res : listdlg.rc
    rc -r listdlg.rc

!if "$(MAKEPCH)"=="1"       # make pre-compiled header for afxwin.h
listdlg.obj : listdlg.cpp listdlg.hpp
    cl /f /c /Zi /Od /W3 /GD /G2 /ALw /YcAFXWIN.H listdlg.cpp
!else                       # use pre-compiled header
listdlg.obj : listdlg.cpp listdlg.hpp
    cl /f /c /Zi /Od /W3 /GD /G2 /ALw /YuAFXWIN.H listdlg.cpp
!endif
```

you examine the .MAK files created by PWB, you will get an idea of just how complex NMAKE files can become. PWB makes full use of the NMAKE macro language.

Bibliography

BOOKS ON C++

For a readable introduction to the C++ langauge:

> *Object Oriented Programming With Microsoft C++*
> Robert Lafore
> The Waite Group Press, 1992

The standard reference for C++ was written by Bjarne Stroustrup. This book is best used as a complete description of the language, not as a tutorial.

> *The C++ Programming Language*
> Bjarne Stroustrup
> Addison-Wesley, 1987

For an interactive, disk-based tutorial that takes you step by step through the C++ language and monitors your progress:

> *Master C++*
> Rex Woolworth, Robert Lafore, and Harry Henderson
> Waite Group Press, 1992

James O. Coplien's book covers advanced features of the C++ language, and how they can be applied to common programming problems. This book is appropriate once you have mastered the basics of C++ and want to improve the style and efficiency of your programming.

> *Advanced C++, Programming Styles and Idioms*
> James O. Coplien
> AT&T Bell Telephone Laboratories Inc, 1992

BOOKS ON WINDOWS

Most books on Windows assume that you are using the C language, not C++. Nevertheless, the documentation of Windows functions is useful to C++

programmers because all Windows functions are available as global functions within your C++ program. *The Waite Group's Windows API Bible* is organized by subject, with example code in C for every function.

> *The Waite Group's Windows API Bible*
> Jim Conger
> The Waite Group Press, 1992

Charles Petzold wrote the classic book on Windows programming using the C language. This book covers all of the basics, and several more advanced topics which are not covered in *Microsoft Foundation Class Programming*.

> *Programming Windows 3.1*
> Charles Petzold
> Microsoft Press, 1992

Jeffrey Richter's book covers advanced Windows programming techniques, including dynamic dialog boxes, custom controls, printer setup, and program installation.

> *Windows 3: A Developer's Guide*
> Jeffrey M. Richter
> M&T Books, 1991

ARTICLES

Adapt Your Program for Worldwide Use With Windows Internationalization Support, William S. Hall, Microsoft Systems Journal, Nov.–Dec. 91, Vol. 6, No. 6.

Screen Capturing for Windows 3.0, Jim Conger, Dr. Dobb's Journal, February 1991, No. 173.

Subclassing Applications, Mike Klein, Dr. Dobb's Journal, December 1991, No. 183.

Undocumented Functions in Windows, Part1, Part2, Andrew Schulman, PC Magazine, January 28, 1992, February 11, 1992.

Glossary

Accelerators • Keyboard accelerators provide key combinations that will generate a WM_COMMAND message with a specified ID value for the keys depressed. This is a quick way to add keyboard functionality to a program.

Alignment • See Text Alignment.

Allocate • To set aside a block of memory for use by the program.

API • Application Programming Interface. The collection of functions and messages that allows the programmer to create new Windows applications using the built-in features of Windows.

Application • A program that can be executed (run) under Windows.

Automatic Variables • Variables that are declared within the body of a function, without the "static" prefix. Automatic variables use the program's stack, so the data is lost as soon as the function terminates.

Batch File • An ASCII text file with the file name extension ".BAT." Used to execute a series of MS-DOS commands in sequence.

Binary Flags • Coded on/off values that are stored together in a single variable. Each bit specifies a different on/off condition. The values are combined using binary operators such as |, &, and ^.

Bitmap • A picture image consisting of each dot (pixel) of the image. Windows supports two bitmap formats, the old device dependent bitmap (DDB) and the newer device independent bitmap (DIB).

Caption • The title area at the top of a parent, child, or pop-up window.

Child Window • A window that is created with the WS_CHILD style. Child windows are only visible inside the client area of their parent. Child windows can be the parents of other, lower level child windows.

Class • (See also window class) A C++ class is a collection of functions and data in a single object. The members of the class can be private to the class, public (accessible outside of the class definition), or protected (providing limited access to other classes). Classes are the basis for *object-oriented* programming using C++.

Client Area • The center part of a window. This is where drawing activities take place.

Clipboard • A memory area maintained by Windows to allow different applications to exchange data. Usually the data is exchanged as part of cut-and-paste operations.

Compiler • A program that reads a text file containing the program statements, and creates an object file (".OBJ" file extension). The object file contains the low-level computer instructions, but the memory addresses are not set until the object file is linked with a linker.

Constructor • All C++ classes have a constructor function. The constructor function is called when an object of the class is created. Constructor functions provide a place to do initialization activities. The compiler will generate a default constructor function if none is defined for the class.

Cursor • The small image (usually an arrow) that moves on the screen when the mouse is moved.

DDB • Device dependent bitmap. This is the "old" bitmap format that encodes the color value of each pixel (dot) of an image. The color palette used to create the bitmap is not included with the data, so different colors may be displayed if the DDB is displayed on different devices.

DDE • Dynamic Data Exchange. Windows applications can exchange data in memory by sending each other messages. The DDE protocol describes a standard set of messages for data exchange.

Declaration • Functions are declared using a prototype called a "function declaration." The prototype informs the compiler which data types are passed as parameters, and specifies each function's returned data type. This allows the compiler to check that the correct data types are passed to functions as parameters, and the values returned when the function returns.

Delayed Rendering • A clipboard technique where the data is not loaded into the Clipboard unless an application requests the data.

Destructor • When a C++ class object is destroyed, the class destructor function is called. Destructor functions provide a place to do cleanup activities, such as freeing memory used by the class object.

Device Context • Windows programs output text and graphics data to a logical device, called the Device Context or DC. Windows then does the conversion from the DC to a real device, such as a video screen or printer.

Device Units • The physical system of units used by the device, such as pixels for a video screen, or dots for a laser or dot matrix printer.

DIB • Device independent bitmap. This is a bitmap data format that encodes both the pixel data and the color palette used to create the picture.

DISCARDABLE • Program code or data that can be purged from memory when Windows needs more room. DISCARDABLE blocks are always moveable.

DLL • Dynamic Link Library. DLLs contain common functions that are used by more than one application program. The Windows functions reside in DLLs, and you can create your own DLLs to add other functions that can be called by any number of applications in the same Windows session.

Driver • A program (actually a DLL) that converts Windows function calls to machine instructions that a particular device will understand. Windows uses drivers to interpret information from the mouse, control the speaker or sound device, control printers, and so on.

Far address • An address that uses both the segment and offset value, suitable for specifying an address in the global heap, outside of the program's local memory heap.

Fixed • Code or data that cannot be moved in memory. Fixed blocks get in the way of Windows' ability to optimize memory, so MOVEABLE and DISCARDABLE blocks are used whenever possible.

Flags • See Binary Flags.

Focus • The window with the focus is highlighted, and receives keyboard input. Normally, the user changes the window with the focus by clicking a window with the mouse. The **CWnd::SetFocus()** function can also be used to change which window has the focus.

Font • A letter typeface. Font data defines the shape of each letter of a character set.

Global Heap • The memory area outside of any program's code or data. This is the free memory space that a program can access with **::GlobalAlloc()**. This area requires *far* pointers to specify an address.

Global Variable • A variable declared outside of the body of any function. These variables can be referenced within any function following the declaration of the variable's type and name in the source code file.

GUI • Graphical User Interface. Windows' appearance to the user is based on GUI concepts. It is graphical, as all of the screen is drawn in graphics mode, not in a video character mode.

Heap • Memory available to the program. Under Windows, programs can access a local data segment, containing the "local heap," and unused memory outside of any program or data, called the "global heap."

Import Library • A file that contains the addresses of exported functions in one or more DLLs. Import libraries are included in the linking step when creating a program that calls functions in a DLL.

Input Focus • See Focus.

Instance • Windows allows several copies of the same application program to be run at the same time. Each running copy is given a unique ID value called the *program instance*.

Keyboard Accelerators • See Accelerators

Linker • A program that reads both objective files and runtime library files and creates an executable program.

LOADONCALL • Data or program code that is not loaded into memory when the program starts, but is only loaded when needed by the program.

Local Variable • A variable declared within the body of a function, and not preceded by the word "static." Local variables (sometimes called "automatic" variables) use the program's stack. The variable can only be used within the body of the function. The variable's value will not be saved after the function returns.

Locked Memory Block • A locked block cannot be moved in memory. Programs call **::LocalLock()** and **::GlobalLock()** to lock blocks before the data is accessed, and then unlock the blocks using **::LocalUnlock()** and **::GlobalUnlock()** when done, so the blocks can be again moved in memory.

Logical Font • A font interpolated from existing font data to create a size or style that is not exactly specified in the font data. The **CFont::CreateFont()** function creates logical fonts.

Logical Units • The system of units used to specify a location on the screen or another device that uses a mapping mode other than MM_TEXT. Typical logical units are MM_LOMETRIC with each unit equal to 0.1mm, and MM_LOENGLISH with each unit equal to 0.1 inch.

Make Program • A compiler utility (such as Microsoft's NMAKE) that helps automate the running of the compiler and linker tools to create finished programs.

Mapping Mode • The system of units used by a device context to convert from a logical X,Y position to a physical location on the device.

Memory Device Context • A device context that is not tied to a physical device, such as the screen or printer. Memory device contexts are used to convert bitmap data to a format that can be displayed on a physical device.

Message • An 18-byte chunk of data sent from the Windows environment to an application program. Windows messages typically notify the application program of some action, such as the user pressing a key or using the mouse. Different applications can also exchange messages. See DDE.

Module • An executable program in memory. This includes both application programs and DLLs.

Moveable • Code or data that can be moved in memory if Windows needs to make room for other objects. The opposite of moveable is fixed.

Near Address • An address within a single data segment. Data stored in the program's local data segment, such as static variables, variables on the stack (automatic variables), and blocks allocated with **LocalAlloc()**, all use near addresses.

Offset • The 80x86 family of microprocessors use what is known as "segmented" addressing. Each location in memory is defined by a combination of a segment and an offset. Locations within one segment can be specified with only the offset value. These locations are called "near" addresses. Locations that occupy more than one segment are called "far" memory addresses, and require both the segment and offset to be specified.

OLE • Object Linking and Embedding. OLE documents allow the user to activate the editor that created a graph, text, or other image by simply double-clicking the portion to be edited. This "object-oriented" behavior is formalized in Microsoft's Windows 3.1 documentation.

Origin • The 0,0 point for a coordinate system. The default origin for a device context is the upper left corner.

Overloaded Function • In C++, a function with the same name can be defined more than once if the list of parameters for each function declaration is different.

Owned Window • A window that has the *hWndParent* parameter set to another window's handle when **CWnd::Create()** is called to create the owned window. Owned windows are either child windows or pop-up windows. The owner of an owned window is the parent window.

Parent Window • A window that has one or more child windows. The child windows will be automatically redrawn if the parent is redrawn. Child windows are only visible if they are within the client area of their parent's window.

Pixel • One dot on an image. Pixel usually refers to a dot on a computer screen, although it can apply to any graphics device that has dot (raster) output.

Pointer • A variable that contains the address of another object in memory. For example, the declaration "char * cp" creates the pointer *cp* that will hold the address of another memory location that contains character data.

Pop-Up Window • A window that is owned by the parent window and has the WS_POPUP flag set when **CWnd::Create()** is called. Pop-up windows disappear when the top-level window that owns them is minimized or terminated. Otherwise, pop-up windows behave independently from the window that owns them, and are visible outside of the owner's client area.

Preload • Data or program code that is loaded into memory when the program starts.

Printer Driver • See Driver.

Private • A private member of a C++ class can only be accessed from within the class definition. Private functions and data members are used to manipulate data that external parts of the program do not need to see. This is sometimes called "data hiding" when applied to data members.

Protected • Protected members of a C++ class are only available within the class and to other classes derived from the class. This is an intermediate level of protection between *public* and *private*.

Pseudo Code • A technique of writing a program outline without using the details of a specific computer language. This is done during the design of a program to think through the overall structure of the program before any detailed coding is done.

Public • Public functions and data members of a C++ class can be accessed from ouside of a class definition. These members are sometimes called the "class interface."

Rendering • See Delayed Rendering.

Resource • Static data that is included with the application program. Resource data typically includes icons, menus, strings, and bitmaps. This data does not change as the program is executed.

Resource Compiler • A program that combines the resource data with the application program to make a finished Windows application.

SDK • The Microsoft Windows Software Development Kit. This contains the Windows resource compiler, CodeView for Windows debugger, other development tools, and full documentation of all Windows messages and functions. The SDK is now bundled with the Microsoft C++ 7.0 package.

Segment • The 80x86 family of microprocessors uses what is known as "segmented" addressing. Each location in memory is defined by a combination of a segment and an offset. Locations within one segment can be specified with only the offset value. These

are called "near" addresses. Locations that occupy more than one segment are called "far" memory addresses and require both the segment and offset to be specified.

Sibling Windows • If a parent has more than one child window, the child windows are siblings.

Static Data • Data in a program that does not change as the program is executed. Windows programs usually store static data as resource data.

Static Variable • A variable declared within the body of a function and preceded by the word "static." Static variables only have meaning within the body of a function, but retain their value between calls to the function. They are stored in the program's local heap, not on the program's stack. Static variables are typically used within functions to save variables that need to be "remembered" between calls to the function.

System • The running Windows environment. This includes all of the running application programs.

Termination • A program is terminated when the program finishes executing and returns control to the Windows environment. Windows removes the terminated program from memory.

Text Alignment • Used to specify the location of the string on the device context. The default alignment places text at a location based on the upper left corner of the first character of the string.

Top-Level Window • The main application window for the program. Top-level windows are never children of other windows.

Viewport • The logical area on the screen or device for which a single device context operates.

Window Class • Before a window can be created, the window's class definition is registered with the Windows environment using the **AfxRegisterWndClass()** function. This sets a number of basic parameters for all windows created from the class. Control classes, such as BUTTON and LISTBOX are predefined, and do not need to be registered. Window classes are not related to C++ classes.

Index

continued

continued

continued

continued

continued

continued

continued

Books have a substantial influence on the destruction of the forests of the Earth. For example, it takes 17 trees to produce one ton of paper. A first printing of 30,000 copies of a typical 480-page book consumes 108,000 pounds of paper which will require 918 trees!

Waite Group Press™ is against the clear-cutting of forests and supports reforestation of the Pacific Northwest of the United States and Canada, where most of this paper comes from. As a publisher with several hundred thousand books sold each year, we feel an obligation to give back to the planet. We will, therefore, support and contribute a percentage of our proceeds to organizations which seek to preserve the forests of planet Earth.

WINDOWS API BIBLE:

The Definitive Programmer's Reference

Jim Conger

A single, comprehensive, easy-to-use reference with examples for the over-800 Windows Application Programming Interface (API) functions. Like all Waite Group bibles, API functions are organized into categories, preceded by lucid tutorials, and feature Windows version compatibility boxes.

Available Now, ISBN 1-878739-15-8, 1,014 pages

$39.95 US/$55.95 Canada

WINDOWS PROGRAMMING PRIMER PLUS

Jim Conger

The friendliest entry-level book for Windows programmers. It flattens the Windows learning curve, keeping the programs small while gradually stepping up the pace. Requires some familiarity with the C language. Both Microsoft and Borland programming tools are demonstrated in 80 example programs that are easy to follow and to the point. Coverage is also provided for the Windows Software Development Kit and Borland C++.

Available Now, ISBN 1-878739-21-2, 714 pages, companion disk available

$29.95 US/$41.95 Canada

OBJECT WINDOWS HOW-TO

Gary Syck

The easy-access question and answer problem-solving guide to Borland's ObjectWindows Library. Get up to speed on OWL and harness the power of object-oriented programming to add buttons, scroll bars, floating menus, dialog boxes, and other Windows elements to programs with ease. The book is designed for the programmer with some C experience but little or no experience with C++ or Windows programming.

Available Now, ISBN 1-878739-24-7, 425 pages, companion disk available

$29.95 US/$37.95 Canada

Send for our unique catalog to get more information about these books, as well as our outstanding and award-winning titles, including:

C++ Primer Plus: Teach Yourself Object-Oriented Programming. Stephen Prata. Teaches "generic" AT&T C++ 2.0 and 2.1 in gentle, step-by-step lessons that teach the basics of OOP. No C programming experience needed.

Master C: Let the PC Teach You C and **Master C++: Let the PC Teach You Object-Oriented Programming**: Both book/disk software packages turn your computer into an infinitely patient C and C++ professor.

Workout C: Hundreds of C projects and exercises and a full-featured compiler make this an unbeatable training program and value.

Windows API Bible: The only comprehensive guide to the 800 instructions and messages in the Windows Application Programming Interface.

Borland C++ Developer's Bible: Strips away the mysteries of using Borland's compilers, linkers, debuggers, assemblers, libraries, and utilities for C and C++ programs in both DOS and Windows.

Image Lab: This unique book/disk set is a complete PC-based "digital darkroom" that covers virtually all areas of graphic processing and manipulation.

Virtual Reality Playhouse: Jack-in to the world of Virtual Reality with this best-selling book/disk package.

Ray Tracing Creations: With this book/disk combination you can immediately begin rendering beautiful 3D graphic objects like the ones in computer movies.

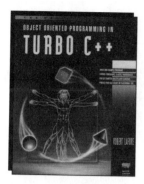

Waite Group Press, Inc.
Attention: *Microsoft Foundation Class Primer*
200 Tamal Plaza
Corte Madera, CA 94925

- **FOLD HERE** -